Creative Living Skills

Eighth Edition

Sue Couch, Ed.D.
Texas Tech University
Lubbock, Texas

Ginny Felstehausen, Ph.D.
Texas Tech University
Lubbock, Texas

Patricia Clark, M.Ed., CFCS
Professional Writer
Mahomet, Illinois

McGraw Hill Glencoe

New York, New York   Columbus, Ohio   Chicago, Illinois   Peoria, Illinois   Woodland Hills, California

Safety Notice

The reader is expressly advised to consider and use all safety precautions described in this textbook or that might also be indicated by undertaking the activities described herein. In addition, common sense should be exercised to help avoid all potential hazards and, in particular, to take relevant safety precautions concerning any known or likely hazards involved in using the procedures described in *Creative Living Skills*.

Publisher and Authors assume no responsibility for the activities of the reader or for the subject matter experts who prepared this book. Publisher and Authors make no representation or warranties of any kind, including but not limited to the warranties of fitness for particular purpose or merchantability, nor for any implied warranties related thereto, or otherwise. Publisher and Authors will not be liable for damages of any type, including any consequential, special or exemplary damages resulting, in whole or in part, from reader's use or reliance upon the information, instructions, warnings or other matter contained in this textbook.

Brand Name Disclaimer

Glencoe/McGraw-Hill does not necessarily recommend or endorse any particular company or brand name product that may be discussed or pictured in this textbook. Brand name products are used because they are readily available, they are likely to be known to the reader, and their use may aid in the understanding of the text. The publisher recognizes that other brand name or generic products may be substituted and work as well as or better than those featured in the text.

The McGraw·Hill Companies

Send all inquiries to:
Glencoe/McGraw-Hill
3008 W. Willow Knolls Drive
Peoria, Illinois 61614-1083

ISBN 0-07-861581-X (Student Edition)
ISBN 0-07-861582-8 (Teacher Wraparound Edition)
Printed in the United States of America
6 7 8 9 10 027 09 08 07

Contents in Brief

Reviewers

Martha A. Campbell, CFCS
Family and Consumer Sciences Educator
Hendry County Schools
Clewiston, Florida

Brenda Hall Ferguson
Family and Consumer Sciences Teacher
Greenville County Public Schools
Greenville, South Carolina

LaDonna K. Forester, CFCS
Family and Consumer Sciences Teacher
Colbert High School
Colbert, Oklahoma

Deb Garbe
Family and Consumer Education Teacher
Neenah Joint School District
Neenah, Wisconsin

Lela G. Goar
New Mexico FCCLA State Advisor
Eastern New Mexico University
Portales, New Mexico

Elaine McLaughlin, M.S., RD
Community Nutritionist
Arlington, Virginia

Nisa Moore
Family and Consumer Sciences Teacher
Tuscaloosa County School System
Tuscaloosa, Alabama

Reeta A. Moore
Family and Consumer Sciences Department
   Chair
Beavercreek City School District
Beavercreek, Ohio

Marjorie Patton
Retired Family and Consumer Sciences
   Teacher and Department Chair
Ben Davis High School
Indianapolis, Indiana

Lynne G. Pritchett
Family and Consumer Sciences Instructor
Gilmer High School
Ellijay, Georgia

Amy Reyna
Career and Technology Counselor
Hillsboro Independent School District
Hillsboro, Texas

Contents

Unit 2—Management Skills

Unit 3—Pathways to Career Success

Unit 4—Interpersonal Skills

Unit 5—Relationships in Your Life

Unit 7—Consumer Skills

Unit 10—Housing and Transportation Choices

HIGHLIGHTED TOPICS

FINDING CREATIVE SOLUTIONS

Viewpoints

TIPS FOR *Success*

More to Explore

Character IN ACTION

Career Options

UNIT 1

Personal Growth

Making the Most of Your Life

Key Terms

- personality
- self-concept
- self-esteem
- potential
- procrastination
- personal growth
- competence
- resilient
- persevere

Objectives

- **Describe** characteristics of personality.
- **Distinguish** between self-concept and self-esteem.
- **Suggest** strategies for boosting self-esteem.
- **Explain** the connection between competence and confidence.
- **Identify** the benefits of a positive attitude.

Who are you? Jot down five things you might say if you needed to introduce yourself to someone. What do these tell about who you are?

*H*ave you ever been sailing or watched someone sail? People who sail use many skills as they set the sails and steer the ship. They must learn how to use the winds and currents to get to where they want to go. They chart their course and then adjust it as the conditions change. Despite all the effort, sailing enthusiasts say the exhilaration and joy they experience is well worth it.

Life is like sailing. It takes skill and effort to navigate the waters. Sometimes the waters are calm; sometimes they're rough. If you just drift along wherever the wind and currents take you, you don't know where you'll end up. In fact, you may go nowhere at all.

You don't have to just drift through life. You can decide where you want to go and then chart your course and steer your way. In life, you steer by making positive choices and learning skills. These choices and skills will help you get where you want to go and enjoy the process of getting there.

Fig. 1-1. Do you know who you are and what is important to you? Why is a better understanding of yourself beneficial?

Getting to Know Yourself

Your journey through life begins with understanding who you are right now. You can then build on this understanding to become the kind of person you want to be in the future. Take a look at yourself to see who you are and what you're capable of becoming. See Fig. 1-1.

Your Personality

People come in all shapes and sizes. They also come with distinctive personalities. Your **personality** is the combination of characteristics that makes you different from every other person. Because of your unique personality, you have your own strengths and weaknesses, needs, and ways of expressing yourself.

Many characteristics are part of personality. In general, they fall into three categories:

- **Emotional.** Every person feels the same basic emotions, such as happiness, love, fear, and anger, yet each responds to them individually. When Kara's grandmother died, Kara expressed her sorrow through tears. Another person might show sorrow in a quiet, less obvious way.

- **Social.** People are also different in the ways they relate to others. Some people prefer the company of others and dislike being alone. Others are just the opposite. Some find it easy to relate to others; others are shy and find it difficult to connect. What social characteristics are part of your personality?

- **Intellectual.** When it comes to the mind and how it works, people have different strengths. Esteban, for example, expresses himself best in words. He has a knack for writing song lyrics that touch others. His friend Derek creates melodies to go with the lyrics, expressing the mood and feeling. The combination of their different intellectual strengths results in a dynamic songwriting team.

The emotional, social, and intellectual characteristics of personality become apparent to others through behavior. It takes time to get to know a person well and see the full depth of that person's personality.

Your Self-Concept

Suppose that you had to complete this sentence: "I am…." What would you say? You might use many, or just a few, words to describe yourself. The way you see yourself is your **self-concept**. Sometimes people call this *self-image* or *identity*. It's based on your perception of your strengths and weaknesses, skills and talents, and many other qualities that make up your unique personality.

Your self-concept is influenced by the experiences you have, by what people say to you, and by what you say to yourself. New experiences and interactions may cause you to revise the way you view yourself. What's important in the end, though, is that you have a realistic self-concept. That means being honest about who you are and what matters to you. When you are realistic about yourself, you can take pleasure in your strengths and good qualities, acknowledge your weaknesses and limitations, and work on those areas that you can improve.

Your self-concept influences your life in many different ways. It affects the way you feel about yourself, your relationships, the goals you set for yourself, and your effectiveness in school and the workplace. If you have a positive self-concept, you are more likely to look for opportunities and accept new challenges. The words you use to describe yourself will tell you if you tend to be more positive or negative about who you are.

Character IN ACTION

Accepting Others People want to be loved and accepted for who they are. Don't criticize others because they don't think the same way you do. Instead, try to understand their needs and point of view. Focus on what makes them special. Rather than struggling to mold others into who *you* want them to be, encourage them to become who *they* want to be. Describe how you can support and encourage one of your friends.

Negative Messages ~ Some people focus too heavily on their weaknesses and lose sight of their strengths. They might see themselves as too lazy, or too shy, or a failure. When people give too much attention to negative messages, they lose confidence in themselves. They may stop trying to improve. All her life, for example, Amelia heard that she was "no good." In time, she gave up trying to be any different. Then her foster mother helped her recognize her good qualities. When her self-concept changed, so did her behavior, and that changed her life.

This doesn't mean that you should just ignore negative messages. You need to evaluate them for any truth that they offer. Malcolm didn't like hearing from his friend that he was acting like he was better than everyone else. When Malcolm thought about this, he realized that some of his behavior *could* be interpreted that way. In reality, his actions were a cover-up for feeling insignificant and unimportant. His friend's comment helped him realize there were better ways to deal with his negative self-concept.

Positive Messages ~ Focusing on the encouraging and positive messages you receive from people you trust helps you build a positive self-concept. Look at your personality, talents, and skills. What are some of the qualities that you like about yourself and value? Are you a good friend? Do you make people laugh? Can people rely on you? When you remind yourself of your positive qualities, you're more likely to try new things. You will be realistic about your successes and failures. Having a positive self-concept does not mean you're perfect. No one is perfect. However, a positive self-concept will increase your ability to achieve and to improve. See Fig. 1-2.

Fig. 1-2. Focusing on the qualities you like about yourself helps you develop a positive self-concept. What are your best qualities?

Building Self-Esteem

Your self-concept is the picture you have of yourself. Your **self-esteem**—the value or importance you place on yourself—reflects how you feel about that image. Self-esteem can be high, low, or anywhere in between. If you like yourself and have a positive self-concept, you will have high self-esteem. People who dislike the picture they have of themselves have to struggle with low self-esteem. Self-esteem can be higher at some times than at others.

Self-esteem matters because it has a strong influence on your behavior and your well-being. When you feel good about yourself, you have more confidence. You're more likely to build healthy relationships. You avoid taking risks that would harm your health. High self-esteem gives you a positive outlook and enables you to make the best of your life.

If your self-esteem is lower than it should be, work on developing a more positive view of yourself. Give your self-esteem a boost by trying these ideas:

- **Learn to accept praise.** When someone compliments you, don't put yourself down. People praise you because they feel that you really deserve it.

- **Focus on your strengths.** Everyone has talents. Remind yourself of the things you do well.

- **Accept yourself as you are.** Don't compare yourself to others. Accept the fact that you're not perfect and that you have some faults. Simply work to improve them.

- **Learn from your mistakes.** Don't label yourself a failure. Instead, see mistakes as opportunities to figure out how you can do things differently in the future.

- **Use your strengths to help others.** Helping others shows you can accomplish something important. It also helps you feel good about yourself. See Fig. 1-3.

- **Take responsibility for your own life.** Learn how to deal with the different demands that are made of you. Managing your own life successfully will spur you to greater achievements.

Your self-concept and self-esteem affect every aspect of your life. Choosing to be a person with a positive outlook will help you set a good course and navigate your own rough waters.

Fig. 1-3. Your self-esteem gets a boost when you help others develop a new skill. What are some ways you could use your strengths to help others?

Aspiring to Be Your Best

Where are you headed in life? You've left childhood behind, and you're well on your way to being an adult. Soon you'll be responsible for making your own way in the world. Now is the time to think about what you hope your adult life will be like and what you want to achieve.

Realizing Your Potential

Like every other person, you have great **potential**—the capability of becoming more than you are right now. You were born with potential. You have strengths that can be developed. The challenge you face is to identify those strengths and make use of them. See Fig. 1-4.

Like every other person, you can also be sidetracked from reaching your potential. This happens when certain attitudes or circumstances block progress.

What problem can you identify in these phrases? "I'll start later." "I've got plenty of time for that." "This will be more fun." It's **procrastination**—the tendency to put off doing something until later. Procrastination may reflect an inability to set priorities and to be self-disciplined. People who constantly procrastinate often fail to make use of their potential.

How far you go is up to you. Things don't have to get in the way if you don't let them. Realizing your potential is a lifelong journey, one that many people fail to take. The time to start is now.

Personal Growth

If Cassidy has the potential to be a veterinarian, does that mean she is certain to become one? The answer is no. Potential is simply the capacity you have. What matters

Fig. 1-4. This teen has the potential to be a great athlete. She knows that it's up to her to make the effort to reach her potential.

is how you use that capacity. The key is to strive for **personal growth** by working toward your potential.

Personal growth involves learning and practicing new skills. Growth has a mushrooming effect. The more you learn, the more you are able to learn, and the closer you move toward your potential. Personal growth is a lifelong process. You're never too old to change and learn.

You have an important asset—yourself. By developing the qualities, skills, and attitudes you need, you can have a positive effect on the world. What's more, you will always be able to look back knowing that you made the best of your life.

Making Positive Changes

Nearly everyone would like to change some things in their lives. Some changes can be made quickly and easily. Most, however, are gradual, taken one step at a time. For example, Jaleesa wants to overcome her shyness. As a first step, she's resolved to speak to someone new every day for one week. Philip is tired of being unable to find things in his cluttered room. He's committed to a major cleaning this weekend and to putting things away every night. Change can involve difficult or simple things. The ability to make and adapt to changes is an essential life skill.

Viewpoints

Attitudes Toward Change

Change is the one constant in everyone's life, yet people greet it with different attitudes and responses.

Sydney: I guess you'd call me impatient, but I get bored when things stay the same for too long. I don't even like taking the same way to school each day. To me, change is opportunity. Think of the great inventions and discoveries we would have missed if people weren't willing to try something new. Think of the fun and excitement we'd miss. Everything that grows, changes.

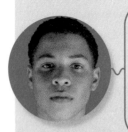

Chad: Have you ever noticed that "change" is one letter away from "chance"? Making a change is risky. I don't have any trouble with losing something to gain something better. But I like to be sure that what I gain is worth more than what I'm giving up—not only now, but in the long run, too. I'd also like to know that it's worth the trouble. I don't want to go through the hassle just to be disappointed.

Seeing Both Sides ~ What words tell you the feelings behind each attitude expressed above? What advice would be helpful for both points of view?

Barriers to Change

Trying to make a positive change isn't necessarily easy. Some people don't want to make the effort or fear they won't be successful. Other barriers to change include thinking you have to do it all yourself, forgetting that change takes time, and procrastinating. Making a plan for change, setting goals, and becoming accountable to someone are ways to overcome these barriers.

Opportunities for Change

Some people look for opportunities to change in order to make life better or more interesting. Maybe you want to expand your talents and skills by learning to play a sport or a musical instrument. Maybe you want to tackle something more personal, like starting a relationship with someone. If you're dissatisfied with some aspect of your life, look for ways to change it. Ask others who have made a similar change how they went about it. Develop a plan of action. Ask someone you trust to hold you accountable to the changes you want to make. All you need then are two special qualities: competence and confidence. They work hand in hand.

Developing Competence

An Olympic athlete, a top musician, an inspiring teacher—all are highly competent people in their area of expertise. **Competence** means having the qualities and the skills needed to perform a task or participate fully in an activity. You can, of course, be a

Fig. 1-5. To gain competence in driving, you need opportunities to learn and practice the skills involved. The same is true of many other areas of life.

competent hurdler without being an Olympic champion. There are degrees of competence.

Making a change requires developing or improving your competence in related areas. Once you've committed to a change, brainstorm ways you can gain the competence needed. The people around you—or people they know—may be willing to help you. School, of course, is an obvious resource. Books, newspapers, and Web sites may have useful information. There are many opportunities for learning, if you recognize them. See Fig. 1-5.

You are already competent in some areas. Continue to improve those skills as well as develop new ones. Doing so can enrich your life and help you improve the lives of others.

- **Willingness to take reasonable risks.** Confident people are willing to take risks to achieve their goals, but they know where to draw the line. A skateboarder who wants to improve skills may try new twists and turns, but knows better than to skate in traffic.

- **Positive self-concept and high self-esteem.** Confident people know that they are not perfect, but they don't dwell on their weaknesses. Instead, they feel good about what they have learned and achieved and keep trying to do better.

Confidence grows stronger each time you succeed. Your increased confidence makes you more willing to work toward building and strengthening your competencies. In other words, competence builds confidence, and vice versa. You see this principle in action all the time. A winning team is inspired to practice harder to win again. Making a high grade in class gives a student the encouragement to strive for other high grades. You can put this cycle to work in your own life, making the changes that you want to make. See Fig. 1-6.

Gaining Confidence

Confidence means believing in yourself and your abilities. People who have this positive attitude display it in their actions. Luisa, for example, wondered if she could get a part in the school play. Though she worried about stage fright, her confidence won out, and she decided to audition. Her positive attitude showed and helped her win a part.

Think about the confident people you know. What qualities do they have that make you see them as confident? You can identify certain common characteristics in confident people:

- **Self-assurance.** Because they believe in themselves, confident people stand up for themselves and for what they believe.

- **Self-control.** Since they realize that their actions affect their own life and the world around them, people with confidence consider carefully what they will do. They use reason, rather than their emotions, to decide what to do and when to act.

Setting Goals for Change

Feeling confident and competent provides a sense of power and purpose. You begin to realize that you can become the person you want to be and work toward the kind of life you want for yourself. Taking action that will lead you in these directions begins with setting goals and continues with making those goals a reality.

To give yourself a chance, make sure that you set goals that can be attained. When you set goals and successfully achieve them, your confidence will build. You'll likely discover that you can make things happen in your life when you're willing to try. For now, remember that change is a gradual process. It can be worked on one step at a time. Be patient with yourself.

TEXTLINK≈

You will learn more about *setting goals* in Chapter 5.

Meeting Life's Challenges

Change isn't always something you work toward. Some changes happen whether you want them to or not. You might have to move to a different city and go to a new school, for example. Then you face the challenge of settling in, making new friends, and building a different life.

Even changes that you initiate yourself can be challenging. Imagine that you take a part-time job working three evenings a week. You'd have to learn the job, make an effort to

More to Explore

Challenges of the Teen Years

The changes that occur during adolescence can make any teen feel uneasy. One teen struggles to fit in at school. Another is uncomfortable with a changing body. Still another feels especially sensitive about what people say. If any of this sounds familiar, don't worry. You can take steps to make things easier. Here are some ideas:

- **Look ahead.** People sometimes look longingly at the past, wishing that changes had not happened. Turning back the clock, however, is simply impossible. Those who look ahead realize that the changes of adolescence are moving them in an exciting direction.

- **Think positive.** Changes present opportunities. They can also signal personal growth. The strong emotions that sometimes hit you, for example, are a sign of deepening feelings that will help you form strong relationships.

- **Take advantage of new abilities.** As a teen, you're developing a greater sense of concern for others. You can use this to make positive changes in your family, school, and community.

- **Get help when you need it.** Almost everyone needs help at one time or another. Adults have lived through adolescence themselves and can often suggest ways of handling its challenges.

get along with your coworkers, and find a way to get your homework and chores done with less time available.

Challenges are a part of life, and everyone has to deal with them. Some people, however, face more serious challenges than others. The challenges presented by disabilities, discrimination, and poverty sometimes seem impossible to overcome, yet there are many examples of people who conquer them. In general, a person's attitude toward challenges makes all the difference between giving up and achieving success.

A Positive Attitude

Few people go through life without hitting a few bumps along the way. Some people hit more bumps than others. Those bumps can either get you down or get you going. What keeps some people going while others give up? It's all a matter of attitude.

Some people develop qualities that enable them to meet life's challenges head on. They are adaptable—willing to make changes as necessary. They are **resilient**—able to recover from or adjust to change or misfortune. They are also willing to **persevere** when necessary—to work patiently to overcome challenges. Adaptability, resilience, and perseverance, along with a positive attitude, help people keep going even when they feel discouraged.

There will be times, of course, when you feel discouraged and overwhelmed. Those are the times when you need to work on keeping a positive attitude. Accept that some things cannot be changed. Work on those that can. Don't focus on your negative feelings; focus on what you can achieve instead. A positive attitude is a powerful ally.

TIPS FOR *Success*

Developing a Positive Attitude

A positive attitude can make the difference between giving up and achieving success.

- **Count your blessings, not your misfortunes.** Focusing on the positives gives a brighter outlook.
- **Work with what you have.** Make the most of your skills and talents.
- **Welcome change.** Don't be afraid to try something new.
- **Find the right opportunity.** If you keep looking, you'll find someone who will give you a chance.
- **Don't fear failure.** Failure is a natural part of success. It helps you to learn and become a winner.

Sources of Support

No one needs to feel alone. As you look toward the future, realize that others are willing to help you meet your challenges in life. Family, friends, religious leaders, school counselors, and teachers are all possible sources of support. Don't be afraid to ask for help if you need it. Others know what it's like to make changes and face challenges. See Fig. 1-7.

Remember, too, that others need your help. Be ready to listen and encourage friends and family. Giving to others benefits you, making you feel more confident and competent as you see what you can contribute to another person's life.

Fig. 1-7. As you face the challenges of the future, remember that you're not alone. If you need help, ask for it.

Building Lifelong Skills

Think about your future. What information and skills do you need to face life's challenges and reach your potential? That's what this textbook is about. You will read about management, interpersonal skills, consumer skills, wellness, and careers. By learning how to manage time, money, and technology, you will make better decisions and solve problems more effectively. Improved interpersonal skills will help you better communicate with your family, friends, and coworkers. Consumer skills will help you use your money wisely, especially when making choices related to food, clothes, transportation, and housing. By learning to create a healthy lifestyle, you will gain lifelong skills needed for wellness. As you explore career options and learn what contributes to success in the workplace, you will develop ideas about careers that might be right for you. This course will teach you skills that will help you make positive choices throughout life.

It's Up to You

You're about to embark on a new phase in the journey of your life. Soon you'll be a young adult, responsible for yourself. Your journey will be satisfying—if you make it so. The choices you make along the way will either positively or negatively affect your life, both now and in the future.

Now it's time to get started. Take charge of your life and make necessary changes happen. Don't just drift along through life. Set your own course and take responsibility for following it. Large or small, challenges await you. Are you ready to accept them? Sail on!

Review & Activities

Chapter Summary

- Personality is the combination of characteristics that make you unique.
- Your self-concept and self-esteem affect every aspect of your life.
- Strategies for boosting your self-esteem include focusing on your strengths and using your strengths to help others.
- You have the potential to become more than you are right now. The process of personal growth helps you reach your potential.
- Competence and confidence give you the power to make changes and achieve goals.
- A positive attitude and support from others help you meet life's challenges.

Reviewing Key Terms & Ideas

1. What are the three main characteristics of **personality**?
2. What is the difference between **self-concept** and **self-esteem**?
3. What are two advantages of having high self-esteem?
4. Name five ways to boost self-esteem.
5. What is **potential**?
6. How does **procrastination** keep people from reaching their potential?
7. How is **personal growth** accomplished?
8. What are two common barriers to making positive changes?
9. What is the connection between **competence** and confidence?
10. How does success contribute to confidence?
11. How can a positive attitude help you meet life's challenges?
12. What does it mean to be **resilient** and to **persevere**?

Thinking Critically

1. **Making Predictions.** Predict what your future will be like based on your current self-concept. What thinking patterns do you need to change to have a more positive self-concept?
2. **Understanding Cause and Effect.** How does the confidence of someone affect his or her self-esteem? Can the confidence of someone with high self-esteem be misused? Explain your answer.

Applying Your Knowledge

1. **Sending Positive Messages.** Make a list of statements you made to friends or family recently commenting on their actions. Evaluate each message. Which ones enhanced the person's self-esteem? Which ones did not? Rewrite each negative message to make it more positive without making it untrue.

2. **Describing Confidence.** Write a want ad that begins "Wanted: Confident Person." Describe what kind of person would be able to fill this job. Use characteristics described in the text and others you think of on your own.

3. **Identifying Strengths and Weaknesses.** List your personal strengths and weaknesses. Make a bookmark or locker sign highlighting one or more of your strengths. Create a plan to improve one of your weaknesses.

Making Connections

1. **Language Arts.** Write a short story or poem about two people, one with high self-esteem and the other with low self-esteem. Show how their level of self-esteem affects their actions.

2. **Social Studies.** Read about a person in history who faced a long-term challenge, such as a physical disability or discrimination. Summarize the ways the person met the challenge he or she faced.

Managing Your Life

Building Sources of Support

Knowing who you can turn to for support when meeting life's challenges is important. However, supportive relationships take time to develop. List your current sources of support and the kinds of support each person or group offers. Identify the types of support you might be lacking, such as people who hold you accountable or challenge you to excel. Then list some ideas for how you might develop these sources of support.

Using Technology

1. **Video Presentation.** Work with two or three other students to make a video on the topic of self-esteem. You might identify common causes of low self-esteem in teens and suggest ways teens can overcome low self-esteem.

2. **Library Technology.** Using an electronic catalog in a library, search for books on personal growth and change. Outline your search process, noting the number of entries for each part of your search. Print the title, author, and other pertinent information for at least four of the books that sound most helpful and interesting.

Taking Care of Yourself

Key Terms

- wellness
- stress
- roles
- defensive driving
- abstinence

Objectives

- **Define** the concept of wellness.
- **Discuss** ways to promote physical, mental/emotional, and social health.
- **Propose** strategies for managing stress.
- **Describe** safety precautions appropriate for various situations.
- **Explain** the connection between abstinence and wellness.
- **Identify** sources of information about health.

QUICK WRITE

What actions do you take to protect your health? Write down at least five things you do regularly to stay healthy. Add to your list as you read this chapter.

Kevin prides himself on being healthy and in great shape. He's on the basketball team, lifts weights, and bikes to his part-time job when he can. He tries to eat only healthful foods and to get eight hours of sleep. Lately, Kevin has been so focused on fitness that his family and friends complain that they never see him. Last month he resigned from the student council to add a weekly workout at a local gym. Now Kevin's grades are starting to slip. His parents are worried about these changes, but Kevin doesn't want to talk about them. Actually, he's unhappy about the tension at home, and he misses his friends. Is Kevin healthy?

Health and Wellness

Kevin may be in excellent physical shape, but he's not necessarily in good health. That's because health has three main aspects: physical health, mental/emotional health, and social health. Thus, physical fitness is part of health, but so are feeling good about yourself, being able to cope with everyday problems, and having satisfying relationships. See Fig. 2-1.

The different aspects of health are interrelated. Kevin focused so heavily on his physical health that it caused problems with his social and mental/emotional health. Often, one aspect of health does affect others.

What can Kevin do to improve his health? A good start would be to adopt a philosophy of wellness. **Wellness** is an approach to life that emphasizes taking positive steps toward overall good health. It includes taking responsibility for your own well-being, becoming informed about health, and making decisions that will improve the quality of your life.

Fig. 2-1. Health has many dimensions. *What signs of health do you see in this teen?*

Physical Health

When you were a child, others made sure that you ate the right foods and got enough rest, and they decided whether you needed medical care. Now you have more responsibility for your own physical health. You make choices about what to eat and when to work, relax, and sleep. It's you who must pay attention to any symptoms of illness. Some of the decisions you make can have a long-term effect on your life. For example, skipping sunscreen during outdoor activities may not seem like a big deal now, but it could lead to skin cancer later on. Learning more about developments and issues in physical health will help you make informed decisions.

Nutrition ~ The expression "You are what you eat" holds a lot of truth. Every meal and snack is an opportunity to choose foods full of the nutrients you need for physical and mental energy. Healthful eating can also reduce the risks of weight problems, heart disease, diabetes, and some forms of cancer. Eating wisely helps you look and feel your best. See Fig. 2-2.

With the flood of conflicting nutrition information available today, perhaps it seems hard to know what to eat. In reality, it doesn't need to be. Eating a wide variety of nutritious foods, including plenty of fruits and vegetables, helps you achieve wellness.

Physical Activity ~ After a day of classes and an evening at the computer, Gabriela was stiff and her muscles ached. "Why am I so sore?" she thought. "I haven't done anything!" Part of Gabriela's problem was lack of exercise. The body is designed for movement and needs regular physical activity. It's not hard to find ways to be more active. Exercising and playing sports are obvious examples, but everyday movements, such as climbing stairs, also count.

Regular physical activity benefits all aspects of health—physical, mental/emotional, and social. Making physical activity a part of your daily routine helps you:

- Look and feel healthier.
- Have greater strength and endurance.
- Maintain an appropriate weight.
- Manage stress effectively.
- Feel more alert.

Fig. 2-2. *Making wise food choices will help you achieve wellness. What healthful snacks do you enjoy?*

Fig. 2-3. There are many fun ways to get moving. What kinds of active games, sports, and pastimes do you enjoy?

If you need to be more active, start by looking for everyday opportunities. Walk to a friend's house instead of asking for a ride. Choose more physical chores at home, like mowing the lawn. Try doing sit-ups or leg lifts while watching television.

Make time for regular exercise, too. You may like the convenience of activities you can do alone, such as jogging or biking. It's also fun to get together with others for activities such as dancing, soccer, or tennis. Choosing activities that you enjoy will help you stick with them. See Fig. 2-3.

Rest ~ When you stay up late, how do you feel the next day? You probably feel tired and perhaps a little grouchy. You may have trou-ble concentrating. Maybe you feel less coordinated than usual. Along with good nutrition and regular physical activity, your body needs adequate rest.

During a good night's sleep, your body systems are able to repair and revitalize themselves. Your skin takes on a healthy glow, and you have the energy you need to get through the day. An occasional late night won't hurt you, but make it a habit to get enough rest. On average, most people need eight hours of sleep each night. How you feel will indicate whether you need more or less.

Hygiene ~ To look your best and feel more confident, it's important to pay attention to your personal hygiene. Good hygiene,

Fig. 2-4. Personal cleanliness is particularly important during the teen years. How does good hygiene affect the way you feel about yourself?

or cleanliness, is also basic to overall wellness. It helps you manage acne, oily skin and hair, increased perspiration, and other common problems. Hygiene is really a matter of just a few simple habits, such as a daily bath or shower, regular brushing and flossing, and keeping your hair, hands, and nails clean. See Fig. 2-4.

Medical Care ~ You probably see a doctor when you're sick, but it's also important to have checkups when you feel fine. Regular checkups help detect problems early. They are also a good time to discuss any questions you have about health. Many experts recommend annual physical and eye exams and twice-yearly trips to the dentist.

Mental/Emotional Health

People who are mentally and emotionally healthy think clearly, feel good about themselves, and are able to cope with the demands of life. They welcome change and enjoy developing new skills. They learn from their mistakes and deal with frustrations without feeling overwhelmed.

While some aspects of mental/emotional health may be linked to heredity, you control many others. When you have problems in this area, it can affect your physical and social health as well. Here are some suggestions for maximizing your mental/emotional health:

- Challenge yourself to learn new information and skills.
- Put your talents and abilities to good use.
- Learn from your mistakes.
- Focus on your strengths, not on your weaknesses.
- Take responsibility for your choices and actions.
- Be open-minded and flexible.
- Develop positive ways to handle your emotions.

There may be times when you feel unable to cope with mental/emotional health issues. Talking to an adult, school counselor, or mental health professional can help. It's important to ask for help when you need it.

Social Health

Your social health concerns the relationships you have with the people around you—your family, friends, neighbors, teachers, classmates, and so on. People with good social health have positive, supportive relationships. They treat others with kindness and respect. They have good communication skills that enable them to make and keep friends and to give and ask for support when it is needed.

Social health also includes your role within society as a whole. By getting involved in your community, you make it a better place. At the same time, you boost your own wellness.

TEXTLINK≈

Unit 5 focuses on the different kinds of *relationships* in your life.

Managing Stress

Giving a class presentation, going on a date with someone new, taking a driving test—what do these experiences have in common? They can all produce stress. **Stress** is your body's response when you feel overwhelmed by responsibilities and demands. It makes you feel tense and can affect all aspects of your health. The key to dealing with stress is to learn how to manage it effectively.

More to Explore

The Body's Response to Stress

Stress is a good example of the mind-body connection. Stress is an emotional response that can cause many physical reactions. The trigger is a hormone called adrenaline. A body under stress releases adrenaline into the bloodstream, where it increases the heartbeat and breathing rate. This is part of the "fight-or-flight" response, which allows the body to react quickly in an emergency by supplying a boost of strength and energy. To primitive humans, who relied on physical abilities for survival, this could be the difference between life and death.

Today, "fight-or-flight" is more an annoyance than a matter of survival. For example, the first-date jitters produce a dry mouth, sweaty palms, and "butterflies" in the stomach. However, negative or prolonged stress can cause more severe symptoms, including upset stomach, difficulty sleeping, loss of appetite, and headaches. Like the instinctive "fight-or-flight" response, these physical effects remain until the danger passes—that is, until the stress that causes them is reduced or managed.

Causes of Stress

You experience stress when pressures seem to exceed your ability to cope with them. Family and friends may make demands that produce stress. Perhaps a friend expects you to take part in a charity event even though you have several school assignments due. Sometimes you are the one who puts pressure on yourself. You might push yourself to do well in a test or to take first place at a track meet. Major life events, such as a death or divorce in the family or a serious illness or injury, cause significant stress. Then there are the daily hassles—you miss the bus; you delete a computer file by mistake; you have an argument with a friend.

In spite of its reputation, not all stress is bad. Sometimes it has a positive effect. For example, the stress of a gymnastics meet or a choir recital can motivate you to do your best. In a crisis, stress helps focus the mind and body to act.

More often, though, people feel the negative effects of stress. When these accumulate, they can affect all aspects of your health. Physically, you might lose your appetite, develop headaches, or have trouble sleeping. Emotionally, you might feel nervous or drained. Stress can cause tension in your relationships with others. How are you usually affected by stress?

Managing Multiple Roles

One potential cause of stress is the challenge of managing your various roles in life. **Roles** are the parts you play when you interact with others. For example, you might be a son or daughter, sister or brother, friend, student, team member, and community volunteer. As an adult, you may add the roles of employee, coworker, husband or wife, and parent. Each role brings its own responsibilities. At times, they can make you feel like you're being pulled in too many different directions. That's where the stress comes in.

Good management skills help you juggle your roles. For example, learning to manage your time can help you fulfill your obligations and still have time for yourself. Relationship skills, such as communication and negotiation, can help you work with others to find solutions. You'll learn about these and other skills in later chapters.

TEXTLINK≈

Chapter 13 offers more ideas for *managing multiple roles.*

Stress Management Techniques

Although stress is a normal part of life, it's important to recognize and manage the negative effects of stress before they become too troublesome. When you feel stressed, do you have a mental/emotional reaction, physical symptoms, or both? Depending on your answer, try some of these coping strategies:

- **Get moving.** If you start to feel overwhelmed, find a physical activity that will help you unwind and refocus. You might go for a run, shoot baskets, or clean your room.

- **Make time for yourself.** Schedule some "you time" every day. Just relax or do something you enjoy—write in a journal, listen to music, or work on a hobby.

- **Talk to someone.** Share your thoughts and feelings with someone you trust. Support from people who care can be remarkably reassuring.

Viewpoints

Dealing with Stress

Is stress always something to be minimized? The way you feel about stress affects your response to it.

Jerome: I look at stress like a pulse: it's a sign of life. Stress shows you're involved in things, like your job or relationships, not just going along for the ride. It comes from being in the middle of the action. For me, life without stress would be a life of boredom.

Chris: People make life too stressful by getting involved in too many things. Maybe they want to be successful at everything, or involved in everything, so they take on too many responsibilities and take them too seriously. Then they get upset with themselves for failing, and with the rest of us for not following their example.

Seeing Both Sides ~ What assumptions about the cause and effect of stress underlie each point of view? Do you think Jerome and Chris could work on a task together successfully? Why or why not?

- **Plan ahead.** If you're nervous about an upcoming event, such as a job interview, take time to prepare for it and rehearse. You will feel more confident.

- **Be realistic.** Expecting a perfect outcome adds as much stress as expecting the worst. Don't demand perfection from yourself or others.

- **Learn from experience.** If you're frustrated because things didn't go the way you hoped, try to figure out what went wrong. Decide what you could do better next time.

- **Learn to say no.** Do you already have too much on your plate? If so, it's better to say no to another commitment than to let yourself and others down by making promises you can't keep.

Staying Safe

Taking responsibility for your health includes assuming responsibility for your safety. Many teens see themselves as invulnerable—accidents, injuries, and violence affect only others' lives. It only takes reading a newspaper or watching a newscast to know that these problems can and do happen all too often. The guidelines that follow will help keep you safe.

- **Be aware of the risks.** In everyday activities, these can range from slipping in the shower to having your wallet stolen on a crowded street. Athletic activities from biking to swimming have their own risks. Learn about such risks and consciously decide which are reasonable and which should be avoided. Whatever the situation, stay aware of your surroundings and possible safety concerns. See Fig. 2-5.

- **Be prepared.** When you know what risks you face, you can plan how to avoid or minimize many of them. For example, taking lessons before scuba diving will teach you safety procedures as well as basic diving skills. In any situation, think of what might go wrong and mentally rehearse how you would react. Ask yourself: "If a fire broke out at the concert, what are two ways I could get out?" "If my ride drinks at the party, how can I get home?" The situations you imagine might never occur, but thinking through the possibilities keeps you on your toes and ready to act.

- **Stay within your limits.** Be realistic about your abilities and be firm about your values. When it comes to your safety, resist pressure from others and make your own decisions. Don't let anyone talk or dare you into doing something that is beyond your capabilities or personal limits. Remember, you will be the one who must deal with the consequences of your actions.

Fig. 2-5. Knowing how to protect yourself from accidents is the first step. Acting on that knowledge comes next. How is this teen practicing safety?

- **Follow the rules.** While safety rules may seem boring, they are based on analyzing years of accident and injury information. Wherever you are—on the road, at the pool, in the gym, on the soccer field—know the rules and follow them. They are designed to protect you. A "No Diving" sign, for instance, is meant to protect people from paralysis or death caused by diving in shallow water.

Safety on the Road

Did you know that injuries kill more teens than all diseases combined? The largest proportion of teen deaths and injuries result from motor vehicle crashes. Following basic safety precautions can help prevent accidents and injuries on the road.

Fig. 2-6. There's no doubt about it, safety belts do save lives. Why do you think teens are less likely than all other age groups to wear safety belts?

- **Wear a safety belt.** Teens are least likely to wear safety belts, yet they also take the greatest risks when driving or riding in a car. Always wear a safety belt and insist that others "buckle up" too. The odds of dying or suffering brain damage or paralysis skyrocket when safety belts aren't worn. See Fig. 2-6.

- **Follow traffic laws.** Speeding, running red lights, making illegal turns, and driving while intoxicated are all against the law. So is crossing a busy street in the middle of the block rather than at a crosswalk. Whether you're driving, walking, or biking, take traffic laws seriously. They protect you and others on the road.

- **Never mix alcohol and vehicles.** Don't ever drive after drinking alcohol. Never let someone who has been drinking alcohol drive you. Take away the keys to prevent the person from driving. Alcohol is involved in more than a third of deaths involving teen drivers.

- **Stay focused.** When driving, concentrate on what you are doing and on the traffic and road conditions. Eating, changing music, talking to friends, and using a cell phone are all potentially dangerous distractions.

- **Drive defensively.** When you practice **defensive driving**, you take steps to minimize the chances of an accident. For example, keep a safe distance from the vehicle ahead of you so that if it stops suddenly, you'll have enough time to stop too. Anticipate dangerous situations and be ready to react.

Protecting Yourself from Violence and Crime

No matter where you live, you can't assume that you are safe from crime. What you can do, though, is take precautions that will help protect you. Wherever you are, stay aware of your surroundings. Don't put yourself in harm's way unnecessarily.

- **At home.** Your home should feel like a place where you are safe. You can help keep it that way through simple steps such as keeping doors and windows locked. Some families experience violence within the home. If that happens to you, seek help from a counselor or other trusted adult.

- **Online.** Internet safety is a major concern. Be smart! Never give out personal information to strangers you meet online. If someone you know only through the Internet wants to meet you in person, tell an adult in your family.

- **At school.** School safety is essential for learning. If you know of situations that may produce violence or are aware of crimes, it's your responsibility to let administrators know. Start or join a committee to improve harmony at school, and do your part to keep relationships positive.

- **In the community.** Some places may be known for high crime rates. Avoid them if you can. On public transportation, be alert for dangerous situations. On the street, walking with confidence and scanning the area as you walk will help keep you from being a victim of crime. If you must walk at night, walk with someone. Choose a well-traveled and well-lighted route. If you get lost in an unfamiliar area, ask a police officer for help or stop at a store or restaurant. Keep your wallet or purse and other valuables out of sight. If someone demands your money or car keys, throw the items away from you and run in the opposite direction. See Fig. 2-7.

Fig. 2-7. Recognizing potentially dangerous situations is a key to protecting yourself from crime. *Why do you think teens who know better sometimes accept rides from strangers?*

Avoiding Risky Behaviors

It's easy to assume that bad things won't happen to you, but certain behaviors greatly increase the odds that they will. These risky behaviors include using alcohol, using illegal drugs, and participating in sexual activity. Other examples of risky behaviors include reckless driving and participating in extreme sports and foolish stunts. All of these behaviors can put people's health—and, in some cases, their life—at risk. When people combine risky behaviors, such as driving too fast while not wearing a safety belt, they increase their chances of suffering the consequences.

The most effective way to stay safe and protect yourself from harm is to practice abstinence. **Abstinence** means refusing to engage in high-risk behavior, including sexual activity and the use of tobacco, alcohol, and other drugs. Choosing to abstain from risky behaviors will help you achieve and maintain wellness.

Resources for Health

To make responsible decisions about your health, you need sound information. Some questions can be answered by a parent, grandparent, or other trusted adult, such as a teacher, school nurse, or guidance counselor. For further information, check your school or public library for books, newspapers, magazine articles, and other print sources. The Internet can also be useful, but keep in mind that not all Web sites give accurate

information. Generally, the Web sites of government agencies and professional health groups are the most reliable places to start.

Most communities have agencies that help individuals and families with health issues. Local police departments sometimes offer programs in violence and injury prevention. Treatment programs and support groups can help people overcome alcohol or drug problems. No-cost or low-cost options may be available for medical care or counseling for those who qualify. Often local groups provide information, assistance, and support for people with specific disabilities or conditions, such as diabetes or birth defects. Find out what your community does to promote wellness, then take advantage of programs that will help you reach your goals. If you need help or support, don't be afraid to ask.

Review & Activities

Chapter Summary

- Wellness focuses on enhancing your overall well-being, including physical, mental/emotional, and social health.
- Nutrition, physical activity, rest, hygiene, and medical care promote physical health.
- Signs of good mental/emotional health include a positive outlook and the ability to cope with the demands of life.
- Social health involves your relationships with the people around you and your role within society as a whole.
- Stress management strategies help prevent the harmful effects of stress.
- You can take steps to prevent traffic accidents and to protect yourself from violence and crime.
- Many sources of health information and assistance are available.

Reviewing Key Terms & Ideas

1. Explain the meanings of **wellness**.
2. Give four suggestions for improving and maintaining physical health.
3. Name three ways that regular physical activity benefits your overall health.
4. Why is it particularly important for teens to pay attention to hygiene?
5. Give three suggestions for enhancing mental/emotional health.
6. Name three examples of ways people demonstrate good social health.
7. Is eliminating **stress** one goal of wellness? Explain.
8. What are two strategies that will help you manage multiple roles?
9. How does **defensive driving** protect you and others?
10. Give three precautions for avoiding crime when away from home.
11. How is **abstinence** related to wellness?
12. Suggest four resources for sound information about health.

Thinking Critically

1. **Recognizing Relationships.** Describe a situation that shows how the three aspects of health influence one another.
2. **Drawing Conclusions.** What do you consider to be the main causes of stress in teens today? Why?

Applying Your Knowledge

1. **Identifying Wellness Behavior.** Study newspaper stories, magazine articles, and television reports to find at least two examples of people who work to improve their own wellness or the wellness of others. Write a summary of these efforts.

2. **Managing Stress.** Use what you have learned in this chapter to develop stress management guidelines that will work for you. List at least six strategies that you could use in times of stress. Keep your list handy and use it when you need it.

3. **Safety Tips.** In groups, choose one aspect of safety that is relevant to teens in your school, such as Internet safety, driving, sports, or school safety. Brainstorm practical ways to stay safe. Make a list of your top ten tips to present to the class.

Making Connections

1. **Science.** Choose a health fad or product to analyze. Find background information from both scientific studies and magazines or ads. Based on your research, draw conclusions about the product claims. How does the information from the two types of sources compare?

2. **Language Arts.** Choose a character from a short story, novel, TV program, or movie. Identify ways this person did or did not take responsibility for his or her own health. What health-related choices did the character make and why? What were the results?

Managing Your Life

Maintaining a Balance

Taking time for yourself can be difficult, especially as you take on more responsibilities and enjoy many activities. Personal time is important, however, for reducing stress and improving emotional health. Take stock of all the demands placed on your time by school and other activities. On a day planner or weekly schedule, block out all the time periods that are not available because of existing commitments. Then identify at least 15 minutes every day that you can call your own. Jot down some low-stress ideas for how you will spend this free time.

Using Technology

1. **Word Processing.** Use appropriate software to create a personal wellness log. Create a table with one column for each day of the week. In the left-hand column, list 5 to 10 wellness goals. Examples might include: "Exercise four days a week" or "Spend 30 minutes a day relaxing." Print out your table, and check off the goals you meet or take steps toward each day. After one week, use the software to write an analysis of your efforts and the results. Include ideas for how you can continue to meet your goals.

2. **Internet.** Use the Internet to find out more about the long-term effects of stress. Share your findings in a brief report.

CHAPTER 3

Developing Character

Key Terms

- character
- mentor
- values
- personal standard
- peer pressure
- proactive
- ethics

Objectives

- **Explain** how character impacts individuals and society.
- **Analyze** the relationship between values and character.
- **Compare** ways people acquire values.
- **Explain** the importance of living according to one's personal standards.
- **Describe** how people can make ethical choices.

QUICK WRITE

Choose a person you truly admire. Write about the personal qualities this person has that have earned your respect. Briefly explain why you look up to this person.

Whom do you admire—your parents, certain relatives, some of your friends or neighbors? Maybe you think highly of some teachers, world leaders, or entertainers. The more important question is, *why* do you admire these people? Do they set an example for others to follow? Do they inspire you to achieve more? Do they strive to make a difference in others' lives? If so, the people you admire are probably people of character.

What Is Character?

People who have **character** possess moral strength and integrity. They understand the difference between right and wrong and are committed to doing what is right. They accept—and live by—principles such as honesty, respect, and caring. They demonstrate responsible behavior. These are the main components of character. See Fig. 3-1.

Can you think of a time when you were faced with a choice between right and wrong, or selfish and unselfish? People face those types of choices every day. What they choose to do shows their character. André, for example, paid cash for a pair of jeans and pocketed the change without looking at it.

When he got home, he realized the sales clerk had given him a ten-dollar bill instead of a one-dollar bill. André went back to the store with his receipt and corrected the mistake. What does that tell you about his character?

André understood that it would be wrong to keep money that was not his. He knew that the honest thing to do was to return the money. By going out of his way to do the right thing, he proved that he is responsible. In all these ways, André demonstrated his character.

Fig. 3-1. People reveal their character by their words and actions. What character traits do you admire most? Why?

Character and Responsibility

Developing character is an important responsibility. Character promotes your well-being. When you abide by the expectations, rules, and laws of your family, school, and community, you stay out of trouble. Behaving responsibly means you are less likely to take dangerous risks that could hurt you or others.

In addition, character promotes the well-being of society. Most people wouldn't want to live in a world in which lying, stealing, and cheating were considered normal behavior. In order for society to function well, people must cooperate with one another. Character traits such as responsibility, respect, and mutual trust are essential to that process. See Fig. 3-2.

Developing character is something you must consciously work at. It doesn't just happen. Families, teachers, friends, and people in the community can all help you develop character. When they model character, you are likely to make the same traits a part of who you are. They can also provide support and set expectations that encourage you to build your character.

You might also have a special person who helps you develop character by being a mentor to you. A **mentor** is someone who acts as a teacher and a guide. This person—perhaps a relative or a friend—takes a special interest in you, investing time and energy in helping you grow. Kalinda, for example, mentors her niece Tammy twice a week. She encourages Tammy to make positive choices and do well in school.

The choices you make and their consequences will give you lots of experience in developing character. Take Brandon, who learned the hard way that lying doesn't pay. When in middle school, he started to lie to his parents about his homework. He would say he was finished so that he could practice

Fig. 3-2. People with character help make the world a better place to live. *How could you help to improve your community?*

his soccer drills. Eventually his parents found out, and he was disciplined. Moreover, low grades prevented Brandon from playing on the school soccer team. Today, as a high school student, Brandon is honest with others and responsible about doing his schoolwork. He learned from his poor decisions. Like Brandon, as you continue to mature, your struggles and trials will help you strengthen your character.

Developing character is a lifelong process. It began in childhood when you started to learn from your family. It will continue as you learn more about what is important in your life and the world around you.

Fig. 3-3. *This family makes a special effort to spend quality time together. What does that tell you about their values?*

The Importance of Values

Values are the foundation upon which character is built. **Values** are beliefs and ideas about what is important. Your actions, the decisions you make, and the kind of person you are all reflect your values. Your values influence all aspects of your life, including your relationships, decisions, and goals.

As people live each day, they turn to their values to guide them. A teen who values trustworthiness and responsibility will keep promises and admit to his or her mistakes. A coach who values respect and fairness will encourage good sportsmanship. A family that values togetherness can show it by making an effort to spend time with one another. See Fig. 3-3.

Universal Values

Some values are universal to all societies. In other words, nearly all people accept them. Universal values include respect, fairness, responsibility, caring, and honesty. Fig. 3-4 on the next page lists common universal values and gives examples of them in action. Values like these guide people and help them live together in society.

Acquiring Values

You began learning values as soon as you were born. Values are learned both directly and indirectly. For example, when a father tells his children to solve disagreements peacefully, rather than by hitting people, this is direct teaching. Values can also be learned indirectly, by observing the behavior of others. When Jaime was in the eighth grade, his

Examples of Universal Values

VALUE	THE VALUE IN ACTION
Trustworthiness	■ Keep promises and fulfill commitments. ■ Be dependable. ■ Stand by your family, friends, and country.
Respect	■ Show high regard for yourself and others. ■ Be tolerant of differences. ■ Deal peacefully with anger, insults, and disagreements.
Fairness	■ Treat others equitably. ■ Take turns and share. ■ Practice good sportsmanship.
Responsibility	■ Stand behind your words and actions. ■ Complete your work. ■ Accept the consequences of your actions. ■ Admit your mistakes and correct them.
Caring	■ Be kind and compassionate. ■ Express gratitude and offer encouragement. ■ Help people in need.
Honesty	■ Tell the truth and admit wrongdoing. ■ Be authentic and sincere. ■ Don't cheat or steal.
Integrity	■ Stand up for your beliefs about right and wrong. ■ Resist social pressure to do what you think is wrong. ■ Live according to your values.
Self-discipline	■ Exercise self-control. ■ Demonstrate hard work and be self-directed. ■ Give your best effort. ■ Show determination in pursuing worthy goals and activities.
Citizenship	■ Respect authority and obey laws and rules. ■ Volunteer at school and in the community. ■ Vote. ■ Conserve natural resources.

Fig. 3-4. These values are accepted by nearly everyone. Why is it important for people to have common values?

mother went back to school at night, eventually earning a college degree. Jaime and his sisters were proud of her. Her graduation was a very special event. Through the indirect teaching provided by his mother's example, Jaime saw the value of his own educational opportunities.

The family home is usually the first place where values are taught and observed. Families often teach one another to share, show respect, and care for one another. You also learn values in school and in your community. What values have you noticed in the behavior of a teacher, coach, Scout leader, or neighbor? What values do friends and classmates show? See Fig. 3-5.

Religion and culture also play a major role in the formation of values. For many people, religious beliefs and teachings provide guidelines to live by. Likewise, cultural traditions teach people what is important in a particular culture. In many Asian cultures, for example, children are taught that respecting their grandparents and other elders is especially important. Can you think of other examples of values that are emphasized in a particular culture?

Society teaches values in many ways as well. Laws, for example, very clearly set forth what is important and what isn't. You learn that safety is valued because of laws that set speed limits and require people to wear safety belts. You know that honesty is valued because people who steal or lie are punished.

Media messages, too, can influence how values are formed. For example, some advertisements imply that having fun and looking good are more important than values such as respect for yourself and others. Some movies and TV shows reinforce the values that you have learned elsewhere, while others do not. Can you think of some examples?

Living by Your Values

All your life you will be examining your values and living by them. Having strong values helps you make wise choices when faced with negative influences and pressure to go against what you know is right. Here are some guidelines that will help you act according to your values:

- **Consider the consequences**. Ask yourself: "Will taking this action result in harm to me or to anyone else? Will it cause me to do anything illegal? Will it lead me to regrets?" A yes to any of these questions means that the action you're considering is not the right choice.

Fig. 3-5. This coach makes a point of offering positive encouragement. What might the team members learn from his example?

- **Listen to your conscience.** Your conscience is the inner voice that tells you what is morally right. Often that nagging feeling that you have when you are about to do something wrong is your conscience trying to steer you in the right direction.

- **Turn to your family.** Family is often the first source of values. When faced with a difficult situation, many people think about what they have been taught and then live by those values.

FINDING CREATIVE SOLUTIONS

Imagining "What If?"

Sometimes the best way to approach a problem or resolve a dilemma is to use your imagination! Imagining what might happen if you take a particular course of action will help you make decisions that reflect your values.

How It Works

The "what if?" approach encourages you to think through the consequences of your actions before you take them. Suppose you have promised a neighbor that you will babysit next Saturday. Now a friend has asked you to help out at a benefit dinner on the same day. You'd really like to help your friend, so you start to use your imagination:

"What if I tell the neighbor I can't babysit?" (She might not be able to find someone else in time.)

"What if I tell the neighbor I'm sick?" (She'll be sympathetic.)

"What if she finds out I'm lying?" (She'll never hire me again, and she'll tell my parents.)

"What if I just tell my friend I'll help her another time?" (Far better to tell the truth.)

The "what if?" approach is particularly helpful when you face a dilemma that causes a conflict of your conscience. Other "what if" questions that you may find helpful at such times include: "What if someone gets hurt?" "What if my parents find out?" "What if our friendship suffers?"

Try It Out

You've been invited to a party next weekend, and would really like to go. However, you've heard rumors that some people will be bringing alcohol and drugs to the party.

▶ **Your Turn** *Think of at least three "what if?" questions that would apply to this situation. Choose one of your questions and describe the thought process that it sets in motion. In what other situations might your questions be helpful?*

- **Gain knowledge.** When faced with a decision involving values, learn more about the situation. Get the facts before you act.

- **Evaluate the source.** Before accepting what others encourage you to do or believe, look at the source. Is it reliable? For example, which is more likely to promote values that are worthwhile: an adult whom you know and trust, or an advertisement that's trying to sell you something? Use reason and logic to reach your decision.

- **Talk to others.** When you have doubts or concerns, talk to adults you trust and respect. Responsible people can help you sort things out. See Fig. 3-6.

Setting Your Standards

Your values are the basis for many decisions in your life. You already understand that actions resulting from your decisions bring positive or negative consequences. As you mature, you're more able to project what those consequences might be. It's time to begin setting personal standards for how you will behave in certain types of situations.

A **personal standard** is a rule or principle you set for yourself. It guides your behavior by defining what you do and don't do. Your personal standards are like your own code of conduct—a promise to yourself about how you will act.

For example, one of Blake's personal standards is a rule that he won't get into a car with someone who has consumed alcohol. At a party one night, his friend had a beer right before he was to drive Blake home. Blake chose not to ride with his friend and called his parents instead.

A couple of people teased him, but he just shrugged it off. He had already decided how to handle such a situation and had simply followed through.

As Blake's situation shows, it helps to think about your personal standards before you're in a situation you might not be ready to handle. Personal standards prevent you from making choices based on the mood of the moment or on **peer pressure**, the influence of others in your age group. Setting personal standards ahead of time is a way of being proactive. **Proactive** people take the initiative to think and plan ahead for situations they might encounter. They take control of life experiences rather than letting life experiences control them.

Fig. 3-6. Talking things over with a trusted adult can help you figure out what to do. *Who helps you when you need guidance?*

At the heart of each of your personal standards are your values. If you value responsibility, your personal standards will reflect responsibility. When setting personal standards, ask yourself:

- What situations tend to put your values in conflict with others?

- When do you feel uncomfortable in what you think people expect of you?

- In what situations do you tend to feel pressured into being someone you don't want to be or doing something you don't want to do?

- What types of situations make you feel like you are compromising yourself?

Next, imagine how you might respond in each situation you identified. Think of various responses and their consequences. Which responses have the most positive outcome for you and others? Which best reflect your values and the character you want to show? Based on your values, set your own rule, principle, or guideline by which to act. Then when you find yourself in this type of situation, remind yourself of your personal standard and act accordingly.

Making Ethical Choices

Besides defining your values and setting your personal standards, you also develop your character by making ethical choices. Ethical choices are the choices you make based on your **ethics**—the principles and values that guide the way you live. They are based on what is fair, right, just, caring, and best for all people involved.

Sometimes ethical choices are clear-cut—you have no doubt about the right thing to do. At other times they can be very challenging. They often require you to solve a problem that impacts others. Making the right choice based on your values and standards is a true indication of your character.

Francisca faced an ethical choice when she was working on the final term paper for her history class. She couldn't understand why her friend Gayle, who was taking the same class, had time to party on the weekends. "I'm not even halfway done with my research," Fran thought. "Can Gayle be finished already, or is she waiting until the last minute?" Finally she asked Gayle about it.

"You mean you're actually writing your own term paper?" Gayle replied. "I bought mine on the Internet. Everyone does. It doesn't hurt anything, and you're guaranteed to get a good grade. Of course, I could write my own paper if I wanted to, but why bother?"

That night, Fran lay awake thinking about what Gayle had said. Was it true that everyone else bought their term papers? If so, why should Fran do all that work and risk getting a bad grade? In the end, though, Fran's conscience led her to the right decision. She knew that the paper she turned in was supposed to be her own work. Putting her own name on a paper that she hadn't written would be cheating. She was even more glad of her decision when, a week later, her history teacher announced that all term papers submitted would be checked for material copied from other sources. Students caught cheating would fail the course.

You will experience similar types of problems throughout your life. As you mature, some problems will become easier to solve, while others may not. However, the better you know your values, standards, and ethics, the more likely it is that you will make good choices. See Fig. 3-7.

Fig. 3-7. Sometimes it may seem difficult to do the right thing—for example, tackling a tough school assignment rather than taking the easy way out. When was the last time you made the right choice even though it was difficult to do?

Character in Action

When you develop positive values, set personal standards, and make ethical choices, you show your character in action. Neenah, for example, does her part to make sure that students with physical disabilities feel included rather than left out. Her peers have come to admire Neenah for her caring and respect for others. Neenah puts her values, words, and actions together to make a difference for others.

You, too, can put your character into action. The "Character in Action" features throughout this text present different character traits and suggest actions to take for situations you might experience. They present opportunities for you to develop your character.

Developing character is a learning process. There are times when you will make a poor choice and fail to act on your values and standards. Learn from the experience and move on. Be careful, but give yourself room to grow.

Character is rooted in positive values and exhibited in a person's actions. It withstands the tests of time, and it's always there—even when no one else is looking.

Chapter Summary

- Good character is important for individuals and for society as a whole.
- Values are the foundation upon which character is built. They influence all aspects of your life.
- Universal values are those that are accepted by nearly everyone.
- Values are learned directly and indirectly through family, religion, culture, society, and the media.
- Personal standards are your own code of conduct.
- Ethical choices require you to face problems that impact the values held by you or others.

Reviewing Key Terms & Ideas

1. What is **character**? How do people show that they have character?

2. Why is it important for people to develop character?

3. In what ways might a **mentor** help you develop character?

4. What are **values**? How are they related to character?

5. How do universal values help societies function?

6. What is the difference between acquiring values directly and acquiring them indirectly?

7. How might your conscience help you act according to your values?

8. What is the purpose of a **personal standard**? Give an example.

9. How does being **proactive** help you deal with difficult situations?

10. Define **ethics**. How are ethical choices made?

Thinking Critically

1. **Understanding Cause and Effect.** How do personal standards help people resist negative peer pressure? How can anticipating peer pressure situations help you deal with them?

2. **Defending Your Position.** Explain why you agree or disagree with this statement: "Character can be developed to a degree, but for the most part, you're either born with it or you're not."

Applying Your Knowledge

1. **Analyzing Trends.** Select a trend of negative behavior in today's society, such as bullying or vandalism. Use library or Internet resources to gather information on the trend. Suggest ways that people might change the trend by demonstrating character.

2. **Developing Character.** Ask an adult to share memories of a time when he or she experienced difficulties in life that helped develop his or her character. Write a few paragraphs describing how the person's experiences led to character development.

Making Connections

1. **Social Studies.** Select a specific culture to research. What values does that culture consider particularly important? Explain how people in that culture directly and indirectly teach those values to their youth.

2. **Language Arts.** Read about the life of someone who brought about social change. For example, you might choose a suffragist, a civil rights leader, a politician, or an educator. Write a brief essay about this person's achievements. Explain how the person's values and character affected his or her life.

Managing Your Life

Identifying a Mentor

A mentor is someone you look up to and who will support and encourage you. To identify a good mentor for you, consider the talents and skills that you would like to observe and learn. Think about the people you admire and respect who have those talents and skills. Decide if you have a healthy relationship that you could build on. Once you've identified several people who might be good mentors, explain what qualities would make each one effective. Identify the person you think might be most effective, and arrange to meet with him or her to discuss the possibility of mentoring you.

Using Technology

1. **Photography.** Find and photograph objects, people, or scenes that symbolize each of the universal values listed in Fig. 3-4. With your classmates, use the photos to create a display that visually interprets each value.

2. **Desktop Publishing.** Use appropriate software to write and illustrate a story that tells how one of your friends has demonstrated character.

CHAPTER 4

Making a Difference

Key Terms

- accountable
- leadership
- collaboration
- service learning

Objectives

- **Defend** the position that your actions can make a positive difference in others' lives.
- **Suggest** ways of showing responsibility in everyday life.
- **Explain** how people in leadership roles affect an organization.
- **Identify** the benefits of volunteering and how to choose a volunteer experience.
- **Discuss** responsibilities of being a citizen.

Think of someone who has made a difference in your life. Write a note of appreciation to the person.

*W*hy are you here on earth? What is the purpose of your life? What should you do with your life? These are important questions.

Life is more than discovering who you are, taking care of yourself, and developing your character. Although these personal growth activities take a major portion of your time and energy, they are not your only purpose. You can also make a difference in the lives of others. Emma, for example, helps at the food pantry once a week. Ramon tutors at an adult literacy program twice a month. Liang and other members of his 4-H club walk a mile of highway every month to pick up litter.

As you have been growing, you have gradually been developing your capacity to think of others. As a preschooler, you were probably taught to share. Throughout your childhood, you learned that your actions impacted others. Now you are learning to reach out to help others improve their lives. Your world is expanding as you move toward adulthood.

Many opportunities exist for you to make a difference at home, at school, at work, and in the community. Start by looking around you, and then do your part.

Doing Your Part

As you think about making a difference, remember this important point: every effort counts. Whether you pick up the clutter around your home or organize a community fundraiser, you are doing your part to make a difference. Sometimes you may work alone; sometimes with others. You may have total responsibility for a task or play a supporting role. At times you may be the leader and at other times a follower. In whatever way you are involved, you will have a positive impact on the people you are working with and working for, and on society as a whole. See Fig. 4-1.

Fig. 4-1. By collecting recyclables, this teen is raising funds for a community service project while at the same time helping the environment. What can you do to make a difference in your community?

Showing Responsibility

No matter how you choose to make a difference, you will be expected to be responsible, do your share, and support others. Being responsible means you are both reliable and **accountable**—willing to accept the consequences of your actions and words.

How can you convince others that you have these qualities? You can show that you are reliable by keeping your word and doing what you say you will do. To show that you are accountable, don't blame others if something goes wrong and it's your fault. Instead, acknowledge your mistakes and take steps to correct them and learn from them. For example, when only two students showed up at a committee meeting, Holly realized that she had forgotten to make the reminder phone calls. She apologized to the committee chair and to the students who showed up. That evening she noted on her calendar when she should call members about the next meeting.

You have many opportunities to show responsibility. For example, you can show personal responsibility by wearing a seat belt. You can show responsibility to your family by following family rules. You can show responsibility to society as a whole by taking action in your community to make life better for all. You can let friends, classmates, teammates, and coworkers know they can count on you by sticking to your commitments. See Fig. 4-2.

Fig. 4-2. Team members are accountable to their teammates. How would you feel if other team members didn't show up to practice?

At Home

There are many opportunities to demonstrate responsibility at home. Many teens slide by, assuming the fewest family responsibilities possible. Others try to complete their assigned chores more or less on time. That shows some responsibility. A more adult approach is to go beyond the minimum. Do your jobs willingly, and take on other things that need doing without being asked. Offer to lend a hand when someone needs help. Be willing to listen if someone has a problem and needs to talk. You may already have discovered how much these little things are

Fig. 4-3. Many families share household responsibilities. How do you fulfill your responsibilities at home?

appreciated. A teen who readily contributes to the family earns the respect, gratitude, and cooperation of others in the family. See Fig. 4-3.

At times, however, showing responsibility requires something more. Caring about your family can mean taking risks. For example, Neva listened as her stepsister Carley talked about "borrowing" their mother's car. Their mother was out of town for a couple of days, and Carley thought it would be exciting to take some of her friends out for a ride. Neva grew concerned. Carley did not have a driver's license and had very little driving experience. Although she knew her message would not be welcomed, Neva trusted in the strength of their relationship. She decided to say something.

"What if you have an accident?" she asked. "What if somebody gets hurt?" As they talked, Neva brought up other possible consequences. At first, Carley was irritated. Eventually, however, she realized that Neva was right, and she abandoned her plan. Both girls showed responsibility.

In School

Showing responsibility at school means more than going to class and doing your homework. It also means doing your part to make your school a safe and supportive environment. When students and staff work together to make a difference in their school, it usually becomes a better place to learn and achieve.

How can you make a contribution? Here are a few ideas. What others would you add to the list?

- **Support school events.** Your presence helps others do their best.

- **Show your school spirit in positive ways.** Putting down another school at a game or competition only gives your school a negative reputation.

- **Protect school property.** Students in many schools have curbed graffiti and vandalism. They know an attractive school is better for everyone. When money must be used for repairs, other programs, such as athletics, clubs, and music, suffer.

- **Help others having difficulty.** Everyone is stronger in some subjects than others. When classmates help one another, everyone benefits. Sometimes just listening can make another's situation better.

- **Treat everyone with respect.** Disrespect, bullying, and harassing others lower morale and negatively impact learning. Respect lifts morale and encourages learning.

Fig. 4-4. Responsible, enthusiastic employees help to create a pleasant working atmosphere. How does this benefit a business?

- **Work to improve your school.** By participating in student government, you can work toward goals that benefit the entire student body.

On the Job

It's not surprising that employers value responsibility so highly. They need employees who arrive at work on time, follow directions, work efficiently, follow workplace rules, and are dependable. Responsible employees feel personally accountable for the tasks assigned to them and do what is necessary to accomplish those tasks. See Fig. 4-4.

Employees who demonstrate responsibility are more likely to receive positive reviews, raises, and promotions. Those who don't may be disciplined or fired. Alex, for example, habitually shows up late at the fast food restaurant where he works. His coworkers are upset at having to work longer and harder because they are short-staffed. After many warnings, the manager has now told Alex that if he's late one more time, he will be fired.

Showing responsibility on the job also benefits others. When all workers are reliable and have a positive attitude, morale is high. By pitching in to help one another, employees create a spirit of cooperation. Those who do business with such a company or organization are more likely to be satisfied customers.

TEXTLINK≈

You will learn more about *responsibility on the job* in Chapter 12.

Participating in Organizations

One effective way to make a difference is to become involved in an organization that interests you. Members of an organization can accomplish much more than they could as individuals. They develop a sense of responsibility and obligation to the organization's mission or purpose. By combining their individual talents, skills, energy, and resources, they work to attain the organization's goals.

Many types of organizations try to make a difference in the lives of their members, others, and society as a whole. School organizations such as Family, Career and Community Leaders of America (FCCLA) and community outreach organizations are two possibilities. Scouts, 4-H, and religious youth organizations encourage teens to help others. As you enter adulthood, you may become interested in civic organizations such as the Lions and Kiwanis. Some professional organizations, such as the American Association of Family and Consumer Sciences, have service and outreach projects.

Taking on Leadership Roles

After you have some experience participating in an organization, you may be asked to take on a leadership role. **Leadership** involves giving people the direction they need to achieve their goals. Leaders influence the actions of a team or group. In essence, they show others the way to go by leading the way.

There are many opportunities for leadership roles in organizations, teams, and groups. You might be a committee chair in a school club, captain of a sports team, or crew leader of employees. Organizations look for people who have the right skills for specific leadership roles. For example, a caring individual would be a good choice to lead a team reaching out to help others. Strong organizational and math skills would be needed for the position of finance committee chair.

Having capable leaders helps organizations keep and attract members and make a difference. Typically, people in leadership roles coordinate their group's efforts, making sure every member is headed in the same direction and focused on the same objectives. They guide and motivate members to reach the organization's goals.

TIPS FOR *Success*

Becoming Actively Involved

If you join an organization, you'll make more of a difference if you become actively involved. Encourage yourself and others to:

- Attend meetings regularly.
- Understand the mission, goals, and activities of the group.
- Participate on a committee.
- Follow through with assigned tasks and responsibilities.
- Develop leadership skills.
- Improve teamwork skills.
- Recruit new members.
- Promote the organization to people you know and meet.

More to Explore

Leadership in FCCLA

Participating in an organization is an ideal way for people to develop leadership skills. For more than 50 years, the organization now known as Family, Career and Community Leaders of America (FCCLA) has allowed students to do just that. FCCLA helps students who are interested in careers in family and consumer sciences. Participating in the group allows teens to build job skills by taking leadership roles.

In FCCLA, opportunities for leadership are limited only by your abilities and energy. You might work as a committee chairperson or a chapter officer, coordinating projects and managing people. If selected by the nominating committee, you can run for office at the district, regional, state, or national level. If elected, you'll participate in planning and work groups and gain experience in public speaking.

Becoming a leader in organizations such as FCCLA provides valuable experience. Interviewing with the nominating committee is good preparation for a college or job interview. Speaking in front of large audiences, managing projects, and dealing with people are skills you can use in your future career. Meeting new people enables you to make connections with others in your field and to exchange ideas and grow as a professional.

Many students don't get this experience until they enter the working world. Organizations like FCCLA give their members a head start.

In any group, success comes from **collaboration**, the cooperative efforts of everyone. Leaders set the example of collaboration. They make sure each person's ideas are welcomed and respected. Every person is encouraged to participate and contribute. How well would groups you belong to score on collaboration?

Most leadership positions last for a specified time period, such as a year or season. At the end of that time period, another person may take over the role. Rotating leadership positions allows an organization, team, or group to fulfill its mission and meet its goals without placing too much pressure on individual members. New leaders bring fresh ideas, and more people are given the chance to develop leadership skills. Everyone benefits.

For some teens, taking on a leadership role is scary and uncomfortable. For others, it's a natural next step in their personal growth.

Whether you are new to leadership roles or have much experience in them, consider their benefits. They give you experience in communicating your ideas to a variety of people in a variety of ways. You learn to resolve conflicts. You develop competence and confidence as you lead and guide others.

Overall, leadership roles help you learn and practice skills that will be useful at work and in your family throughout your life.

TextLink≈

You will learn more about *leadership* in Chapter 16.

Viewpoints

Leaders and Followers

"Leaders are born, not made." Is leadership something that comes easily to some and not at all to others, or can anyone take on a leadership role?

Denyse: Every person has certain talents, and you're happier and more effective if you stick with what you're good at. If you're not comfortable as a leader, you won't enjoy it or feel confident. On the other hand, if you're willing and able to lead, you'll feel frustrated as a follower. Either way, you should use your strongest talents. That's what's best for you and the group.

Leona: I think you limit people by calling them either leaders or followers. Everyone has leadership skills. Some people just aren't comfortable using them. They should be encouraged, even pushed a little. Leading a group builds a special sense of pride. It helps people gain confidence. And that helps everyone, because we need all the good leaders we can find.

Seeing Both Sides ~ What different ideas might people have about leaders and their duties? How might these ideas affect how a person feels about assuming this role?

Volunteering in Your Community

In communities everywhere, people make a difference in the lives of many through volunteering. A volunteer is someone who puts caring into action by offering services free of charge. When you volunteer, you offer your talents, skills, and time to improve the lives of others.

Some people volunteer from a sense of duty; others do so because they care deeply about a cause. Lionel, for example, is a college senior majoring in architecture. He's determined to become a Peace Corps volunteer and work to help needy people construct decent homes. Lionel is willing to put a promising career on hold to make a difference across the world. People who are committed to a cause—as Lionel is—give more, expect less, and sacrifice much. They tend to be more involved and dedicated in donating their time and energy.

Benefits of Volunteering

Every community has many needs. Community programs meant to meet those needs often have low operating budgets and must rely on the work of volunteers to be effective. How much they can do is directly linked to how many willing hands are extended. Volunteers with enthusiasm, talents, skills, and time make the difference.

Although you receive no money for volunteer work, it brings many rewards. You learn job skills and gain valuable work experience. You can also develop a network of people who share your interests. This network may lead to friendships, further training and skill development, or information about job opportunities. You will likely work with people of different ages and from different areas of the community. This enables you to interact with a variety of people and learn more about the community you live in. Finally, one of most rewarding benefits is that helping others brings you feelings of self-worth and fulfillment.

Ways to Help

Many teens want to volunteer, but aren't sure how to start. They might not know how or where to direct their efforts. A good way to begin is by taking a look at yourself. What are you interested in? Are there any causes that particularly concern you? What issues or problems have touched your life or the lives of people you know? Have you been moved by news stories about a particular need in your community or the larger world?

Also think about what activities you like to do and what you're good at. You'll want to choose a volunteer activity that you not only believe is worthwhile but also will enjoy. That way you will be more likely to stick with it. For example, do you prefer working inside or outside? Do you enjoy talking with older people or playing with young children? Consider the skills you would like to share or learn and the amount of time you have to give. See Fig. 4-5.

Now you're ready to start looking for a volunteer opportunity that matches your interests, skills, and schedule. You can find ideas for volunteering by talking to a school counselor, reading the newspaper, or checking your community's Web site. Some communities have an agency that keeps track of opportunities for volunteers in the area. Here are just a few of the many ways you might volunteer:

- Help at a local food bank, senior citizens' center, or animal shelter.

Fig. 4-5. *This teen helps older adults who want to improve their computer skills. How could you use your skills to help others in your community?*

- Participate in a charity walkathon or race.
- Join Habitat for Humanity, which helps build or renovate houses for low-income families.
- Coach a Special Olympics team.
- Help beautify your community by planting flowers or building bike trails.
- Take part in a neighborhood cleanup campaign.
- Counsel others on a teen hot line.
- Help with a campaign to combat violence, drunk driving, or drug abuse.
- Work with a recycling or hazardous waste removal program.

Service Learning

An effective way to help others is through a service learning project. **Service learning** involves taking what you learn in the classroom and using it to meet a community need. Students often choose and plan their own service learning experiences in partnership with their school and a community agency or organization. Many times students receive classroom credit for their work. Service learning also provides opportunities for students to learn new skills and to explore and investigate various careers.

Check to see whether your school already has a service learning program in place. If you find that your school doesn't have a program, a school counselor or teacher may be willing to help you develop a service learning project that will meet a community need. For example, if you are studying horticulture, you or your class might work with the park district to design plantings for a new park. Your involvement can help make your community a better place to live.

Becoming a Responsible Citizen

Volunteering is one way to show responsibility as a citizen. You are a citizen of your country, your school, and your community. As a citizen, you have certain rights, including the right to receive an education and to be protected by the police. Citizenship also brings with it certain responsibilities:

- **Respect others' rights.** Treat other people as you expect to be treated. Show respect for their individuality, their needs, and their property.

- **Obey laws.** Communities and countries make laws for the good of all. You have a responsibility to obey the laws, including traffic laws. See Fig. 4-6.

- **Prevent and report crime.** Fighting crime means more than avoiding criminal activity. It begins with prevention. Neighborhood watch programs are one example. You have a responsibility to report crimes you are aware of and to cooperate with police investigations. In these ways, you help prevent further crimes, protecting yourself and others.

- **Comply with emergency and security procedures.** In a severe drought, for example, citizens may be asked to restrict their water usage. Cooperating with security measures, such as allowing your bags to be searched, helps keep everyone safe.

- **Pay taxes.** Many government services are financed by taxes. Citizens are obliged to pay their full share or risk punishment. Once you begin earning a certain level of income per year, you will pay taxes on it.

Fig. 4-6. By obeying traffic laws, you can make the roads safer for everyone—and avoid violations and fines.

- **Stay informed.** By keeping up with the local, national, and international news, you stay aware of what is going on around you. This helps you make informed decisions and take responsible actions.

- **Participate in government.** When you and others attend meetings and voice your opinions, you can change government policies. What the public says influences those in leadership positions.

- **Take part in elections.** When you reach age 18, you will be eligible to vote in national, state, and local elections. If you feel that a person in office is not doing a good job, you can vote for somebody else. Even before you can vote, you can help candidates you believe in campaign for election. You might even run for office yourself one day.

- **Perform jury duty when called.** You may be called to serve on a jury after you reach age 18. The jury system is basic to our form of justice. Jurors listen to evidence presented in a trial and then, in consensus with other jurors, reach a verdict based on the evidence. See Fig. 4-7.

- **Serve in the military if called.** Young people in the United States can volunteer to serve in the military, but they are not required to do so in times of peace. However, there have been times of war and crisis when people have been called to serve in the military. At those times, if you are called to serve, it is important that you do so in some way.

Fig. 4-7. Jury duty is a responsibility of citizenship. Why would it be important to serve on a jury?

Citizens who truly care about their communities actively work to make them better for all. They are willing to volunteer to help others, and they accept responsibility for their civic duties.

Whatever you do, don't just sit back and do nothing, thinking that the actions of one individual don't matter. They do, to yourself as well as to others. As a family member, student, employee, leader, volunteer, and citizen, whatever constructive steps you take are significant. When you develop the habit of helping, you cultivate the attitude of caring. Then you discover what a difference you really can make.

Review & Activities

Chapter Summary

- Throughout life, you will have many opportunities to make a difference in the lives of others.

- You can show responsibility by being reliable and accountable at home, in school, and on the job.

- Getting involved in an organization is an effective way to make a difference.

- Leadership roles present opportunities to build skills and confidence.

- Capable leaders encourage the participation and cooperation of everyone.

- Volunteering to improve the lives of others brings many rewards.

- As a citizen, you have certain rights and responsibilities. Taking an active role in your community helps make it a better place to live.

Reviewing Key Terms & Ideas

1. If you do something wrong, how can you show that you are **accountable** for your mistake?

2. Give two examples of ways you can show responsibility at home.

3. How does a school benefit when students and staff work together to make a difference?

4. Why is joining an organization often more effective than working as an individual?

5. What does **leadership** involve? How do organizations benefit from having competent people in leadership roles?

6. Why is **collaboration** important to the success of group activities?

7. Give three examples of benefits people get from volunteering.

8. Identify at least three things to consider when choosing a volunteer experience.

9. What does **service learning** involve?

10. Why do citizens need to stay informed?

Thinking Critically

1. **Inferring Meaning.** Discuss the meaning of the saying, "Bloom where you are planted." How might it be applied to the idea of making a difference?

2. **Analyzing Behavior.** After reviewing the responsibilities of citizenship, determine which three are taken most seriously by teens you know and which three are taken least seriously. Explain your reasoning. What are the effects of these trends, short-term and long-term?

Applying Your Knowledge

1. **Finding a Volunteer Match.** Evaluate your talents, skills, and areas of concern. Research community volunteer needs. Identify at least two volunteer opportunities that might be a good match for you, and explain why.

2. **Creating a Leadership Description.** Identify a leadership role of an organization, team, or group you participate in. Create a job description of the leadership role.

3. **Recruiting Volunteers.** Identify a need for volunteers in a school or community organization. Write a school announcement or student editorial aimed at persuading students to volunteer for the identified need.

Making Connections

1. **Math.** Tally the number of volunteer hours per week the students in your class perform. Based on the total for this sample, predict the number of volunteer hours logged by students in your school. Describe the impact those volunteers have on the community.

2. **Social Studies.** Review a historical document or famous speech given by a national leader (such as the Declaration of Independence or a presidential or civil rights leader's address). Describe how the document or speech inspires citizens to make a difference.

Managing Your Life

Planning for a Leadership Role

Think about a leadership role that you believe you are qualified to hold in your school or in an organization to which you belong. Possibilities include class treasurer, student council representative, or officer in FCCLA. Write and record a speech in which you identify your leadership skills, explain why you would be a good choice for the position, and urge others to vote for you. Make use of your speech when you find the right opportunity.

Using Technology

1. **Spreadsheet.** Create a spreadsheet for logging your volunteer activities and the hours you contribute. Enter enough data (real or sample) to demonstrate how it works. Keep the spreadsheet updated for future use in completing college, scholarship, and job applications.

2. **Internet.** Conduct an Internet search for service learning ideas. Create a page in Web browser (HTML) format with links to the best sites. If possible, get permission to post your page on the school Web site.

Career Options
Health and Medicine

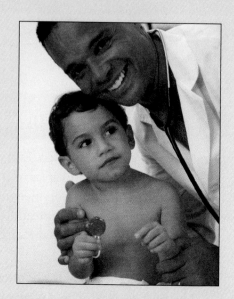

Health and medicine is one of the largest industries in the country, providing health care services to millions. Although many career opportunities in health and medicine require advanced education and training, some entry-level positions are available. The field can be divided into three broad sectors: Medical and Dental, Nursing, and Administration. For most occupations in this career cluster, employment opportunities are expected to rise steadily.

Main Employers

- Hospitals
- Clinics
- Medical offices
- Dental offices
- Nursing homes
- Home health care services
- Medical laboratories

Health and Medicine Job Opportunities

Industry Segment	Entry Level	Additional Education and/or Training	Advanced Education and/or Training
Medical and Dental	- Medical Assistant - Receptionist	- Dental Assistant - Dental Hygienist - Dental Lab Technician - Physical Therapy Assistant - Emergency Medical Technician	- Surgeon - Dentist - Orthodontist - Physical Therapist - Chiropractor - Dietitian - Physician
Nursing	- Nursing Aide - Nursing Orderly - Home Health Aide	- Licensed Practical Nurse (LPN) - Registered Nurse (RN)	- Nurse Practitioner - Certified Nurse-Midwife
Administration	- Medical Records Clerk - Admitting Clerk - Billing Clerk	- Medical Secretary - Admitting Manager - Health Services Manager	- Hospital Administrator - Public Health Administrator

| Karen O'Neill, **DIETITIAN**

Growing up, I thought that I would be happy with almost any nine-to-five job. After graduation, I started working at a local store. Eventually, I was promoted to assistant manager. I liked my job and had no intention of going to college.

Then my father was diagnosed with diabetes. The doctor sent him to a dietitian to help him learn how to eat better and lose weight to manage his disease. My mom and I went with him. The dietitian helped us understand the importance of following a healthful eating plan. At that meeting, I realized that I had found a career that I was really interested in.

I needed a college degree to become a dietitian. I found that a career in dietetics required so much knowledge of science. I had courses not only in nutrition and foods but also in biology, microbiology, chemistry, and physiology. I completed my internship at a local hospital. After earning my degree and dietitian license, the hospital hired me full-time. I'm still there!

I work with patients with health problems such as high blood pressure, heart disease, and diabetes. I assess their nutritional needs and develop nutrition programs to help them manage their conditions and improve their health. I also work with doctors to coordinate the patients' care. I really enjoy my work, and I have my dad to thank for helping me to find my career path!

Check It *Out!*

Choose three health and medicine occupations that require advanced education and training. Using print or online resources, learn about the qualifications needed for each, including degree, license, certification, and/or practical experience. Compile a chart of your findings.

2

Management Skills

Learning to Manage

Key Terms

- prioritize
- short-term goal
- long-term goal
- resource
- resourceful
- contingency plans

Objectives

- **Discuss** reasons for and influences on priorities.
- **Explain** the benefits of setting goals and the different types of goals.
- **Identify** resources that help people achieve their goals.
- **Compare** strategies for making the most of resources.
- **Outline** the four steps of the management process.

What does the word *manage* mean to you? Write a brief definition, then explain why everyone needs to learn how to manage.

*O*ne of the many challenges of the teen years is to learn to manage your own life. Over the next few years you will need to decide how you will earn a living, spend your time, use your resources, and reach your goals. Sounds pretty daunting, doesn't it? Fortunately, managing is just like many other life skills: it's something you can learn, practice, and get better at.

Learning the basics of managing now will help you in the short term and the longer term. It will help you determine your priorities, set career and personal goals, use your time, money, energy, and other resources effectively, and find ways of balancing your work and social life. You will get more out of your life. Managing your life starts with determining what your priorities are.

Establishing Priorities

What dreams and plans do you have for the years ahead? Perhaps you have so many ideas about what you want to do that sorting them out seems overwhelming. Accomplishing everything you want to do may not be reasonable or even possible.

That's why you need to prioritize. When you **prioritize**, you decide which goals and activities are most important to you. Identifying your priorities gives you a direction to follow as you learn to manage your life. See Fig. 5-1.

Fig. 5-1. Your priorities affect many choices that you make, from how you spend your free time to the goals you set for the future.

Needs and Wants

Establishing your priorities starts with taking a close look at your needs and wants. Needs are those things you must have for survival, such as basic food, clothing, and shelter. Wants, on the other hand, are things that you desire but that aren't essential. It's easy to fall into the trap of thinking that certain wants are needs. If you already have several pairs of jeans, do you really *need* another pair, or do you just *want* them? Being able to tell the difference between needs and wants is essential to setting priorities. Good managers focus on meeting needs before wants. See Fig. 5-2.

The Role of Values

When setting priorities, also examine your values—the beliefs and ideas that guide your life. They help you determine what is more important, less important, and unimportant. If you value good health, for instance, good nutrition and exercise may be priorities. If you value education, then getting good grades, graduating, and being accepted into college may be priorities. Your values help steer you toward what is right for you and away from activities that are not in your best interest.

Differing Priorities

Priorities differ from person to person. Dylan's life revolves around sports—playing on the basketball and soccer teams, joining in pick-up games, and following teams on TV. His brother Justin, on the other hand, thinks sports are boring. He would rather play his guitar or write songs for his band. In spite of those differences, spending time together is a high priority for both of them. They like to talk, watch science fiction movies, and go fishing.

Figuring out your priorities isn't a one-time job. Right now, your list might include getting your driver's license or finding a part-time job. When you graduate, what do you think your priorities will include? How might they change if you get married and start a family? Life changes cause priorities to shift.

Fig. 5-2. You might need transportation to get to work, but having the sports car of your dreams is a want that you can live without. *Name other examples of needs and wants.*

Viewpoints

Different Priorities

Everyone makes their own choices. What happens when people have different priorities? Is there any way to reach an understanding?

Nick: My friends don't understand why I won't go out with them more often. Sure, I like to have fun, but right now my schoolwork and my part-time job have to come first. I just wish I could make my friends understand my priorities. I don't mean to hurt their feelings, but sometimes when they ask me to go to a movie or a party with them, I have to say no.

Jonathan: It's true that things like school and jobs are important. But it's not healthy to spend all your time on serious stuff. Other things in life are important, too. If you never spend time with your friends, they won't be there for you when you need them.

Seeing Both Sides ~ Do you think Nick and Jonathan have each based their priorities on their values? What tells you this? Why is awareness important for getting along with people who have different priorities?

Setting Goals

Once you know your priorities, you can set appropriate goals. A goal is something you consciously aim to achieve and are willing to plan and work for. The ability to set and meet goals is a basic tool for managing your life.

Like priorities, your goals are personal. You and your friends probably have a common goal of graduating, but may have very different career goals. That's because the goals you choose are influenced by your own particular needs, wants, values, and priorities.

It's not just individuals who set goals. Families, businesses, communities, and other groups or organizations often set them as well. One family's goal might be to save enough money for a down payment on a home. Another family might focus on helping an elderly relative stay in her own home as long as possible. A business might set a goal of increasing production or sales by 10 percent. A community might set a goal of building a new recreation center.

Even though people and groups have different goals, they set them for the same reasons. Goals give direction and a sense of purpose. Without goals, it's easy to just drift along, not really making progress. If at age 50 you realized that you had accomplished very few of the things you wanted to do in your life, how would you feel? By starting now to become comfortable with setting and working toward goals, you can make your whole life more fulfilling. Achieving goals gives you a sense of accomplishment, boosts your self-confidence, and improves your self-esteem. See Fig. 5-3.

Short-Term and Long-Term Goals

A **short-term goal** is something you want to accomplish soon. Examples of short-term goals are baking brownies for tomorrow's bake sale, fixing your brother's bike, reading a favorite author's new book, and learning a software application. A **long-term goal** is something you plan to accomplish further in the future, perhaps in six months, a year, or after you finish high school. Long-term goals might be to make the debate team next spring, win a gymnastics competition in two years, or become a graphic designer.

A long-term goal can seem overwhelming if viewed as a single task. Breaking it down into short-term goals will make it seem much more manageable and attainable. Mario's church youth group learned this when they took up the challenge of beautifying a nearby vacant lot. When the teens real-

Fig. 5-3. *Having a goal can motivate you to work harder and reach higher than you thought possible.* How do you feel when you succeed in reaching a goal?

ized how much work needed to be done, they nearly gave up. Their leader suggested breaking the project into three phases: planning, cleaning up the lot, and installing new landscaping. They decided what they had to accomplish in each phase and set weekly goals. They asked friends, neighbors, and local businesses to help. By the time school was out, the lot had flowers, some new trees, benches, and individual garden plots for nearby residents. Whatever the long-term goal, thinking it through and identifying specific short-term goals can help you achieve it.

Fixed and Flexible Goals

A fixed goal is one that can be met only at a certain time. If you want a part in the school play, for instance, you will need to be ready for tryouts. Fixed goals are often tied to specific dates over which a person has no control.

Flexible goals, on the other hand, have no definite time limit. Building your savings is an example of a flexible goal. It's ongoing, and the amount of money saved can vary from time to time. However, if you're saving to buy a computer before the new school year begins, then it becomes a fixed goal.

Fixed and flexible goals can be either short- or long-term goals. Preparing to take the SAT test in six months is a fixed, long-term goal. Preparing for next week's history test is a fixed, short-term goal. Distinguishing between fixed and flexible goals helps you better manage your time in order to meet them. See Fig. 5-4.

Aiming for Success

When it comes to goals, some people never get beyond the dreaming stage. To make your goals a reality, you need to stay focused and motivated. Many people have found these suggestions helpful:

- **Analyze your goals.** Begin by weighing a possible goal against your needs, wants, values, and priorities to decide if it's really worthwhile. If so, analyze further. Is the goal short-term or long-term? Is its timing fixed or flexible? Do you need to break the overall goal down into smaller short-term goals? Should you tackle this goal immediately or put it aside for later?

- **Be realistic.** Goals that are challenging can spur you to learn, grow, and seek new experiences. They are likely to be more

satisfying than goals that are too easy to achieve. However, if your goals are too hard to reach, or if you set too many, you might give up on them in frustration. It's best to be realistic. Choose goals that challenge you, but that can be reached with a reasonable amount of effort.

- **Be specific.** State goals in specific terms that will enable you to measure your progress. For instance, which of these goals is worded more effectively: "Be more

Fig. 5-4. Learning a new piece for a piano recital is a fixed goal. Why?

physically active" or "Work out at least 30 minutes five days a week"? With the second goal, you know exactly what action to take, and you can easily determine your progress and level of success.

- **Put goals in writing.** Once you choose a goal, write it down. Try posting some of your goals where you will see them often, maybe on your mirror or inside your locker door. This can help you stay on track. Some people record their goals and progress in a notebook. They find that doing so makes them more likely to achieve the results they want.

- **Follow through.** It's all too easy to set goals and then abandon them for one reason or another. When you set a reasonable goal that is well thought out, believe in yourself. Know that you can accomplish it, and then set out to do so.

Identifying Your Resources

In order to reach your goals, you need to manage your available resources. A **resource** is something you can use to achieve a goal. Although there are many types of resources, they fall into four main categories: human, material, community, and natural. Everyone has these resources, though in varying amounts. Learning to recognize the resources available to you is the first step in managing them. See Fig. 5-5.

Human Resources

Human resources are found within yourself and other people. They include *knowledge* and *skills*. Knowledge consists of everything you read, observe, learn, and remember. Your skills might range from

Fig. 5-5. You make use of resources every day. A museum is a community resource. *What other examples of resources can you identify in this scene?*

using a computer to swimming, playing a musical instrument, or making things from wood.

Creativity is another human resource. Your creativity is what enables you to come up with original solutions to problems and unique ways of expressing yourself. To accomplish tasks and achieve goals, you also need two other human resources: *time* and *energy*.

Family and friends are also human resources. You might be able to call upon their knowledge, skills, creativity, time, and energy in addition to your own. Of course, you can do the same for them.

Material Resources

Material resources are all the physical objects you can use to accomplish your goals. Money is perhaps the most obvious example. If your goal is to learn how to play tennis, money can help you reach that goal by enabling you to pay for a tennis racket, shoes, and lessons.

Material resources also include tools, equipment, and other possessions. Serena is using one of her family's possessions—a sewing machine—to make bright fleece hats and mittens that she sells at craft shows. She is saving the money she earns to get a fashion merchandising degree after graduation. In what ways have you used material resources to reach goals?

Technology has expanded both the variety of material resources that are available and their capabilities. Think of all the ways in which computers, cell phones, satellites, and lifesaving medical equipment—to name just a few examples—have impacted people's lives.

Fig. 5-6. Community resources, such as a public library, benefit everybody. *What community resources are available to you?*

Community Resources

Communities also offer resources that can help you enjoy life, improve your skills, and solve problems. They include facilities such as schools, libraries, hospitals, museums, parks, and theaters. Places of worship, shopping malls, and public transportation are other examples of community resources. See Fig. 5-6.

The businesses in your community provide access to many additional resources. Through them, people are able to learn new skills, earn money, and purchase products they need or want.

People in the community can also provide valuable help. Teachers can expand your learning. School counselors and religious leaders can help you deal with problems. Doctors, dentists, and other medical professionals can help you stay healthy. Perhaps there's someone who is an expert on a topic that interests you and is willing to share that knowledge or skill.

Natural Resources

The resources found in nature include air, water, soil, plants, and minerals. Some, such as clean air and drinking water, are necessary for survival. People have also come to depend on sources of fuel such as gas, oil, and coal. Without natural resources, your options would be severely limited. For these reasons and more, natural resources, like any other resources, need to be used wisely.

Using Resources Wisely

To make the best use of the resources available to you, you need to understand their limits and know how to make the most of them. In other words, you need to be resourceful. People who are **resourceful** are able to use creative problem solving to manage available resources wisely. The ability to come up with creative, efficient ways to manage resources helps them deal with both everyday situations and unusual challenges.

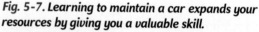

Fig. 5-7. Learning to maintain a car expands your resources by giving you a valuable skill.

Resourceful people use several strategies to make the most of their resources. These strategies include expanding, exchanging, conserving, and substituting resources.

Expanding Resources

Some resources, such as your knowledge and skills, can be expanded—you can add to your supply. To improve your drawing skills, for example, you might take lessons and practice drawing every day. To learn more about car care and repair, you could read books, do online research, take a class, or work with someone who knows how. See Fig. 5-7.

TIPS FOR Success

Maximizing Your Creativity

The ability to think creatively is a valuable resource. Sometimes creative thinking is referred to as "thinking outside the box" because it isn't constrained by conventional rules or solutions. Think of your imagination as a muscle, one that can gain strength and flexibility through workouts. Build this muscle by brainstorming, either alone or with friends or family. Challenge yourself to find unique solutions to problems. Often just letting a problem "sit" in your mind—instead of forcing an immediate answer—allows you to come up with a more creative solution.

Personal energy is another resource that you may be able to increase. Energy comes from eating nutritious foods, being physically active, and getting enough rest. Your energy level also depends on your attitude. A positive attitude gives you more energy and enthusiasm. That makes it easier to overcome obstacles and get things done.

Conserving Resources

Some resources can't be increased because the supply is fixed. In that case, you need to make the most of what you have. You can do this by conserving, or saving, resources. When you conserve resources, you use them in the most efficient way possible.

Time is a good example. Everyone has the same 24 hours each day. Why is it that some people seem to get everything done on time with ease, while others struggle with deadlines? There are lots of reasons, including personality and other responsibilities. However, anyone can take better charge of time through planning and wise choices. You will learn the ins and outs of time management in Chapter 7.

Some natural resources, such as oil and coal, are also in limited supply. Once they are used up, they can't be replaced. Conserving these resources will allow them to last as long as possible. People can conserve by reducing consumption, reusing, and recycling whenever possible. Conserving also means protecting resources such as air and water from becoming polluted.

TEXTLINK≈

You can learn more about *conserving natural resources* in Chapter 50.

Taking care of your possessions is another way to conserve resources. Giving possessions the right care will keep them usable as long as possible. You'll save money and have more options for reaching your goals. Like possessions, community resources also need to be cared for so they remain available for others. Whenever you use a community resource, that care becomes your personal responsibility. Whether it's cleaning up after a picnic or returning library books on time, do your part.

Exchanging Resources

Have you ever exchanged resources with someone else? Perhaps you've traded clothes with a family member or offered your skills and time to help a friend. This can be another useful way to manage resources.

Matt wants to learn how to play the guitar. His sister Katelyn, who has been playing for several years, has loaned him her guitar and is teaching him the basics. Katelyn knows she can count on Matt to help her with any computer problems she has. Each has resources to offer the other.

Your family, friends, and people in the community may have resources that they're willing to share with you. Don't be afraid to ask for help when you need it. You, in turn, should be ready to return the favor.

Substituting Resources

In some situations, resources that are plentiful can be substituted for others that are in short supply. Suppose that your grandmother's birthday is next week, and you don't have much money to spend on a gift for her. You do, however, have the time, skills, and creativity to make a gift yourself. You might decide to frame a photo that you took, create a personalized screensaver, or make a book of coupons for household tasks that you're willing to do. By substituting the resources that you have in place of the money you lack, you can accomplish your goal.

Fig. 5-8. In the working world, good managers learn to make the best use of their resources. The same skills can help you manage everyday challenges in your own life.

The Management Process

By now you know the importance of establishing priorities, setting goals, and maximizing resources to meet those goals. But how do you put it all together? How can you bridge the gap between just thinking about your goals and making them happen?

What you need is a systematic way of working toward your goals. Fortunately, people experienced in good management have come up with just such a system. It's called the management process, and it's useful for all kinds of situations. See Fig. 5-8.

The management process involves four steps:

1. Planning
2. Organizing
3. Implementing
4. Evaluating

Keep in mind that this management process doesn't define everything included in management. Being a good manager involves a variety of skills, including decision making, problem solving, communication, leadership, organization, critical thinking, and creative thinking. You will learn about management skills throughout this book.

Think of the management process as a road map. It helps you find the most effective ways to use your resources in order to achieve your goals. You are more likely to reach any significant goal—short-term or long-term—if you use this process. It works whether you're trying to accomplish goals on your own or as part of a group. The more complex the task or project, the more important the management process becomes.

Character IN ACTION

Fulfilling Commitments When you make commitments to yourself and others, you are promising that you can be relied on. Management skills can help you fulfill those commitments. When you set priorities, use resources wisely, and plan and organize your work, you increase your ability to achieve what you have promised. Give an example of a commitment you have made and the management skills that you use to meet it.

Planning

There's an old expression, "If you fail to plan, you plan to fail." Do you often find yourself scrambling to finish a big project at the last minute? Lack of planning might be the reason. When you take time to plan, you can get more done and use your resources more effectively. Successful planning includes these steps:

- **Identify your goals.** What do you want to accomplish? Put it into words and write it down. Besides your primary goal, identify the secondary goals that fill in the specific details. For example, if you're planning an anniversary party for your aunt and uncle, some of your goals might be to invite relatives and friends, to provide food, and to present the couple with a gift from the whole family.

- **Establish your priorities.** While you're thinking about your goals, consider which ones matter most to you. In case you're not able to accomplish everything you hope to, you will need to make choices. Use what you've learned about setting priorities to decide which of your goals are most important.

- **Assess your resources.** What resources are available to help you meet your goals? Make a list. If you include family and friends as resources, make sure they are able and willing to help.

- **Create a task list.** Based on the resources you have available, decide how you'll accomplish each goal. Will you buy food that's already prepared, make it yourself, or ask everyone to bring something? Then make a list of all the steps you will need to complete. Try not to leave anything out, down to the smallest detail. If you're planning to make food yourself, for instance, remember to include shopping for ingredients, preparing the food, and cleaning up.

As you plan, anticipate possible problems that could occur. Then develop **contingency plans**—alternative courses of action that could help you overcome potential obstacles. If you plan to serve food outdoors, what will you do if it rains? In case something goes wrong, having contingency plans will help ensure success. You'll know how to achieve your goals in a different way.

Organizing

After you make your plans, the next step is to get organized. Good organization is essential to making tasks go smoothly. To get organized, you need to:

- **Create a schedule.** How much time will you need to perform each task on your list? Which tasks must be completed first? Develop a sequence of events that charts your course of action. If you're trying to meet several goals, look for efficient ways to juggle the various tasks required. For example, buying party supplies and shopping for a gift might be combined into one errand.

Fig. 5-9. The organizing phase is especially important when you're working with others. What might happen if the members of a group didn't coordinate their efforts?

- **Gather your resources**. Are all the resources you will need ready to use? Check that any required equipment is in good working order. If other people will be working with you, get together and decide how to coordinate your efforts. See Fig. 5-9.

Implementing

Now that your planning and organizing is complete, it's time to carry out, or *implement*, your plan. Use the resources you have gathered and follow the task list according to your schedule. See Fig. 5-10.

As you work through your plan, track your progress. If you're experiencing problems or something unexpected comes up, consider turning to an appropriate contingency plan. For example, if you're not completing tasks on schedule, you may need to ask for additional help or reexamine your priorities.

Evaluating

You might think that after planning, organizing, and implementing, the management process is complete. One final step remains, however. After you have finished your work, you need to take stock of your plan and how well you carried it out. Doing so will help you manage more successfully in the future.

Start by evaluating your results—did you accomplish your goals? Don't stop there, however. Evaluate the process you used, too. If you met your goals, what enabled you to succeed? What could you have done to make things work even more smoothly?

If some goals didn't get accomplished, try to analyze what happened. Did you set goals that were too ambitious? Did you fail to

Fig. 5-10. A plan does no good unless you put it into action. Once you do, all your planning and preparation will pay off.

make the best use of your resources? Did you forget to include something in your task list or schedule? Did a problem arise that you didn't anticipate? Sometimes people have a perfectly good plan, but don't follow it. If that's what happened to you, think about what you can do next time to track your progress and stay motivated.

Evaluating helps you learn from your experiences. Each time you use the management process, you will get better at it. By the time you have more responsibilities and more complicated goals to meet, managing will become second nature.

Review & Activities

Chapter Summary

- When establishing priorities, consider your needs, wants, and values.
- Goals may be short-term or long-term, fixed or flexible.
- Goals that are well thought out are more likely to be achieved.
- Human, material, community, and natural resources can all help you meet goals.
- Resourceful people know how to expand, conserve, exchange, and substitute resources.
- The management process involves planning, organizing, implementing, and evaluating.

Reviewing Key Terms & Ideas

1. Why is it necessary to **prioritize**?
2. How does examining needs, wants, and values help you set priorities?
3. Why do you need to set goals? What might happen if you had no goals?
4. Give an example of a **short-term goal** and of a **long-term goal**.
5. What is the difference between a fixed goal and a flexible goal?
6. How can you increase your chances of successfully achieving your goals? Give at least three guidelines.
7. Give an example of each of the four main categories of **resources**.
8. What does it mean to be **resourceful**?
9. Why is it important to conserve natural resources?
10. What is the difference between exchanging resources and substituting resources?
11. What is the purpose of **contingency plans**?
12. Describe what happens in each of the four steps of the management process.

Thinking Critically

1. **Defending Your Position.** Identify a goal, then determine what you think is the most important resource for accomplishing that goal. Be prepared to defend your choice.
2. **Drawing Conclusions.** Can planning help you achieve more in the same amount of time? Why or why not?

Applying Your Knowledge

1. **Identifying Short-Term Goals.** Choose a long-term goal. Identify at least six different short-term goals that could contribute to the long-term goal.

2. **Creating a Task List.** Choose a simple task, such as replacing a light bulb or making a sandwich. List all resources needed and the sequence of steps. Then team up with a partner. As you describe each step, your partner will act out the task. Evaluate the results. What have you learned from this exercise?

Making Connections

1. **Math.** Because resources can be exchanged for one another, the time, energy, and skills used to accomplish a task can be assigned a monetary value. To demonstrate this, choose a task such as mowing a lawn or knitting a sweater. Establish the scope of the task (for example, the size of the lawn), then estimate the amount of time required. What would you consider a fair hourly rate for the labor involved? What would be the total labor cost? Be prepared to explain your estimates and calculations.

2. **Social Studies.** Choose a government program that interests you—either local or national. Find out what the priorities are, what goals have been set, and what is being done to manage available resources. Prepare a brief report of your findings.

Managing Your Life

Making the Most of Human Resources

Like everyone, you have resources that are found within yourself: knowledge, skills, creativity, and energy. It's easy to take these resources for granted, yet they can be very valuable in helping you meet your goals. In writing, assess your own human resources. What are the areas in which you have knowledge? What skills and talents do you possess? How have you shown your creativity and energy? Think of as many examples as you can. Then write down at least ten specific ways in which you could expand those resources. Save your list for future use.

Using Technology

1. **Presentation Software.** Use appropriate software to create a presentation for the class on the wise use of resources. Include both visual images and text to demonstrate the concepts of expanding, conserving, exchanging, and substituting resources.

2. **Management Software.** Learn about a software program that is designed to help businesses manage tasks and resources. You might gather information from the Web site of the software company or from product reviews in magazines, for example. Prepare a report that explains how the software could be beneficial to the management process.

Making Decisions and Solving Problems

Objectives

- **Analyze** influences on people's choices.
- **Explain** how choices impact you and others.
- **Demonstrate** the decision-making process.
- **Identify** the characteristics of practical problems.
- **Apply** methods for solving practical problems.

QUICK WRITE

List five decisions that you made in the last week. Which ones were hardest to make? Why?

*H*ave you ever watched a carpenter or a mechanic select a tool or combination of tools for a particular job? Because of their skills and experience, these workers know which tools they need. Just as a carpenter or mechanic selects the right tools for the job, you need to select the best processes to help you make decisions and solve problems. This chapter will give you several approaches for your tool kit. With practice, using these "tools" will become second nature.

Looking at Decisions and Problems

Every day you face decisions and problems. Some are so routine that you may not even be aware that you're making them. Others are difficult dilemmas that could have serious consequences. These situations may seem so complicated that it's hard to know where to begin. Sometimes you may think it would be easier if someone else would just make the choices for you!

You're more likely to make good choices if you are proactive. **Proactive** people anticipate future decisions or problems and take action. They don't ignore a problem, hoping that it will go away. They act as soon as they realize that something needs to be done, and they don't let fear of making a wrong decision stand in their way. Nor do they let others make decisions for them. Proactive people recognize and accept their responsibility for their own decisions and actions. See Fig. 6-1.

Fig. 6-1. Submitting an application as soon as you hear about a job opening would be proactive. What are some other ways you could be proactive?

Influences on Choices

Whether you're faced with a decision or a problem, you don't make choices in a vacuum. Many factors influence the choices you make—some from within yourself and others from outside. Some influences promote wise choices; others can get in their way.

- **Attitude.** How do you react when confronted by decisions or problems? Do you view them as unwelcome obstacles or as opportunities for growth? Facing decisions and problems doesn't have to be a negative experience. With a positive attitude, you can often see more options. Keeping an optimistic outlook can help you approach

Viewpoints

Approaches to Making Decisions

"Think it through." "Just decide!" These attitudes certainly reflect different approaches to decision making. Can only one be right? How can you decide how to decide?

Gina: The best decisions I've made came after I learned the facts and thought things through. In fact, if I can't decide about something, it's usually a sign that I need more information. Sure, it takes time, but it saves time in the end—time spent trying to undo bad decisions. When you think about the cost of making a bad decision, you know it's worth the effort and patience.

Melissa: If you take too long figuring out what you want, the opportunity may be gone. Another person involved might take back an offer or ask someone else, leaving one less option for you. And if you try to look at every angle and get every opinion, you're almost asking other people to choose for you. Either way, you limit your options, and that doesn't lead to the best decision.

Seeing Both Sides ~ Do Gina and Melissa seem to take decision making seriously? How do you know this? What might explain their differing approaches? What compromise regarding making decisions might they agree to?

Fig. 6-2. Even though you are striving for independence, you can still ask your family for advice when you need it.

decisions and problems as interesting challenges and learning experiences.

- **Emotions.** Have you ever made a decision on impulse because of how you felt at the time—hungry, bored, irritated, elated? Your emotions can have a powerful effect on the choices you make. They can sometimes lead to poor decisions or stand in the way of solving a problem. The strategies explained in this chapter will help you avoid these pitfalls.

- **Values, goals, and priorities.** These are the foundation upon which wise choices are made. You'll want to make decisions and solve problems in a way that reflects the values you hold, the goals you want to achieve, and the priorities you have set.

- **Ethics.** Your **ethics** are the principles and values that guide the way you live, based on what you believe to be just and fair. For example, one of your ethical standards might be "I won't hurt others by spreading gossip." Ethics help you make choices that are best for everyone involved, not just for you.

- **Family.** Your family has guided your development, taught you values, and modeled ways to make decisions and solve problems. Their influence continues as you make more decisions for yourself. You can turn to them when you have trouble making choices. See Fig. 6-2.

- **Peers.** Your peers also influence your choices, though their influence may not always be positive. As you make choices about what to do or how to behave, be

your own person. You don't have to do something just because everyone else is doing it. Distinguish between positive and negative peer influence. You are always personally responsible for the choices you make.

- **Media.** A great deal of information comes to you through the **media**—channels of mass communication. Newspapers, magazines, radio, television, movies, and Web sites all present facts, fiction, and opinions. Much of the information is intended to influence your thinking and your choices. Awareness will help you stand up to media influence.

- **Society and culture.** Your family, peers, and the media are just part of the larger society and culture in which you live. Cultural traditions, religious beliefs, societal expectations, current trends—all have an influence on the choices you make.

- **Economic factors.** When making decisions or solving problems, the options that families and individuals have may depend in part on their financial resources. Choices about how to spend and save money, in particular, are influenced by how much money there is to work with. Good management can help you make the most of your financial resources.

The Impact of Choices

Every choice has consequences. Sometimes the consequences are immediate and affect only you. Other times, they last a long time and also affect others. The consequences can be positive, negative, or a combination of the two. Before you make choices, think about their impact. The stronger the potential impact, the more thought you should put into the choice.

It's easy to overlook the impact of your choices on others. You want to act independ-

Fig. 6-3. Developing strong decision-making skills can boost your confidence. *What major decisions are you facing in the next few years?*

ently and make your own decisions. Though this is normal, remember that nearly every choice you make impacts others in some way.

Losing sight of this concept can cause you to hurt others, even if it's unintentional. Christa, for example, decided to take a part-time job so that she could earn some money. She kept her goal a secret until she landed a job at the supermarket, working two afternoons a week. Her mom pointed out that taking the job meant that Christa no longer could pick up and watch her younger sister after school. As a result of Christa's decision, her mother had to cut back her working hours two days a week. She now gets less money in her paycheck.

Considering the impact of your decisions on others will help you make better choices. You are more likely to think through the consequences, weigh the possible outcomes, and make the wisest choice. If Christa had thought through the impact of her choice, she might have arranged to work evenings or weekends instead of afternoons.

The Decision-Making Process

Making decisions is a part of life. Some of the decisions you will make over the next few years are crucial because they will give your life direction and purpose. As you enter adulthood and become responsible for all your decisions, your ability to make good ones can significantly impact the quality of your life. See Fig. 6-3.

Fortunately, there's a process you can follow to help you make the best choices for each situation. The **decision-making process** is a six-step procedure for making thoughtful choices. The six steps are:

1. **Identify the decision to be made.** You're more likely to make a good choice if you can clearly spell out what you're trying to decide. Why do you need to make a decision? What do you hope to accomplish? Who else will be affected by the decision?

2. **List possible options.** Gather the information and other resources that will help you make a good decision. You might want to do some research or ask for advice from someone you trust. Then think of as many possible courses of action as you can.

3. **Evaluate the pros and cons of each option.** What would be the positive and negative results of each alternative? Remember to consider how others will be affected, not just yourself.

4. **Make a choice.** After carefully weighing the options, select the one that will have the most positive outcome overall.

5. **Act on your decision.** Identify what you need to do in order to put your decision into action. Then do it.

6. **Evaluate your choice.** Afterwards, look back at the results of your decision. Did you make the best choice? How did your decision affect others? Accept responsibility for the results and learn from them.

The decision-making process helps you focus on the main issue. It reminds you to identify possible courses of action and to analyze each one. Finally, by evaluating the decision you made, you can improve your decision-making skills. See Fig. 6-4.

Fig. 6-4. After a few weeks of music lessons, this teen evaluated her decision to learn an instrument. She decided it was the right decision, even though it meant many hours of practice.

Practical Problems

The decision-making process is useful when you have a specific choice to make. Sometimes, however, you're dealing with more than just a single decision. You may be facing a **practical problem**—a complex situation that has many aspects and involves making several interrelated choices. Practical problems require thinking about values and ethics, not just facts. Learning how to solve practical problems is one of the most valuable life skills that you can learn.

Jamal's dilemma is a good example of a practical problem. He feels that his dad and his stepmom, Julie, expect him to do too many chores around the house. He works hard to keep his grades up, is on the baseball team, and has a part-time job. It seems like

whenever Jamal tries to relax, his dad or Julie finds some other chore for him to do. What's more, they often expect him to look after his stepbrother and sister at a moment's notice. Jamal usually does what his parents ask, but he feels like retorting, "Why do all these chores have to be done right now? Why can't I have a little time to myself?" Jamal feels trapped and overwhelmed by his parents' expectations. However, he doesn't know how to deal with the issue. He realizes that his dad and Julie work very hard and need to rely on him. He wants to keep the peace by pleasing his parents. At the same time, he also feels that he has a right to some free time.

Characteristics of Practical Problems

Have you, like Jamal, faced complicated problems that left you feeling overwhelmed and confused? You will certainly face more as you confront challenging aspects of your future, such as college, career, relationships, marriage, and family. See Fig. 6-5.

Although practical problems are unique, they have certain common characteristics:

- **Practical problems are complex.** They usually involve several different issues, and the way to deal with them is not clear. To find a solution, you need to sort out and examine those issues. Jamal, for instance, is dealing with home, school, and job expectations, time issues, and family relationships.

- **Practical problems have unique circumstances.** Even two people with the same problem will approach the problem from different perspectives and may arrive at two different solutions.

- **Practical problems affect others.** They may involve family, friends, classmates, and even members of the community. Thus, you need to consider others' needs and feelings when resolving such problems. Jamal recognizes that his dad and stepmom work long hours. He has to consider the rest of the family as he works through his problem.

- **Practical problems involve ethical choices.** You must consider your ethics in order to determine the right thing to do. What ethical principles might affect Jamal's situation?

- **Practical problems require action.** They don't resolve themselves. You need to identify and weigh both the positive and negative consequences of each possible option. Only then can you make the best choice. After a choice is made, you must act to set the solution in motion.

Fig. 6-5. Deciding where to go to college and what courses to take is an example of a practical problem. What makes this a complex issue? Who else might be affected by the decision?

More to Explore

Ethical Decision Tests

Practical problems involve ethical choices—decisions about what is right and fair for all who are involved. How can you determine whether a decision is ethical? Try using the questions below. They apply an ethical standard to your choice or action.

- **What would happen if everyone made this choice?** This question helps you decide if you would be willing to accept the consequences if others made the choice or took the action.

- **What would happen if I were the person being affected by this choice?** This question encourages you to switch roles with other people involved in your decision. If you were the person being affected by your choice or action, would you still see the choice or action as being fair and caring?

- **What would happen if my circumstances were slightly different and I made this choice?** This question checks to see whether the choice or action would be justified under other circumstances. If it is, the choice or action is probably ethical.

- **Which choice will have the most positive consequences for the most people involved?** This question focuses on what will happen to everyone involved as a result of your choice or action. The most ethical decision is usually the one with the most positive consequences for the most people.

Examining Practical Problems

When you're faced with a practical problem, start by examining the situation and asking yourself questions about it. As you do, pay attention to the following four aspects of the problem. You can't get a complete picture of the situation unless you look at it from all four angles.

- **Context.** Just as no two people are exactly alike, no two practical problems are identical. Each problem has its own context to consider. **Context** refers to all of the conditions surrounding the problem or situation. To examine the context of the problem, ask yourself questions such as: What factors are at work here? What aspects of this situation do I need to be aware of? How do they affect the problem? In Jamal's case, he is dealing with a situation in which both parents work and his siblings need care. He needs to consider those circumstances as he resolves the problem.

- **Desired ends.** Also think about what ends, or outcomes, are desired. What conditions must be met in order for everyone involved to feel that the problem has been successfully solved? Keep in mind that your values influence what outcome you desire. The same is true of the others who are involved.

- **Means.** Consider the means or methods that might be used to reach the desired ends. What are possible ways to achieve the desired outcome? For each possible strategy, think about who would take action, what resources could be used, and what steps would need to be taken.

- **Consequences.** The actions taken will affect you and others. Ask yourself: What might be the positive and negative results of the actions I'm considering? Who will be affected and how? What are the risks and benefits of each possible course of action?

This process of examining and asking questions about a practical problem is known as *practical reasoning*. Unlike the decision-making process, practical reasoning is not a step-by-step method. Rather, you are likely to move back and forth among the four aspects as you work through the problem. The process requires time and thought. Only after you have considered all four aspects thoroughly will you be ready to choose the most appropriate course of action. See Fig. 6-6.

The REASON Process

Once you've examined a practical problem, you may find it helpful to use another problem-solving tool, the REASON process. It's similar to the decision-making process, but is meant to help you think through and solve practical problems. You can remember the elements of this process by thinking of the word *REASON*. Each letter in the word represents one element in the process:

- **R**ecognize the primary problem.
- **E**valuate information.
- **A**nalyze alternatives and consequences.
- **S**elect the best choice.
- **O**utline and take action.
- **N**ote the results of actions taken.

The best way to understand the REASON process is to see it being used. As you read about how Jamal solved his problem, notice how the different elements in the process relate to one another.

Fig. 6-6. *You may want to make notes as you think through the problem. What are some advantages of putting your thoughts in writing?*

Fig. 6-7. *Where you turn for information will depend on the type of problem you're tackling.* What sources of information have you found helpful and reliable?

Recognize the Primary Problem

A practical problem may involve several issues that are all tangled together. Try to identify the main issue or the root cause. Once you've identified it, make that your focus. Take the other factors into consideration, but don't get sidetracked by issues that aren't really related to the main problem.

When Jamal tried to analyze his situation, it took him awhile to find the real issue. "This problem is really confusing," he thought. "It's not just the chores they ask me to do. I feel like I'm continually racing around trying to keep up with homework, the team, my job, and my responsibilities at home. Maybe the problem is that I don't have time for everything."

As he thought about the time issue, he considered dropping baseball or his part-time job. Then he asked himself why he was always so frustrated and angry at home. Finally he realized that the main issue was really deeper. "I just want to be treated with respect and have Dad and Julie understand some of my needs. It's really more about that than the other stuff."

Evaluate Information

Next, think about what information you need to solve the problem. Look for information from reliable sources. You don't need every available piece of information—just enough solid information to better under-

stand your situation and make a choice. See Fig. 6-7.

Jamal thought about what information might help him see the problem more clearly. He grabbed a pen and paper and jotted down the following notes:

- Keep track of how much time I spend each week doing chores and helping out with the kids.
- Write down how much time I actually do spend relaxing.

Analyze Alternatives and Consequences

Think of what options you have. What are the short-term and long-term consequences of each option? How do your options fit in with your values, goals, priorities, and ethics? Consider both the positive and negative consequences for you and for others.

Jamal continued making notes, listing alternatives:

- Not do anything now, just keep up the best I can.

- Ignore some of Dad and Julie's requests and start living my own life.

- Talk with Dad and Julie about negotiating new guidelines.

Over the next week, Jamal gathered information and continued to think through his alternatives. He made a chart showing the consequences of different options. Fig. 6-8 shows what his chart looked like.

Select the Best Choice

Which is the wisest choice for you? There may be more than one acceptable solution to the problem. Select an option that has a positive outcome for both you and others. Make sure it's workable for your situation and resources.

As he reflected on his options, Jamal said to himself, "The best and right choice is to talk with Dad and Julie. It won't be easy, though. I need to explain that with baseball and work, I have more demands on my time than I had last fall. The information I've gathered will help them see that. I hope

Jamal's Alternatives

ALTERNATIVE	POSITIVE CONSEQUENCES	NEGATIVE CONSEQUENCES
Not do anything now, just keep up the best I can.	**+ Me:** Not much. I'll learn how to do various chores. **+ Family:** They will reap the benefits of my work.	**– Me:** Anger and frustration; tension will increase and communication decrease. **– Family:** Won't understand my anger and tension; problems could get worse.
Ignore their requests and start living my own life.	**+ Me:** Do what I want when I want. **+ Family:** None.	**– Me:** Get into trouble for not doing chores when they want; constant conflict. **– Family:** Frustrated and angry; increased tension.
Talk with Dad and Julie about negotiating new guidelines.	**+ Me:** I voice my concerns; can show I'm maturing and becoming more responsible in making decisions; family might understand and know me better. **+ Family:** They accept that I'm growing up; we all work on relationship as well as expectations.	**– Me:** Time and energy needed to have conversation and work out solution. Solution might not be acceptable to me. **– Family:** Might resent my asking for time for myself.

Fig. 6-8. A chart like this can help you analyze the consequences of the alternatives you are considering.

they'll understand that I'm responsible and do help out, but I need more control over how I plan and use my time. I know it's tough for Dad and Julie having to care for three of us and make enough money, but I'm sure we can work something out. I'm still willing to help, but things need to be handled differently."

Outline and Take Action

Once you've chosen an option, create a step-by-step plan to solve the problem. Identify and gather the resources you need to carry out your plan. Think about possible barriers to your plan and options for overcoming them.

Jamal decided to talk to his dad and Julie on Sunday. That was usually the day they were most relaxed. He thought, "I'll have to think through how to tell them about my feelings so they won't get defensive. That will be my biggest challenge. I don't want to look like I'm complaining, but that I want to solve this problem."

Note the Results of Actions Taken

Finally, look back on the outcome of your actions. Did they have positive results? If the results were not what you expected, think about how you could achieve a better outcome next time. See Fig. 6-9.

Several weeks after talking with his parents, Jamal looked back on how it went. "Dad and Julie really listened to what I had

Fig. 6-9. No matter how things turned out, give yourself credit for facing up to your problem and taking steps to solve it.

to say," he thought. "Now we have a plan for my weekly responsibilities. I make sure I get my chores done, and Dad and Julie make sure I have some time to relax. I don't feel nearly as stressed and frustrated anymore. All of us are doing better."

Jamal found that the REASON process was an effective tool for solving his practical problem. He also realized that resolving a problem can be satisfying in itself.

Whenever you work through a decision or problem, use the tools you have learned about to make the wisest choice for yourself and others. You'll build character, gain knowledge and wisdom, and develop competence in making wise choices for now and the future.

Review & Activities

Chapter Summary

- You are more likely to make wise decisions if you are proactive and anticipate what needs to be done.
- Your choices are influenced by many factors from within and without.
- Considering the impact of your choices will help you make better decisions.

- The six-step decision-making process can help you choose among different options.
- Learning to solve practical problems is a valuable life skill.
- When examining practical problems, consider the context, desired ends, means, and consequences.
- You can use the REASON process to think through and resolve practical problems.

Reviewing Key Terms & Ideas

1. What are the characteristics of people who are **proactive** in their decision making?

2. How does a positive attitude help with decision making?

3. What are **ethics**? Why are ethics important in making choices?

4. Name four other factors that influence choices.

5. What are the different types of consequences that a choice can have?

6. Identify the six steps of the **decision-making process**.

7. What does the term **practical problem** mean?

8. Summarize the characteristics that practical problems share.

9. What questions can help you examine the **context** of a problem?

10. Identify the six elements of the REASON process.

Thinking Critically

1. **Analyzing Influences.** Think of a purchase you made recently, such as buying jeans or a CD. What factors influenced your decision to buy that particular item instead of other options? Explain how each factor influenced you.

2. **Making Predictions.** How does the way you go about making choices as a teen impact the way you might go about making choices as an adult?

3. **Making Comparisons.** How are the decision-making process and the REASON process similar and different? Identify situations in which one of the processes would be a more effective tool to use than the other.

Applying Your Knowledge

1. **The Impact of Choices.** Choose five decisions you have made in the last week. For each, make a list of all the people affected by that decision, including yourself. Put a plus next to each name if your decision had a positive impact or a minus for a negative impact. Based on your findings, rate yourself on how well you routinely consider the effects of your choices. Give a rationale for your rating.

2. **Using the Decision-Making Process.** Imagine that you've just transferred to a new school. You would like to get to know people by getting involved in a school club, team, or other organization. Describe how you would apply each step of the decision-making process in this situation.

Making Connections

1. **Language Arts.** Select a short story, novel, or play and identify the primary problem the main character faces. Describe how the character goes about solving the problem. Based on what you learned in this chapter, suggest other, more effective ways for approaching and dealing with the problem.

2. **Social Studies.** Use newspapers or news programs to identify at least three practical problems faced by government leaders. Be ready to explain how these situations demonstrate the characteristics of a practical problem.

Managing Your Life

Solving a Practical Problem

Identify a practical problem you are experiencing. Use practical reasoning, the REASON process, or both to work through the problem. Keep a journal of your thinking process and actions. After you have resolved the problem, reflect on the process you used. What worked well? What didn't work well? How might you adapt or change how you solve future problems based on this experience?

Using Technology

1. **Technology in Problem Solving.** Give examples of how technology helps people in specific jobs identify and solve problems. In what ways have you used technology as a resource for problem solving? How did it help you?

2. **Web Page.** In Web browser (HTML) format, explain one of the processes for decision making or problem solving. On the main page, outline the steps of the process. Provide a link from each step to a separate page on which you give more information and examples. Use visual and/or audio elements to add interest.

Managing Time and Money

Key Terms

- deadline
- procrastination
- overscheduling
- dovetail
- budget
- income
- expenses

Objectives

- **Create** a to-do list and identify priorities.
- **Explain** how to avoid common time management problems.
- **Identify** strategies for managing time effectively.
- **Determine** how attitudes, priorities, and goals affect money use.
- **Develop** a budget for managing income and expenses.

Which do you find harder to manage—your time or your money? Write a paragraph explaining what you find particularly challenging.

*T*ime and money are valuable—and limited—resources. Both can be used wisely, and both can be squandered. Learning to manage your time and money is an essential part of taking responsibility for your own life. Making the best possible use of these resources will improve your life and your outlook.

Time is especially limited. No one has more than 24 hours a day to work with. How people use those 24 hours affects what they accomplish, the relationships they develop, their health and wellness, and how they feel about themselves.

Unlike time, money is a resource that varies from person to person. Some people don't have enough money for food, clothing, and shelter. Others have so much that they can spend freely. For most people, the amount of money available is somewhere in between. No matter how much money a person has, good management practices will help it go further. See Fig. 7-1.

Right now is the time to learn and practice skills for time and money management. By establishing good time and money management habits today, you are more likely to prevent disappointments in the future.

Taming the To-Do List

Have you noticed that some people always seem to have more time than others? That's because they have learned about time management and know how to make the best possible use of their time. Experts in time management have developed techniques that work. These can be learned and used by anyone. Even if you manage time well already, you can probably improve. The benefits will make the effort worthwhile.

Fig. 7-1. Shopping for bargains on the Web is one way to save money. How might it also save time?

Part of time management is task management—keeping track of the tasks you need and want to accomplish, then making sure you get them done. That means creating a to-do list, or task list, and keeping it under control. By studying time management and learning from others, you can quickly learn how to tame your to-do list.

Fig. 7-2. Having a goal to work toward—such as earning enough money to pay for a trip—provides an incentive to use time wisely. How do your goals influence the way you spend your time?

Identify Responsibilities and Goals

Before making a to-do list, look at the big picture and think about what you need and want to accomplish. Consider different areas of your life, such as home and family, school, job, friends, and personal life. For each area, identify your responsibilities and your goals.

Your responsibilities are the tasks you are required to do. Responsibilities at home might include preparing dinner, caring for a sibling, or helping with household chores. You also need to schedule time for school responsibilities, such as homework and studying. Maintaining friendships and family relationships takes time, too. Personal care responsibilities, such as getting enough sleep, eating well, and exercising regularly, also impact your daily and weekly schedule. All these responsibilities will guide the way you use your time.

You also have goals that you want to accomplish in the different areas of your life. These, too, can guide you in managing your time. For example, someone who wants to maintain a strong relationship with a far-away friend finds time to stay in touch through letters, phone calls, or e-mail. A person who wants to become a better swimmer schedules time for practice. A student whose goal is to achieve a high test score will spend time preparing for the exam. In each situation, a goal is the underlying motivation for the activity. See Fig. 7-2.

Make a To-Do List

A to-do list helps you keep track of your responsibilities and goals. How and when you make your list is entirely up to you. Megan updates her list on her electronic planner every morning as she eats breakfast.

Willis writes his list on a notepad each evening before he goes to bed. Many families maintain a to-do list on a bulletin board or on the refrigerator door.

Whatever method you choose for creating your list, be sure to do it regularly. Some people update their list daily; others maintain a weekly list. Write down everything that you need to accomplish for the day or week. You may wish to organize your list into categories, such as phone calls, school assignments, chores, and so on. See Fig. 7-3.

If a project on your list seems too big or overwhelming, break it down into smaller tasks. For example, Alita wants to redecorate her room. She has limited time, so she breaks the project into smaller steps. Early in the week she'll decide what paint colors to use. Later in the week she'll prepare the room for painting. On the weekend, she'll do the painting with the help of some friends.

Establish Priorities

Few people have time to do everything they would like to do. That's why they set priorities. They decide which tasks are more important than others and focus on them first. For example, a task with an immediate **deadline**—a time or date by which the task must be completed—usually has higher priority than those with later deadlines or no fixed schedule.

A simple way to prioritize is to assign one of these categories to each task on your list:

- **A**—tasks that must be done.
- **B**—tasks that should be done.
- **C**—tasks that you hope to do.

Do the A items first because they have high priority. Then, as time permits, you can

Fig. 7-3. To-do lists are valuable management tools, provided you update them regularly. You might want to revise your list every Friday evening, for example.

work on B items and then C items. Low-priority items that don't get done may eventually be given a higher priority on future lists. For example, washing a sweater may not be a high-priority item until you want to wear it for a certain occasion.

Plan Your Schedule

Once you have identified your responsibilities and goals, made your to-do list, and established your priorities, you can plan your schedule. Use a calendar or planner to keep track of things that must occur at specific times, such as a dentist appointment, team practice, or a part-time job. Plan each day by looking at both your calendar and your to-do list. First see what's scheduled on your calendar. Then choose one or more tasks from your list to accomplish, based on priorities and time available. Plan a specific time to do them. Try to give yourself some flexibility in case some tasks take longer than you expect.

After you have completed a task, check off the item on your to-do list. You'll feel good when you see how much you are accomplishing. See Fig. 7-4.

Using Time Wisely

Keeping track of tasks is just one part of time management. You also need to make the best use of the time you have. Not every day needs to be loaded with accomplishments, but too much wasted time can keep you from reaching goals. Try to identify your personal time wasters. Do you spend too much time talking on the phone or sitting in front of the television? Do you spend more time with friends than you should and then have to rush through your homework? It's okay to include relaxing activities in your routine, but when they interfere with the rest of your life, you may need to make some changes. That means avoiding time traps and using strategies that work.

Time Traps to Avoid

Time traps prevent you from using your time effectively. Two of the most common time traps are procrastination and over-scheduling.

Procrastination ~ People often put off doing tasks that they dislike, even important ones. Why is **procrastination**—the tendency to put off doing something until later—a problem? When you put things off, you are more likely to have to rush through them at the last minute. When you rush, you're more likely to make mistakes or do a poor job. Here are some tips that will help you avoid procrastination:

Fig. 7-4. Completing the tasks on your to-do list gives you a sense of accomplishment.

FINDING CREATIVE SOLUTIONS

Setting Deadlines

When you have a task to complete, do you start it early or leave everything until the last minute? Some people find it hard to get motivated to do something until they absolutely have to. Then they run the risk of having too little time to do a good job. If you are one of those people, you might find that setting deadlines will help.

How It Works

Deadlines help you pace yourself and give you targets to aim for. Some projects have built-in deadlines: you must hand in your homework assignment by a specific class period. Many tasks or projects, however, have no particular time limit. It's easy to put them off unless you set a deadline yourself.

For a long-term project, you might set interim deadlines. Suppose you want to sew a quilt to give as a wedding present in four months' time. Aim to have a quarter of it completed by the end of the first month, half by the end of the second month, and so on. For shorter projects, just set a date to complete them and let the pressure of the deadline motivate you.

Try It Out

Tiffany's room is so cluttered that even she can't stand it. Clothes hang from the door-knob and bedpost; piles of magazines litter the floor. There are CDs on every available surface. Shoes have been stuffed under the bed. Tiffany has reached the point where she can never find anything.

▶ **Your Turn** *What interim deadlines could help Tiffany get this mess under control? List some specific deadlines in the most useful order.*

- **Do unpleasant tasks first.** They will seem easier if you do them when you're fresh, and you'll feel better knowing they're out of the way.

- **Avoid distractions and interruptions.** These can often be hard to resist. Make an effort to stay focused on the task at hand.

- **Set up a schedule.** Having a daily routine for such tasks as studying can help you beat the urge to put them off.

- **Take a small step to get started.** If you're putting something off because it seems overwhelming, divide it into smaller steps and take one step at a time.

Overscheduling ~ As a musician, Geoff was always eager to get involved in anything musical that was going on. At the beginning of the school year, he joined the orchestra and also signed up for keyboard lessons. Later, when some classmates were auditioning for a musical and asked him to accompany them, he agreed to do so. Soon Geoff realized that it was all too much.

Overscheduling, or trying to accomplish too many things in a limited amount of time, is a problem for many people. They wind up with so much to do that they can't do anything well. They feel overwhelmed and stressed out. It's better to be realistic about how much you can do with your time than to find yourself overloaded. If overscheduling is a problem for you, learn how to say no. Practice responses that allow you to decline gracefully. You might say something like, "I'm sorry, but I can't take on another project right now." Then stick to your decision.

Time-Tested Strategies

Efficient time managers avoid the troublemakers you have just read about. Here are some other strategies they practice and recommend:

- **Be prepared and organized.** Before you begin a task, think about what resources you need to accomplish it. If you're cleaning your room, take the vacuum cleaner and dusting supplies with you on one trip. Making several trips for supplies slows you down.

- **Allow enough time.** Mistakes are more likely when you rush through tasks. Doing a task right the first time usually takes less time than doing it over again.

- **Dovetail activities.** When you **dovetail** activities, you overlap them in order to save time. For example, if you have to return a video and buy groceries, do both errands in one trip.

- **Be realistic about what you can accomplish.** Don't set impossible goals. Schedule tasks that can be accomplished in the time you have available.

- **Be flexible.** Not everything goes as planned. If you are flexible, you can adjust your schedule to include unexpected events.

Managing Leisure Time

You might think that leisure time needs no management. It's easy to have fun, right? Yet many people are so busy that they don't relax. Leisure is an important part of a balanced lifestyle, and good time managers make sure that they include relaxation in their schedule. Not only that, they make sure that they get the most out of their leisure time. If you've ever spent an afternoon lazing in front of the television but later wished that you had done something more fulfilling, you'll understand the need to manage leisure time.

When planning your leisure time, include time to spend alone as well as time with family and friends. Then figure out how to spend the time. Choose activities that relax and refresh you. You may need to set aside a couple of hours for some activities, such as a game of chess or a bike ride. Others can be done in smaller slices of time. The key to managing leisure time is balance: give yourself enough time to relax, but not so much that you fail to meet your responsibilities.

Money Matters

When you manage your time wisely, you seem to have more hours in a day. The same is true of money: when you manage your money wisely, you seem to have more of it. Right now you might not have much money to manage, but it's not too early to start learning. See Fig. 7-5.

Careful money management enables you to:

- Live within your means.
- Meet goals to purchase special items.
- Prepare for financial emergencies.
- Gain and maintain a sense of financial independence.

Attitudes Toward Money

Personality and attitude affect the way people manage money. People who are cautious by nature are careful about spending and find that saving is easy. Those who are more spontaneous may spend very freely and save little. Many people fall somewhere in between.

Fig. 7-5. Learning the basics of money management now will help to prepare you for the time when you have greater financial responsibilities.

For some people, money provides a sense of security. Knowing that money is there to pay bills and cover emergencies is comforting. This is a useful feeling, as long as it doesn't become extreme. If money is hoarded while basic needs are not met, that can be a problem.

People who want the feeling of power or status may use money to satisfy their desires. They use money to acquire more money and possessions. If this focus becomes an obsession and other dimensions of life are ignored, these people may continually struggle to be happy.

This is only a sampling of how attitudes affect the way people manage money. You may be able to think of others.

Understanding your own attitudes toward money will allow you to plan better and help prevent you from making inappropriate financial decisions. When you need to make money decisions jointly—with family, friends, or in the future with a spouse—it's important to recognize and respect other people's attitudes, especially when they differ from your own.

Financial Priorities and Goals

Managing your money effectively starts with examining your priorities and goals. When it comes to priorities, needs must always come first. As a teen you probably don't have to pay for groceries, utilities, and housing, but once you live on your own, you will have to meet those needs.

If you have money left after meeting your needs, you can decide on your next priorities. To do that, you must consider your values. Which is more important to you, saving for college or buying a used car? Would you rather buy new clothes or save for a vacation? Would you prefer to spend less on rent by sharing an apartment or spend more to have a place of your own?

Looking at your values and priorities helps you establish financial goals. You will have both short-term and long-term goals. Short-term goals are less expensive and can be met in a short period of time. Manuel, for example, saved his weekly allowance for a month so that he could buy a wedding gift for his sister. Long-term financial goals are more costly and may take months or years to meet. Chantal started saving for college when she got her first babysitting job at age 12.

TEXTLINK≈

More information about *financial management* can be found in Chapter 31.

One Step at a Time

Every day you're bombarded with inducements to spend. Advertisers work hard to persuade you to buy things you don't need. It may be tempting to wear the latest fashions or to see new movies as soon as they're released. Right now, with few financial responsibilities, you may be able to spend freely on such wants. Once you're living on your own, though, you might have to do without them. Developing financial discipline now will make it easier for you to manage your money later.

What does financial discipline mean? It means taking care of needs before wants. It means being patient and thinking carefully about your purchases. When you are disciplined, you acquire wants gradually and thoughtfully. By going one step at a time, you can focus on what is important to you and save money for future needs.

Using a Budget

Good money managers use a **budget**—a plan for spending and saving money. If you have a weekly or monthly budget, you're more likely to spend and save money wisely. A budget will also help you avoid running out of money between allowances or paychecks. You can use a computer and financial software for budgeting, but pencil, paper, and calculator work just as well. To create a budget, you need to estimate your income, estimate your expenses, and bring them into balance.

Estimate Income

Your **income** is the money you take in and have available to spend. It might come from an allowance, a part-time job, or odd jobs such as babysitting or running errands. List all your sources of income and the amount for each. Be sure all the amounts are for the same period of time—either weekly or monthly. If your income varies, estimate the average amount. If you have a part-time job, your employer might take out money for taxes. In that case, list your take-home pay.

Estimate Expenses

The second step in creating a budget is to determine your expenses. **Expenses** are the items that you spend your money on. The best way to be sure you don't overlook any expenses is to track where your money goes for a period of time. Use a small notebook to record every item you spend money on and how much you spend. See Fig. 7-6.

There are two basic types of expenses:

- **Fixed expenses.** These are expenses that don't vary in amount and that you have to pay regularly. Examples of fixed expenses are car payments, insurance premiums, and payments for lessons.

- **Flexible expenses.** These expenses vary in amount and are less predictable than fixed expenses. They include money for necessities such as school supplies and clothes and for optional items such as movies and popcorn. You usually have more control over flexible expenses than fixed expenses.

After you have kept track of your expenses for a week or month, group them into categories such as clothing, entertainment, and gifts. Find the total in each category. Use this as a basis for deciding how much to allow for each spending category in your budget. Remember, however, that the expenses you recorded during one week or month might not reflect all your expenses over time. It's a good idea to build some extra room in your budget for expenses that come up only once in a while.

Fig. 7-6. Recording every item that you buy enables you to analyze your spending patterns. What do you spend most of your money on?

Fig. 7-7 shows a sample budget sheet. Notice how income, fixed expenses, and flexible expenses are listed.

You may be surprised at how much you spend on certain items. Aaron, for example, discovered that he spent about $1.50 a day on snacks during the school year. At $30 a month, he was spending $270 in a school year. He decided that there were other things he would rather do with $270. Becoming aware of how you spend your money can help you decide which expenses to continue and which ones to change.

Plan for Savings

Notice in Fig. 7-7 that "Savings" is listed as an item under expenses. Many people say they are going to save, but they never get around to it. Others say they will save whatever they have left over at the end of a week, but then find that nothing is left over. The best way to create savings is to treat them just like any other expense. By setting aside money for savings each week or month, you create a fund that will be available in case you have unexpected expenses. If you have an expensive goal in mind, such as college or a vacation, you will need to save even more.

Sample Monthly Budget

INCOME	
Allowance	70
Paycheck	250
Total Income	$320
EXPENSES	
Savings	30
Fixed Expenses	
Charity	15
Payment to parents for guitar	15
Guitar lessons	50
Car payment to parents	100
Flexible Expenses	
School lunches	30
Food away from home	20
Entertainment	20
Gifts	10
Clothing	30
Total Expenses	$320

Fig. 7-7. A simple budget enables you to plan your income and expenses and keep the two in balance.

Balance the Budget

To balance your budget, compare your total income with your total expenses. If your income is greater than your expenses, you can spend or save the excess. If your income is less than your expenses, look for ways to increase your income or reduce your expenses.

As part of preparing a budget, ask yourself whether you're satisfied with the way you have been spending your money. You may decide that you should reduce the amount of one of your flexible expenses so that you can put away more money toward reaching a long-term goal. See Fig. 7-8.

A realistic budget is one that you can actually follow. When Aaron decided to save more money, he didn't cut out all snacks. He simply reduced the amount he allowed himself to spend. He avoided the vending machines by bringing snacks from home. In this way, he saved money without putting unrealistic expectations on himself.

Follow Your Plan

A budget is useful only if you follow through with it. Once you've set up your budget, continue to track and record your income and expenses. Set aside time each week or month to compare your actual income and expenses with the budgeted amounts.

If you can't stay within the budgeted amount for one of your expenses, decide how you will deal with the problem. Can you come up with a way to cut back on future spending in that category? Perhaps you need to increase the amount you've budgeted by cutting back on a different expense.

Fig. 7-8. Budgeting is all about choices. Cutting back on other expenses enabled this teen to save toward the down payment on her first car.

Reviewing your income and expenses regularly makes it easier to stay in control of your spending. It helps you see where your money goes and determine just how much you're willing to spend on specific items. By following your budget plan, you can make sure that you don't live beyond your means and that you save for future needs.

Maintaining a budget is easy once you get used to it. By learning budgeting and money management skills now, when you have fewer funds to manage, you will be well prepared for the more serious money management you will need to do in the future.

Review & Activities

Chapter Summary

- A to-do list and a calendar can help you plan each day.
- Procrastination and overscheduling are time traps to avoid.
- You can apply strategies for managing time more effectively.
- Good time managers include time for relaxation in their schedule.
- Careful money management enables you to live within your means.
- To manage money effectively, you need to examine your attitudes, priorities, and goals.
- You are more likely to spend and save wisely if you use a budget.

Reviewing Key Terms & Ideas

1. What are the benefits of using time and money wisely?
2. What is the purpose of a to-do list?
3. How does a **deadline** help you prioritize the tasks on your to-do list?
4. Describe how to plan your daily schedule.
5. Why is **procrastination** a problem? Suggest a way to avoid it.
6. How can you avoid **overscheduling**?
7. How does finding ways to **dovetail** help you save time?
8. Why is it important to manage leisure time?
9. What are four benefits of managing your money effectively?
10. Why do you need to understand your own attitudes toward money?
11. Explain how priorities and goals influence the way money is managed.
12. What is the purpose of a **budget**?
13. Give examples of **income** and **expenses**. Why do they need to be balanced?
14. Over which expenses do you have greater control—fixed or flexible? Why?

Thinking Critically

1. **Making Predictions.** What might happen if someone with an already overloaded schedule takes on still more responsibilities? What might happen if someone goes through his or her day simply doing the next thing that comes to mind?
2. **Categorizing Information.** Make a list of the categories you would use in preparing a personal budget. Identify whether each expense category is fixed or flexible.

Review & Activities CHAPTER 7

Applying Your Knowledge

1. **Using a To-Do List.** Make a to-do list for tomorrow. Set your priorities for the day by assigning A, B, or C to each task. Cross off each task as you complete it. At the end of the day, evaluate your list. Write a paragraph about how this time management tool worked for you.

2. **Identifying Time Management Strategies.** Reflect on the past 24 hours. Identify strategies you could have used to manage your time more effectively. Write a paragraph explaining how these strategies might have changed your day.

3. **Identifying Financial Goals.** Identify two short-term and two long-term financial goals. Estimate how much money and time you would need to reach these goals.

Making Connections

1. **Social Studies.** Investigate the ways that time management techniques are used in business and industry. Choose one technique that could be applied in your home or school. Prepare a diagram or a description to present to the class.

2. **Math.** Assume that you want to buy a bike that costs $300. If you were to save for your bike at the rate of $5 a week, how long would it take you to save the full amount? How long would it take if you saved $10 a week? What might you do to get the bike sooner?

Managing Your Life

Create a Personal Budget

Make a weekly budget for yourself by following the suggestions in the chapter. Live on your budget for at least two weeks. Keep track of your actual income and expenses, and compare them to your budget. Write a short report describing any difficulties you had in preparing or living on your budget and any problems you anticipate in staying within it. Discuss how you expect to handle these difficulties, including any revisions you propose in your budget.

Using Technology

1. **Technology Evaluation.** Research one or more technology products designed to manage time and schedules, such as personal organizers. Evaluate them according to features, ease of use, and cost.

2. **Spreadsheet.** Use appropriate software to create a budget spreadsheet. Include formulas for totaling income, totaling expenses, comparing income and expenses, and comparing budgeted amounts to actual figures. Enter sample data to show how the spreadsheet works. Use it over a period of time and refine it as necessary to meet your needs.

Managing Time and Money **CHAPTER 7** 123

CHAPTER 8

Managing Technology and Information

Key Terms

- technology
- identity theft
- obsolete
- critical thinking
- copyright
- plagiarism

Objectives

- **Compare** the benefits and drawbacks of technology.
- **Describe** strategies for managing technology.
- **Evaluate** the reliability of information.
- **Give guidelines** for using information effectively.
- **Explain** the importance of respecting ownership of information.

Write about three ways technology makes life easier for your family. Then describe three ways it makes life harder.

*T*echnology and information are both valuable resources. They impact your family life, school life, and social life in countless ways. In the future, they will affect your career choices and your working life. The challenge for you, and for everyone else, is to learn to manage these resources effectively.

The Impact of Technology

In a broad sense, **technology** is the application of science to help people meet their needs and wants. Technology has revolutionized the way people live and work. In the home, modern equipment can raise and lower temperatures automatically, cook meals in minutes, and answer the telephone when you're eating dinner. You can chat with your friends online, send photos and other documents over the Internet, and send text messages using your cell phone. See Fig. 8-1.

In the workplace, many tasks once done by hand have been automated. Others have been made easier and faster with the use of computers. Many occupations, such as computer programming, did not even exist until technological advances created a demand for them.

Technology will continue to affect people's lifestyles and their quality of life. New products, as well as improvements of existing products, will become available. New ways of doing things will be developed. New jobs will be created; some existing jobs will be phased out. The only thing that's certain in this rapidly changing world is that it will continue to change.

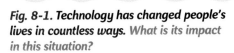

Fig. 8-1. Technology has changed people's lives in countless ways. What is its impact in this situation?

Technology has an impact not only on individuals and families but also on society as a whole. It makes it possible for people to live more comfortably. It reduces the need for physical labor, giving people more time for enjoyment. It contributes to better health and longer life spans. It enables people to feel more connected with the wider world. Does that mean that technology makes people happier and more contented? Not necessarily. As you will see, technology affects people in both positive and negative ways.

Benefits of Technology

Most people would agree that the benefits of technology vastly outweigh its drawbacks. Technological advances have had a positive impact on many aspects of everyday life. Here are some examples:

- **Communication.** Modern communication technology started with the telephone. Today, you can also send and receive e-mails, text, photographs, and video images. You can fax documents and leave voice mail messages. There have never been so many options for communicating with others.

- **Transportation.** The vast, complex systems of air travel and mass transit that exist today would be difficult to coordinate without the help of computers. Cars and other vehicles also contain computers that keep them functioning properly and warn drivers of problems. Some vehicles have global positioning systems that display maps and give drivers directions.

- **Health care.** Individuals can use the Internet to access information about a variety of medical conditions. Health care professionals use CAT scans, MRIs, and other sophisticated techniques to detect and diagnose diseases. Lasers and other high-tech instruments make faster, less invasive surgery possible. See Fig. 8-2.

- **Safety and security.** Many devices help protect people and property. Examples include vehicle air bags and anti-theft devices, home security systems, smoke detectors, and airport screening systems. Monitoring systems allow many older people with health problems to live independently.

- **Production.** Robotics has revolutionized manufacturing, increasing efficiency and

Fig. 8-2. Electronic scanning equipment enables doctors to make accurate diagnoses. This is just one example of how technology has revolutionized medicine.

Fig. 8-3. Many people do part of their banking and shopping electronically. What are some possible drawbacks of automated transactions?

quality. Computers are used to design and assemble products and to track shipments. Agricultural technology has helped increase the production and safety of food products.

- **Personal productivity.** Think of all the ways technology helps you get more done in less time. How much time and effort have you and your family saved because of home appliances? What tasks can be completed faster or more easily with computer software?

- **Education.** Distance learning and online classes allow students to earn degrees without attending regular classes. Through online discussion boards, students and teachers can interact at their convenience.

- **Finance and retail.** Many supermarkets and other retail stores have electronic checkout scanners, which also help them track inventory. Online shopping enables you to make purchases without leaving home. You can make financial transactions at any hour of the day using computers, a phone, or automated teller machines (ATMs). See Fig. 8-3.

- **Entertainment.** Technology places a world of entertainment options at your fingertips. On-demand TV, digital video, gaming stations, digital music players, and a host of other electronic devices bring entertainment into the home.

Drawbacks of Technology

Despite its many benefits, technology can have negative side effects. Chief among these are the stress and frustration associated with rapid and continual change. People sometimes find it hard to keep up with technology and to learn new ways of doing things. Some fear or resist the changes that technology brings.

There's no doubt that technology can be frustrating. Just when you master one device or process, something new replaces it. Moreover, new methods aren't always user-friendly. Have you ever tried to call a company for information, only to find that you must work your way through several menus before you can talk to a real person? Malfunctions occur; computers crash; viruses spread. Even something as seemingly minor as a temporary power failure can cause major frustrations for people who have become dependent on their electronic systems.

Fig. 8-4. Surfing the Web can be fun, but it's often a solitary pursuit. How might this affect personal relationships?

Other drawbacks of technology include the negative effects it can have on people's physical and social health. Hours spent working at a computer can result in back problems, eyestrain, and wrist injuries. Poor health caused by lack of physical activity is another risk. Spending hours watching television, playing computer games, or surfing the Web can keep people from interacting face to face. See Fig. 8-4.

The complexity and expense of new technology can make it hard for consumers to make buying decisions. When you don't understand the features on competing products, choosing the right one is difficult. The costs of some technology can be high, especially when it is first introduced.

Technology has also caused many people to worry more about their privacy and their job security. It has become increasingly necessary to guard against **identity theft**, the illegal use of an individual's personal information. In the workplace, jobs continue to be eliminated by technology that replaces human labor.

TEXTLINK≈

You can learn more about *identity theft* in Chapter 28.

Managing Technology

Managing technology can help you enjoy the benefits and minimize the drawbacks. A good way to start is by examining the relationship between technology and other resources.

Like any resource, technology can be used to improve your life and meet your goals. You can use the Internet, for example, to gather information about competing products before deciding what to buy. You can use instant messaging to communicate with a friend who has moved far away.

In addition to being a resource in itself, technology is also a tool for managing other resources. Financial software helps families manage their money. Databases enable people to manage large amounts of information. Voice mail helps you manage your time.

On the other hand, technology can be a drain on other resources, especially time and money. Many high-tech devices and services are expensive. It takes time to figure out what technology you might need and to learn how to use and maintain it.

Fortunately, there are resources to help you manage the use of technology. Many manufacturers and suppliers offer technical support to help you install new equipment or solve problems. Books and training programs present information and encourage skill development through practice exercises. Knowledgeable friends and family can often share their experience and expertise. See Fig. 8-5.

Strategies for Managing Technology

How can you avoid the pitfalls associated with technology? How can you stay in control of the technology in your life and use it to your advantage? Here are some suggestions:

- **Keep a positive attitude.** A positive attitude helps you see that the benefits of technology are real, despite occasional snags. For example, using a computer for word processing saves time overall, even if you occasionally lose your work because of a software problem.

Fig. 8-5. Learning a new program is much easier if you have a friend who can point out the main features. What other resources can help you manage technology?

- **Be patient.** Set aside time for learning about new equipment or software. Don't expect to master it immediately. Be patient if you have to wait for files to download or for answers from technical support. Ask yourself what difference a few seconds or minutes will make.

- **Maintain healthy work habits.** When working at a computer, sit with your shoulders straight and your back supported. Take regular breaks and do stretching exercises. Compensate for the time you spend at a computer by being physically active at other times.

- **Maintain interpersonal relationships.** Guard against the isolation that can result from too much time spent with television, computers, and video games instead of people. Make sure you include time in your life for family and friends.

- **Make wise consumer choices.** Buy new technology when you need it, not because there's a new version of last year's product. Some manufacturers want you to think that as soon as a new product comes out, the old version is **obsolete**—out of date and no longer useful. In reality, there may be only a few new features or design changes in the latest version. Consider your priorities and budget, and determine to what extent the product or service will improve your life. See Fig. 8-6.

- **Protect your privacy.** Don't give out personal information over the phone, by e-mail, or on the Internet except to people you know you can trust. When buying online, make sure you are at a secure site before giving credit card information. Share your e-mail address only with family and trusted friends.

- **Help others develop technology skills.** When family, friends, and coworkers help one another develop technology skills, everyone benefits. Jordan gave his grandmother his old computer and taught her how to use e-mail. Now she has an easier way to keep in touch with distant family and friends.

By following these strategies, you can make the most of technology. You can enjoy its benefits, knowing that it enhances the quality of your life instead of detracting from it.

Fig. 8-6. Don't buy a new product simply because it has new features. First find out how useful the new features will be to you.

Evaluating Information

You are living in what has been called "the information age." More people have access to more information than ever before. Much of this information explosion is due to communication technology. Television brings news from around the world as it happens. The Internet puts information from countless Web sites at your fingertips. In addition, traditional sources of information such as newspapers, magazines, and books continue to flourish.

Having access to so much information is beneficial in many ways. It also presents challenges. How do you know whether information is reliable? How can you judge its significance? How can you avoid being overwhelmed by too much information?

Viewpoints

Caught in the Web

The Internet has been called a superhighway. To some people, however, it's a road without a map. For every person who "surfs the Net" with ease, it seems that there's another person getting lost.

Brianna: The Internet is incredible. Whatever information you need, you can find it there. Learning and researching is so much easier. I can gather more facts and opinions, compare different sources, even connect with people to share ideas and get more answers. I especially like sites with lots of links. They help you view one topic from different angles.

Nicole: I dread looking things up online. I spend hours wading through useless information and visiting unhelpful sites. When I do find what I need, I worry about whether it's trustworthy. I can find just as much information at a good library with the help of a reference librarian, and without all that frustration and wasted time.

Seeing Both Sides ~ Have you ever shared the experiences described by Brianna and Nicole? What strategies can help you identify the most useful Web sites with a minimum of searching?

Critical Thinking

To evaluate information, you need to use critical thinking. **Critical thinking** means applying reasoning strategies in order to make sound judgments. For example, one such strategy is distinguishing fact from opinion. A fact can be verified by research; an opinion is what someone thinks or believes. If you recognize that a statement is opinion, how does that affect the way you interpret it? In most cases you will want to consider the opinion, but make up your own mind based on the facts. Critical thinking is an essential skill for the information age.

Identifying Reliable Sources

One key aspect of critical thinking is assessing whether information comes from a reliable source. Don't just assume that all the information you receive is true. Reading something in a book doesn't guarantee that it's correct. Anyone can create a Web site— the information on it may or may not be accurate. A neighbor may tell you something that he or she believes is true but that turns out to be incorrect.

Before you allow information to influence your judgment, check it out to make sure it's reliable and true. Use these strategies for evaluating the reliability of information:

- **Determine the source.** If you read something in a magazine, check to see who wrote the article and what sources the author cites. If you're using a Web site, find out who runs the site. If a friend passes information on to you, ask where it came from. Be suspicious of information that doesn't have a source that you can check.

- **Evaluate the source.** Look for details about authors or others cited as sources.

Are they qualified? Make sure they are legitimate experts in their fields. Try to determine whether the information might be biased, perhaps to promote a product or way of thinking.

- **Confirm the information.** Check the information against other sources. See if they give similar information.

- **Be skeptical.** Phrases such as "scientists have discovered" or "doctors believe" don't mean anything unless they are backed by hard facts. If an article mentions a scientific study, find out who conducted the study and who paid for it. When you find information that makes you suspicious, trust your instincts. Look for supporting information from other sources.

Using Information Effectively

Once you have found reliable information, you must determine how you can use it most effectively. Often you will need to organize and summarize the information so it is useful to you. For instance, if you're researching competing products, you might want to list the advantages and disadvantages of each according to their features, use, care, and costs. See Fig. 8-7.

Sometimes you may not know how much information to gather. Avoiding "information overload," yet obtaining enough information to make an informed decision, can be tricky. Be sure to obtain several credible, reliable sources and check them against one another before you stop gathering information. However, don't try to get *all* the available information on a particular topic—your task would never end.

Fig. 8-7. *Organizing information from various sources can help you make comparisons. What are some ways of organizing information?*

Respecting Ownership Rights

Even though the information you find in published works and on the Web is freely available, it's not necessarily free to take and use. Music files, pictures, articles, and other materials are all created by someone. In many cases, that person owns the copyright to the information. **Copyright** gives legal rights to the people and companies that produce original works. It gives them control over the way their works are used and the right to profit from their efforts.

Using copyrighted material without permission is a form of plagiarism. **Plagiarism** occurs when someone takes part of another person's original work and uses it as if it were his or her own work. If you copy a passage from an online site and paste it into an essay without citing the source, you are pla-

giarizing. Plagiarism is illegal because it violates copyright law. It's also unethical. If you plagiarize, you are taking credit for something you did not create.

Plagiarism is an increasing problem because so much information is available in electronic format. New technologies are being developed to catch people who steal copyrighted material.

Respect the ownership rights of people who create original works. If you use information from someone else's work, give that person credit. Summarize the information in your own words, or quote short extracts and clearly indicate the source. By respecting ownership rights, you help ensure that creative people will continue to provide new works that enrich everyone's life.

Review & Activities

Chapter Summary

- Technology and information are valuable resources that need to be managed effectively.
- Technology impacts everyday life in both positive and negative ways.
- Strategies for managing technology help you benefit from its advantages while minimizing its drawbacks.

- Thanks to communication technology, people have access to a vast amount of information.
- Critical thinking skills enable you to evaluate information.
- Not all information comes from reliable sources.
- Finding reliable information is not enough; you must also use it effectively.
- Plagiarism is an increasing problem.

Reviewing Key Terms & Ideas

1. What is **technology**?
2. Give five specific examples of ways that technology has had a positive impact on everyday life.
3. What are three drawbacks of technology?
4. Identify four different resources that can help you manage technology.
5. How can a positive attitude and healthy work habits help you manage technology effectively?
6. Why might some manufacturers want you to think that a product is **obsolete**?
7. Why do you need to use **critical thinking** when evaluating information?
8. Give two guidelines for using information effectively.
9. What rights do **copyright** holders have?
10. What is **plagiarism**? Why should you avoid it?

Thinking Critically

1. **Making Predictions.** What kinds of jobs in today's workplace are most likely to be eliminated by technology? What kinds are least likely to be eliminated? Why do you think so?
2. **Defending Your Position.** Should people who fear or resist new technology be left alone, or should they be encouraged to understand and use new equipment and methods? Give reasons for your answer.
3. **Drawing Conclusions.** Why is it more important than ever before to evaluate the reliability of information? What are the best ways to do this?

Applying Your Knowledge

1. **Benefits and Drawbacks.** Choose a relatively recent technology that you have used. What are its benefits and drawbacks for you? Do the benefits outweigh the drawbacks? Why or why not?

2. **Evaluating Reliability.** Find information on the same topic from two different sources, one that you consider reliable and one that you consider unreliable. Explain how you analyzed the reliability of each source.

3. **Ownership Rights.** Research the legal and ethical issues related to plagiarism. Write an article for the school newspaper explaining the meaning of copyright and discouraging students from plagiarizing.

Making Connections

1. **Science.** Many times, new technology has resulted from an accidental discovery made while researching some other topic. Find an example and report on what led to the discovery. What can you conclude about the relationship between science and technology?

2. **Language Arts.** Write two essays, each trying to persuade the reader to accept the same viewpoint. In one essay, base your arguments on reason; in the other, on emotions. Exchange essays with a classmate, and analyze the essays you receive. What words and phrases signal the use of reason or emotion? Which essay is more persuasive? Why?

Managing Your Life

Maintain Healthy Work Habits

Extended time in front of a computer can cause eyestrain, back problems, and wrist pain. Research how to avoid these problems. Address both the work environment (such as lighting, positioning of equipment, and appropriate seating) and worker habits (such as proper posture and stretching). Analyze your work environment at home and your own work habits. If possible, make appropriate changes. Create a file folder of the information you obtain for use in the future.

Using Technology

1. **Researching New Technology.** Choose a new technology that interests you. Research how it works, what it replaces, what its advantages are, and the implications of its use. Prepare a report for the class.

2. **Presentation Software.** Using appropriate software, prepare a presentation for classmates in which you explain and illustrate how to manage technology effectively. Use the ideas in the chapter as a starting point, but add ideas and examples from your own experience.

Career Options

Agriculture and Natural Resources

$\mathbf{A}$griculture and natural resources is one of the oldest industries. It includes people who work the land to provide consumers with food, energy, and other products. This career cluster offers job opportunities for people of all levels of education and experience, including many entry-level positions. The industry can be divided into five broad sectors: Agriculture; Forestry; Fishing; Mining and Quarrying; and Oil and Gas. Employment opportunities for many occupations are declining, though some in agriculture are expected to increase.

Main Employers

- Farms
- Landscape companies
- Logging companies
- Fishing companies
- Mines and quarries
- Oil and gas companies
- Government agencies

Agriculture and Natural Resources Job Opportunities

Industry Segment	Entry Level	Additional Education and/or Training	Advanced Education and/or Training
Agriculture	• Farmworker • Meatpacker • Groundskeeper	• Farmer, Rancher • Farm Manager • Agricultural Technician	• Agricultural Inspector • Landscape Designer • Food Scientist • Soil Conservationist
Forestry	• Logger • Forest Worker • Lumbermill Worker	• Forestry Technician • Logging Machinery Operator	• Forester • Conservation Scientist
Fishing	• Fisher • Deckhand	• Boatswain • First Mate	• Fishing Vessel Captain
Mining and Quarrying	• Miner • Rock Splitter	• Mining Supervisor • Machinery Operator	• Mining Engineer • Safety Engineer
Oil and Gas	• Extraction Worker • Rigger	• Derrick Operator • Drill Operator	• Petroleum Engineer • Petroleum Geologist

I've always been fascinated with science. My parents bought me a chemistry set when I was ten, and I played with it endlessly. In high school, I took every science class I could—including biology, chemistry, and physics—and loved all of them.

I went to college wanting to study science, but I didn't know which aspect to focus on. A professor suggested that I look into food science. I didn't even know what a food scientist did. I checked it out, though, because I love food almost as much as science! The more I learned about the field, the more interested I became. After taking courses in food analysis, food chemistry, and food microbiology, among others, I earned a bachelor's degree in agricultural science.

Now I work as a food scientist for the Department of Agriculture, a federal government agency. I help research new food sources and products. Other food scientists analyze foods to determine their nutrient levels. Still others look for better ways to process, package, and store food. Our work benefits the agriculture and food industries, as well as consumers.

I am now taking night classes to earn my master's degree. This helps me stay current in my field and could also lead to a promotion. You need a master's degree or a doctorate to advance in this field. For now, I'm happy combining my interest in food with my love of science.

Check It *Out!*

Technological changes have had a huge impact on the agriculture and natural resources industry. Choose one industry segment, such as mining. Find out how technology has changed the nature of the work and required job qualifications. Prepare an oral report on your findings.

UNIT

3

Pathways to Career Success

Careers in a Changing World

Key Terms

- career
- career path
- lifestyle
- entrepreneur
- global economy
- downsizing
- outsourcing
- apprenticeship
- internship
- employability skills

Objectives

- **Examine** reasons why people work.
- **Explain** the impact of career decisions.
- **Compare** different types of employers and employment.
- **Analyze** changes affecting the workplace.
- **Propose** ways to develop skills needed for the workplace.

In what ways will your life change when you enter the working world full time? Write about the impact—both positive and negative—that working will have on the way you live.

Have you decided what you will do when you leave school? Some people seem to know from an early age what kind of work they want to do. Others take a while to figure out what's right for them. Whether you've already made a decision or are still exploring your options, it's helpful to think about the impact that your choice of occupation will have on your life. Deciding what work to do is one of the most significant decisions you will make.

Why People Work

If you were to ask your classmates why they want a job, most would probably answer, "To make money." Most teens look forward to earning cash for new clothes, movie tickets, or perhaps gas and car insurance. Later, as you gain more independence, you'll use your money for food, housing, and much more. Eventually you may need to support a family of your own.

Earning a living is an important reason for working, but it's not the only reason. In addition to meeting basic physical needs, work can satisfy certain emotional, intellectual, and social needs. Here are some ways that work contributes to your overall sense of well-being:

- **Achievement.** Supporting yourself helps you feel proud and competent.

- **Fulfillment.** You gain satisfaction from doing a job well and from contributing something to society. See Fig. 9-1.

- **Personal growth.** Working helps you develop your skills and gain knowledge.

- **Sense of belonging.** Many people build satisfying relationships with coworkers and enjoy being part of a team.

Fig. 9-1. Many people look for a line of work that will bring personal satisfaction. What rewards do you think this preschool teacher gets from his work?

- **Approval.** Performing a job well gains the approval of others and boosts your self-esteem.

Jobs vary in the degree to which they meet a person's physical, emotional, intellectual, and social needs. No job can satisfy all of a person's needs. Still, most people want to work not only for the money but also for the opportunity to experience other benefits. That's one reason why it's important to think carefully about the work you will do.

The Impact of Career Decisions

As you begin thinking about career decisions, keep in mind that a career is more than just a job. A job is a specific position with a particular employer. A **career**, on the other hand, is a series of related jobs in a particular field. See Fig. 9-2.

Maria, for example, currently has a job as a hostess in a restaurant. This is just the first step in her plan to build a career in the food service industry. Looking ahead, Maria sees herself working at many different jobs in a variety of food service establishments. Along the way she'll learn about the business, build her skills, and take on increasing responsibility. Her goal is to open her own restaurant someday.

Most people change jobs from time to time in order to gain more experience, earn more money, or simply to do something dif-ferent. Most people also have more than one career in their lifetime. Usually people start new careers in response to economic conditions or because they seek greater satisfaction from their work.

Career Paths

When you've set a career goal, you need to map out the path that will take you there. A **career path** consists of the steps you take to reach your career goal. Often the steps include education, training, and job experience. To reach her goal of opening her own restaurant, Maria plans to go to college and major in the hospitality program. Then she'll look for jobs that give her experience in many aspects of food service.

Fig. 9-2. Some jobs offer little in the way of advancement, while others are clearly stepping stones to a more successful future. What jobs might be part of a career in the journalism field?

For some careers, you can choose from a variety of paths. You might, for example, get a job as soon as you graduate from high school, working up to your chosen occupation by changing jobs and getting promotions. Or you might attend college first, then start out at a higher level. Another option might be to take college courses at night while working during the day. Whatever path you choose, the main thing is to make sure it leads to your goal.

In a forest, some paths are straight and easy to follow, but most have twists and turns. Career paths are just the same. Some people follow a straight line. They know what they want to do, they get the education or training that they need, and they get jobs that move them forward along their path. In many cases, however, people follow a less direct route. They may have to try different options before finding a good fit. They may also find that their goals change over time. Mapping out a career path is wise, but it's also wise to keep your plan flexible. See Fig. 9-3.

Fig. 9-3. Career paths sometimes take an unplanned detour. This landscaper originally planned on a computer programming career before discovering he preferred to work outdoors.

Careers and Lifestyle

The work you choose will shape your **lifestyle**, or the way you live, in many ways. It will be a key factor in:

- **How much you earn.** Although pay varies, it's a fact that some career areas and occupations have more earnings potential than others.

- **Where you live and work.** Certain types of jobs are found everywhere, but others exist only in rural settings or large cities. Some are more plentiful in a specific part of the country.

- **Your schedule and free time.** In some jobs, working long hours is expected. Your job might require you to work nights, weekends, and holidays, adjust to a constantly changing schedule, or be on call 24 hours a day. Extensive travel might limit the amount of time that you can spend at home.

Your career choices will influence these factors not just in the short term but for years to come. For these reasons, you need to think carefully about your values and decide what is important to you. Consider how you would honestly answer questions like these:

What type of family life do I envision in my future? Where do I want to live? What level of material comfort and status will I be satisfied with? Do I want to take an active role in community life? What kind of balance do I hope to achieve between my work and other areas of my life?

With your answers to these questions in mind, you'll be able to evaluate career options based on how well their characteristics match your values. Deciding what kind of lifestyle you would like does not guarantee that you will achieve it, of course. But it will help you narrow down your career choices and eliminate those that are clearly unsuitable. See Fig. 9-4.

Fig. 9-4. A flight attendant's job involves frequent travel. *Would everyone find this lifestyle appealing? Why or why not?*

The World of Work

Before you begin to explore specific career options, it's helpful to understand some general characteristics of the world of work. Most career fields include various types of employers and employment. Factors such as pay, benefits, and the work environment may depend in part on which type you choose.

Public and Private Sectors

The world of work is divided into two broad sectors. The *public sector* is funded by tax dollars. It consists of local and state governments and federal government agencies. Police officers, firefighters, teachers in public schools, and park rangers are examples of people who work in the public sector. The *private sector* is the part of the economy that is not controlled by the government. Businesses that produce and sell goods and services to make a profit—such as department stores, automakers, and insurance companies—operate in the private sector. People in some occupations may have a choice of working in the public or private sector. For example, a chemist might work for the U.S. Department of Agriculture or for a food processing company.

Types of Businesses

Businesses in the private sector range from small, family-owned operations to vast enterprises employing thousands of people. Every product you use—computer, jeans, bicycle, shampoo, soda, you name it—was produced by a business. Businesses also provide the services that you purchase, such as haircuts, dry cleaning, car insurance, and so on.

Viewpoints

Large and Small Companies

Like a small town and a big city, a small business and a large company have obvious differences. Yet they can be thought of as different paths to similar goals.

Dale: Working in a big corporation is where the action is. All the resources are there. You have experienced people to teach you and help you make the right moves, plus access to the latest technology. You can learn from the ground up and go as far as your talents take you. You might even find yourself opening a new branch office in another country.

Grace: Working in a small company gives you a better idea of what business is all about. Each employee gets to make more decisions, and each decision may have a direct impact on the company's success. It gives you a great sense of power, and also of responsibility. You feel more connected to your coworkers and the company.

Seeing Both Sides ~ What opportunities do both Dale and Grace see in their work situations? Could either person feel successful in the other's work environment? Explain.

In the United States and countries with a similar economic system, there are three main types of business organizations. *Individual proprietorships* are owned and controlled by one person, known as the proprietor. The proprietor is entitled to all the profits if the business is successful, but risks losing money if it fails. *Partnerships* are owned and controlled by two or more people. They share the profits and the risks. *Corporations* are owned by many people. The owners are called shareholders because they own shares in the company. They make money if the corporation is successful and lose money if it is not.

Fig. 9-5. This bank teller enjoys the flexibility that her part-time job allows. Why might some people prefer part-time instead of full-time work?

Types of Employment

Just as there are different types of businesses, there are also different employment options. You need to be aware of the advantages and disadvantages of each when considering the type of job you will take.

- **Full time.** Working full time generally means spending at least seven or eight hours at work each day, five days a week. It is a major commitment. In return, you may receive benefits such as paid vacations and health insurance and have a chance to advance in your career.

- **Part time.** If you work part time, you may work a few days each week or a few hours each day. This arrangement allows more time off to do other things. However, part-time workers earn less than full-time workers and do not usually receive benefits. See Fig. 9-5.

- **Contract.** Contract work involves working on a specific project for a specified period of time. When the project is over, the workers need to find another assignment. Contract work offers flexibility, but it can result in periods of unemployment between projects.

- **Temporary.** Some employers hire temporary workers to help out during busy seasons or to fill in for vacationing employees. Temporary work may be attractive to those who don't want to make a long-term commitment, but it offers no security or benefits.

- **Freelance.** Freelance workers are self-employed and usually work for a number of different clients. Many work from home. They can choose the hours they work, so they enjoy a degree of flexibility. On the other hand, they may have periods of down time, and they receive no benefits.

Entrepreneurship

An **entrepreneur** is someone who sets up and operates a business. Do you think you have what it takes to be an entrepreneur? Before you answer, consider the rewards and risks of entrepreneurship.

The main reward is that you are your own boss. You decide how the business will be run, what hours you will work, who you will hire, and so on. Some people thrive on these challenges and gain great satisfaction from being in charge. If their business is successful, they may also make a lot of money.

The biggest down side to being an entrepreneur is that you risk losing the money you invest in the business if it fails. More than two-thirds of new businesses do fail within their first four years, so this is a serious risk. Many entrepreneurs also find that they need to work long hours. Running a business takes a lot more time and effort than many people realize.

Changes in the Workplace

Today's workplace is constantly changing. Developments around the world affect the demand for certain goods and services. Economic trends influence consumer spending. Technology changes the way some work is done. Companies have to adapt to such changes in order to stay in business.

You can follow the changes in the world of work by staying informed. Use the news media to find out which industries are growing and which are in decline. Learn about the fastest growing occupations. Talk to people who work in an industry that interests you and ask what changes they anticipate. Be aware of events and trends that could affect the industry. The workers who are best able to anticipate and prepare for change are most likely to be successful. See Fig. 9-6.

Economic Factors

When the United States was founded, almost all the people worked on farms. Then, during the late 1800s and early 1900s, more and more workers left the farms for better-paying jobs in factories. The focus of the U.S. economy shifted from agriculture to manufacturing. In recent years, the focus has shifted again, and today the United States is primarily a *service economy*. This means that more people work at producing services than goods. These services include health care, child care, education, tourism, food service, banking, and insurance.

The shift in emphasis results from the fact that the United States is part of the global economy. The **global economy** refers to the way national economies around the world are linked by trade. Some economic, political, and social barriers among nations are being removed. As a result, goods, services, information, and technology are traded in a global market. Some goods that were once manufactured in the United States are now produced less expensively in other countries.

Fig. 9-6. Recently, one of the fastest growing occupations has been that of medical assistant. What is the advantage of choosing an occupation for which demand is high?

More to Explore

Employment and Health Insurance

Not all of the changes taking place in the world of work are for the better. At one time, most employees could assume that they would receive health insurance, at little cost to themselves, as one of their benefits. That is no longer the case. Rising costs have caused some companies to drop coverage for their employees altogether. Companies that continue to offer insurance require their employees pay a higher share of the costs.

You may think that, as a young person, you don't have to be concerned about health insurance. Not true. If for no other reason, you need health insurance because people in your age group are at high risk for accidents. When researching jobs, find out about the coverage you can expect, if any, and the costs. Factor your findings into your decision making.

It is more economical for the United States to import them than to make them. That is one reason why jobs in manufacturing have declined.

Companies are also affected by economic conditions at a local, regional, national, and international level. Some economic ups and downs are general and affect all industries. Others may affect only a few specific industries, such as the automobile industry or the airline industry.

When times are hard, companies look for ways to reduce their costs. Some resort to **downsizing**, which involves laying workers off in order to reduce costs. Another strategy for containing costs is **outsourcing**, which involves contracting out certain tasks to other companies. A hospital, for example, may hire a laundry service instead of hiring, training, and supervising an in-house laundry staff.

Staying informed about economic conditions will help you make wise career choices. It will help you take advantage of new developments and steer clear of industries that are in decline.

The Role of Technology

Millions of workers in all kinds of industries use computers and other forms of technology to do their work. In offices, stores, factories, and warehouses across the nation, technology enables people to work more quickly and efficiently.

To compete and prosper in today's marketplace, companies must constantly adapt to changing technology. They must invest in equipment and software that will enable their employees to be more productive. They need employees who are flexible and willing to learn new ways of doing things.

No matter what career field you enter and what jobs you hold, you'll probably use technology in some form. It's also likely that you'll need to keep up with changes in technology throughout your working life. Taking the time to master current technology is time well spent.

Preparing for Your Future

Most jobs today require some kind of education or training after high school. Depending on the type of work, the education or training period may last from a few weeks to many years. When researching occupations, learn about the time and effort needed to prepare for them. Once you have a clear idea of the requirements, you can explore specific education or training options.

Education and Training

Further education and training is provided in a variety of schools and colleges throughout the country. Some employers also offer training opportunities. Options to explore include:

- **Apprenticeships.** An **apprenticeship** combines classroom instruction with on-the-job learning. Apprenticeships are most common in skilled trades, such as carpentry and electrical work. They usually take several years to complete, but apprentices are paid during the training period. See Fig. 9-7.

- **Internships.** An **internship** involves short-term work for little or no pay in exchange for an opportunity to work and learn. Employers gain willing workers, while interns gain valuable experience. Interns who demonstrate strong skills may be offered the chance of a full-time position after they complete their schooling.

- **Vocational-technical centers.** These schools and colleges offer training for skilled occupations in a variety of fields such as health care, computer technology, and automotive technology. Most vo-tech centers offer evening as well as daytime classes. Courses may last from one to three years.

- **Trade schools.** Trade schools offer training for specific professions ranging from machining and plumbing to graphic design and computer programming. Most trade schools are privately run and tend to be more expensive than vocational-technical centers. However, they may offer specialized courses that are not available in other types of institutions.

Fig. 9-7. An apprenticeship provides an opportunity to learn from more experienced workers.
What are other advantages of on-the-job learning?

- **City or community colleges.** These colleges offer two-year associate degree programs in a wide range of occupational areas. Many have evening and weekend classes. Students who graduate usually have the option of transferring credits to a four-year degree program.

- **Colleges and universities.** These institutions offer four-year courses of academic study leading to a bachelor's degree. A bachelor's degree is the minimum requirement for many higher-paying professions. Colleges and universities also offer graduate programs leading to advanced degrees.

- **Armed forces.** The armed forces offer training in more than 1,500 different fields, including electronics, engineering, mechanics, and computer technology. To receive training, you must enlist for a minimum of four years of active duty. Later you can use the training in a civilian occupation.

- **Distance learning.** If you can't attend traditional classes, you might be able to enroll in a distance learning program. These programs use the Internet, videos, and other forms of communication technology to teach students in their homes or in other off-campus locations.

Paying for Education

~ It's one thing to decide what kind of education or training you need, but another to figure out how you're going to pay for it. Education and training costs can be expensive. Depending on what you decide to do, you may have to pay for tuition, books and supplies, room and board, and transportation. Where's the money going to come from?

It's a good idea to face this question while you are still in high school. You might need to start saving money now. Consider taking a

TIPS FOR *Success*

Cutting Education Costs

Here are some ideas for cutting education and training costs:

- Take advanced placement courses while you're in high school. You may be able to convert them into college credits and save tuition costs.
- Improve your chances of getting financial aid by getting good grades.
- Reduce tuition costs by attending a college in the state where you live.
- Take as many classes as you can handle so that you can graduate early and enter the workforce sooner.

part-time job after school and a full-time job during school breaks. Start a savings account, and don't use this money for any other purpose. Talk to your family. Depending on their income, they may be able to set money aside for your education in a special, tax-free account.

Many students receive financial aid for their education in the form of grants, scholarships, or loans. Grants are usually given on the basis of need, while scholarships are usually awarded on the basis of academic achievement, athletic skill, or special talents. Grants and scholarships do not have to be repaid. Loans, on the other hand, which are offered by colleges and banks, must be repaid over a period of time. Education loans are usually offered at a lower interest rate than most other loans.

When considering loans and other options, remember that money spent on education and training is an investment in your future. In general, the more education and training you receive, the more money you'll be able to earn.

Employability Skills

Education and training can help you learn the skills needed to perform a specific job. However, there's another set of skills that you need no matter what career field you enter. These are **employability skills**—the skills that help you fit into the workplace and be a valuable team player. Employers need people who can demonstrate basic academic skills, thinking skills, technology skills, interpersonal skills, and management skills. See Fig. 9-8.

By developing a wide variety of skills and abilities, you'll perform better in whatever career path you follow. What's more, whenever you change jobs or careers, you'll be able to transfer these skills to your new work situation.

Basic Academic Skills ~ Employers expect workers they hire to have basic academic skills. If yours aren't strong, you'll be at a disadvantage.

- **Reading** is as critical at work as it is in other aspects of daily life. To do your job correctly, you'll need to read and understand letters, manuals, reports, schedules, and other information.

- **Writing** skills enable you to communicate clearly when you write letters, memos, and reports, fill out forms, and send e-mails.

Fig. 9-8. The classes you're taking right now are building your employability skills.

- **Math** skills are needed for tasks such as counting change, tallying sales figures, and understanding graphs and charts. While calculators and computers make it easier to do calculations, you still need basic math skills to use these tools properly.

Thinking Skills ~ Sports fans know that successful athletes need more than just physical skills. They need to be able to concentrate, take initiative, and make quick decisions. Similarly, thinking skills will help you get ahead in the workplace. You need:

- **Critical thinking** skills to judge the reliability of information.
- **Reasoning** skills to draw conclusions and apply what you learn to new situations.
- **Creative thinking** skills to solve problems and come up with new ideas.

Interpersonal Skills ~ To work effectively with others, you need good communication skills and the ability to work as part of a team. Communication skills include listening actively, giving feedback, and speaking clearly. Teamwork involves working toward a common goal, putting the team before self, and being willing to compromise.

TEXTLINK≈

You can learn more about *communication skills* in Chapter 15 and about *teamwork* in Chapter 16.

Technology Skills ~ As you learned earlier, most jobs today require the ability to use computers and the software programs needed to perform specific operations. At the very least, you should be familiar with the basics of word processing. You're more likely to get ahead if you know how to use spreadsheet, database, and scheduling programs.

You should also be able to send and receive e-mail and use the Internet to find information. See Fig. 9-9.

Management Skills ~ Management skills aren't just for managers. All workers can use skills such as planning, setting priorities, organizing, and managing resources to do their work more effectively. Management skills are essential if you want to get ahead in your career.

Workplace Readiness

You may not be ready to move out into the workplace just yet. Fortunately, there's a lot you can do while still in school to build your workplace readiness. Here are a few suggestions:

- Work on your basic skills. Ask your teacher to tell you what you most need to improve, and work on that area first.
- Strengthen your technology skills. Take advantage of every available opportunity to become familiar with high-tech equipment and to learn new software programs.

Character IN ACTION

Improving Talents and Skills Use the many opportunities you have now to improve your talents and skills for future employment needs. It takes time, effort, and self-discipline. Commit yourself to a plan to learn and master talents and skills over time. Don't be afraid to ask others to help you. Know that your efforts and success will pay off. From time to time, reflect on how you have improved, and celebrate your progress. What could you do to help others develop their talents and skills?

Fig. 9-9. More and more jobs require computer skills. Dry cleaners, for example, use a computer to tag garments.

- Strengthen your communication skills. At school and at home, practice listening and speaking one-on-one and in a group. Focus on organizing your thoughts and expressing yourself clearly.

- Take advantage of classroom activities that will make you more marketable. You might, for example, take an active role in mock interviews or act out work-related situations.

- Get direct experience of the workplace by volunteering or taking a part-time job. Notice what it takes to get the work done. Be aware of the different roles people play.

- Talk to people who have jobs. Find out what skills they use and how they use them.

The more you prepare for your role in the workplace, the more comfortable you'll be when you start your first job. Just don't expect to stop learning once you receive that first paycheck. Education, training, and skill development will be a continual part of your career development in the changing world of work. Learning is a lifelong process.

Review & Activities

Chapter Summary

- People work to satisfy physical, emotional, intellectual, and social needs.
- Your career will influence significant aspects of your lifestyle.
- Employment options include full-time, part-time, contract, temporary, and free-lance work.

- Entrepreneurs enjoy rewards but must accept risks and hard work.
- The world of work is constantly changing in response to political, economic, and social events.
- Most jobs require education and training after high school.
- Employability skills include basic, thinking, technology, interpersonal, and management skills.

Reviewing Key Terms & Ideas

1. Give two examples of how working can contribute to emotional health.
2. What is the difference between a job and a **career**?
3. What aspects of **lifestyle** are impacted by career decisions?
4. Does a clerk in the county courthouse work in the public sector or the private sector? Explain.
5. Compare full-time and part-time work. What are the advantages and disadvantages of each?
6. What are some rewards of being an **entrepreneur**? What are some possible drawbacks?
7. What is the **global economy**? What are its implications for U.S. manufacturers?
8. Why do companies need to adapt constantly to changing technology?

9. Explain the difference between an **apprenticeship** and an **internship**.
10. Give four examples of costs that you might incur if you go to college. What kind of financial aid might be available to meet those costs?
11. Why should you develop **employability skills**? Which of these skills can you practice while still in school?

Thinking Critically

1. **Understanding Cause and Effect.** Why is it important to consider the lifestyle you would like when planning your career?
2. **Drawing Conclusions.** What actions can you take now that will give you a more competitive edge when you start interviewing for a job?

Applying Your Knowledge

1. **Why People Work.** Interview three people you know who appear to be happy in their jobs. Ask them to describe the rewards and satisfactions of their work. Take notes and write a brief report on your findings.
2. **Building Employability Skills.** Make a list of the employability skills you need to focus on. Draw up a plan for working on those skills. In your plan, include short-term goals and steps for reaching the goals.

Making Connections

1. **Social Studies.** Research how the global economy has affected employment patterns around the world. Choose a specific product, such as steel or cars, and find out where the product is now produced and where it used to be produced. If there has been a change, find out why.
2. **Math.** Use an almanac or a government Web site to obtain employment figures by occupation for the United States. Look for broad categories such as Service Occupations, Manufacturing, Farming, and so on. Use a calculator to add up the totals and determine percentages. Then prepare a circle graph that presents your findings.

Managing Your Life

Researching Financial Aid

It's not too soon to start finding out what kind of financial aid you might receive if you decide to go to college. Ask your school guidance counselor for a list of sources of aid. Search the Internet by keying in terms such as "financial aid" or "scholarships." Contact your state's education department to find out if you might qualify for state funding. Prepare a chart on which you can record and compare your findings.

Using Technology

1. **The Impact of Technology.** In a small group, discuss ways in which specific technologies may have contributed to the following trends: downsizing; outsourcing; the growth of freelance opportunities; the increasing intrusion of work on personal time. Share your group's ideas with the class.
2. **Distance Learning.** Find a Web site that gives information about a specific distance learning program. In your own words, summarize how the program works. How do students interact with the instructor and with one another? Do they ever meet face-to-face? How are assignments given and turned in? How are tests taken? Based on this program, what do you see as the main advantages and disadvantages of distance learning?

CHAPTER 10

Exploring Career Paths

Key Terms

- aptitudes
- career cluster
- job shadowing
- career plan

Objectives

- **Assess** personal qualities that influence career choices.
- **Explain** the purpose of career clusters.
- **Evaluate** career options using information gathered from appropriate sources.
- **Compare** ways of getting firsthand work experience.
- **Describe** the components of a career plan.

If you could choose any job in the world, what would it be? Write a few sentences explaining why that job appeals to you so much.

A hundred years ago, career choices were not as complex as they are today. There were fewer occupations to choose from, and most people understood what the work involved. Everyone knew, for example, what a farmer, a shopkeeper, a seamstress, or a factory worker did for a living.

In the United States today, there are more than 20,000 occupations to choose from, and new ones emerge every week. Job titles such as systems analyst, desktop publisher, and software engineer were unheard of a few decades ago. Now these are among the fastest growing occupations. Many jobs are also less "visible" than those of yesteryear. People pour into vast office skyscrapers every day, but what do they do once they get inside? To add to the confusion, many jobs are so technical that they're hard to explain to someone outside the profession.

With all this complexity, how can you possibly know which career field to enter? Some people don't make a choice. They just take the first job that comes along, then drift from one job to another without a clear sense of direction. If you want a satisfying career, that's not the right approach. You need to examine your options, make the best choice for you, and set out along your chosen path.

Personal Assessment

The average person in your generation can expect to work until beyond age 67. That's a big chunk of time! With all those working years ahead of you, you'll want to choose work that is challenging and enjoyable. How do you do that? You can start by examining who you are and what's important to you. That means looking at your aptitudes, skills, interests, personality traits, and values. See Fig. 10-1.

Fig. 10-1. You're more likely to make wise career choices if you think carefully about your personal qualities, such as how you like to spend your free time.

Your Aptitudes and Skills

From the time she was a child, Stacey loved to take things apart and put them back together. Her friend Geraldo, in contrast, jokes that he has trouble replacing a light bulb. However, speaking in front of a group seems to come naturally to him.

Like Stacey and Geraldo, you have certain **aptitudes**, or natural talents, that you were born with. In addition, you have skills that you've developed through training and practice. For example, being good with numbers is an aptitude; knowing how to solve a trigonometry problem is a skill. Together, your aptitudes and skills form a valuable package that you can build on and that you can offer an employer. See Fig. 10-2.

Choosing a line of work that matches your aptitudes and skills is a good idea. It lets you use your strengths and increases your chances of success. To identify your aptitudes and skills, ask yourself:

- What school subjects are easiest for me?
- What do I do well?
- What could I probably learn to do well?
- Which of my skills were easiest to learn?
- What aptitudes and skills do my teachers, family, and friends think I have?

Your Interests

Interests that you enjoy in your free time might suggest a satisfying career direction. Leo, for example, enjoys taking photos, playing soccer, collecting baseball cards, and watching sports on television. Do you see a way to link these interests to an occupation? One possibility for Leo is working as a sports photographer.

Getting involved in after-school activities can help you develop current interests and discover new ones. Your school and community offer many opportunities in such areas as sports, music, drama, science, and debate. An interest that starts out as a hobby might lead to a fulfilling career.

Your Personality

If you're shy, you probably would not enjoy working as a salesperson. If you enjoy being outdoors, you might feel stifled if you took an office job. Consider the kind of person you are when exploring your career options. You'll be far happier in a career for which your attitudes, characteristics, and other personality traits are well suited. See Fig. 10-3.

Fig. 10-2. Throughout your life, you continue to develop a variety of skills. What are some occupations in which woodworking skills would be an asset?

Fig. 10-3. Your personality will give you clues to the occupations that will suit you. What personality traits would help this teacher to be successful at his work?

To learn more about your personality traits, ask yourself:

- Do I prefer working alone or with others?
- Do I look for stability or do I enjoy taking risks?
- Am I careful and methodical or do details annoy me?
- Do I dislike stress or do I thrive on it?
- Am I good at concentrating or do I need distractions?
- Do I prefer working indoors or outdoors?
- Do I prefer to lead or to follow?

Awareness of your personality traits and personal preferences will be valuable as you research career fields. It will help you focus on the right ones for you and steer clear of those for which you are clearly not suited.

Your Values

Your values are your beliefs, feelings, and ideas about what is important. They will guide you in your career choices. For example, if you feel called to help others, you might consider professions such as nursing, counseling, or social work. If you care deeply about the environment and want to make a difference, look into occupations that focus on protecting natural resources. If you strongly believe in the importance of education, consider teaching.

Other, more practical, values will also have a bearing on your career choices. For example, is it important that you work regular hours? Do you want to make a lot of money? Do you want to stay close to home? Following a career path that reflects your values will help ensure that you enjoy your work and find it worthwhile.

Assessment Tools

Identifying your aptitudes, skills, interests, personality traits, and values is not always easy. Fortunately, assessment tools are available to help. They include questionnaires, tests, and surveys that help you discover more about your strengths and weaknesses and what is important to you. Your school guidance counselor can tell you more about these tools.

Researching Career Fields

Once you have a clearer understanding of yourself, you can start to identify career fields and occupations that might be a good fit for you. To do that, you'll need to do some research.

Career Clusters

When you go to a bookstore, you don't have to look at every book to find the one you want. Instead, you look at signs that direct you to the right section. Similarly, you don't have to research 20,000 occupations to find the best one for you. You can narrow down your search by using a career cluster system. A **career cluster** is a group of occupations that have certain characteristics in common. Often these occupations require many of the same types of skills. If you have the skills to be successful in one occupation, there are likely to be other occupations in the same cluster that you might like.

Ten Career Clusters

- Health & Medicine
- Agriculture & Natural Resources
- Government, Law & Public Safety
- Arts & Communication
- Human Services
- Education & Training
- Business & Finance
- Hospitality & Tourism
- Manufacturing & Engineering
- Housing & Construction

The ten career clusters used in this text are listed in Fig. 10-4. You may come across other cluster systems as you research careers. The U.S. Department of Education, for example, identifies 16 career clusters. No matter what system is used, the goals are similar: to simplify your career search.

Career clusters can also help you plan a career path. Within each cluster, you'll find occupations that require different levels of education and training. You can use this information to chart a progression through a series of jobs that will advance your career. The "Career Options" features in this book show sample job opportunities at different levels. Those features also relate the career paths of specific individuals.

Sources of Information

Locating information about career fields and occupations is easy once you know where to look. The library in your school is a good place to start. Most school libraries have a careers section where you will find reference books, magazines, videos, and other information sources, as well as Internet access.

Print Sources ~ Two valuable resources published by the U.S. Department of Labor are the *Career Guide to Industries* and *Occupational Outlook Handbook*. Both are updated every two years. The *Career Guide to*

Fig. 10-4. You'll learn more about these career clusters as you read the "Career Options" features found in this textbook.

Fig. 10-5. Start your review of printed career information in your school library. The librarian will know which titles will help you most.

Industries looks at whole industries, while *Occupational Outlook Handbook* explores occupations within those industries. Complementing these two works is the *Occupational Outlook Quarterly*. Updated every three months, it covers topics such as new and emerging occupations, training opportunities, and salary trends.

If you have an idea of the industry you would like to work in but no specific occupation in mind, the *Career Guide to Industries* would be a good place to start. It describes more than 40 industries, explaining the nature of each industry, the working conditions, the occupations included, and the outlook for that industry. It also gives information on training, advancement prospects, and earnings. Once you have a particular occupation in mind, go to

Occupational Outlook Handbook. It gives detailed information on thousands of occupations, including the nature of the work, the working conditions, average earnings, and job outlook.

You'll find many other books about career planning on the library shelves. Ask your librarian to direct you to the ones most relevant to your search. Be sure to check the publication date of any book you use. Out-of-date books could give misleading information. See Fig. 10-5.

Online Sources ~ The *Career Guide to Industries, Occupational Outlook Handbook,* and *Occupational Outlook Quarterly* are all available online. Using them as online resources makes it easy to move from one to another and back. At the end of each industry profile and occupation profile, you will find links to other Web sites that provide additional information.

Another valuable online resource is the Department of Labor's Occupational Information Network, or O*NET. This online database offers information on more than 950 occupations. You can use it to research career clusters and fields and to find out which occupations match your skills and interests.

Interviewing People ~ You can also find out about different occupations by locating people with careers that interest you and asking them about their work. This is not always possible, of course, but such interviews are worthwhile if you can arrange them. Before meeting with the person, prepare a list of questions you want to ask. Most people are happy to tell you about their work, and an insider's view will tell you far more than pages of print. See Fig. 10-6.

Information to Gather

You've decided to look into some career fields or occupations that interest you. What do you need to find out? Here are some topics to research:

- **Nature of the work.** What are the main tasks and responsibilities? What skills are required? Who would you interact with? What equipment would you use?

- **Working conditions.** What hours are involved? Would you work indoors or outdoors? Alone or as part of a team? Would you be exposed to noise or dirt? Does the work involve physical labor? Would you be expected to dress in a certain way?

Fig. 10-6. You'll gain a lot of valuable information by talking to someone who has a career that interests you.

- **Qualifications.** What level of education is required? What other skills and training are needed? What high school courses would be useful?

- **Employment patterns.** How many people are employed in this line of work? What types of organizations or industries employ them? Are the jobs concentrated in certain geographic areas?

- **Earnings.** What are the average earnings for this occupation? What accounts for differences in earnings? What kinds of benefits are usually offered?

- **Future prospects.** What is the outlook for this occupation or career field? Is it growing fast, slowly, or not at all? What impact might technology have on future prospects?

Looking at Trends

Given the rapid pace of change in today's world, it's important to look at issues and trends that may have an impact on your career plans. Technology, for instance, will continue to have a huge impact on career trends. It has eliminated some jobs while creating others. It has also changed the way people do their jobs. For example, secretaries who used to take shorthand and work at typewriters are now administrative assistants, working at computers and handling a wider variety of tasks.

Population patterns also affect employment trends. Since the number of older Americans is growing, the demand for services targeted at them is likely to grow too. By anticipating employment and social trends, you can focus on career areas that have a promising future.

Getting Firsthand Experience

One of the best ways to find out about career options is to get actual work experience. Here are some options to consider:

- **Part-time work.** You may be able to work evenings, weekends, or during the summer while you're still in school. See Fig. 10-7.

Fig. 10-7. Doing part-time work is one way to gain experience and learn how a business operates. What might this theater usher learn from her part-time job?

- **Volunteer work.** Helping out in your community benefits you as well as others. Although you aren't paid for the work, the experience is valuable.

- **Youth employment programs.** Some communities create work opportunities for teens, especially during the summer months. For example, they might hire teens to help with the preparations for a parade or festival.

- **Job shadowing.** Spending time in the workplace with someone who has a job that interests you is called **job shadowing**. You follow the person as he or she goes through a normal workday. By watching and listening, you learn what the work involves.

- **Work-study programs.** In some communities, schools and businesses work together to provide on-the-job training for teens. Students spend part of their week in school and part at work.

- **Internships.** Companies that hire interns offer them an opportunity to work and learn at the same time. Interns are usually assigned specific tasks. They may be unpaid or may receive minimum wage.

Firsthand work experience is valuable for several reasons. It helps you learn more about possible career areas, the drawbacks and rewards of particular jobs, and how businesses operate. You'll also be able to discover what kinds of work you most enjoy. On-the-job experience gives you a chance to develop valuable skills and positive work habits, a selling point when you apply for jobs in the future. The supervisor you work for may be willing to recommend you to other potential employers—or even hire you for a full-time job someday.

Developing a Career Plan

At this stage in your life, you may or may not have a clear idea of what career path you plan to follow. It's not necessary to make a firm decision now. What's more important is to gather ideas of what you might like to do and to learn as much as you can about your options.

Eventually, however, you'll need to focus on the one career area that seems to be the best match for you. Use your decision-making skills to evaluate the pros and cons of each option and narrow down your choices. Consider both what you know about yourself and the information you have gathered about career areas and occupations.

TEXTLINK ≈

The *decision-making process* is discussed in detail in Chapter 6.

When you have chosen a direction for your career, you're ready to start developing a **career plan**—a plan for the career path that you will follow. A career plan includes a long-term goal and the short-term goals that will enable you to reach it.

Here's an example. Anisa's long-term goal is to be a high school family and consumer sciences teacher. Her short-term goals include:

- Taking family and consumer sciences courses in high school.

- Getting involved in Family, Career and Community Leaders of America (FCCLA).

- Applying to colleges with degree programs in family and consumer sciences education.

FINDING CREATIVE SOLUTIONS

Listing Pros and Cons

Problem solving often involves weighing several alternatives before deciding on the best solution. One way to evaluate your options is to list the pros and cons of each.

▶ How It Works

Writing down pros and cons, rather than just thinking about them, will help you see them more clearly. Use a separate sheet of paper for each option you're considering. Make two columns, one for positive aspects and one for negative aspects. Remember to consider consequences for other people as well as yourself, and for the future as well as the present.

Ideally, the option you choose will have more pros than cons, and more pros than the other options. However, you should go beyond looking at which list is longer. Some pros and cons may be more important to you than others. It's up to you to weigh the factors that you list.

▶ Try It Out

John has decided he wants to be an electrician. Now he needs to choose a training option that will provide him with the experience and knowledge needed to pass the state licensing exam and become a skilled and trusted professional. A local contractor offered John an unpaid opportunity for full-time, hands-on training. The nearest junior college offers a two-year program with apprenticeship opportunities. John is also considering a military program that provides extensive training for future electricians.

▶ **Your Turn** *If you were in John's position, what factors might you consider as you made your list of pros and cons? Which of these factors would carry the most weight for you? Why?*

- Getting firsthand work experience by working part-time and summer jobs.

As you follow your chosen career path, you may discover that your interests or priorities change or that the opportunities in your chosen field are too limited. For these and other reasons, it's a good idea to keep an open mind and be prepared to change course. People tend to change careers more often now than in the past, and that trend is likely to continue. Your main task, at this stage in your life, is to get started along the road to success in whatever you decide to do.

Chapter Summary

- A personal assessment can help you choose a career area that is right for you.

- Career clusters make it easier to explore career options.

- You can gather information about occupations from print and online sources and by interviewing people who have careers that interest you.

- You can get firsthand work experience through part-time work, volunteering, job shadowing, a work-study or youth employment program, or an internship.

- Once you narrow down your options, the next step is to develop a career plan.

Reviewing Key Terms & Ideas

1. What should you examine when conducting a personal assessment?

2. What is the difference between **aptitudes** and skills? Give two examples of each.

3. What types of assessment tools can help you with career planning?

4. What are **career clusters**? How can they help you plan a career path?

5. What is the difference between the *Career Guide to Industries* and the *Occupational Outlook Handbook*?

6. What information should you look for when researching a potential career field?

7. Why do you need to investigate employment trends when looking into career options?

8. What is **job shadowing**? How does it differ from an internship?

9. Name three advantages of getting first-hand work experience while you are still in school.

10. What is a **career plan**? What should be included in it?

Thinking Critically

1. **Making Comparisons.** How might making career choices be different for you than it was for your parents or grandparents?

2. **Understanding Cause and Effect.** Why are people more likely to succeed in a career that reflects their interests and values?

Applying Your Knowledge

1. **Personal Assessment.** Make a list of the aptitudes, skills, interests, personality traits, and values you possess that might influence your career choices. Identify at least three in each category. Give examples to illustrate how you know that you possess each.

2. **Evaluating Career Options.** Use the information sources mentioned in the chapter to research three occupations that interest you. Create a table comparing key facts about the occupations. Based on your findings, which of the three occupations currently seems to be the best choice? Why?

Making Connections

1. **Math.** Create a graph that shows one recent or projected change in the employment market. Examples are the increase in service jobs and the decline in jobs in manufacturing. Use the references identified in this chapter, as well as the latest edition of the *World Almanac and Book of Facts*. Share your results with your classmates.

2. **Language Arts.** The increased percentage of older Americans in the population will affect employment patterns. Write a brief essay describing the kinds of jobs that are likely to increase as a result of this population change.

Managing Your Life

Creating Career Exploration Files

It's easy to become overwhelmed when you start researching career areas. There's so much information available, both in print and on the Web. You'll find your task easier if you create special files where you can keep track of the sources you used and the information you found most helpful. In a file folder, keep a list of each book, magazine, pamphlet, and Web site you use. Note where the print sources are located and what they are useful for. For Web addresses, keep a list of the sites you found most helpful along with their URLs and any relevant notes.

Using Technology

1. **Internet.** Find the O*NET Web site. Locate the search option that lets you select skills from a list and search for related occupations. Conduct a search based on your ten strongest skills out of those listed. Choose skills from at least four areas. Report on the results.

2. **Multimedia Presentation.** Choose one of the ten career clusters identified in Fig. 10-4. Imagine that you have been hired to recruit people into this field or a particular aspect of it. Create a ten-minute multimedia presentation that emphasizes the challenges and rewards of this career area.

CHAPTER 11

Finding a Job

Key Terms

- résumé
- references
- portfolio
- job leads
- networking
- cover letter
- compensation package

Objectives

- **Prepare** documents needed for a job search.
- **Compare** ways of finding job leads.
- **Demonstrate** how to complete a job application.
- **Propose** strategies for a successful job interview.
- **Describe** how to evaluate a job offer.

If you started looking for a job tomorrow, where would you begin? Jot down your ideas for starting a job search. Add to your list as you read this chapter.

Ask ten different people how they got their job, and you'll probably get ten different answers—everything from "A friend told me her company was hiring" to "I found it on the Web." One thing everyone will tell you, however, is that you have to make an effort. Employers won't come looking for you. You have to find the opportunities and pursue them. First, though, you need to get prepared. There's a lot you can do to ensure that your job search goes smoothly.

Organizing a Job Search

If you were going to make a pizza from scratch, how would you start? You wouldn't just pull random items out of the refrigerator and cabinets and set them in the oven. Instead, you'd make sure you had the right ingredients and that you knew what to do with them. The same is true of a job search. Before you start making calls or filling out applications, take time to prepare the documents you'll need and to do the necessary research.

Preparing a Résumé

Most employers ask job applicants to provide a résumé. A **résumé** is a written summary of a job seeker's work experience, education, skills, and interests. Think of it as a written portrait of your qualifications for

the job. You'll find that this organized list of skills and experience is also helpful for filling out applications and preparing for interviews.

Your résumé may determine whether or not you will be interviewed, so you should spend some time on it. Think carefully about what you will include and how you will organize the information. See Fig. 11-1.

Fig. 11-1. Brainstorming a list of your skills and accomplishments is a good way to begin writing your résumé. *What would you put on your résumé?*

There are several possible ways to organize a résumé. Fig. 11-2 on the facing page shows one example. Notice the categories of information that are included, such as work experience, educational background, and skills. You might also want to highlight honors and awards, membership in professional organizations, and other relevant information.

Many employers ask for **references**, the names of people they can contact to learn more about you. You can list the names on your résumé, or simply write "References available on request" and provide them at a later date. Before giving anyone's name as a reference, be sure to ask the person's permission. Choose people such as former employ-ers, teachers, or religious leaders. Ask those who can honestly give a positive recommen-dation of your abilities and character.

Use a computer to prepare your résumé. Make sure it is neat and that there are no spelling or grammatical errors. Once you are happy with it, print it out and have someone check it for you. Another pair of eyes may spot an error that you missed.

Electronic résumés are increasingly common. These are computer documents that can be e-mailed to potential employers and posted to online job search databases. Before preparing an electronic résumé, find out what guidelines the employer or job search site wants you to follow.

Compiling a Portfolio

Depending on the type of job you're looking for, you might want to prepare a **portfolio**. This is a collection of work samples that demonstrate your skills. For example, someone who wants to work at a newspaper might have a portfolio of writing samples or artwork. The samples should be placed in some type of folder that will both protect them and present them attractively.

Whether or not you prepare work samples, you'll want to have certain other documents with you when you apply for a job or go for an interview. It's a good idea to compile a special folder for these items. In it, place copies of your résumé, a list of references, letters of recommendation from former employers, award certificates, and any other relevant information.

TIPS FOR *Success*

Résumé Writing

A résumé is a tool for selling yourself. For a successful résumé:

- Keep it brief—ideally one page.
- Include an employment objective that fits the job you're applying for.
- When listing work experience and education, start with the most recent experience and work backward.
- If you've never been employed, highlight experiences such as volunteer work, school activities, and neighborhood jobs.
- Focus on your strengths. Include any awards or honors you've received.
- Above all, make sure everything on your résumé is accurate and honest.

Emily Nichols
510 Chestnut Street
Springdale, GA 33333
020-555-7890
enichols@xyz.com

EMPLOYMENT OBJECTIVE
To obtain a position as a teacher's aide in a preschool program.

WORK EXPERIENCE
Teacher's Aide. Carmine College. Have worked with the children of students and faculty in this preschool program for an average of 8 hours a week since August 2004.

Child Care Assistant. Valley Child Care Center. Worked as an aide from June through August 2003 and 2004.

Babysitter. Have been a neighborhood babysitter for five years. Clients have included many families with infants and young children.

EDUCATIONAL BACKGROUND
Delany High School, graduated May 2006
CPR training, Springdale YWCA, July 2006

SPECIAL SKILLS
- Proven ability to teach young children new skills and lead them in games.
- Organized Little Brother/Little Sister Day at Delany High School in 2005 and 2006.
- Can sight read music and play the piano.
- Can speak and write some Spanish.

HONORS
National Honor Society, 2004–2006

ACTIVITIES AND INTERESTS
Have had roles in class plays at high school; member of the school choir for three years; enjoy playing the piano, camping, and singing.

REFERENCES
Available on request.

Fig. 11-2. Notice how this résumé is organized. Why do employers prefer résumés that are brief and easy to read?

More to Explore

Creating an Electronic Portfolio

You may want to develop an electronic portfolio—one that is created and viewed on a computer. Like its paper counterpart, an electronic portfolio is designed to help employers learn about your strengths and personal qualities. But instead of putting the information in a paper folder, you place it on a CD or DVD, or perhaps create a Web page to which you direct prospective employers.

One advantage of an electronic portfolio is that it allows a multimedia approach. Here are some ideas for what you might include:

- **Text.** Your electronic résumé; writing samples; a personal statement of your strengths.
- **Images.** Photos of you participating in a volunteer project; scans of your artwork; photos of items that you've made or built.
- **Audio.** An audio file that demonstrates your fluency in a second language.
- **Video.** A brief segment that demonstrates your public speaking ability or other special skills.

Each time you share your electronic portfolio, update it with new information and samples if needed. Remember, the creativity and quality of your portfolio presentation will help make a positive impression.

Finding Job Leads

You've written your résumé and assembled your portfolio. Now the question is, who will you show them to? You need to identify employers that might want to hire you. **Job leads**, or information about specific job openings, may come from many sources. Exploring different sources of job leads will increase your chances of finding a job that's right for you.

Networking ~ Networking involves using personal contacts to find a job. Your network may include relatives, friends, neighbors, local business owners, former employers, members of your place of worship, and members of any clubs you belong to. Let these people know what kind of job you're looking for. One of them might know of a suitable job lead. Pay particular attention to people who work in companies where you would like to work. These people may be able to provide you with not only job leads but also useful information about the company.

Don't feel embarrassed about asking personal contacts for help in finding a job. Most people are happy to assist in such an important matter. Networking is an effective way to locate job leads. In fact, it may be the only way to learn about the many job openings that are not advertised.

School Resources ~ Be sure to take advantage of your school's efforts to help students find jobs. Your school career counselor will have useful information and may also post notices of available jobs. Perhaps your school organizes an annual job fair, at which local businesses give information and applications to interested students. Attending a job fair is a great way to learn about employers in your community and the job opportunities they offer. Your school may also organize work-study programs that can lead to full-time job opportunities.

Printed Ads ~ You'll find ads for jobs in the classified section of most newspapers. The ads are usually organized into different categories, such as "Industrial/Technical," "Medical/Dental," and "Office/Clerical." Certain magazines that focus on specific industries also carry job ads.

Internet Resources ~ Many Web sites post job listings. These sites typically let you search by job title, employment location, and other criteria. You can also post your résumé online so that potential employers can access it.

If there's a particular company that you'd like to work for, visit its Web site. Job openings may be posted there, and you'll also be able to learn about the company. See Fig. 11-3.

Employment Agencies ~ Employment agencies bring together job seekers and employers. The job seekers fill out agency applications, employers describe their openings, and the agency tries to match them up.

There are two main types of employment agencies. Public employment agencies, operated by state governments, usually have offices in large cities and towns. They also post job openings on their Web sites. Their services are free. Private employment agencies charge a fee for their services. The employer or person hired pays the fee. Some agencies specialize in certain career fields, such as health care or technology.

Fig. 11-3. Many companies post job openings on the Internet. What are some advantages of using the Internet as a job search tool?

Emily Nichols
510 Chestnut Street
Springdale, GA 33333
020-555-7890
enichols@xyz.com

June 11, 20—

Mr. Alex Sanchez, Principal
The Willow Preschool
320 David Road
Springdale, GA 33333

Dear Ms. Sanchez:

Donna Mulvaney, whose daughter Courtney attends your preschool, suggested that I contact you about a position as a teacher's aide at the Willow Preschool. I understand that one of your aides is about to leave and that you plan to replace her.

Please consider me for this position. I worked as a part-time teacher's aide for two years while I was finishing high school. Now that I have graduated, I would like to work with children full time. I believe that I have had enough experience working with children to know that I enjoy this kind of work, and that children respond very positively to me. Please review my enclosed résumé. It provides more details about the skills and experience I can bring to your preschool program.

I am especially interested in working at the Willow Preschool because I have heard many positive things about it from parents in my neighborhood. I hope you will find that I have the necessary skills and background to be considered for the position.

I would be happy to attend an interview at any time. Thank you for your consideration.

Sincerely,

Emily Nichols

Emily Nichols

Fig. 11-4. A cover letter is another opportunity to highlight your strong points. *What qualifications did Emily point out in her cover letter?*

Fig. 11-5. A well prepared application can be your "ticket" to an interview.

Applying for a Job

When applying for a job, remember that you may be one of dozens or even hundreds of applicants. To improve your chances of being chosen, you need to "sell yourself" by highlighting your best qualities. Employers will be interested in the skills you have to offer, of course. But they will also be influenced by what you write or say, how you dress, how you speak, and how you behave. Whether you apply in writing, in person, or by telephone, making a good impression is essential.

Writing a Cover Letter

When you learn about a job opening, the first step in applying is usually to send your résumé. Along with it, you'll need to send a **cover letter**, a brief letter in which you introduce yourself. An effective cover letter tells why you are interested in the job and summarizes your main qualifications. Your goal is to convince the employer that you are enthusiastic, qualified, and worth interviewing. A sample cover letter is shown in Fig. 11-4 on the facing page.

Completing an Application

Many employers require applicants to complete an application form. It asks for personal information, such as your address, phone number, and Social Security number. It also asks for information about your education and work experience.

When completing an application form, have your résumé and other job search documents handy. That way you will have most of the information you need. Read the instructions before you start to fill in the form. Write as neatly and clearly as you can. If a question doesn't apply to you, write NA, for "not applicable." When finished, check over the form to make sure it's complete, accurate, and neat. If the application has misspelled words or other errors, the employer might assume that you are careless or sloppy. See Fig. 11-5.

Interviewing for a Job

The majority of job applicants never get past the initial screening, so being asked to an interview is a good sign. It means that you've made a strong enough impression to be considered a serious candidate. The interview is probably the most important part of the job-seeking process. It's well worth spending time to prepare for it.

Preparing for the Interview

A good way to start preparing for an interview is to learn about the company. If the company has a Web site, check it out. If you know someone who already works there, talk with that person. Find out more about what the company does, what's going on in the industry as a whole, and how current market trends may affect the company. Knowing about the company will help you ask intelligent questions and create a good impression.

Another way to prepare is to anticipate the questions you might be asked and plan how you will answer them. It's likely that you will be asked about your education, your work experience, your career goals, and your interest in the job. You might also be asked about your strengths and weaknesses. You might want to arrange for a family member or friend to ask you some typical questions so that you can practice your answers.

Decide ahead of time what you will wear for the interview, and make sure the clothes you want to wear are clean and pressed. Plan to be well groomed, too. Remember that the first thing your interviewer will notice is your general appearance. A clean and neat appearance make a more favorable impression. See Fig. 11-6.

Make sure you know the exact place and time of the interview and the interviewer's name. If you're not sure how long it will take you to get there, do a trial run. On the evening before the interview, gather all the items you'll need, including a pen and note pad, and get a good night's sleep.

Making a Positive Impression

During the interview, you will be judged on more than your résumé and your answers to questions. The interviewer will be observing the way you conduct yourself. By giving the impression that you are a confident and capable person, you can increase your chances of being hired. To create a good impression:

Fig. 11-6. A few days before an interview, try on the outfit you plan to wear. Make sure it is clean and wrinkle-free. What else can you do to improve your general appearance?

FINDING CREATIVE SOLUTIONS

Anticipating Possible Problems

Realizing you have a problem is the first step in solving it. However, you don't always have to wait for the problem to occur before considering plans of action. Anticipating possible problems can help you prepare for them.

How It Works

It often pays to think ahead. For instance, when driving in heavy traffic, defensive drivers don't assume that everyone around them will behave as expected. They try to anticipate potential problems. What if the car ahead brakes suddenly? What if the truck approaching the intersection tries to beat the red light? Drivers who "expect the unexpected" will be better prepared to react.

You can do the same in many types of situations. Anticipation leads to preparation. By considering what problems might arise, you can take steps to prevent or solve them.

Try It Out

You're preparing for your first interview for a full-time job. You've heard that there will probably be some tough questions intended to test your composure under pressure. You're worried that you might give the "wrong" answer—or worse yet, draw a blank.

▶ **Your Turn** *Brainstorm a list of ten tough questions that an interviewer might ask. Then write down answers that you think would make a good impression. Practice them. How can the process of preparing this list increase your chances of a successful interview?*

- Arrive on time, or even a little early.
- Be friendly but businesslike.
- Sit up straight.
- Speak clearly; don't mumble.
- Maintain eye contact.
- Think positively about yourself.

Answering and Asking Questions

When the interviewer asks questions, listen carefully and avoid interrupting. Try to keep your responses brief, focused, and positive. Show an enthusiastic interest in the job and a sincere desire to learn.

After the interviewer has finished questioning you, he or she will probably ask whether you have any questions. This is the time to bring up the questions that you prepared ahead of time, as well as any others that have come to mind during the interview. Your questions will help the interviewer evaluate your interest in the position. They will also help you get the answers you need in order to make a decision in case you're offered the job. See Fig. 11-7.

Discussing Pay and Benefits

Should you discuss pay at your interview? That depends on the situation. Some employers provide full details of pay and benefits to the applicants they interview.

Others prefer to discuss that information only with the person to whom they make an offer. You should let the interviewer take the lead.

If the subject does come up, remember that the **compensation package** includes pay and any additional benefits that the employer offers. You'll want a clear understanding of both before making a decision about any job offer. Information about pay includes how much you will be paid, how often, and how the rate of pay is figured. Benefits vary from company to company, but may include paid vacations, paid sick days, health insurance, and other extras. Good benefits can add significant value to the compensation package.

Fig. 11-7. It's best to save your questions regarding a position until after the interviewer's questions. What questions would be appropriate to ask?

Following Up

It's courteous to send a follow-up letter shortly after the interview. In your letter, thank the interviewer for taking the time to talk with you. If you still want the job, emphasize your continued interest and restate the skills you could bring to it. Use language that conveys enthusiasm and confidence. Your letter will help the interviewer remember you.

If, after the interview, you decide that you really aren't interested in the job, you should still send a follow-up letter. Express your appreciation for the interview, then simply say that you no longer wish to be considered for the position.

Evaluating a Job Offer

You may have to go through several interviews before you receive a job offer. Eventually, though, you'll hear, "We'd like to hire you." Your first impulse may be to say, "Great! When can I start?" However, a job offer, especially for a full-time position, deserves careful thought. Instead of accepting immediately, politely thank the employer and ask whether you can take a day to decide. See Fig. 11-8.

A job offer indicates that the employer has decided your skills and abilities are a good match for the company's needs. Now it's your turn to decide how well the job fits you. Consider more than just pay and benefits. Will this job give you the opportunity to learn valuable skills? Do you have the feeling that you'll fit in well and enjoy working there? If your answers are "yes," you have good reasons to accept the job offer.

Fig. 11-8. *If you receive a job offer, consider it carefully before accepting.*

Handling Rejection

If an interviewer calls to tell you that you have not been accepted, try to treat it as a learning experience. Ask politely why you were not hired. Some interviewers will take the time to explain what skills you were lacking or why you did not make a good impression in the interview.

Sometimes you won't hear anything after an interview. Not all employers are willing to spend the time making follow-up calls. The best you can do on such occasions is look back at the interview, try to decide what you did well and not so well, and practice again so that you will do better next time.

Review & Activities

Chapter Summary

- A résumé summarizes your qualifications for a job.

- For some jobs, you might provide samples of your work organized in a portfolio.

- You can find job leads by networking, using school resources, reading classified ads, using the Internet, or contacting employment agencies.

- Applying for a job often involves preparing a cover letter and completing an application form.

- If you are asked to a job interview, take steps to prepare for it and to make a positive impression.

- If you receive a job offer, evaluate it carefully before you accept it.

Reviewing Key Terms & Ideas

1. What types of information should be included in a **résumé**?

2. What is the purpose of giving **references** to a prospective employer? Name three examples of possible references.

3. What does **networking** involve? How might it help you find a job?

4. Describe three different ways you can use the Internet to find a job.

5. What is the purpose of a **cover letter**?

6. Why should you check a completed application form carefully before returning it?

7. Why is it a good idea to research a company before you go for an interview there?

8. Give three examples of behaviors that would give a positive impression at an interview.

9. Should you ask about your **compensation package** if the interviewer does not mention it? Why or why not?

10. Name three factors you should consider when evaluating a job offer.

Thinking Critically

1. **Comparing Alternatives.** Five different sources of job leads are described in this chapter. What are the advantages of each? What disadvantages might there be?

2. **Understanding Cause and Effect.** What might happen if you didn't prepare carefully for a job interview? Be specific.

5

Applying Your Knowledge

1. **Preparing a Résumé.** Create your own résumé, following the guidelines and example given. Exchange résumés and critique one another's work.

2. **Job Application.** Complete a job application form from a local employer as if you were applying for a job. Fill in all blanks, but don't reveal private information. (For example, instead of your actual Social Security number, use all zeros.)

3. **Mock Interviews.** With a partner, choose an advertised job opening. Work separately to research the company and develop interview questions. Take turns playing the job candidate and interviewer. Evaluate your own and your partner's performance as the candidate.

Making Connections

1. **Language Arts.** Practice using language effectively to convince an employer to interview you. Write two different cover letters. In each, express enthusiasm for the job and "sell" yourself as the ideal candidate, but use different words to express your thoughts.

2. **Math.** Assume that you list ten people as possible contacts for your job search. Assume that each of those ten suggests two additional people who might help. Half of those people suggest one more person each. How many people will you have in your network?

Managing Your Life

Keeping Track of a Job Search

When you start to look for a job, you will need to keep track of the companies you contact, the phone calls you make, the letters you send out, the people you interview with, and so on. You might set up a manual tracking system or use a computer. Choose one of these two methods and describe the system you would use. Explain why it is important to keep track of your progress. What might happen if you don't?

Using Technology

1. **Internet.** Do a job search on the Internet. Choose a job that interests you and a city you'd like to work in, then visit at least two Web sites designed for job seekers. Compare the sites for ease of use and number of openings in the category you are investigating. Compare your findings with those of other students.

2. **Word Processing.** Use a computer to design two versions of your résumé—one that you can print and mail out with a cover letter, and another that you can send as an e-mail attachment. Make the first one look attractive by using different typefaces and styles. In the second, do not use italics, underscores, bullets, or any other fancy formatting, since these features might get "garbled" when the document is transmitted. Make both versions of your résumé well organized and attractive to potential employers.

CHAPTER | 12

Success in the Workplace

EMPLOYEE
Of the Month

Objectives

- Describe personal qualities that indicate a desire to succeed on the job.
- Explain guidelines for understanding one's role as an employee.
- Demonstrate how to handle workplace situations with an appropriate attitude.
- Identify ways to prepare for a performance evaluation.
- Describe strategies that can improve an employee's chances of advancement.
- Discuss guidelines for leaving a job.

What does it take to succeed in the workplace? List the personal qualities you think successful workers need.

*R*amona always arrives at work a few minutes early. As a sales associate in a busy department store, she knows that she must be ready to work as soon as customers start to arrive. She checks her appearance, makes sure her department is tidy, and reviews prices of items that are on sale. After a few weeks on the job, she knows some of the regular customers by name and makes a point of greeting them with a friendly smile. Ramona enjoys helping her customers find the items they want, and she takes pride in giving them first-rate service.

By her behavior, Ramona is showing that she takes her work seriously and wants to succeed in her job. Her supervisors, as well as her customers, will notice her positive attitude. If she keeps up the good work, in time she will likely be offered a higher position.

Fig. 12-1. Employers look for people who can work well with others. Name another employability skill that these workers are using.

What Employers Look For

Succeeding at work means more than simply showing up and doing the job you are paid to do. Employers look for people who, like Ramona, bring a positive attitude to their work and a willingness to "go the extra mile." They look for many other qualities, too.

When employers hire new employees, they look first for the employability skills that people need to function effectively in the workplace. They include reading, writing, and math skills. They also include thinking skills, technology skills, management skills, and interpersonal skills. See Fig. 12-1.

Beyond these skills, employers look for personal qualities or character traits that tell them a person wants to succeed.

TEXTLINK≈
To review information about *employability skills*, see Chapter 9.

Employees who demonstrate the following traits are more likely to get noticed and get ahead:

- **Responsibility.** Responsible employees show, through their actions, that they can be relied on. They arrive at work on time, follow directions, and obey workplace rules. They manage resources wisely instead of wasting time, money, or materials. They accept responsibility for completing the tasks assigned to them.

- **Work ethic.** Employees who have a strong **work ethic** recognize that they have an obligation to work hard and to complete tasks efficiently and well. They are motivated by a desire to do their best and help the company succeed. These workers don't need constant supervision. They use their **initiative**—their willingness to do what needs to be done without being asked.

- **Professionalism.** Employees demonstrate professionalism by being loyal to their company. They promote the interests of the company and avoid saying or doing anything that might reflect negatively on it.

- **Honesty.** Honest employees put in the hours required of them and do not conduct personal business on company time. They don't lie, and they don't steal supplies or other company property.

- **Flexibility.** People with **flexibility** are willing to adapt to new or changing requirements. The modern workplace is fast-paced. It needs employees who can "think on their feet" and switch priorities when necessary. Workers today may need to learn new ways of working that involve new technology and new skills. They must also be ready to pitch in to help others when there's a tight deadline or some other urgent need.

Character IN ACTION

Workplace Confidentiality As an employee, you gain access to certain information about the company and about other people who work there. Much of this information is not meant to be public knowledge. Show you can be trusted by keeping such information to yourself. Avoid discussing company business with people outside the company, and avoid gossiping about coworkers and supervisors. If you accidentally see or hear information not intended for you, ignore it. Give three examples of the kind of information that should be kept confidential.

Understanding Your Role

When you start a new job, you want to do well. Your employer wants you to be successful too. You're more likely to succeed if you understand your role and what is expected of you.

Your Role Within the Company

Some employers provide new workers with a written job description. Others give a spoken description of what the job entails. In either case, make sure you understand your responsibilities. Don't be afraid to ask about anything that is not clear to you.

Fig. 12-2. This company encourages employees to be creative and share ideas openly. What other clues to the company's workplace culture do you see?

In addition to knowing what your responsibilities are, you need to know how you fit in. Who is your immediate supervisor? Whom will you be working with? What are their responsibilities? Whom should you ask if you need help with a minor problem?

In order to fit in, you need to understand the **workplace culture**, which is based on the attitudes, behavior, habits, and expectations of the company's owners and employees. Every workplace is different. Some companies promote a casual, informal atmosphere in which ideas are readily exchanged. Others have a more rigid structure in which ideas are exchanged only in formal meetings. The workplace culture is also reflected in the way employees dress and relate to one another. See Fig. 12-2.

You can figure out the culture of the place where you work by watching, listening, and asking questions. Your coworkers will guide you in appropriate behavior and will let you know what to expect in specific situations. Once you understand the culture of your workplace, you will know how best to make your own contribution.

Your Role as a Company Representative

If your work involves contact with outsiders—such as customers, clients, or suppliers—be aware that you are acting as a company representative. Take care to dress appropriately and act in ways that reflect positively on the company. Do everything you can to meet or exceed customers' expectations for quality of service.

Even when you are out with friends, or talking with your family, be aware that they will judge your company by the things you say about it. By showing respect in what you say, you earn respect for the company and, possibly, additional business.

The Importance of Attitude

Your attitude is your outlook on life. Your attitude toward your job shows in the way you behave and relate to others. You're more likely to succeed in your work if you have a positive attitude that encourages others and contributes to a pleasant work environment. A positive attitude will also help you handle difficult or uncomfortable situations.

Showing Enthusiasm

You're more likely to succeed in the workplace if you know how to show enthusiasm. That means taking pleasure in what you do and communicating it to others. Enthusiastic employees help to make teamwork exciting and fulfilling. Their enthusiasm is infectious and has a positive effect. That's why employers value them so highly. See Fig. 12-3.

Of course, it's easy to be enthusiastic when things are going well. It's harder to be a cheerleader during the rough times—but that's also when cheerleaders are most needed. You may have to push yourself more than usual, but remember: your upbeat attitude may be just what is needed to help people get back on top of things.

Handling Problems Positively

When a problem arises, how do you respond? Keeping a positive attitude is more beneficial than giving in to feelings of anger or frustration. A positive attitude is a "can-do" attitude. It focuses on what can be done to resolve a problem rather than on the problem itself.

Imagine, for example, that you're printing out letters that need to be mailed today. Suddenly the printer stops working. Someone with a negative attitude would think, "Now I'll never get the job done." Someone with a positive attitude would focus on finding another printer to use.

How can you develop a positive attitude? Start by recognizing that every problem can be solved. It's just a matter of exploring possible solutions and choosing the one that works best. Nobody expects you to have all the answers, but if you have a positive attitude you're halfway toward solving most problems.

Fig. 12-3. Employers look for a positive attitude that will translate into positive results. *How does a positive attitude help you achieve more?*

Fig. 12-4. Even experienced workers occasionally make errors. Don't be afraid to admit a mistake and to accept help in correcting it.

Handling Pressure

You're almost certain to experience pressure in the workplace from time to time. The best approach is to stay calm and figure out a plan. If you have so many tasks that you don't know where to start, make a list and decide on priorities. If you have a tight deadline, plan a schedule to see how it can be met. Be prepared to put in extra time, but ask for help if you need it.

Any time you experience pressure or other problems, try to work out your own solutions first. If you need additional help, talk to your supervisor. He or she will appreciate your effort to deal with the situation and may be able to offer additional suggestions.

Dealing with Mistakes

Everyone makes mistakes from time to time. The key is knowing how to handle them. If you make a mistake, try to figure out what can be done to fix it. Then speak to your supervisor. Explain the situation and suggest your solution. Your supervisor may accept your suggestion or may have another idea. See Fig. 12-4.

Never try to hide a mistake. Doing so could cause additional problems. It might also cause people to distrust you. Instead, own up to what you have done, accept responsibility for it, and move on. Try to learn from your mistake and think of ways to keep it from happening again.

More to Explore

Workplace Safety

No matter where you work, you have a right to a safe environment and a responsibility to follow safety regulations. The Occupational Safety and Health Administration (OSHA) is the branch of the U.S. Department of Labor that works to prevent job-related injuries, illnesses, and deaths.

OSHA sets standards for safety and carries out inspections to make sure companies meet the standards. All employers must place an OSHA poster in the workplace to provide their employees with information on their safety and health rights. Companies that fail to meet OSHA standards face fines and other penalties.

Employees have a responsibility to follow the safety procedures of their workplace. They should know how to perform their work safely and how to operate and maintain any equipment needed to perform their work. They should also report any unsafe conditions to their supervisor.

Responding to Criticism

Nobody likes to be criticized, but in the workplace you have to learn to accept criticism gracefully. It's easier to do this if you remember that people criticize you because they want to help you do your job better. Your supervisor has the right and responsibility to offer criticism when your work needs improvement. He or she will probably offer **constructive criticism**—feedback that suggests ways you can learn and improve. Such criticism is intended not to put you down, but rather to build you up. Focus on the supervisor's suggestions, and discuss specific actions you can take to address the problem.

Handling Successes and Disappointments

You're the only one of five coworkers to receive a promotion. How do you react? What if you're the only one to be passed over for promotion? People experience successes and disappointments of all kinds in the workplace. Try to deal with them in a mature and responsible way.

It's fine to express your happiness if you receive a promotion or raise. Remember, however, that other people may be disappointed that they did not receive the same treatment. Likewise, if you experience a great disappointment, don't let your emotions take over. Try to stay positive and look toward the future.

Evaluating Your Performance

Daniel has been working as an administrative assistant for almost a year. Last week his supervisor informed him that he would receive a performance evaluation in a month's time. He will be given a written evaluation two weeks beforehand and will have an opportunity to discuss it when he meets with his supervisor. Daniel is a little nervous about the evaluation, but mostly he looks forward to it. He thinks he has been doing a good job and welcomes the opportunity to discuss how he can improve and move ahead.

Most companies use performance evaluations to recognize employee accomplishments and point to areas that need improvement. Some, like Daniel's company, have a formal procedure that includes a written evaluation. Others have a less formal process. In most cases, employees receive feedback on the specifics of their work and on personal qualities such as initiative, attitude, and reliability.

Bear in mind that performance evaluations are important to your future success. Management decisions about promotions, pay increases, and new responsibilities are often based on these evaluations. It is well worth your time to prepare thoroughly for an evaluation and to take seriously any advice you are given. Before the evaluation, jot down questions you want to ask and ideas you want to discuss.

As part of your evaluation, you might be asked to explain what you think your strengths are and how you might improve. To prepare, think back on your recent job performance. What goals were you given or

TIPS FOR *Success*

Tracking Workplace Achievements

To help you prepare for performance evaluations, keep good records throughout the year. Record information about specific tasks and accomplishments, such as:

- **Projects you worked on.**
- **Responsibilities on each project.**
- **New skills you acquired.**
- **Technology you used.**
- **Achievements that you would like to bring to your supervisor's attention.**

did you set for yourself? What steps did you take to achieve them? What challenges and obstacles did you face, and how did you handle them? Even if you are not asked to evaluate your own performance, thinking about questions like these may help prepare you for what your supervisor has to say.

Advancing on the Job

Most people expect to advance in their career. As they gain more skills, they hope to be promoted to a position that involves more responsibility and pays more money. Employers, too, want workers whom they can promote. It's in a company's interest to retain good employees and help them develop their potential.

Opportunities to Grow

You are more likely to advance in your career if you take advantage of opportunities to expand your skills and knowledge. Some companies offer seminars and training classes to help employees learn more about their industry, get up to speed on new technology, and become more effective in their jobs. The company may ask for volunteers to work on special projects or to serve on interdepartmental teams. Take advantage of opportunities such as these.

Some companies provide or fund **continuing education**—courses geared toward working adults. Employers may pay tuition fees for approved courses that will help their employees gain relevant work skills. Even if you must pay your own way, taking courses or getting a degree can help you advance.

Mentoring

You are more likely to advance if you have a **mentor**—someone within the company who acts as a teacher and a guide. Mentors give support and advice based on experience. They can help you understand the workplace culture, suggest ways to improve your skills, and introduce you to others in the company who can help you advance.

Many people who have succeeded in their careers have had mentors who counseled them along the way. Some companies have formal mentoring programs that arrange for promising employees to be teamed with mentors. Often, though, a mentoring relationship develops naturally when people work together. See Fig. 12-5.

Fig. 12-5. The guidance of a mentor is one of the best resources for learning on the job. How might you find a mentor?

Leadership in the Workplace

Another way you can advance in your career is by demonstrating that you have leadership qualities. Employers are more likely to promote workers who have the ability to guide and motivate others.

How can you demonstrate leadership skills? You can do this by showing, in your day-to-day work, that you know how to make decisions, solve problems, and manage resources. Take advantage of opportunities to organize meetings or other company events. Volunteer to work on committees. Show that you know how to communicate and get things done.

> **TEXTLINK≈**
> *Leadership skills* are discussed in detail in Chapter 16.

Changing Jobs

Few people stay with the same company all their working life. Most change jobs from time to time. Some people move on because they seek new opportunities or new challenges with a different employer. Others move on because they are unhappy in their present job or cannot see a way of advancing. Some have no choice. A job change is forced upon them when they are laid off because their company downsizes, relocates, or goes out of business.

If you are unhappy in your present job and want to look for another one, don't act too hastily. Few people can afford to live without a paycheck, so don't hand in your notice until you have found another position. Usually, it's best not to tell coworkers of your decision to leave until you have another job.

Fig. 12-6. *Thanking your employer for the experience you gained is one way to leave a job on a positive note.*

When you leave your present job, make a point of leaving on good terms. After all, you may want to ask your employer for a reference. Also, there's always the possibility that you might want to return and work for this employer again in the future. Even though you are going your separate ways, your former employer and coworkers can remain part of your network as you continue on your career path. See Fig. 12-6.

Chapter Summary

- Employers look for employability skills and for qualities that tell them a person wants to succeed.
- To understand your role in the workplace, you need to know what your responsibilities are and what is appropriate behavior for the workplace culture.
- A positive attitude can help you handle difficult situations and succeed on the job.
- Performance evaluations are used to recognize accomplishments and identify areas that need improvement.
- Look for opportunities to expand skills and knowledge, benefit from a mentor, and demonstrate leadership qualities.
- When changing jobs, try to leave on a positive note.

Reviewing Key Terms & Ideas

1. How can one tell whether an employee has a strong **work ethic**?
2. How do employees show that they have **initiative**?
3. Why is **flexibility** particularly valued in the modern workplace?
4. As a new employee, what would you need to find out in order to understand your role within the company?
5. What does the **workplace culture** tell you about the place where you work?
6. What are two advantages of having a positive attitude in the workplace?
7. Why should you not try to hide mistakes you make at work?
8. What is the goal of **constructive criticism**?
9. What should an employee do to prepare for a performance evaluation?
10. What are **continuing education** courses and why might it be advisable to take them?
11. How might a **mentor** help you advance in your career?
12. Why is it advisable to leave a job on good terms?

Thinking Critically

1. **Understanding Cause and Effect.** Why do employers look for people who want to succeed in their work?
2. **Analyzing Behavior.** How does a positive, enthusiastic attitude contribute to effective teamwork?

Applying Your Knowledge

1. **Handling Success and Disappointment.** With a partner, write two scenarios: one in which an employee is given a promotion or award, and one in which an employee experiences a disappointment. Role-play two versions of each scenario, showing an inappropriate way of handling the news and a more mature approach.

2. **Self-Evaluation.** Practice for future workplace evaluations by writing a self-evaluation of your performance in school over the past six months. Create an evaluation sheet with at least six categories, such as *grades, attendance, attitude,* and so on. Then rate yourself in each category on a scale of 1 (poor) to 5 (excellent). Under a section labeled *Constructive Criticism,* suggest ways you could improve your performance in school.

Making Connections

1. **Math.** Research three occupations, each in a different career cluster (see page 160 in Chapter 10). Give examples of how math might be used in each occupation.

2. **Language Arts.** Imagine that you are a customer service representative. Write a letter responding to a customer's complaint about a defective product. Make sure your letter is clearly worded, respectful, and free of grammar or spelling errors.

Managing Your Life

Adjusting Your Attitude

You have learned that employers look for a positive "can-do" attitude. If you think you need an attitude adjustment, it's not too soon to start practicing. In the next few days, focus on applying a positive attitude to all the problems you experience—at school, at home, in your social life. Write a brief account of how this process helped you deal with the problems. Be prepared to discuss your experience in class.

Using Technology

1. **Presentation Software.** Prepare a presentation that you might use to convince an employer that you have the qualities that lead to success in the workplace. Include photos and other visuals. Write notes that you can use when giving the presentation.

2. **Audio Equipment.** Create a public service announcement designed to educate students about success in the workplace. Choose one of the topics in the chapter, such as "What Employers Look For," "The Importance of Attitude," or "Advancing on the Job." Write a script, then use audio technology to record and deliver your announcement.

CHAPTER 13

Balancing Multiple Roles

Key Terms

- role conflict
- personal boundaries
- support system
- flextime
- job sharing
- telecommute

Objectives

- Analyze the negative effects of role conflicts.
- Explain the need for balance as you manage multiple roles.
- Analyze strategies for achieving balance in life.
- Describe support systems that help families manage multiple roles.
- Discuss family-friendly workplace policies.

List the various roles you have in your life. Which do you enjoy the most? The least? Why?

*T*eresa sat Carlos in his high chair with a bowl of dry oat cereal. It was 6:00 p.m., the kitchen was full of clutter, and she was exhausted. She held her head in her hands as flashes of her day raced through her mind. Her boss had complained about her team being behind schedule. Her coworker had called in sick, leaving Teresa with an extra meeting to lead. Then the sitter had called in the afternoon to ask her to take Carlos because he had a fever.

Teresa knew her husband would be home shortly and would need dinner before leaving in an hour for his night class. First, though, she had to call the organizer of the hospital fundraiser to discuss her role on the committee. As Teresa reached for the phone, Carlos began to fuss and squirm, wanting her attention. Teresa picked him up and sang to him softly. The phone call would have to wait. *I feel like I'm being pulled in a million different directions,* she thought.

Challenges of Multiple Roles

Have you ever felt like Teresa? Sometimes too many demands clamor for your attention, and it seems like you just can't do it all. Like Teresa, you have many roles. Hers include parent, employee, spouse,

and volunteer. Your roles might include son or daughter, student, part-time worker, friend, hospital volunteer, and team member. When you start your career, and perhaps a family of your own, you'll take on some new and expanded roles. See Fig. 13-1.

With so many roles in your life, they're bound to conflict with each other at times. A **role conflict** occurs when one role has a significant negative impact on another role.

Fig. 13-1. Taking on several demanding roles at once is an enormous challenge. What roles do you see in your future?

Another word that describes this situation is *spillover*. One role "spills over" into another, affecting your ability to fulfill it as well as you would like.

Roland can tell you about spillover. He had really been looking forward to the birthday party for his favorite little cousin, T.J., who thinks Roland is the coolest person ever. The weekend of the party, however, Roland was hard at work on a major school project that was due on Tuesday. By Sunday, he realized that unless he skipped the party, he didn't have much chance of finishing the project on time.

Roland knew that if he chose to stay home and work on his project, he'd miss the fun and disappoint T.J. He decided to go to the party for just a little while. However, he found it hard to relax and enjoy himself because he kept thinking about the unfinished project. His role as student was spilling over into his role as a family member. How might attending the party cause spillover in the other direction, affecting Roland's role as a student?

The Impact

As Teresa's and Roland's situations show, role conflicts can affect you in many ways. You may experience:

- **Internal effects.** When the demands of your roles clash, it's natural for stress to build. Like Teresa, you may feel distracted, exhausted, and unable to think clearly.
- **Interpersonal effects.** Relationships often carry the brunt of role conflicts. Spillover affects not only you but also your family, friends, coworkers, and others.
- **External effects.** Role conflicts can sometimes keep you from participating in activities that are important to you. Disarray—like the clutter in Teresa's

kitchen—is another common external effect. It results when some tasks get pushed aside in the effort to juggle many roles.

These three types of effects are interrelated. Can you see how a disorderly home could lead to still more stress and a greater strain on relationships?

Looking to the Future

Like Roland, you probably experience role conflicts right now. Like Teresa, you'll find that as you enter adulthood and add still more roles to your life, the challenges will become even greater. More than ever, you'll have to find ways to strike a balance between your work life, family life, community involvement, and personal needs.

Role conflicts are an important issue in the workplace. Spillover from family stress is a major cause of absenteeism, tardiness, inefficiency, and distraction at work. The spillover of work stress also has a negative effect on family life. People who are under stress at work tend to argue with their spouses more and participate in family activities less. You can see why learning to manage multiple roles is a key skill for both workplace success and family harmony.

Adding to the Challenge

Role conflicts can occur under the best of conditions. Certain factors, however, can make them more likely and harder to deal with. These factors include:

- **Difficult situations.** People who have erratic work schedules or who hold multiple jobs may find it especially difficult to fulfill their family roles. Even more stress is added if a family has to deal with challenges such as finding reliable child care, coping with an extended illness, or caring for an older family member. What are some other situations that could make it more difficult to manage multiple roles?

- **Unrealistic expectations**. A college student who must work long hours to earn money should not expect to also take extra courses and graduate early. New parents who are trying to function on little sleep should not expect to keep their home spotless. Sometimes lowering your expectations is a healthy thing to do.

- **Overcommitment**. Many people agree to more obligations than they can handle. Making too many commitments often stems from a desire to please everyone and an inability to say no. It's also easy to underestimate the time and energy needed to fulfill certain roles. After trying out for the school play, for example, you may find that rehearsals take up more time than you expected and interfere with getting your homework done.

The Need for Balance

There's no way to avoid role conflicts completely. You can, however, minimize the negative effects of spillover. Management skills can help you balance your multiple roles effectively.

What does "balancing multiple roles" mean? It's not that you put each of your roles on a scale and expect them to weigh the same. Not all roles are equal in their importance to you. Nor does it always mean dividing your time and energy in proportion to how much you value each role. Many adults spend most of each workday at their job, but that doesn't necessarily mean they value that time more than the time they spend with their families.

Balancing multiple roles is really about maintaining a sense of balance within yourself. Have you ever seen a circus performer walking a tightrope? An internal sense of balance allows the tightrope walker to move steadily along the rope without falling. He or she is able to stay calm and focused while shifting weight smoothly from one foot to the other. In the same way, a sense of balance can steady you as you shift from role to role. See Fig. 13-2.

Fig. 13-2. Balance is what keeps you calm and steady in a hectic world.

A sense of balance won't eliminate role conflicts or make your life perfect. However, when you have balance in your life, you feel in control. You can enjoy your roles as much as possible rather than feeling overwhelmed by them. You're able to stay focused on your goals.

Achieving Balance

How can you achieve the balance that will help you manage your various roles? While there's no easy answer, three strategies can help: setting priorities, managing your time, and reducing stress.

Setting Priorities

One of the biggest challenges of balancing multiple roles is choosing where to focus your time and energy. To make choices that are right for you, consider your values—your beliefs, feelings, and ideas about what is important. Then set priorities based on your values and your responsibilities. You may not always be able to do everything you want to do, and that can be hard to accept. But you'll feel better knowing that your choices are in harmony with your values.

Setting priorities can help you put your roles in perspective. You may be able to reduce the time spent on some roles that are less important. However, if you're like most people, you'll always have more than one high-priority role. Balancing these roles is a matter of give and take.

During a particularly busy week at work, Becky's role as an employee required more of her time and energy than usual. Other roles temporarily received less attention. When things eased up at work, the balance shifted back. Give yourself the flexibility to adjust your roles as needed. Just make sure you're not consistently neglecting important areas of your life. See Fig. 13-3.

Fig. 13-3. Although he has a busy schedule, this teen enjoys spending time with his little sister. What might happen if he neglected this part of his life?

Changing Priorities ~ In his twenties, David went through a stage of focusing on career advancement. To meet the demands of his job, he often worked late or on weekends. From time to time he took college courses at night to learn new skills. After he married and had children, however, David's priorities changed. His career was still important, but he was no longer willing to give up evenings and weekends for it. He wanted, and needed, to spend as much of that time as possible with his family. Your choices might be different from David's. Still, like him, you will find that your priorities change as you go through life.

Setting Boundaries ~ Establishing your priorities will help you set **personal boundaries**. These are limits you set for yourself based on your values and priorities. They enable you to control the number of roles you play and to focus on what matters most to you.

Whenever you're given the opportunity for a new activity or are asked to take on another role, ask yourself, "Do I have room in my life for this right now? How will it affect my other roles? Does it fit with my values and priorities?" Careful consideration, rather than a quick response, can help you say yes to those opportunities that best fit and no to those that don't.

Managing Time

The ability to manage your time effectively is a key skill in balancing multiple roles. Time management helps you focus on your priorities and use your time effectively. Here are some tips for making the best possible use of your time:

- Make a daily or weekly to-do list. Use a calendar to keep track of appointments and special events.

- Plan each day by checking your calendar and your to-do list.

- Be realistic about what you can accomplish in any given day. Plan for things to take longer than you predict.

- Build flexibility into your schedule so that you can make changes.

- Learn to say no. It's better than letting someone down later.

- Plan for some free time. Don't schedule every hour of the day.

TEXTLINK≈

Time management is discussed in more detail in Chapter 7.

Fig. 13-4. Working out is one way to manage stress. *What helps you relax?*

Reducing Stress

As you've learned, stress often results from role conflicts. Too much stress can knock you off balance. It can also pull you into a downward spiral: the more stress you feel, the more difficult it is to manage multiple roles. That can lead to more role conflicts and still more stress.

Take steps to reduce stress before it becomes a problem. No matter how busy you are, set aside time to relax and calm your mind. Enjoy some fun activities, too. Take care of yourself by eating right and getting enough sleep. Stay physically active—just taking a walk is a great stress reducer. Stress management techniques like these will help you keep your balance. See Fig. 13-4.

TEXTLINK≈

Review the discussion of *stress* in Chapter 2.

Developing Support Systems

Managing multiple roles is easier with a good **support system**—all the people and organizations a person can turn to for help. A typical support system might include family, friends, and coworkers, as well as professional and community services. Think of all the roles you have. Who interacts with you in those roles and how can they support you? Talk with those people to see how you can help one another.

At Home

Many families call on their extended family for support. Working parents, for example, often find that juggling child care and transportation is easier with help from grandparents or other relatives. These arrangements are often more convenient and less expensive than other options. They also give family members the chance to spend time with one another and grow closer.

Good communication helps family members understand each other's roles and the demands of those roles. If you want your family to support you, be open about the role conflicts that you experience. Talk about your various roles. Let your family know when you have scheduling conflicts or important deadlines to meet. Help them understand the demands you face in balancing your life. Sharing these concerns with your family not only enhances understanding, but may give you a new perspective and lead to new solutions. In return, be willing to listen to the concerns of family members and offer your support.

At Work

Just like at home, it helps to have a support system at work. Perhaps you and some of your coworkers can get together for lunch, share concerns, and encourage one another. Your supervisor may be willing to lend a helping hand at appropriate times. Having support at work can make the difference between enjoying a job and feeling constant stress due to role conflicts.

Family-Friendly Policies ~ Employers know that their employees have personal lives and family obligations. They're aware of the challenges that a single parent faces when a child is sick. They know about the demands on parents when school is out and the concerns of employees caring for aging relatives.

Of course, employers can't allow workers unlimited time off to deal with personal issues. However, some employers have introduced family-friendly policies that make it easier for employees to balance their lives. These policies include:

- **Flexible work hours.** Some companies have introduced **flextime**, a system that allows workers to choose when they will begin and end their working day. Some people, for example, prefer to start at 7 a.m. and leave at 3 p.m. That way they can be home when their children return from school. Others prefer to start later and stay later. See Fig. 13-5.

- **Compressed schedules.** An employee who works a compressed workweek might work four ten-hour days and then have three days off. This option is often used in hospitals or in schools and universities during the summer months.

- **On-site child care.** Companies that provide on-site child care facilities make it possible for employees to stay close to their children while they work. Parents can visit their children during their lunch break, and they're on hand if there is any kind of emergency.

Fig. 13-5. Flexible hours allow this worker to avoid the rush hour when traveling to and from work. What are some other advantages of flexible hours?

Viewpoints

How Much Flexibility Is Fair?

In any workplace, there will be times when family commitments interfere with the job, and vice versa. How much flexibility and understanding is it fair to expect in such situations? The answer may depend on whose shoes you're standing in—the employer's or the employee's.

Angela: I'm sympathetic when one of my employees has a problem at home—I have a family, too. I make as many allowances as I can, but I can't give people time off every time their kids get sick. That's not fair to the other workers. Besides, I need people here, every day, to get things done. If I lose business and have to lay people off—well, should everyone pay for the problems of a few people?

Paul: I take my job seriously. It's how I support my family. But supporting my family also means being there when they need me. I know what it costs my boss to give me time off. But I don't do my best work when my mind is on my family and the things I should be doing for them. My family is my first responsibility, and if I need time off to care for them, I'll take it.

Seeing Both Sides ~ Why do Angela and Paul have different viewpoints about conflicts between work and family? What might be done to help resolve such differences?

- **Job sharing.** Under a system called **job sharing**, two part-time workers share one full-time job. They split the hours and the pay. One might work in the mornings and the other in the afternoons, or one might work two days a week and the other three. Job sharing offers flexibility to people who don't need or want to work full time.

- **Telecommuting.** Technology makes it possible for some employees to **telecommute**, or work from home using communication links to their job. They may communicate by telephone, fax, or e-mail, or they may be able to log on to their office computer network from home. Telecommuting is ideal for people who don't need daily face-to-face contact with their coworkers. It saves travel time and allows flexible work hours. See Fig. 13-6.

- **Family and medical leave.** Companies with more than 50 employees are required by law to allow workers to take time off to deal with family and medical emergencies. The Family and Medical Leave Act guarantees up to 12 weeks of leave for workers who get sick, need to care for relatives, or need time off for the birth or adoption of a child. Employers are not required to pay employees during their time off, but the employees have the assurance that they will have a job to return to.

In the Community

Friends and neighbors often join together for mutual support and assistance. For example, neighborhood parents may take turns waiting with young children for the school bus.

Many communities offer programs and facilities to help families balance their multiple roles. Some schools and places of worship offer after-school programs for children, as well as family activities that encourage all family members to draw closer. Some community service organizations also arrange for supervised after-school programs.

Help with caring for older family members may also be available from the community. Some communities have day care centers for seniors, offering lunches and a range of activities and outings. For older people who cannot get out, Meals on Wheels provides daily hot lunches. Social service agencies can arrange for other needed care.

Fig. 13-6. By telecommuting, this woman is able to work from home several days a week. *How might this help her balance multiple roles?*

Regaining Lost Balance

Everyone experiences role conflicts and loses balance from time to time. If you find that one of your roles is taking too much time and energy and is spilling over into other important roles, try to keep things in perspective. Remember that you don't have to be perfect. Use your support system. Re-examine your priorities and look for ways to regain the balance in your life. The more you practice maintaining balance, the easier you will find it becomes.

Chapter Summary

- Role conflicts occur when one role spills over into another.
- Difficult situations, unrealistic expectations, and overcommitment increase role conflicts.
- An internal sense of balance helps you to manage multiple roles.
- To achieve balance, try to set priorities, manage your time, and reduce stress.
- Support systems are available to help people manage multiple roles.
- In the workplace, family-friendly policies help employees balance work and family life.

Reviewing Key Terms & Ideas

1. What are **role conflicts**? What kinds of negative effects can they have on a person's life?
2. Name four ways in which role conflicts can affect performance in the workplace.
3. Give two reasons why people tend to make more commitments than they can handle.
4. How does balance help you manage role conflicts?
5. Describe how to set priorities in a way that helps you achieve balance in your life.
6. How does setting **personal boundaries** help you manage multiple roles?
7. Give three examples of time management strategies that would help you avoid overcommitment.
8. Suggest four ways to manage stress.
9. What kinds of people might a typical **support system** include?
10. How do **flextime** and **job sharing** benefit employees?
11. What does **telecommute** mean? How do workers benefit from this arrangement?
12. Give two examples of support systems offered by communities.

Thinking Critically

1. **Drawing Conclusions.** Why do you think many people find it hard to achieve balance in their lives?
2. **Making Generalizations.** What aspects of modern society contribute to the increased need for support systems for balancing multiple roles?
3. **Analyzing Behavior.** Which of the three strategies for achieving balance do you need to use more? How, specifically, can you do so?

Applying Your Knowledge

1. **Examining Commitments.** Make a list of all your commitments for the next two weeks. Include family events, after-school activities, meetings with friends, part-time jobs—everything that you have already agreed to do. Examine your list critically. Do you need to cut back on your commitments? Highlight the items on your list that are least important to you. Use this activity to plan future commitments more carefully.

2. **Effects of Role Conflicts.** Think about a time when you experienced role conflict. What were the internal, interpersonal, and external effects of that experience?

Making Connections

1. **Language Arts.** Write a story that illustrates the negative effects of role conflict and that presents a solution for handling the situation that created the conflict. Be prepared to read your story to the class.

2. **Social Studies.** Do research to find out more about the Family and Medical Leave Act in the United States. Determine how employees become eligible for leave under the terms of the act. Do they continue to receive health benefits while they are on leave? Summarize your findings in a chart.

Managing Your Life

Balancing Roles at Home

Could your family—or a family that you know well—use a little help with balancing roles at home? Make a list of the household management roles that each person in the family plays. Who does most of the shopping, cleaning, child care, cooking, maintenance, and so on? Do some people have more roles than others? Is there an imbalance that could be fixed? Based on your findings, suggest ways that the family might achieve a better balance in the home.

Using Technology

1. **Presentation Software.** Use appropriate software to create a brief presentation—targeted at teens—describing the negative effects of overcommitment. You might use humorous or exaggerated photos or drawings to make your points. Show your presentation to classmates.

2. **Telecommuting.** Use the Internet or conduct interviews to learn more about the advantages and disadvantages of telecommuting. What kinds of equipment do telecommuters need to buy? What effects does telecommuting have on family life? How do telecommuters adapt to working alone for long stretches of time? Do the benefits outweigh the drawbacks? Prepare a brief report on your findings.

Career Options

Government, Law, and Public Safety

*G*overnment, law, and public safety provide jobs at the federal, state, and local levels. Workers in this field enforce laws, protect citizens, provide community services, and administer a variety of programs and agencies. Job opportunities in government, law, and public safety are varied and require wide-ranging levels of education and experience. The career cluster can be divided into four broad sectors: Federal, State, and Local Government; Law and Legal Services; Criminal Justice and Law Enforcement; and Fire Protection. Because budgetary issues affect many occupations in this cluster, employment opportunities are somewhat unpredictable and vary greatly by location.

Main Employers

- Government agencies
- Law firms
- Private industry
- Police departments
- Fire departments

Government, Law, and Public Safety Job Opportunities

Industry Segment	Entry Level	Additional Education and/or Training	Advanced Education and/or Training
Federal, State, and Local Government	■ Office Clerk ■ Postal Clerk ■ Census Taker ■ Legislative Aide	■ Court Clerk ■ Lobbyist ■ Social Security Administrator	■ Urban Planner ■ Legislator ■ IRS Agent ■ Employment Counselor
Law and Legal Services	■ Office Assistant	■ Legal Secretary ■ Paralegal ■ Law Clerk	■ Lawyer ■ Judge ■ Magistrate
Criminal Justice and Law Enforcement	■ Security Guard ■ Police Dispatcher	■ Police Officer ■ Sheriff ■ Parole Officer ■ Correctional Officer	■ Police Chief ■ Detective ■ Customs Agent
Fire Protection	■ Dispatcher	■ Firefighter	■ Fire Captain ■ Fire Inspector ■ Fire Investigator

I consider myself a "people person," and I've always wanted a career in which I could help others. By middle school, I had decided to become a police officer. By high school, I was sure I wanted to be a teacher.

I went to college and majored in education. After earning my bachelor's degree and my teaching certificate, I taught high school English. I enjoyed teaching, but it never seemed like the perfect fit. With large class sizes, I couldn't give my students much individual attention. One day, when I was helping some students with their résumés, I realized that I would like to be an employment counselor.

I always enjoyed talking to students about careers and helping them with college choices. As an employment counselor, I could work one-on-one or in small groups. While still teaching, I took classes to earn a master's degree in counseling.

When I heard about a job opening for an employment counselor with the county government, I applied and got the job. I've never regretted my decision to switch from teaching to counseling. Now I help people make career decisions. I learn about my clients' interests, skills, education, training, and work history. Sometimes I give them aptitude and achievement tests to identify their skills and abilities. I also help them with their interviewing and job search skills. When my clients tell me that they've been offered a job, I feel good knowing that I've played a role in their success.

Check It *Out!*

Choose one government, law, or public safety occupation that interests you. Locate someone who works in this field. Find out how the person got the job, what qualifications and training were required, and skills developed on the job.

UNIT 4

Interpersonal Skills

Successful Relationships

Objectives

- **Distinguish** among different kinds of relationships.
- **Identify** benefits of good relationships.
- **Analyze** factors that influence relationships.
- **Describe** ways to build and maintain strong relationships.
- **Identify** characteristics of unhealthy relationships.

QUICK WRITE

What is it that draws you to certain people and not to others? Write about the qualities you admire in your friends. What traits cause you to stay away from some people?

*H*ow many people will you interact with before the day is over? Probably quite a few. Your contacts during a typical day are likely to include family, classmates, teachers, friends, and a variety of others. Are your interactions with these people mostly positive, or do you have problems getting along with some? The answer depends largely on your relationship skills. The better those skills become, the more satisfying your relationships will be.

Kinds of Relationships

You will have many different kinds of relationships in your life. **Relationships** are the connections you have with other people. They vary in three basic ways—in their degree of closeness, their purpose, and their form.

Some relationships are very close, while others are casual. There are many variations in between. Close relationships are supportive and fulfilling. You may enjoy a close relationship with a parent, a sibling, another relative, or a friend. These close relationships give you someone to confide in and to share special times with. Casual relationships, on the other hand, are often linked to certain activities or interests and have a different level of importance.

Many relationships exist for a specific purpose. Your relationships with your teachers are based on your need to learn. Members of a soccer team form relationships so that they can play well together. Coworkers form relationships that enable them to work together and share ideas. See Fig. 14-1.

Fig. 14-1. Relationships are formed for many reasons. How might the way you interact with a coworker be influenced by the purpose of the relationship?

Relationships come in many forms. Your relationships with children are different from those that you have with other teens, your parents, or with older people. You may have relationships with people from different kinds of backgrounds as well. Building relationships with people from a variety of cultures and age groups adds flavor to life.

Rewards of Relationships

Relationships bring many benefits and rewards. Here are some of them:

- **Companionship.** When you're with people you like, you have fun spending time together. You may share your experiences, feelings, and ideas.

- **Love and affection.** Your relationships with your family and friends give you a sense of belonging and acceptance. You know that other people care about you. See Fig. 14-2.

- **Support.** One of the most valuable rewards of relationships is knowing that people will be there when you need them. If you have a problem, your family and friends are willing to help. For example, when Estella's father was hospitalized, friends and neighbors brought meals and drove Estella to school.

- **Positive self-concept.** When people show that they respect and care about you, you see yourself in a positive way. Feeling good about yourself helps you reach out to others, which brings its own rewards.

- **Expanded interests.** Relationships expose you to new ideas. You have opportunities to develop new interests and learn from others. The more diverse your relationships, with people from a variety of backgrounds, the more this is true.

Fig. 14-2. Family relationships provide love, affection, and support.

Influences on Relationships

Think of all the different ways you address the people in your life. You may have a nickname for a friend. When addressing a teacher, you may use "Mr.," "Mrs.," or "Ms." You might address a police officer, or other authority figure, as "sir" or "ma'am." This difference illustrates the fact that you have more than one kind of relationship. Read on to learn about some of the factors that influence the kinds of relationships you have and how you relate to different people.

Roles and Expectations

Your role in a relationship is one factor that influences your behavior. Everyone has many different roles. Barry is a son, brother, friend, neighbor, student, pep band member, and hospital volunteer. What would your list include? What roles are you likely to add in the future?

Every role carries with it certain **expectations**, the wants and needs each person hopes to gain from the relationship. Expectations affect how people act in their different roles. For example, children look to their parents to take care of them. Parents, in turn, expect their children to follow family rules and help around the house. Members of a debate team are expected to practice, follow the coach's instructions, and do what is best for the team. In turn, members expect the coach to provide leadership and treat members fairly. See Fig. 14-3.

Sometimes roles and expectations are in conflict. For example, a friend may have different expectations for your relationship than you do. If you have younger sisters or brothers, they may expect you to spend more time with them than you're willing to give.

Fig. 14-3. Teachers and students have certain expectations based on their roles. *What do you expect of your teachers? What do you think they expect of you?*

Personal Qualities

The qualities that make you unique influence the relationships you form. Examples of these personal characteristics include:

- **Values.** Your personal values, and your beliefs about what is right and wrong, are major influences on your relationships. Friendships with people who have similar values and beliefs are likely to involve less conflict. Best friends often have similar values.

- **Needs.** Most people expect relationships to fulfill certain needs, such as companionship, love, belonging, and acceptance. Consciously or unconsciously, you seek relationships with people who seem most able to meet your needs.

- **Interests and abilities.** Many of your relationships will be with people who share some of the same interests. Others will give you the opportunity to develop new interests. If you have particular abilities you may seek out people who can help you develop them.

Self-Esteem

Self-esteem—the value or importance you place on yourself—influences your relationships. High self-esteem gives you the confidence to meet new people and try new experiences. When you feel good about yourself, you find it easier to make friends and build worthwhile relationships. Self-esteem also helps you steer clear of relationships that may harm you.

Good relationships, in turn, enhance your self-esteem. Sometimes you may think you don't care about other people's opinions. However, what people think of you and the way they treat you have a strong effect on how you feel about yourself. When people accept you and treat you with respect, it helps reinforce that you're a valuable person.

What happens to people who don't feel accepted by others? Their self-esteem is likely to be low. They find it more difficult to be confident about themselves and their abilities. Sometimes they act as if they don't care what others think of them. If that describes you or someone you know, remember that self-esteem can grow. Everyone has personal strengths that should be recognized and celebrated. Everyone has the ability to improve.

Make it a habit to give sincere compliments each day—especially to those who seem to need it most.

Stereotypical Thinking

Some people make assumptions that get in the way of healthy relationships. They may assume, for example, that all teens are irresponsible, or that all older people are forgetful. These are examples of stereotypes. A **stereotype** is an expectation that all people in a particular group will have the same qualities or act the same. Stereotypes are often based on characteristics such as gender, age, race, religion, and nationality. They usually result from limited contact with members of the group about which the assumption is made.

Some stereotypes are just annoying. Krista, who is over 6 feet tall, dreads the "You play basketball, don't you?" question. Others are more harmful. Some people are denied certain opportunities because of others' stereotypical thinking. Some people who

Character IN ACTION

Combating Stereotyping One of the best ways to overcome stereotyping is to get to know people as individuals. Look for opportunities to interact with people who are different from you—those who are older or younger, have a disability, or come from a different background, for example. Simply starting a conversation could open the door to better understanding. Brainstorm more ways to help stamp out stereotyping.

hold stereotypical views avoid contact with anyone who fits into a particular group. They lose the chance to get to know some interesting people and develop rewarding relationships.

Personal contact with different kinds of people is one way to overcome stereotypical thinking. Challenging such assumptions when they come to mind is another.

Building Positive Relationships

Good relationships don't just happen. People who enjoy positive relationships are willing to put in the necessary time and effort to build a strong foundation. They find ways to work through problems and disagreements. Through their actions, they show that they are committed to the relationship. Some of the qualities found in strong relationships are shown in Fig. 14-4.

Qualities in Strong Relationships

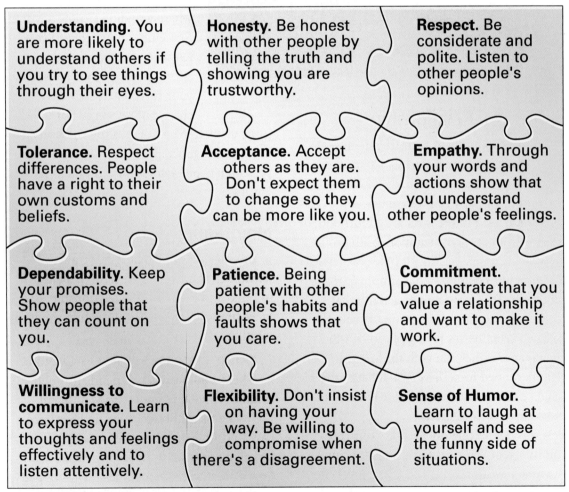

Understanding. You are more likely to understand others if you try to see things through their eyes.

Honesty. Be honest with other people by telling the truth and showing you are trustworthy.

Respect. Be considerate and polite. Listen to other people's opinions.

Tolerance. Respect differences. People have a right to their own customs and beliefs.

Acceptance. Accept others as they are. Don't expect them to change so they can be more like you.

Empathy. Through your words and actions show that you understand other people's feelings.

Dependability. Keep your promises. Show people that they can count on you.

Patience. Being patient with other people's habits and faults shows that you care.

Commitment. Demonstrate that you value a relationship and want to make it work.

Willingness to communicate. Learn to express your thoughts and feelings effectively and to listen attentively.

Flexibility. Don't insist on having your way. Be willing to compromise when there's a disagreement.

Sense of Humor. Learn to laugh at yourself and see the funny side of situations.

Fig. 14-4. Just as the pieces of a puzzle fit together to reveal the whole picture, these qualities fit together to build relationships that last.

Fig. 14-5. Don't let fear of rejection stop you from talking to someone. Most people welcome getting to know new people.

Are you nervous about starting a conversation with someone you don't know? Perhaps you're afraid that you'll be rejected. Keep in mind that many others have the same fear. Think about a time when you went to a party or event where you didn't know anyone. Remember how relieved you felt when someone made the effort to talk to you? Now it's your turn. There's always a chance of rejection, but it's a small chance. Why not take the risk and talk to someone you'd like to get to know? The person may be grateful that you did. See Fig. 14-5.

Starting a Relationship

Think about one of your friendships. Do you remember how it started? Chances are you and your new friend had something in common. Perhaps you were in the same class at school, lived in the same neighborhood, or belonged to the same team or youth group.

Starting a new relationship doesn't have to be difficult. The first step is simply to make an effort. Try a new club or activity that sounds interesting, perhaps one at your school. Whether it's taking photos for the newspaper or helping with the Spanish Club's canned food drive, you'll have a chance to meet and spend time with others who share your interests.

Consider getting involved in your community, too. You might join a health club, learn a new sport, or try out for a local choir or drama group. Part-time paid work and volunteer jobs both provide opportunities to meet new people.

Maintaining a Relationship

You may discover that starting a new friendship is the easy part. The challenge is to build and maintain the relationship. It takes time and effort, but the results are well worth it.

Making Time for Others ~ Chandra and Kelly had been good friends through middle school, but ended up at different high schools. Although it would have been easy to drift apart, they tried to stay in touch by calling or instant messaging each other at least once a week. Sometimes they shopped together. Each met the other's school friends. Through their efforts, they were able to maintain a bond.

Just as plants need water in order to thrive, relationships need frequent doses of attention to stay strong. You can keep in touch by telephone and e-mail, but relationships also need "face time." Here are some suggestions for making quality time for your family and friends:

- Make an effort to plan activities with people you care about. Spend less time on solitary activities such as watching TV, playing video games, and surfing the Internet.

- Plan ahead to avoid conflicts with important family activities.

- Eat meals with your family as often as possible. Ask whether you can invite friends from time to time.

- Recognize that good relationships are worth the effort.

Giving and Receiving ~

Emilio tells this story about his friend Isaac: "It was Saturday morning after a big storm. There were tree branches all over the lawn, and I knew I had a lot of hard work ahead of me. Then Isaac came from his house across the street carrying a rake and work gloves. I had offered to drive us to the out-of-town football game that afternoon, and he didn't want either one of us to have to miss it. The two of us got the yard cleaned up in record time. Isaac's a great guy. He's always doing things like that."

Isaac demonstrated one of the basic principles of a strong relationship: both sides give as well as receive. This principle of giving and receiving applies not just to friendships, but to all relationships. For example, if your supervisor lets you have the day of the homecoming dance off work, you could volunteer to fill in for an absent coworker the next week. See Fig. 14-6.

In a strong relationship, giving and receiving go on all the time. Giving boosts your self-esteem. Having something to offer and being appreciated makes you feel good about yourself. By the same token, when you receive help, you have an opportunity to show your appreciation.

Showing Tolerance ~

An important key to getting along with others is to show tolerance. **Tolerance** means respecting other people's beliefs and customs. When you show tolerance, you recognize that other people, like you, have a right to their own personal values and beliefs. They are free to make their own choices. Tolerant people don't assume their way is the only right way.

Tolerance is essential to getting along with people, from family to casual acquaintances. As society becomes more diverse, tolerance becomes even more important. Only with widespread tolerance can people from different backgrounds live together peacefully and productively.

Fig. 14-6. Successful relationships maintain a balance of giving and receiving. *What can you do to ensure that your relationships are balanced?*

People who lack tolerance may develop **prejudice**, an unfair or biased attitude toward an individual or group. Prejudice involves prejudging, or forming opinions about people without really knowing them. These negative attitudes can, in turn, lead to acts of **discrimination**—treating certain people differently as a result of prejudice. Examples of discrimination include refusing to rent a home to someone because of skin color, preventing an individual from joining an organization because of ethnic identity, and refusing to hire a worker because of age. Discrimination on the basis of age, gender, ethnic background, or certain other factors is illegal. It's also destructive to individual people and to society as a whole.

Prejudice and discrimination, like stereotypes, often grow out of ignorance. People who have little exposure to other ways of life are more likely to see differences as negative or alarming. You can help combat prejudice and discrimination by making an effort to increase your understanding of all people. See Fig. 14-7.

Fig. 14-7. "Ageism"—prejudice against certain age groups—is a form of intolerance. By refusing to let such attitudes become part of your thinking, you can help create a better society.

Understanding Authority

Throughout life you will have relationships with **authority figures**—people who have the right and responsibility to influence your behavior. Most authority figures are adults. They include parents, teachers, coaches, supervisors, and law enforcement officials. Expect your relationships with such people to be somewhat different from those you have with others.

Relating to Authority Figures ~ Now that you're close to becoming an adult yourself, you probably spend more time with adults than in the past. That interaction can be rewarding. Drawing on their experience, responsible adults can give advice on everything from everyday problems to choosing a career. You, in turn, can share your own view of life and help adults keep in touch with the way the world is changing.

While most relationships with adults are positive ones, there may be times you resent certain authority figures. As you move toward adulthood, you want to make more of your own decisions. Your desire to have more control is normal, but it may sometimes strain your relationships with some of the adults in your life. In order to keep the peace, try to strike a balance between asserting your independence and respecting those in authority.

Have you ever been in charge of children? If so, you know what it's like to be an authority figure. It was your responsibility to enforce the rules and keep the children safe. Your actions, regardless of how the children viewed them, were aimed at living up to the responsibilities of your role. That's the way it is for anyone in authority. Teens who realize this are better able to get along with authority figures. Like you, people sometimes make mistakes in the way they handle situations. Being in charge can be difficult at times. Looking at situations from both sides builds understanding, as well as the ability to get along.

You spend a lot of time with teachers and other authority figures at school. Here are some guidelines that will help you make relationships with authority figures positive:

- Be courteous and respectful.

- Practice self-discipline. Obey the rules.

- Tell the truth.

- Listen to what you are told. Ask questions if you don't understand.

- Accept responsibility for your behavior. Admit your mistakes. See Fig. 14-8.

- When you have a problem, talk to a person in authority.

Remember that people in positions of authority are there to help you. Often, they can give you good advice and help you avoid mistakes. Good relationships with parents, teachers, and school officials will help you build positive relationships in the future with employers and other authority figures.

Fig. 14-8. Authority figures have to give honest evaluations. *Would you blame the messenger, or take this opportunity to learn from your mistakes?*

Unhealthy Relationships

No one who truly cares about you would threaten you, pressure you to do something wrong, or ask you to go against your values. A relationship with someone who does these things is unhealthy. Here are some characteristics of unhealthy relationships:

- **Physical abuse.** No one has the right to harm you physically or threaten to do so. If any relationship includes fear of harm,

Fig. 14-9. Don't waste your time in an unhealthy relationship. Surround yourself with people who help you feel good about yourself.

ask a trusted adult for help now. Physical abuse can't be explained away and is *never* acceptable.

- **Controlling behavior.** It's unhealthy to be around a "friend" who always wants to control what you do, where you go, and with whom you spend your time. Don't confuse controlling behavior with caring. In a healthy relationship, you are in control of your own actions.

- **Isolation.** A relationship that isolates you from other friends and your family is harmful and headed in the wrong direction. It causes you to miss out on activities and the company of others. No single person can bring the rewards that come from healthy relationships.

- **Low self-esteem.** Feelings of depression, inadequacy, or low self-esteem when you are around another person are clear signs the relationship isn't a positive one. See Fig. 14-9.

- **Dependence.** Feeling like you are totally dependent on another person and that you couldn't function on your own are not good signs. It's far better to be with someone who encourages you to act independently and make decisions for yourself.

- **Bullying.** If someone bullies you or threatens to harm you, walk away from the relationship. Such behavior is unacceptable.

- **Dishonesty.** Lies and deceit have no part in a healthy relationship. You can't be yourself if you feel that you need to lie about your actions or feelings, or if you believe the other person is dishonest with you.

- **Irresponsible behavior.** A relationship with someone who encourages you to take unnecessary risks or behave in ways that could get you into trouble can jeopardize your health and future.

- **Illegal activity.** If someone influences you to steal, drink alcohol, use drugs, or engage in other illegal activities, end the relationship. Look for friends who respect you and the law.

Almost everyone has had to deal with an unhealthy relationship, but some people are more vulnerable. Recognizing the signs of an unhealthy relationship is the first step toward dealing with it. Stand up for yourself. In most cases, the best course of action is to end the relationship before the situation worsens.

Ending a Relationship

Relationships end for a variety of reasons. You may need to end a relationship because it is unhealthy. You may feel that you have outgrown the other person and no longer have anything in common. Dating relation-

Viewpoints

Ending a Relationship

"All good things must come to an end." That saying is true of some relationships. When a relationship ends, how should the people involved respond?

Connor: I hate it when people let a relationship just die out. If you think a relationship is ended, you should say so. Otherwise, the other person is left wondering, "Did I do something wrong?" and wasting time trying to make plans together. Then you start to feel annoyed and the other person gets angry. It's kinder to just say, "It's over."

Ann: Unless a relationship is really unhealthy, there's no need to "end" it. It's obvious, when two people start to have different interests or different feelings, they naturally don't want to spend as much time together. There are no hard feelings on either side. To tell someone your relationship is over makes it sound like you don't want anything to do with the other person. That could really hurt.

Seeing Both Sides ~ How do both views show consideration for "the other person"? If you sensed a relationship might be over, how could you explain your feelings without suggesting that you definitely wanted to end it?

ships often end because both people realize they are not compatible. Some relationships end for practical reasons, such as when people move to another city.

Ending a relationship is never easy. If you want to explain your reasons, try not to be accusing. You might say "I don't think we have much in common" rather than some-thing hurtful like "You're boring." Let the other person know that you still value him or her as a person.

No matter who ends the relationship, try not to dwell on the loss. Be grateful for the other valuable relationships in your life, and look ahead to the new ones that may be just around the corner.

14 *Review & Activities*

Chapter Summary

- Relationships vary in their degree of closeness, their purpose, and their form.
- Positive, healthy relationships bring many benefits and rewards.
- Factors that influence relationships include roles and the expectations they carry, personal qualities, self-esteem, and stereotypical thinking.

- Maintaining positive relationships takes time and effort, give and take, and tolerance.
- Teens need to strike a healthy balance between asserting independence and respecting authority figures.
- Certain signs warn that a relationship is unhealthy and should be ended.

Reviewing Key Terms & Ideas

1. Define **relationships** and explain the difference between a close relationship and a casual relationship.
2. Give at least three examples of the benefits that good relationships can bring.
3. Explain the connection between roles and **expectations**.
4. Why are you more likely to get along with someone whose values are similar to yours?
5. Why is high self-esteem important to relationships?
6. What is a **stereotype**? How does stereotypical thinking harm relationships?
7. Give six examples of qualities needed for strong relationships.
8. What can you do to meet people and make new friends?

9. How can you show **tolerance** toward people with different customs?
10. What is the connection between **prejudice** and **discrimination**?
11. Why are relationships with **authority figures** different from those with others?
12. Describe at least four characteristics of unhealthy relationships.

Thinking Critically

1. **Drawing Conclusions.** Why are roles and expectations sometimes in conflict during adolescence? What can you do to keep such conflict to a minimum?
2. **Understanding Cause and Effect.** Identify at least two aspects of modern life that tend to perpetuate stereotypes. Why is such stereotyping harmful?

Applying Your Knowledge

1. **Qualities of Strong Relationships.** Review the qualities needed for strong relationships in Fig. 14-4. Select one of the qualities that you feel you need to work on. Identify some specific actions you can take to improve on that quality.

2. **Giving and Receiving.** Give examples of how the principle of giving and receiving works in your relationships with family and friends. How can you strengthen your relationships by improving the balance between giving and receiving?

3. **Promoting Tolerance.** Create a plan for a campaign to promote tolerance in your school. Your plan might include encouraging student organizations to sponsor tolerance projects, inviting guest speakers, or other strategies. Explain how you would work with teachers, administrators, and other students to organize and implement your plan.

Making Connections

1. **Social Studies.** The U.S. population is the most diverse in the world. Research one of the waves of immigration in U.S. history to discover the reasons behind it. What are some ways in which American culture benefited as a result?

2. **Language Arts.** Write down at least three ways of opening a conversation with someone new. Then jot down some topics you could discuss once you get the conversation going.

Managing Your Life

Initiating Relationships

If you are like many people, you want to make new friends, but you usually wait for someone else to make the first move. Taking the initiative yourself could result in some rewarding relationships. Identify at least two school or community activities that interest you and would be new to you. Find out how you can get involved. Using that information, develop specific, measurable goals that will help you take the initiative and broaden your relationships.

Using Technology

1. **Internet.** Research how people can use the Internet and other communication technology to maintain relationships with friends and relatives who live far away. What options are there for exchanging messages? For sending and receiving photos? For exchanging video images? Summarize your findings in a brief report.

2. **Video Presentation.** Work with two or three other students to make a video on the topic of gender stereotypes. You might identify common assumptions about males and females and tape interviews with individuals to show that the stereotypes are not supported by the facts.

CHAPTER 15

Communication Skills

Key Terms

- communication
- verbal communication
- nonverbal communication
- "I" messages
- body language
- eye contact
- mixed message
- assertive
- aggressive
- passive
- active listening
- feedback

Objectives

- **Define** verbal and nonverbal communication.
- **Distinguish** between "I" messages and "you" messages.
- **Explain** how tone, body language, and image send messages to others.
- **Demonstrate** active listening techniques.
- **Give** guidelines for communicating by phone and in writing.

When you have something important to say, how do you get started? Write down three different ways to open a conversation about a serious topic.

Sharleen gripped the weights and prepared to lift. Watching from across the weight room, her friend Natalie called, "Sharleen, you can't do that."

Sharleen's face reddened as she hoisted the weights with determination. She didn't like being told "you can't," especially when she knew she could. Suddenly she felt a sharp pain in her back. Sharleen lowered the weights and grimaced.

Natalie came to her friend's side. "See, I told you. You're bound to hurt yourself when you lift weights that way."

Poor communication can cause much confusion. Do you see what happened with Sharleen and Natalie? Sharleen misinterpreted what Natalie was saying. Natalie wasn't trying to tell Sharleen she wasn't capable. She just wanted to say that her technique wasn't correct. Unfortunately, the words she chose were unclear, and Sharleen took them the wrong way.

The Process

Communication is the process of sending and receiving messages between people. Often people use **verbal communication**, which means sending messages with words. You use words to communicate face to face, on the phone, and in writing. When you're talking to someone, you send messages in other ways too. **Nonverbal communication** involves sending messages without words through the use of facial expressions and gestures. People combine verbal and nonverbal messages to communicate their thoughts and feelings.

Communication is a two-way street—one person sends messages and another receives them. When all goes well, messages are sent and received correctly. All too often, though, messages aren't transmitted or interpreted as intended, and the kind of confusion Sharleen and Natalie experienced is the result. Making a serious effort to polish your communication skills can help you avoid such situations—as well as more troublesome ones. See Fig. 15-1.

Fig. 15-1. Good communication skills help ensure that messages get through clearly. Have you ever misunderstood what someone said to you? What caused the problem?

More to Explore

Overcoming Communication Challenges

It's easy for most people to take the ability to communicate for granted. Some people, however, have disabilities that makes communication challenging. Adaptive techniques have

been developed to help overcome these challenges. For example, people who are blind can use the Braille alphabet to read with their fingertips. Sign language allows people who are deaf to communicate with one another and with hearing people. These techniques have been in use for many years.

More recently, technology has greatly expanded the methods for overcoming communication challenges. Speech synthesizers convert written text into the spoken word. Screen magnification software helps the visually impaired use computers. Text telephones enable the hearing impaired to use the phone to send typed messages. These and other devices have helped people with communication disabilities gain greater independence.

Devices such as a Braille printer make it possible for people with impaired vision to use a computer.

Barriers to Communication

To communicate effectively, you need to be aware of barriers that can prevent messages from being sent and received as intended. Unclear messages and misunderstandings are two of the most common barriers to communication. If you've ever arrived at an event at the wrong time or on the wrong day, you know how easy it is for messages to get confused.

Poor listening skills are another barrier to communication. Some people don't listen because they're too focused on their own thoughts. Others don't concentrate. It's easy to get distracted when someone is speaking to you. Learning to block out distractions and focus on what someone is saying is an important communication skill.

Language and culture can also interfere with clear communication. People who have limited language skills may find it hard to say exactly what they mean. Their listeners need to make an extra effort to understand. A person's culture—the beliefs, values, and customs of a particular group—can also influence the way messages are interpreted. For example, you might hug someone as a sign of affection, but another culture might find the gesture offensive. The best way to overcome cultural misunderstandings is to learn about and respect cultural differences.

The Messages You Send

To express yourself clearly, you need to be aware of what you say and how you say it. Effective communication is a skill that can be learned, practiced, and improved. Here are some ideas that will help you.

Sending "I" Messages

Rico wanted to play a video game, but his older brother Ben was using it. "You can have it when I'm finished," he said.

Rico was annoyed. It seemed to him that Ben always had the first chance at everything. "You always have things your way," he accused. "You're so selfish!"

"That's not true," Ben shot back. "You're just being impatient!"

Rico and Ben's disagreement could have been resolved. Instead, it produced hurt feelings because they both sent the wrong kind of messages. Rico accused his brother of treating him unfairly; Ben felt he had to defend himself. The dispute turned personal and destructive.

Both would have been better off using "I" messages. With **"I" messages**, you say how you feel and what you think, rather than criticizing someone else. "I" message have three parts:

- "I feel …" (here you name an emotion—anger, fear, disappointment)
- "when you …" (here you say what behavior bothers you)
- "because …" (here you explain why it bothers you)

For example, instead of attacking his brother, Rico could have said, "I feel upset when you play our new video games first because I'd like to be first once in a while." That way, he would have communicated his point of view to his brother. "I" messages work because they are less likely to cause negative feelings, which interfere with communication. Using "you" messages dooms a disagreement to attacks and accusations. "I" messages help keep a conversation reasonable. They enable both people to stay focused on the underlying problem and to solve it together. See Fig. 15-2.

Fig. 15-2. Disagreements don't have to turn into arguments. Why are "I" messages better than "you" messages in a disagreement?

Using the Right Tone

People send messages with their tone of voice. Imagine that a young child says to you, "Look at the picture I drew!" You might answer, "That's terrific." Your words contain a positive message, but the way you say those words is the key to your message. If your voice shows enthusiasm, the child knows you like the drawing. If your tone of voice is insincere or bored, however, the child will know that you don't really care.

Be aware of how your words sound. If you want to express sympathy, use a gentle tone. If you're asking someone to help you, use a polite tone. Knowing how you sound helps ensure that you send the messages you intend to send.

Using Body Language

Has someone ever asked you "What's wrong?" before you even said a word? How did the person know that something was wrong? He or she probably sensed that something was different about you. You may have been walking more slowly than usual or staring into space. Maybe you just didn't say hello. Somehow you sent a message that you weren't even aware of.

Body language refers to a person's posture, facial expressions, gestures, and way of moving. Body language affects not only how others see you, but also how they react to your verbal message. Imagine that you want to persuade your friends to take part in a charity walk. If you stand up straight, smile as you speak, and use persuasive gestures, you're more likely to gain your friends' support. See Fig. 15-3.

An important element of body language is **eye contact**—direct visual contact with another person's eyes. Using eye contact shows that you're interested, confident, and friendly, and that you mean what you say. Be aware, though, that in some cultures it's considered rude to look someone directly in the eye while speaking.

Controlling body language is one way to manage the image that you project to others. Attending to your appearance is another. How people act and what they say is more important than how they look, but clothes do send a message. When you choose clothes that go together and are appropriate for a situation, you show that you care.

Fig. 15-3. The way you carry your body, your facial expressions, and your gestures all send messages, just as your words do.

Fig. 15-4. Some conversations can be held almost anywhere. For others, you may need to find a quiet, private place to talk.

Good grooming plays an important role in the image that you project, too. Washing your face, combing your hair, and wearing clean clothes contribute to a neat, healthy appearance. These actions communicate to others that you respect and care about yourself. They also show respect for others.

Avoiding Mixed Messages

Sometimes you might say one thing but your body language says another. You might say "I don't mind," for example, but your tense body and sad expression communicate that you feel hurt and that you *do* mind. When your words and body language don't communicate the same thing, you send a **mixed message**. Mixed messages cause confusion. People won't know whether to believe what you say or what they see. Practice thinking about what message you want to send and making sure your body language matches your words.

Choosing Time and Place

Knowing when and where to communicate can make communication positive as well. Sometimes it's best to speak your mind immediately. At other times it's wiser to wait. In choosing when and where to talk to someone, keep these tips in mind.

- Be sure that the other person is willing and able to listen. Asking your mother something serious the minute she walks in the door from work probably isn't a good idea.

- Avoid times when emotions will hinder the message. If you're angry, calm down before talking. If you're confused, take time to figure out what you want to say. Consider your listener's emotions, too. You're more likely to communicate effectively if both of you are calm and focused.

- Make sure the other person isn't distracted. Choose a time and place when the receiver can concentrate on the message and when you are unlikely to be interrupted. See Fig. 15-4.

Communication Styles

The *way* you speak can be just as important as *what* you say. You're more likely to get your message across if you're assertive. Being **assertive** means that you express your ideas and opinions firmly and with confidence. You show, through your communication style, that you mean what you say. People are more likely to listen to assertive speakers and to take them seriously.

Being assertive is not the same as being aggressive. People who are **aggressive** are overly forceful and pushy. They are often angry or frustrated. They think that by being aggressive they will persuade others to their point of view. Often, the opposite happens. Many people react to aggressive behavior by rejecting the message and walking away.

People who have a **passive** communication style keep their opinions to themselves and give in to the influence of others. Some passive people are too timid to express an opinion. Others don't know what their opinions are. They find it easier to follow the crowd. This communication style can lead people to make unwise choices.

The Messages Received

Just as important as sending clear messages is accurately interpreting the ones you receive. Other people want you to pay attention to and understand what they have to say. In that way, they are no different from you.

Active Listening

"I heard you; I heard you," Angelo grumbled to his friend, Tanya.

"Yes, I know you heard me talking, but did you really *listen*?" Tanya asked in exasperation.

Hearing is just a physical action—receiving sound waves. **Active listening**, on the other hand, is concentrating on what is said so that you understand and remember the message. See Fig. 15-5.

Active listening helps strengthen relationships because it promotes real understanding. People who make an effort to listen are less self-absorbed and more likely to learn from others. Active listening boosts self-esteem in others, too. When you show an interest in what people have to say, you help them feel that they have something worthwhile to offer.

Fig. 15-5. Your body language and facial expressions can show that you're paying attention. What clues tell you that this teen is actively listening to what the other has to say?

Here are some techniques for active listening:

- **Keep an open mind.** Be prepared to accept the other person's point of view.
- **Eliminate distractions.** For example, if the music or TV is too loud, turn it off or move to a quieter place.
- **Listen with a purpose.** Think about why you're listening. For example, you listen to your friends' problems to let them express their feelings.
- **Make eye contact.** Look the speaker in the eye, and keep your expression open and interested.
- **Focus your attention.** Think about what's being said, not how you'll respond.
- **Control negative emotions.** If the speaker's message upsets you, focus on staying calm and listening. Then you can present your views.
- **Don't cut the speaker off.** Let the person who is speaking finish at his or her own pace.

Feedback

Part of any two-way communication is giving **feedback**. Feedback occurs when a listener lets a speaker know that he or she is trying to understand the message being delivered. You can give feedback in many different ways:

- Interject a comment when the speaker pauses.
- Express your interest by asking questions that lead to more conversation.
- Restate what the other person said in your own words. Then ask whether you understood the message correctly. See Fig. 15-6.

Fig. 15-6. Giving feedback is a way of confirming that you have understood a message correctly. Why is this particularly important when someone gives you directions or explains a process?

- When the other person is upset and needs to unload negative feelings, show empathy. Use such phrases as "That sounds unfair" or "You must have been so hurt." Don't feel you need to solve the problem. Having someone to listen may be all that the speaker needs.

FINDING CREATIVE SOLUTIONS

Reaching a Compromise

Communication involves expressing your own point of view and listening to the views of others. But what happens if you disagree? What if you need to reach an agreement in order to move forward? In such situations, you may need to compromise.

▶ How It Works

When people compromise, they each give up something in order to reach a solution that's acceptable to all concerned. The art of compromise is to find areas on which people *can* agree, and then to resolve the differences.

▶ Try It Out

You are chair of the five-person committee charged with creating a poster for the school musical. You've called a meeting to discuss people's ideas.

Mark begins by explaining his idea. Paige reacts first: "That will never work. Nobody will notice it," she says.

"It isn't clear and engaging enough. It's too busy," adds Rashon.

Mark starts to protest, but Paige cuts him off. "We need something catchier, Mark, something more creative." Then she and Rashon started discussing a poster they had seen that they really liked.

Mark is embarrassed and says nothing. Meanwhile the last member of the group, Keiko, starts to sketch a version of Mark's idea that is simpler and more focused.

▶ **Your Turn** *You need to find a way to keep your team together and get the job done. Suggest some possible approaches to solving the problem. How might you reach a compromise that everyone would agree to? What communication skills are particularly important in a situation like this?*

Dealing with Criticism

One kind of feedback that you might not welcome is criticism. Perhaps you give a class presentation and a friend says it was too long-winded. Friends and family might also criticize your clothes, your appearance, your food choices, your movie choices, the way you speak, or the way you spend your time. How do you deal with this criticism?

The first thing to remember is that criticism is often well meant. People are trying to help you by offering criticism. In fact, if you're honest with yourself, you might agree with some of the criticism you receive. Keep an open mind and consider comments that seem intended to help you. The opinions of others can be helpful. In fact, it's a normal part of workplace routine.

What about criticism that is spiteful or inaccurate? Ignore it. People have a right to express their opinions, just as you do. You don't have to respond to negative comments. Nor is there anything to be gained from dwelling on personal attacks. Learn to distinguish between helpful and unhelpful criticism and focus your thoughts on what's helpful.

Communicating by Phone

When you talk on the phone, you can't see the person you're speaking to, and you can't be seen. That means neither of you can "read" facial expressions or other body language. Neither of you can use eye contact to emphasize a point. Nor can you nod or smile to encourage the person to keep talking.

You need to make more of an effort, then, to express yourself clearly and make sure the person has understood you. Using active listening and providing feedback become more essential in phone conversations. Here are some other tips:

- **Find a convenient time.** When you call someone, ask, "Do you have time to talk?" If someone calls you when you're busy, ask if you can call back. If you're rushed or

distracted, you won't be able to give your attention to the caller.

- **Find a convenient place.** When you use a cell phone, try to find a quiet place to make your call. Calling from a busy mall could make it hard for your listener to hear you.

- **Avoid disturbing others.** A ringing cell phone can be intrusive, especially in a theater, library, classroom, or quiet restaurant. In such situations, turn off the phone or set it to vibrate or flash instead of ring. If you need to make or answer a call, step outside first. See Fig. 15-7.

- **Leave clear messages.** If you need to leave a voice mail message, think carefully about what you want to say. Let the listener know when you called and the reason for your call.

Fig. 15-7. When using a cell phone, find a place where you won't be distracted and where you won't disturb others.

Viewpoints

Cell Phones

There's no doubt about it: cell phones are handy and convenient. But not everyone is pleased about this modern communication tool.

Tyler: I couldn't manage being without my cell phone. I use it to arrange for a ride to my after-school job. I also use it to call my friends and plan activities. My parents like me to have my phone with me. That way they can check in with me if they need to. If there was any kind of emergency, I'd be able to contact them. Cell phones are much more convenient than other kinds of phones—wherever you are, you can make and receive calls.

Sara: Cell phones don't belong in public places! I hate it when people make calls in the supermarket line, or on the bus, or in a restaurant. Why should I have to listen to their conversations? Sometimes they're standing less than two feet way from me, talking really loudly. It's also very irritating when a cell phone rings in the middle of a concert or movie. Cell phone users need to be more sensitive to other people.

Seeing Both Sides ~ Do you think these viewpoints are valid? What can cell phone users do to avoid irritating others? Write a list of five rules that you think all cell phone users could easily follow and that would show courtesy to others.

Remember that it's easy to get distracted when you're talking on the phone. You've probably had the experience of talking with a friend and realizing that he was giving you only part of his attention. Perhaps he was watching TV at the same time, or playing a computer game. That's when misunderstandings can occur.

Communicating in Writing

Throughout history, people have communicated by writing letters. Today, sending e-mail is a popular alternative. Good writing and reading skills help you communicate with your friends and family. These skills are also essential in the workplace. Many jobs require you to write memos and reports, or to read and understand written instructions.

Whenever you communicate in writing, the same guidelines apply: consider whom you are writing to, the purpose of your message, and the subject you're writing about. Keep these suggestions in mind:

- Organize your thoughts before you start. Make notes, list the points you want to cover, and decide on the sequence you want to follow. See Fig. 15-8.

- Pay attention to the tone you use. A letter of application requires a formal, respectful tone. You can be more casual when writing to a friend.

- Keep it simple. Use straightforward language and make your points clearly. Don't make it hard for your reader to understand the reason for your message.

- Check that you have made all your points.

- Proofread your work before you send it. Check your spelling and grammar, and make sure you didn't leave out any words or letters.

When you receive written messages, read them carefully. When you read with purpose, you focus on the reason for the message. Try to understand what the person is saying. Follow up with any questions you have.

The Impact

Without good communication, relationships can't thrive. This is true on a personal level, in the workplace, and in society in general. In fact, diplomats from different countries must have excellent communication skills in order to do their work and to improve international relations.

In the workplace, you need to get along with people of different ages, genders, cultures, backgrounds, and abilities. That requires strong communication skills. Communicating effectively increases understanding and cooperation—at home, with friends, at work, and in the community. Understanding fosters good feelings, promoting even better communication.

Fig. 15-8. *Before you respond to a letter or an e-mail, take a moment to highlight the points you want to cover.* What are some other ways to organize your thoughts before you communicate in writing?

Chapter Summary

- Communication involves sending and receiving verbal and nonverbal messages.

- "I" messages, in which you say how you feel and what you think, are more effective than "you" messages.

- Body language, eye contact, and personal appearance all contribute to the messages you send.

- When you listen actively and concentrate on what is said, you're more likely to understand and remember a message.

- Telephone etiquette involves choosing an appropriate time and place to call and avoiding distractions.

- When communicating in writing, you need to consider whom you are writing to, the purpose of your message, and the subject you're writing about.

Reviewing Key Terms & Ideas

1. What is the difference between **verbal** and **nonverbal communication**?

2. Give four suggestions for sending effective messages.

3. Describe the three parts of an **"I" message** and give an example.

4. Why are "I" messages more effective than "you" messages?

5. Give two examples of **body language** and the message each sends.

6. What is a **mixed message**? Why does it cause problems in communication?

7. Which communication style is more effective: **assertive** or **aggressive**? Why?

8. How does **active listening** differ from simply hearing a message?

9. Describe three ways to improve your listening skills.

10. What is the purpose of **feedback**?

11. What disadvantage does speaking on the telephone have compared with speaking face to face?

12. What are two guidelines to follow when using a cell phone?

13. Why should you read through any message that you write before you send it?

Thinking Critically

1. **Making Comparisons.** Why is written communication sometimes less effective than talking in person? Is it ever more effective? Explain.

2. **Recognizing Assumptions.** Why do what you wear and your grooming have an important effect on the image you present to others?

Applying Your Knowledge

1. **Creating "I" Messages.** Turn the following "you" messages into "I" messages:

   A. "You never pick up your things."

   B. "You're always late."

   C. "You don't give me a chance to talk."

   D. "You won't let me decide for myself."

2. **Active Listening.** With a partner, plan and act out a situation to demonstrate active listening and giving feedback.

3. **Improving Communication.** Working in a small group, write a scene in which two teens have trouble communicating in a specific situation, such as choosing where to eat out or working together on a school assignment. Then rewrite the scene to show positive communication.

Making Connections

1. **Social Studies.** Read a famous speech, such as Abraham Lincoln's Gettysburg Address or "I Have a Dream" by Martin Luther King, Jr. In small groups, discuss the purpose of the speech and how specific words and phrases helped get the message across. Report your group's findings to the class.

2. **Language Arts.** Practice changing the tone of a message to suit your audience. Write two letters—one to your supervisor at your part-time job and one to a close friend—in which you explain that your family will be moving to another state in a few weeks.

Managing Your Life

How to Communicate?

With so many communication options to choose from, how do you decide which is most appropriate? When is it better to phone rather than to e-mail? When is a handwritten letter preferable? Choose three of the following communication options: face-to-face meeting; telephone call; e-mail message; printout of a letter; handwritten letter; card with handwritten note. Describe a situation for which each option would be most appropriate, and explain why.

Using Technology

1. **Internet.** Use the Internet to learn more about communication technology designed for people with disabilities such as blindness and deafness. Focus on a device that particularly interests you and prepare a short report to share with your classmates.

2. **Presentation Software.** Use appropriate software to create a brief presentation explaining the dos and don'ts of phone etiquette. If possible, include photos of people using phones in various situations. (You might use a digital camera or scan photos from magazines.) Share your presentation in class.

Teamwork and Leadership Skills

Objectives

- **Summarize** benefits of teamwork.
- **Describe** characteristics of a good team player.
- **Contrast** positive and negative teamwork processes and roles.
- **Analyze** characteristics of effective leadership.
- **Explain** the importance of resolving group conflict.

QUICK WRITE

Write about a team that you have worked or played with. In what ways did you work well together? What didn't go so well? What do you think it takes for teams to be successful?

Amy, Shamara, Luis, and Kyle were assigned to work together on a history project. When the team met for the first time, Amy was ready to get to work. "Okay, we only have two weeks. Let's decide how we're going to get this project done," she said. Then she suggested some ideas for getting started. "Wait a minute," said Shamara. "We've never worked together before. I think we'd do a better job if we spent some time getting to know each other first." At that, Kyle headed for the door. "I'm really busy. You guys let me know what you decide, and I'll try to make the next meeting." As they watched him go, Luis shook his head. "I've worked on teams before where one person did all the work. We need to make sure everyone contributes."

Many teams find themselves in situations like this. Amy, Shamara, Luis, and Kyle have started out with some good ideas, but they also face challenges in learning to work together effectively. Teamwork and leadership skills can help them succeed.

What Is Teamwork?

Think about places you've been in the past week, such as home, school, the mall, or the gym. No matter where you went or what you did, you probably saw teamwork in action. **Teamwork** involves working with others to achieve a common goal. It's based on the principle that people working together can accomplish more than individuals working alone. See Fig. 16-1.

Teamwork is a key to the success of families, schools, workplaces, and communities. In your family, you might work together to clean up the kitchen after a meal so that

Fig. 16-1. When individuals come together and work in harmony, they can create a whole that is greater than the sum of its parts. What do musicians need to do in order to work well as a team?

everyone gets to his or her next activity on time. Maybe you've worked on a group project in school, like Amy, Shamara, Luis, and Kyle. Your local school board and city or town council are examples of teamwork in your community. What other examples of teamwork can you think of?

Benefits of Teamwork

Learning to be an effective member of a team is a skill that will always be useful. In the workplace, employers recognize that many goals can only be accomplished through teamwork. Some businesses depend almost entirely on a teamwork approach. In these companies, managers do not tell employees what to do. Instead, teams of employees are responsible for choosing their own methods of reaching the goals that have been set. Teamwork on the job helps people to be productive and builds loyalty to the company.

Because teamwork is so important in the workplace, now is the time to learn and practice teamwork skills. School provides many opportunities. You can participate in class projects, sports, and organizations such as Family, Career and Community Leaders of America (FCCLA). These experiences can help make you both a productive student and a desirable job candidate.

Teamwork has many benefits, both for the group as a whole and for individual team members. These benefits include:

- **Efficiency.** Projects can be completed in less time if people work together.

- **Combined strengths.** The variety of skills that various team members bring to a project is a plus. Sometimes one person has skills that others lack. Combining those strengths enhances the quality of the results.

- **Mutual support.** Think of a time when you worked alone on a difficult project. It's easy to procrastinate or become discouraged. On team projects, team members can support and encourage one another. See Fig. 16-2.

- **Job satisfaction.** By giving and receiving positive feedback, team members help each other feel that they're making a worthwhile contribution.

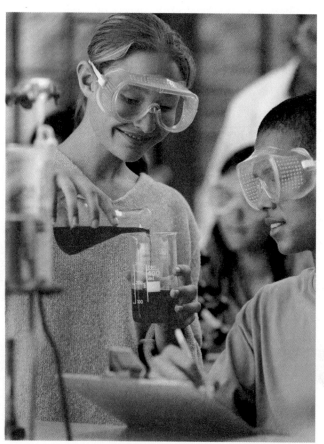

Fig. 16-2. Many tasks are easier and more enjoyable when you work with others. Why do you suppose this is true?

How to Be a Team Player

Be willing to contribute. Let the team know how you can be most useful. Team success depends on using members' knowledge, skills, and ideas effectively.	**Use good communication skills.** In team meetings, express your ideas clearly and listen attentively. Communicate effectively between meetings.	**Respect differences.** Show respect for every team member, regardless of age, abilities, gender, and culture. Everyone can contribute.
Avoid competing with other team members. There is no "I" in teamwork. Teamwork is about what *we* can achieve.	**Do your fair share.** Take on as much as you can handle and accept responsibility for the tasks assigned to you.	**Focus on team goals.** The team's goals are your top priority. Don't get sidetracked by something unrelated.
Work to resolve conflicts. If team members disagree, help find a workable solution while respecting others' opinions.	**Support team decisions.** Accept responsibility for carrying them out, even if you don't agree with them.	**Pitch in to help others.** If someone on the team has a tough job or falls behind, be supportive and lend a hand.

Fig. 16-3. Putting these ideas into practice will help make you a valued member of any team.

- **Personal development.** Teamwork helps you develop skills, gain self-confidence, and learn from others. Rachel served as student council representative for her homeroom during freshman year. That gave her the confidence to run for treasurer of her sophomore class.

- **Improved relationships.** Teamwork offers opportunities to build and strengthen relationships. Working together can lead to lasting bonds among team members.

Characteristics of Team Players

What does it take to be a good team player? In a word: cooperation. Imagine trying to pull a huge, heavy box by tying ropes to it. If everyone grabs a rope and pulls in a different direction, nothing is accomplished. Only by pulling together will the team achieve its goal.

Cooperative team members coordinate their efforts. They are willing to do what is necessary to complete a job, and they accept responsibility for team results. Fig. 16-3 describes ways team members can show cooperation.

How Teamwork Works

Teams work together for a common purpose. That purpose may be to complete a class assignment, solve a problem, produce a product, raise money for an organization, or prepare for competition. A group in your literature class may work as a team for just a few weeks, or even a few days. The track team may work together for a season. In a large corporation, team projects often require weeks, months, or years to complete. Regardless of the team purpose or the time frame, successful teams use similar processes to achieve their goals.

Dividing Tasks

Teams function best when all team members understand what is expected of them. Everyone should be asked to contribute, and responsibilities should be distributed fairly. If people feel they're expected to do too much, resentment can build. If they're asked to do too little, they may feel they are not a valued part of the team.

Successful teams assign tasks in ways that make the best possible use of the knowledge and skills of all team members. For example, the prom committee asked Elena to present its plans to the entire junior class. They knew her specialty on the speech team was persuasive speaking. Other team members took on tasks that suited their abilities, too.

Making Group Decisions

When teams are faced with important decisions, they must find a way to reach agreement. Team members must be willing to listen and consider different points of view. See Fig. 16-4.

The method used to reach a decision will depend on the group and the situation. Possible methods include:

- **Majority rule.** This is a democratic process in which decisions are made by voting. All team members are allowed to vote on an issue, and the majority opinion must be accepted. One disadvantage of this process is that it creates winners and losers.

Fig. 16-4. Reaching a group decision may not be easy, but it's an important process. What are the advantages of involving the whole team in decision making?

More to Explore

Using Parliamentary Procedure

Parliamentary procedure is a set of rules for conducting meetings in an orderly way. This democratic method ensures that even though the majority rules, the rights of the minority are protected. Many government bodies, professional associations, and student organizations use parliamentary procedure. Here are some of the basic rules:

- **Motion.** A method of bringing business before the group for consideration. For example, a member might say, "I move that we hold a fundraising car wash next Saturday."

- **Second.** If another member agrees that the motion should be considered, he or she says, "I second the motion."

- **Debate.** Members can present their opinions for or against the motion. Those who wish to speak must first ask to be recognized by the *chair*, or leader of the meeting.

- **Motion to amend.** During debate, a member can propose changes to the original motion. After the proposed changes are voted on, debate on the main motion continues.

- **Division of a question.** This is a way to break up the motion so that each part can be considered and voted on separately.

- **Vote.** When debate is concluded, the chair restates the motion, calls for a vote, and announces the results. The group is now ready to consider the next item of business.

- **Compromise.** When team members compromise, they each give up some of what they want. The result is a solution that's not totally satisfying to anyone, but that everyone can live with.

- **Consensus building. Consensus** means agreement by the entire group. Building consensus is a process in which everyone's ideas are taken into account. The final decision must be agreeable to everyone. If any member of the team has a strong objection, an alternative must be found.

Consensus building may take a long time, or it may not be possible at all. Even if the team doesn't reach a consensus, the process can help clarify the issues being discussed.

Avoiding "Groupthink"

Sometimes groups work well together, yet make poor decisions. Irving Janis, a researcher who studied how groups work together, coined the term "groupthink" to explain why this can happen. **Groupthink**

Roles of Team Members

POSITIVE ROLES	NEGATIVE ROLES
Initiator: a person who gets things moving. **Coordinator:** a person who organizes team resources. **Leader:** a person who takes responsibility for moving the team forward. **Harmonizer:** a person who tries to build good relationships among team members. **Encourager:** a person who praises other people's ideas. **Seeker:** a person who asks questions. **Innovator:** a person who has creative ideas. **Peacemaker:** a person who helps the team deal with conflict.	**Avoider:** a person who refuses to actively participate. **Dominator:** a person who tries to control other team members. **Blocker:** a person who rejects everyone else's ideas. **Distracter:** a person who turns attention away from the team's primary goal.

Fig. 16-5. Not every team includes these roles, but you may recognize them in team members you have worked with. *Which roles have you played?*

refers to a faulty decision-making process caused by a strong desire for group agreement. When teams experience groupthink, they consider only a few alternatives before selecting a course of action. They ignore information that does not support the action they decide to take. Team members with opposing opinions are pressured to agree with the majority.

Groupthink is a barrier to effective teamwork. Teams can avoid groupthink by being open and accepting of diverse opinions and by encouraging critical evaluation of all ideas. Teams made up of people with diverse backgrounds and experiences are less likely to engage in groupthink.

Taking on Roles

A football team does not need eleven quarterbacks. An orchestra does not need forty conductors. Members of a team play different roles to help achieve the team's goals. You need team members who have different skills and contribute them to the team's success. The situation described at the beginning of this chapter illustrates some of the roles team members play. See if you can match each team member to one of the roles described in Fig. 16-5.

When you participate in a team, ask yourself what role or roles you are playing. Are they positive, or do they impede the team's progress?

Effective Leadership

To be effective, teams need good leadership. **Leadership** provides the direction and motivation that helps a team or group achieve their goals. Every team needs a leader, whether the goal is to plan a class project, organize a family reunion, or run a small business.

Some leaders are chosen or elected. Others take a leadership role when they see a need to do so. For example, Ryan heard that a fire had destroyed the home of a friend in his math class. He wanted to help, but he knew he couldn't provide the new home or clothes the family needed. Instead of giving up, Ryan brainstormed with some of his classmates about ways they could help. Together they organized a school-wide fundraiser to help the family. In this case, Ryan's leadership made things happen.

Leadership Skills

People like Ryan serve as role models. A **role model** is a person who sets an example for others. When you serve as a role model and others follow your example, your ability to make a difference extends beyond your own actions. See Fig. 16-6.

What leadership skills did Ryan demonstrate in helping his classmate's family? First, he had the *vision* to imagine what he wanted to achieve. He could see that while he alone could do little to help the family, he could make a difference by persuading others to help too. In addition, Ryan demonstrated the *commitment* to take action. His skill in *persuasion* convinced others to share his vision. Without these leadership skills, Ryan couldn't have achieved his goal.

The list that follows describes other important skills leaders need. As you read about them, ask yourself which skills you already have and which you need to work on.

- **Communicating clearly.** Good leaders consciously choose what they say and how they say it. They understand the importance of body language and avoid sending mixed messages. Good leaders are active listeners and provide feedback to show that they are sincerely trying to understand other people's points of view.

- **Motivating others.** Effective leaders offer guidance, praise, and encouragement to

Fig. 16-6. A good leader knows how to guide and motivate others. What might happen if a group had no leader?

FINDING CREATIVE SOLUTIONS

Using Humor

As team members work to achieve their goals, many challenges can arise. A team meeting might be called to discuss a problem and consider possible solutions. When a problem proves especially tough, frustration can build and tempers can flare. The resulting conflict distracts the team's focus away from solving the original problem. Using humor to lighten the team's mood can help calm nerves and open lines of communication.

How It Works

When the situation is already tense, use humor like hot sauce—with a light touch and in the right places. Never make fun of other team members or laugh at their ideas. Your goal is to unite the group, not divide it. Try making a silly suggestion: "It looks like we're not making any progress in reaching a decision. Shall we use the 'rock, paper, scissors' method or 'one potato, two potato'?" You might let the joke be on you: "Whose dumb idea was that? It was mine? I take that back—it's the best idea I've ever heard!" Gently pointing out the humorous side of the situation can break the tension, allowing the team to refocus on solving the problem at hand.

Try It Out

You're the leader of a group that will plan and build a float for the homecoming parade. You don't have much money to work with, and the parade is just two weeks away. So far, every idea suggested for the float has been voted down as being either too difficult, too expensive, or not good enough. Some committee members are becoming angry and blaming one another. Some seem disgusted and are about to walk out of the meeting.

▶ **Your Turn** *Come up with a way to lighten the mood of this meeting. How could you help committee members see the humor in the situation? How could doing so help the team work together more effectively?*

motivate team members. When it comes to motivation, people are not all the same. Some appreciate public recognition for their efforts, while others might be embarrassed by it. Leaders must try to learn what approach each person responds to best.

- **Managing.** Good leaders understand the "big picture." They are skilled in planning, organizing, and implementing a project. They know how to make the best use of the skills and resources of the team members to get the job done.

- **Delegating.** Effective leaders avoid the temptation to do all the work themselves. Instead, they **delegate**, or assign tasks to other team members. They try to match the abilities of team members to the tasks to be accomplished. By delegating, effective leaders help other team members gain experience and strengthen skills.

- **Making decisions.** Leaders must understand and use the decision-making process. They involve others in identifying and evaluating alternatives and selecting the best course of action. They are willing to reconsider when decisions don't work out.

- **Solving problems.** Good problem-solving skills help effective leaders face up to challenges. They work with their team to analyze alternatives and find creative solutions.

Leadership Qualities

Think about some of the leaders you know—classmates, teachers, coaches, family members, community leaders. What personal qualities do they share? In addition to leadership skills, successful leaders need personal qualities that encourage people to follow their lead. Chances are that the leaders you know are dependable, enthusiastic, and honest. These are qualities common to many successful leaders.

Leaders also need the courage to face difficulties and take risks. A positive attitude is helpful, too. Leaders must believe that they can reach their goals and communicate that belief to their team. A sense of responsibility is essential. Leaders must accept responsibility for their actions in order to gain the respect of others. A sense of humor also helps. Team members may be more willing to make an effort for a leader who makes the work enjoyable.

Ethical Leadership

Leaders must do what's needed to get a job done. However, there's more to leadership than just doing things right. Leadership is also about *doing the right thing*. An effective leader practices **ethical leadership**—leadership based on moral principles.

How do leaders demonstrate ethical principles? They tell the truth and keep their promises. They have respect for themselves and for others, including people different from them. Ethical leaders accept responsibility for the consequences of their actions. They play by the rules and treat people fairly. Many work to make a difference in their communities. See Fig. 16-7.

Fig. 16-7. Taking the lead in cleaning up your community is one way to make a difference. What are some other examples of ethical leadership?

Teens in positions of leadership must remember their ethical responsibilities. As a leader, you must be concerned about your behavior not only for yourself, but because of the example you set for others. Remember that leadership is not about seeking recognition for yourself. True leadership involves serving other people and working to make life better for all.

Leadership Styles

Think about some of the political leaders you have seen on television. Some have an energetic style of speaking, while others are more low-key. If you could observe these leaders as they work with others behind the scenes, you'd find that they don't all use the same style of leadership, either. **Leadership style** refers to a leader's pattern of behavior when directing a team. The style that is chosen may depend on the leader's personality as well as the situation.

Four Styles of Leadership

STYLE	CHARACTERISTICS	ADVANTAGES	DISADVANTAGES
Authoritarian	Leader makes decisions using his or her own judgment, then tells others what to do.	The team process is efficient and orderly. Decisions can be made quickly.	Ideas and experiences of team members are not utilized. Without input into decisions, members may lack commitment to goals.
Democratic	Leader encourages team members to express their opinions. Decisions are made by the majority.	Everyone is welcome to contribute. Team members support decisions and work to carry them out.	Team process is inefficient. There are more disagreements and decisions take longer.
Integrated	Leader emphasizes maintaining group harmony and helping team members build good relationships.	Team may reach better decisions. Decisions are more likely to be based on consensus.	Team-building process is time-consuming.
Laissez-faire	Leader takes a "hands-off" approach and lets the group function on its own.	Leaders may emerge from the group.	Team process lacks organization and is inefficient.

Fig. 16-8. There's more than one approach to leadership. What might leaders take into account when choosing which style to use?

Sharing Leadership Sometimes you might find yourself sharing a leadership position, such as co-chairperson. To minimize conflict, start by getting to know each other. Learn how you each communicate, delegate tasks, and solve problems. Discuss the team's goals to make sure you're in agreement. Look for ways to distribute the work and leadership, capitalizing on each of your strengths. Think of a specific classmate. If you were sharing leadership, what strengths might each of you bring to the partnership? How might this affect the way you divide responsibilities?

The four most common leadership styles are authoritarian, democratic, integrated, and laissez-faire. (*Laissez-faire* [leh-zay-FAIR] is a French term meaning "leave alone" or "let people do as they choose.") Fig. 16-8 summarizes these four leadership styles and their advantages and disadvantages.

Different styles of leadership are appropriate for specific situations. For example, in a crisis, an authoritarian style would allow for quick decisions. In a situation in which team members have never worked together before, an integrated style might be more appropriate. If a team task is particularly complex, a democratic leadership style would encourage everyone to contribute. Laissez-faire leadership might work best with team members who are highly motivated and capable of moving forward independently. Successful leaders are able to vary their leadership style to suit the situation.

Resolving Group Conflict

Conflict is a natural part of teamwork. When people work together, there will always be opposing ideas and interests that lead to disagreements. If team members have very different personalities, maintaining harmony can be especially challenging.

Whatever the source of conflict, the important thing is how team members respond to it. Facing up to conflict and working through the issues can have positive results. It can bring problems into the open, strengthen relationships, and lead to better team decisions. On the other hand, unresolved conflict is a major obstacle to team progress.

When conflict occurs, team members must work together to find a solution while maintaining good relationships. The conflict resolution strategies explained in Chapter 18 will help you resolve conflicts in positive ways.

TEXTLINK≈

Negotiation is one of the conflict resolution strategies discussed in Chapter 18.

As a team member, there are ways you can help prevent some conflicts and keep others from escalating.

- Focus on trying to understand other people's ideas.

- Give people credit for having good ideas, even when you don't agree with them.

- Use differences of opinion as an opportunity to examine creative new alternatives.

- Don't get irritated about things that don't matter. Ask yourself, "How important is it?"

- Maintain a positive attitude.

- Above all, stay focused on the team goals. They're the reason your team exists.

Chapter Summary

- Teamwork skills are valuable throughout life and yield a variety of benefits.

- By cooperating, team players can accomplish more than they can as individuals.

- Teams must find ways to divide tasks fairly and make effective group decisions.

- The different roles that team members play can help or hinder the team's success.

- Effective leaders often have certain skills and qualities, and they practice ethical leadership.

- Different leadership styles can be useful depending on the situation.

- Most groups face conflicts that they must work to resolve.

Reviewing Key Terms & Ideas

1. Why are **teamwork** and **leadership** both needed if a group is to meet its goals?

2. How will teamwork skills benefit you now and in the future?

3. List six characteristics of cooperative team players and briefly describe the importance of each.

4. Explain why **consensus** is desirable, but **groupthink** is not. How can teams avoid groupthink?

5. Contrast two positive roles and two negative roles that team members can play.

6. How do leaders serve as **role models**?

7. Identify eight skills important for leadership.

8. Why is it important for leaders to **delegate** responsibilities to team members?

9. Give two examples of ways people can demonstrate **ethical leadership**.

10. What is meant by **leadership style**?

11. Explain the difference between authoritarian and laissez-faire leadership.

12. Why do team members need to know how to resolve conflict?

Thinking Critically

1. **Defending Your Position.** Is there such a thing as a "born leader," or must people learn to be leaders? Give reasons for your answer.

2. **Analyzing Viewpoints.** Which style of leadership do you prefer to use when taking on a leadership role? Why? Which style do you prefer when someone else is leading you? Why? Explain how your preference is affected by your perspective as a leader or team member.

Applying Your Knowledge

1. **Teamwork Skit.** Working with a group of classmates, write and act out a short skit illustrating the characteristics of a good team player. Then evaluate the teamwork that your group used in the process of creating the skit.

2. **Demonstrating Leadership.** You have been asked to lead a meeting for a school club. When the meeting is due to start, several people continue talking to one another instead of paying attention. Explain how you, as the leader, would deal with this situation.

3. **Skills Rating.** In a group, devise a rating sheet that can be used to evaluate teamwork and leadership skills. Be ready to explain the purpose of your rating sheet, how to use it, and the rationale for its design. Try it out by evaluating your own teamwork and leadership skills.

Making Connections

1. **Social Studies.** Choose a well-known leader from American history. Analyze the skills and qualities that helped that person be an effective leader. Give examples that illustrate each skill or quality.

2. **Science.** Investigate the role of *collaboration*, or teamwork, in scientific research. What methods of collaboration are used? How does collaboration enhance the pursuit of scientific knowledge? Present a report of your findings.

Managing Your Life

Building Teamwork and Leadership Skills

Make a plan for improving your teamwork and leadership skills. Start by listing the skills and qualities that team members and leaders need. Evaluate yourself honestly in each area, then identify the one in which you need the most improvement. What resources could help you build this skill or quality? What specific steps could you take?

Using Technology

1. **Video Presentation.** Work with classmates to make a video demonstrating the use of parliamentary procedure. Refer to *Robert's Rules of Order* to be sure your video correctly demonstrates at least ten parliamentary rules.

2. **Desktop Publishing.** Use your computer skills to produce an attractive poster publicizing a student organization such as Family, Career and Community Leaders of America (FCCLA). Focus on the leadership opportunities that are available.

Peer Pressure and Refusal Skills

Objectives

- **Describe** internal and external influences on decisions.
- **Compare** positive and negative peer pressure.
- **Analyze** the consequences of giving in to negative peer pressure.
- **Evaluate** ways to manage peer pressure.
- **Give examples** of refusal skills.

QUICK WRITE

Think back to a time when someone tried to persuade you to do something you felt uneasy about. Write about how you handled the situation.

Raul was getting his books out of his locker when his friends, Charlie and Antonio, stopped by. "Today's the day!" Charlie whispered. "We're cutting classes this afternoon to go to the lake. You're coming, aren't you?" Raul grinned. Cutting class sounded fun and daring. He was about to say yes, then hesitated. He'd miss art, his favorite class, and history, his hardest subject. If he was caught skipping, he'd get a Saturday detention, and he'd be punished at home, too.

Raul thought about his choices. He wanted to go and have fun with his friends. Maybe cutting a few classes wasn't such a big deal. On the other hand, he wasn't obligated to do what they wanted. Their friendship shouldn't depend on that. He made his decision. "Not this time, guys," he said as he headed toward the art room.

Influences on Decisions

Like Raul, you have probably been tempted to do things that weren't in your best interest. Making decisions in such circumstances isn't always easy. You feel pressure because you want to please your friends, yet you also want to do what's right for you.

Decisions are actually influenced by a number of pressures, both internal and external. Understanding these pressures and their effects on you can help you make better choices.

Internal Pressures

Internal pressures come from within you. They are the result of the expectations that you set for yourself. See Fig. 17-1.

Trevor works hard to excel at school. Although his teachers and family expect a lot from him, Trevor tries to exceed those expectations. He gets high grades and is involved in school activities. However, this year Trevor is struggling in his physics course. His perfect grade point average is

Fig. 17-1. Your own expectations for yourself can sometimes be tougher to meet than anyone else's. What are some of the internal pressures that affect your decisions?

sliding. He doesn't want to ask for help from the teacher or other students because they might think less of him. Trevor is dealing with internal pressures to be perfect, smart, and successful without any help. These internal pressures are influencing his decisions.

External Pressures

External pressures come from outside sources. Three of the most influential are the media, your family, and your peers.

- **Media.** Think about all the messages you receive from the **media**, channels of mass communication such as newspapers, magazines, radio, television, movies, and Web sites. You are bombarded by these messages on a daily basis. Advertisements, in particular, can influence your decisions about everything from the jeans you wear to the shampoo you choose. You will make better choices if you realize how strong an influence the media is.

- **Family.** Your family can help you make important decisions. Even when they're not around, they are a strong influence on you. When faced with an important decision, you probably ask yourself what your family would think. That's because your family has your best interests in mind. See Fig. 17-2.

- **Peers.** As a teen, you probably feel strong external

TEXTLINK≈

The influence of *advertising* is explored further in Chapter 29.

pressure from other teens. The influence of people in the same age group is called **peer pressure**. Teens tend to be more sensitive to it than adults. One reason is that in your teen years, you are still discovering who you are and what's important to you. It's natural to look for approval and acceptance from other teens. Peer pressure can be open and direct, like the pressure Raul felt to skip classes. It also can be more subtle, like being influenced to listen to the same music as your peers.

Positive Peer Pressure

Peer pressure isn't necessarily bad. Peers can encourage each other to develop new skills and get involved in worthwhile activities. Perhaps you can remember a time when friends gave you the confidence to try out for the school play or cheered you on in a sports event. See Fig. 17-3.

Fig. 17-2. Your family is likely to have a major influence on your decisions, whether or not you talk things over with them. What kinds of decisions would you discuss with your family?

Celeste's efforts are an example of positive peer pressure. She heard about a project to build a playground for children in a neighborhood that didn't have one. She not only volunteered to help, but also called some of her friends and encouraged them to sign up as well. Some of her friends recruited other friends. Before long, 34 teens had volunteered to help with the project, all because of Celeste's initiative.

Negative Peer Pressure

Peer pressure is negative when it influences you to do something that's not in your best interest or that conflicts with your values. Teens who start to use alcohol, tobacco, or drugs often do so because of peer pressure. Similarly, negative pressure pushes some teens into joining a gang, shoplifting, driving recklessly, or becoming involved in a sexual relationship. They know that these activities are risky and dangerous, even destructive. They know that giving in to such pressure affects their health and their future. What they don't know is how to resist.

Resisting pressure from peers can be difficult. Sometimes peers can be forceful in pressuring you. They might use insults, threats, or other forms of intimidation. Aggressive behavior like this is a sign that peer pressure is negative rather than positive. After all, if someone wants you to do something that's in your best interest, threats aren't needed.

Facing the Consequences

It's easier to resist negative peer pressure if you know the risks attached to it. Giving in to negative peer pressure can have serious consequences that can affect you, and others, for years to come.

Fig. 17-3. Positive peer pressure is a motivating force that rewards people with feelings of acceptance and belonging.

- **Emotional consequences.** When people do something that goes against their values, they usually feel guilty. They might experience low self-esteem because they realize they failed to stand up for their beliefs. Often they worry about the results of their actions.

- **Physical consequences.** People who allow others to pressure them into using alcohol, tobacco, or other drugs pay for it with their health. Many drugs are linked to serious health problems such as heart disease, cancer, and harmful changes in the brain. Teens who allow themselves to be pressured into sexual activity run the risk of contracting a sexually transmitted disease, perhaps even AIDS. There is also the possibility of pregnancy, which poses health risks—as well as many others—for teen mothers and their children.

- **Social consequences.** Those who give in to negative peer pressure run the risk of losing friendships that they value. Teens who join a gang, for example, will find that the gang takes over their life. Sometimes it may seem as though giving in to pressure is the way to make friends. However, people who have the strength to stand up to peer pressure may actually look down on those who are easily swayed. See Fig. 17-4.

- **Educational consequences.** Negative peer pressure leads some teens to do things that affect their academic lives. Doing something you know is wrong can result in stress that causes your grades to suffer. Cheating on a test or copying a research paper can impact not only grade point averages, but graduation and future educational opportunities.

- **Legal consequences.** When peer pressure leads to illegal acts, the consequences can be severe. If you break the law and are caught and arrested, you may be convicted and even sentenced to jail. A criminal record can interfere with your future educational and work opportunities.

- **Consequences for others.** Most decisions you make affect not only you, but other people as well. Actions that are harmful to your health have emotional, and sometimes financial, consequences for your family. Doing something that is dishonest or illegal causes friends and family to feel betrayed. When you weigh your choices and make decisions, make it a point to consider how others could be affected.

Managing Peer Pressure

By learning to manage peer pressure, you can benefit from its positive effects and avoid its negative consequences. You'll know when to go along with the crowd and when to hold back. Refusing to go along may not be easy, even when you know it's the right choice. In the end, though, you'll feel better about

Fig. 17-4. Giving in to negative peer pressure could result in the loss of positive friendships that you value.

yourself and avoid the consequences of unwise choices. Your stand might also set an example for others. Some teens go along with the crowd because they don't know how to say no. Your refusal might give others the courage to make better decisions.

People who are able to resist negative peer pressure have a strong sense of what's right for them. They also know how to be assertive. You may need to improve your strength in these areas, but understanding their importance can help you do so.

FINDING CREATIVE SOLUTIONS

Examining Values

Some problems have easy, obvious solutions, but others can make you feel as though you're caught in a trap. That can be the case when you're feeling pressure from others to go in a direction that, deep down, you're not comfortable taking. Reflecting on your values can help you look beyond outside pressures and solve problems based on your beliefs.

How It Works

When you're faced with a tough problem, think about how values such as honesty, loyalty, respect, and fairness apply to the situation. What's the honest thing to do? How can you show respect for others? Examining your values can give you the insight you need to find a solution.

Try It Out

Jill and her two best friends have been teasing Leah, a new classmate. At first it seemed like harmless fun. Lately, though, Jill has noticed some changes in Leah. She keeps her head down in class and hardly says a word unless called on. In the halls between classes, she shrinks away from people. Yesterday Jill saw Leah hurry out of the restroom, her eyes red and puffy.

Jill is starting to feel that things have gone too far. She's stopped teasing Leah, but her friends haven't. When Jill tried saying something to them about it, they brushed her off. Jill doesn't know what to do next. She wonders if she should tell one of the school counselors what's going on. At the same time, she doesn't want to get her friends in trouble.

▶ **Your Turn** *What values might lead Jill to talk to a counselor about her friends' actions? What values might lead her to seek another solution? If you were in Jill's situation, how would you weigh these conflicting values? What solution do you suggest and why?*

Know Yourself

To deal with negative peer pressure, you need a firm sense of your values, priorities, and goals. What matters to you? What do you want your life to be like? When you know these things, you'll find it easier to make decisions and stick to them. This, in turn, will give you confidence to stand up to your peers, no matter how much pressure you feel. Here are some of the qualities that indicate a firm sense of self:

- **A strong value system.** Having a strong set of values will help you recognize and deal with difficult situations. For example, if your health is important to you, it should be easier to resist any pressure to use tobacco. Use what you have been taught by your family and other responsible adults to develop a value system that will guide your decisions and actions.

- **Confidence in your own judgment.** Trust your own judgment and instincts. When you're pressured to do something that you feel is wrong, remember that you are more qualified than your peers to determine what's right for you. If an inner voice tells you to say no, listen.

- **High self-esteem.** When you feel good about yourself, you're less concerned about gaining the approval of others. You can be more confident in saying no when people pressure you.

- **Clear priorities.** When you focus on your priorities, you are less likely to be influenced by negative peer pressure. Become involved in positive activities that will help you achieve the personal goals you have set.

Practice Assertiveness

Knowing what's important to you gives you the confidence to be assertive. People who are assertive state their positions firmly but respectfully. They don't waver when other people pressure them. Learning to be assertive will help you say no and make it stick.

Maggie's boyfriend, Lucas, tried to persuade Maggie to go to a party at his friend's house. She knew that there had been drugs and underage drinking at a party there last year. "No, I don't want to go," she told Lucas. "If there's trouble, we could be arrested and I won't take that risk. Besides, I'd have to lie to my parents, and I won't do that." Maggie's assertiveness makes her position clear. Her self-esteem, strong values, and knowledge of the risks made it easier for her to be assertive. Lucas showed he was a true friend by accepting Maggie's answer rather than pressuring her to change her mind.

TIPS FOR *Success*

Prepare for Peer Pressure

You will be better able to resist negative peer pressure if you plan ahead for it. Here are some ways to prepare:

- Identify the people and situations most likely to give you trouble. Avoid them as much as possible.

- Choose a situation that you anticipate might occur. Write down your reasons for saying no.

- On your own, or with a friend, practice different ways of responding to the situation. Then decide which method is likely to work best.

Using Refusal Skills

As a teen, you want to fit in and be part of the group. At the same time, you need to be true to yourself and maintain your individuality. That's why refusing to do something your peers pressure you to do is never easy. You need to know not only when to say no, but *how* to say it with conviction.

Fortunately, you can benefit from the experience of others. Many people have developed effective ways to say no. These **refusal skills**, or techniques for resisting negative peer pressure, are simple but powerful. Arming yourself with good refusal skills will prepare you to manage negative peer pressure effectively. Fig. 17-5 describes some refusal skills you can use.

Skills for Life

Peer pressure doesn't disappear when you become an adult. The refusal skills that you learn now will be useful throughout your life. There will always be people who pressure you to go against your better judgment. You may encounter them in the workplace, in your personal life, and in the community. Learning how to stand up to negative peer pressure will protect you from the consequences of poor decisions and help you get where you want to go in life.

Refusal Skills

Plan ahead. Decide in advance what you will do when faced with problem situations.	**Take your time.** Don't be rushed into a decision. Take time to collect your thoughts.	**Say what you mean.** State your position clearly and firmly. "No, I don't want to" can't be misunderstood.
Avoid mixed messages. Make sure your body language reinforces what you say.	**Make eye contact.** Look straight at the other person to show that you mean what you say.	**Don't apologize.** You don't need to explain or justify your decision. Just take a stand and stick to it.
Stay in control. Try not to get angry or upset. You can better control the situation if you stay calm.	**Change the subject.** Deflect the pressure by talking about something else that is important to you.	**Suggest an alternative.** Reverse the pressure. Suggest an alternative that is safer and more fun.
Reject the action, not the person. You can refuse to go along without putting other people down.	**Use humor.** Say something like "You can't be serious" to let people know you're not interested.	**Walk away.** If someone refuses to take no for an answer, make your point by walking away from the situation.

Fig. 17-5. You have many different options for dealing with peer pressure situations.

Chapter Summary

- Decisions are influenced by both internal and external pressures.

- Positive peer pressure helps you develop new skills and gain confidence.

- Negative peer pressure can influence people to participate in activities that conflict with their values.

- Giving in to negative peer pressure can have serious consequences, both for you and for others.

- Managing negative peer pressure requires a strong sense of self and the ability to be assertive.

- Arming yourself with good refusal skills will help you resist negative peer pressure.

Reviewing Key Terms & Ideas

1. Explain why people's decisions are influenced by internal pressures.

2. Describe how the external pressures of the media and the family influence decisions.

3. What is **peer pressure**? Why does it have an especially strong influence on teens?

4. How does positive peer pressure differ from negative peer pressure?

5. In what ways might giving in to negative peer pressure affect your health? Your relationships?

6. How can a strong value system help you deal with negative peer pressure?

7. Why does high self-esteem help you resist peer pressure?

8. What are the characteristics of an assertive person?

9. Define **refusal skills** and give at least three examples.

10. Why will you still need refusal skills when you are an adult?

Thinking Critically

1. **Recognizing Relationships.** How can learning to resist pressure from peers help you deal with pressure from the media?

2. **Predicting Possible Outcomes.** What are the likely outcomes of an assertive and a nonassertive response to negative peer pressure? What does each tell about the person giving the response?

Applying Your Knowledge

1. **Analyzing Media Influence.** Study the ads in a magazine geared toward teens. What kinds of techniques are used to pressure you to buy the advertised products?

2. **Suggesting Assertive Approaches.** Work in small groups to develop a list of at least ten negative pressures that teens often face. Then describe possible assertive approaches to handling each one.

3. **Using Refusal Strategies.** Suppose a friend is trying to persuade you to get a tattoo, but you don't want to. Choose two strategies from Fig. 17-5 that you think would be particularly effective in this situation. Explain how you could apply them.

Making Connections

1. **Social Studies.** Think of a project that you and your peers could do to help your community. Brainstorm a list of ways you could use positive peer pressure to get others in your school to help with the project. Choose the five best strategies and justify your choices.

2. **Language Arts.** Write a skit in which one teen tries to persuade another to steal something from a store. The other teen successfully refuses *and* convinces the first teen not to steal.

Managing Your Life

Choosing Friends Wisely

One way to reduce the amount of negative peer pressure you will experience is to choose friends whose values and interests are similar to your own. Using that as your goal, identify ways to meet and make such friends. Make a list of the qualities you would look for in a friend, and rank them in order of importance. Try out at least one of your strategies for finding new friends who would enrich your life.

Using Technology

1. **Video Presentation.** Work in groups to make a video illustrating the influence of the media on teens. For example, you might tape several television commercials that target teens, followed by interviews with students on their responses to the commercial messages.

2. **Internet.** Use the Internet to search for information about programs designed to help teens deal with peer pressure and develop refusal skills. Analyze two of these programs. Who sponsors them? Were teens involved in planning the programs? Do the programs include ideas and techniques you think would work in your school or personal life? Report your findings.

Conflict Resolution Skills

Objectives

- Explain why conflicts occur.
- Describe some positive and negative results of conflict.
- Suggest strategies for preventing conflict.
- Evaluate different ways of resolving conflicts.
- Explain the benefits of mediation.
- Determine ways to prevent violence.

QUICK WRITE

Write a description of a situation in which you, or someone you know, managed to resolve a conflict peacefully. What caused the conflict? What skills were used to resolve it?

*C*assie was fuming as she called her older brother Steve on his cell phone. "Where are you? I have to leave for work in ten minutes, and you promised to drive me."

"Sorry, Cassie," came Steve's reply. "I'm across town with some friends. You'll have to find another way to get there." Cassie was furious. She knew she could take the bus, but she would be late for work. Her supervisor would be annoyed, her pay would be docked—and it was all Steve's fault. "Just wait till I see him tonight," Cassie muttered.

Why Conflicts Occur

Cassie's situation has the makings of a conflict. A **conflict** is a clash among people who have opposing ideas or interests. Some conflicts are trivial and quickly resolved. Others are serious and take time and effort to resolve. The worst kinds of conflict are those that lead to violence.

Knowing why conflicts occur can help you avoid or prevent them. Here are some of the basic causes:

- **Poor communication.** Cassie's conflict with Steve could be the result of poor communication. She may not have made it clear that she needed a ride. He may not have realized that she was relying on him. Misunderstandings of this kind lie at the heart of many conflicts.

- **Power struggles.** Power struggles occur when individuals or groups feel a need to be in control. Many families experience trivial power struggles over the TV remote control every evening! More serious power struggles can occur in the workplace, where coworkers may clash over roles and responsibilities. See Fig. 18-1.

- **Personality differences.** People who have very different values and attitudes from one another are more likely to clash than those who agree on basic issues. If you're a careful and methodical person, for example, you might clash with someone

Fig. 18-1. A power struggle on the basketball court is part of the game. In real life, disputes over who's in control can lead to conflict.

working on the same project who rushes through the work and pays little attention to detail.

- **Jealousy.** This powerful emotion can cause feelings of resentment or hostility. Jealousy is often associated with romantic relationships, but it can occur in other situations as well. You might feel jealous when another student receives an award that you felt you deserved.

- **Prejudice.** Prejudice involves prejudging or forming negative opinions about people without knowing them personally. People who are prejudiced lack tolerance for people whose values and beliefs are different from their own. Prejudice has been a major cause of conflict throughout history.

Results of Conflict

Conflict is a fact of life and is not always a bad thing. Disagreements occur in almost all relationships. When you know how to deal with a conflict and move toward a solution, you benefit in a number of ways. Poorly handled conflicts, on the other hand, can have long-term harmful effects.

Positive Results of Conflict

Think about the last time you settled a disagreement with a family member or friend. Did you learn something that was helpful? Working to resolve a conflict is a valuable experience. It helps you develop your problem-solving skills and communicate effectively. You also learn to get along with people who don't agree with you—a skill that will help you now and in the future. See Fig. 18-2.

Making an effort to resolve a conflict strengthens a relationship, too. When you explain your views and learn how the other person feels, you get to know each other better. Accepting joint responsibility to resolve the conflict shows that each person values the relationship.

Working to resolve a conflict can bring issues to light and help people identify alternative ways of resolving a situation. Cooperating with someone often produces a more acceptable solution than insisting on having your own way.

Fig. 18-2. Accepting joint responsibility to deal with a conflict can be a valuable experience. *What do you gain from resolving a disagreement with a friend?*

Fig. 18-3. Conflicts that result in angry words can be especially damaging. Try to avoid saying anything you will later regret.

Negative Results of Conflict

As Tyrone thought about a recent disagreement he had with a friend, the angry feelings returned. His muscles tightened and his stomach felt queasy. The argument had never been settled, and he wasn't sure it ever would be. Can you relate to the way Tyrone felt? If so, you know that unresolved conflict can have some serious negative effects.

- **Negative emotions.** Think about a time when you experienced a serious disagreement with someone. Did you feel anger, frustration, fear, pain, humiliation, sorrow, distress? All of these unpleasant emotions are associated with conflict.

- **Stress.** Conflict causes stress. Stress in turn can cause headaches, digestive problems, anxiety, and other physical and mental problems. People who experience stress caused by serious conflict may have difficulty sleeping, feel extreme fatigue, and find it hard to concentrate.

- **Hurtful words.** In the heat of anger, it's easy to say the wrong thing and hurt another person's feelings. Remember that once something has been said, it can't be "unsaid." See Fig. 18-3.

- **Damaged relationships.** Conflicts can break up families and friendships. Some family feuds never get resolved and last a lifetime. In the workplace, conflicts can cause difficulties for coworkers and may cause people to lose their jobs.

- **Violence.** When tempers flare, an argument can escalate to produce physical violence. The result may be serious injury or even death. All negative effects of conflict are troubling, but violence is the most serious, both for the individuals involved and for society as a whole.

Preventing Conflicts

The best way to deal with conflict is to prevent it from happening in the first place. If you know someone who purposely tries to provoke you into an argument, stay away from the person if you can. If you get involved in a minor disagreement, try to maintain a sense of perspective. Don't start arguing about something that you will have forgotten by tomorrow. Keep your sense of humor and let the other person see that you're not rising to the bait. See Fig. 18-4.

Adapting Your Behavior

Sometimes the easiest way to prevent a conflict is to adapt to the other person's behavior. This approach works best when a situation bothers one person more than the other. Riley, for example, was annoyed that his friend Tim was late almost every time they went somewhere together. Instead of confronting Tim and causing a possible conflict, Riley decided to plan for Tim being late. If he was supposed to pick Tim up, Riley asked him to be ready ten minutes sooner than they really needed to leave. That way, Tim could be late and they would still get where they were going on time.

Examining Your Attitude

Some people project an attitude that invites conflict. Lori, for example, feels that people are always criticizing her and doing things to annoy her. When she complained to her friend Marisa about it, Marisa told her, "I think you need an attitude adjustment."

Marisa was probably correct. People like Lori are always on the defensive. They take even the mildest remark as a personal insult. Often they misinterpret and distort other

Fig. 18-4. Don't let minor disagreements become major ones. *How might a sense of humor help you deal with minor disputes?*

people's words and actions. The result can be constant conflict and unhappiness.

Lori decided to take a closer look at herself and examine her attitude. She realized that her defensiveness was related to her own negative feelings about herself. She began to work on improving her self-esteem and developing a more positive attitude. Gradually, she learned to react to people differently and avoid focusing on things that cause conflict.

If you feel that other people are often in conflict with you, ask yourself: Am I overly defensive? Do I misinterpret other people's words and actions? Do I have an attitude that invites conflict? Thinking about questions like these can lead to greater self-awareness and help you adjust your attitude, if necessary.

Resolving Conflicts

If a conflict does develop, you need to resolve it. You can start by using the problem-solving process described in Chapter 6. When trying to reach a positive resolution, keep in mind these two goals:

- To agree on a solution that is acceptable to all parties.
- To preserve or strengthen the relationships involved.

Negotiation

Conflict resolution involves **negotiation**—communicating about a problem to try to reach an acceptable solution. Negotiation is used at all levels of society. Friends negotiate when deciding which movie to see. Labor unions negotiate employment contracts. Nations negotiate peace agreements.

For negotiation to be successful, all those involved in the conflict must be willing to participate. They must be open to considering other viewpoints, and they must be willing to accept responsibility for achieving a solution and making it work. Good communication skills are basic to negotiation. Just as poor communication can cause conflict, effective communication is an essential part of resolving it.

The ideal outcome of negotiation is a **win-win solution**, a solution that benefits everyone involved and has no real drawbacks for anyone. Finding a win-win solution requires creative thinking and a willingness to explore options. Suppose a family is planning where to go on a weekend trip. If one member of the family insists on a destination that the others won't enjoy, that person wins and the others lose. A win-win solution would be to find an alternative that the whole family finds appealing.

When a win-win situation is not possible, other outcomes need to be explored. Here are some other ways to resolve a conflict:

- **Compromise.** In a compromise, each party agrees to give up something in order to reach a solution that satisfies everyone. Compromise is sometimes called the "fair-fair" solution. Each side gets something they want, but not everything. When two children agree to take turns playing with a toy instead of having it all to themselves, that's a compromise.

- **Agree to disagree.** Some differences cannot be resolved because it's clear that the parties will not change their point of view. If you and your uncle hold strongly opposing political views, trying to convince each other to change is probably pointless. Agreeing to disagree may be the best solution. Simply accept that you have a difference of opinion rather than arguing about it.

TIPS FOR *Success*

The Art of Negotiating

Negotiating skills will be useful to you throughout your life. Here are some suggestions for effective negotiation:

- Choose the right time and place.
- Explore the issues and feelings behind each person's position.
- Listen more than you talk.
- Be open to other points of view.
- Avoid blaming and name-calling.
- Attack the problem, not each other.
- Look for creative win-win solutions.

Fig. 18-5. Mediators encourage people to find a fair solution to their conflict. Why do mediators need to avoid making judgments or suggesting solutions?

- **Withdraw.** Dealing with conflict is never easy. Sometimes a solution seems impossible to find. Tempers get frayed. Negotiations go nowhere. In such cases, it may be best to withdraw for a while. Walking away from the situation gives both parties time to calm down and collect their thoughts. They can resume their negotiations later, when they have new ideas to discuss or are more willing to reach a compromise.

Mediation

When other attempts to settle conflict are not successful, mediation can help. **Mediation** involves settling a dispute with the help of an impartial third party. This process is widely used to resolve conflicts in families, the workplace, schools, and communities.

The word *mediate* literally means "to be in the middle." As a person in the middle, the mediator does not make judgments or decide how to resolve the conflict. Instead, the mediator helps people find a fair solution that satisfies both sides. Mediators are concerned with the process; the parties involved in conflicts are responsible for finding the solutions. See Fig. 18-5.

Formal mediation, involving a trained mediator, should be considered when a conflict persists for a long time or threatens to interfere with normal living. For example, a serious conflict between family members may be a suitable case for formal mediation.

Mediation can also be informal. For example, you might ask a family member to help if you have a disagreement with a friend. Sometimes just talking things over with a third party can help people involved in a conflict reach a solution.

Peer Mediation ~Many schools use peer mediation to settle differences among students. **Peer mediation** is a process in which specially trained students help other students resolve conflicts peacefully. Peer mediators remain neutral. They often see solutions that those involved in the conflict are too upset to see. One of their goals is to keep everyone calm. Peer mediators are trained to see things through the eyes of those involved in the conflict. They learn to ask questions that help students clarify their feelings and thoughts.

Like other forms of mediation, peer mediation is voluntary and confidential. To be successful, the students involved in the conflict must be willing to participate. Confidentiality encourages students to speak freely by assuring them that no one else will know what is said.

Peer mediation is effective partly because the mediators are students themselves. They understand their peers' attitudes and viewpoints. They can relate to the issues involved. When stating the problem, they use language that students can understand. The widespread success of peer mediation programs illustrates the value of this conflict resolution technique.

More to Explore

Mediation in the Workplace

Employers, like schools, have discovered that mediation is a good way to resolve conflicts. What kinds of conflicts occur in the workplace? Many complaints involve perceived discrimination. For example, workers who feel that they have been treated unfairly because of age, race, marital status, religion, or disability may file a complaint. Other workplace conflicts involve disputes about responsibilities, space, and equipment.

Workers can request mediation whenever they believe it will help resolve a dispute. All parties involved must agree, voluntarily, to mediate. The mediator then arranges a session in which the parties try to resolve their differences. Information shared during the session is confidential.

Employers believe that mediation offers several benefits. It allows people to be heard and to develop ways of dealing with a dispute by creating their own solutions. Equally important, it clears the air and reduces workplace stress.

Violence

If everyone were skilled in conflict resolution, violence might not be a problem in modern society. Unfortunately, that's not the case. From armed robberies to fights between rival gangs to violent acts on school grounds, violence is a distressing reality.

Factors Affecting Violence

Why do some people resort to violence? Sometimes it's because they don't know how to solve problems in constructive ways. Violence may be the only way they know how to express anger. Such behavior may be acquired during childhood. Children learn violence from adult role models, sometimes adults in their own families. They see violence on television and in sports, video games, movies, and other forms of media. Some people believe that violence in the media contributes to violence in society.

Teen violence often involves gangs. Gang members are more likely than other teens to participate in illegal activities, engage in violent behavior, and become victims of violence themselves. Once a person is in a gang, it's hard to get out. Gang leaders demand loyalty and use threats and fear to keep members from leaving.

Easy access to weapons contributes to violence. To prevent weapons from being brought onto school property, many schools have installed metal detectors and other security devices.

Yet another contributing factor is substance abuse. Drug addicts often use violence when they need money to support their drug habit. In addition, people under the influence of alcohol or other drugs are less able to control their emotions and more likely to become violent if they get involved in a disagreement.

Preventing Violence

The first step in preventing violence is to recognize that it's never an acceptable way to settle differences. Choose nonviolent attitudes and actions for yourself, and encourage your peers to make positive choices. If you find yourself in a confrontation involving threats, violence, or weapons, value your own safety and walk away. It takes a strong person to walk away from a situation like this, but your life and well-being are worth more than winning any argument.

You also can work with others to reduce violence in your school and community. One of the most effective strategies for reducing youth violence is **peer education**, a program based on the principle of teens teaching teens. Like peer mediation, peer education works because young people are more likely to listen to their peers than to adults.

Here are some other examples of ways to take action against violence:

- **Educate yourself about youth violence.** Knowing what youth violence "looks like" in your community can motivate you to take action. Find out how many teens have been arrested for violent crimes or weapons possession. How many have been victims of violence? How many are members of gangs?

- **Identify violence prevention resources available in your community.** These might include school officials, community leaders, law enforcement officials, parent-teacher groups, and social service organizations.

- **Learn to recognize the warning signs.** People who are at risk for violent behavior almost always show warning signs. These signs include drug and alcohol use, intolerance for differences, social withdrawal, and threats of violence.

Viewpoints

Violence in the Media

Is violence in the media a cause or an effect of violence in real life? Is it possible to make such a clear distinction?

Dennis: If society is a more violent place, the media is partly to blame. News shows lead with the most violent stories, especially if they have it on tape. Murder trials make the headlines. Popular shows and movies are full of people getting shot—and worse. After you see so much of this, you start to think that this is how the world works: if you want something, you can get it through violence. How can we teach kids to settle problems peacefully? They never see it on TV.

Andrea: The world is a violent place, even without TV crews or reporters to tell us about it. If anything, seeing the effects of real-life violence is the best argument for avoiding it. Violence in entertainment is nothing new. Some great books and movies revolve around a murder or war. To reduce violence in the media, you have to get rid of the causes of violence in the real world.

Seeing Both Sides ~ Might Dennis and Andrea agree on some responsible ways for the media to depict violence? What can individuals do to balance the possible negative impact of violent images?

- **Report situations that have the potential for violence.** When you become aware of threats of violence or observe other warning signs, tell a responsible adult. Not all threats of violence translate into violent acts, but sharing your concerns will help protect yourself and others.

- **Avoid gang influence.** Don't be lured into a gang. Gang membership puts you at greater risk of inflicting, or being a victim of, violence. Encourage your peers to avoid gang influence too.

You can do your part to reduce the incidence of violence in your community. Remember that violence is never an acceptable way to resolve a conflict. Everyone has a stake in curbing and preventing it.

Review & Activities

Chapter Summary

- Knowing why conflicts occur can help you avoid or prevent them.

- Being able to handle conflict can produce positive results. Unresolved conflict can produce negative results.

- You can prevent some conflicts by maintaining a sense of perspective, adapting your behavior, or choosing to have a positive attitude.

- Negotiation and mediation are strategies for resolving conflict.

- Violence is associated with an inability to express anger in another way; exposure to violence in the media; gangs; access to weapons; and substance abuse.

- You can work with others to reduce violence in your school and community.

Reviewing Key Terms & Ideas

1. What is **conflict**? Explain five reasons why conflicts occur.

2. Why is working to resolve a conflict a valuable experience?

3. Give two examples of ways conflict affects people in negative ways.

4. How does a defensive attitude contribute to conflict?

5. What conditions must be met for **negotiation** to be successful?

6. How does a **win-win solution** differ from a compromise?

7. In what kinds of circumstances might people agree to disagree?

8. Explain why **mediation** is a good approach for resolving a conflict.

9. Describe how **peer mediation** works.

10. What should you do if you are involved in a conflict that may result in violence?

11. Why might people who abuse drugs become violent?

12. Describe three actions you can take to help prevent violence in your community.

Thinking Critically

1. **Making Judgments.** When you compromise, you agree to give up something. In what kinds of conflicts would you refuse to compromise? Why?

2. **Drawing Conclusions.** What advantages for teens does peer mediation have over mediation involving an adult? What special skills do peer mediators need?

Applying Your Knowledge

1. **Analyzing Conflict.** Keep a log in which you list all the events and incidents that caused conflict in your life during one week. Write down how each event made you feel and what you did to handle it. At the end of the week, analyze your entries to see what patterns emerge. Summarize what you learned about the way you deal with conflict.

2. **Promoting Nonviolence.** Create a promotional campaign to promote the idea of settling disputes in nonviolent ways. You might use posters, videos, exhibits, flyers, public service announcements, and articles in the school newspaper.

Making Connections

1. **Language Arts.** Think about a recent conflict you had with a friend or family member. Write a paragraph explaining your side of the conflict. Then write a second paragraph summarizing the other person's point of view.

2. **Social Studies.** Cultural differences can lead to prejudice, which in turn can lead to conflict. Focus on ways to resolve this problem by completing this sentence: "When conflict is a problem between people of different cultures, they need to…"

Managing Your Life

How Do You Manage Conflict?

The way you manage conflict is more important than conflict itself. To evaluate how you deal with conflict, ask yourself these questions: Do I listen and try to understand other people's points of view? Am I tolerant and accepting of people who are different? Do I get to know people before I form opinions of them? Am I willing to negotiate and compromise? Do I avoid trying to prove I am always right? Consider your answers to the questions. What do they tell you about the way you manage conflict? Write a paragraph about managing conflict. Explain what you think you do well and what changes you need to make.

Using Technology

1. **Internet.** Use the Internet to learn more about the work of the United Nations in resolving international conflicts. Focus on the how the UN tries to achieve the goal of keeping conflicts from developing into wars.

2. **Multimedia Presentation.** Work with two or three other students to prepare and present a multimedia presentation on the topic of violence prevention. You might use presentation software, the Internet, videos, videoconferencing, or other options.

Career Options
Arts and Communication

many careers in this cluster require creativity and artistic abilities. Others are technical. As a group, these careers focus on designing and producing media that inform and entertain the public. There are career opportunities for people of differing levels of education and experience, although many require a college degree. This career cluster can be divided into the four broad sectors shown below. There is keen competition for many of the available jobs in this cluster.

Main Employers

- Television and radio stations
- Film companies
- Dance companies
- Theaters
- Newspapers
- Magazines
- Publishing companies
- Advertising agencies

Arts and Communication Job Opportunities

Industry Segment	Entry Level	Additional Education and/or Training	Advanced Education and/or Training
Television, Radio, Film, and Internet	■ Production Assistant ■ Radio Operator ■ Audio Technician	■ Film Editor ■ Recording Engineer ■ Announcer ■ Web Site Designer	■ Television Producer ■ Movie Director ■ Cinematographer ■ Animator
Dance, Theater, and Music	■ Stagehand ■ Lighting Assistant ■ Ticket Seller	■ Actor ■ Makeup Artist ■ Costume Designer ■ Publicist	■ Dancer ■ Musician ■ Playwright ■ Theater Manager
Art and Photography	■ Photo Finisher ■ Photographer's Assistant	■ Art Gallery Manager ■ Museum Curator	■ Photographer ■ Artist ■ Sculptor ■ Illustrator
Books, Magazines, Newspapers, and Advertising	■ Printing Press Operator ■ Advertising Assistant ■ Assistant Copywriter	■ News Editor ■ Managing Editor ■ Graphic Designer ■ Desktop Publisher	■ Editor in Chief ■ Publisher ■ Art Director

When I was six years old, my mom bought me a pack of 64 crayons and a big notepad full of blank paper. From that day on, I was sure I wanted to be an artist. I soon moved on from crayons to colored pencils and pastels. By the time I was in high school, I was working with watercolor and oil paints.

Back then, I didn't take art lessons because I already knew that I had a talent for drawing and painting. I figured that there wasn't much else I needed to know. I thought I could earn a living by selling my artwork. I took some of my paintings and drawings to a bunch of art galleries, but none of the owners was interested in selling my work. Several of them told me that I had talent but that I needed formal training.

My parents encouraged me to go to college and study art. I took courses in all aspects of art, including art history, principles of design, and even computer-aided design. I was surprised to find out what an important role computers play in the field of art and design. I decided to major in graphic design. This field allows me to use my creativity as an artist, yet gives me the practical skills I need to earn a good living.

After graduating from college with a Bachelor of Arts degree, I got a job as a graphic designer for a magazine. I use a computer to design and lay out the pages for the magazine, including choosing the colors, typefaces, and illustrations, then organizing the elements on the page. After a few more years of honing my artistic and computer skills at the magazine, I'd like to venture out as a freelance graphic designer. Being on my own would allow me more artistic freedom. Either way, though, I'm fulfilling my childhood dream of being an artist!

Check It Out!

Choose three arts and communication occupations that interest you. Use print or online resources to find out about the education and training requirements. Summarize your findings in a brief report.

UNIT 5

Relationships in Your Life

CHAPTER 19

Your Family Ties

Key Terms

- nuclear family
- single-parent family
- blended family
- extended family
- nurture
- socialization
- family life cycle
- support system

Objectives

- **Compare** different family forms.
- **Explain** the primary functions of families.
- **Describe** the traditional family life cycle and its variations.
- **Assess** the effects of current social trends on family life.
- **Give** examples of ways to strengthen families.

QUICK WRITE

What does the word *family* mean to you? Write at least six words that come to mind when you think about families.

"Okay everyone, it's time for the family photo!" The Mulvaney family—three generations of them—had gathered for a holiday dinner. As family members began to line up for the portrait, Anna Mulvaney noticed that Vincent, her foster son, was hanging back. "I didn't know if you wanted me in the photo," he explained. "After all, I'm not really family."

"Vincent," said Anna gently, "as long as you live under our roof, you're part of our family. So come up here with the rest of us, and get ready to smile for the camera!"

Families Today

All families share certain things in common, such as the basic responsibility of caring for their members. Yet families differ in many ways, too. When you think about families you know, you can probably recognize several different forms of families. See Fig. 19-1.

The most basic family form is the **nuclear family**, consisting of a husband, wife, and their children. A **single-parent family** is headed by one parent. Some single parents have never been married; some are widowed.

Most single-parent families, however, are formed when parents are separated or divorced from one another. If a single parent remarries, a **blended family** is formed. Blended families can include children of each spouse, plus new children of the couple.

There can be variations within these family forms. For example, children may join the family by either birth or adoption. Some families, like Anna's, include foster children who have been temporarily placed in their care.

Fig. 19-1. Families differ in size and in the people they include. However, all families fulfill a similar role in their members' lives.

The Mulvaney family that gathered for the portrait is an **extended family**. This term describes a larger family group—not only your parents and siblings but also your grandparents, uncles, aunts, and cousins. In some cases, members of an extended family share a home together. A family that includes children, parents, and one or more grandparents living under the same roof might be referred to as *intergenerational*, since it includes three generations.

Whatever their form, all families share certain characteristics. Learning about families—their purpose, what impacts them, and how members interact—can help you understand the influence families have and how you can contribute to family strength.

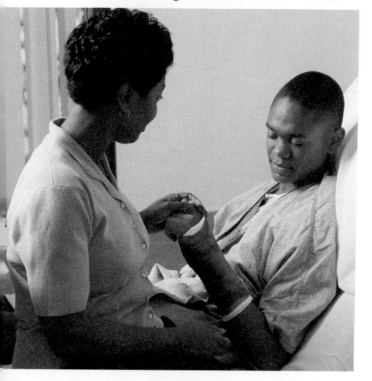

Fig. 19-2. All family members have physical needs that the family is responsible for meeting. *What needs are being met in this situation?*

Family Functions

Throughout history and in every society, families have served an important purpose. They **nurture** family members by providing the care and attention needed to promote development. That's quite a responsibility, with impact far beyond the family itself. Families provide the structure in which children learn to become independent and to live successfully in society. The characteristics and qualities of these new adults influence what society as a whole is like.

Meeting Physical Needs

The most basic responsibility of families is to provide for family members' physical needs, such as food, clothing, and shelter. Infants and young children are entirely dependent on the physical care provided by families. They couldn't survive without it. At times, others in the family may also need special physical care due to an illness, accident, or disability. See Fig. 19-2.

Physical needs include responsibility for health and safety. Parents must make certain their children eat nutritious foods and receive appropriate health care. Parents also need to set rules for children to keep them safe and teach them responsible behavior.

Promoting Intellectual Development

The family is a child's first teacher—sharing knowledge, stimulating thinking, and encouraging creativity. Parents, siblings, and other family members can all help a young child learn. Even after the child is in school, the family needs to remain actively involved in his or her learning. Taking the child to a zoo and planting a garden together are just two examples of family teaching and learn-

Fig. 19-3. Family members can be a source of advice and strength. How do you provide your family with emotional support?

ing opportunities. What others can you remember from your childhood?

Parents can learn from children, too. Alicia taught her father how to use his new computer. Her brother, Miguel, taught the whole family the basics of sign language, something he learned in fourth grade.

Meeting Emotional Needs

Families nurture emotional development by showing love and acceptance. Being loved and accepted by your family helps you develop a positive self-image and high self-esteem. It enables you to show love and affection for others. Families also teach children how to express their emotions in acceptable ways.

In a strong family, emotional bonds last for a lifetime. Whenever family members are facing difficulties, they feel confident their family will be willing to listen and help. See Fig. 19-3.

Encouraging Social Skills

The process of socialization begins in the family. **Socialization** means learning how to interact with other people. The family teaches basic social skills such as communication, cooperation, and respect for others. The social skills that children learn in the family carry over into their other relationships throughout life.

Some social skills are taught directly, such as when parents teach young children to say "please" and "thank you." More often, children learn social skills by observing and following the examples set by others. Even very young children pay attention to how adults in the family interact with each other and with people outside the family. Everything children hear or see—words, tone of voice, body language—helps form their idea of appropriate behavior. That's why being a good role model is such an important parental responsibility.

Instilling Moral Values

Families help children develop values that will be a basis for their actions and decisions throughout life. Children need to learn the importance of honesty, respect, fairness, and other values. Individuals and society benefit when people have a healthy sense of right and wrong.

As with social skills, families teach moral values both directly and by example. With very young children, teaching focuses on behavior. The parent of a two-year-old might say, "In this family, when we want something, we ask nicely." Two-year-olds follow the rules because it helps them get what they want. When they are older, they learn the reasons for the rules. By age ten or twelve, children have learned to show respect and consideration for others.

Fig. 19-4. A marriage marks the beginning of a new family. What adjustments must the couple and their parents make?

The Family Life Cycle

Family researchers know that families go through a process of growth and change over the years. They have named this process the **family life cycle**. Keep in mind that families vary significantly. The life cycle model can't reflect all variations, but it does give a general picture of how families must adapt to changing situations and priorities.

- **Beginning stage.** Traditionally, the family life cycle begins when two people marry. The couple establish a home and learn to live together. Priorities at this stage include building their relationship, working out their respective roles, and setting goals for the future. See Fig. 19-4.

- **Parenting stage.** When the couple become parents, their priorities focus on raising children. As they devote time and effort to caring for children, they have less time for activities as a couple.

  - **Launching stage.** This time of transition occurs as the children begin to leave home and become independent. They must adjust to new responsibilities, just as their parents must learn to relate to them as adults.

  - **Middle-age stage.** After children leave home, parents have more time to focus on being a couple again. They may reassess their careers, take up new hobbies, and become more involved in community activities. Preparing for retirement becomes a more immediate concern.

  - **Retirement stage.** Retirement gives more time for leisure activities. A couple may move to a smaller home or to a retirement community. In this

Viewpoints

Moving Back Home

Living with parents as a young adult means redefining the roles of parent and child. Seeing one another in a new light can be a challenge for both sides.

Carl: My son Keith lived with me while he trained to be an electrician. It was hard at first. I was still "Dad." I had my rules. But Keith was eager to lead his own life and didn't always want to do things my way. So we agreed: instead of rules, we would live by values. Respect, responsibility, courtesy—the things that help everyone get along. That's what I tried to teach Keith all his life. He's learned, and I'm proud of that.

Jennifer: To save money, I moved back with my parents after college. After four years on my own, I was looking forward to being looked after again. Fortunately, they expected more from me. I didn't always like it, but they insisted that I pay my way and take care of myself. You might say they pushed me out of the nest. But that's what I needed.

Seeing Both Sides ~ How did earlier views of their roles affect the relationship of the parents and children in these situations? Imagine you are either Keith or one of Jennifer's parents. Explain how you grew or what you learned from this experience.

---

stage, aging-related issues such as health and independence are more likely to be major concerns.

These stages are typical, but not universal. Some couples don't have children; some marry and become parents later in life, when most people become grandparents. In families with several children, the parenting and launching stages may overlap. Divorce and remarriage cause some families to repeat certain stages. Long after the traditional launching stage, parents may still have adult children living with them or may serve as substitute parents for their grandchildren. Some people of retirement age keep working and perhaps even start new careers.

Trends Affecting Families

Jesse tossed his backpack on the kitchen table. "Hi, Dad. When's dinner?"

"You'll have to wait a little longer," his father replied as he stirred the spaghetti sauce. "I need you to pick up your sister at the pool. Mom has to work late."

As Jesse headed out the door, he thought about how things had changed during the past year. Since his mother had accepted a promotion and was working longer hours, he didn't see her as much. Still, he liked having his dad around more now that he was working only part time.

Every family experiences changes, and many of the changes result from social trends. Here are some of the trends affecting family life today:

- **Roles and responsibilities.** Years ago, more families followed a traditional model: the father earned the family income, and the mother took care of the home and family. While that's still true in many families, couples today often opt for different roles. Both may work outside the home and share household and family responsibilities. Jesse's family illustrates yet another option. His mother is the main wage earner, and his father assumes most of the home responsibilities.

- **Smaller families.** In 1800, the average family included seven children. The population was more rural, and families needed children to help with farm work. Today, many couples postpone or pass up having children, sometimes to establish their careers or to save more of their earnings. One result is that the average number of children per family is currently less than two. See Fig. 19-5.

- **Divorce and remarriage.** Compared to 50 years ago, more marriages today end in

Fig. 19-5. On average, today's families have far fewer children than families in the 19th century did. *What are some possible effects of this trend?*

divorce. When people with children remarry, everyone in the blended family must adjust to new relationships. You'll read more about the challenges faced by blended families in Chapter 20.

- **Single-parent households.** Most single-parent households are headed by women, although the percentage headed by men is increasing. Single parents face the challenge of raising their children alone while working to support the family. Having sole responsibility for their children also makes it hard for single parents to spend time with friends or build new relationships.

- **Longer life spans.** People are living longer than in the past. While many older people are healthy and active, others are not able to live independently. An increasing number of adults are now the primary caregivers for both their aging parents and their own children. People in this situation are often referred to as the "sandwich generation." See Fig. 19-6.

- **Increased mobility.** If your family has moved in the last five years, you are an example of today's highly mobile society. It's not uncommon for a family to relocate several times. The most common reason is a parental job change or promotion. A major disadvantage for families who move a long distance is being separated from members of their extended family.

- **Advances in technology.** Technology such as cell phones, e-mail, and instant messaging makes it easier for families to stay connected, even when they live far apart. Technology has also allowed more people to work from their homes rather than an office. However, technology can also isolate family members. Spending more time on electronic entertainment leaves less time for real family interaction.

Fig. 19-6. *Many people in middle adulthood find themselves caring for the generation on either side of them.* How might this affect family life?

Strengthening Families

Imagine walking through a park on a summer day and coming across an ancient oak tree. Its trunk is so massive that you can't circle it with your arms. It reaches up toward the sky and spreads its limbs in all directions. Even the branches that are farthest away have green, healthy leaves.

A strong family is similar to this ancient oak tree. Both are deeply rooted in a nourishing environment. Both have a solid base with branches going off in various directions. No matter how far the branches of a tree—or a family—go, they stay connected to their roots.

Fig. 19-7. Family members may be very different from one another in some ways, yet share common bonds. Why is it important to respect one another's differences?

You know what a tree needs in order to thrive: soil, water, air, and sunshine. Similarly, a family needs certain elements to keep it strong. These elements provide a sense of stability and security and help make family life satisfying and fulfilling. As you read about the qualities of strong families, ask yourself how you can make a greater contribution in your family.

Respect

People in strong families respect each other's abilities, needs, and opinions, even if they don't share them. They accept and appreciate their differences. For example, Dana is very outgoing, while her brother Donovan is more reserved. Although the two siblings have very different personalities, each values and respects the other's unique qualities. See Fig. 19-7.

Here are some other ways you can show respect for your family:

- Listen to and consider others' points of view.
- Follow the rules your family sets for you.
- Ask before you borrow someone else's property.
- Give others the privacy they need.
- Be considerate of others' feelings. Avoid negative comments.

Communication

Effective communication is basic to all relationships, and family relationships are no exception. On a practical level, clear communication is essential for anyone sharing a home because schedules and plans must be coordinated. On a deeper level, it's impossible to develop closeness without open, honest communication.

Good communication can be simple and informal. Consider posting a family calendar or message board to keep track of everyone's schedule. If you have a change in plans, call to let others in the family know.

Family meetings can be another useful tool. Some families have regular meetings to keep up with family news and plan their schedules. Others have meetings only when there is a need to solve a specific problem, handle a crisis, or make decisions that affect the whole family.

Sometimes family members have something on their mind, but aren't sure how to bring up the subject. Be sensitive to signs that someone in your family needs to talk, and let the person know you're there to listen. Just as important, stay in touch every day. Simple gestures, like asking "How are you doing?" and being genuinely interested in the answer, help ensure that lines of communication stay open.

Trust

Family closeness is also built on trust. When there's trust, you can count on your family's help and support. When you confide in a parent or sibling, you can trust that the information will remain confidential. Young children trust their parents to take care of them and meet their needs. As they get older, they trust parents to make decisions that are in the best interests of the family. Parents trust teens to do what they are supposed to do, even when the parents are not around to enforce the rules. Building trust in families is a two-way street. If you want your parents to give you their trust, you must show them that you are trustworthy. See Fig. 19-8.

Fig. 19-8. In order to receive driving privileges, teens must show they can be trusted to drive responsibly. What are some ways you can build trust in your family?

Emotional Support

Michi recalled her first piano recital. "I was so nervous performing in front of all those people. Then I saw my brother Hiro sitting there in the front row with my parents. He's really not that interested in music, so I didn't expect him to come. Knowing he was there just to support me gave me a lot of confidence. I forgot all about being nervous and played my best."

Michi's experience shows how emotional support contributes to strong families. Emotional support includes words and actions that are positive and reassuring. When people face challenging situations and need confidence, knowing that someone believes in them makes a difference. You can show emotional support in little ways every day. Here are a few suggestions:

- Tell a family member who is facing a challenge, "I know you'll do well."

- Give hugs for no special reason.

- Make a habit of giving compliments.

Character IN ACTION

Valuing Older Family Members When you make an effort to connect with your older relatives, both they and you benefit. Make a point of finding time to talk with older family members. Ask them what their life was like when they were younger. Their experiences may help you see your own life in a different light. By listening to them and treating them with respect, you remind older people that they are valued. Think of three things you'd like to ask an older relative about his or her life.

- Find ways to help others without being asked.

There are countless ways to show people that you care for them and value them simply because they are family. Think of the ways you support your family. How could you increase your support?

Sharing

Sharing is one of the first lessons that children learn, and it remains an important tool for strengthening family ties. One way of sharing is to work together toward common goals. Dividing responsibilities helps a family function efficiently and lets everyone make a contribution.

Family traditions can help create a sense of shared identity and history. Some of your family traditions may have been passed on from previous generations. For example, you might know that holiday meals in your family always include a certain special dish made from your great-grandmother's recipe. You can also start new traditions of your own, such as picking apples every fall or playing games together every Sunday evening.

Perhaps the most important way of sharing, though, is simply to spend time together as a family. Whether you're doing something special or just telling one another about your day over dinner, sharing helps form strong and lasting bonds.

Support Systems

Even strong families need outside help from time to time. A **support system** consists of all the people and organizations a family can turn to for help. Having a support system is especially important when challenging situations arise.

For many families, the support system begins with the extended family. A grandparent may be willing to stay with a sick child so a parent can go to work. The support system might also include neighbors and friends who are willing to help out. For example, friends may take turns caring for each other's children. See Fig. 19-9.

Families can also rely on community resources for support. Social service agencies can provide help when special problems arise. Libraries are great sources of information. Parks and recreational facilities help families meet their needs. Schools and places of worship may offer after-school programs for young children, as well as family activities that help families grow closer.

Your Role in the Family

As a teen, your role in the family is changing. You may be expected to help more around the home, to take part in family decisions, and to accept more responsibility. At the same time, you have more activities and obligations outside the family. You may want to spend time with your friends, participate in school activities, and pursue personal hobbies. Perhaps you have a part-time job as well.

Finding time for family can be challenging when there are so many demands on you, but it's worth the effort. You'll need to plan ahead and set priorities so that you can be sure of spending quality time with your family. Making the effort will bring many rewards. You will play an important role in your family in the years to come, helping to

Fig. 19-9. A group of parents might take turns caring for their children after school. Why are support systems more important today than in the past?

keep it strong and contributing to its enduring traditions. When you work to make your family strong, the benefits reach beyond the family and make your community a better place. Strong families are the foundation for strong communities.

Chapter Summary

- Although families come in many forms, they all have similar functions.
- Families are responsible for the physical, intellectual, emotional, social, and moral development of family members.
- At each stage of the family life cycle, families must adapt to changing situations and priorities.
- Societal trends bring changes that affect families.
- Families are strengthened by respect, communication, trust, emotional support, sharing, and support systems.
- You have an important role to play in helping to keep your family strong, now and in the years to come.

Reviewing Key Terms & Ideas

1. What is the difference between a **nuclear family** and an **extended family**?
2. Explain how a **blended family** is formed.
3. How do families **nurture** their members? Why is this such an important function?
4. How do families meet the physical, intellectual, and emotional needs of their members? Give two examples for each.
5. What does **socialization** involve? How do children learn social skills?
6. Give three examples of moral values that families teach their children.
7. Describe the five stages of the traditional **family life cycle**.
8. Give two examples of variations on the family life cycle pattern.
9. What does the term *sandwich generation* mean? Why has the number of people in the sandwich generation increased?
10. How does the trend toward increased mobility affect families?
11. Why is good communication important for developing a strong family?
12. Explain why trust is a two-way street.
13. Give four examples of family **support systems**.
14. What are the benefits of finding time to spend with your family?

Thinking Critically

1. **Recognizing Cause and Effect.** Review the list of trends affecting families on pages 284-285. Suggest positive and negative consequences of each trend.
2. **Identifying Alternatives.** How can family members make sure they communicate with one another on a regular basis? Give at least three suggestions not mentioned in the text.

Applying Your Knowledge

1. **Family Functions.** Identify some of the ways that a family might fulfill its five different functions when family members share a meal. Record your ideas in a chart with a column for each type of function.

2. **Family Life Cycle.** In a small group, discuss a specific stage of the family life cycle as assigned by your teacher. What adjustments and challenges must families face at this stage? Brainstorm ideas for helping families successfully adapt and meet the challenges. Share your ideas with the rest of the class.

Making Connections

1. **Math.** Obtain data from the latest census about the size and structure of families in your state. (Census Bureau data is available on the Internet or in your local library.) Create a graph to describe your findings.

2. **Language Arts.** Select a tradition that is important in your family. Write a short story or essay describing the tradition and explaining how it helps promote family strength through sharing.

Managing Your Life

Strengthening Your Family

Every family member shares responsibility for strengthening family bonds. Think about your own family. In what ways does it already show the qualities of a strong family? What areas could be improved? Identify a goal for enhancing the strength of your family. Then identify three actions you could take that would contribute toward that goal. Develop a plan for making your ideas a reality.

Using Technology

1. **Presentation Software.** Choose a current societal trend affecting families. Conduct research to find specific information and statistics about the trend and its effects. Using appropriate software, create an electronic presentation that summarizes your findings.

2. **Photography.** Select one of the qualities of strong families, such as respect or trust. Using family members or friends as models, take photos that symbolize your chosen quality or show it in action. Choose your best photos and use them to create a poster or electronic slide show.

CHAPTER 20

Challenges for Families

Key Terms

- crisis
- custody
- joint custody
- grief
- substance abuse
- alcoholism
- abuse
- neglect

Objectives

- Explain how changes and crises affect families.
- Identify strategies that help families cope with challenges.
- Describe specific challenges often faced by families.
- Suggest sources of help for families facing challenges.

Families need support when times are tough. List some ways you could reach out and help a family that is experiencing problems.

*M*aya fought back tears as she flopped down on her bed. She still couldn't believe what she and her sister had just been told. "I've accepted a job offer, but it will mean a big change for us," their mother had said. The whole family would be moving to another state in the summer. When she heard the news, Maya felt her heart sink. Moving would mean leaving all her friends behind. Instead of spending her senior year with them, Maya would be a "new kid" in a strange school. "Isn't there some way to keep this from happening?" she thought desperately. "Why do things have to change?"

Changes and Crises

Change is a fact of life, something that families experience all the time. When changes occur, everyone in the family is affected, although in different ways. Maya is concerned about leaving her friends and fitting in at her new school, while her mother is concerned about the demands of a new job. See Fig. 20-1.

Most changes cause stress, though the degree of stress varies. A job change that requires the family to adjust to a new morning routine might cause short-term stress that's relatively easy to handle. In Maya's situation, a job change is causing significantly more stress. Then there are family challenges so serious that they constitute a **crisis**—an event or situation that overwhelms usual coping methods and causes severe stress. A home fire or a life-threatening illness would be considered a crisis. Many of the challenges discussed in this chapter can be a crisis, depending on their seriousness and the individual family's situation.

Fig. 20-1. When their older sister returned home after college, these brothers had to learn to share a room again. *What are some changes you have had to adapt to at home?*

Change always presents challenges because it requires adapting to a new situation. Even when the change is a positive event, such as the adoption of a child, a family needs to modify its established routines and adapt to a different meaning of "family." Sometimes families face several challenges at the same time. For example, a serious illness may lead to job loss and financial difficulties. How a family deals with challenges depends on the circumstances of the challenge, the strength of the family as a unit, and the coping skills of family members.

Coping Strategies

Challenges of any type require families to adapt, make decisions, and learn to cope. The first step is to acknowledge the difficulties that the family is facing. Sometimes people don't even realize how much stress they're under. They feel they should be able to take everything in stride. In some cases, family members may deny that there's a problem or try to hide it from others. Denial, however, doesn't make a problem go away—it only makes it harder to solve.

Once a family has recognized and agreed to deal with a specific challenge, it can use a number of coping strategies.

- **Communicate.** Talking things over helps family members get to the root of problems and begin to solve them. Be willing to listen or just give a hug to show how much you care.
- **Cooperate.** Working together will bring family members closer. You can help by taking responsibility for things that need to be done without being asked.
- **Follow routines.** Maintain some stability by continuing to follow familiar routines

as much as possible. Try to make time for some of the activities you enjoy.

- **Use problem-solving skills.** The problem-solving strategies explained in Chapter 6 can help you and your family clarify the situation and evaluate possible solutions.
- **Ask for help when needed.** Don't be afraid to ask for help in dealing with difficult issues. You can find suggestions for sources of help at the end of this chapter.

Character IN ACTION

Standing by Family When times are tough, people often turn to their family for comfort. When you stand by people in your family, you show your love for them. You let them know that you're there when they need you. When family members have problems, take time to learn about what they are dealing with and the best ways to help them. Identify ways you have reached out to help someone in your family.

Challenges Families Face

Each family faces unique situations and challenges. Still, it helps to realize that many other families have faced similar problems before. Their experiences can help you learn what to expect. When you're aware of the adjustments and difficulties that each type of situation brings, you are better able to recognize and respond to problems as they arise. As you read about the following challenges, think about how the coping strategies you have just learned might be applied in each situation.

Moving

In today's mobile society, most families face moving, perhaps once or many times. Even a move within the same community changes daily life. If a move involves relocating to another community or state, the family must adjust not only to a new home but also to a whole new set of people, places, and activities. See Fig. 20-2.

If your family moves, you will adapt more quickly if you resolve to keep a positive attitude. If you will be attending a new school, learn as much as possible about it ahead of time. Find out what courses are offered and what school activities are available. Joining in activities can help you meet teens with similar interests. Volunteering is another excellent way to make new friends and become a part of a new community. Remember, too, that moving doesn't have to mean losing all your current friendships. Make plans to keep in touch through e-mail, phone calls, and letters.

Changes in Employment

Whenever people change jobs or lose a job, their families face adjustments. Job-related changes often involve financial adjustments as well. This is a time when a family needs to pull together to work through the situation in a positive way.

In the past, people often stayed in one job their entire working life. Now most people change jobs—and even careers—several times. Job changes can affect family life in a variety of ways. For example, a promotion might mean more income, but also more

Fig. 20-2. *Moving to a new home is exciting, but also stressful. What would you find most difficult about moving to a different community?*

responsibility and job stress. If the new job requires longer work hours, household routines and responsibilities might need to be altered, and finding time for family activities can be more difficult.

The challenges are greater if a family member loses a job. People can lose their job for many reasons, often through no fault of their own. Sometimes a business downsizes or an employer simply moves operations elsewhere. Whatever the reason, it's common for people who lose their job to experience feelings of rejection and failure. It can be hard for them to keep a positive attitude about finding a new job, especially if the unemployment lasts a long time.

When a job loss occurs, it's important that the family's words and actions encourage and show confidence in the job seeker. That's not always easy. During a prolonged job search, family members may become more irritable or communicate less. Health problems are more likely to occur. Getting through such rough times depends on the family's ability to support one another and their belief that the situation will improve.

Financial Problems

Families can experience financial problems for many reasons. Losing a job means a reduction in family income. Some families experience similar financial hardship after a divorce, during a prolonged illness, or after a disaster such as a flood. Some families overspend and find themselves deeply in debt.

Fig. 20-3. Babies are cute and loveable, but they take up a lot of time. What kinds of adaptations do people have to make when there's a new baby in the family?

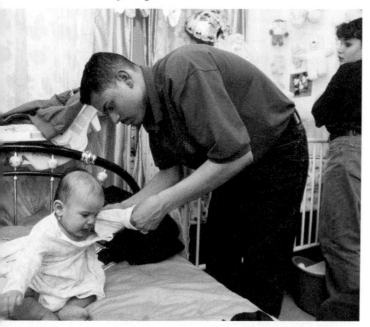

Whenever a family is facing financial pressures, all family members need to understand that sacrifices must be made. Necessities such as food, housing, and health care take priority. Wants may have to be postponed to ensure needs are met. Each person in the family can help in some way. It might be by postponing purchases, taking on more responsibilities around the house, finding a part-time job, or just being patient and supportive.

Additions to the Family

One of the most common changes that families experience is the addition of a new member. Whether the new arrival is a baby or an aging grandparent, life changes for everyone. Family priorities and schedules change, and family members often have to take on new responsibilities. Financial resources may be strained.

The arrival of a baby is usually a happy event. However, taking care of a newborn is a 24-hour-a-day responsibility. Parents get less sleep and have less time for themselves and each other. For children, there's less opportunity for one-on-one time with their parents. At the same time, young children often must learn to be more independent, and older children must help out more. See Fig. 20-3.

Some families adopt an older child or care for a foster child. These children require a period of adjustment, especially if they have lived in several previous homes. They need time to get used to their new surroundings and reassurance that they are welcome. Foster children present unique challenges for families because foster care is usually temporary. That means that families face two adjustments: one when foster children join the family and another when they leave.

Simplifying a Problem

Some problems involve so many different aspects that they can seem overwhelming. It's hard to figure out what to do because you don't know where to start. To make such problems more manageable, you need to simplify them.

▶ How It Works

When emergency workers arrive at the scene of an accident, they must quickly determine how many people are injured and who needs attention first. In the same way, if you encounter a complex problem, you first need to break it down into its various parts. Once you've identified the components of the problem, decide how they rank in urgency or importance. Then tackle one part at a time in order of priority.

▶ Try It Out

Jeff's parents recently divorced. Now he divides his time between two homes—Sunday through Wednesday at his mother's home and Thursday through Saturday at his father's home in the same community. Jeff is glad that he gets to spend time with both parents. On the other hand, he's finding life more complicated now—he has two addresses, two phone numbers, and two places to store his belongings. Often he doesn't have something he needs because it's at the other home. Constantly switching back and forth is making him feel unsettled, and he's not sure his friends will know where to find him on any given day.

▶ **Your Turn** *Identify the different aspects of Jeff's problem. If you were in his position, how might you prioritize them? Why? What solutions can you suggest for each?*

In some cases, an adult joins the family. An adult child may return home after a divorce or a job loss. An older relative who can no longer live alone may come to live with the family. In such cases, more people will be living in the same space. New relationships are formed. What other adjustments would be needed?

Divorce

Divorce is one of the most painful changes a family can go through. Children experience a wide range of emotions when they learn that their parents are getting a divorce. Some feel angry or resentful toward one or both parents. They may fear that their parents will no longer love and care for them. Some children withdraw from friends or lose interest in schoolwork.

Young children, especially, tend to blame themselves for the breakup of their parents' marriage. They may feel that their behavior caused the divorce. On the other hand, children sometimes feel a sense of relief when their parents separate or divorce. This is especially true when family life has been troubled by constant arguments.

Divorcing parents must reach agreement about custody of their children. **Custody** is legally assigned responsibility for making decisions that affect children and providing for their care. In some cases, one parent has custody and the other parent is allowed to see the children at specified times. In other cases, divorced parents have **joint custody**—they share legal responsibility for the children. With a joint custody arrangement, children have the advantage of regular contact with both parents. However, children's routines can be disrupted if they have to move back and forth between their parents' homes.

It's essential that parents work together to provide their children with a sense of stability and knowledge that they are loved. Children shouldn't be forced to take sides or to listen to negative comments about either parent. As much as possible, both parents should continue to be involved in children's lives. Counseling can be useful to help children and parents make the transition.

Remarriage and Blending

When Preston's mother told him that she was going to remarry, he was happy for her and Ron, but also apprehensive. "Will Ron expect me to call him 'Dad'?" he wondered. "How will my real father react? What will having a new stepbrother be like? Will I still have my own room? Will things change between me and Mom?"

If you are part of a blended family, you may be able to relate to questions such as these. Blended families face many challenges. Adults have to learn to live together as marriage partners while adjusting to new parenting relationships. Children gain stepparents,

Fig. 20-4. It takes awhile for stepbrothers and stepsisters to become comfortable with one another. What strategies could help make the adjustment as smooth as possible?

and often stepsisters and stepbrothers, plus a new extended family. They have to abandon any lingering hope that their divorced parents will get back together. Rivalries over territory and possessions may develop.

It takes time for a blended family to adjust and get organized. It's not realistic to expect stepparents and stepchildren to love and accept each other immediately. Given time, however, blended families can build caring, supportive relationships. Flexibility, communication, and patience will help. See Fig. 20-4.

Teen Pregnancy

An unplanned pregnancy creates many challenges for teens and their families. Teens need the support and guidance of their parents as they consider options such as adoption or marriage. Parents can also help the teen couple plan strategies for the future, such as how to complete school while supporting and caring for the baby.

When teens become parents, many lives are changed. Whether or not they marry, both teens have financial and practical responsibilities for the baby's care. Those responsibilities last until the child reaches adulthood, or even beyond. The teen parents are not the only ones whose lives are affected. Their parents and other family members also face adjustments and, in many cases, take on added responsibilities.

Being a good teen parent isn't easy. It is possible, however, with the help of a strong support system.

TEXTLINK≈
You can read more about *teen parenthood* in Chapter 27.

Fig. 20-5. When someone is sick or injured, the family can help by showing love and support. What else could you do to help at such a time?

Health Challenges

When Maggie's father was injured in a car accident, she had trouble coping. At first she didn't want to visit him in the hospital. She didn't want to see what he was going through. She finally realized, however, that her parents needed her. Maggie's support helped her mother manage the crisis, and her encouragement helped her father through his long recovery.

Many families have to face the challenge of caring for someone who is seriously ill, injured, or disabled. It's natural for family members to be worried and upset in such situations. It can be difficult to deal with uncertainty and to make medical decisions. In addition to the emotional effects, family life is disrupted and financial difficulties may arise. See Fig. 20-5.

Mental illness can also challenge families. Depression is one of the most common types. It is more than just feeling disappointed or "down." People with depression have difficulty carrying out daily activities, such as getting out of bed, going to work, or performing routine tasks. Recovery from depression usually requires medical treatment. Other mental illnesses can be even more serious. Accurate diagnosis and treatment are vital.

If your family experiences a health challenge, find out more about the condition so you know what to expect. It also helps to meet with others who have dealt with similar situations. Joining a support group may be beneficial, especially when health problems are long term.

Death

Rita's Aunt Consuelo had lived with the family since Rita was a child, and the two were very close. When her aunt died, Rita was not prepared for the conflicting emotions that she felt. At first she tried to deal with her grief by not thinking about it. Later she began to feel guilty about the times when she and Aunt Consuelo had argued. She wished she had reacted differently.

Sometimes Rita even felt angry at her aunt for leaving her, but mostly she just felt sad and lonely.

Rita's feelings of denial, guilt, anger, and loneliness are all natural. Everyone who is close to someone who dies has these conflicting emotions as they go through the process of grief. **Grief** is the sorrow caused by the death of a loved one and the emotional adjustment to that loss.

Here are some suggestions for coping when someone close to you dies:

- **Accept the reality of the situation.** Participating in the funeral or memorial service helps you avoid denial.

- **Accept and express feelings.** It's natural for your own and others' feelings to last a long time. Let yourself cry, talk, and share sad feelings.

- **Share happy memories.** Reach out to others close to the person. Share your memories and the good times you had together. See Fig. 20-6.

Fig. 20-6. Sharing memories of happier times can help family members cope with the loss of a loved one.

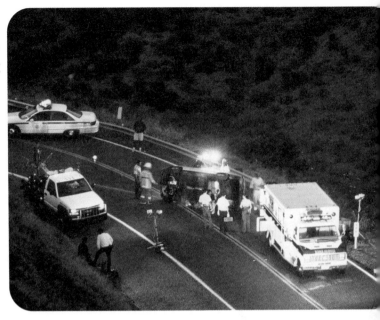

Fig. 20-7. Accidents are just one of many problems associated with substance abuse. People who use drugs become a threat to themselves and to others.

- **Find ways to help**. Be aware of others' needs. Besides listening, look for practical ways to help. Perhaps you could prepare meals or take care of younger children.
- **Spend time with the family**. To deal with a death, family members often find strength in one another and close friends.
- **Seek help, if needed**. Sometimes it's helpful to talk to someone outside the family who understands the situation, especially if grief lasts and lasts. Religious leaders, counselors, and those who have adjusted to a death are often good choices.

Suicide

Suicide—the taking of one's own life—is an act of desperation and despair. Signs that someone might be considering suicide include depression, mood swings, giving away favorite possessions, and talking about death or suicide. If you suspect that someone you know is considering suicide, tell an adult who can intervene. Suicide is never a solution to a problem.

Unfortunately, people who are considering suicide don't always show signs. Even if they do, it's not always possible to prevent them from carrying out their intentions. When a person does commit suicide, family members and friends often feel guilt that they weren't able to prevent the tragedy. They need reassurance that they are not to blame. Counseling often helps people work through their feelings after a suicide.

Drug and Alcohol Problems

Problems related to **substance abuse**—the use of illegal drugs or the misuse of legal drugs or substances—afflict many families. Alcohol is the most commonly abused substance. Prolonged use of alcohol can lead to **alcoholism**, a disease in which a person develops a physical and mental need for alcohol. Other substances that can be abused include illegal drugs, legally prescribed medicines, and even some common household products.

Substance abuse is linked to many problems. It can create a mental or physical dependence that leads to regular cravings for the drug or substance. Both physical and mental health can deteriorate. Some people who abuse drugs lose their jobs because they are not able to work effectively. Some commit crimes to support their habits. Accidents, violence, and suicide can also result from substance abuse. All of these problems harm both the abuser and the abuser's family. See Fig. 20-7.

If someone in your family has a substance abuse problem, learn what you can about the problem and how best to deal with it. People who want to stop using drugs or alcohol often need to enter treatment programs to overcome their problem. However, no addict will stop using drugs or alcohol until he or she is ready. Nagging won't help. Seek help and support for yourself so that you can cope with the situation.

TEXTLINK≈

Chapter 33 provides more information about *substance abuse.*

Family Violence

Sometimes the home becomes a dangerous place because of violence in the family. **Abuse** occurs when one person threatens the physical or mental health of another. It can be directed against any member of the family—including children, spouses, or older family members—and it can take many forms. Beatings are a form of physical abuse. Constant threats, ridicule, and criticism are forms of emotional abuse. Sexual abuse occurs when an adult forces sexual activity on a child or another family member. Another form of abuse is **neglect**, the failure of parents to meet a child's basic needs. Those who are unable to care for themselves, such as some elderly or disabled people, may also suffer from neglect.

Signs of abuse may be physical or emotional. Victims of physical abuse may have unexplained injuries, such as bruises in unusual places. Victims of emotional abuse often suffer from low self-esteem. Their abusers may have told them that they deserve to be punished. Sometimes victims see abuse as normal because it's all they have ever known.

Some abusers are themselves victims of abuse. Growing up in an abusive household, they learn these behaviors. Later they repeat them with their own children, creating a cycle of abuse. Counseling can help abusers learn positive ways of dealing with stress and anger. Victims of abuse may also need counseling to help them deal with the emotional scars.

Abuse is never justified. It takes courage for family members to admit that there's a problem and to seek help, but it's essential that they take action. That's the only way to protect against further abuse and prevent the cycle from repeating itself. If you or someone you know is in an abusive situation, find out what help is available in your community. Taking steps to stop abuse can make a real difference.

Major Disasters

If you watch the news, you know that any family can be the victim of a disaster. Hurricanes, tornadoes, floods, and fires are just some of the disasters that can strike people's homes or communities, with or without warning.

Dealing with the aftermath of a major disaster can be extremely difficult. If a family's home is severely damaged or destroyed, everything changes. Sometimes a place of employment is damaged, affecting work and income. Public agencies and private organizations, such as the American Red Cross, often provide some aid. However, overcoming the emotional effects of a disaster can take a long time. Some people have more difficulty than others. They may need to seek help in order to get life back to normal.

Sources of Help

Families sometimes manage to find their own solutions to their problems, but often they need outside help. It's not a sign of weakness to ask for help. Rather, it is a sign of courage and maturity to admit that you cannot handle a problem alone. See Fig. 20-8.

Here are some suggestions for sources of help:

- **Family.** If you're faced with a problem, often another family member who understands the problem can be of help. Other times it's best to talk to someone outside the family who is not involved in the situation.

- **Other adults you trust.** When you need to seek help outside the family, talk to a teacher, counselor, or religious leader. A trusted adult will guide you to the help you need.

- **Friends.** Sometimes talking a problem out with a trustworthy friend can give you new insights and help you find a solution.

- **Support groups.** Groups of people going through a similar challenge provide a forum to discuss specific problems and give and receive support.

- **Agencies and organizations.** Many local, state, and national groups provide support services for families. Look for a guide to human services in your telephone directory or on the Web, or ask for information at the library.

- **Professional counselors.** Psychologists, therapists, and other mental health professionals are trained to help individuals and families solve problems. If a problem involves a whole family, everyone may need to work together to find a solution.

Families with problems have a valuable resource in one another. They may find that responding to a change or a crisis brings them closer together. When families face difficulties, they can put aside small differences to focus on what is important—preserving the family and supporting those they love. By pulling together, families can survive and thrive.

Fig. 20-8. A professional counselor can help family members work through a crisis situation. Why might some people be reluctant to seek professional help?

Chapter Summary

- Nearly all families experience changes and crises that require them to adapt to new situations.
- The first step in dealing with a challenge is acknowledging the problems it creates.
- Coping strategies, such as communication and problem-solving skills, can help families handle changes and crises.
- Challenges faced by families can range from common situations such as moving to serious crises such as death, drug and alcohol problems, violence, and major disasters.
- Seeking help from outside sources when needed is a sign of courage and maturity.

Reviewing Key Terms & Ideas

1. In general, how are families affected by change?
2. Under what conditions would a family change be considered a **crisis**?
3. Name four general strategies for coping with challenges.
4. Describe three ways a family might be affected when a parent changes jobs.
5. What are some actions families can take when they experience financial problems?
6. What unique challenges do families have when they care for foster children?
7. Describe three reactions children may have when their parents get divorced.
8. Why must divorcing parents reach an agreement about **custody**?
9. Describe the adjustments necessary in a blended family.
10. Give two suggestions that could be helpful for families who have a child with a disability.
11. What does the process of **grief** involve?
12. Identify four problems that are associated with **substance abuse**.
13. Why is **neglect** considered to be a form of **abuse**?
14. Suggest three sources of outside help for families facing a challenge.

Thinking Critically

1. **Drawing Conclusions.** Why is it essential for families to learn to deal with change?
2. **Summarizing Information.** What are some of the most important actions family members can take when dealing with a change or a crisis?

Applying Your Knowledge

1. **Welcoming Newcomers.** In a small group, develop a "Welcome Kit" for families who move into your community. Provide useful information and advice that will make it easier for these families to adjust to their new environment.

2. **Suicide Warning Signs.** Do research to learn more about the warning signs of suicide. Create a poster that highlights the signs and tells teens how to respond if they notice these signs in others.

3. **Researching Challenges.** Choose one of the challenges for families discussed in the chapter. Do some research to find out more about how the challenge affects families. Prepare a brief presentation in which you outline the effects of the challenge and possible approaches to dealing with it.

Making Connections

1. **Language Arts.** Imagine that you write a newspaper advice column. Write a letter from a fictitious teen describing a serious problem that his or her family is facing. Then write a reply that offers encouragement, suggests coping strategies, and recommends sources of help.

2. **Social Studies.** Research recent trends in the unemployment rate. Over the past few years, has unemployment risen or fallen? What economic factors have influenced the unemployment rate? How has this trend affected families?

Managing Your Life

Resources for Families

Every community has sources of help and support for families in crisis. These support systems are valuable resources for managing challenges. Even if you don't need their services now, you may someday. Prepare now by investigating the services available in your community. In particular, find out what agencies or organizations provide help at little or no cost to families. Make a list of these community resources, organized by the type of challenge they can help families manage. Share your list with your family, and keep it for future reference if a need should arise.

Using Technology

1. **Audio.** Arrange to record an interview with someone who has been through a change in employment. Ask the person to talk about the adjustments that were necessary and the coping strategies that he or she used.

2. **Internet.** Use the Internet to locate information about an organization or agency that offers support services to families. Examples include Alateen, Children's Protective Services, and Consumer Credit Counseling Service. Prepare a fact sheet about the agency that you can post on your class bulletin board.

CHAPTER 21

Your Friendships

Key Terms

- reciprocity
- diversity
- clique
- harassment
- sexual harassment

Objectives

- **Identify** qualities of strong friendships.
- **Describe** ways to meet people and make friends.
- **Explain** the benefits of diversity in friendships.
- **Give guidelines** for strengthening friendships and handling changes in friendships.
- **Discuss** problems that may occur in peer relationships.

306

QUICK WRITE

There's an old saying, "To have a friend, be a friend." Write about what this means to you.

$\mathcal{F}$riends are an important influence on your life. They open you up to new interests and help you develop socially and emotionally. It doesn't matter how many friends you have or whether other people think they are the "right" friends. What does matter is choosing friends who are right for you.

Qualities of Friendship

Ask ten different people what they like most about their closest friend, and you might get ten different answers. If you examined their answers carefully, though, you would discover that certain qualities are basic to all strong friendships. These qualities include:

- **Common interests.** Whether it's a favorite sports team or an enthusiasm for astronomy, similar interests encourage communication and give friends a basis for spending time together. See Fig. 21-1.

- **Caring.** Friends care about each other. They are kind, considerate, and concerned about the other person's well-being. Real friends don't ask each other to do anything wrong or harmful.

- **Empathy.** Friends show empathy when they understand and identify with what the other person is feeling. Empathy lets them share the joy of good times and ease the pain of difficult times.

- **Respect.** Friends respect each other's opinions, even if they don't always share them.

- **Dependability.** Friends know they can depend on each other to keep their promises and do what they say they will do.

Fig. 21-1. Friends show that they care by taking an interest in each other's lives. What are some other ways to show a friend that you care?

- **Forgiveness.** Friends understand that nobody is perfect. They are willing to forgive each other's mistakes and say "I'm sorry" when they make mistakes of their own.
- **Reciprocity.** Friendships rarely last when one person does most of the giving. **Reciprocity** means that there is a mutual exchange—each person gives as well as receives.

Making Friends

It's one thing to know the qualities you look for in a friend, but quite another to find someone who has those qualities. How do you make new friends? Your first step is to take advantage of opportunities to meet people.

Meeting People

Friendships usually begin because people have something in common. If you want to make new friends, think of ways to meet people who share your interests. Getting involved in school activities is one good way. Molly made friends quickly after she joined the volleyball team. Daryl met one of his best friends while working as an aide in the school library.

Volunteering in your community lets you meet people of different ages and backgrounds while helping others. You might participate in a food drive or help with a holiday parade. As with school activities, your participation can help you discover and develop your talents and skills. That makes you a more interesting and well-rounded person—qualities people look for in friends.

Starting a Conversation

Maybe starting up a conversation with someone you don't know comes naturally to you. More likely, doing so feels uncomfortable, as it does for many people. With practice, though, approaching and talking with people becomes easier.

When you want to start a conversation, don't worry about coming up with something original to say. Most people are pleased that you speak to them at all. They may feel just as nervous about starting a conversation as you do. See Fig. 21-2.

Here are some tips for starting a conversation and keeping it going:

- Show an interest in the other person. Most people like to talk about themselves—after all, it's a topic they are experts on!
- Don't do all the talking yourself. Good conversation requires a give and take of speaking and listening.

Character IN ACTION

Helping a New Student It's tough to start out at a new school. When you see a new student, go out of your way to be friendly. Invite the person to sit with you at lunch or go to a game with you. Introduce the new classmate to your friends and to people in other social groups. Take the initiative to help the new student feel at ease. Think of three activities that you might invite a new student to join in.

Fig. 21-2. Everyday topics are fine for getting a conversation started. You might break the ice by talking about a class assignment or a new movie that just came out.

- Ask open-ended questions that require more than a yes or no answer. This encourages the other person to respond in a way that will keep the conversation going.

- Pay attention to what the other person says, and give feedback. This shows your interest and may lead to other topics.

- Avoid personal or controversial topics. When you're getting to know someone, keep the conversation casual and low-key. Save serious discussions for people you know better.

Taking the Next Step

Meeting people and engaging them in conversation can be the start of a friendship, but it's only a beginning. For a friendship to develop, someone has to take the next step. If you enjoy your first conversation with a person, be the one to take that step. You might follow up with a phone call or find a way to talk to the person at school. Suggest doing something together so you can get to know each other better. If you spend time together and discover common interests, the friendship will grow. Don't try to rush things. Strong friendships grow over time.

Handling Rejection

Whenever you make the effort to reach out to another person in friendship, you risk being rejected. Not every person you want for a friend will want to be your friend. Being rejected can be painful, and it may shake your confidence. Remember, however, that everyone experiences rejection at times. It usually isn't personal, so there's no reason to think less of yourself. People have all kinds of reasons for accepting and rejecting others. Focus on building relationships with those who do want your friendship.

Some people try to put on an act to get others to like them and lessen their chances of rejection. That's not a good idea. You need friends who accept you for who you are.

On the other hand, change for the right reasons can improve your life and your friendships. Rejection can sometimes alert you to the need for such a change. When Dominic and Jake started to spend time together, Dominic tried to take charge of everything. He always decided what they would do and rarely listened to any of Jake's suggestions. When Jake began to avoid him, Dominic was hurt and asked Jake what was wrong. After they talked, Dominic saw himself through Jake's eyes. He began to share decisions and tried to be a better listener. Jake and others began to enjoy spending time with him.

Fig. 21-3. If most of your friends are your age, you're a typical teen. *Why are people likely to have a greater variety of friends once they start working?*

Diversity in Friendships

Most of your friends are probably similar to you in some ways, but different in other ways. In fact, some of your friends may be quite different from you. That's a plus. **Diversity**, or variety, in friendships can enrich your life.

Friends Like You

It's natural for most of your friends to be other teens. Among people your own age, you're more likely to find friends who like the same things you do and who face similar concerns and problems. That makes it easier to talk about what's going on in your lives. Friends of the same age can often help each other gain confidence and develop a positive self-concept. See Fig. 21-3.

Friends Who Are Different

Do you have friends who are younger than you, and some who are older? Carla found a friend in Mrs. Jandacek, who lives in her apartment building. Carla enjoys hearing her neighbor tell stories about what life was like for her in Eastern Europe and how she came to this country. Carla also values her friendship with Tanisha, the five-year-old daughter of another neighbor. Carla has fun playing with Tanisha and hopes that she can be a good role model for her.

Throughout your life, you'll have friendships with many different people—some older and some younger; some male and some female. Some may have a different cultural background or belong to a different ethnic group than you. Some of your friends may have different religious beliefs or may have grown up under very different circumstances. You'll find, though, that people are more alike than they are different.

Fig. 21-4. True friends help each other any way they can. These friends have made a pact to work together on improving their grades.

Having diverse friendships will help you accept and respect differences and avoid conflicts that can arise from lack of understanding. Appreciating the benefits of diverse friendships is a sign of maturity. When you are friends with a variety of people, you learn to understand yourself and others better. That helps you live successfully in a diverse society.

Strengthening Friendships

It takes effort to maintain a friendship. Fortunately, you already know a lot about the qualities and skills that strengthen friendships, because they are the same ones that make any relationship strong. Think back on what you have learned in previous chapters about communicating, cooperating, and resolving conflicts. These and other relationship skills will help you maintain lasting friendships.

One key to maintaining strong friendships is not taking them for granted. Good friends continue to show the qualities that helped them become friends in the first place. They make time for each other, confide in each other, and communicate openly and hon-

estly. They admire each other's strengths and accept each other's weaknesses. When they make mistakes, they forgive each other. Because they value the friendship, they will do whatever is needed to keep it strong. See Fig. 21-4.

Changes in Friendships

Friendships change over time, just as people do. You may feel closest to one friend for a while and then build a closer friendship with someone different. You might remain friends with someone for years, but the nature of your friendship might change. When Diego and Bruce were in high school, they were best friends who spent time together almost every day. Today, ten years later, they are still close, but fill a different role in each other's lives. They live in different states, write to each other regularly, and visit twice a year. Each has new friends who fill the need for day-to-day companionship.

More to Explore

Online Friendships

Online chat rooms provide a convenient way to meet people and form friendships without ever leaving home. You can chat about similar interests and share ideas with people almost anywhere in the world.

Online relationships have some drawbacks, however. All you know about the people you meet online is what they choose to tell you. How do you know if they are telling the truth? How do you know that you can trust them? You don't—so it's wise to be cautious about what you say online. Don't reveal personal information, such as your address, your telephone number, or where you go to school. You'll find more Internet safety tips on page 412.

Remember, too, that you should balance the "virtual time" you spend with online friends and the "face time" you spend with other friends. Technology can enhance the process of meeting people and developing friendships, but it can't replace it.

Growing Apart

Although some friendships last a long time, others grow more distant and eventually end. You may simply find that you no longer have anything in common with certain friends. If that happens, chances are you won't have to do anything to end the friendship. You'll simply spend less and less time together.

If you and a friend seem to be drifting apart, try to figure out why. Is this a friendship that you both still value, but that is suffering from neglect? If so, look for ways to strengthen the relationship. However, if it seems that you no longer share common interests, it may be time to let go.

Don't be discouraged when you and a friend grow apart. As you move toward adulthood, you are developing new interests and gaining new experiences. Some of your

friendships may not survive these changes. Growing apart from some of your friends is part of growing up. You will have opportunities for new friendships as you move in new directions.

Ending a Friendship

While sometimes friendships end on their own, there may be other times when you choose to end a friendship deliberately. You may realize that you no longer enjoy a person's company, or you may feel that someone does not treat you with the respect that you deserve. Don't be afraid to end a friendship that you consider to be unhealthy. It's far better to focus your efforts on mutually rewarding and satisfying friendships. You may want to review the suggestions for ending a relationship found on pages 220–221 in Chapter 14.

Peer Relationship Problems

Although peer relationships can be a source of friendships, they can also be a source of problems. You may have already faced situations with cliques, gangs, harassment, or negative peer pressure. If not, chances are you will someday. Knowing how to deal with these situations can help you be prepared.

Cliques

A **clique** is a small, exclusive group that restricts who can join. Cliques are formed by people who want to set themselves apart. Belonging to a clique gives its members a sense of identity and importance that they might otherwise be lacking. In that way, cliques are somewhat like security blankets. Their members feel more secure when surrounded by others just like themselves.

While cliques give their members security, they have obvious downsides. When cliques develop an "us versus them" attitude, they create barriers to relationships with other people. Cliques may pressure their members to ignore people who don't "fit in." That hurts everyone involved. See Fig. 21-5.

Cliques are signs of immaturity. Avoid cliquish attitudes and behaviors. Practice including other people, not excluding them—your life will be richer.

What if you're on the outside of a clique looking in? If a group is so exclusive that they won't take you as a member, it's their loss. People who can't accept you for yourself aren't worth looking up to.

Gangs

A gang is a clique that goes far beyond excluding people. Gangs do more than limit membership; they promote distrust and hatred of outsiders. They engage in antisocial, and often unlawful, behavior. Gang members are more likely to participate in, or become victims of, violence.

If you're approached about joining a gang, simply say no. Studies show that if you turn down the invitation in a way that doesn't show disrespect—for example, "My mom wouldn't approve"—chances are you won't be harmed. For more ideas, review the refusal skills listed in Fig. 17-5 on page 259.

Fig. 21-5. Cliques lose out by excluding others.
What actions can you take to show that you prefer to include, and not exclude, other people?

Teasing and Harassment

Many teens experience teasing from their peers. Sometimes friends tease each other in a joking way that's not intended to be taken seriously. As long as it doesn't go too far, this kind of teasing is harmless. It helps to have a sense of humor and know how to laugh at yourself.

In other cases, teasing is intended to irritate, anger, or embarrass someone. If teasing stops being funny and starts to bother you, the best response is usually to ignore it.

FINDING CREATIVE SOLUTIONS

Brainstorming

When it comes to solving problems, it's often true that "two heads are better than one." A group of people working together may be able to come up with a solution that one person alone would have missed. One of the most familiar and useful techniques for solving problems as a group is brainstorming.

How It Works

Brainstorming involves getting together with other people and suggesting any ideas that come to mind. The idea is to generate as many ideas as you can, without stopping to evaluate them.

Assign one person in the group to write down everything that is suggested. Agree ahead of time that all ideas are welcome—even ones that may seem silly or impractical at first. Sometimes those "wild" ideas are the most valuable because they lead you in a new direction of thinking. Often you'll find that other people's ideas help you come up with new ideas of your own.

Brainstorming sessions are often used in business. Many companies recognize them as productive ways to encourage creative ideas and to get people to think in new ways.

Try It Out

In the past few months, reports of harassment in your school have increased. The school administration has decided to form a task force of students and staff members to address this problem. You have volunteered for the task force.

▶ **Your Turn** *In small groups, brainstorm ideas for combating harassment. Consider how to discourage the behavior as well as how to deal with incidents that occur.*

When possible, stay away from people who engage in this kind of behavior.

Hurtful teasing that continues can be a form of **harassment**—persistent hostile behavior directed at a specific person. Bullying is another form of harassment that can be particularly harmful. Bullies seek power and attention by being intentionally cruel. The bullying may take the form of pushing, kicking, or other physical harm, or it may involve taunting and intimidation. Bullies want their victims to be afraid of them. In fact, one of the best ways to stand up to a bully is to show that you are not afraid.

Sexual harassment is annoying behavior of a sexual nature. Sexual remarks, gestures, and touching are considered forms of sexual harassment. Other examples include sexual name-calling, telling sexual jokes, making comments about another person's body, spreading sexual rumors about another person, and pressuring someone for sexual activity.

Harassment in any form should not be tolerated. If you experience or observe such behavior, let the harassers know that their behavior is cruel and offensive. If the harassment continues, tell your parents and seek help from a teacher or counselor. When harassment occurs at school, teachers and school officials have a responsibility to put a stop to it.

Peer Pressure

Pressure from your peers is not necessarily a problem. In fact, good friends can have a positive influence on you. However, at times your peers may pressure you to do things that make you uncomfortable.

Sometimes negative peer pressure is easy to recognize. When someone tries to get you to do something that's illegal or obviously

Fig. 21-6. Feeling good about yourself gives you the confidence to resist negative peer pressure.

wrong, you know it. Other times, you may not fully realize the consequences of what you are being pushed to do. When you're not sure, think about your values. Doing something that goes against them is never a smart decision.

Having a strong self-concept and trusting your own judgment will help you resist negative peer pressure. Make your own decisions and stand up for what you believe. You never have to go along with the crowd. See Fig. 21-6.

TEXTLINK≈

Peer pressure is discussed in greater depth in Chapter 17.

CHAPTER 21 Review & Activities

Chapter Summary

- Qualities such as caring, empathy, and respect are common to strong friendships.
- Look for ways to meet people who share your interests.
- To start a conversation, show an interest in the other person and ask open-ended questions.
- Diversity in friendships brings many benefits.
- Some friendships grow stronger over time; others become more distant or end.
- You can show maturity by avoiding cliques and stay safe by avoiding gangs.
- Harassment is harmful and should never be tolerated.
- Be prepared to recognize and resist negative peer pressure.

Reviewing Key Terms & Ideas

1. How can friends show empathy to one another?
2. Why should friendships be based on **reciprocity**?
3. Describe two ways to meet new people who might become friends.
4. Why is it a good idea to ask open-ended questions when trying to start a conversation?
5. What should you keep in mind if someone does not accept your offer of friendship?
6. Explain two benefits of **diversity** in friendships.
7. Describe three actions you can take to keep a friendship strong.
8. If you and a friend seem to be spending less and less time together, what might this mean? What should you do?
9. What is a **clique**? How are cliques harmful to their members?
10. What risks are associated with gang membership?
11. What's the best way to respond to teasing if it is not too serious?
12. Describe bullying behavior. Why is it considered **harassment**?
13. Give four examples of behavior that would be considered **sexual harassment**.
14. Explain how you can stand up to negative peer pressure.

Thinking Critically

1. **Making Comparisons.** How do childhood friendships differ from those that develop during the teen years?
2. **Drawing Conclusions.** Why do you think it often takes many months to build a strong friendship?

Applying Your Knowledge

1. **Icebreakers.** Imagine that you would like to start a conversation with a new student in your class. Think of three conversation starters that would be appropriate for this situation. Pair up with another member of the class and practice your conversation starters on one another. After each conversation, give one another feedback to improve your conversation skills.

2. **Code of Conduct.** Write a code of conduct for students that addresses teasing, bullying, and other forms of harassment. Be prepared to explain why you included the specific guidelines you did.

Making Connections

1. **Language Arts.** Many plays and novels explore the nature of friendship. Choose a fictional friendship from a play or novel that you have read. Prepare a brief report on the nature and strength of the friendship.

2. **Social Studies.** In the United States, people who are meeting someone for the first time often introduce themselves and shake hands. In other cultures, the etiquette might be different. Find out about three cultures in which a different custom is followed. Be prepared to demonstrate the customs to the class.

Managing Your Life

Qualities of Friendship

Which qualities of strong friendships do you value most in your friends? Think about the qualities described in this chapter, as well as other qualities that make friendships strong. Rank the qualities from most important to least important. Why are some qualities more important to you than others? Of the qualities most important to you, which do you think are *your* strongest qualities? Which qualities do you need to work on? Identify some ways to work on the qualities you need to improve. Put your plan into action over the next few days, and then evaluate the results.

Using Technology

1. **Communication Technology.** In small groups, discuss the effects of communication technology on friendships. Consider technology such as voice mail, caller ID, e-mail, and instant messaging. In what ways do they make it easier to form and maintain friendships? What negative effects might they have on friendships?

2. **Video.** Select one of the peer relationship problems discussed in the chapter. Prepare a 60-second public service video that encourages teens to take action against this problem. Present your video to the class, and make it available to school administrators.

CHAPTER 22

Dating and Marriage

Key Terms

- sexually transmitted diseases (STDs)
- abstinence
- infatuation

Objectives

- Explain reasons for dating.
- Give guidelines for responsible dating relationships.
- Suggest ways of handling emotions in romantic relationships.
- Discuss factors that contribute to marital success and failure.
- Identify reasons some people remain single.

QUICK WRITE

List ten qualities you would look for in a marriage partner. Rank them in order of importance.

*J*ackee and Morgan have been dating for about a year. The relationship has been a positive one for both of them, but now things are about to change. Morgan will be going away to college next month, and Jackee still has a year of high school to go. Jackee feels torn. She really likes Morgan, but one of the great things about being a couple is the security of always having someone to go out with. It won't work that way when Morgan is 300 miles away. Morgan, too, is unsure about the future of their relationship. So far, neither of them has brought the subject up, but both know that they have to make a decision.

Starting Out

Jackee and Morgan have developed a close, romantic relationship, but it didn't happen overnight. The process that led them to this point began years ago. It started when each first became interested in members of the opposite sex as more than just friends. This happens at different ages for different people.

Before Jackee and Morgan even met, they each began going out on dates with some of their friends. Spending time going out with others has several benefits. It gives you opportunities to improve your interpersonal skills, such as making conversation and practicing give and take. You learn to better understand yourself and the people you go out with. In the long run, going out helps you discover which characteristics you want to look for when you choose a partner for life. See Fig. 22-1.

Fig. 22-1. Going out on dates helps you develop your ability to relate to others.

Going Out as a Group

Many teens prefer to go out in groups, especially when they begin dating. Going to a game or movie as part of a group lets you have a good time with less pressure than going out as a couple. In a group, it's easier to learn to feel comfortable with the opposite sex. There are more people to keep the conversation going, and everyone helps make sure the group has a good time. Some teens continue group dating throughout high school, whether or not they also date as couples. See Fig. 22-2.

Going Out as a Couple

Going out on a "couple date" gives you a chance to practice relating to a dating partner one-on-one. It doesn't necessarily mean that you have a serious relationship with that person. Many teens go out on casual dates with different people that they enjoy spending time with. This lets them get to know a variety of people.

After they've been going out together for a time, some couples decide to date each other exclusively. Going out with just one person helps you to get to know that person well. It can also create a sense of security. It's comfortable to know that you always have a date for the weekend and for special events. However, spending all your time with one other person has its drawbacks. You may come to rely too much on that relationship, and you miss opportunities to meet other compatible people.

Family Rules

Many families have rules about dating. For example, some parents don't allow dating one person exclusively. They may believe that teens need opportunities to socialize with lots of different people. Some may fear that their son or daughter will get too involved in a relationship and lose sight of important long-term goals, such as getting a good education. Cultural or religious beliefs, too, may influence a family's rules about dating.

Parents often have rules about where their teens may go and what they can do on a date. Their concerns about drugs, alcohol, unsafe driving, and sexual pressures are valid ones. By setting restrictions, they try to keep teens out of potentially harmful situations. Even if you don't agree with your family's rules, remember that their purpose is to protect you.

Fig. 22-2. Many teens are more comfortable going out in a group. What types of activities would be good choices for group dating?

Fig. 22-3. Planning ahead for a date helps ensure you will both have a good time. What are some other ways to show responsibility when dating?

Responsible Relationships

Going out can be fun, but it has a serious side. When you start going out with someone, you take on new responsibilities. You need to establish boundaries for your new relationship. It's important to plan ahead so that you're prepared to handle situations that may arise.

Personal Responsibility

In a healthy dating relationship, you show respect for yourself by staying true to your personal values and following family rules. You also show respect for your partner's values and rules. If your partner has a curfew, you are both responsible for making sure it's kept.

Communication is an important part of any relationship, but it's a key to responsible dating. Talk with your partner about where you will go, how you will get there, who will pay, how you will get home, and similar issues. Agreeing on what you will do ahead of time eliminates uncertainty and helps you both have a good time. It also establishes an understanding of what you expect from the date. See Fig. 22-3.

When you go out on a date, your goal is to enjoy each other's company. That means accepting each other's wishes and feelings. Remember that a person who cares about you would not pressure you to go against your values. Trying to control another person's behavior in a dating situation is a sure sign of an unhealthy relationship.

Sexual Responsibility

Media often send the message that sex is an expected part of any dating relationship. That's simply not true. Shelly learned the lessons of sexual responsibility the hard way. In her words: "I thought we were in love and that being in love made it okay to have sex. What a mistake! Soon after I said yes, he seemed to lose interest. It really wasn't love at all. I feel like such a fool."

Fig. 22-4. Teens who become parents miss out on many of the activities that their peers enjoy. What are some other difficulties of teen parenthood?

As Shelly discovered, sexual activity can be emotionally damaging. Teens who become sexually active often experience regrets and guilt. Although they may think sex is a private matter, word gets around and reputations suffer. They may lose the respect of their friends and find it harder to form new relationships. They also lose the peace of mind and self-respect that comes from living according to one's values.

In some ways, Shelly was fortunate. She only had to deal with her feelings. Sexual activity, even one time, opens you to other serious risks.

The Risks of Sexual Activity ~ Teens who become sexually active face serious consequences that could have long-term effects on their lives.

- **Unintended pregnancy.** Pregnancy changes teens' lives dramatically. Both parents must assume responsibility for their baby—physically, emotionally, and financially. Sometimes one or both parents drop out of school. This is a very short-sighted solution that severely limits job opportunities and long-term earning potential. The resulting financial problems add stress to the relationship. Some teens think having a child will guarantee someone will love them. The reality is that teen parents often feel trapped by the responsibilities of parenting and resent missing out on the normal activities of other teens. See Fig. 22-4.

- **Sexually transmitted diseases.** Sexual activity carries the risk of contracting a serious disease. **Sexually transmitted diseases (STDs)** are diseases spread through sexual contact. Most STDs are treatable but, if left untreated, can cause lifelong health problems. Many teens don't want to admit they may have such a disease, so they don't get help. In the meantime, they may pass their STD on to others. AIDS is the most devastating STD because there is no cure. Caused by a virus and spread primarily by sexual activity, AIDS weakens the body's defense system and eventually causes death.

TEXTLINK≈

More information about *STDs* can be found in Chapter 33.

Handling Sexual Feelings ~ Because of the many risks associated with sexual activity, you need to know how to handle your sexual feelings. Having such feelings is normal, but letting your feelings control your actions is a mistake. It's important to think ahead and make decisions about your behavior before a difficult situation occurs.

Millions of teens gain peace of mind by practicing abstinence. **Abstinence** means refusal to engage in high-risk behavior. Abstaining from sexual activity is the only sure way to avoid the risks. Some teens reinforce their decision by joining an abstinence campaign and signing a pledge to delay sexual activity until they are married.

The choice not to engage in sexual activity is easier when you talk to your dating partner about your decision. Many teens are relieved to learn that the other person agrees. Even if your partner doesn't agree, you have the right to make your own choices, and your partner must respect your decision. Being willing to communicate honestly about avoiding sexual activity is a sign of maturity.

Going out in a group and in public rather than spending time alone as a couple helps relieve the pressure for sexual activity. Avoid inviting a dating partner to your home unless your parents or other adult family members are there. Above all, don't fall for arguments such as "If you loved me…" or "Everyone is doing it." Lines such as those show lack of respect. Taking sexual responsibility seriously allows you to remain in control of your life and become the kind of person you want to be.

Resisting Sexual Pressure ~ Effective refusal skills will help you say no to pressure to engage in sexual activity. Refusal skills start with a firm sense of who you are and what is important to you. That way you can be confident and assertive in communicating your wishes. In addition to planning ahead, here are some other suggestions for handling sexual pressure:

- State your position. Don't apologize or try to justify your decision.

- Avoid mixed messages. Make sure your body language matches your words.

- Keep your values and your long-term goals in mind.

- If someone won't accept "no" for an answer, leave. Call someone to come and get you, if necessary.

TIPS FOR *Success*

Practicing Abstinence

Abstinence brings peace of mind and self-respect. Here are some suggestions to help you keep your commitment to abstinence:

- Set limits on the kinds of people you will date and the places you will go.

- Plan ahead when you go on a date so that you know what you will do.

- Avoid risky situations, such as parties where people might be drinking alcohol.

- Spend your time with people who share your beliefs.

- Join a program that encourages and supports abstinence.

- Learn to show affection without being sexually active.

Handling Emotions

By nature, the teen years are a time of emotional highs and lows. Learning to handle your emotions and express them appropriately are vital skills. Romantic feelings are especially complex and challenging. To complicate matters, often one person has stronger feelings of attachment than the other.

Crushes and Infatuation

Before they develop a deep, long-term relationship, most people experience less fulfilling ones. These first relationships are sometimes painful, but they are necessary learning experiences.

Many people's first romantic experience comes when they develop a crush on someone. Crushes are usually directed toward a person with whom a real romantic relationship is not possible. For example, a young teen might have a crush on a friend's older sibling or on a movie star. Usually the other person is not even aware of the feelings. A crush can be difficult to deal with because the feelings are so strong. Fortunately, crushes are usually temporary, and the feelings eventually subside. See Fig. 22-5.

You probably know people who began a relationship based on **infatuation**, an intense romantic attraction. Like a crush, infatuation often is idealistic and unrealistic. People tend to focus on physical attraction and other qualities they like in the other person. They ignore characteristics or behaviors that might cause problems. Infatuation also tends to be self-centered—people are more concerned about their own happiness than about the other person's feelings. Infatuation can fool people into thinking they love someone. When people make a commitment based on infatuation, however, they usually regret it.

Fig. 22-5. Most people go through a phase of having a crush on someone. The best way to get over a crush is to develop more realistic relationships with people your own age.

Fig. 22-6. Breaking up is never easy. How can you show respect for a person when ending a relationship?

Jealousy

Jealousy is the feeling that the person you care about is more interested in something or someone else than in you. For example, Marcelo was upset when his girlfriend Abby started to spend hours working on projects with the other members of the homecoming committee.

When you care about another person, it's normal to feel jealous at times. However, intense or prolonged jealousy is destructive to a relationship. Extremely jealous people are usually insecure. They may resent any situation that seems threatening and become possessive and controlling.

Frequent attacks of jealousy call for self-examination. The jealous person may be expecting too much. Remember, no relationship can fulfill all of a person's needs. It's best for couples to balance the time they spend together and apart. Having other friends and separate interests helps people develop as individuals and puts less pressure on the relationship.

Breaking Up

It usually takes much time and many relationships before you find a person that you're truly compatible with. Consequently, most relationships have to end. Ending a relationship on a friendly note is ideal, but that doesn't always happen. Telling someone that you want to end a relationship, or hearing this message from another person, can be painful. See Fig. 22-6.

If you are the one ending the relationship, make a clean break. Don't just drift away or stop calling. Talk to the person and explain why you want to end the relationship. Be firm but fair. Remember the positive emotions you felt in the past, and be sensitive to the other person's feelings.

If the other person wants to end the relationship, don't try to prevent the breakup. Clinging to a relationship with an unwilling partner is unhealthy and just postpones the inevitable. No matter who ends the relationship, avoid saying negative things to or about each other.

After a breakup, give yourself time to recover. Don't be in a hurry to start a new relationship. Instead, reflect on the one that ended. What was good about it? What went wrong? What you learn may help you develop more fulfilling relationships in the future.

Love and Commitment

Eventually, you may find someone special and feel ready to make a commitment to the relationship. Making a commitment means you both accept that you have an obligation to one another. There are different levels of commitment. At first, a couple may simply agree not to go out with others. In time, the commitment may become a plan for marriage.

How Do You Know It's Love?

People have long struggled with the question, "How can I be sure it's love?" They may have believed themselves in love in the past, only to discover that their feelings changed. Learning from past relationships will help you recognize the kind of love that makes a relationship last.

Real love is based on caring and trust. It requires giving as well as receiving. People who love each other have mutual interests and a desire to work together toward common goals.

How do you know whether the love you feel is the kind that will last? Ask yourself whether you have enough in common with the other person. Do you have similar values and compatible goals for the future? Does your love motivate you to take action to benefit the person you love? Does the relationship make you a better person? It's important to give a relationship enough time to develop and to learn all you can about the other person. One way to tell whether love will last is simply to give it time and find out whether it endures.

Marriage

When two people determine that their love is the kind that makes for a lasting relationship, they usually start thinking about marriage. Plans for marriage typically begin with an engagement period.

Getting Engaged

When people get engaged, they make a promise to marry. The engagement period—which may last a few months, a year, or longer—serves several useful purposes. Getting engaged communicates to family and friends that the two people have made a commitment. The engagement period gives the couple time to plan for their wedding and for their married life. It also gives them a final opportunity to test the relationship and make sure that marriage is the right decision.

Here are some of the questions that couples need to ask and answer during their engagement:

- Where will we live?
- What do we want our daily life to be like?
- How will we manage household tasks and finances?
- Will either of us continue our education? If so, how will we pay for it?
- Will we both have careers? What if a career change requires relocation?
- Do we want to have children? If so, how many? How will we raise them?
- Do we agree on religious matters? If not, how will we handle religious differences?
- How will we observe family holiday traditions?

At one time, engagements were considered legal contracts and were rarely broken. Today, broken engagements are not unusual. Why do people change their minds? Some people realize that they rushed the decision to get engaged. They decide to slow down and give the relationship more time to develop. Some find that their feelings for their partner have changed over time. Others discover they are not ready to take on the responsibilities of marriage.

A broken engagement brings a sense of loss and can be very painful. However, it's better to call off an engagement than to ignore the warning signs that the marriage won't last.

Marriage Laws

Every state has laws governing marriage. Marriage laws serve to legalize the couple's agreement, regulate property rights, and provide protection for children. Because the laws differ from state to state, engaged couples need to check the laws for the state in which they will marry. Examples of the legal requirements for marriage are shown in Fig. 22-7.

Examples of Marriage Laws

Mutual consent. All states require mutual consent for marriage. If either party is against the idea, the marriage is not valid.	**Monogamy.** All states have laws that require monogamy—marriage to only one person at a time.	**Marriage age.** Most states allow people to marry after they reach 18. Parental consent is needed for marriages below that age.
Physical requirements. Most states require a blood test shortly before marriage to show that the partners do not have certain communicable diseases.	**Waiting period.** Most states give couples time to "think it over" by requiring a waiting period of one to five days before or after the license is issued.	**Marriage license.** All states require couples to obtain a license in order to marry. The license serves as a legal record of the marriage.
Marriage officials. State laws identify officials who may perform a marriage ceremony. Officials include members of the clergy and civil authorities such as judges and mayors.	**Prohibited marriages.** All states prohibit marriage between close blood relatives, such as sisters and brothers, uncles and nieces, and aunts and nephews. Some prohibit marriage between cousins.	**Annulment.** State laws allow annulment of a marriage if the legal requirements for marriage were not met. An annulment means that no valid marriage ever existed.

Fig. 22-7. The marriage laws of each state are similar in some ways, but vary in certain details.

What Makes a Marriage Strong?

Choosing the right person does not guarantee that a marriage will succeed. Life brings constant challenges—career changes, the birth of children, illness, financial problems, and other events—that can test a marriage. Dealing with such issues while maintaining a close, caring relationship requires effort. When deciding whether to marry, you'd be wise to consider how well a potential partner deals with change and difficulty.

One of the keys to a strong marriage is communication. Partners who express their feelings, discuss issues, and make decisions together will have a happier relationship. Another key is sharing. When couples share responsibilities so that neither partner feels overburdened, their marriage will be stronger. Couples also need to be able to resolve conflicts. Even the most devoted partners don't agree on everything. Above all, the couple must be committed to making the marriage work. See Fig. 22-8.

Fig. 22-8. Communication and sharing are two of the keys to a strong marriage. What other qualities contribute to marital harmony?

When Marriages Fail

Marriages are more likely to end in divorce today than in the past. Almost half of first marriages in the United States end in divorce. Marriages fail for many different reasons. Some people don't take the commitment seriously and bail out at the first sign of trouble. Some have unrealistic expectations. In some marriages, the partners change in ways that make them less compatible. Disagreements about money are often cited as a factor contributing to divorce. Another major reason for divorce is the tendency for some people to get married before they are ready to take on adult responsibilities.

The high divorce rate does not necessarily mean that there are more unhappy marriages. In the past, people often stayed in a troubled marriage for financial reasons, because society disapproved of divorce, or "for the sake of the children." Today, people are more likely to give up on an unhappy marriage. Most divorces occur during the first few years of marriage.

Teen Marriage

Even for mature adults, marriage presents enormous challenges. For teens, the problems can be even more difficult. Teen marriages do not have a high rate of success. The pressures are greatly increased when teens marry because of a pregnancy. More than three-fourths of these marriages end in divorce.

Some teens do build successful marriages, but most feel it's better to wait until they are older. Delaying marriage gives them a chance to pursue their education and career goals. Marrying later also brings more maturity. Partners have had time to learn more about themselves. This helps them make smarter decisions about who they want to marry and what they want in a marriage. See Fig. 22-9.

Remaining Single

In the past, everyone was expected to get married, and most people did. Today, a large percentage of people remain single. Some have always been single; others are single again following a divorce or the death of a spouse.

People stay single for a variety of reasons. Some have not yet met a person they want to marry. Others prefer the independence and freedom of single living. They choose to focus on other fulfilling aspects of life, such as a career, travel, or community service. Some people remain single so that they can care for aging family members. Many people expect to marry someday, but delay marriage in order to complete their education or make progress in their career.

Whatever the reasons for remaining single, it's important to recognize that marriage is a choice, not an obligation. Getting married because your family expects it or because all your friends are getting married is not a good idea. The decision to marry should be based not on what others expect of you, but on what you want for yourself.

Fig. 22-9. Many teens believe that they will make better decisions about marriage if they wait until they are older and have had more time to learn what is important to them.

22 *Review & Activities*

Chapter Summary

- Going out in groups has benefits, as does going out as a couple.

- When you start going out with someone, you take on new responsibilities.

- Sexual responsibility includes understanding the risks, handling sexual feelings, and resisting sexual pressure.

- Crushes, infatuation, jealousy, and breakups bring difficult emotions.

- An engagement period gives a couple time to prepare for marriage.

- Every state has laws governing marriage.

- Not all marriages succeed, but communication, sharing, and commitment help create a strong marriage.

- There are many possible reasons for staying single.

Reviewing Key Terms & Ideas

1. What benefits can be gained by going out with others?

2. What are two advantages of going out in a group rather than as a couple?

3. Explain how respect relates to responsible dating.

4. Why should you agree on what you will do on a date before you go out?

5. In what ways is sexual activity emotionally damaging for teens?

6. How are **sexually transmitted diseases** spread? Why must they always be treated?

7. What is the benefit of practicing **abstinence**?

8. What is the difference between **infatuation** and real love?

9. If jealousy is a problem for a couple, what advice should they follow?

10. Give three guidelines for ending a relationship.

11. Give five examples of topics couples should discuss during their engagement.

12. How does communication contribute to a strong marriage?

13. Name four reasons why some marriages fail.

14. Give three examples of why someone might choose to remain single.

Thinking Critically

1. **Analyzing Viewpoints.** Knowing the dating situation at your school, what would your chief concerns be if you were the parent of a teen who was starting to date? What rules would you set for your son or daughter?

2. **Drawing Conclusions.** How do crushes and infatuation help prepare people for real love?

Applying Your Knowledge

1. **Dating Etiquette.** In groups, discuss guidelines for dating etiquette. What actions can show your date, and your date's family, that you are a thoughtful, considerate person? What are the benefits of making a good impression? Share your group's conclusions with the class.

2. **Abstinence Pledge.** Write a pledge for teens that promotes abstinence. In your pledge, include at least three reasons for choosing abstinence.

3. **Breaking Up.** Work with a partner to act out ending a relationship in a clear but tactful way. Use what you learned in the text to guide you.

4. **Readiness for Marriage.** Complete the sentence, "People are not ready for marriage until they…" List as many signs of readiness as you can think of. Be prepared to explain the items on your list.

Making Connections

1. **Math.** Find a reliable source of statistics related to marriage. Choose a specific set of statistics to illustrate (for example, the number of teen marriages per year over the last ten years). Create a graph that illustrates your data. Be prepared to explain why the type of graph you chose is appropriate for your purpose.

2. **Social Studies.** In a small group, research marriage customs in another culture. Report your findings to the class.

Managing Your Life

Rules to Live By

Going on a date is easier if you know ahead of time what the rules are. Make a list of the rules that your family has set. These may cover where you are (and are not) allowed to go, what time you must be home, and so on. Add to that list the rules that you make for yourself. These may include rules about paying your own way, being involved in decision making, knowing how you will get home after a date, and so on. Include rules for specific situations that you might encounter, such as being invited to a party where alcohol and drugs are available. Save your list and refer to it before going out. Add to the list when new situations require additional rules.

Using Technology

1. **Desktop Publishing.** Use appropriate software to create a brochure giving teens advice for dating responsibly and avoiding the risks of sexual activity. Include guidelines given in the text, but add your own ideas as well.

2. **Presentation Software.** Research the marriage laws in your state. Find out what the law says about the minimum age for marriage, the waiting period, marriages that are prohibited, and other legal requirements. Using appropriate software, prepare an electronic presentation that summarizes your findings.

People in the Workplace

Key Terms

- sociability
- tact
- stereotype
- initiative
- constructive criticism
- rivalry

Objectives

- **Explain** how workplace relationships differ from friendships.
- **Describe** strategies for getting along with coworkers.
- **Give guidelines** for getting along with supervisors.
- **Suggest** positive responses to relationship problems in the workplace.
- **Discuss** the need to keep work life and personal life separate.

Imagine that you're looking back on your first six months on the job. Write a journal entry that explains how you went about establishing good relationships with your coworkers and supervisor.

By the end of his first week at work, Manny had finally learned the names of his coworkers and had a pretty good idea of what was expected of him. He was part of a large team working on a project that would last several months. Already Manny realized that if he wanted to succeed, he would have to get along with the others on the team. They were all different ages and had different backgrounds, personalities, and attitudes. Manny knew that building good working relationships would take time, but he was excited to be working with such an interesting variety of people.

Workplace Relationships

In some ways, workplace relationships are different from the relationships you have with friends. You can't choose your coworkers—they come with the job. You may have little in common with some of your coworkers except that you work at the same place. Similarly, you can't end a workplace relationship the way you can end a friendship if it doesn't work out. You have to find ways to get along with everyone at work, even people you don't particularly like. See Fig. 23-1.

Because the main focus is getting the job done, workplace relationships tend to be less close than friendships. Of course, some of your coworkers might also be friends. That's fine, as long as you remember to keep your friendship separate from your working relationship. That means when it comes to job-related matters, such as dividing tasks or coordinating work schedules, you must treat your friends just the same as other coworkers. Showing favoritism to your friends is a sure way to cause resentment among other employees.

Fig. 23-1. Although you can't choose your coworkers, you can choose to get along with them. What are some advantages of working with people of different ages and backgrounds?

Viewpoints

Friends at Work

If getting along with coworkers is good, being friends with them would be better—or would it? Some people have problems with that idea.

Gerald: I always work better with people when we're friendly, but not friends—not the way I'm friends with people outside of work. At work, friendship can interfere with doing your job. Suppose you get promoted. Could you give orders to a friend? Could you report a friend to a supervisor if you had to? It causes too much conflict for everyone. The whole place suffers.

Suzanne: I don't push it, but I always try to make friends with people at work. I think it's a bonus. A job can get tough and stressful. When you like and care about the people you work with, it gives a feeling of "we're all in this together." It motivates you. And it's great to find people to enjoy things with outside of work. I mean, you can never have too many friends, right?

Seeing Both Sides ~ What qualities are common to friendships and good workplace relationships? How would a friendship with a coworker need to be different from other friendships in order to succeed?

You and Your Coworkers

Good working relationships make your job more enjoyable. Just as important, they contribute to a positive and productive work environment. The qualities listed here are among those that can help you work effectively with others and avoid friction. No matter where you work, now or in the future, you'll find them useful.

- **Sociability.** You don't have to be friends with everyone on the job, but you need to be sociable. **Sociability** means behaving in a friendly manner and enjoying other people's company. Smiling, saying hello, and being pleasant to people on the job are ways to be sociable. See Fig. 23-2.

- **Tact.** People who have **tact** know what to do or say in order to avoid offending others. Saying "You might find it works better if you do it this way" is more tactful than saying "You're doing that all wrong."

- **Fairness.** Always treat coworkers fairly. Recognize the efforts of others and give credit where it's due. If you're involved in assigning tasks, do so in a way that distributes the workload as evenly as possible.

- **Patience.** After you've been on the job awhile, you might be asked to teach a coworker a skill or to train a new employee. Have patience with the other person's learning process and mistakes. Remember, you were new on the job once too.

- **Sense of humor.** A sense of humor contributes to good workplace relationships. In a tense situation, laughter can lighten things up and relieve stress.

Combating Stereotypes

The American workplace is highly diverse. It presents you with an opportunity to work with people of different ages, genders, cultures, backgrounds, and abilities. Such diversity enables you to observe and understand other people's customs, beliefs, and ways of doing things.

For a diverse workplace to succeed, workers must avoid thinking in terms of stereotypes. A **stereotype** is an expectation that all people in a particular group will have the same qualities or act the same. Stereotypes are harmful and unfair because they don't acknowledge individual differences.

The best way to combat stereotypes is to treat people as individuals rather than as part of a group. Don't form an opinion of anyone before you get to know the person. Keeping an open mind and treating everyone fairly will help you build good working relationships.

Fig. 23-2. Breaks and lunch hours provide opportunities to be sociable. Why is it a good idea to take advantage of these opportunities?

Doing Your Part

You're more likely to get along with your coworkers if you do one simple thing: pull your own weight. That means knowing what is expected of you and doing it. Your coworkers—as well as your supervisor, customers, and anyone else you interact with on the job—must be able to depend on you. Doing your part is especially important on a team project. If one person falls behind, the whole team suffers.

Doing your part also means putting in extra effort when needed. If someone calls in sick, you might have to take on some of that person's work. If your team is behind schedule and facing a crucial deadline, you might have to work late. When you show that you're willing to do what is needed to get the job done, others will notice and appreciate it.

Fig. 23-3. Arriving on time for a meeting is a sign of respect. What are some other simple ways to show respect at work?

Working Cooperatively

In any job, you have to work cooperatively with others to achieve common goals. You and your coworkers must coordinate your efforts so that everything goes smoothly. You can't each go off in your own direction.

Cherie discovered this the hard way. She was assigned to a project with four coworkers and was eager to do a good job. Her piece of the project seemed quite separate from the others, so she didn't see the point of going to team meetings. She thought she could put the time to better use by concentrating on her own tasks. In the end, because Cherie didn't understand what the others needed, parts of her work were off target and had to be redone. Cherie realized that instead of saving time, she had wasted it—and annoyed her coworkers in the process.

Workplace Etiquette

Good manners are as important in the workplace as in any other area of life. Workplace etiquette is simply a matter of showing consideration and respect. For example, listen to other people's ideas, even if you don't agree with them. In meetings, give people a chance to be heard without interrupting.

Another way to show respect is to value other people's time. Don't disturb others when they are busy unless absolutely necessary.

If you need to discuss something with your supervisor or a coworker, ask when it would be convenient to meet. Be on time for meetings, and keep discussions brief and to the point. See Fig. 23-3.

You should also respect other people's space and privacy. If you share a work area, keep your part of it tidy. Don't snoop in a coworker's desk, file cabinet, or locker. Avoid listening to other people's telephone calls and private conversations or looking at their computer screens. Treat other people's computer files the way you would treat personal letters—don't open them unless they are addressed to you. If you do accidentally read or overhear something not intended for you, ignore it. Remember, respect is a two-way street. When you show respect for your coworkers, you'll gain their respect in return.

Communicating on the Job

Communication is an important part of any job. When you work as part of a team, speaking and listening are especially important. You need to be able to provide information that the team needs and receive feedback and information from other team members.

In most jobs, the ability to write is also a key skill. Whether you're writing a business letter, a memo, or an e-mail, good writing helps you get your point across clearly and concisely. A poorly written document could cause confusion and misunderstanding.

Communication at work also means asking for help when you need it. Don't be afraid to ask questions or to admit that you don't understand something. To be effective, you need a clear idea of your tasks and responsibilities. Most supervisors are happy to provide guidance. Coworkers can also be a source of advice and tips.

You and Your Supervisor

The same qualities that enable you to get along with your coworkers will help you get along with your supervisor. You must remember, though, that supervisors play a different role than coworkers. Supervisors are responsible for making sure that people do their work and that projects get completed. That means assigning tasks, checking progress, and resolving problems. Getting along with supervisors requires that you recognize their authority, take initiative when appropriate, and accept criticism when it is offered.

Fig. 23-4. By asking for guidance when needed, you can benefit from your supervisor's knowledge and experience.

Accepting Authority

Supervisors have special knowledge, training, or experience that gives them the right to oversee the work of others. You are accountable to your supervisor for the quality of your work, and your supervisor is responsible for evaluating your performance and giving you feedback.

As an employee, you need to respect and accept your supervisor's authority. Recognize that your supervisor has knowledge and experience that you don't have. Follow the instructions you are given, and ask for clarification or advice when you need it. Keep your supervisor informed about your work at all times. If any problems arise, discuss them with your supervisor and offer suggestions for solving them. See Fig. 23-4.

Taking Initiative

Although following instructions is important, supervisors also appreciate **initiative**—willingness to do what needs to be done without being asked. The key to taking ini-

tiative is knowing when it's appropriate to move ahead on your own. Ask yourself:

- Is this task within the scope of my job?
- Do I have the knowledge and skills to do this task on my own?
- Have I handled similar tasks successfully in the past?
- Would my supervisor appreciate not being bothered with the details of this task?
- Has my supervisor encouraged me to take initiative?

If the answers are "yes," this is probably a good time to show initiative. Even so, it's best to inform your supervisor about what you plan to do. You might say, "I noticed the stockroom shelves have gotten pretty disorganized. I'll straighten them up tomorrow if it's all right with you." When you use your initiative, you show that you take your work seriously and have your employer's interests in mind. Your supervisor will notice and appreciate your effort.

Responding to Criticism

Your supervisor is responsible for making sure you do your work correctly. If you make mistakes, or if the quality of your work is poor, your supervisor will talk to you about it. Good supervisors don't just tell you what you're doing wrong. They offer **constructive criticism**, feedback that includes suggestions for ways you can learn and improve.

If you receive criticism, try not to be defensive or take it personally. Be objective and professional. Remember that your supervisor wants you to succeed. The goal of the criticism isn't to put you down, but to correct your mistakes and improve your performance. See Fig. 23-5.

Problems in Workplace Relationships

Problems can arise in workplace relationships just as in other types of relationships. Short of quitting your job, you can't walk away from your relationship with a coworker. Instead, you have to confront the problem and find a way to deal with it. Common problems that impact workplace relationships include conflicts, rivalries, and harassment. As you read about these problems, consider how you could respond to each.

Conflicts

Workplace conflicts can result from personality differences, poor communication, jealousy, and other factors. Conflicts are most likely to flare up when people are under stress. A tight deadline or an especially busy period can cause tempers to become short.

If the conflict is minor, you may be able to resolve it simply by talking things over. Try using the conflict resolution skills explained in Chapter 18. If the conflict is serious or prolonged, talk with your supervisor. Unresolved workplace conflicts can poison the atmosphere for everyone and must be dealt with as quickly as possible.

Some companies have formal policies and procedures for resolving employee conflicts. If the conflict persists, mediation by a neutral third party may be necessary.

Fig. 23-5. When you receive criticism of your work, be appreciative, not defensive. Remember that constructive criticism can help you improve and succeed.

Rivalries

Rivalry, in which people compete against each other to gain an advantage, is to be expected in the workplace. It's natural for people to compete for recognition or to get ahead. Some companies encourage rivalry by offering rewards and incentives. Such rivalries can have both positive and negative effects on coworker relationships. Ideally, rivalries among individuals or teams motivate people to do their best without causing hard feelings. Sometimes, though, workplace rivalries get out of hand and cause anger and resentment.

Some employers work to minimize rivalries by emphasizing cooperation rather than competition. Coworkers who see themselves as members of a team are less likely to compete just to gain an advantage over someone else. Good team players are more concerned about achieving team goals than about who gets the credit. See Fig. 23-6.

Harassment

Workplace harassment can take many forms. Taunting, intimidation, and threats are all examples of harassment. Sexual harassment involves unwelcome behavior of a sexual nature, whether physical or verbal.

Any kind of harassment in the workplace is unacceptable. It should not be tolerated, nor should it be ignored. Unless someone takes action to stop the behavior, it is likely to continue. If you experience or observe harassing behavior, tell the harasser to stop, then report the situation to your supervisor. If the harasser *is* your supervisor, talk to the next higher manager. Workplace harassment is offensive and violates people's rights. All companies have policies to prevent such behavior and procedures for dealing with people who break the rules.

Fig. 23-6. In a cooperative work environment, team members celebrate successes together. Why might some employers prefer a competitive working atmosphere?

Work Life and Personal Life

Have you ever had to wait in a store or other business because the person who was supposed to be helping you was chatting on the phone or with a coworker? How did that make you feel? Such situations are a good reminder that while you're at work, you should stay focused on the job that you're being paid to do. Keep personal and family matters out of the workplace as much as possible. You'll be a better employee and get along better with your coworkers.

Sometimes personal distractions come from within the workplace. A coworker might come by your work area and start a conversation that's not work-related. It's fine to make small talk with your coworkers occasionally, but keep it brief. After a minute or two, say something like, "I'd like to talk more, but I really need to get back to work now." If you want to continue the conversation, you might offer to meet for lunch or after work.

More often, distractions come from outside the workplace. Everyone has family responsibilities and personal matters that they need to attend to. Responsible workers make the necessary arrangements so that these matters won't disrupt the workplace. For example, working parents arrange for child care or after-school activities. They have a backup plan in case the children can't go to school or to their regular care provider.

As much as possible, deal with personal and family matters outside working hours. If you must make a personal call, do it during your lunch hour or break. Follow any rules about using the company's phones or e-mail system for personal matters. Discourage family members and friends from contacting you at work unless there's an emergency. Help them understand that you have an obligation to your employer and your coworkers.

TEXTLINK≈

Chapter 13 provides more advice for *balancing multiple roles.*

While the goal is to keep work life and personal life separate, it's not always possible. If personal or family matters arise that can't wait, deal with them, but take as little time as possible. If there's a continuing concern in your personal life that may impact the job, talk to your supervisor. Together, try to work out a solution that's fair to both of you.

Character IN ACTION

Sensitivity to Personal Problems
Keep in mind that your coworkers also have personal lives. If a coworker seems distracted, anxious, or short-tempered, consider the possibility that personal or family issues may be the cause. You shouldn't try to pry into his or her personal life to find out. Just be sensitive to the possible need for a little extra tact and understanding. How might you show support for a coworker while respecting his or her privacy?

Chapter Summary

- Workplace relationships differ from friendships in several ways.
- Qualities such as sociability, tact, and fairness improve workplace relationships.
- Stereotypes are harmful and unfair.
- Doing your part, working cooperatively, and communicating clearly can help you get along with coworkers.
- Workplace etiquette is a matter of being respectful and considerate.
- To get along with your supervisor, you need to accept authority, take initiative, and respond appropriately to criticism.
- Conflicts, rivalries, and harassment are examples of workplace problems that you may have to deal with.
- Responsible employees recognize that work and personal life are separate.

Reviewing Key Terms & Ideas

1. Name three ways in which workplace relationships differ from friendships.
2. How can you demonstrate **sociability**?
3. What is **tact**?
4. How can a sense of humor help you get along with coworkers?
5. Why are **stereotypes** harmful? What can you do to overcome them at work?
6. Why is doing your part particularly important when you are part of a team?
7. Give four examples of workplace etiquette.
8. Name three ways to show that you accept your supervisor's authority.
9. What is **initiative**? What does taking initiative indicate to others?
10. What is the purpose of **constructive criticism**? Explain how an employee can respond to it positively.
11. What should you do if you experience a serious workplace conflict?
12. Give an example of workplace **rivalry**. How can it be minimized?
13. Why should you take action to prevent any kind of harassment in the workplace? What actions should you take?
14. Why should you keep work life and personal life separate?

Thinking Critically

1. **Making Predictions.** What kinds of situations would be especially difficult to deal with if you became best friends with one of your coworkers? Why?
2. **Making Judgments.** Give examples of the kinds of situations in which it would be appropriate to take initiative. In what kinds of situations would it be better to be guided by your supervisor?

Applying Your Knowledge

1. **Wanted: Interpersonal Skills.** Examine advertisements for job openings in the newspaper or on the Internet. Keep notes on what interpersonal skills are mentioned in the ads. Share and discuss your findings with the class. Which interpersonal skills were mentioned most often? Why do you think employers emphasize them?

2. **Accepting Criticism.** Working in pairs, take turns giving and responding to constructive criticism. Afterwards, discuss what specific types of criticism were most helpful and what responses were most appropriate.

3. **Work and Personal Life.** Ask adult friends or family members who work outside the home to describe their experience of trying to keep work and personal life separate. What kinds of situations are hardest to deal with? How are such problems resolved?

Making Connections

1. **Social Studies.** Use the Internet to gather information about federal and state laws concerning discrimination and harassment in the workplace. Summarize the main provisions of each law you find. Share your findings with the class.

2. **Language Arts.** What's your opinion of workplace rivalry? Write a brief essay explaining why you think it should be encouraged or discouraged.

Managing Your Life

Practicing Sociability

Sociability in the workplace requires being friendly but not intrusive. Sociable people feel comfortable greeting others and making small talk. Why not start practicing your sociability skills now? In your encounters with neighbors and acquaintances, practice making the kinds of conversations you would have with coworkers. Keep a journal of your experiences. If some attempts don't go well, identify ways you can improve next time.

Using Technology

1. **Telecommuting.** Technology allows many employees to work from home, communicating with coworkers by e-mail, telephone, or other means. Interview an employee or employer who has experience with telecommuting to learn how it affects workplace relationships. Do telecommuting employees feel isolated? Is teamwork affected? What strategies can help? Report your findings to the class.

2. **E-mail.** With a partner, practice writing business e-mails. Assume the roles of a supervisor and an employee. The first e-mail should be from the employee to the supervisor regarding a conflict with another worker. Reply to one another's messages for a total of four e-mails. Follow the guidelines in the chapter.

Career Options
Human Services

*H*uman services is a vital and thriving career field. Workers in this area care for children, families, and consumers, helping them get through daily life and resolve problems. This field offers career opportunities for people of varying levels of education and experience. Human services can be divided into three broad sectors: Child Care and Development; Family Services; and Consumer Services. For most occupations in this career cluster, the employment outlook is good.

Main Employers

- Child care centers
- Schools
- Guidance agencies
- Nursing homes
- Home care agencies
- Social service agencies
- Consumer agencies

Human Services Job Opportunities

Industry Segment	Entry Level	Additional Education and/or Training	Advanced Education and/or Training
Child Care and Development	▪ Child Care Worker ▪ Camp Counselor	▪ Child Welfare Worker ▪ Parent Educator ▪ Preschool Teacher	▪ Child Care Center Director ▪ School Social Worker ▪ Child Development Specialist
Family Services	▪ Nursing Home Aide ▪ Home Care Aide ▪ Community Service Worker	▪ Caseworker ▪ Recreational Therapist ▪ Vocational Counselor ▪ Social Services Assistant	▪ Marriage Guidance Counselor ▪ Family Counselor ▪ Social Services Director
Consumer Services	▪ Product Safety Tester ▪ Personal Shopper	▪ Consumer Advisor ▪ Consumer Credit Counselor	▪ Consumer Education Specialist ▪ Consumer Fraud Investigator

When I was 13 years old, my parents got divorced. They explained that it wasn't my fault, but I still felt maybe something I had done had caused their breakup. As an only child, I didn't have anyone to talk to about my concerns. I really could have used a sympathetic listener.

As I grew up, I wanted to help other children and families get through tough times. I wanted to be that sympathetic listener I once so desperately needed.

Today, I work as a family counselor in private practice. Married couples and families come to me for a variety of reasons, including marital problems, substance abuse, physical abuse, and emotional disorders. I help them understand their problems, how they affect relationships, and how they can be resolved. When I help families make positive changes, it's very rewarding.

Becoming a family counselor required education beyond four years of college. After college, I spent two years completing a master's program in marriage and family therapy. During that time, I volunteered at a women's shelter and at a crisis hotline to get required experience working directly with clients. After receiving a master's degree, I continued my education for an additional four years and earned a doctorate (Ph.D.) in marriage and family therapy.

Check It *Out!*

Choose an occupation of interest in human services. Contact someone in your community in this field and arrange to observe the person at work, or conduct a telephone interview. Report what the job involves, working conditions, and its plusses and minuses.

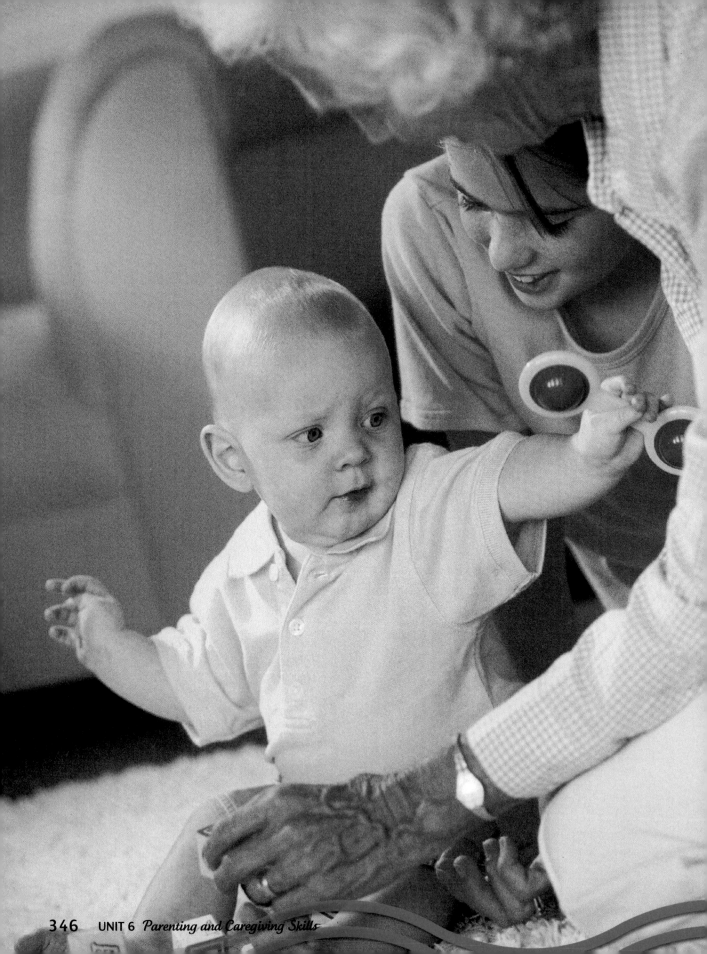

6

Parenting and Caregiving Skills

CHAPTER 24

Life Span Development

Key Terms

- large motor skills
- small motor skills
- heredity
- environment
- developmental tasks
- prenatal
- embryo
- fetus
- reflexes
- eye-hand coordination
- parallel play
- cooperative play
- hormones

Objectives

- **Discuss** reasons for studying human development.
- **Describe** the five areas of development.
- **Give examples** of how heredity and environment influence development.
- **Explain** changes that occur at different stages of development.
- **Discuss** the special needs of people with disabilities.

Humans go through many stages between infancy and old age. Which stage do you think is the most interesting? Write a paragraph explaining why.

*S*onia has been away at college for almost a year and hasn't seen her baby cousin Max since he was a young infant. Back then he was a baby who drank from a bottle, slept a lot, and could barely sit up. Now he's a little dynamo. He can walk across the room, feed himself, play with his toys, and charm his older cousin. Sonia can't believe what a difference a few months can make.

The Journey of Development

What Sonia witnessed was just the beginning of a long journey. Human development is a process that continues throughout the life span. From the phenomenal growth that takes place in infancy to the more gradual transitions of the later years, change is one of the constant features of life's journey. Consider the many ways that you have changed just in the past few years. This fascinating process will continue through the rest of your life. See Fig. 24-1.

Studying human development will help you better understand yourself and those around you. It helps prepare you to care for children—perhaps as an older sibling, cousin, babysitter, parent, or even teacher. An understanding of human development also helps you relate to people at other stages, such as your parents or older relatives.

Areas of Development

Human development is an amazing, complex process. Each person develops into a unique individual with his or her own appearance, abilities, and personality. Nevertheless, certain general patterns can be seen in the development process. The changes that take place as you develop can be grouped into five areas. In each area, changes continue throughout life.

Fig. 24-1. Human development is an amazing journey of constant change. Some of these changes are easier to see and measure than others, but all are significant.

- **Physical development.** Changes in appearance, strength, and coordination are all part of physical development. Physical development involves large and small motor skills. **Large motor skills** use the large muscles in the arms and legs. You use these skills to walk, run, swim, and lift things. **Small motor skills**, involving smaller body parts such as the hands and fingers, are needed for tasks such as writing, playing a musical instrument, and using tools. See Fig. 24-2.

- **Intellectual development.** This area of development involves your ability to think, understand, reason, and communicate. Young children first experience the world through their senses. Gradually they learn to organize the information their senses give them and put it into words.

- **Emotional development.** Infants have limited ways of expressing their emotions. They cry if they are displeased and smile if they are happy. As children mature, they learn to recognize and express more complex emotions and to handle them in socially acceptable ways.

- **Social development.** Children start to develop social skills at an early stage. They learn to get along with other children, share, and make friends. More complex social skills, such as cooperating, negotiating, and building different kinds of relationships, develop over time.

- **Moral development.** With guidance, children learn to understand right from wrong. Once they understand the difference, they develop a conscience that will eventually guide their behavior and help them develop moral standards.

The five areas of development are interrelated. For example, think of the development required to be able to speak. Physically, children need to have developed good hearing as well as control of the muscles used for speech. Intellectually, they need the mental capacity to communicate. Socially, they need to interact with others and imitate role models.

Nearly all children follow the same *sequence* of development, building on what they learn. They babble before they speak, for example, and crawl before they walk. What differs markedly from individual to individual is the *rate* of development. Some children develop more rapidly than others. One child begins to walk at ten months; another does so at 15 months. One child may use ten words at 18 months of age; another may use 50 words by that age. Each person develops in his or her own time.

Fig. 24-2. Physical development includes progress in motor skills. *What type of motor skills are these children demonstrating?*

Fig. 24-3. Through heredity, children inherit some of the characteristics of both biological parents.

Influences on Development

What makes development so highly individual? The source of your uniqueness is a complex interplay between the traits that you inherit and the environment you grow up in. The combination of these influences is different for every person.

Heredity

Heredity refers to the set of characteristics that you inherit from your parents and ancestors. You inherit these characteristics through *genes*, the basic units of heredity that are passed on from parents to their children. The genes determine physical traits such as eye color, hair color, height, and build. They may also help to determine your emotional makeup. For example, the tendency to be easygoing or shy may be inherited. See Fig. 24-3.

Environment

Your **environment**—everything that surrounds you—also has a profound impact on your development. Your environment includes your family, friends, home, school, neighborhood, and community.

Environmental influences are strong and complex. Home life, for example, influences children's development as they grow. A loving and supportive home environment will have positive effects on emotional development. A family's living conditions, economic status, culture, traditions, level of education, access to health care, and involvement in the community are other environmental aspects. All can influence a child's development.

Even technology affects development. Technological advances can bring a higher standard of living through better health care and more widespread education. Television and computer technology enable people to learn more about their world and expand their knowledge. On the other hand, spending too much time in front of a television or computer could cause people to miss out on social interaction. How might development be affected as a result?

Stages of Development

Humans develop in distinct stages that correspond roughly to chronological age. Each stage of development, from infancy onwards, is marked by certain **developmental tasks**—skills and abilities that are mastered as part of the maturing process. Some of these tasks are obvious, such as learning to walk. Others are more subtle, such as learning to think logically and reason. The very first stage of development takes place before a baby is born.

Prenatal Development

Prenatal means "before birth." Prenatal development refers to the process that begins with conception and ends with the birth of a baby. During the first eight weeks of pregnancy, the developing baby is called an **embryo**. During the embryo phase, all the major body structures and internal organs form and the heart begins to beat. From the ninth week until birth, the developing baby is referred to as a **fetus**. During these months, the bones harden, the muscles grow strong, and the body systems reach full development.

Good prenatal care is vital to healthy development of the unborn baby. Pregnant women need good nutrition, regular exercise, and proper medical care to give their baby the best possible start in life.

Infancy

In their first year of life, infants undergo dramatic changes in every area of development. The changes that take place during infancy occur more rapidly than at any other stage of life.

Physical Development ~ Newborn babies are entirely dependent on others, yet they have many inborn abilities that enable them to interact with their world. Madison was a typical newborn. She could use her five senses, although her vision was blurred until she was several months old. She also had several **reflexes**—automatic, involuntary responses. For instance, she could suck on a nipple and grasp a finger placed in her palm.

At first, Madison would simply gaze at her surroundings when she was awake. Soon she started to pick things up and put them in her mouth. This activity helped her develop **eye-hand coordination**—the ability to make precise movements with the hands in relation to what the eyes see. As her large motor skills developed, she learned to roll over, sit up, crawl, and eventually stand.

Intellectual Development ~ From the start, infants are eager to explore their world and learn about it. Soon after birth, Madison could follow the movement of objects and people with her eyes, and she would turn her head toward a sound. Gradually she learned to communicate vocally with others. She cried in different ways to express her hunger, anger, and discomfort. At three months, she could babble and coo at familiar people and toys. She began to imitate other people's actions, waving bye-bye and playing peekaboo. She also learned to respond to simple requests, such as "Point to your nose" or "Where are your shoes?"

Emotional Development ~ An important emotional task of infants is to develop trust. Through daily contact with her parents and caregiver, Madison learned that they would meet her needs for food, safety, cleanliness, and closeness. This gave her the security to learn and thrive.

More to Explore

Brain Development

The brain develops more rapidly during the first few years of life than at any other time. Babies are born with most of the brain cells they will need. However, their brains are "unfinished" and must make connections between the cells.

These brain connections are established and strengthened through stimulation. Looking into a baby's eyes, stroking, talking, and singing all stimulate the brain to release hormones that promote growth. Infants who are *not* exposed to stimulating sights, sounds, and experiences are more likely to have difficulty mastering language and learning other basic tasks. Early stimulation, therefore, is essential for brain development.

Social Development ~ Infants quickly develop basic social skills. Like most infants, Madison began to smile when she was three months old. By seven months, she was able to recognize familiar faces and voices and could respond to her name. At about the same time, she became fearful of people she did not recognize, showing that she knew the difference.

Toddlerhood

Physical growth usually slows as infants become toddlers. During this stage, which lasts from about age one to three, children master an amazing number of skills.

Physical Development ~ Most toddlers are walking by 15 months. José took his first steps at 13 months and was toddling everywhere soon after. By the time he was two,

José could run, climb, and walk up and down stairs by himself. His parents encouraged his efforts, but watched him constantly to prevent accidents. They also put a gate across the stairs.

As his small motor skills developed, José learned to feed and dress himself. He liked toys that he could take apart and put back together.

Intellectual Development ~ José's language skills grew from a few simple words to short phrases to complete sentences as he learned to express his needs, thoughts, and ideas. He began to grasp basic intellectual concepts, such as cause and effect. He knew, for instance, that if he dropped something, it would fall. He learned about size and space, and discovered that small objects could go on top of larger ones. José also enjoyed looking at books with colorful pictures and short, repetitive sentences. He could point to and name familiar pictures and objects. See Fig. 24-4.

Emotional Development ~ As José learned to do things for himself, he began to think of himself as a capable individual, separate from his parents and caregivers. His self-esteem grew as the people around him encouraged him. José often expressed strong emotions, but his moods changed quickly. For instance, he would scream while being bundled into his outdoor clothing, but clap his hands and laugh once he was in the car for a ride.

Fig. 24-4. As he plays with blocks, this toddler is learning about the size and shape of objects. What can toddlers learn from playing with water or sand?

Social Development ~ Toddlers tend to engage in **parallel play**, in which they play alongside other children but not with them. José's parents knew that this is a natural phase and did not yet expect him to share with other children.

Around the age of two, toddlers struggle to assert their independence—they want to do everything themselves. José's favorite words became "Me do!" Yet he still wanted reassurance that his parents were ready to help him. Toddlers often experience frustration at this stage, which may result in temper tantrums.

Moral Development ~ Toddlers begin to develop a sense of right and wrong. Through the reactions of caregivers to what they do, they discover that some behaviors are acceptable while others are not. Sometimes José would test the limits. By being patient but firm, his parents helped him learn the difference between right and wrong on a very basic level.

The Preschool Years

Preschoolers—children between the ages of three and five—are more independent than toddlers and have better control over their bodies. They are beginning to build skills in many areas that will help prepare them for school.

Physical Development ~ Preschoolers' large motor skills are well developed. They can hop, run in even strides, pedal a tricycle, and throw and catch a ball. Their small motor skills, too, are better developed than they were in toddlerhood. When Claire was a preschooler, for example, she could draw recognizable objects, print the letters in her name, and use scissors to cut paper. See Fig. 24-5.

Fig. 24-5. In small motor skills, this preschooler has made a lot of progress in a short amount of time. How will these skills help her when she starts school?

Intellectual Development ~ Most preschoolers begin to learn to count, identify colors, and recognize the letters of the alphabet. As their vocabulary grows, they learn to express more complex ideas. A typical preschooler, Claire was curious about everything around her and asked a lot of "how" and "why" questions. Her active imagination showed in her love of playing dress-up and pretending to be different characters.

Emotional Development ~ Because preschoolers have better language skills than toddlers, they can express themselves more easily and don't get so frustrated. Children in this stage are also less self-centered. Claire, for example, started to show empathy for others—that is, to understand that others have thoughts and feelings.

Preschoolers experience a full range of emotions, from fear and anxiety to joy and pride. They may display many fears because they can't always distinguish between fantasy and reality. For a while, Claire was afraid to go to bed at night because she feared that a monster would come out of her closet.

Social Development ~ During the preschool years, children move from parallel play to **cooperative play**, in which they play together in small groups. These play activities help them learn to take turns, share, and solve problems together. Around age four or five, a child is likely to choose another child, usually of the same sex, as a best friend.

Moral Development ~ Preschoolers have a rigid sense of right and wrong. They know that adults set rules, and they get upset when someone doesn't follow those rules. When something didn't go the way she thought it should, Claire could often be heard lamenting, "It's not fair!" Some people believe that preschoolers behave well simply in order to be rewarded or avoid punishment. However, others believe that they are beginning to understand basic moral concepts such as fairness and justice.

The School-Age Years

When children reach school age, they begin to spend large periods of time in a structured setting away from home. Interaction with other adults and with peers helps them build on their skills.

Physical Development ~ Children continue to grow physically at this stage, but the rate of growth slows down. Their baby teeth are replaced by permanent ones. School-age children can ride a bicycle and participate in games that involve more skillful running, jumping, and throwing. The continued development of small motor skills allows them to write and draw more precisely.

Intellectual Development ~ School-age children continue to be curious about their world. They ask many questions and acquire reasoning skills as they think about why and how things happen. They build on these skills to master more complex tasks. They learn to use symbols such as numbers and letters, which enables them to read and do simple arithmetic. See Fig. 24-6.

Emotional Development ~ As children develop intellectually, they outgrow their preschool fears. However, school-age children are more prone to feelings of stress caused by academic pressures or events at home, such as divorce or a major move. Children with high self-esteem and a supportive family are more likely to handle stress effectively.

Social Development ~ School-age children generally have more social opportunities outside the family. They form peer groups that help them learn how to negoti-

Fig. 24-6. The ability to do math problems requires symbolic thinking. *What can caregivers do to encourage children's math skills?*

Fig. 24-7. Like any stage of life, the teen years have their ups and downs. A positive attitude helps you enjoy the good times and cope with the challenges.

ate and compromise in group settings. During this stage, children also continue to develop skills that society values, such as sharing and considering the feelings of others.

Moral Development ~ School-age children begin to understand that many rules are flexible and can be changed. They care deeply about what other people think, and most want to be thought of as "good." Children's consciences take on a stronger role at this stage.

Adolescence

Adolescence is a time of exciting changes in all areas of development. It is the period in your life when you prepare for adulthood. Responding to the changes in a positive way eases the transition. See Fig. 24-7.

Physical Development ~ Adolescence begins with the onset of *puberty*, the bodily changes that indicate sexual maturity in the physical sense. These changes are triggered by **hormones**—natural chemicals that are released within the body and affect its systems. The age when this process begins and ends varies greatly among individuals, but the process is similar for everyone. One of the most obvious changes is the shape of the body as it takes on the characteristics of a man or a woman. Some changes, such as outbreaks of acne or the squeakiness of a developing male voice, can be awkward but are usually temporary. A sense of humor is helpful for dealing with the physical changes of adolescence.

Intellectual Development ~ During adolescence, new intellectual skills enable you to imagine the consequences of different actions and to think about alternatives. Equally important, you develop the ability to reflect on the results of your decisions and to learn from your mistakes. At this stage, you are also better able to reason and to think in abstract terms. You can think things through, consider different solutions to a problem, test new ideas, and form your own judgments.

Emotional Development ~ Hormones also affect emotions. Mood swings are common during adolescence, and many teens experience stress related to the changes they are going through. You may wrestle with the desire to be treated as an independent adult in some situations and to have someone take care of you in others. Adolescence also brings increased sexual awareness.

Social Development ~ As you move toward greater independence, it's typical to spend more time with your peers and less time with your family. Family is still important, though, and most teens continue to look to parents for advice. Friendships become deeper and more stable. Romantic feelings often develop during this stage. Still, many teens are not ready for one-to-one relationships and prefer to spend time with a group.

Moral Development ~ Most teens know the difference between right and wrong, but don't always act accordingly. Because you want to fit in and please others, you may feel pressured to go along with the crowd, even when doing so is not in your best interest. One of the responsibilities of becoming an adult is to examine your beliefs and traditions and develop a strong value system of your own.

Early Adulthood

Early adulthood stretches from the late teens to the late thirties, and can be an exciting time marked by many changes. This is when individuals determine who they are and what they want to do. For many people, these are some of the busiest years of their life, as they complete their education, establish a career, gain financial independence, and build long-term relationships.

Physically, young adults are at their peak. They have finished growing and have the potential to enjoy a high level of fitness. However, because many work in jobs that don't require much physical activity, they need to make an effort to stay active and fit to prevent later health problems.

Intellectually, young adults can enjoy the mental stimulation that comes from establishing a career and working toward career

Fig. 24-8. Young adulthood can be a busy and fulfilling stage of life. Developing relationships with friends and coworkers, and perhaps with one special person, is often a priority.

goals. Learning is a lifelong process, and those who recognize this and create opportunities to learn will benefit from it over the years.

Young adulthood is often a very sociable time. Many people enjoy exploring new interests and spending time with a variety of people. It is during this stage, too, that many people marry and start raising a family of their own. See Fig. 24-8.

Middle Adulthood

Middle adulthood, from the forties to the mid-sixties, is often a period of reflection. Many people at this stage of life take stock of their lives and reexamine their priorities. Some face major life events—perhaps divorce and remarriage, children leaving home, the birth of grandchildren, or the illness or death of parents. For many people in middle adulthood, life becomes a balancing act between work, family, and social commitments. Those in the so-called "sandwich generation," who care both for children and for aging parents, can be particularly stretched by conflicting demands.

Adults can remain physically fit during these years if they stay active and eat a healthy balance of nutritious foods. Still, sooner or later some physical changes associated with aging become noticeable, such as gray hairs or a need for reading glasses. Some respond to the signs of aging with alarm and a flurry of attempts to slow the process down. Others accept that they are growing older and concentrate on enjoying their families, careers, and involvement in their community.

Many adults realize their professional goals during this stage. Some decide to seek fulfillment and intellectual stimulation in a different field of work. Pursuing new challenges and keeping the mind active can help maintain mental fitness.

Late Adulthood

People are living longer than they used to. Thanks to advances in health care and medicine, many enjoy active and productive lives in their seventies, eighties, and beyond. It's not uncommon for older people to work beyond the normal retirement age, either because they want to or because they can't afford to stop working. Whether they are working or retired, people in this stage of life can find these years enjoyable—or not. A lot depends on a person's health, financial situation, and attitude.

It's true that this time of life has its drawbacks. Physical changes during the later years may cause people to slow down. The joints often become less flexible, and muscles may be weaker. Many older people experience some loss of vision or hearing. Other health problems associated with old age may develop. Sometimes mental abilities also decline with age. It may take longer to learn new tasks or to recall facts, and short-term memory loss often occurs. Emotionally and socially, many people in their later years have to deal with the death of a spouse and other loved ones.

In spite of these challenges, the majority of older people are able to lead active, fulfilling lives. A positive attitude is the key. Many seniors make a choice to stay as physically active as possible, to continue learning new things, and to maintain social relationships. They keep up with what is going on in the world and stay involved in their community. Older people who feel they are still making a useful contribution are most likely to gain satisfaction from their later years. See Fig. 24-9.

Fig. 24-9. Many older people enjoy reaching out to others by doing volunteer work. How do they benefit from such work?

Special Needs

Up to now, this chapter has focused on the typical pattern of development. Of course, no one follows the "typical" pattern exactly, since every person is unique. Some people, however, have special needs that must be recognized and met if they are to reach their full potential.

There are many possible kinds of special needs. Children who are gifted, for example, need challenging opportunities to develop their special abilities and talents.

Most special needs involve a disability of some kind. Disabilities can be present from birth, although they might not be recognized right away. In other cases, people become disabled later in life due to disease, injury, or problems of aging. There are many different types of disabilities, but they can be grouped into general categories. Here are some examples:

Fig. 24-10. This child has Down syndrome, a birth defect that leads to mental retardation. An encouraging approach will help her make the most of her abilities.

- **Physical disabilities** include disabilities that limit movement, vision, or hearing.

- **Mental disabilities** affect intellectual development and everyday life skills. There are many possible causes.

- **Learning disabilities** affect the ability to understand or use language. People with learning disabilities often have average or above average intelligence, but have difficulty with certain tasks—perhaps listening, reading, spelling, or doing math problems, for example.

- **Emotional problems** may be indicated by withdrawal from others, aggressiveness, or violence, especially if these behaviors are extreme or repeated.

Recognizing and meeting special needs is essential at any time of life. However, it's especially important during childhood, since the early years are such a crucial time for development. Fortunately, much is known today about appropriate support for children with special needs. Children with learning disabilities, for example, *can* learn. They just need instruction that is tailored to their needs. When a disability is correctly diagnosed and treated, much can be done to help the person reach full potential.

People with special needs are like everyone else in most ways. They have the same basic needs for friendship, respect, and dignity. Children with special needs, like all children, need love and guidance. The greatest desire of most people with disabilities is to fit in with others and be as independent as possible. See Fig. 24-10.

Chapter Summary

- Humans develop physically, intellectually, emotionally, socially, and morally.
- Heredity and environment combine to make each individual unique.
- Each stage of development is marked by the mastery of developmental tasks.
- During infancy and toddlerhood, dramatic changes take place.

- During the preschool and school-age years, children develop greater strengths in all areas.
- Adolescence is a transition stage between childhood and adulthood.
- Early, middle, and late adulthood each have their own rewards and challenges.
- Some people have special needs because their development does not follow the typical pattern.

Reviewing Key Terms & Ideas

1. Name three benefits of studying human development.

2. Briefly describe what's involved in each of the five areas of human development.

3. What is the difference between **large motor skills** and **small motor skills**?

4. What is **heredity**? Give two examples of traits that are influenced by heredity.

5. Give four examples of factors in a person's **environment** that might influence development.

6. What role do **developmental tasks** play in the maturing process?

7. What is the **prenatal** stage?

8. What are **reflexes**? Give two examples of reflexes that newborns have at birth.

9. What is **eye-hand coordination**?

10. What is the difference between **parallel play** and **cooperative play**?

11. Compare the moral development of preschoolers and school-age children.

12. How do **hormones** relate to the onset of adolescence?

13. Give examples of challenges that people often face in middle adulthood.

14. Describe four types of disabilities.

Thinking Critically

1. **Drawing Conclusions.** Why do you think some researchers are interested in studying twins who were separated at birth and grew up in different homes?

2. **Identifying Alternatives.** Suppose two children want the same toy. If you were the caregiver, how would you respond if the children were both infants? Both toddlers? Both preschoolers? Explain why each response would be appropriate.

Applying Your Knowledge

1. **Understanding Development.** In a small group, discuss the benefits of knowing what to expect of children and adults at each stage of development. Determine ways that you can put this knowledge to good use in your current life.

2. **Identifying Developmental Tasks.** Create a chart showing developmental tasks in each area of development from birth to age 12. Use additional sources of information if necessary.

3. **Aging Well.** Many people have made significant contributions to society late in life. Choose one such person and learn more about him or her. Focus on how the person's attitudes and actions can serve as a role model for aging well. Share your findings with the class.

Making Connections

1. **Science.** A number of scientists have developed significant theories of child development. They include Maria Montessori, Arnold Gesell, Jean Piaget, Lev Vygotsky, Erik Erikson, B. F. Skinner, Albert Bandura, and Robert Coles. Choose one to investigate. Summarize the person's contribution to the understanding of child development.

2. **Language Arts.** Coping with fear is a common theme in many picture books for preschoolers. Write a review of one such book that describes how it can help children learn to handle their fears.

Managing Your Life

Preparing for the Next Stage

You are about to begin the next stage of your development—early adulthood. Think about the changes it will bring. How can you prepare for those changes? For each area of development, write down your goals for maximizing your potential during your young adult years. Make sure each goal is specific and realistic. If necessary, break long-term goals into short-term goals. Then identify resources that could help you reach those goals. Save your notes and use them to guide your decisions and actions as you move into adulthood.

Using Technology

1. **Presentation Software.** Choose one of the developmental stages from infancy through the school-age years. Using appropriate software, prepare a presentation that summarizes what caregivers can expect of a child at that stage. Include suggestions for promoting healthy development in all areas.

2. **Internet.** Choose a specific disability that interests you. Use the Internet to gather information about it from reliable sources. Find out what special needs people with this disability might have. What strategies can help meet those needs? Share your findings with the class.

Providing Care

Objectives

- **Summarize** children's basic physical needs.
- **Describe** ways to keep children safe.
- **Explain** basic first aid and emergency procedures.
- **Compare** different types of child care services.
- **Discuss** care options for older adults.

Write about a time when you helped care for a young child or an older person. What did you learn from the experience?

*H*ave you ever been a caregiver? Anyone who is responsible for taking care of an infant or young child—on a long-term or short-term basis—is a **caregiver**. So is anyone who provides care for an older adult or a person with a disability who needs assistance.

Most children have several caregivers. Their primary caregivers—those who have the main responsibility for raising children—are usually the parents. Since taking care of children is an enormous job, parents usually need the help of others. Relatives, babysitters, and child care professionals may be among those who provide care occasionally or on a regular basis. All of these caregivers need parenting skills. **Parenting** means providing care, guidance, and support in order to promote a child's development. See Fig. 25-1.

Caring for anyone—children, older adults, or others—is a serious responsibility. You can prepare yourself by gaining the knowledge and skills you need to be an effective caregiver. This chapter and the ones that follow will help you get started. You can continue to learn more about caregiving by reading other books and articles, asking experienced caregivers for advice, and gaining experience of your own.

Meeting Children's Physical Needs

The most basic responsibility of caring for children is meeting their physical needs. Infants and young children depend on their caregivers for food, clothing, health care, and other requirements. If physical needs are not met, overall development may suffer.

Fig. 25-1. Parents and other caregivers are there to guide and protect children as they grow, learn, and explore the world around them.

- **Food.** Children need nutritious foods to promote healthy growth and development. Caregivers need to learn about appropriate foods and portion sizes for different ages. Food habits develop early in life, so caregivers play an important role in establishing healthful habits. For example, toddlers who are given fresh fruits instead of cookies and sweets may be less likely to have a "sweet tooth" as adults.

TextLink≈

You can learn more about *food for children* in Chapter 36.

- **Sleep.** Infants and young children need more sleep than teens and adults. Most infants and toddlers take one or two naps during the day and sleep as long as 12 hours at night. However, getting children to bed can be a challenge! Young children may resist going to bed, and older children often find creative reasons for staying up past their bedtime.

- **Clothing.** Infants need basic garments such as shirts and sleepers—and of course, lots of diapers. Toddlers and preschoolers are active and can get dirty quickly, so their clothes should be comfortable, durable, and easy to care for. Clothes that slip on and off easily encourage young children to learn to dress themselves.

- **Cleanliness.** Infants explore their world by touching and putting objects in their mouths, so be sure to keep toys and other favorite objects clean. Infants and children also need daily baths. Always check the water temperature before placing or allowing a child in the water, and never leave a young child alone in a bathtub.

- **Health care.** Infants need regular checkups during their first year to make sure they are developing normally. After the first year, children need less frequent checkups. Caregivers should make sure that children get **immunizations**—vaccines that prevent specific diseases. Health care providers can tell you what vaccines are recommended at what ages. Many child care centers and schools require proof of immunization before enrollment.

More to Explore

Preventing Abuse

Keeping children healthy and safe includes protecting them from abuse. Child abuse can take several forms, including physical abuse, emotional abuse, and sexual abuse. Neglect, another form of abuse, occurs when parents fail to meet children's basic needs. Of course, children are not the only ones who can suffer from abuse—its victims may include people of any age. Older adults, like children, are especially vulnerable to abuse.

No matter what form it takes, abuse is inexcusable and illegal. If you notice signs of possible abuse, such as unexplained injuries, take action to protect the victim from further harm. Every state has a hotline number to report suspected cases of abuse. You do not have to give your name. The people who answer have special training that enables them to assess the situation and determine what to do.

Keeping Children Safe

Safety should be a top priority for every caregiver. Accidents and injuries can have tragic results, but most can be avoided by taking some simple precautions.

Safety for Young Infants

You might think that a baby who is just a few weeks or months old couldn't get into much trouble. However, even very young infants can wriggle out of your grasp in an instant, and they love to put all sorts of things in their mouths. To prevent injuries, follow these safety rules:

- Keep small objects and all plastic bags away from the baby. They can cause choking or suffocation.

- Never leave a baby alone on a bed, dresser, or changing table, even for a moment. The baby could roll over and fall.

- Choose toys that are labeled safe for the baby's age. Inspect them regularly for loose pieces and other damage.

- Make sure the baby's crib and other equipment meet current safety standards.

Childproofing the Home

When babies learn to pull themselves up, crawl, and then walk, their world expands—and so do the potential hazards. Children this age are very curious and love to explore. They are often unaware of dangers around them. It's up to caregivers to provide a safe environment.

You can start by **childproofing** the home—identifying potential hazards and taking steps to keep them from causing harm. One good way to identify hazards is to explore on your hands and knees. At that

Fig. 25-2. Safety gates can be used to keep young children away from hazards. *Besides stairways, where might they be needed?*

level, it's easier to see potential dangers that you might not otherwise spot. Here are some steps to take when childproofing a home:

- Put plastic caps over electrical outlets that are not being used.

- Install safety gates at the top and bottom of stairs. See Fig. 25-2.

- Keep scissors, matches, lighters, and other dangerous objects out of children's reach. Store poisonous substances—such as cleaning products, chemicals, paints, and medicines—on high shelves, preferably behind doors that lock or have childproof latches.

- Make sure there is no risk of furniture, such as a dresser or television stand, toppling over on a climbing child. If necessary, secure the furniture to the wall.

- Make sure all windows that can be opened have secure screens.

- Move small appliances such as the toaster and iron out of reach. Unplug them when not in use.

- Teach children that heaters and the range are hot and must not be touched. Keep the handles of pots and pans turned toward the center of the range so that children can't grab them.

TEXTLINK≈

See Chapter 48 for more on *home safety.*

Safety Away from Home

Caregivers need to be equally concerned about children's safety when they are away from home. For any car journey, no matter how short, secure infants and children in approved safety seats that are installed in the back seat. See Fig. 25-3.

If you take children to a park or other public place, don't let them out of your sight. Be especially vigilant if you are near a swimming pool or other body of water. Choose playgrounds that have well-maintained equipment and soft ground cover.

When children are old enough to understand, teach them about "stranger danger." Tell them that they must never get into a car or agree to go anywhere with someone they don't know.

Fig. 25-3. The type of safety seat needed depends on the child's age and weight. Be sure you know the correct way to install and use any safety seats you have.

Dealing with Emergencies

No matter what precautions are taken, injuries can occur that need prompt action. Some are serious enough to require emergency procedures. The first rule for dealing with any emergency is to stay calm. When you do, you can more easily assess the situation and determine what needs to be done. Remember, too, that children are more likely to remain calm if you do.

Providing First Aid

To deal with common injuries, caregivers need to know the basics of first aid. **First aid** is emergency care or treatment given right away to an ill or injured person. Some common first aid procedures are described in Fig. 25-4.

Basic First Aid Procedures

PROBLEM	WHAT TO DO
Bites (animal or human)	Wash the wound with water. Cover it with sterile gauze. Call a physician for advice.
Bites (insect)	*For minor bites:* Wash the area and apply antiseptic. *For ticks:* Use tweezers to pull out the tick, then treat as a minor bite. *For bee, hornet, or wasp stings:* Scrape against the stinger with a flat object, such as a credit card, until you pull out the venom sac. Wash the area thoroughly and apply ice to prevent swelling. Some people are highly allergic to stings. If the victim is short of breath, feels faint, or has stomach pain, seek medical help immediately.
Broken bone	Seek emergency medical care. Do not try to straighten the limb.
Bruises	Wet a clean washcloth in cold water and wring it out. Gently apply it to the bruise.
Burns	*For minor burns:* Immediately run cold water on the burn for about five minutes. *For serious burns:* Go to the hospital or call an ambulance. Do not try to remove burned clothing.
Cuts and scrapes	Apply direct pressure to stop bleeding. Wash the wound, then apply antiseptic and a bandage. For deep cuts, seek medical help.
Foreign object in eye	Gently pull the lower lid down while the person looks up. If you can see the object, lightly touch it with the corner of a clean cloth to remove it. If you can't remove it, seek medical help.
Nosebleed	Keep the person seated and leaning forward. (Do not tilt the head back, as this may cause choking.) Apply direct pressure on the bleeding nostril for 10 minutes.
Poisoning	Call the poison control center immediately. Report the name of the substance and the amount swallowed. Follow the instructions you are given. If you are told to go to the hospital, take the container along.
Sprains	Apply ice to reduce any swelling. Wrap the injured limb in an elastic bandage and keep it elevated. Consult a physician if necessary.

Fig. 25-4. A course in first aid gives you knowledge and confidence for dealing with emergencies. Where can you get first aid training in your community?

Getting Help

If you are with someone who suffers a serious injury, such as a broken bone or severe bleeding, call the local emergency number immediately. In many areas you can call 911 for emergency assistance. Explain the nature of the emergency and give the location. Keep the victim warm to prevent shock, and offer reassurance until help arrives. In general, don't try to move an injured person.

First Aid for Choking

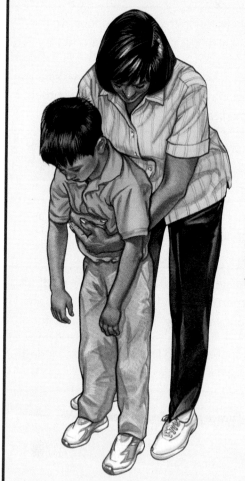

Emergency Procedures

In some situations, performing the right emergency procedures may save a life. Choking is one example of an emergency that needs immediate action. Choking occurs when a piece of food or some other object becomes lodged in a person's airway, preventing the person from breathing. You can save a choking victim by performing the procedure described in Fig. 25-5.

Another emergency procedure is used for someone who has stopped breathing or whose heart has stopped beating. **CPR**, which stands for *cardiopulmonary resuscitation*, combines rescue breathing with chest compressions. Rescue breathing forces air into the victim's lungs, while chest compressions help keep blood circulating. Only people who have been properly trained should perform CPR. If you are interested in learning this lifesaving technique, contact the American Red Cross or the American Heart Association.

Fig. 25-5. Quick action can help save a choking victim.

This technique is for children one year and older and for adults. If the victim is conscious and standing or sitting, but unable to speak, breathe, or cry, follow these steps:

1. Stand or kneel behind the victim and wrap your arms around the victim's waist.
2. Make a fist with one hand. Place the thumb side of your fist just below the victim's rib cage.
3. Use your other hand to grasp your fist. Press your clasped hands into the victim's abdomen with a quick upward thrust. This forces the air in the lungs to expel the object.
4. Repeat if necessary.

Choosing Child Care Services

If you become a parent, one of the many things you will have to think about is making child care arrangements. Parents have many different reasons for using child care services. Some couples decide they will both continue with their careers after their child is born. Many single parents have to arrange for child care so that they can earn a living. Some parents simply want to give their children opportunities to interact with other children. See Fig. 25-6.

Parents who decide to use child care have a number of options to choose from. The quality and availability of these options vary greatly, even within a single community. Parents want what is best for their children, but must also consider factors such as cost and convenience. Here are some of the options they may consider:

- **In-home care.** Parents may arrange for a caregiver to come to their home. This allows the child to stay in familiar surroundings.

- **Family child care.** Some caregivers look after a number of children in their own home. The children can enjoy a homelike setting and develop social skills as they play with one another.

- **Child care center.** This type of facility offer programs of carefully planned activities in an environment designed for children. Centers must meet health and safety standards in order to be licensed. The number of children per caregiver is monitored so that all children receive adequate supervision and care.

Fig. 25-6. Child care services enable parents to hold full-time jobs in the knowledge that their children are being well cared for.

- **Before and after school care.** Working parents of school-age children may need child care for a few hours before and after school each day. Such programs might be offered by community centers, local agencies, schools, or child care providers.

Caring for Older Adults

The percentage of older adults in the population has been rising. Thanks to improvements in health care and the standard of living, people can expect to live longer than ever before. While older adults often stay active and independent for a long time, many eventually need some level of assistance.

The amount of care that is needed depends on the situation. Some older people just need a hand with specific tasks such as cleaning, laundry, meals, and errands. Some need more extensive care for a short time while they recover from an injury or illness. People of any age who develop serious or chronic medical conditions may need long-term care. Those who have suffered severe strokes or who have some form of dementia, such as Alzheimer's disease, need almost constant supervision. The person's specific needs and the resources of the family must be taken into account when choosing care options.

Providing Care at Home

Most older adults prefer to stay in their own home as long as possible. They are more comfortable in familiar surroundings. In many cases, family members are able to provide enough assistance to allow the older person to remain at home. See Fig. 25-8.

For some older people, another option is to move in with family members. When Richie's great-grandfather Harold moved in, it was an adjustment for the whole family. Richie volunteered to give up his bedroom and share a room with his younger brother.

Fig. 25-7. Parents should talk with the director of any child care center that they are considering. If you were a parent, what questions would you want to ask?

Many parents spend a good deal of time choosing the right setting and the right caregivers for their children. They get recommendations, interview caregivers, and ask for references. They ask questions such as:

- How many children are assigned to each caregiver?

- What training and qualifications do the caregivers have?

- What activities are offered? How will they benefit my child?

Parents should also visit any child care facility that they are considering. They should observe how the caregivers relate to the children, inspect indoor and outdoor equipment for safety and cleanliness, and generally get a feel for the atmosphere of the place. See Fig. 25-7.

His dad built a ramp to the front door and installed grab bars in the bathroom. Everyone pitched in to help with chores and the new responsibilities that came along with the change. The house was more crowded than before, but Richie found that he didn't mind. He enjoyed spending time with Harold and getting to know him better.

Sources of Assistance

In many communities, programs and services are available to assist older people. For example, Meals on Wheels is a volunteer program that delivers hot meals to older people in their homes. Some communities have senior transportation services that provide rides to doctors' offices and other places. Older people who are looking for recreation and companionship may find that their local senior center meets their needs. Most senior centers offer social activities and nutritious meals.

Arrangements can often be made for older people to receive care services in their own home. A *home care aide* is someone who provides help with bathing, dressing, and other aspects of personal care. A *home health aide* is a health care professional who can give medicines and perform other health care tasks in addition to providing personal care.

Resources like these are especially useful for older people who live alone and don't have family nearby. They can also provide much-needed support for family caregivers. After her grandmother had knee replacement surgery, Mai stayed with her for a week, but then she had to go back to work. She arranged for someone from a home health care agency to check on her grandmother every day. Mai came back on weekends until her grandmother was up and about again.

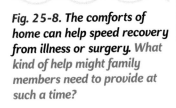

Fig. 25-8. The comforts of home can help speed recovery from illness or surgery. What kind of help might family members need to provide at such a time?

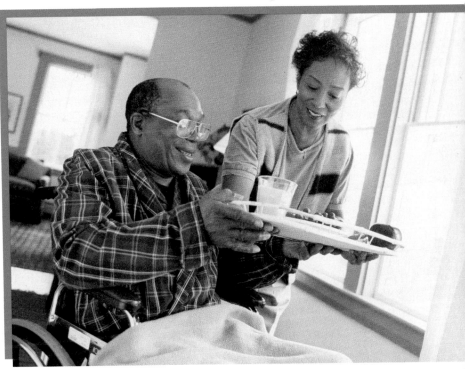

Sometimes, by choice or out of necessity, family members take on the role of full-time caregiver. Dealing with someone who needs constant care is very demanding, and caregivers are at high risk for stress and depression. Some nursing homes offer **respite care**—temporary care that relieves caregivers of their responsibilities for a short period of time. Older people who receive respite care know that they will return home again, and their caregivers get a much-needed break.

Residential Options

Even with outside help, it's not always possible for older people to live on their own or with family members. If this is the case, a number of residential care options can be explored.

- **Retirement communities.** Older adults who need minimal assistance might benefit from living in a retirement community.

Residents have their own apartments or houses and generally care for themselves. They may have the option of going to a central dining hall for meals. Services such as transportation and social activities are usually offered.

- **Assisted living facilities.** These provide personal care services, social activities, and some health services. They are appropriate for people who need help with meals, bathing, dressing, and so on but do not require round-the-clock care. See Fig. 25-9.

- **Nursing homes.** For individuals with physical or mental disabilities that need round-the-clock care, a nursing home may be necessary. Nursing homes—also called extended care facilities—are licensed by the state to provide nursing care, personal care, and medical services.

- **Continuing care facilities.** These facilities provide different housing options to meet people's changing needs. For example, a resident may start out in an independent living unit and move into an assisted living unit when it becomes medically necessary.

Fig. 25-9. Assisted living is a good option for older adults who can no longer live independently but who don't need nursing care. What kinds of services do assisted living facilities offer?

As when choosing child care, family members need to devote time and effort to finding the right care for older relatives. They should also involve the older person in the decision whenever possible. Older people who participate in decisions that concern them, and who feel that their wishes are respected, are better able to adapt to their changing circumstances.

FINDING CREATIVE SOLUTIONS

Changing Perspectives

When a solution seems obvious, you might tell someone, "It's as plain as the nose on your face." From that person's perspective, however, his or her own nose is far from plain—it's practically invisible! To come to an agreement about the solution to a problem, sometimes you need to look at the situation from a different perspective.

How It Works

To appreciate someone else's perspective, try to put yourself in his or her place. What are the other person's concerns and needs? For example, Dario was annoyed that his friend Laurence spent too much time studying instead of having fun. But when he looked at the situation from Laurence's perspective, he realized that Laurence wanted to set a good example to his siblings and be the first in his family to go to college.

When you change your perspective, you can see why other people's priorities are different from yours. You develop greater empathy and become more willing to compromise. You can start working toward a real solution, one that you both agree on.

Try It Out

At age 78, even Kris's strong-willed Aunt Dorothy admits she's starting to feel her age. Arthritis and failing eyesight make working in her kitchen and negotiating the stairs in her home difficult, perhaps even dangerous. Kris's family wants Dorothy to move into an assisted living community, but Dorothy won't hear of it. "I can still do for myself," she maintains. "And I could never live in two little rooms."

▶ **Your Turn** *Take the part of either Dorothy or a member of Kris's family. Write a paragraph explaining your concerns. In small groups, identify differences in the two parties' perspectives. Focus on outcomes both parties want, and suggest a workable solution.*

Chapter Summary

- Children depend on caregivers to meet their physical needs.
- Taking steps such as childproofing the home will help keep children safe.
- Caregivers need to know what to do in an emergency.
- Before making child care decisions, parents should explore their options carefully.

- Older adults may need some level of care depending on their health.
- Family members may be able to provide care for older adults at home. Community programs and services can help.
- Residential care options for older adults include retirement communities, assisted living facilities, nursing homes, and continuing care facilities.

Reviewing Key Terms & Ideas

1. What is a **caregiver**?
2. What does **parenting** refer to?
3. What are the basic physical needs of infants and young children?
4. What is the purpose of **immunizations**?
5. What should you do if you suspect that a child has been abused?
6. How does **childproofing** a home help to keep children safe?
7. How can caregivers protect children when taking them on a car journey?
8. What is the purpose of **first aid**?
9. How can you tell if someone is choking? What should you do?
10. What two actions are performed in **CPR**?
11. What is the difference between in-home care and family child care?

12. How can parents assess a child care facility that they are considering?
13. Name three types of community programs or services that provide support for older people.
14. What is the purpose of **respite care**?
15. What kinds of care services are provided in an assisted living facility?

Thinking Critically

1. **Making Comparisons.** Who has a more challenging job—a parent caring for a child, or an adult child caring for a parent? Give reasons for your answer.
2. **Defending Your Position.** Do you think parents and other caregivers should be required by law to learn first aid techniques? Why or why not?

Applying Your Knowledge

1. **Infant Care Skills.** Using books on baby care, learn how to perform one of the following tasks: give a bottle to an infant, change a diaper, or give a baby a bath. Practice the skill on a doll, then demonstrate it to the class.

2. **Childproofing Your Home.** Make a list of the changes you would need to make in order to childproof your home for an infant who has just learned to crawl.

3. **Care Options.** Investigate the child and adult care options available in your community or nearby area. Categorize them according to the type of facility, the age group served, and so on. If possible, compare prices. Summarize your findings in a chart. How would you rate the availability of care options in your area?

Making Connections

1. **Language Arts.** Write a children's story to help preschoolers learn when they may talk to strangers and when they should not.

2. **Social Studies.** Research what life is like for older people in another country. What living arrangements are most common? What government or community services are provided for older adults? How do societal attitudes toward aging compare to those in the United States? Prepare a brief report.

Managing Your Life

Organizing a Babysitting Service

Babysitting for family members, friends, and neighbors can help you gain practice in caring for children. Running a successful babysitting service, like any other job, requires good management skills. To get organized, create systems for keeping track of the information you need, such as:

- Your schedule, showing jobs you have accepted and dates when you are available.
- Facts about each family that hires you: address and phone number, names and ages of children, household rules, and so on.
- A record of the jobs you have taken, including the rate you charged, the number of hours, and the total pay.

Getting organized will help you run a more successful service. You will also build management skills that will come in handy in the working world.

Using Technology

1. **Video.** Use a video camera to "tour" a typical living room or kitchen from a toddler's point of view. Narrate the tour by explaining the hazards and/or safety precautions you encounter.

2. **Technology for Safety.** Find examples of relatively new technology that can enhance the safety and security of children or older adults. Share your findings with the class.

CHAPTER 26

Nurturing and Guiding

Key Terms

- nurture
- age appropriate
- quiet play
- active play
- attention span

Objectives

- **Discuss** children's intellectual, emotional, social, and moral needs.
- **Give guidelines** for effectively guiding children's behavior.
- **Explain** how children's play contributes to development.
- **Compare** different types of play.
- **Describe** how caregivers can promote play and provide learning opportunities.

378

QUICK WRITE

Write a description of an incident—real or imaginary—that shows why every young child needs individual attention and encouragement.

Five-year-old Tiffany came into the kitchen to ask if she could play outside with her friend. Her stepmother Joanne said, "You may, if you can tell me the rules."

Tiffany hopped up and down as she chanted, "Stay in the back yard. Come inside if a stranger comes near. Share and take turns."

"That's right," Joanne smiled. "Now, would you like to take your ball and glove with you, or will you be having a tea party today?"

Nurturing Children

When you **nurture** children, you provide the care and attention needed to promote development. In the previous chapter, you learned about some of the physical needs of infants and children. However, those needs are just the beginning. For children to develop their full potential, they need not only physical care but also a loving, stimulating environment. They need caregivers who provide for their intellectual, emotional, social, and moral needs.

- **Intellectual needs.** Research about how the brain develops shows the importance of an environment that stimulates all five senses. You can create such an environment without buying expensive toys. A variety of simple toys, everyday objects, and enriching experiences help children develop their senses and learn about the world around them. Even more important, children need interaction with others. When you talk with children, read to them, play with them, and share interesting activities with them, you help stimulate intellectual development. See Fig. 26-1.

Fig. 26-1. Children are like sponges: they absorb information from everything in their environment. What might this child be learning?

- **Emotional needs.** All young children need to feel loved and valued. They need people in their lives who will listen to them, give them smiles and hugs, cheer their accomplishments, and comfort them when they are upset or afraid. Children who feel loved and successful have greater confidence and higher self-esteem. These qualities provide strength and resiliency to overcome disappointment and stress. See Fig. 26-2.

- **Social needs.** Children need to learn how to make friends and get along with others. They must also learn to express their thoughts, feelings, and desires in socially acceptable ways. To develop these social skills, they need both opportunities to be around other children and guidance from caregivers. As they learn to play with others, share, and take turns, children gain valuable skills that will help them get along with people throughout life.

- **Moral needs.** Children also need to develop a sense of right and wrong. Consistent, loving guidance helps them do so. Basic values such as fairness, justice, and empathy are best taught by example. When you listen carefully while a child explains something, you model respect. When you show sympathy for a child who is upset over a lost pet, you demonstrate compassion. What are some other ways you can model values for young children?

Fig. 26-2. Having someone to share their successes with helps children feel valued. If this child had not won a trophy, how would you respond if you were the caregiver?

Guiding Behavior

Children aren't born knowing how to behave. It's the responsibility of parents and other caregivers to teach them. Children need guidance so that they can learn what behavior is expected of them.

As they guide children toward appropriate behavior, caregivers need to be patient, understanding, and gentle. Another important quality is consistency. If the rules for good behavior constantly change, children won't know what's expected of them. If you respond to misbehavior one day but overlook it another day, they will be confused.

Guiding children starts with promoting good behavior and setting clear limits. Since children aren't perfect, you also need to respond appropriately when they misbehave.

Promoting Good Behavior

Modeling appropriate behavior is the best way to promote it in children. Children imitate what they see and hear. If they hear "please" and "thank you," they are more likely to use these words themselves. If they experience shouting or swearing, they may imitate this too.

Responding to children's positive behavior encourages them to repeat it. When a child does something well, offer specific praise: "You put away your toys all by yourself! That's a big help." Simple comments like this encourage the child to repeat the behavior.

Setting Limits

Children need to know what they may and may not do. Although they will sometimes complain about rules, they actually feel more secure when they know what is expected of them.

Limits should be **age appropriate**, or suited to a child's developmental stage. Reasonable limits protect children from harm and prevent them from hurting others, yet still allow them to explore and learn. As children grow, limits should gradually become less restrictive.

State limits clearly and positively. Telling children what they may do is more effective than telling them what they may *not* do. For example, "You may ride your bike to the corner" is clearer than "Don't go too far."

Handling Misbehavior

From time to time, most children do things they shouldn't. Sometimes they have not been told that something is wrong. It's not fair to punish children in that situation. Nor should they be punished for actions that they can't help, like accidentally knocking over a glass of milk.

Sometimes, however, children know the rules but forget to follow them. Other times they may challenge their limits to see what will happen. In such situations, caregivers need to respond immediately and appropriately. Here are some options for dealing with misbehavior:

- **Redirect behavior.** With infants and toddlers, misbehavior can often be avoided or stopped by redirecting the child's attention. For example, if a toddler is trying to reach for a breakable object, offer a safe toy instead.

- **Give reminders.** All children make mistakes. Reminding the child of the desired behavior—"Use your quiet voice in the house, please"—may be all that is needed in some cases.

- **Remove the child from the situation.** While playing with toy trucks, Emilia became upset and hit one of her playmates. Her father told her to sit quietly away from the others for a short time.

Fig. 26-3. A short "cooling-off" period helps a child settle down after misbehaving. It also reinforces the idea that the child must learn self-control.

The Importance of Play

When children play, they are doing much more than having fun. Play has as much purpose for children as work does for adults.

Play and Development

When children play, they learn about the world, themselves, and others. Play promotes progress in all areas of development.

- **Physical development.** Physical activities such as playing tag or riding a bike help develop motor skills. They strengthen muscles and improve coordination.

- **Intellectual development.** Play is how young children learn. For example, playing with puzzles helps children learn about shapes and sizes and how things fit together. Reading to children teaches them about letters, words, and ideas. Storytelling, pretend play, and drawing encourage creativity.

- **Emotional development.** If you've ever watched a grandparent play peekaboo or pat-a-cake with a baby grandchild, you know that play can be a way to build bonds. Playing with children lets them know that they deserve your time and attention. This boosts self-esteem and helps children learn to give and receive love.

- **Social development.** When children play with others, they learn how to develop and maintain friendships. Playing board games

This gave Emilia a chance to calm down and regain her self-control. After she did, Emilia's father reminded her that she should ask politely for what she wants instead of hitting. He then let her rejoin the others. See Fig. 26-3.

- **Enforce consequences.** When Antoine refused to pick up his toys, his mother reminded him that he would not be allowed to play with something else until the toys on the floor were put away. It would not have been appropriate to punish Antoine by canceling a planned trip to the zoo next week. Such punishment is too far removed from the present time and is unrelated to Antoine's behavior.

and group games promotes social skills such as sharing, taking turns, resolving conflicts, and compromising.

- **Moral development.** Playing with others also helps children understand how their actions affect those around them. For example, through play, children gradually learn that cheating is wrong because it is unfair to others.

Quiet and Active Play

Young children need a balance of quiet play and active play. **Quiet play** involves activities that engage the mind and use small motor skills. Making things out of clay and putting a puzzle together are examples of quiet play. This type of play helps children learn to sit still and focus on an activity. **Active play** involves physical activities that employ large motor skills. Climbing a jungle gym and riding a tricycle are examples of active play. This type of play provides healthy exercise and lets children work off their energy. Since each type of play has different benefits, it's important to encourage both. See Fig. 26-4.

Promoting Children's Play

Caregivers should encourage play that is age appropriate. Activities that are within a child's skill and interest level are the most fun and the most stimulating.

Fig. 26-4. Children are more likely to sleep well at night if they have had opportunities to be active during the day. What are some other benefits of active play?

Infants and Play

Because infants explore the world through their senses, they need toys that stimulate the senses with different textures, shapes, sounds, and colors. Mobiles, rattles, and teething rings are examples of toys that infants enjoy playing with.

Fig. 26-5. Babies are delighted by simple games like peekaboo. *How do traditional infant games positively affect development?*

ers, fitting toys together, and stacking blocks. These activities help them learn about size, space, and balance. Sensory activities—such as sand and water play, making things out of clay, and painting—encourage creativity and help children develop small motor skills. Toddlers also like to imitate adults by "helping" with simple household chores.

Toddlers tend to have a short **attention span**. In other words, the length of time they are able to concentrate on one task is not very long. To keep play stimulating and interesting, offer a new activity as soon as the child appears to lose interest in the current activity. Individual activities are best, since toddlers have not yet learned to take turns or share.

Preschoolers and Play

Play becomes more complex in the preschool years. Children's large and small motor skills are becoming more developed. Their artwork begins to look more realistic; they build more elaborate block towers; they can manipulate smaller puzzle pieces. Preschoolers are developing their imagination, too. They love pretend play, such as dressing up and playing house. Pretend play helps them express their feelings and practice the behavior they see in adults.

At this age, children often look to caregivers for approval. You will hear them say "Watch me!" and "Look at what I made!" Showing genuine interest and appreciation for children's efforts will help build their self-esteem.

The best plaything for infants, however, is an interested adult. Babies want attention. They love to be held, to see faces, and to hear voices. Since infants are somewhat limited in how they can play with toys, they get more out of playtime when an adult interacts with them. This interaction also builds a connection between infant and caregiver. See Fig. 26-5.

Toddlers and Play

Toddlers are very active. They enjoy running, jumping, climbing, dancing, and swinging. They also love to explore the physical world by filling and emptying contain-

Providing Opportunities

Responsible caregivers enrich children's lives by providing opportunities to play and learn. You can make everyday events, such as a trip to the supermarket or the bank, into fun learning experiences. At the supermarket, for example, you might talk about why the freezer section is cold or encourage a child to count the cans of soup in the cart. See Fig. 26-6.

Materials for play don't have to be fancy. To a toddler, an empty margarine tub might be a drum to bang on or a boat to float in the tub. To a preschooler, it can be a prop for playing store. A large empty box, clean paintbrushes and water, old clothes to dress up in—all provide opportunities for play.

Keep in mind that the role of the caregiver is to encourage play, not control it. Offer play materials and suggest activities when needed, but avoid telling the child what to do. For example, if you give a child paper and a brown crayon and say "Draw a horse for me," you are in control. Instead, set out a variety of drawing materials and say, "I thought you might like to make something with these." This gives the child the power to choose.

As children grow older, they need less guidance and encouragement to play. Still, they benefit when caregivers become involved in their play from time to time. Look for appropriate opportunities to suggest ideas, provide materials, and join in the fun. Children who spend time with interested, creative caregivers gain much from the experience.

Reading Books

Taking the time to read with children is rewarding. Young children love to cuddle in a caregiver's lap to listen to a story. They enjoy asking questions and sharing the funny, happy, scary, or sad feelings that the story describes. Such experiences fulfill many of their developmental needs. Here are some tips for making reading an enjoyable learning experience:

- **Choose age-appropriate books.** Stories should be suitable for the child's age and interests. Let the child share the experience of choosing books.

Fig. 26-6. Everyday experiences like shopping for groceries can become fun activities for a young child. What is this child gaining from the experience?

- **Discuss the story.** Talk about the pictures, what the characters are feeling, and what the child thinks will happen next. Make connections to the child's own life when possible. See Fig. 26-7.

- **Be prepared to read the same story many times.** Children often ask to hear a story over and over again. This is a sign that they find the story especially enjoyable.

- **Encourage children to "read" themselves.** Children interact with books in many different ways before they are actually able to read. Even infants and toddlers like to hold a book, turn the pages, and look at the pictures. After hearing a favorite story repeated many times, a child may "read" it from memory or learn to associate certain words with certain pictures.

When children are old enough to read simple books themselves, encourage them to read to you. Help them with words they don't know, and praise them for the parts they read well. Make a point, too, of letting children see you read and write in your everyday life. This helps them see that reading and writing are useful and enjoyable.

Electronic Entertainment

Children love to be entertained, and some caregivers are happy to let television do the entertaining. Many child care experts believe, however, that too much television can be harmful to children's development. Watching television requires very little interaction or thought and does not promote physical activity. What's more, many programs and commercials are inappropriate for young children. Computer and video games are more interactive than television, and some can stimulate learning. Still, playing these games is an inactive and often solitary pastime, as is surfing the Internet.

How can parents and other caregivers make the most of what television and electronic games have to offer? Here are some suggestions:

- Balance electronic entertainment with active and social play. Limiting your own TV and computer use will set a good example.

Fig. 26-7. Talking with children while you read to them helps them get involved in the story. What else can caregivers do to make reading an enjoyable experience?

Viewpoints

Organized Activities for Children

As anyone who has observed children can tell you, a small child can be just as pleased with a tiny caterpillar as with an expensive toy. When it comes to learning experiences, however, some parents think that one is better than the other.

Sharona: I'm glad the school has programs like the one my four-year-old is in. He gets to meet other kids his age in a safe setting, and the atmosphere is more enriching than I could make at home. He takes part in lots of organized activities and might even find something he has a special talent for. It's good for young children to try lots of different things so that they build different skills in different areas.

Patrick: I love to watch our three-year-old play with her friends. They learn so much on their own, just using their imagination. In fact, I think they learn more when they have to make their own fun without a lot of help from adults. There's no pressure, no schedule. No one tells them what they have to do or for how long. They'll get enough of that in school. For now, the only rules are "Play nice" and "Ask Mom or Dad first."

Seeing Both Sides ~ What elements are essential to a learning environment for children? Describe a positive setting for children that reflect both Sharona's and Patrick's points of view.

- Choose appropriate programs and games. Most have ratings to help you decide.
- Keep televisions and computers in areas used by the entire family, not in children's rooms.
- Monitor children's computer activities.
- Watch television programs with the child and talk about what is happening. If the child loses interest, turn the set off.
- Consider using filtering software to prevent access to inappropriate Web sites.
- Teach children not to give out personal information to strangers online.

Chapter Summary

- Caregivers need to understand and meet children's intellectual, emotional, social, and moral needs.

- Guiding behavior involves promoting good behavior, setting reasonable limits, and handling misbehavior.

- Children's play is purposeful and promotes progress in all areas of development.

- Children need a balance of active play and quiet play.

- Different types of play activities are appropriate for each stage of a child's development.

- Effective caregivers provide a variety of opportunities for play and learning.

Reviewing Key Terms & Ideas

1. What do you do when you **nurture** children?

2. What two things do children need in order to develop intellectually?

3. How does feeling loved and successful benefit children?

4. Name three social skills that children need to learn.

5. How can caregivers teach children basic values?

6. What does **age appropriate** mean?

7. Describe four ways to respond to misbehavior.

8. Give examples to show how play contributes to each area of a child's development.

9. Explain the difference between **quiet play** and **active play**.

10. Why do caregivers need to be aware of a child's **attention span**?

11. Give two examples of age-appropriate play activities for preschoolers.

12. How can caregivers encourage play without controlling it?

13. Explain two guidelines to follow when reading books to children.

14. What are the disadvantages of television as an activity for children?

Thinking Critically

1. **Making Comparisons.** What do you see as the benefits and drawbacks of competitive games and sports for children compared to noncompetitive play? How can caregivers help children learn to handle the disappointment of losing?

2. **Understanding Cause and Effect.** Many parents have learned to offer children choices when possible rather than telling them what to do. Why would this technique help reduce misbehavior?

Applying Your Knowledge

1. **Everyday Learning.** Think of a household task that is done regularly, such as meal preparation, laundry, food shopping, or cleaning. Describe how this activity could be made into an enjoyable learning experience for a toddler or preschooler.

2. **Television Observation.** Observe a child or group of children viewing a television program. Notice their body language, their state of alertness, and their emotional reactions to the program. Record your observations and draw conclusions.

Making Connections

1. **Language Arts.** Imagine you are a toddler or a preschooler. Write a letter to your caregiver telling how you would like to spend your time and how you would like to be treated. Incorporate the information you've learned about the needs and development of toddlers and preschoolers.

2. **Social Studies.** Interview older relatives to discover what kinds of toys and games children had 50 or more years ago. Ask how the toys and games were used and what children learned from them. Compare the ways children learned from play in that time period with the ways they learn today. What is similar about the two time periods? What is different?

Managing Your Life

Resources for Nurturing Children

Whether or not parenthood is in your future, you will have opportunities to interact with children. How will you nurture their development? Begin now to collect ideas that can help you provide creative, enriching activities for children. Possible resources include books, magazines, and Web sites related to parenting and child development. Look for ideas for simple games, creative ways to use everyday objects, and so on. Place the materials in a file organized by age group.

Using Technology

1. **Internet.** Evaluate three different Web sites that offer games or other activities for preschool or school-age children. Rate the sites on educational and entertainment value. Write a review that summarizes your evaluation of the sites and gives recommendations.

2. **Desktop Publishing.** Use appropriate software to prepare a booklet that gives suggestions for modeling moral behavior and values to young children. Illustrate your booklet with photographs or drawings.

CHAPTER 27

Responsibilities of Parenthood

Key Terms

- emotional maturity
- premature
- low birth weight

Objectives

- **Summarize** the rewards and responsibilities of parenting.
- **Distinguish** between unrealistic and realistic reasons for wanting a child.
- **Discuss** emotional, financial, and personal readiness for parenthood.
- **Describe** the process of adjusting to parenthood.
- **Explain** challenges faced by teen parents and their children.

Write a letter of encouragement, from an infant's point of view, to a couple in their first year of parenthood.

As Jamie cradled her newborn son in her arms, she felt a mixture of joy, apprehension, and awe. She knew that her life had changed forever. She looked up at Dave, her husband, who was gazing intently at the baby's face. "I can't wait to start teaching him how to catch a ball and ride a bike," Dave said.

Jamie laughed. "Well, I'm afraid you're going to have to wait. Our little boy has a lot to learn first."

"You're right," said Dave, "and so do we." Jamie and Dave looked at their son in wonder. They were excited—and nervous—about being parents, but they looked forward to sharing the rewards and responsibilities of their new roles.

However, most new parents don't realize how hard parenting is. It takes responsibility to provide constant care, love, security, shelter, guidance, and financial support. Moreover, parenting is a responsibility that continues for many years. Each stage of childhood—and each child—is different, requiring parents to constantly meet new challenges.

Fig. 27-1. Many parents enjoy keeping family and cultural traditions alive by passing them on to their children. *What traditions have been passed on in your family?*

Rewards and Responsibilities

Welcoming a child into the world can bring great joy. It's just one of the rewards of parenting. Raising children gives parents a chance to experience the world through the wonder of a child's eyes. Parents develop new skills, strengths, and understanding of their child and themselves. They experience a sense of accomplishment, pass on family traditions, and forge deep bonds of love. See Fig. 27-1.

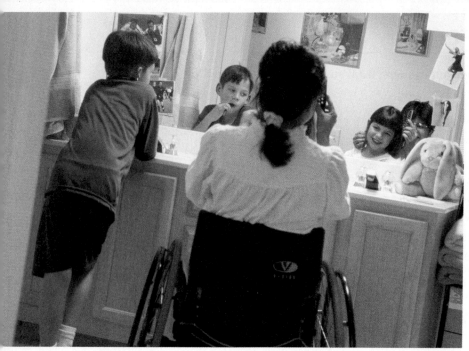

Fig. 27-2. Parents care for their children in many different ways. *What might happen if children's needs in each area were not met?*

Caregiving Responsibilities

If you've studied the previous chapters, you know that parents must meet the physical, emotional, intellectual, social, and moral needs of their children. Providing love, attention, and guidance are just as essential as providing food, clothing, and shelter. See Fig. 27-2.

Caring for a child is a 24-hour-a-day job. Parents can't just set the responsibilities aside for a while. Somebody has to be responsible for a young child at all times. Parents who have an outside job must make arrangements for child care while they are at work.

Parents also have a responsibility to be good role models. Whether they realize it or not, their children are constantly observing the values, character traits, and skills that they demonstrate in their everyday actions. For better or worse, children will pattern themselves after the example set by their parents.

Financial Responsibilities

The cost of raising a child begins even before the baby is born. As soon as a woman knows or suspects she is pregnant, she should see a doctor. Regular medical care is needed throughout the pregnancy to monitor the health of both mother and baby. It gives the baby the best possible start in life—something that every child deserves.

For someone so tiny, a new baby brings many expenses. Parents may need to buy equipment such as a car seat and crib. The baby will need food, diapers, and clothes, which are quickly outgrown. Even parents with health insurance usually have to pay for routine medical exams and immunizations. Child care can be another major expense.

As children get older, the costs of food and clothing increase. School, sports, and other activities add still more expenses to the list. Parents' financial responsibilities continue until the child earns a living and becomes independent.

Readiness for Parenthood

Despite all the responsibilities, many people still want to have children. Just the sight of an adorable infant can bring out these desires. Sometimes, however, the motives behind the desires don't make good sense. Some people have unrealistic ideas about what having a child might mean to them. Compare the different ideas about parenthood shown in Fig. 27-3. Which show more maturity?

Parenting is a lifelong, life-changing commitment. The decision to have a child needs to be backed up by sound reasoning. No one should have a child just to make someone else happy. A child can't fix other problems or weaknesses in your life or strengthen a weak relationship.

How do people know when they are ready to become parents? They can start by recognizing that parenthood is a serious decision that requires serious effort. Then they need to honestly analyze their emotional, financial, and personal readiness.

Emotional Readiness

People who want to become parents need to be emotionally mature. **Emotional maturity** is the ability to understand and act on one's emotions in ways that are appropriate for an adult level of development. With emotional maturity comes the ability to understand one's feelings and to act on them appropriately. Emotionally mature parents have the inner resources to put the needs of their child before their own needs. They have patience, sensitivity, self-control, and self-confidence. Their expectations about raising a child are realistic, not idealistic. They know that their lives will change the moment they become parents, and they truthfully believe they can handle the demands and responsibilities of parenting.

Ideas About Parenthood

UNREALISTIC IDEAS	REALISTIC IDEAS
■ I'm lonely. A child will love me. ■ I feel unimportant. A baby will attract attention and I'll be noticed. ■ My parents (or in-laws or friends) want us to have a child. ■ My relationship with my spouse is shaky. A child will make it stronger. ■ I'm afraid of the future. A child will care for me when I'm old.	■ Our marriage is strong, and we're ready to become parents. ■ I am willing to put someone else's needs ahead of my own. ■ I'm secure in who I am and will work hard to be a good parent. ■ We know what we're taking on, and we accept the responsibility.

Fig. 27-3. People who are considering parenthood should take an honest look at their reasons. What other unrealistic ideas might some people have about parenthood?

Financial Readiness

Because raising a child is expensive, couples should assess their financial readiness to become parents. They need to determine how they will manage the immediate and longer-term costs of raising a child. That means examining their current income and expenses. Are spending cuts needed to increase savings or to meet additional expenses? Will a larger living space be needed? If so, how much will housing costs increase? If both parents have jobs, will one stay at home to care for the child? Can the family manage on one income? If both parents continue working, how much will quality child care cost? Such questions help couples review the financial realities of raising a child and make a decision that is right for them. See Fig. 27-4.

Personal Readiness

A child gives a family a new and different focus. Couples must be ready to put the needs of their child first, delaying some of their personal needs and wants. They must also assess whether they have the skills and qualities they will need for raising a child. While parenting is somewhat of a "learn as you go" process, some parenting skills can be developed ahead of time. Couples with the following characteristics are more likely to be successful parents:

- **Management skills.** Parents need to know how to use their money, time, and energy wisely. They must be able to stretch the family budget, juggle tasks, and care for themselves and their children.
- **Flexibility.** Parents who are flexible are better able to meet daily challenges. At a moment's notice, parents may have to change their focus or their plans in order to clean up a spill, give a mud-caked child a bath, or take care of a sick baby.

Fig. 27-4. Before deciding to have a baby, couples should develop a plan for meeting the financial costs of parenthood.

Viewpoints

Evaluating Readiness for Parenthood

Docs evaluating readiness before becoming a parent making parenting any easier? That depends on whom you ask.

Antonio: Some people are so casual about becoming parents. Maybe they don't realize how big a commitment it is. Before our son was born, my wife and I weighed all the factors—our finances, our careers, our relationship—to see if we were ready and willing to be good parents. When Tomas was born, we felt more confident because we knew we had what a child needs for a good start.

Eva: Some people talk about parenting readiness like it's a math equation: a good income plus maturity plus a good marriage equals good parents. But when our baby was born, we discovered that those things just scratch the surface. Even though we thought we were "ready," we had no idea how demanding the job would be. Readiness is good, but it doesn't guarantee that you'll have an easy time.

Seeing Both Sides ~ Overall, what role do the readiness factors you've studied play in good parenting? How do they relate to other considerations and qualities that are important to good parenting?

- **Willingness to sacrifice.** Parents often need to sacrifice their time, money, and personal interests for the sake of their children. Being willing to make such sacrifices helps to create a healthy, nurturing family environment.

- **Consistency.** Parents need the maturity to behave consistently. Establishing and enforcing routines, rules, and limits help children feel secure and understand their boundaries.

Adjusting to Parenthood

No matter how ready they are, new parents face major adjustments. Months after a baby is born, they are still getting used to their new roles. A mother's physical recovery from giving birth may take longer than expected. It's not uncommon for new mothers to experience periods of depression and anxiety. A father may worry about finances or feel like an outsider when the mother and baby get lots of attention. Studies show that marital satisfaction often decreases after the birth of a baby. Spouses tend to argue more and to show less affection to one another.

All of these possible results are normal adjustments to parenthood and family life. It's how the couple handles them—as individuals and together—that makes the difference in the outcome. Couples who can acknowledge and deal with the challenges are more likely to experience personal growth and a stronger marriage.

TIPS FOR *Success*

Walking in a Parent's Shoes

Do you want to test your readiness to have a child? Try spending a day with friends or relatives who have young children. Lend a hand with feeding, bathing, and dressing. Go along on outings to the supermarket or park. Notice how much time and energy the parents devote to their children and how little time they have to relax. Then ask yourself whether you're ready to take on those responsibilities every single day for years to come.

Teen Parenthood

Adjusting to parenthood is difficult for anyone, but it can be especially hard for teens. Teen parents face difficulties that parents in their twenties and thirties usually don't. Most teens are not mature enough—physically, emotionally, or financially—to take on the responsibility of caring for a child.

Teen parenthood has predictable consequences. The lives of both the child and the parents are affected in many ways.

Effects on the Child

Teen mothers are often not fully developed physically. As a result, they face special risks with pregnancy. Babies born to teen mothers are more likely to be **premature**—born before 37 weeks of development. They are also more likely to have **low birth weight**, which means weighing less than 5½ pounds at birth. Babies who are premature or have low birth weight are more likely to experience blindness, deafness, respiratory problems, mental disabilities, and other disabilities. A significant percentage of these babies die before their first birthday.

Because of the increased risks, good prenatal care is essential for teen mothers. Many teens put off getting medical care because they don't want to face the fact that they are pregnant. However, those who take proper care of themselves greatly increase the chances of having a healthy baby.

Babies born to teen parents often have less supportive and stimulating home environments than those born to older parents. They tend to have higher rates of behavioral problems. They are more likely to be neglected or abused because their parents don't know how to deal with stress. Years later, they are more likely to be teen parents themselves. All of these effects have long-term consequences for the children and for society as a whole.

Effects on the Parents

The teen years are an important stage of mental, emotional, and social development. Having a child interferes with this development. As a teen, you're still discovering yourself and trying to decide what you want out of life. It's hard enough to get through this confusing time without complicating it with a child or two.

Having a child changes your entire lifestyle. Teens who must put time and energy into caring for a child have fewer resources for other pursuits and interests. They don't have the freedom or the money to go out and have fun with friends.

Teen mothers are often single mothers. By law, teen fathers are required to provide financial support for the child. Not all fulfill this responsibility, however. Some end their relationship with the mother as well. Even when teen parents do marry, the marriage is more than likely to fail.

A significant number of teen parents don't complete their education. They drop out of school to support themselves or to care for their child. Without a high-school diploma, these parents have little hope of getting a job that pays much more than minimum wage.

Teen parents who succeed do so against great odds. Usually they have support systems that help them complete their education and earn a living while raising and caring for their child. They persevere when life is tough and hold tightly to their hopes for a better future. See Fig. 27-5.

Fig. 27-5. Teen parents have a difficult path ahead of them. Those who are exceptionally mature and get lots of support have the best chance of success.

Planning Ahead

The decision to become parents deserves careful thought and discussion. A couple considering parenthood should talk seriously about whether they are prepared for such a major step. They should discuss how they will handle the demands of parenting along with their other responsibilities and goals. Above all, they should remember that the happiest and healthiest children are born to parents who are ready for them.

Chapter Summary

- The rewards of parenting are significant, but require hard work and sacrifice.
- Parents have specific caregiving and financial responsibilities.
- The decision to have a child should be based on sound reasoning.

- People considering parenthood should evaluate their emotional, financial, and personal readiness.
- Parenthood requires a couple to make many adjustments.
- Teen parenthood has negative effects on both the child and the parents.

Reviewing Key Terms & Ideas

1. Identify three rewards of parenting.
2. What types of caregiving and financial responsibilities do parents have? Give three examples for each.
3. Name two unrealistic reasons for wanting a child and two realistic reasons.
4. What are some signs of **emotional maturity**?
5. How can a couple assess whether they are financially ready for parenthood?
6. Name three personal characteristics that parents need.
7. What challenges might a new mother face when adjusting to parenthood? What challenges might a new father face?
8. Under what circumstances are babies considered to be **premature** or to have **low birth weight**?

9. What health risks are associated with premature birth?
10. Why are teen parents less likely than older parents to finish school?

Thinking Critically

1. **Recognizing Assumptions.** Read the list of unrealistic ideas about parenthood in Fig. 27-3. What assumptions are being made in each case? Are they valid? Why or why not?

2. **Making Predictions.** What do you think your life would be like in five years if you had a child? What would it be like if you did not have a child?

3. **Distinguishing Fact from Opinion.** Is the statement "Teen parents are not capable of being good parents" fact or opinion? Why do you think so?

Applying Your Knowledge

1. **Exploring Parenting Decisions.** Talk with several adults about their decision to become parents or not to become parents. What influenced their decision? How has the choice they made affected their lives? Summarize the insights you gained from this activity, but change the names of the people you interviewed to protect their privacy.

2. **Teen Pregnancy.** Find out what programs are available in your local area to help pregnant teens get good prenatal care and stay in school. Be prepared to report your findings to the class.

Making Connections

1. **Math.** Choose one category of expenses related to caring for an infant, such as food, clothing, medical care, furnishings, or equipment. Estimate the amount that parents would typically have to spend in that category through the baby's first birthday. Use books, Web sites, store ads, and other sources to identify the items needed and their cost. Share your results with the class.

2. **Science.** Investigate the reasons that teen parents tend to have babies that are premature or have low birth weight. Prepare a brief report on your findings.

Managing Your Life

Preparing for Parenthood

Make a list of personal characteristics that you believe a person should have before becoming a parent. Be as specific as you can. Then assess yourself on each characteristic. Which are you already strong in? Which would you need to acquire or improve in order to be a responsible, effective parent? Think about how those qualities would be helpful even if you don't become a parent. Choose one characteristic that you would like to work on, and make a plan for improving in that area. Include ways to evaluate your progress over time.

Using Technology

1. **Internet.** Find two Web sites that offer advice and resources for parents. Write a review that compares the two sites and evaluates their usefulness.

2. **Spreadsheet.** Gather statistics about teen pregnancy rates over the past 20 years. Input the data into a spreadsheet. Use the spreadsheet program to create a graph that illustrates overall trends. What are some possible explanations for these trends?

Career Options
Education and Training

*E*ducation and training is the largest service industry in the United States. Workers in this segment provide academic, vocational, and technical instruction and training throughout the lifespan. The majority of career opportunities in this field require advanced education and training, such as a bachelor's degree or master's degree. The education and training industry can be divided into two broad sectors: Teaching/Training and Administration. For most occupations in this career cluster, employment opportunities are on the rise.

Main Employers

- Schools
- Colleges
- Universities
- Trade and technical schools
- Departments of education

Education and Training Opportunities

Industry Segment	Entry Level	Additional Education and/or Training	Advanced Education and/or Training
Teaching/Training	▪ Teacher Assistant ▪ Student Teacher	▪ Preschool Teacher ▪ Coach	▪ Kindergarten Teacher ▪ Elementary Teacher ▪ Middle School Teacher ▪ High School Teacher ▪ College and University Teacher ▪ Vocational/Technical Teacher ▪ Corporate Trainer
Administration	▪ Administrative Assistant ▪ Office Clerk	▪ Test Developer ▪ Instructional Media Designer ▪ Computer Specialist	▪ Principal ▪ Dean ▪ Preschool Lead Teacher ▪ Director of Admissions ▪ Curriculum Specialist

I come from a large family. Because I was the oldest of six children, my parents relied on me to help take care of my younger brothers and sisters. Those experiences convinced me that I wanted to become a teacher.

To teach, I needed a bachelor's degree. When I started in the elementary education program at the state university, I wasn't sure at which level I wanted to teach. During summer break after my freshman year, I worked at a child care center, and I really enjoyed working with four- and five-year-olds. The next summer I was a camp counselor for eight- and nine-year-olds. I found out that I preferred working with the younger children. After graduating and receiving my teaching license, I was fortunate to find a job as a kindergarten teacher.

If you were to visit my classroom, you might see the children learning their alphabet and beginning to read, singing songs, or learning about weather. Because young children learn mainly through play, I include lots of it in my teaching program. It's through such activities that students learn language skills, social skills, and preliminary math and science concepts. I know I play an important role in helping my students develop the basic skills they need for first grade.

Check It Out!

Requirements for teaching licenses vary by state. Choose a specific teaching level that interests you. Use library or online resources to learn about the licensing requirements for teachers at that level in your state. Present your findings in a brief oral report.

Consumer Skills

CHAPTER 28

Consumer Issues

Key Terms

- consumer
- redress
- small claims court
- identity theft
- fraud
- pyramid scheme
- chain letter
- return policy
- shoplifting

Objectives

- **Explain** the role, rights, and responsibilities of consumers.
- **Evaluate** sources of consumer information.
- **Outline** the process of making a consumer complaint.
- **Identify** ways to protect your privacy and prevent identity theft.
- **Describe** common types of consumer fraud.
- **Give** guidelines for being a responsible, considerate consumer.

What makes a wise consumer? Why do some people always seem to get better deals than others when shopping? Write a paragraph expressing your thoughts.

Jesse hung up the telephone and looked in dismay at the figure he had written down. The dealership where he had bought his car had just quoted him $750 to replace a broken fender. He couldn't afford that much, but he had to get it fixed. He talked it over with Brian, his older brother. Brian suggested that Jesse shop around for a better price. "After all," said Brian, "there's no law that says you have to take it to the dealer. Another repair shop might give you a much better price."

Your Role as a Consumer

Brian was right: there is no law that says that Jesse must go to the original dealer. However, there *are* laws that protect his right to choose another service provider. Jesse is learning about his role as a **consumer**, someone who buys and uses products and services. He is discovering that consumers have rights—in this case, the right to choose. They also have responsibilities—he is responsible for making his vehicle safe. Just as important, they have power—the power to influence the marketplace. See Fig. 28-1.

You may not think that you're exercising power every time you buy shampoo or make some other consumer decision. However, the fact is that consumers collectively have a great deal of power. Through their buying decisions, they determine which goods are produced and which services are offered. If

Fig. 28-1. Consumers have power! Your buying decisions help influence what goods and services are made available.

too few consumers buy a certain product, it will be taken off the market. The manufacturer will have to offer better choices or risk going out of business.

At the same time, consumers play a significant role in the economic system as a whole. When consumers feel optimistic about the economy, they are more likely to spend money on goods and services. When consumers spend more money, employers hire more workers to keep up with demand. When more workers are employed, more people have money to spend on goods and services. In these circumstances, the economy grows. The opposite is also true, of course. When consumers lack confidence, they spend less and economic growth slows. See Fig. 28-2.

Teens make up an important segment of the consumer population. In addition to spending their own money, they influence their parents' purchases on everything from groceries to home entertainment systems to vacation destinations. So although you may not always realize it, your opinion matters!

Influences on Consumer Spending

You don't make your consumer decisions in a vacuum. Many factors influence the choices you make. Chief among them are your own needs, wants, and values. They guide you toward spending on the goods and services that matter most to you. Your family is another major influence. Just as Brian influenced Jesse's decision to shop around for a better price for his car repair, you may find that family members guide your decision making both directly and indirectly.

Advertising is another major influence on your consumer decisions. In Chapter 29, you'll learn how to think critically about its messages. Other influences include the society you live in, the culture you grew up in, your financial resources, your friends, and your interests. Technology also plays a role. When you have access to a computer and the Internet, you have access to a wide and ever-growing range of products and services.

Consumer Rights and Responsibilities

The government has enacted many laws to protect consumers. These laws regulate the sale of goods and services ranging from food and cars to health insurance and home loans. They ensure that businesses treat

Fig. 28-2. Economists closely watch data about consumer spending. *Why might consumers spend more when they feel optimistic about the economy?*

consumers fairly. They also give consumers the right to **redress**—to seek legal remedy when laws are violated. Consumer protection is provided at the federal, state, and local levels by agencies set up specifically to enforce the laws.

Along with each of a consumer's legal rights comes a responsibility. To benefit from their rights, consumers must stand up for themselves and take appropriate action. Fig. 28-3 explains the basic consumer rights and the corresponding responsibilities.

Consumer Rights and Responsibilities

RIGHTS	RESPONSIBILITIES
Right to safety. Consumers should be protected against being harmed by a product.	**Responsibility to use products safely.** Consumers should use products as directed by the manufacturer.
Right to be informed. Consumers should be given the facts about goods and services and should be protected against false and misleading advertising.	**Responsibility to use information.** Consumers should obtain information about the goods and services they intend to buy and use it to make evaluations.
Right to choose. Consumers should have access to a variety of goods and services at competitive prices.	**Responsibility to choose carefully.** Consumers should use their intelligence when choosing products and services.
Right to be heard. Consumers have the right to speak out and to help shape consumer laws and regulations.	**Responsibility to speak up.** Consumers should let their opinions on consumer issues be known.
Right to redress. Consumers are entitled to refunds or replacements of unsatisfactory products and to take legal action when laws are violated.	**Responsibility to seek redress.** Consumers should seek remedies for unsatisfactory products or services.
Right to consumer education. Consumers have the right to learn about consumer issues.	**Responsibility to learn.** Consumers should use the information available to them to become more effective consumers.
Right to service. Consumers have the right to expect courtesy and responsiveness from businesses.	**Responsibility to reward good service.** Consumers should show appreciation for businesses that provide good service and merchandise.

Fig. 28-3. For every consumer right, there is a corresponding responsibility. Which right protects you against buying harmful products?

Gathering Information

As Fig. 28-3 shows, consumers have the right to be informed about products and services and the responsibility to use the information that is available to them. That raises two questions: "Where do you find the information you need?" and "How can you judge its usefulness and reliability?"

Sources of Consumer Information

You can gather information from a wide variety of sources. Some are more likely to be reliable than others.

- **Government agencies.** The Federal Trade Commission, the Federal Consumer Information Center, and the Consumer Product Safety Commission are among the federal agencies that assist consumers. In many states, the attorney general's office handles consumer affairs.

- **Consumer organizations.** Nongovernment consumer groups include the National Consumers League, Consumers Union, and the Better Business Bureau. Like the government agencies, they offer consumer education, protection, and other services.

- **Media sources.** An abundance of consumer information is found on television, radio, and the Internet. Magazines and newspapers also carry information about products and services. The quality of the information will vary. Consumer magazines such as *Consumer Reports*, published by the Consumers Union, generally provide the most objective information.

- **Advertising.** You can learn about product availability, price, and main selling features from advertisements. However, since they're trying to sell you something, advertisements are not a good source of objective information.

- **Packaging.** Product packaging generally provides information on the contents of the package and instructions for use. Inserts may also provide information.

  - **Salespeople.** Customer service representatives and salespeople are often a good source of information about the products or services that they sell. You need to be aware, however, that they may be more interested in selling than in giving unbiased information. See Fig. 28-4.

Fig. 28-4. Knowledgeable salespeople can point out the features of a product and help you make comparisons. For what kinds of products would you seek the help of a salesperson?

Fig. 28-5. When you're gathering information, look for reliable sources. What signs might indicate that a source is reliable?

■ **Research studies**. Study findings are often reported in the news. Although this information can help you make decisions about products, you need to examine its accuracy. Studies or reports may be biased or may simplify results and give only partial information.

■ **Other consumers**. Among the most useful sources of information are people you know who have used a service or product you are interested in. As you consider their recommendations, remember that your needs and standards may differ from theirs.

Evaluating Information

As you are aware, not all consumer information is provided with consumers' best interests in mind. You should, therefore, carefully evaluate any information that you obtain. Here are some ways to do so:

■ **Consider the source**. What authority or expertise does the source have? Expert sources are more reliable than anonymous sources or people who are not qualified. See Fig. 28-5.

■ **Look for signs of bias**. Does the source seem to be favoring a particular product or service? Is there a reason for bias? A product review in a magazine, for example, might be biased because the manufacturer advertises in the magazine.

■ **Distinguish between opinion and fact.** Opinions about a product might include that it is easy to use, will perform better than competitors' items, and will enhance your life. Facts, on the other hand, provide detailed information that can be verified.

■ **When in doubt, check it out**. If something sounds too good to be true, it probably is. If you have doubts about the claims made for a product or service, check other sources. You may find that someone is "bending the truth" or making exaggerated claims.

Resolving Consumer Problems

Sometimes, despite all your best efforts, you end up buying something that is unsatisfactory in some way. Perhaps the CD changer on your new stereo system doesn't work, or the cordless drill was missing a part when you took it out of the box. Maybe a sweater shrank when you washed it, even though you followed the care instructions. These kinds of consumer problems can be resolved. Businesses want satisfied customers and will usually work to settle a complaint.

Making a Complaint

Before you make a complaint, determine what you want to achieve. Do you want a defective item to be replaced or repaired, or would you prefer a refund or a merchandise credit? If a service was performed poorly, do you want the provider to do it over or to refund your money?

Next, decide how and to whom you will make your complaint. Depending on the situation, you might contact the company that makes a product or the retailer that sold it to you. You might make a complaint in person, by phone, or in writing.

In Person ~ If you purchased an item at a store, you can make your complaint in person. You might start with the sales clerk who helped you originally, or you might ask for a manager. Many stores have customer service departments to handle customer complaints.

Make sure that you have your receipt. Explain exactly what is wrong with the product, and propose your solution for dealing with it. Be polite but firm. Remember that you have bargaining power and that stores usually want to settle consumers' complaints.

By Phone ~ Making a complaint by phone is similar to doing it in person. Have all the necessary information ready: what the problem is, when and where you purchased the item, and what solution you want. Describe the problem clearly. Write down the name of the person you speak to, the date, and the action discussed. Keep this information in case you need to follow up on your call.

In Writing ~ If complaining in person or by phone doesn't work, you can write a letter. Clearly and politely state the problem, what you have done so far to resolve it, and what solution you're looking for. Again, keep your tone polite and reasonable. Enclose copies of the sales receipt and other relevant documents; keep the originals for yourself. Also keep a copy of the letter.

Taking Further Action

If your first attempt to resolve a complaint is unsuccessful, try again. For example, if speaking to a store clerk does not bring the desired results, you might ask to see a manager. If a phone call is ineffective, write a letter. If after several attempts you are still unable to settle the problem, there are sources you can turn to for assistance.

Business Groups ~ Perhaps the best known of many business and industry groups that assist consumers is the Better Business Bureau (BBB). The BBB is an organization of businesses that promises to follow fair business practices. It provides reports on local businesses and helps resolve consumer complaints against its members and other businesses in the community. To find a branch near you, refer to the main BBB Web site. You might also ask your local chamber of commerce to help you with a consumer complaint. This organization represents and serves businesses in a particular town or city.

Government Agencies ~ The same agencies that offer consumer information also help protect consumers and handle complaints. You can contact the nearest Federal Information Center to learn which federal agency can best help with your particular problem. State and local agencies are listed in the phone book.

Legal Action ~ If a complaint is not settled, you may wish to take legal action. Minor complaints can be settled in **small claims court**—a court in which claims under a certain amount are settled by a judge. Although you have to pay a minimal fee to file a claim in small claims court, you do not have to hire a lawyer and pay legal fees. See Fig. 28-6.

If you have a serious complaint that cannot be heard in a small claims court, you may wish to hire a lawyer and file a lawsuit. This can be an expensive and time-consuming process. Local legal aid agencies may be able to assist you if you can't afford a lawyer.

Fig. 28-6. Consumers with complaints may find that a small claims court suits their needs. It allows them to bring their case without having to pay for a lawyer.

Protecting Your Privacy

Consumers give out personal and financial information in many situations—when applying for a credit card, opening a bank account, and making certain purchases, for example. You might also give out personal information when you complete a product registration form, answer a telephone survey, or fill out a form on a Web site. Many consumers are concerned about how their personal and financial information is used and who has access to it. They want to protect their privacy and avoid having personal information fall into the wrong hands.

More to Explore

Internet Safety

When you use the Internet, take steps to protect yourself from harassment in the form of unpleasant or threatening messages. Safety is a particular concern in situations such as Internet chat rooms and forums. Remember that information you give in such settings is available to just about anybody. Follow these guidelines:

- Use your primary e-mail address only with trusted friends and family. Use a different address for communicating with people you don't know.

- Keep your passwords private.

- Don't give out personal information such as your name, address, or phone number. Use only a screen name or an e-mail address.

- Be careful what you say online. Nothing on the Internet is completely private.

- Remember that people are not always as they represent themselves online. You know only what they choose to tell you.

- Use the preference options to block e-mails, chat messages, or instant messages from anyone who bothers you.

- If someone is harassing you, save the messages and any information that might help identify the person. Tell a trusted adult, and contact the police.

To address concerns about privacy, the government has enacted laws to restrict what companies can do with the information they collect from you. Companies involved in financial activities must send their customers privacy notices, explaining company policy regarding the sharing of information. Customers have the right to opt out of having their information shared in certain ways. When you receive privacy policies in the mail or are notified about them by e-mail or on the Web, read them. Find out how your information is shared and what choices you have. If you don't receive a privacy policy from a company you deal with, ask for it.

Identity Theft

Rosa became alarmed when she started getting calls and notices from credit card companies saying she was behind in making payments. When she checked, she discovered that someone else had used her Social Security number and date of birth to open accounts in her name, then had charged over

$20,000 worth of goods to them. Two years later, Rosa is still trying to sort out the nightmare caused by a complete stranger.

Rosa is a victim of **identity theft**—the illegal use of an individual's personal information. Identity theft can have serious and long-lasting consequences for victims. They may spend months or years—and a great deal of money—trying to set the record straight. In the meantime, they may find it difficult or even impossible to get credit cards, car loans, or home loans.

How Does It Happen? ~ Identity theft begins when someone gains access to personal information such as your name, address, date of birth, Social Security number, and bank or credit card account numbers. They might do this by:

- Stealing your wallet or purse containing identification, credit cards, and checkbook.

- Stealing your mail, including pre-approved credit offers, bank and credit card information, tax information, and new checks.

- Completing a change of address form to have your mail sent to another location.

- Retrieving discarded papers, such as checks, credit card bills, or bank statements, from trash cans or dumpsters.

- Watching over your shoulder as you sign a check at a store or use an automated teller machine. See Fig. 28-7.

- Obtaining your account number from receipts you leave behind.

- Stealing personal information from the Internet.

- Stealing records from a business or gaining access to its computer system.

- Posing as representatives of banks or government agencies and getting you to reveal information over the phone or by e-mail.

Once thieves have this information, they may use it in a number of ways. In addition to using your credit or debit account to run up charges, they may open a new credit account in your name. They may also change the mailing address on credit card accounts so that the bills go elsewhere, delaying your discovery of the theft. If the thieves have your checkbook, they may forge checks and empty your bank account.

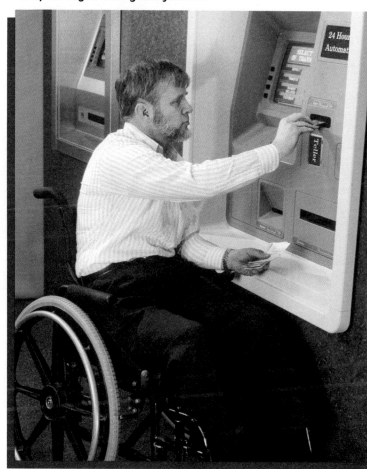

Fig. 28-7. *When you use an ATM, make sure others aren't watching you enter your personal identification number. Remember to take your card and receipt with you when you're finished.*

What You Can Do ~ As you can imagine, identity theft can be a devastating experience. Take these precautions to reduce the chances that it will happen to you:

- Don't give out your Social Security number unless absolutely necessary.

- Don't give personal information over the phone, by mail, or by e-mail except to people you know you can trust.

- When you need to give personal information over the Internet, make sure you are at a secure site.

- Tear up or shred documents such as bank statements and credit card statements before you throw them away. Cut up expired credit cards. See Fig. 28-8.

- Change computer or online passwords frequently. Don't share them with anyone, and don't write them down where someone has access to them.

- Keep items with personal information locked away.

- Make sure nobody is watching when you use an automated teller machine.

If you suspect that your identity has been stolen, take immediate action. File a police report, and keep a copy of it as proof. Call your bank and credit card companies, tell them what has happened, and ask what steps you should take. Contact the major credit bureaus—including Equifax, Experian, and Trans Union—to place a fraud alert on your credit file. Finally, contact the Federal Trade Commission for information about other steps you should take.

Fig. 28-8. Destroying financial documents by shredding them is one way to protect your identity. What might you do if you don't have access to a shredder?

Guarding Against Fraud

Identity theft is just one example of **fraud**—deceitful conduct for personal gain. People who engage in fraud may lie, make misleading statements, divert money from a legitimate cause, sell a worthless product, or engage in some other practice that persuades victims to part with their money. Fraud is illegal, but it is common. Every year, millions of people become victims of fraud. Many of them never recover their money.

Telemarketing Fraud

In one of the most common types of fraud, deceitful sellers use the telephone to make their "offers." Some persuade victims to buy expensive goods or services. Instead of the promised items, victims who send money receive an item of far less value or nothing at all. Some fraudulent telemarketers talk victims into investing money in phony schemes that "can't fail." Others persuade people to send money for charity, but then keep the money for themselves.

Pyramid Schemes and Chain Letters

A **pyramid scheme** is a get-rich-quick plan based on recruiting more and more participants. People pay a fee to join, and then recruit others. The other people also pay a fee and bring in still more participants. In theory, people who stay in the pyramid long enough receive the money paid in by new recruits. In fact, pyramid schemes can never work in the long run because they are impossible to sustain. The people who start them often make money, but the later recruits lose everything that they paid in. Pyramid schemes are based on false promises and are illegal. See Fig. 28-9.

Fig. 28-9. Don't let the promise of easy money lure you into a pyramid scheme. It will collapse sooner than you think, giving you nothing in return.

One type of pyramid scheme is the **chain letter**—an e-mail or mail message that encourages people to send copies of the letter to additional people, along with money. Participants are promised that they will in turn receive money as the number of participants multiplies. Chain letters, like other pyramid schemes, depend on continuously recruiting new members. Most collapse after a short while, robbing most participants of their money.

Fig. 28-10. *Fraud has been around for centuries, but the methods have changed to keep up with new technology.* **What might cause you to suspect Internet fraud?**

Internet Fraud

Internet fraud uses some aspect of the Internet—e-mail, chat rooms, Web sites—to conduct fraudulent transactions and solicit money from victims. Some online auction and retail sites are fraudulent, sending consumers items worth far less than what was promised. Other schemes charge a fee for information on starting a home business but never send the materials. Still others claim to be verifying credit card information when in fact they are stealing that information. See Fig. 28-10.

Taking Action

How can you recognize a fraudulent offer? Look for these warning signs:

- Individuals or businesses that will not reveal their location or give an address.
- Insistence that payment be made before information can be sent out.
- High-pressure offers that are "good for today only."
- Any offers that seem too good to be true.

If you think you have been a victim of fraud, report the incident. Contact the Federal Trade Commission or the National Fraud Information Center. Even if you just suspect that an offer may be fraudulent, report your suspicions. You may save others from becoming victims.

Acting Responsibly

Just as you expect a business to act honestly and fairly, a business expects you to do the same. Your actions toward other consumers and toward the businesses you deal with affect far more than just yourself. They also affect the welfare of other people, businesses, and even the economy. Make sure that you act in a responsible manner.

When you shop or use a service, be considerate. Wait your turn and respect the rules of the establishment. Be courteous when you interact with employees, whether in person, by phone, or by e-mail. See Fig. 28-11.

Would you want to buy clothes that had been torn when someone tried them on, or a household item that had been dropped and damaged? Neither do your fellow consumers. Treat merchandise with care. If you decide not to purchase an item, put it back where it belongs.

Make sure you are aware of and follow a store's **return policy**—the rules for returning or exchanging merchandise. Some stores give store credit only, not refunds. Most stores set time limits for the return of items and expect returned items to be undamaged and unused. Consumers who wear an item of clothing and then return it are dishonest.

Dishonesty costs business owners, and ultimately consumers, millions of dollars a year. **Shoplifting**—the theft of merchandise from a store by shoppers—is a particularly serious problem. Stores not only lose income because of stolen items but also must spend money to prevent theft. The costs of security guards, cameras, and anti-theft tags are passed on to consumers in the form of higher prices. Shoplifting has serious consequences for anyone who attempts it, including arrest, fines, imprisonment, and a criminal record.

Responsible consumers are aware of the important role they play in the marketplace and in the economy. They understand their rights; they expect to be treated fairly; they are fair and honest themselves. You can enjoy your power as a consumer by choosing goods and services that meet your needs, by showing courtesy, and by doing your part to avoid and prevent crime against consumers.

Fig. 28-11. Shopping is more enjoyable for all when customers make an effort to be polite and pleasant. What are some other ways to show consumer courtesy?

Chapter Summary

- Collectively, consumers influence the marketplace and the economy as a whole.

- Consumers have legal rights in the marketplace and responsibilities that go with those rights.

- Consumer information is available from many sources, but should be evaluated carefully.

- Before making a consumer complaint, determine what you want to achieve, whom you will contact, and how.

- Protect your privacy and your identity by being cautious about giving out personal information.

- Fraud occurs when people deceive consumers into paying for useless products or services.

Reviewing Key Terms & Ideas

1. Explain the power that **consumers** have in the marketplace.

2. Identify at least six different influences on consumer spending.

3. Explain seven consumer rights and their corresponding responsibilities.

4. Under what circumstances might you use your right to **redress**?

5. Name five types of sources for consumer information.

6. How can you evaluate consumer information?

7. What is the advantage of using a **small claims court** to settle minor complaints?

8. What is **identity theft**? Give an example of how it might occur.

9. Explain how a **pyramid scheme** works. Why is it considered **fraud**?

10. What should you do if you suspect fraud?

11. Give three guidelines for being a considerate, responsible consumer.

12. What are two reasons why **shoplifting** results in higher prices for consumers?

Thinking Critically

1. **Analyzing Behavior.** Think of an item that you purchased recently. What or who influenced your decision? Based on what you have learned in this chapter, would you use a different process another time? Why or why not?

2. **Recognizing Bias.** Of the consumer information sources listed in the chapter, which are least likely to be biased? Why? For each of the other types of sources, give an example of why bias might occur.

Applying Your Knowledge

1. **Consumer Information.** Find three sources of consumer information about a specific product or service. Each source should be a different type. Evaluate the reliability of each source and explain how you reached your conclusions.

2. **Consumer Complaint.** When you pick up your shirt from the dry cleaner, you notice a hole that was not there before. Explain the process you would follow to make a complaint. Specify to whom you would complain, how you would make contact, and what you would say or do. Include a plan for making a second and third complaint in case the first attempt was not successful.

3. **Fighting Fraud.** Research some schemes, pitches, or phrases that might be used by fraudulent telemarketers. Make a brochure or poster that could be used to educate others about these tactics.

Making Connections

1. **Language Arts.** Write an article for the school newspaper giving teens some guidelines on protecting their privacy online.

2. **Math.** Research current statistics about the costs of shoplifting to businesses and/or consumers. Create two different types of graphs that highlight statistics you feel are especially significant. Explain why each type of graph is an appropriate way to present the information.

Managing Your Life

Preventing Identity Theft

Discuss the problem of identity theft with family members. What activities put you and your family most at risk? Identify everyday actions that might enable someone to gain access to personal information. For example, do family members take precautions when using an ATM or making Internet purchases? How do you, as a family, dispose of documents containing personal information? Where do you store personal documents? Based on your discussion, work together to create a plan for reducing your family's risk. Identify specific steps to take and who will take them. After implementing the plan, meet again to evaluate how well it is working.

Using Technology

1. **Internet.** Compare the privacy policies of two or three online stores. What are the similarities and differences? What do they say about sharing your information? What choices do consumers have about how their information is shared? Prepare a brief report.

2. **Video.** With one or two classmates, create a video demonstrating appropriate and inappropriate ways to interact with store personnel and fellow customers when shopping.

CHAPTER 29

Advertising

Objectives

- **Compare** benefits and drawbacks of advertising.
- **Describe** various types of advertisements.
- **Give examples** of persuasive advertising techniques.
- **Evaluate** advertising messages.
- **Describe** deceptive advertising practices.

QUICK WRITE

Think of an ad that you consider especially memorable and effective. Write a paragraph explaining why it made an impression on you.

*H*ow do you choose the products you buy? Whether you're aware of it or not, many of your purchasing decisions are influenced by advertising. Every day you are exposed to dozens—perhaps hundreds—of ads. Small wonder, then, that those ads help to determine the products and services you choose.

The Role of Advertising

Most advertising is designed for one main purpose: to make people want to buy what the advertiser is trying to sell. Businesses spend billions of dollars each year to promote their products and services. It's true that not all ads are trying to sell something. Some promote various political, social, and charitable causes. However, all ads have a common goal: to influence people's opinions and behavior.

Most advertising is meant to appeal directly to consumers. Advertisers use a variety of techniques to persuade consumers to choose one product or service over another. When there is little difference in quality between competing brands, the effectiveness of an advertising campaign might determine whether a product succeeds or fails. See Fig. 29-1.

For advertisers, an effective ad campaign has obvious benefits, and the drawback is the cost. For consumers, too, advertising has both benefits and drawbacks.

Fig. 29-1. Companies spend large amounts of money and effort on creating ads that will persuade people to buy their products. *What kinds of ads do you find most effective?*

Benefits of Advertising

Advertising can be helpful to consumers when it provides information about products and services. Ads can inform you about product features and benefits, make you aware of new or improved products, and tell you about sales and special promotions. Often you can use ads to compare different products.

Advertising also makes it possible for information and entertainment to be provided at little or no cost to the public. Most newspapers, magazines, radio and television stations, and Web sites rely on advertising. Advertisers pay large sums to buy space or time for their messages. If they didn't, you would have to pay much more for your favorite magazine, for example.

Drawbacks of Advertising

The benefits of advertising must be weighed against the drawbacks. Many people find ads annoying, especially when they interrupt a favorite television program. More seriously, ads can persuade people to spend money they can't afford on goods or services that they don't really need. Some advertising is misleading, suggesting benefits that a product is unlikely to deliver.

Advertising also increases the prices that consumers pay for goods and services. In fact, advertising and other forms of promotion can add as much as 75 percent to the cost of a product. That's the main reason why unadvertised store brands are less expensive than nationally advertised brands. See Fig. 29-2.

The Power of Advertising

Few people admit to being significantly influenced by ads. However, surveys and sales figures show that well-designed advertising is powerfully persuasive. You have only to examine your own family's buying habits to understand the power of advertising. Consider the foods you eat, the places you go, and the movies you watch. Chances are that advertising plays a significant role in your family's consumer choices, as it does for millions of other families. Knowing how powerful advertising is should motivate you to become more aware of how it works.

Fig. 29-2. When comparing products, remember that prices reflect not only the cost of the goods, but also the cost of advertising them.

Types of Ads

Advertisers have numerous ways to reach consumers. As new technology develops, new methods of advertising will develop also.

Advertisements are communicated through numerous **media**, or channels of mass communication. Some of the media that advertisers use to capture consumers' attention are:

- **Newspaper and magazine ads.**
  Newspapers are especially useful to local advertisers trying to reach consumers in the community. Magazines generally reach a wider national audience. Some have a general readership and carry ads that appeal to many people. Other magazines target specific groups of readers—such as teens, gardeners, or cooks—and carry ads designed to appeal to those readers. See Fig. 29-3.

- **Radio and television commercials.**
  Advertisers usually purchase 30 to 60 seconds of air time during or between programs. In general, the more popular a program is, the more expensive the ad time. Ads during major sports events are usually the most expensive to air because they are seen by a huge audience.

- **Infomercials.** Some television or radio ads, called paid programming or **infomercials**, last 30 minutes or more. They are designed to seem like regular programming, such as a talk show or news program. Their real purpose is to sell a product. A typical infomercial might include information, product demonstrations, and praise from satisfied customers.

- **Internet ads.** Thousands of companies advertise their products and services on the Internet. They use their own Web

Fig. 29-3. All of these magazines will bring advertising messages to their readers. What kinds of products are advertised in the magazines that you read?

pages or purchase ad space on other Web sites. E-mail is also a powerful advertising tool.

- **Direct mail.** The practice of delivering ads to consumers' homes by mail is called **direct mail advertising**. The ads may be in the form of letters, brochures, catalogs, or coupon booklets, for instance.

- **Outdoor advertising.** Examples of this type of advertising include billboards, neon signs, and posters plastered on the sides of buses and buildings.

- **Other advertising formats.** Many other media, from cell phone start-up screens to blimps floating in the sky, carry ads. You might even be carrying ads yourself! Check out your clothing—are any company names or logos visible?

Information vs. Image

No matter what media they use, ads can be divided into two basic types based on the kind of message they convey. *Information ads* supply facts that help you learn about and compare products or services. An example might be an ad for athletic shoes that explains how they are designed and constructed to improve performance. *Image ads* focus not on facts but on the image of the product they are promoting. An image ad for the same shoes might show them being worn by an athlete, with no facts given except the name of the brand. Image ads are designed to make you associate the product with positive feelings. Which type of ad do you think is more useful for consumers?

Fig. 29-4. Advertisers don't hesitate to exploit people's insecurities—such as concern about whether their breath is fresh enough.

Persuasive Techniques

Advertisers use a variety of techniques to persuade consumers to buy their products. Understanding these techniques can help you analyze ads and your reaction to them. Here are some commonly used persuasive techniques. Can you think of others you've seen?

- **Positive images.** Advertisers often try to show how happy, healthy, smart, good-looking, or popular you will be if you use their product. For example, an ad might suggest that people who wear a certain brand of swimwear get invited to great beach parties.
- **Hidden fears.** Some ads play on consumers' fears. An ad for a cleaning product might suggest that a home will be unsanitary without it. See Fig. 29-4.

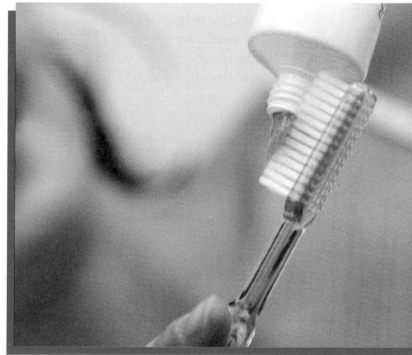

Viewpoints

Celebrity Endorsements

A celebrity endorsement can help sell a product to consumers. Endorsements can also enhance a celebrity's image—or diminish it, depending on whom you ask.

Vince: I don't like to see my favorite actors or athletes in ads, even if they really use the product they're selling. I don't think it's fair to use their popularity that way. I know they get paid to make the commercial, but fans don't see a paid performer—they see a hero. It abuses my loyalty as a fan. It makes me think less of the celebrity.

Greg: Celebrity endorsements have been around for ages, and I don't see what's wrong with them. Celebrities work hard for their success, and endorsements are some of the rewards. Besides, it's fun to see my favorite stars in commercials. I just have to remind myself that they're getting paid to say they like a product.

Seeing Both Sides ~ What are some special concerns about using a well-known person in an advertisement? Give two guidelines to help separate a celebrity's appeal from a product's value when judging a celebrity ad.

- **Bandwagon.** These ads try to convince you that everyone else has "jumped on the bandwagon" and is enjoying this product, so you should too.

- **Testimonials.** Celebrities, famous athletes, and consumers often make **testimonials**, or positive statements about a product based on personal experience. Keep in mind that in most cases, these people are paid to **endorse**, or give their approval to, the product.

- **Demonstrations.** Some ads use demonstrations to show the advantages of a product, such as the strength of paper towels or the effectiveness of a razor.

- **Slogans and jingles.** Advertisers hope that clever slogans and jingles—those catchy tunes in some ads—will lodge in your memory and come to mind when you're shopping.

- **Putdowns.** Advertisers may make negative statements about a competitor's product to make their own product seem better.

- **Before and after.** You've probably seen them: the overweight woman in drab clothes (before) transformed into a swim-suit beauty (after). How about the sad-looking young man with acne (before) who is now clear-skinned and smiling (after)? Keep in mind that advertisers use all sorts of tricks to exaggerate the differences in the two photos.

Evaluating Ads

Once you're aware of the techniques that advertisers use, you can recognize how an ad is trying to manipulate you. Don't just take ads at face value. Use your critical thinking skills to analyze their messages and the way they are presented. Here are some suggestions:

- **Look for facts.** Separate emotional appeals and opinions from facts. Use the facts to make decisions.

- **Check the fine print.** Look for the details of special offers. For example, if a fitness club is promoting a "special introductory price," it probably means you pay the advertised price for only a month or two. Look for details that explain how much the price goes up and when.

- **Analyze what's being said.** "Recliners from as little as $99" means that $99 is the *lowest* price at which a recliner is being sold. It doesn't mean that *all* the store's recliners are that price. How high do the prices go from there? Who knows—you can't tell from the ad.

- **Watch out for vague claims.** Suppose an ad says "Doctors agree that …." Who are these doctors? How many of them were consulted? Are they medical doctors or some other kind? A statement like this may be technically true, yet almost meaningless.

Deceptive Advertising

A certain amount of exaggeration and hype is expected in ads. However, some ads go too far—they make false statements or omit information in order to mislead consumers. That's deception, and it's illegal. Here are some examples of deceptive practices:

- **False claims.** Advertisers who make specific claims for their products, such as "reduces the risk of skin cancer" or "twice as powerful as other leading brands," must be able to back up their claims with scientific evidence. If they can't, they are being deceptive.

- **Hidden catches.** An ad that does not clearly disclose important details, such as restrictions or extra fees, is deceptive. So is an ad that offers a "free gift" without revealing that you have to purchase something to get it.

- **Deceptive pricing.** Suppose a store's ad for jeans says, "Sale! $34.99." If the store always sells that brand of jeans for $34.99, then the use of the word "Sale" is deceptive. Items on sale are supposed to have a lower price than usual.

- **Bait and switch.** Advertisers who use **bait and switch** lure buyers by advertising an unusually low-priced item that they have no intention of selling. That's the "bait." When shoppers try to buy the advertised item, they might be told, "We just sold the last one." In reality, the bargain item may never have been in the store.

The salesperson then tries to "switch" the shopper to a higher-priced item. See Fig. 29-5.

The Federal Trade Commission (FTC) regulates advertising and can require advertisers to prove their claims. If the FTC rules that an ad is deceptive, the advertiser must stop using it and in some cases must pay a fine. Consumers can report suspected cases of deception by calling the FTC or visiting its Web site.

Advertising is here to stay, and it's up to you to make wise use of it. Use critical thinking skills to evaluate ads. Look for facts, analyze information, recognize emotional appeals, and be skeptical of promises that seem too good to be true. Learn to separate the truth from the persuasive techniques. When you know how to evaluate ads, you can benefit from them—and enjoy the creativity that goes into an effective advertising campaign.

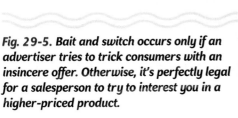

Fig. 29-5. Bait and switch occurs only if an advertiser tries to trick consumers with an insincere offer. Otherwise, it's perfectly legal for a salesperson to try to interest you in a higher-priced product.

Chapter Summary

- Advertising has power to influence people's opinions and behavior.
- Consumers benefit from advertising in several ways, but must also guard against its drawbacks.
- Advertising includes information ads and image ads in many different media.
- Advertisers use a variety of techniques to persuade consumers.
- Use your critical thinking skills to evaluate ads.
- Laws against deceptive advertising are enforced by the Federal Trade Commission.

Reviewing Key Terms & Ideas

1. What is the main purpose of advertising?
2. Describe two ways in which advertising benefits consumers.
3. How does advertising affect the price you pay for products?
4. Give five examples of advertising **media**.
5. What are two differences between **infomercials** and regular commercials?
6. Give three examples of **direct mail advertising**.
7. Explain the difference between image ads and information ads.
8. What are **testimonials**? Give an example.
9. How and why might a celebrity **endorse** a product?
10. Give three guidelines for evaluating advertising.
11. What is **bait and switch**? Why is it deceptive?
12. Describe two other deceptive advertising practices.

Thinking Critically

1. **Making Comparisons.** Do you think advertising's benefits to consumers outweigh the drawbacks? Why or why not?
2. **Distinguishing Fact from Opinion.** Select five ads that each make several statements about the product being advertised. Which statements give specific facts that the advertiser could be asked to prove? Which statements are opinions or vague claims that do not have to be proven?

Applying Your Knowledge

1. **Persuasive Techniques.** For each of the persuasive techniques described in the text, find one or more examples in current advertising. Bring copies or descriptions of the ads to class. In small groups, share your examples. Be prepared to explain how the persuasive techniques are used.

2. **Evaluating Ads.** Write a set of guidelines for evaluating ads. Include the suggestions given in the text plus additional ideas of your own. Use your guidelines to evaluate four ads in different media. In writing, explain how you evaluated each ad and what conclusions you reached.

3. **Creating an Ad.** Write an ad to promote a school fundraiser or a community function. Use persuasive techniques to create interest in the event.

Making Connections

1. **Social Studies.** Research examples of political ads. Prepare a report describing the techniques that politicians use in their advertising campaigns.

2. **Language Arts.** Use newspapers and magazines to analyze the language used in ads. Make a list of commonly used words and expressions. Discuss with classmates the intent and effectiveness of these words and expressions.

Managing Your Life

Smart Buying Decisions

You'll make better buying decisions if you establish criteria for your purchases before you shop. By determining ahead of time what you require of a product, you can use advertising to your advantage and resist appeals to your emotions. Identify a product you plan to buy in the near future. Make a list of criteria the product must meet, based on your needs, wants, values, goals, and resources. Prioritize your list. Then use ads as a resource to help you determine which products come closest to your requirements. Keep your research materials, and update them when you're ready to make the purchase.

Using Technology

1. **Internet.** Find out what the government has done to regulate intrusive forms of Internet advertising, such as pop-up ads and spam. Prepare a report of your findings. Do you think that more regulation is needed? Why or why not?

2. **Presentation Software.** From newspapers and magazines, cut out ads that illustrate the advertising techniques described in the chapter. Use scanning equipment and presentation software to create a presentation for your classmates. Write speaker's notes that describe each technique, and use them as you make your presentation.

CHAPTER 30

Shopping Skills

Key Terms

- impulse buying
- irregulars
- seconds
- warranty
- rebate
- bonded

Objectives

- **Identify** the benefits of planning and researching purchases.
- **Compare** various shopping options.
- **Give guidelines** for shopping from home.
- **Explain** strategies for evaluating quality and finding good buys.
- **Describe** steps to take when shopping for a service.

430

QUICK WRITE

In writing, describe some of your favorite places to shop. Why do you prefer those places over others?

*N*ick studied the inline skates in front of him at the sporting goods store. He was looking to buy his first pair, but there were so many options. He knew he didn't need speed skates or hockey skates, but that still left many choices. Did he want plastic, nylon, or metal frames? Did he need one brake or two? What kind of brakes? What about wheel size?

Nick's friend Gabe saw his hesitation. "You know, you don't have to decide right now," Gabe said. "Maybe you should read up on the different kinds of skates before you spend a lot of money."

Nick nodded. "You're right. And I'm starting to think it would be a good idea to buy used skates to start with. They'll cost a lot less. After I've had them for a while, I can think about buying new ones. By then I'll have a better idea of what I want."

Planning Purchases

Have you, like Nick, ever felt overwhelmed when shopping? Consumers today have so many choices of goods and services. Those who plan their purchases before they shop usually get better value for their money and are more likely to be satisfied with what they buy. Of course, you don't need to spend a lot of time planning every purchase. Buying a pen or a pair of socks usually doesn't require much research. However, if you're in the market for a computer, a tennis racquet, or some other major purchase, you will want to plan carefully. See Fig. 30-1.

Start by thinking about your needs, wants, values, goals, and resources. They will affect the choices you make all through the shopping process. Imagine, for example, that

Fig. 30-1. Investigating products before you buy will help you make wise purchasing decisions.

you're shopping for a sleeping bag. The more expensive ones have extra insulation for added warmth. Will you need that extra warmth, or would a lower-priced sleeping bag with less insulation suit your needs? Knowing which features are important to you will help you determine what to look for and how much you're willing to pay.

Research Products

To find out what features and options are available for the product you're planning to buy, you may have to do some research. By investigating the products that are on the market, you can also get a feel for price ranges and begin to make comparisons.

Fig. 30-2. Displays like this one encourage impulse buying. *How might recognizing these merchandising efforts help you resist them?*

There are many ways to research products. You might ask friends and family members who have bought similar items to tell you about their experiences. You can study product reviews in consumer magazines and search the Internet for product and pricing information. Start visiting stores—not necessarily to buy, but to gather information. Examine the merchandise and read labels, tags, and instruction booklets. Ask sales clerks to explain or demonstrate products. Take their recommendations into consideration, but also check other sources. The better informed you are, the more likely that you will be satisfied with your purchase.

Avoid Impulse Buying

Planning your purchases can help you avoid **impulse buying**—making unplanned purchases with little or no thought. Retailers have many ways of tempting you to buy more than you intended. They make attractive offers, such as "Buy one, get one free." They suggest additional items to go with what you're buying. They provide demonstrations and free samples to interest you in a product you may not have considered. They display tempting items in noticeable locations, such as in center aisles and checkout lanes. See Fig. 30-2.

Sellers know that these methods often succeed in getting you to make additional purchases. That's good for the seller, but not for you. Impulse buying is like a leak that drains dollars from your wallet and your budget. To avoid impulse buying, keep these suggestions in mind:

- List what you want to buy before you shop, and stick to those items.
- Take only as much money as you think you will need for the items on your list.

Fig. 30-3. You can find real bargains at a neighborhood yard sale. Sellers are often more interested in getting rid of unwanted items than in making money.

- If you see something you hadn't planned to buy but that looks like a good bargain, wait and think it over. Return to the store later if you still want it.

Shopping Options

When it comes to shopping, you have many choices. You can shop in a variety of stores or use technology to shop from home.

Stores and Outlets

Stores offer several advantages. You can see and examine items and compare different brands. You can get information and advice from sales clerks. If you want to return an item, you can simply take it back to the store.

Choosing the right type of store can help you make the purchase that best suits your needs. Here are some of the many available options:

- **Department stores** carry a wide selection of goods in different price ranges. Some offer their own credit cards and provide additional customer services.

- **Discount stores** carry nationally advertised brands at reduced prices.

- **Specialty stores** sell a particular type of merchandise, such as clothing, office supplies, or electronics. Selection and price vary, often depending on whether the store is a small operation or part of a national chain.

- **Factory outlets** sell merchandise from one manufacturer, usually at lower prices than other retailers. Some of the goods are **irregulars**—items that are slightly imperfect. You may also find **seconds**, which have more noticeable flaws.

- **Warehouse clubs** offer a large range of products—such as groceries, clothing, and home furnishings—at discounted prices to customers who pay a membership fee. Many of the products are sold in bulk.

Secondhand Sources

Bargain hunters can save money by shopping at places where used items are sold. At yard sales and garage sales, for example, people sell items that they no longer need or want for low prices. At flea markets, people rent tables to sell new or used goods at low prices. See Fig. 30-3.

You can also pick up bargains at auctions, where items go to the highest bidder, and in secondhand stores. Yet another source of previously owned goods—from furniture to cars—is the classified ads section in your local newspaper.

When buying from any of these sources, inspect items carefully before making your purchase. You probably won't be able to return items for a refund.

Shopping from Home

Instead of going to a store, would you rather shop from your easy chair? No problem. Technology offers many ways to shop from home by telephone, television, or computer.

- **Catalogs** are as varied as stores. Some specialize in a particular type of item, such as clothes or electronics. Others offer a wider variety. When buying from a catalog, you can order by phone, by mail, or in many cases from the company's Web site.

- **TV shopping** channels sell products ranging from collectibles to jewelry to household items. The products are explained or demonstrated by a presenter. Customers pay by credit card over the phone or send a check. Infomercials, too, present opportunities to buy items seen on TV without leaving home.

More to Explore

Internet Auctions

An Internet auction site that offers a wide variety of new and used items can be a wonderful source of bargains. Sellers provide a description, and often a photo, of the item they are putting up for auction. Prospective buyers have a certain number of days to view the item and place bids. When the auction closes, the highest bidder and the seller arrange for payment and shipping.

To make your Internet auction experience pleasant and worthwhile:

- Read the feedback provided by other buyers who have dealt with a particular seller. Look for comments about whether items were described accurately, shipped promptly, and packaged carefully to arrive in good condition.

- Examine the descriptions and pictures carefully before you bid. You generally cannot take back a bid once you place it.

- Ask the seller questions by e-mail if you want more information. You might request proof that an item is authentic.

- Since it's easy to get caught up in bidding, set a limit on your spending before you begin. Remember to factor in shipping charges.

- **Internet shopping** is increasingly popular. You can buy just about anything imaginable, from anywhere in the world, day or night. You can use search sites to find the item you are looking for, or you can visit your favorite stores' Web sites. The Internet makes it easy to compare prices and products from different suppliers.

Pros and Cons ~ More and more people are discovering the advantages of shopping from home. When you order by phone, mail, or the Internet, you avoid the hassle of crowded stores and parking lots. Often you can order at any time of day or night. In addition, you generally have a wider selection of products to choose from, including hard-to-find sizes and items. See Fig. 30-4.

Shopping from home does have some drawbacks, however. Because it's so convenient, it's easy to buy on impulse and spend more than you planned. You can't see, handle, and compare items directly, so you risk being disappointed when they arrive. Often you must pay a shipping and handling charge in addition to the cost of the item. If you're not satisfied with the item when it arrives, you may have to pay an additional shipping charge to send it back.

Guidelines for Home Shopping ~
For your protection and satisfaction when shopping from home, follow these guidelines:

- Make sure the company you are ordering from has a good reputation. If you're not familiar with it, ask people who have ordered from that company for their input.

Fig. 30-4. Home shopping makes it possible to buy items that are not available in local stores. What types of items might you buy this way? Why?

- Look carefully at the pictures and descriptions of items to be sure you know what you're getting. Check with a company representative if you have questions.

- Read through the terms and conditions of sale. They should include the price, applicable taxes, delivery options and costs, and return policies. Also look for warranties and company contact information.

- Compare the prices of products you want to order with those of similar products carried in local stores. Remember to include taxes and shipping.

- Find out how long it will take to deliver the items. If you need them by a certain date, be sure they will arrive in time.

- When shopping online, don't provide your credit card number unless you know you are on a secure site. Secure sites use safeguards to keep your personal information from being intercepted. The letters "shttp" or "https" in the Web address at the top of your screen indicate that the site is secure.

- To keep from overspending, use a shopping list and set a spending limit. Before you place your order, add up the total charges including shipping and tax. Resist the temptation to spend more than you planned.

Viewpoints

At-Home Shopping

With catalogs, the Internet, shopping networks, and infomercials, a world of goods comes to you instead of the other way around. It's a big change from traditional shopping. Is it a change for the better?

Lynne: Shopping from home is fast and efficient. You look through a catalog, see what they have, then decide if you want to buy something. When you shop online, you can do a search to find out who sells an item and get the best deal. And you do it all when it's convenient for you. When you shop in a store, it takes time to find what you want, and then you have to wait in line to pay for it.

Adrienne: You miss a lot when you shop at home. Shopping can be a fun experience, especially when you go with friends. Friends will give you an honest opinion, and I value that more than a catalog description. Sometimes my friends find good bargains or suggest things that I wouldn't have considered. Shopping at home takes all the fun out of the experience.

Seeing Both Sides ~ Does shopping at home have to be a solitary experience? Is shopping with friends always time consuming? Describe two ways to combine the benefits of shopping with friends with the advantages of shopping at home.

- Keep a record of what you order, including the order number, price, and the date of the order. Also make a note of the online merchant's site address and other contact information. If the merchant sends you an e-mail confirmation of your order, keep a copy.

- When your items are delivered, make sure they are exactly what you ordered and are in good condition. If not, contact the company immediately.

Finding Good Buys

If you want to get the most for your money, you'd be wise to comparison shop. That means comparing similar products to one another, as well as comparing prices offered by different sellers. You can comparison shop by visiting different stores, looking through ads and catalogs, and searching the Internet. When you do, consider both quality and price.

Evaluate Quality

The lowest-priced product is not the best buy if the quality is too poor for your needs. By the same token, a higher price doesn't automatically mean better quality. Learning to evaluate quality will help you choose products that are right for you.

The quality of an item is determined by factors such as performance, durability, convenience, maintenance, and safety. To check how well a product works, you might ask for a demonstration in the store. This would be appropriate for items such as cameras, computers, musical instruments, or sporting equipment. To test the quality of clothes and shoes, try them on and examine the workmanship.

You can compare the durability and amount of care items need by looking at care labels and service manuals. Labels on clothing tell what fabric the garment is made of and how it should be cleaned. Appliances come with service manuals that describe the kind of care the item requires. If you're buying something that requires assembly, be sure instructions are included.

There are different ways to evaluate the safety of products. You can often find information on product safety in consumer magazines and at consumer Web sites. For items such as clothing and furniture, check the labels to see whether they are made of flame-retardant or flame-resistant fabrics. For electrical products, check for the mark of Underwriters Laboratories (UL), an independent organization that tests electrical products for safety. See Fig. 30-5.

Fig. 30-5. The UL mark tells you that the product has been tested by experts for safety.

Look for Warranties

Many products have a **warranty**—a guarantee that provides protection against faulty products. Often warranties are provided in writing by the manufacturer or seller. Before you purchase an item, find out whether there is a written warranty. Read it carefully and make sure you understand its terms. For example, the warranty might be in effect for two years, cover replacement parts but not labor costs, and exclude certain parts.

Written warranties can be full or limited. A *full warranty* meets certain conditions specified by federal law. For example, it guarantees a refund or replacement if the product is defective and cannot be fixed. A *limited warranty* does not meet all the conditions of a full warranty, but still gives valuable protection. Both full and limited warranties can have time limits and other restrictions.

Even if an item does not come with a written warranty, it may be covered by an *implied warranty*. This protection is provided by state law rather than by the manufacturer or seller. If you buy an item that doesn't do what it is supposed to do—for example, a CD player that won't play CDs—an implied warranty would give you the right to a refund or a replacement.

Identify Hidden Costs

When comparing prices, remember that there may be hidden costs—expenses of time, energy, and money not included in the purchase price. You already know, for example, that shipping costs can be a factor when you shop at home. Other hidden costs can include accessories, batteries, taxes, fees, and maintenance.

When you're shopping, estimate the hidden costs and factor them into your price comparisons. Keep in mind, too, that shopping itself can add hidden costs. Traveling long distances in search of a better bargain costs time and money. If you spend two hours of your time and $5 in gas to save $10 on a purchase, is it worth it? Only you can decide.

Take Advantage of Sales

One way to find good buys is to shop at sales. Retailers often hold sales events at specific times, such as holidays, the end of a season, and the start of the school year. In addition, certain types of items traditionally go on sale at certain times of year. See Fig. 30-6.

Fig. 30-6. You can save money if you shop when items are on sale. What are some disadvantages of sales?

Savings during a sale can be substantial. Just because an item is on sale, however, doesn't always mean that it's a good buy. When shopping at sales, keep these guidelines in mind:

- Be sure you really want and can use the item you're considering. A $15 jacket might seem like a good deal. However, if it doesn't fit well or doesn't go with any of your other clothes, you will have $15 less to put toward another item that you could really use.

- Don't assume a sale price is the best price. One store's sale price might actually be higher than the regular price at another store. Compare to find out.

- Be aware that items marked "As is" or "Final sale" often may not be returned. You need to be completely sure you want the item before paying for it.

- If an appliance is on sale because the model is being discontinued, ask if replacement parts will still be available.

- Notice which items are *not* on sale. Merchants hope that customers will also buy regular-priced items when they are in the store for sales.

Consider Coupons and Rebates

Coupons and rebates are another way to save. Coupons allow you to get a certain amount or percentage off the price of the featured product. You can find coupons in magazines and newspapers, in the mail, and on the Internet. Some coupons are issued by specific retailers; others by product manufacturers.

A **rebate** is a refund of part of the purchase price of a product. Rebates are offered on items ranging from small appliances to cars. To receive a rebate, you have to fill out a form and send it to the manufacturer with proof of purchase. You will then receive a check for the rebate amount.

Coupons and rebates can help you save a significant amount, but only if you use them wisely. If you buy an item you don't need just because you have a coupon, you have wasted your money. Many people fail to follow rebate directions exactly, so they miss out on the promised savings.

TIPS FOR *Success*

Finding Bargains

Many of the ideas in this chapter will help you save money when you shop. Here are some additional tips:

- Ask the store clerk for a discount, coupon, or special deal.

- Consider buying a less popular brand.

- Compare prices on the Internet. Then ask a local retailer to match the lowest price you find.

- Check the classified ads for sales or auctions at storage rental facilities.

- Look for discounted items that may need some repair.

■ You can usually return goods if you're dissatisfied, but you can't return or "undo" an unsatisfactory service.

Comparing Service Providers

For many services, you will want to shop around and compare qualified providers, just as you comparison shop for merchandise. There are several steps to choosing a provider who will meet your needs.

Get Recommendations ~ Make a list of providers who offer the type of service you're interested in. Talk to friends and family who have hired someone to perform similar work. Which provider did they use? Were they satisfied with the experience and the results? Would they recommend the person?

Check Qualifications ~ Once you have a list of possible providers, look into their qualifications. Find out about their experience, skills, reliability, and ethics. Here are some ways to get information:

■ Ask for samples or pictures of providers' work.

■ Request names of previous customers. Contact several and ask them whether they were satisfied with the results. See Fig. 30-8.

■ Check that providers have a legitimate and current license, if it's required for the kind of work you are considering.

■ If the work will be done in your home or on your property, verify that providers

Shopping for Services

Consumers purchase a wide variety of services, from haircuts and dry cleaning to plumbing and car repairs. There are some significant differences between shopping for goods and shopping for services.

■ Goods usually have a set price. The price charged for a service often depends on several factors, making it harder to compare prices from different providers.

■ It's more difficult to evaluate the quality of a service. If you get estimates from carpenters to build bookshelves, for example, how can you determine who will do the best job?

■ Buying goods is generally a simpler process. Hiring someone to provide a service often involves estimates, contracts, and other paperwork. See Fig. 30-7.

have liability insurance. Workers should also be **bonded**, which provides protection against financial loss in case of theft.

- Check with the Better Business Bureau to make sure that no complaints have been filed against any providers you are considering.

Get Estimates ~ Once you've narrowed down your list of possible providers, ask for written estimates of how much it will cost to do the work. This will help you determine how much you can expect to pay and allow you to compare prices from different providers.

Read the Contract ~ Some major jobs, such as home repair or remodeling, require a contract—a legally binding agreement between the service provider and the customer. The contract is signed by both parties and protects both in the event of a dispute. Read any contract carefully to make sure you understand what you are signing. Contracts should provide the following information:

- The name, address, phone number, and license number of the person supplying the service.

- Details of the work to be done.

- An estimate of when the work will begin and end.

- The total cost, along with a payment schedule.

- Information about warranties on materials and services.

Getting the Most for Your Money

Once you have chosen a provider, it's in your interest to do all you can to make the experience positive. Provide any information needed to do the job, and ask questions if you don't understand something. Work with the provider to resolve any difficulties that arise.

After the work is done, evaluate the service you received. Was the provider efficient? Was the work completed on time? Were you satisfied with the overall experience? If so, you may want to use the provider again and recommend him or her to others. If you are dissatisfied with any aspect of the service, discuss the problem with the provider. Service providers want satisfied customers and repeat business, so they will generally try to resolve problems.

Fig. 30-8. A reputable service provider should be able to provide you with the names of previous customers as references. What kinds of questions would you ask them?

Chapter Summary

- Consumers who plan their purchases and avoid impulse buying are usually more satisfied with their purchases.

- You can shop at a variety of stores or use the telephone, television, or Internet to shop from home.

- Shopping from home has advantages, but also drawbacks that require caution.

- When comparison shopping, consider quality and warranties as well as price.

- Wise use of sales, coupons, and rebates can help you save money.

- Shopping for services involves a different process than shopping for goods.

- Before selecting service providers, check out their qualifications, prices, and contract terms.

Reviewing Key Terms & Ideas

1. What are the benefits of planning purchases and researching products before you buy?

2. Why should you take steps to resist **impulse buying**?

3. What is the difference between **irregulars** and **seconds**? At what type of store will you find them?

4. Give five guidelines to follow when shopping from home.

5. What factors determine the quality of an item?

6. What does the Underwriters Laboratories mark tell you?

7. What is the purpose of a **warranty**?

8. Give examples of hidden costs. Why do you need to be aware of them?

9. Are items on sale always a good buy? Why or why not?

10. How does a **rebate** work?

11. How does shopping for services differ from shopping for goods?

12. Describe three ways to determine whether a service provider has the experience and skills to do a good job.

13. When and why should you find out whether workers are **bonded**?

14. What information should be included in a contract with a service provider?

Thinking Critically

1. **Analyzing Behavior.** Why is it often difficult to resist the temptation of impulse buying? What might make it easier?

2. **Understanding Cause and Effect.** What effects, both positive and negative, has the rise of Internet shopping had on traditional retail stores?

Applying Your Knowledge

1. **Researching a Product.** Choose a product that you are interested in buying. Using four sources of information, research the choices that are available. What is the general price range for the product? What are the most popular brands? Which available features are most important to you? What are some signs of quality to look for? Summarize your findings in a report.

2. **Comparing Shopping Options.** Identify three stores or Web sites that carry a specific type of product. Compare the three sellers in terms of selection, price, service, return policies, and other factors. Which seller do you prefer? Why?

3. **Evaluating Warranties.** Read the warranties for two similar products. Make a table comparing their key points. Which offers better protection? Explain.

Making Connections

1. **Language Arts.** Write an article for your school newspaper or Web site giving advice for shopping for a specific type of product or service. Offer at least ten tips, including guidelines for evaluating quality and saving money.

2. **Math.** Find a specific item both at a local store and on the Internet. Calculate the total cost from each seller, including any taxes and shipping charges. What percentage would you save if you bought the item from the lower-priced seller?

Managing Your Life

Improving Your Shopping Habits

Most people have some good shopping habits and some that could be improved. Think back on your recent purchases and the way you approach shopping in general. Do you tend to make impulse purchases? Are you often disappointed with the quality of items you buy? Are you too impatient to wait for sales? After identifying areas that need improvement, make a plan for tackling them. Follow the steps in the management plan described in Chapter 5. Give yourself several weeks to make the needed improvements, then evaluate how well your plan worked.

Using Technology

1. **Online Auctions.** Visit an online auction site. Find information about the safeguards that protect buyers from dishonest sellers. What responsibilities do buyers have? Report to the class.

2. **Internet.** Choose a type of service you might want to hire someone to perform. Using the Internet, research what you should look for in a provider. Identify potential providers in your area. Summarize your findings in writing.

Financial Management

Objectives

- **Explain** types of earnings and deductions found on a pay stub.
- **Identify** the purpose of various tax forms.
- **Apply** strategies for selecting and using bank accounts.
- **Discuss** the role of insurance.
- **Compare** various investment and retirement options.

QUICK WRITE

Write down five questions you have about financial management. As you read the chapter, note the answers to your questions or where you could find more information.

Wanda was sorting through a pile of bills when her cell phone rang.

"Hey, Wanda. Have you looked outside yet? It's a perfect morning for a run! How about meeting me over at the track in 20 minutes?"

"Maybe later, Cheryl. Right now I'm paying my bills."

"Come on, I thought you wanted to stay in shape."

"I do, but I need to keep my finances in good shape too. After I write these checks, I'm going on the Web to find out how I can pay some of my bills automatically."

"Hey, I could use that. Last month I had to pay two late fees on bills. I sure can think of better ways to spend that money."

"Well, why don't you come over? We can check out online banking, then hit the track afterwards."

"Sounds good. We'll get ourselves in shape, and our finances too!"

Fig. 31-1. Soon you'll be a young adult in the working world, responsible for your own financial decisions. What money management skills do you think you need to learn first?

Financial Fitness

Financial fitness, like physical fitness, takes effort. Just as you need to exercise regularly to stay physically fit, you need to attend to your finances regularly to stay financially fit. The key to financial fitness is management. See Fig. 31-1.

So what does financial management involve? In a nutshell, it means understanding your paycheck, using bank accounts, and managing your income and expenses. It also means paying your taxes, buying whatever insurance you need, and investing for your future. Developing financial knowledge now will help you gain control over your life and shape the future you want as an adult. The best place to start is with the main source of the finances you will manage—your paycheck.

Understanding Your Paycheck

Many people get an unpleasant shock when they receive their first paycheck: it's much smaller than they expected. Has this happened to you? To avoid a similar shock in the future, take a look at how pay is calculated and what is taken out of it.

Paycheck Earnings

Workers are paid at the end of each pay period, which is typically one week, two weeks, or a month. Some employees receive a paycheck; others have their pay directly deposited into their bank account. Either way, you'll receive a pay stub similar to the one shown in Fig. 31-2.

Your pay stub will show your earnings for the pay period. The method for calculating your earnings should be explained to you when you take the job. Possible methods include:

- **Hourly wages.** If you're paid by the hour, you receive your hourly wage multiplied by the number of hours worked. If you work more hours some weeks than others, your pay will vary.

- **Piecework.** Often used in manufacturing and assembly work, piecework is based on the number of items you produce. The more you produce, the more you earn.

Fig. 31-2. A pay stub provides important information about earnings and deductions. *How much did this person take home after deductions?*

Identification

WORKER, PAT L		Period Ending 06/01		Check # 1103503		
Employee # 5678		Employee SSN 000-50-1234		Department 425		

Earnings	Hours	Current	Year-to-Date	Deductions	Current	Year-to-Date
REGULAR RATE 7.00	54	378.00	4158.00	DENTAL	5.00	55.00
				FEDTAX	23.03	253.33
				STATE TAX	4.29	47.19
				FICAHI	5.45	59.95
				MED INS	16.50	181.50
				SOCSEC	7.20	79.20
Totals	54	378.00	4158.00		61.47	676.17
Net Pay		316.53				

Earnings   **Net pay**   **Totals**   **Deductions**

- **Salary.** A *salary* is a set amount of income for a year. Salaried employees typically receive the same amount of money each pay period.
- **Commission.** Employees involved in sales work may be paid a *commission*—a percentage of the amount that they sell. Some receive commission in addition to their regular wage or salary. Others, such as those who sell cars or real estate, might receive commission only. See Fig. 31-3.

On a pay stub, you'll see two different listings for pay. **Gross pay** is the total amount you earn. Suppose, for example, your salary is $480 per week and you are paid every two weeks. The gross pay on your pay stub will be $960. That's not how much you'll receive, however. A certain amount of your pay will be taken out for taxes and other deductions. The amount you actually receive after deductions is your **net pay**.

Deductions

A *deduction* is anything that is subtracted from gross pay. Some deductions are required by law; others are optional. Here are some of the deductions that you may see on your pay stub:

- **Federal taxes.** Your employer is required to deduct a certain percentage of your gross pay for federal income taxes.
- **State and local taxes.** The amount withheld for state and local income taxes will depend on where you live.
- **Social Security.** Social Security taxes pay for retirement, disability, and survivors' benefits. They may be listed on your pay stub as FICA (Federal Insurance Contributions Act) or OASDI (Old Age, Survivors, and Disability Insurance).

Fig. 31-3. For someone who works on commission, such as a real estate agent, pay is based on closing the sale. What are the pros and cons of this arrangement?

- **Medicare.** Deductions for Medicare pay for the medical expenses of people aged 65 or older and of younger people with certain medical conditions.
- **Retirement or savings plan.** If your company offers a retirement or savings plan, you may elect to have money deducted from your paycheck so that it can be invested in the plan.
- **Benefits.** Companies that offer benefits such as health and dental plans may require employees to contribute to the plans. These contributions would appear as deductions on your pay stub.

Paying Income Taxes

The biggest deduction on your pay stub is likely to be for federal income taxes. All workers are required to pay their fair share. Many state and local governments also collect income taxes.

In most cases, employers are responsible for withholding, or keeping back, taxes from their employees' paychecks and sending the money to the government. The amount of income tax withheld varies from person to person. It depends on how much you earn, how often you get paid, and other factors. To ensure that your employer withholds the correct amount from your pay, you will need to fill out a Form W-4 (Employee's Withholding Allowance Certificate) whenever you start a new job. The form asks for information about your marital status, number of dependents, and so on.

If you earn enough money, you are required to complete a tax return at least once a year. The purpose of this form is to report your total earnings for the preceding year and to determine exactly how much tax you should have paid on those earnings. Then you compare the amount you should have paid with the amount you actually paid. If you paid too much tax, you can request a refund. If you paid too little, you must send payment for the difference.

The Internal Revenue Service (IRS) is the agency that collects federal income tax. A tax return can be filled out on paper and sent by mail to the IRS, or it can be completed and sent electronically. Either way, you need certain information and forms in order to complete your tax return. The basic ones are:

- **Form W-2.** Your employer is required by law to send you a Form W-2 (Wage and Tax Statement) by January 31. See Fig. 31-4. This form shows your total earnings for the previous year and the total amount of tax that was withheld. When you

a Control number				
	OMB No. 1545-0008			
b Employer identification number 123456-78		**1** Wages, tips, other compensation 9,672.00	**2** Federal income tax withheld 745.00	
c Employer's name, address, and ZIP code ABC STORES 2001 RING ROAD LARGETOWN, NY 10001		**3** Social security wages 9,672.00	**4** Social security tax withheld 599.66	
		5 Medicare wages and tips 9,672.00	**6** Medicare tax withheld 140.24	
		7 Social security tips	**8** Allocated tips	
d Employee's social security number 000-98-7654		**9** Advance EIC payment	**10** Dependent care benefits	
e Employee's name, address, and ZIP code JESSE B. STUDENT 4567 LINCOLN ST. LARGETOWN, NY 10001		**11** Nonqualified plans	**12** Benefits included in box 1	
		13	**14** Other	
		15 Statutory employee ☐ Deceased ☐ Pension plan ☐ Legal rep. ☐ Deferred compensation ☐		
16 State NY Employer's state I.D. no. 00-98765	**17** State wages, tips, etc. 9,672.00	**18** State income tax 345.00	**19** Locality name **20** Local wages, tips, etc.	**21** Local income tax

Form W-2 Wage and Tax Statement

Department of the Treasury—Internal Revenue Service

Copy 1 For State, City, or Local Tax Department

Fig. 31-4. Your Form W-2 summarizes your earnings and taxes for the year. How much federal income tax was withheld from this person's pay?

receive this form, you should make sure that your name and Social Security number are correct and that the figures for income and taxes match the year-to-date figures on your last pay stub of the year.

- **Form 1099-INT.** Your bank will send you a Form 1099-INT that shows the amount of interest you earned during the year. **Interest** is a fee the bank pays you for the opportunity to use your money. Interest counts as income and must be reported on your tax return.

- **Instruction booklets and forms.** Depending on your circumstances, you must complete one of three different forms in order to file your federal tax return. Form 1040 is the longest form and can be used by anyone. Form 1040A is a simpler version for taxpayers who fit certain requirements. Form 1040EZ is the simplest form. If you're single, have a relatively small income, and have no dependents, you can probably use Form 1040EZ. Directions on each form will help you determine which one is right for you. Tax forms are available in most public libraries. You can also download and print forms from the IRS Web site.

Using Bank Accounts

Most people open one or more bank accounts when they start working, if not before. Bank accounts offer several advantages. The money is in a safe, insured place, yet you can withdraw cash whenever you need it. You can also put your money to work for you while you're not using it. Banks offer checking and savings accounts to help people manage their money.

More to Explore

Financial Software

Although you can successfully manage your finances using traditional paper records, financial software can streamline the job. Checking account management, for example, is a basic feature of many financial software products. When you enter information about a check or other transaction, an electronic check register instantly updates your account balance. You can print checks or, in many cases, send payments electronically. Other common program options include creating and tracking a budget, tracking the value of your investments, and setting reminders for paying bills. Some packages can assist you with online banking and income tax planning.

Opening a Checking Account

When you have a checking account, you can use checks instead of cash to buy items or pay bills. Checks are more secure than cash because only the payee—the person to whom a check is made out—can cash or deposit it. Most checking accounts also provide other conveniences, such as the ability to withdraw money at automated teller machines (ATMs).

Before you open a checking account, shop around. Many banks offer more than one type of checking account. Some require a minimum balance. Many charge a monthly service fee, and others charge a fee for each check written. Estimate how much money you'll keep in the account and how many checks you'll write, then choose an account that meets your needs for the least possible cost.

Using Checks

A check is a written order that instructs a bank to pay a certain person a specific amount. Once the check has been cashed or deposited by the payee, it makes its way back to your bank, which deducts the money from your account.

When you write a check, you are responsible for making sure there is enough money in your checking account to cover it. If your account has insufficient funds, the unpaid check will "bounce" back to the payee's bank, and you and the payee will both be charged a fine. To avoid the cost and embarrassment of a bounced check, keep an accurate record of the deposits you make and the checks you write. A booklet called a *check register* is usually used for this purpose. A sample check register is shown in Fig. 31-5.

Making Electronic Transactions

Technology makes it possible for many financial transactions to be done electronically. These options allow people to deposit, withdraw, and transfer money at any time, without the help of a bank teller.

- **ATM transactions.** Automated teller machines, or ATMs, give bank customers electronic access to their accounts. You need an ATM card and a personal identification number (PIN) to use an ATM. Most let you deposit funds, withdraw cash, check your account balances, and transfer money between accounts.

- **Debit cards.** Many ATM cards can also be used as a **debit card**—a card that deducts the cost of purchases from the user's account at the time of purchase. You can make either online or offline transactions with a debit card. With an online transaction, you enter your PIN into a keypad at the place of purchase. The cost of the item is then deducted from your account almost immediately. With an offline transaction, you sign a receipt instead of entering your PIN. The money is deducted

CHECK NO.	DATE	CHECK ISSUED TO	AMOUNT OF CHECK	✓	DATE OF DEP	AMOUNT OF DEPOSIT	BALANCE 556 48	
543	2/8	Pure & Fresh, Inc. (bottled water)	16 50	✓			16 50	
							539 98	
544	2/16	XYZ Center	59 95				59 95	
							480 03	
	2/18	Deposit				400 00	400 00	
							880 03	
545	2/20	City Electric	124 63				124 63	
							755 40	
546	2/21	123 Comm	35 96				35 96	
							719 44	
	2/22	ATM withdrawal	60 00				60 00	
							659 44	

Fig. 31-5. Use your check register to record all checks, withdrawals, and deposits, including ATM transactions. What might happen if you forgot to enter a withdrawal from your account?

from your account when the receipt reaches the bank. Merchants determine whether they will use online or offline debit card transactions.

- **Automated services.** With your permission, banks can automatically transfer money to and from your accounts. Direct deposit of your paychecks is an example. You can also arrange to have certain loans and bills paid directly out of your account each month.

- **Telephone banking.** Many banks allow you to access your accounts by telephone. A recorded message asks you to enter a password or PIN, then gives you a list of options. Typical options include hearing your account balance, hearing recent transactions, and transferring money from one account to another.

- **Online banking.** Bank customers who have Internet access can take advantage of any online banking features that are offered. After you log in with your password, you have access to account information on a secure site. Typically you can view current account balances, see a list of previous transactions, and transfer funds between accounts. You may also be able to print bank statements, order checks, and request other services. If the bank offers online bill payment, you can pay bills electronically instead of mailing a check, saving time and postage.

Reconciling Your Account

Once a month, your bank sends you a statement of your checking account. It tells you the balance at the beginning of the statement period and lists the deposits and withdrawals you made during the month. Any service fees and interest payments are also shown. A typical bank statement is shown in Fig. 31-6.

Fig. 31-6. Your bank statement lists all the transactions you made during a specific period. The entries in your check register should match the statement.

603-130804

MIDSVILLE CITY BANK
MIDSVILLE CO 80000

MIDSVILLE CITY BANK

ACCT 060710

PAT SENIOR
890 N STATE ST
MIDSVILLE CO 80000

PAGE 1 OF 1   THIS STATEMENT COVERS: 1/16/— THROUGH 2/15/—

MIDSVILLE CITY REWARD
603-130804

SUMMARY

PREVIOUS BALANCE	691.20	MINIMUM BALANCE	537.71	
DEPOSITS	400.00+	AVERAGE BALANCE	687.00	
INTEREST PAID	2.27+	AVERAGE RATE	4.000%	
WITHDRAWALS	553.49−			
SERVICE CHARGES	.00−	INTEREST PAID TO DATE	3.54	
NEW BALANCE	**539.98**			

CHECKS AND WITHDRAWALS

CHECK	DATE PAID	AMOUNT	CHECK	DATE PAID	AMOUNT
542	1/30	49.92	543	2/10	16.50
			544	2/14	387.07

EXPRESS BANKING

WITHDRAWAL #036 AT 48 ON 2/06		2/07	100.00

DEPOSITS

	DATE POSTED	AMOUNT
CUSTOMER DEPOSIT	2/03	400.00
INTEREST PAYMENT THIS PERIOD	2/15	2.27

When you receive your statement, you should **reconcile** your account. This process—also known as balancing your checkbook—involves bringing the bank statement and your own record of transactions into agreement. Check the items on the statement against the items listed in your check register. If you find that you forgot to enter a transaction, make an entry in your check register. Also record any service charges and interest payments shown on the statement. Reconciling your account once a month helps you manage your account by correcting any errors before they cause problems.

Building Your Savings

It's always a good idea to save some of your money for emergencies or future use. You can protect the money you save—and have it earn money for you—by putting it into a savings account. Money in a savings account doesn't just sit there. The bank uses it to make loans and investments and pays you interest in return.

Most banks pay *compound interest*—interest that is calculated on the deposits you make *and* on the interest you have already earned. Interest is usually compounded daily or monthly. The more frequently interest is compounded, the more you stand to gain, provided you leave the interest in the account to continue growing. The effect of compound interest adds up over time.

When comparing interest rates offered by different banks, look for the *annual percentage yield* (APY). This figure tells you how much you'll earn, including the effect of compound interest. As with checking accounts, most banks offer different types of savings accounts with different terms. There

Fig. 31-7. *Before deciding which bank to use, spend some time researching and comparing the alternatives.* Do you already have a bank account? If so, why did you choose that bank?

may be minimum balance requirements, transaction limits, and various service charges and fees. See Fig. 31-7.

Traditional savings accounts generally pay relatively low interest rates. Once you build up enough savings, you may want to consider a **money market account**. With this type of savings account, the financial institution pays a higher interest rate because it invests the money you deposit. Most money market accounts also give you the ability to write a limited number of checks each month. However, they often have a higher minimum balance than regular savings accounts, as well as strict limits on the number of withdrawals and transfers you can make.

Learning from Experience

"Live and learn." "Experience is the best teacher." "If I knew then what I know now…" Sayings like these point out that the past can be a valuable problem-solving tool for the present and future. The key is to learn from experience.

How It Works

If you find that a certain problem keeps recurring, perhaps it's because you haven't learned from experience. Suppose, for example, that your checking account is often overdrawn. At first you might think it's because you don't make enough money—a situation that can be difficult to change. However, when you think back on how you manage your checking account, you realize there's another explanation. You often forget to record your ATM withdrawals and automatic payments. If you learn from this experience, you can work on developing better habits so that you avoid bounced checks. If you fail to learn from experience, the problem is likely to continue.

Try It Out

No matter what he did, James never seemed to save anything from his paycheck to put in his savings account. To pinpoint the problem, he decided to keep a spending record. For two months, he wrote down everything he earned and everything he spent. Now he's looking over his notes to see what he can learn from them.

▶ **Your Turn** *Suggest three ways James can use his records to find reasons for his problem with saving money. What can he look at? What questions can he ask himself? What actions can he take, based on his findings, to save money?*

Managing Income and Expenses

A savings account won't do you much good if you spend your money faster than you earn it. To be financially fit, you must learn to manage your income and expenses. You must have the self-discipline to establish priorities, set goals, and work to meet them.

Most people find that the best way to manage income and expenses is to use a *budget*—a plan for spending and saving—as explained in Chapter 7. A budget will help you live within your means and meet your financial goals. Without such a plan, you may live from paycheck to paycheck, with no clear idea of where you want your money to go.

Buying Insurance

Ramon remembers all too clearly the wintry day when he was driving to work and skidded on ice. He lost control and hit an oncoming car head on. Fortunately, no one was hurt. "Good thing I had insurance," says Ramon. "My car was totaled, and the other car needed extensive repairs, but the insurance covered most of the costs. All I had to pay was $500."

As Ramon can tell you, an important part of financial management is making sure you have the insurance that you need. Ramon had no way of predicting that he would have an accident, any more than you can predict what the future holds for you. You do know, however, that anyone—including you—can experience health problems, accidents, natural disasters, and crime. That is why you need insurance. An insurance policy can't prevent these problems from happening, but it can give you financial protection if they do. See Fig. 31-8.

How Insurance Works

An insurance policy is a legal contract that spells out the agreement between the insurance company and the consumer. The consumer, or *policyholder*, agrees to make payments called *premiums*. In return, the insurance company agrees to compensate the policyholder in case of certain events or losses. The policy states the kinds of losses that are covered, the kinds that are excluded, and the limits on what the insurance company will pay for each loss. When buying insurance, be sure you study the policy carefully.

Fig. 31-8. People who experience a disaster like this can gain some comfort from knowing that their insurance company will compensate them for their loss.

Most insurance policies have a **deductible**, a set amount the policyholder must pay for each loss before the insurance company pays out. Suppose you have a $200 deductible on your auto insurance. If your car receives $500 worth of damage, you pay just $200. The insurance company pays the rest. Deductibles keep the insurance company's costs down, limit the number of small claims, and encourage policyholders to guard against loss.

Types of Insurance

The four most common types of insurance, considered the basic minimum for most adults, are health, auto, home, and life insurance. Each covers specific types of risks and losses.

Health Insurance ~ You need health insurance because you can't predict what your future medical needs might be. A major illness or serious accident could result in thousands of dollars in medical bills. See Fig. 31-9.

Health insurance plans vary considerably in terms of what they cost and what they cover. Minimal coverage may include only medical emergencies. Full coverage might include regular doctor visits, routine lab tests, treatment from specialists, and prescription drugs. Some health plans let you use any health care providers you choose. Many, however, won't pay full benefits unless you use certain approved providers.

Many employers offer health insurance for employees and their families. Usually, employees are required to contribute toward the cost of the insurance.

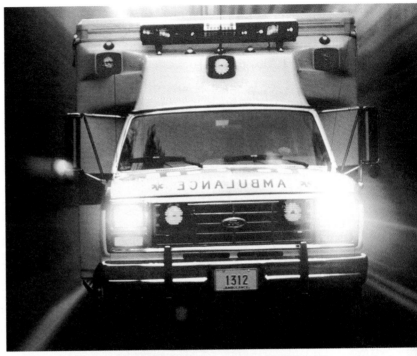

Fig. 31-9. Anyone can have an accident. With good health insurance, you have to worry only about getting better, not about paying the bills.

Auto Insurance ~ Nearly all states require drivers to carry minimum amounts of auto insurance. Depending on your policy, your auto insurance may compensate you if your vehicle is stolen, vandalized, or damaged in a storm or some other natural event. If you are involved in a traffic accident, your insurance may cover damage to your own vehicle, to other vehicles and other property, and injuries to you or others. Insurance requirements and laws vary from state to state, particularly when it comes to motor vehicle accidents.

Home Insurance ~ People buy home insurance to protect themselves from financial loss involving their home and its con-

ber may face financial hardship. There are a wide variety of types of life insurance. Some provide insurance protection only; others combine insurance and investment features.

Insurance Needs

With all types of insurance, many different coverage options are available. It's wise to set aside time to study the options and discuss your needs with an insurance agent.

Insurance needs change as people's circumstances change. If you drive an old car and have only a few possessions, you probably need little insurance. If later on you drive a newer model car and have a home full of furniture, you will need more insurance.

Life insurance needs, in particular, change as you move through the life cycle. A single adult who lives alone and doesn't contribute to anyone else's support may need only enough life insurance to cover funeral expenses. A parent or guardian who has young children to support needs enough life insurance to pay for the children's care, including their education. Older people with grown children typically need less life insurance, but may need long-term care insurance. This type of insurance pays for ongoing care for older people who need it.

tents. Most home insurance policies combine property and liability coverage. *Property coverage* insures against loss resulting from theft, fire, flooding, or other damage. *Liability coverage* insures against losses caused to others while they are in the home. If someone were to fall and break a hip while visiting you, for example, liability insurance would probably pay for the person's hospital bills.

People who own their own home generally purchase policies that cover the building itself as well as the contents. Those who rent need cover only their personal property, since insurance on the building would be the landlord's responsibility. See Fig. 31-10.

Life Insurance ~ Life insurance, in its most basic form, pays benefits to a specified person or persons in the event of the policyholder's death. Without life insurance, those left behind after the death of a family mem-

Investing for the Future

Banking, budgeting, taxes, and insurance are financial topics that impact your life right now or in the near future. There's another piece of the financial puzzle that requires you to take a more long-term view. **Investing** is committing money in the hope that it will make more money over time. It's like planting a seed—under the right conditions, it will eventually grow into a tree that gives you fruit year after year.

If investing is for the future, why think about it now? If you don't plant the seed at the right time, you won't have the tree later when you need it. Investing works the same way. The sooner you begin investing, the more time your money will have to grow.

Investing differs from saving. A savings account is the best place for money that you will need in a relatively short time or that you want to have readily available in case of an emergency. Investing is for money that you won't need to touch for at least several years. See Fig. 31-11.

Investment Risks

Another difference between saving and investing is the amount and type of risk involved. With a savings account, you know that money you deposit will never be lost and that you'll earn interest at a generally steady rate. In contrast, the value of investments can swing up and down in a way that's hard to predict. You might end up with more money than you expected; you might end up with less than you expected, perhaps even less than you started with. The higher the possible return, the greater the risk.

Knowing that, you might be tempted to avoid investing altogether. However, that approach has risks too. Over time, prices tend to rise because of inflation. This causes dollars to lose some of their purchasing power. If you keep all your money in a savings account, chances are it will lose purchasing power faster than it will earn interest. The amount of your savings will slowly grow, but its value will actually decline over the years.

What's the solution? You can manage risk by making smart choices. Save some money, and invest some too—but do it wisely and appropriately. Start by learning a few simple rules.

- **Take care of financial basics first.** Don't consider investing until you have a steady income, a balanced budget, enough money in your savings account for emergencies, and adequate insurance.

Fig. 31-11. Over the long term, investing is likely to earn better returns than keeping your money in a savings account. This person is keeping track of investments with which she hopes to buy a house someday.

- **Get the knowledge you need.** Never invest in something you don't understand. Many books, Web sites, and courses are available to help beginners learn about investing. You may also want to pay for professional advice. Whatever sources of information you use, carefully evaluate their reliability.

- **Diversify and balance your investments.** Putting all your money in a single investment is dangerously risky. It's much safer to *diversify* by spreading your money among several investments. You'll also want to *balance* different types of investments in a way that's appropriate for your goals and timeline. As you learn about investing, pay special attention to these topics.

Investment Options

Anyone who decides to invest money should be familiar with the basic types of investments and the risks they carry. Four of the most popular types of investments are:

- **Certificates of deposit.** When you invest in a **certificate of deposit (CD)**, you deposit money with a financial institution for a specified period of time and receive an agreed-upon interest rate in return. The term, or length of time you leave the money on deposit, may be as short as three months or as long as several years. If you withdraw the money early, you must pay a sizeable penalty.

- **Bonds.** Governments or corporations issue **bonds**, or certificates of debt, as a way of borrowing money. Consumers buy the bonds by paying money to the issuer. The issuer promises to repay the debt, plus an additional amount, by a certain date. The safest and most reliable bonds are *savings bonds* issued by the U.S. Treasury. Other types of bonds vary in risk and return.

- **Stocks.** Corporations can raise money by selling **stock**—ownership interest in the company. They do this by making *shares*, or individual units of ownership, available to investors. Investors who purchase shares of stock receive a portion of the profits if the corporation does well. They also risk losing money if the company does badly or fails.

- **Mutual funds.** A **mutual fund** is a group of investments held in common by many individual investors. Because so many people purchase shares in the mutual fund, it may have millions of dollars to invest. The fund managers use the money to purchase and manage stocks, bonds, and other types of investments. Earnings are divided among the fund's investors. Mutual funds are less risky than some other kinds of investments because they are highly diversified. They also have the advantage of being managed by financial experts.

Planning for Retirement

People may have a variety of investment goals throughout their life. However, one investment goal is shared by almost everyone: building up a retirement fund. After you retire, you'll need one or more sources of income to replace the paychecks you received when you were working.

As you've learned, Social Security taxes are withheld from every worker's paycheck. These taxes go to the Social Security fund, which is administered by the federal government. When people reach retirement age, they are eligible to receive monthly payments from the Social Security fund. However, Social Security payments alone are not adequate to fund retirement. For most people, the solution is to invest money throughout their working years, then draw on that money in retirement. See Fig. 31-12.

There are several ways to invest for retirement. Two of the most common are 401(k) plans and individual retirement accounts. In addition to providing investment opportunities, both also offer tax advantages.

401(k) Plans ~
Many companies offer retirement plans to their employees. A **401(k) plan** is a specific type of retirement plan. Employees who choose to participate have a certain percentage of their pay withheld from each paycheck. This reduces the amount of income tax they owe. The money that was withheld is put into that employee's retirement fund and invested. Often participants can choose their own investment options from a list provided by the plan administrators.

Many companies that offer 401(k) plans make matching contributions. For example, for every dollar that you invest in your plan, the company might contribute 25 cents. This provides a guaranteed return on your investment—almost like getting free money. For this reason, if you have the opportunity to join a 401(k) plan with matching contributions, you'd be wise to sign up.

Individual Retirement Accounts ~
Whether or not your employer offers a retirement plan, you can invest for retirement on your own. An **individual retirement account (IRA)** is a plan that enables workers and their spouses to set aside money for retirement. Banks and other financial institutions can set up IRAs. Contributions to an IRA cannot exceed a certain amount each year. The money can be invested in var-

Fig. 31-12. *People who begin investing for retirement while they are young are more likely to have the money they need to support a comfortable lifestyle in their later years.*

ious ways. There are different types of IRAs, each with different rules and tax advantages.

No matter what types of investments you include in your retirement plan, the important thing is to start early. Planning for retirement while you are still young gives you more years to build funds and more time for your investments to grow. You'll thank yourself later.

Chapter Summary

- Managing your finances can help you gain control of your life.
- A pay stub shows your earnings and deductions.
- Paying your fair share of income tax involves completing the proper forms.
- Checking accounts differ in rates, fees, and restrictions.
- Reconcile your checking account when you receive your bank statement.
- Money in a savings account works for you by earning interest.
- You should have a plan for managing your income and expenses.
- The most common types of insurance are health, auto, home, and life insurance.
- Investments carry risks, but can bring significant rewards in the long run.

Reviewing Key Terms & Ideas

1. What is the difference between receiving a salary and hourly wages?
2. Which is larger—**gross pay** or **net pay**? What accounts for the difference?
3. Name and describe four common types of paycheck deductions.
4. When and why would you be asked to fill out a Form W-4?
5. What is the purpose of a tax return?
6. Describe how to choose a checking account.
7. How does a **debit card** work?
8. What must you do to **reconcile** your checking account?
9. In what ways is a **money market account** different from a regular savings account?
10. Why is it important to have a budget?
11. What is the main reason for having insurance?
12. What is a **deductible**?
13. Name the four basic types of insurance.
14. What are two ways in which **investing** differs from saving?
15. Explain the difference between **bonds** and **stocks**.
16. How is a **401(k) plan** similar to an **IRA**? How are they different?

Thinking Critically

1. **Making Comparisons.** Compare the pros and cons of electronic banking versus making banking transactions in person. Overall, which do you prefer? Why?
2. **Drawing Conclusions.** If someone were to give you $500 to invest for two years, what investment option would you choose? Why?

Applying Your Knowledge

1. **Maintaining a Check Register.** Jean had a balance in her checking account of $150. On June 15 she wrote a check for $41.45. She made a debit card purchase for $33.95 on June 17. On June 20 she deposited $100. On June 21 she wrote a check for $57.19. Calculate Jean's new balance.

2. **Opening a Savings Account.** Assume that you've decided to open a savings account. Make a list of the questions you would want answered when you compare different banks.

3. **Insurance Options.** Research consumer advice related to one of the four main types of insurance. If you were shopping for this type of insurance, what basic choices would you have to make about the kind of coverage you want? Summarize your findings in a brief report.

Making Connections

1. **Social Studies.** Investigate federal income tax rates over the past ten years. When and why did the government raise or lower taxes? What groups of taxpayers were affected? Compare your findings with those of your classmates.

2. **Math.** With a small group, calculate the effects of compound interest on a $500 deposit. Assume that the annual interest rate is 5% and that the interest is compounded monthly. Show your findings in a table.

Managing Your Life

Tracking Electronic Transactions

Years ago, almost all that someone could do with a checking account was write checks. Today, electronic banking options such as ATM and debit cards, direct deposit, automatic payments, and online banking add convenience. However, they also add to the complexity of keeping track of your account balance. What's the best way to remember to record transactions and keep from overdrawing your account? Think of possible strategies for each type of transaction. Then choose the best strategies and create a plan for managing your checking account.

Using Technology

1. **Web Page.** Look for Internet sites that provide reliable financial management information geared toward teens. Create a page in Web browser (HTML) format with links to the best sites. Include a brief description and rating of each site you found.

2. **Financial Software.** Research and compare various types of financial software. If possible, speak to people who use different types of software. Ask them to explain the advantages and disadvantages of the software program that they use.

Using Credit Wisely

Key Terms

- credit
- creditors
- principal
- finance charges
- credit history
- credit report
- credit rating
- annual percentage rate (APR)
- credit limit

Objectives

- **Distinguish** between different types of credit.
- **Summarize** the pros and cons of using credit.
- **Describe** the functions of credit bureaus, credit reports, and credit ratings.
- **Compare** the costs and features of different credit cards.
- **Explain** how to use credit wisely and recognize credit problems.

QUICK WRITE

Write about your opinion of credit cards. Do they make life easier, or do they cause too many people to get into too much debt?

*"H*ere's your mail, Shane," said his friend Leroy, dropping the bundle on the table.

"Thanks, Leroy, I hope it's not all bills. The garage just phoned with an estimate for fixing my car. I need the car for work and school, but I just don't have that kind of money right now."

Shane sorted his mail. "Bill, junk, junk, another bill, magazine, computer catalog." Shane held up the last piece—a long envelope from an address that he didn't recognize. "Hmmm, this looks interesting," he said as he tore open the envelope. Inside was a credit card with his name on it. "Great! Here's that credit card that I applied for. Now I can bail out my car."

"Talk about luck, Shane! Your money problems are over. You can also use that credit card to take me to lunch at that new place I just told you about. Let's take this computer catalog with us and see what goodies you can order."

"No way," laughed Shane. "I plan to use credit to make my financial situation better, not worse."

Understanding Credit

When you use **credit**, you receive money, goods, or services now and promise to pay for them in the future. The idea of credit is summed up in the phrase "buy now, pay later." See Fig. 32-1.

It sounds simple, but in fact, buying on credit is serious business. When you buy on credit, you are committing your future resources. If Shane uses his new credit card to pay for his car repairs, he will owe money to the credit card company instead of the repair shop. What's more, if he takes a while to pay off his debt, he will pay a lot more than the cost of the original car repair.

Fig. 32-1. The idea of buying now and paying later may seem appealing, but you should be aware of what you're getting into.

Banks, finance companies, stores, and other organizations that extend credit are **creditors**. They allow consumers to borrow money on the understanding that the consumer will pay back the loan over a specified period of time. During that period, the consumer will pay back the **principal**—the original amount borrowed—and *interest*, a fee paid for the opportunity to use the creditor's money. Because of interest, you almost always pay more when buying on credit than you would if you paid at the time of purchase.

Types of Credit

Consumers can choose from several types of credit. Each type has advantages and disadvantages and is associated with particular kinds of transactions. Three of the most common types of credit are:

- **Cash loans.** If you're in the market for a car or another large purchase, you may decide to take out a cash loan. If you apply for a loan, you must prove that you can repay it or offer something of value to secure it. People who buy a home, for example, generally offer the home as security. If they fail to repay the loan, the creditor can force the sale of the home to settle the debt.

- **Sales credit.** If you buy something now from a store and pay the store for it over time, you're using sales credit. This kind of transaction is also known as an *installment plan* because the customer pays for the purchase in regular installments. Stores hope that by giving you more time to pay for a purchase, you will buy more than you otherwise would. The amount of interest charged for sales credit varies from business to business.

- **Credit cards.** Businesses, banks, and other financial institutions issue credit cards, the most widely used type of credit. Credit cards offer great convenience. They enable people to buy goods and services without carrying large sums of cash. They also allow people to make purchases by telephone or on the Internet. A downside of credit cards is that most carry higher interest rates than other types of credit.

Pros and Cons of Using Credit

Credit offers several major advantages, in addition to the convenience. It enables you to buy things that you need but cannot yet afford. For example, buying a car on credit allows you to enjoy the benefits of the car while you are still paying for it. Credit also helps you handle unexpected expenses, such as the cost of replacing or repairing a broken appliance. In addition, using credit is a way to build proof of your financial responsibility. Using a credit card and making your payments on time, for example, could help convince a creditor to give you a loan.

The most notable disadvantage of using credit is its cost. When you use credit, you incur **finance charges**. These consist of the interest and any additional fees, such as charges for late payments. With most credit cards, unless you pay the balance in full by the due date, you will incur additional finance charges every month until you pay off your bill. Over time, these charges can add a significant amount to the cost of your purchase.

Credit also tends to encourage impulse buying. It's so easy to hand over a credit card for something that catches your eye. You'd be much more likely to pause and consider your purchase if you had to hand over hard cash instead. Many people also find that

credit encourages them to overspend. Katie, for example, couldn't decide between a blue sweater and a green one. Because she had a credit card, she bought both, even though she didn't need two sweaters and couldn't really afford them. A credit card makes buying seem so easy—until the bill arrives. See Fig. 32-2.

That's why it's important to learn about how credit works and how to use it wisely. With good consumer skills, you can enjoy the benefits of credit and minimize the drawbacks.

Becoming Creditworthy

If you want to use credit, you need to convince creditors that you are creditworthy—that you can be trusted to pay the money back. Lenders have several ways of assessing the risk they are taking before they agree to extend credit. One way is to examine the applicant's finances—past and present.

Applicants who have used credit in the past have a **credit history**, a pattern of past behavior in paying debts. Creditors are more likely to extend credit to those whose credit history indicates that they paid past debts in full and on time. People who have a record of failing to pay debts or of being repeatedly late with payments are considered a high credit risk. They are less likely to be granted additional credit.

The questions on a credit application also help creditors determine your creditworthiness. The creditor may verify your answers by calling your employer and other appropriate people. Here are some typical questions:

- **Employment questions.** Where do you work? How long have you worked there? What is your occupation? How much do you earn?

- **Housing questions.** Where do you live? How long have you lived there? Do you own or rent? What is your monthly housing payment?

- **Financial questions.** Which banks do you have accounts with? How much is in each account? What loans do you currently have? How much do you owe on those loans? What are your monthly loan payments?

When deciding about loans, lenders also use information from *credit bureaus*. These agencies gather information about a consumer's spending patterns from banks, stores, and other sources. They compile the information into a **credit report**, a record of a particular consumer's transactions and payment patterns. They then sell the report to lenders who are evaluating that person's credit application.

Credit bureaus don't make judgments about whether a person is a good credit risk. They simply provide information. The lenders make the decision based on the credit application and credit report. After considering this information, they come up with a **credit rating**—an evaluation of a consumer's credit history. If the credit rating is favorable, the lender approves the credit application.

TIPS FOR *Success*

Establishing First-Time Credit

If you don't have a credit history, how can you get credit? Here are some ways to show that you are creditworthy:

- Open checking and savings accounts. Make regular deposits and avoid overdrawing on the account.

- If possible, put utility bills, such as telephone and Internet service, in your name and pay your bills on time.

- Apply to a local store for a credit card. Pay your credit card bills on time. After a few months, apply for a card from another business, and pay those bills on time as well.

Shopping for a Credit Card

Unless you have a bad credit history, you should not find it difficult to obtain a credit card. What you may find difficult, though, is deciding what credit card to use. There are thousands to choose from. Understanding some basic features can help you choose wisely. See Fig. 32-3.

General purpose cards, issued by major banks and financial institutions, can be used to purchase goods and services at businesses throughout the country and around the world. Most general purpose cards can also be used to obtain cash from automated teller machines. *Private label cards*, issued by chain stores and gasoline companies, are more limited. You can use them only for purchasing from the company that issues them. Some stores may offer special discounts to customers who use their cards.

The credit card business is highly competitive, and card issuers are constantly looking for ways to attract new customers. Some do so by offering *prestige cards*—cards that come in a special color, such as gold or platinum, and suggest that the user has special status. *Co-branded cards* carry the name of the issuing bank and of another company, such as an airline or hotel chain. Users earn rewards for using the card, such as air miles or free nights at hotels.

Smart cards are specially designed for online shopping. A computer chip in the card stores information such as user name, password, and shipping information. To make an online purchase, you insert the card into a special reader, which fills out the Web order form.

Comparing Fees and Terms

In addition to comparing different kinds of cards, you should compare the fees and terms. These are spelled out in the small print of a credit card agreement and can vary considerably from issuer to issuer. Here are some costs and features to consider:

- **Annual percentage rate.** The **annual percentage rate**, or **APR**, is the annual rate of interest that the company charges you for using credit. If you compare the APR of two or more cards, you will likely see significant differences. The lower the APR, the less interest you will pay.

- **Credit limit.** Your **credit limit** is the maximum amount of credit that the creditor will extend to you. If your credit limit is $2,000, you must not run up charges that exceed that amount.

- **Fees.** Some issuing companies charge an annual fee for the use of their card. You might also be charged fees for late payments or for going over your credit limit.

- **Grace period.** Most credit card companies allow a grace period of 20 to 25 days. If you pay the balance on your card during the grace period, you do not have to pay any finance charges.

- **Special features and incentives.** Many credit cards offer incentives to encourage consumers to use their cards. Common incentives include travel insurance, frequent flyer miles, and discounts on car rentals.

When selecting a card, choose the features that most closely match your needs and spending habits. If you intend to carry over a balance, look for low interest rates. If you plan to pay off the balance every month, you might look for incentives that would be useful to you.

Using a Credit Card

When using a credit card, try to follow a few simple rules. They will help you manage your finances, create a good credit history, and protect yourself from fraud.

- Set your own limit on what you will charge each month. If you get close to your limit, stop spending.

- Save your credit card receipts. Use them to keep track of your spending and to check that your bill is correct.

- If possible, pay off the balance on your bill within the grace period. If you can't pay the full balance, don't just make the minimum payment required. Pay the most you can afford.

- Before using a credit card to buy online, make sure you are at a secure site.

- Keep a list of credit card numbers in a safe place. If your card is stolen, notify the credit card company immediately.

FINDING CREATIVE SOLUTIONS

Examining Costs and Benefits

One way or another, everything has a price. That advice is worth remembering when you face a problem or difficult decision. A close examination of your options can reveal which offers the most benefit at the smallest cost.

How It Works

When weighing various options, look at *all* the costs and benefits—money, time, effort, satisfaction, and so on. Keep in mind that some of these will matter more than others, depending on the situation and your priorities. Ask yourself what each cost or benefit is worth to you, both now and over time.

For example, suppose you're trying to decide whether to take music lessons. Paying for the lessons and practicing every day are costs. The skills and pleasure you acquire are probable benefits. How you weigh each item depends on your finances, schedule, and other personal factors.

Try It Out

It's almost spring, and Martin is worried that his old lawnmower won't last the summer in his one-person lawn care business. The new, more powerful model he wants is more than he can afford right now. He could charge the mower on his credit card, but he figures it would take six months to pay off the balance. His other option, saving enough money to pay cash, would take four months. Competition for clients is fierce. Martin knows that if he loses customers, he may not get them back.

▶ **Your Turn** *List two potential costs and two potential benefits for each of Martin's options. Given Martin's situation, what would you advise him to do?*

Credit Problems

Credit is a valuable tool when used wisely. Unfortunately, some people charge too many purchases on their credit cards or borrow too much money. They end up with more debt than they can handle.

A person who cannot make the required payments suffers serious consequences. Goods may be repossessed by creditors, and collection agencies may be called in to claim the unpaid debt. Perhaps most seriously for the long term, the person develops a poor credit history that may make it difficult—or impossible—to obtain a loan in the future. It can take years to improve a bad credit rating.

How can people tell if they are heading toward credit problems? Here are some of the warning signs:

- They worry almost constantly about their debt.
- They routinely spend more than they earn.
- They have reached the credit limit on most of their credit cards.
- They skip payments on some bills in order to pay other, more pressing, ones.

If you think you're getting into credit trouble, take action immediately to recover from the situation. Contact your creditors and see if you can work out a payment plan that will help you. If necessary, get help from a credit counselor. The counselor can help you work out a plan to get out of debt and manage your money. See Fig. 32-4.

If you haven't already, you'll soon be approached by credit card companies eager to have you as a customer. As you consider the credit cards available to you, remember the responsibility that goes with them. You're about to start building your credit history. For years to come, it will be there to help you—or to haunt you. It's up to you to build a history that reflects how well you have managed your use of credit.

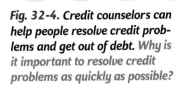

Fig. 32-4. Credit counselors can help people resolve credit problems and get out of debt. Why is it important to resolve credit problems as quickly as possible?

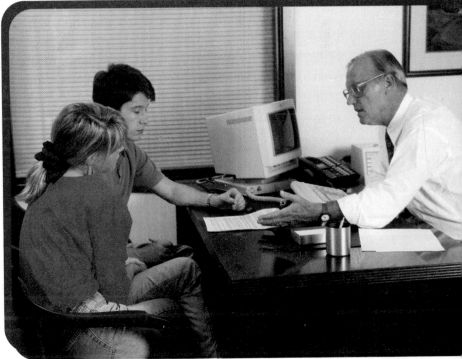

Chapter Summary

- When you use credit, you buy now with the intent to pay later.

- Creditors charge interest for the use of their money.

- The three most common types of credit are cash loans, sales credit, and credit cards.

- The advantages of using credit must be weighed against the costs.

- When you apply for credit, the creditor will investigate your credit history.

- When shopping for a credit card, compare the fees and terms of different cards.

- Following some simple rules about using credit will help you manage your finances.

- People who have credit problems should take immediate action to resolve them.

Reviewing Key Terms & Ideas

1. What do you promise your **creditor** when you buy an item on **credit**?

2. Explain the difference between **principal** and interest.

3. Briefly explain how cash loans, sales credit, and credit cards differ.

4. What are four advantages of using credit?

5. What costs are included in **finance charges**?

6. Name a disadvantage of using credit, other than its cost.

7. Why do creditors examine an applicant's **credit history**?

8. Describe the purpose of credit bureaus, **credit reports**, and **credit ratings**.

9. What is the difference between a private label card and a general purpose card?

10. Why should you compare the **APR** of different credit cards?

11. Why do you need to know what your **credit limit** on a particular card is?

12. Why do you need to know what the grace period on your credit card is?

13. Why should you save credit card receipts?

14. Name three signs of credit problems.

15. What should you do if you think you are getting into credit trouble?

Thinking Critically

1. **Analyzing Behavior.** What is it about using a credit card that makes it so easy to buy on impulse and overspend? What could consumers do to counteract this tendency?

2. **Drawing Conclusions.** Do you think it would be difficult to be without a credit card in our society? Why or why not?

Applying Your Knowledge

1. **Cash or Credit?** Imagine that you're moving into your own apartment and you need to buy a bed. If you pay cash, it will cost you $750. If you use the store's installment plan, you'll pay $50 a month for 18 months. Explain what factors you would consider when deciding how to pay.

2. **Comparing Credit Cards.** Make a chart to compare the costs and features of different credit cards. Research three credit cards and fill in the chart.

3. **Payday Loans.** Find out what a "payday loan" is and why consumers should steer clear of them. (The Federal Trade Commission is one good source of information.) Prepare a brief report of your findings.

Making Connections

1. **Math.** The Andersons took out a bank loan of $8,000 to make renovations on their house. They have to repay the loan in 36 monthly payments of $300. How much will the Andersons pay in finance charges? Show how you arrived at your answer.

2. **Social Studies.** In small groups, discuss the positive and negative effects of the introduction and increased use of credit cards in the United States. Try to reach consensus on whether the effects are mostly positive or mostly negative.

Managing Your Life

A Personal Credit Plan

Credit is a resource that can enhance your life. Like all resources, it must be used wisely. Take some time to reflect on how you will manage the use of credit, now and in the years ahead. Consider questions such as: What are your goals in using credit? How will you set priorities in order to use a limited amount of credit to the best advantage? How will you use the decision-making process to make choices about credit? What will you do if you face credit problems? Write down your ideas and plans. Keep them for future reference to help you manage credit throughout your life.

Using Technology

1. **Internet.** Locate at least three Web sites that feature financial calculators to help you compare the effects of interest rates and other variables on loans or credit cards. Report on the capabilities of the sites you found and how they would be useful to consumers.

2. **Desktop Publishing.** Use appropriate software to create a booklet or brochure educating teens about credit cards. Include suggestions for using credit cards wisely, recognizing credit problems, and dealing with problems if they arise.

Career Options
Business and Finance

*T*hose who work in the business and finance field provide a variety of products and services to consumers. Career opportunities are available for people with wide-ranging levels of education and experience. The industry can be divided into five broad sectors: Management; Marketing and Communications; Administrative and Information Support; Financial Management; and Banking, Insurance, and Investment. For some occupations in this career cluster, employment opportunities are expected to decline, while opportunities are expected to improve for other occupations in the cluster.

Main Employers

- Manufacturing industries
- Service industries
- Retail industry
- Banks
- Insurance industry
- Finance industry

Business and Finance Job Opportunities

Industry Segment	Entry Level	Additional Education and/or Training	Advanced Education and/or Training
Management	▪ Management Trainee ▪ File Clerk	▪ Supervisor ▪ Human Resources Manager	▪ Management Consultant ▪ Chief Executive Officer
Marketing and Communications	▪ Receptionist	▪ Ad Salesperson ▪ Public Relations Specialist	▪ Marketing Manager ▪ Advertising Manager ▪ Public Relations Manager
Administrative and Information Support	▪ Administrative Assistant ▪ Data Entry Clerk	▪ Database Manager ▪ Computer Operator	▪ Information Systems Manager ▪ Computer Programmer
Financial Management	▪ Bookkeeper ▪ Payroll Clerk	▪ Accounting Clerk ▪ Insurance Agent	▪ Credit Counselor ▪ Chief Financial Officer
Banking, Insurance and Investment	▪ Bank Teller ▪ Insurance Claims Clerk	▪ Account Clerk ▪ Insurance Agent ▪ Stockbroker	▪ Bank Manager ▪ Insurance Underwriter ▪ Investment Banker

These days, people say that I've got good "money sense," but I wasn't always this way. In high school, I started borrowing money from my parents and friends. I got a part-time job, but I spent money as fast as I made it. By high school graduation, I was $1,000 in debt.

My parents suggested that I see a credit counselor. I was skeptical, but it turned out to be one of the smartest decisions I've ever made. My credit counselor helped me get control of my finances and out of debt. I decided that becoming a credit counselor myself would give me the satisfaction of helping others.

I went to college and majored in finance, which required courses in math, finance, accounting, and economics. I knew that as a credit counselor, I would deal with people one-on-one, so I also took several psychology courses. My senior year, I volunteered at a nonprofit credit counseling service. After graduation, they offered me a full-time, paid position.

As a credit counselor, I work with people who have debt problems. I help them resolve their financial issues, including paying off their debt. I may negotiate new payment schedules with companies to whom they owe money. By teaching clients good money management skills, I help keep them from repeating their mistakes. We both feel wonderful when they are debt free!

Check It *Out!*

Choose three careers in one industry segment, each requiring a different level of education and training—entry level, additional, and advanced. Use resources to learn the specific requirements of each occupation. Summarize your findings in a three-column chart.

UNIT 8

Wellness, Nutrition, and Food Choices

CHAPTER 33
Health and Wellness

CHAPTER 34
Nutrient Needs

CHAPTER 35
Guidelines for Food Choices

CHAPTER 36
Planning Meals and Snacks

CHAPTER 37
Shopping for Food

CHAPTER 38
Safe Kitchen, Safe Food

CHAPTER 39
Food Preparation Basics

CHAPTER 40
Serving Meals

475

Health and Wellness

Key Terms

- wellness
- aerobic activities
- dehydration
- body image
- calories
- eating disorders
- anorexia nervosa
- bulimia
- binge eating disorder
- substance abuse
- addictive
- sexually transmitted diseases (STDs)
- abstinence

Objectives

- **Discuss** the goals of wellness.
- **Propose** ways to incorporate physical activity into everyday life.
- **Identify** factors that influence body weight.
- **Describe** three different types of eating disorders.
- **Summarize** problems associated with substance abuse.

Why do people today need to make more of an effort to be physically active than they did in the past? Explore this question by writing an imaginary dialogue with a teen who lived 100 years ago.

"What a difference a few weeks can make," thought Ladonna as she pulled herself out of the pool and headed for the locker room. These early morning swims were just one of the changes she had made in her life. She was also eating the right foods, getting enough sleep, and finding ways to be active throughout the day. "Kendra was right," she thought. "I *was* in bad shape."

Kendra was Ladonna's older sister, now away at college. At home during spring break, Kendra had noticed that her sister lived on junk food, got no exercise, and stayed up late playing computer games. She seemed to have little energy for anything, and her grades were slipping. Kendra had a long talk with Ladonna. At first Ladonna was annoyed. She felt she was being criticized. When she realized that Kendra was genuinely concerned, though, she decided to make some changes. "I can't wait till Kendra comes home again," Ladonna said to herself as she got dressed. "I feel so much better, and I know she'll see the difference."

Wellness for Life

Ladonna is discovering the benefits of **wellness**—an approach to life that emphasizes taking positive steps toward overall good health. Wellness encompasses physical, mental/emotional, and social health. The three strands are interconnected, as Ladonna

is learning. Now that she is more physically active, she has more energy and feels better about herself. As a result, she is working harder in school and getting better grades, and her social life is also improving.

When you choose wellness, you choose to take care of yourself. You make the effort to become informed and to make decisions that will improve the quality of your life both now and in the years ahead. See Fig. 33-1.

Wellness has two primary goals. One is to promote health, and the other is to prevent disease.

Fig. 33-1. These friends know that wellness brings many benefits. They encourage each other to continue making choices for good health.

Health Promotion

The way you choose to take care of yourself shows how you value your health. Taking time for physical activity, being thoughtful about the types and amounts of foods you eat, and becoming actively involved in your school and community are all ways you can take care of yourself.

Fig. 33-2. *Making healthy choices in one area of your life can motivate you to improve your health in other ways. Why do you suppose this is true?*

Healthy habits build on themselves. When you get enough sleep, you have more energy. When you have more energy, you tend to be more physically active. When you are physically active, you are more likely to eat the right foods and avoid harmful substances. See Fig. 33-2.

Disease Prevention

Making good health choices can help protect you from disease. When your body is strong and healthy, it's better able to fight off the germs that cause many diseases. More importantly, good health habits reduce your risk of developing certain health problems in your later years. Health problems such as high blood pressure, heart disease, and cancer are sometimes called "lifestyle diseases." That's because they often develop as a direct result of harmful lifestyle behaviors such as inactivity, unhealthy eating patterns, smoking, and drinking alcohol.

It's Up to You

You must take responsibility for your health. No one else can make this commitment for you. You can enjoy the benefits of wellness if you choose to. You might start by setting some personal goals. Here are some suggestions to help you succeed:

- **Set goals that are realistic.** Learn from past experience. If you didn't live up to what you intended, such as jogging every day, set a more reasonable goal. Walking every other day would be a good start and easier to achieve.

- **Write down your goals.** Use specific language that says exactly what you will do, such as "Eat three different vegetables every day." A specific plan will help ensure success.

- **Keep track of progress.** Use a calendar or small notebook to write down what you accomplished and to measure progress toward your goals.

- **Lose the excuses.** Don't say "I don't have time to eat right" or "It's too cold to go walking." Instead, focus on your goals and do what is right for you.

- **Ask for support.** Reach out to your family, friends, and others who share a similar goal. Encourage each other to keep going.

- **Celebrate your successes.** Take credit for reaching your goals. If you fall short, figure out how you can do better next time.

Aim for Fitness

Fitness is important to everyone. When you are fit, you have the strength and energy to handle the demands of everyday life. Your body works at its best, and you look good and feel well. While many healthful habits contribute to fitness, the key is to be physically active.

Benefits of an Active Lifestyle

Regular physical activity promotes your overall physical health and helps you look and feel better. It strengthens your heart and lungs, improves your muscle tone, and helps you maintain a healthy weight. In addition, an active lifestyle contributes to improved balance, coordination, and flexibility. See Fig. 33-3.

Physical activity brings mental/emotional and social benefits, too. It helps you manage stress, build self-esteem, and feel more alert and energetic. You also enjoy a sense of accomplishment as you see the results of your efforts. Because you feel better about yourself, you have more confidence when you are around other people.

The Elements of Fitness

The three main elements of fitness are strength, endurance, and flexibility. To be fit, you need an active lifestyle that promotes all three.

- **Strength** is the ability of your muscles to exert force. You need strength to carry grocery bags or to push a lawnmower. You can build muscle strength by doing activities that involve lifting and carrying. As an

Fig. 33-3. Even short periods of physical activity, worked into your daily schedule on a regular basis, can bring benefits. How much physical activity do you get in a typical day?

Ten Ways to Be More Active

1. **Use your feet.** Walk instead of getting a ride whenever you can. Park further away from the entrance to the mall.
2. **Power your own wheels.** Skating and biking are great ways to spend time with friends.
3. **Take the stairs.** Forget the elevator and escalator—climb stairs whenever you can.
4. **Move to the music.** Dance with friends or by yourself.
5. **Work out at chore time.** Dusting, raking leaves, and taking out trash all get you moving.
6. **Take a class.** Try something you've never done before, such as yoga, karate, or dancing.
7. **Help others.** Volunteer to help older neighbors with household chores, yard work, or shoveling.
8. **Earn money.** Become a part-time pet walker. Offer to wash cars for a small fee.
9. **Play.** Be a kid again. Make a snowman, fly a kite, jump rope, shoot hoops.
10. **Just have fun!** Do whatever you enjoy—Frisbee, handball, swimming—so long as it involves movement.

Fig. 33-4. There are lots of ways to become more active. Which of these suggestions appeal to you most? What ideas can you add?

alternative, you can do push-ups, curl-ups, and step-ups. If you are interested in weight training, ask a qualified instructor to show you some useful exercises.

- **Endurance** is your ability to use energy over a period of time without getting tired. You build endurance by doing **aerobic activities**—sustained, rhythmic activities that improve the efficiency of your heart and lungs. Examples include walking, running, bicycling, and swimming. These activities increase your intake of oxygen and help improve the circulation of blood and oxygen through the body. They also build the endurance of your muscles.

- **Flexibility** is the ability of your joints to make the full range of movements available to them. Being flexible enables you to kneel, bend, turn, and throw. It also reduces your risk of injury. You can improve flexibility by doing activities that involve bending and stretching.

Get Up and Move!

You don't have to be an athlete to be active. You can build physical activity into your everyday routines. In fact, a good way to stay active for life is to make physical activity a normal part of your lifestyle. Aim for at least 60 minutes of physical activity a day. You can do it all at once or spread it out in 15- or 20-minute periods. Fig. 33-4 suggests some ways you can increase your level of activity.

Many people build activity into their lifestyle by participating in a sport such as soccer, basketball, tennis, or swimming. If you believe this would work for you, think about the sports you might like. Do you prefer team sports or sports that you can do on your own? Do you want regularly scheduled activities, or do you prefer more flexibility? Try to choose activities that you will enjoy and that will keep you motivated. See Fig. 33-5.

Avoiding Injury

If you participate in strenuous sports, you need to protect yourself from muscle pulls and other injuries by warming up and cooling down before and after the activity. A *warm-up* is a period of gentle exercise to prepare your body for more vigorous activity. Try gentle stretching exercises or a slow jog. The warm-up gradually increases your heartbeat and your temperature, making your muscles more flexible. A *cool-down* is a period of gentle exercise to help your body recover from exercise. You might cool down by walking or stretching.

Before, during, and after strenuous activity, be sure to drink plenty of water. Drinking water helps prevent **dehydration**, which is excessive loss of body fluids. Dehydration can lead to muscle cramps, dizziness, and nausea.

A Healthy Weight

Regular activity and sensible eating will help you maintain a healthy weight. You also need to know what is a healthy weight for you. Many people are concerned about their weight when they need not be. Weight is a complex issue that involves a number of factors, some of which are beyond your control. These factors include:

- **Height.** The taller a person is, the more he or she can expect to weigh.
- **Age.** Adults typically weigh more than teens of the same height.
- **Gender.** Males generally weigh more than females of the same height.
- **Bone structure.** People with larger body frames usually weigh more than those with smaller body frames.
- **Body build.** People who are muscular tend to weigh more than those who are not.
- **Growth pattern.** Teens mature at different ages and at different rates. Your weight is affected by the stage of physical maturity you have reached.

Fig. 33-5. Choosing an activity you really enjoy will help you stick with it. What kinds of sports activities are most appealing to you?

Your Body Image

The mental concept you have of your physical appearance is your **body image**. Many teens have a problem with their body image. They think they are too fat, or too thin, or too tall, or too something else. Often, they reach this opinion because they are comparing themselves to athletes, movie stars, or fashion models. Trying to look like someone else is not realistic. Like the color of your eyes and hair, your body shape is an inherited trait.

It's normal for people to have different sizes and shapes. What's important is to have a realistic body image. Accept the character-istics that you cannot change, such as height and build. Instead of trying to look like someone else, focus on maintaining a weight that is healthy for your particular body.

Your Appropriate Weight

You can't tell whether your weight is right for you just by looking in a mirror or getting on a scale. You can, however, use the Body Mass Index (BMI) chart shown in Fig. 33-6. The BMI uses weight in relation to height and age to help determine whether you are in an appropriate weight range. It also helps individuals determine whether they are underweight, at risk for being overweight, or

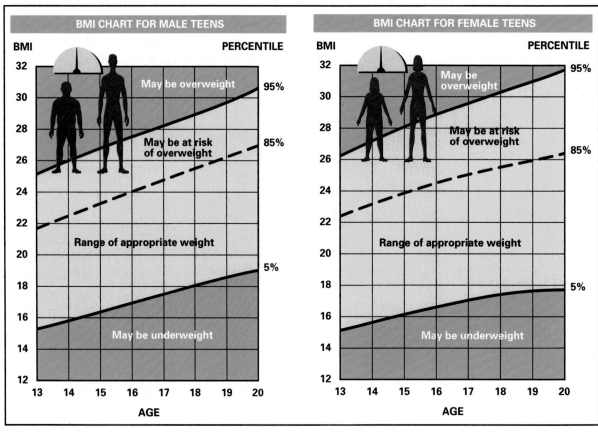

Fig. 33-6. To calculate your BMI, divide your weight in pounds by your height in inches. Divide again by your height in inches. Multiply by 703. The result is your BMI. Now find the point on the chart where your age and BMI intersect. This will help you determine whether you are at an appropriate weight for your age and height.

already overweight. As you can see, there is a wide range of appropriate weights for someone of your height and age.

You can use the BMI to find out where you stand compared to thousands of other teens of your age. As many as half of all female teens, and many male teens, have incorrect ideas about what is an appropriate weight for them.

Smart Weight Management

Some people do weigh more or less than is appropriate for their height, age, and build. Both overweight and underweight are unhealthy. Overweight contributes to heart disease and diabetes, and it puts a strain on muscles and joints. Underweight contributes to anemia, low energy, and other disorders associated with poor nutrition.

Viewpoints

Body Image and the Media

From movies to magazine ads, media sources continue to feature models and others who are razor-thin. How much influence do these media images have? Do people take them seriously? Do they cause any harm?

Terence: Everyone knows those models and TV stars don't look like real people—at least, they don't look like anyone I know. Some might be that thin naturally, but a lot of them starve themselves to get that way. No reasonable person should expect to be as thin as people on TV. That's like expecting your cooking to turn out as perfect as the food on cooking shows. It won't, but you do the best you can.

Cynthia: When you see all these ultra-thin celebrities, that's not just unreal—that's unhealthy. They look like they're starving—and we're supposed to think that's an ideal body? We send food to people who look like that in poor countries. It's especially bad because a lot of these stars are role models for teens. We need to see images of healthy bodies. We need to hear that healthy is cool.

Seeing Both Sides ~ What opinions do Terence and Cynthia share on this issue? Suppose these teens were to collaborate on an article for their school paper. What points would they agree to include?

Weight management is a matter of energy balance. Food supplies your body with energy, and physical activity uses energy. This energy is measured in units called **calories**. When energy taken in and energy used are in balance, body weight remains stable. Using more energy than is taken in results in weight loss. Taking in more energy than is used results in weight gain. Thus, weight can be managed by adjusting eating habits, physical activity, or both.

If you think you might be overweight or underweight, ask your doctor for advice. You might learn that your weight is appropriate after all. If not, a healthy lifestyle that includes sensible eating and regular physical activity may be all you need to reach an appropriate weight.

Losing Weight ~ Very few teens need to lose weight. At this stage of life, weight gain is natural and healthy because of normal growth. Many doctors advise overweight teens not to try to lose weight, but rather to slow down the rate at which they are gaining weight. Over time, even a small decrease in calories consumed and a small increase in physical activity can slow down weight gain.

If at some point your doctor does advise you to lose weight, you'll want to know how to do so safely and successfully. Weight loss should be gradual, no more than 1 to 2 pounds a week. Most successful weight loss programs combine sensible eating with increased physical activity. Here are some guidelines for losing weight safely:

- Follow the tips given earlier for increasing physical activity.

- Choose nutritious foods that are lower in fat and calories. You'll learn more about food choices in the next several chapters.

- Cut back on foods that are high in calories but contribute little to good health, such as potato chips, ice cream, and soft drinks. See Fig. 33-7.

Extreme diets that severely restrict food choices are not recommended. They may not provide the right nutritional balance for good health. Besides, extreme diets rarely work in the long run. They may produce short-term weight loss, but most people gain the weight back. The only way to lose weight and keep it off is to make permanent lifestyle changes.

Fig. 33-7. Regardless of your weight, it's a good idea to choose soft drinks less often. Milk is a better choice because of its bone-building benefits.

Gaining Weight ~ Some of the same cautions that apply to weight loss apply to weight gain as well. Weight should be gained slowly and steadily, and the foods chosen should reflect the nutrition guidelines you will learn in later chapters. Here are some additional tips for those who need to gain weight:

- Plan meals around foods you like.
- Try to eat more frequently and to eat larger portions at each meal and snack.
- Snack on hearty, nutritious foods, such as yogurt, fresh or dried fruit, and sandwiches on whole-grain bread.

Health Concerns

Unfortunately, teens are vulnerable to a number of health concerns. Some are linked to emotional factors such as low self-esteem, unrealistic body image, or depression. Some result from immature decision making. Knowing the risks, and knowing how to avoid them, could protect you from serious health problems.

Eating Disorders

Eating disorders are extreme eating behaviors that can lead to serious health problems and even death. There are several types of eating disorders. All are complex mental health problems that need professional treatment. While eating disorders can affect anyone, they are more common among females than males. They most often occur during the teen years and in young adulthood.

Anorexia nervosa is an eating disorder that involves an extreme urge to lose weight by starving oneself. People with anorexia nervosa drastically reduce the amount of

Fig. 33-8. *This young woman sees her body for what it is. A person with anorexia could weigh much less, yet think she is fat. What challenges does this create for treating the disorder?*

food they eat. They resist the efforts of parents and friends to get them to eat more. At the same time, some greatly increase the amount of physical activity they get. In addition to drastic weight loss, anorexia results in damage to the bones, muscles, skin, and organs. It can even lead to kidney failure or heart failure. Yet even as they starve themselves, people with anorexia nervosa see themselves as fat. This distorted self-image is part of the disease. See Fig. 33-8.

Bulimia is an eating disorder that involves bouts of extreme overeating followed by attempts to get rid of the food eaten. The periods of overeating are often done in secret. Then the person gets rid of the food by using laxatives or vomiting. These practices are very damaging to the digestive tract and other parts of the body. Consequences can include dehydration, irregular heartbeat, and heart failure.

Binge eating disorder, the most common eating disorder, involves compulsive overeating. People with this disorder eat unusually large amounts of food at one time, even though they are not hungry. Unlike people with bulimia, people with binge eating disorder do not attempt to get rid of the food after eating. They often experience feelings of shame or guilt after overeating, which adds to the depression that is associated with the disorder. Binge eating disorder can lead to extreme overweight and related health problems, such as heart disease and diabetes.

Eating disorders are extremely dangerous. They can be life-threatening if left untreated. Most people who have eating disorders need

professional help. They may need a combination of medical, nutritional, and psychological counseling. The support of family and friends is also important to the recovery process.

Substance Abuse

Substance abuse is the use of illegal drugs or the misuse of legal drugs. Substance abuse can damage the body, leading to disease or even death. It is also linked to many social problems, including violence, divorce, and suicide. Many abused substances are **addictive**—they cause a mental or physical dependence that leads users to crave regular doses. Some substance abusers resort to stealing to support their habit. Some lose their jobs because they can no longer work effectively. Relationships suffer. Families suffer. As you can see, substance abuse is a serious problem with serious consequences. You can avoid all these problems by deciding to remain free of alcohol, other drugs, and tobacco.

Alcohol ~ Alcohol is a depressant drug found in beer, wine, and other alcoholic beverages. It slows down the functioning of the brain and can produce mental and physical impairment. People who drink alcohol and then drive a vehicle or operate machinery risk injuring or killing themselves and others. Binge drinking, in which a person drinks large quantities in a short period of time, is especially dangerous and can cause death.

Because alcohol is so readily available in American society, teens need to understand why they should refuse to drink. For one thing, in the U.S., alcohol is illegal for anyone under age 21. For another, drinking causes people to do foolish and sometimes dangerous things that they later regret. It also interferes with healthy development and with

Character IN ACTION

Knowing When to Get Help Friends sometimes trap themselves in lifestyles that will have devastating effects. You can still support your friends even when you don't support their choices. When friends confide in you about serious problems, such as an eating disorder or substance abuse, ask a trusted adult or community agency how you can best help them. Encourage your friends to seek treatment, and support them when they do. Practice ways you can gently, yet assertively, talk with friends about their choices.

healthy relationships. Finally, there is the risk of alcoholism, a serious disease in which people cannot control their drinking.

Other Drugs ~ Drug abuse includes the use of illegal drugs such as marijuana, cocaine, heroin, and others. It also includes the misuse of legal medicines—taking a prescription medicine without a doctor's orders, for example, or taking too much of any medicine. Even certain household products can be abused by taking them into the body instead of using them as directed.

Some drugs, called stimulants, speed up the body's functions. Others, called depressants, slow down the body's functions. Some drugs are swallowed, some are inhaled, some are injected. No matter what their type or their form, all drugs interfere with a user's ability to think clearly and make sound judgments. People who become addicted to drugs risk their health and face a painful withdrawal process.

Tobacco ~ Tobacco contains nicotine, a powerful drug that interferes with the brain's functioning and causes users to want more and more tobacco. Cigarettes, the most common form of tobacco, cause heart disease and cancer and are the leading cause of preventable death in America. Smokeless tobacco, or chewing tobacco, causes many kinds of cancer. In recognition of the many negative effects of tobacco, companies across the nation have introduced smoke-free policies in the workplace.

Choosing to Be Drug Free ~ Teens who choose to be drug free show that they care about their health, their future, and their families. When you say no to drugs, you show that you are capable of making

Fig. 33-9. People who value their health don't even consider using drugs, tobacco, or other harmful substances.

mature decisions and of resisting pressure to do something that is not in your best interest. See Fig. 33-9.

You can use several strategies to protect yourself from exposure to drugs. Start by choosing friends who share your values and avoiding situations where drugs may be available. Practice your refusal skills too. Decide ahead of time what you will say if someone tries to persuade you to use any kind of drug.

Sources of Help ~ Teens who do start using alcohol, drugs, or tobacco need to get help. Asking for help is not a sign of weakness. It shows courage and maturity. Most communities offer support and treatment programs for drug addiction. Trained counselors help users withdraw from their drug habit, and support groups help users stay drug free. Among the organizations that offer support are Alcoholics Anonymous, Narcotics Anonymous, and Cocaine Anonymous. There are also local support groups to help teens who want to quit using tobacco.

Sexually Transmitted Diseases

Sexually transmitted diseases (STDs) are diseases that are transmitted from one person to another as a result of sexual contact. STDs vary in severity and in symptoms. Some STDs have no symptoms in their early stages, while others have painful symptoms. Different diseases need different treatment, so diagnosis is essential. Left untreated, STDs can have serious long-term effects including sterility, brain damage, and heart disease.

Common STDs ~ The most common STD is *chlamydia*. Many people infected with chlamydia have no symptoms, so they can unknowingly pass it on to a sexual partner. Over time the disease can cause sterility in both males and females. *Genital herpes*, another common disease, produces painful blisters in the genital area. *Gonorrhea* is a bacterial infection that can cause inflammation of the joints and, if left untreated, sterility. *Pelvic inflammatory disease*, or PID, is an infection of the female genital area, usually caused by another STD. *Nongonococcal urethritis* is an inflammation of the urinary tract. It is more common in males than

females. Most STDs, if caught early, can be treated with antibiotics. However, some STDs cannot be cured. In those cases, treatment can help manage the symptoms, but the person has the disease for life.

HIV and AIDS ~ Because of its impact, the most talked-about STD is *acquired immunodeficiency syndrome (AIDS)*. HIV, the virus that causes AIDS, attacks a person's immune system—the system that helps the body ward off infection. Eventually the immune system fails to protect the body, and the person becomes increasingly likely to contract a disease that causes death.

HIV can be passed from an infected person to another during sexual activity. It can also be transmitted from a mother to her baby during birth. In addition, drug users who share needles risk contracting the virus. People can be infected with HIV for up to ten years before they develop any symptoms. During that time, they can pass the virus on to others. The only way to determine whether someone has the virus is through a blood test. Medicines can prolong the life of people with HIV and AIDS. So far, though, there is no cure.

Practicing Abstinence ~ The only certain way to avoid contracting an STD is to practice **abstinence**. Refusing to engage in sexual activity of any kind is a mature way of protecting your physical and emotional health. Millions of teens choose abstinence and the peace of mind that goes with it.

Teens who practice abstinence generally choose friends who share their values. They avoid situations that might cause sexual tension, and they make their wishes clear to their partners. Acting according to positive values helps them feel proud that they are in control of their life.

Health Care Decisions

Wellness, as you know, emphasizes taking positive steps toward overall good health. One of those steps is to seek the help and advice of health care professionals. Doctors, nurses, dentists, and dental hygienists are just a few of the health care professionals who can help you make informed decisions about your health.

Using the Health Care System

The United States has the most advanced health care system in the world. It's also the most expensive. Many people have some form of health insurance to help them pay for medical expenses. When you start working, your employer may offer health insurance. Because insurance plans vary widely in what they cover, you will need to study your plan carefully.

For routine medical care, most people go to a *primary care physician*—a doctor who provides general care and conducts checkups. Patients who need specialized care for specific conditions are referred to *specialists*—doctors who are trained to handle particular kinds of diseases or medical conditions. If you broke your leg, for example, you would be referred to an orthopedic surgeon. If you had a serious skin problem, you would see a dermatologist.

Your Health Care Responsibilities

Health care professionals can do only so much. They need your cooperation. They rely on you to schedule checkups, ask questions, make appointments if you have a problem or concern, and follow their advice. See Fig. 33-10.

You are also responsible for maintaining healthy habits and protecting yourself from disease. Perform recommended self-exams, be alert for signs and symptoms of disease, and use health care products wisely. Accepting responsibility for your health is an important step toward the rewards of wellness.

Fig. 33-10. Taking responsibility for your health includes practicing prevention and getting regular checkups. Be sure to ask your doctor about any concerns you may have.

Chapter Summary

- Wellness emphasizes taking positive steps toward overall good health.
- Regular physical activity improves physical, mental/emotional, and social health.
- Aim for an active lifestyle that promotes strength, endurance, and flexibility.
- Instead of striving for the "ideal" body, maintain a weight that's healthy for you.
- People who need to lose or gain weight should do so gradually.
- Eating disorders are serious mental health conditions that need professional help.
- Teens who choose to be drug free show that they care about their health.
- The only certain way to avoid contracting an STD is to practice abstinence.

Reviewing Key Terms & Ideas

1. What are the two primary goals of **wellness**? Give an example of how developing healthy habits can help you meet each goal.
2. In what ways does regular physical activity promote overall physical health?
3. How do **aerobic activities** contribute to fitness?
4. What is the purpose of a warm-up? A cool-down?
5. What is **dehydration**? How can you prevent it?
6. Name six factors that influence body weight.
7. How does a realistic **body image** contribute to good health?
8. What do **calories** measure?
9. Why is losing weight not an appropriate goal for most teens?
10. Describe the main characteristics of **anorexia nervosa**, **bulimia**, and **binge eating disorder**.
11. What is **substance abuse**? Describe four problems that can result from it.
12. What does **STD** stand for?
13. Why do STDs need to be properly diagnosed and treated?
14. Name four ways to take responsibility for your own health care.

Thinking Critically

1. **Recognizing Assumptions.** What assumptions do many teens make that stand in the way of developing healthy habits? What could be done to counteract them?
2. **Understanding Cause and Effect.** What aspects of our society contribute to the negative body image that some teens have? Why do they have this effect?

Applying Your Knowledge

1. **Examining Obstacles to Fitness.** List as many lifestyle factors as you can think of that cause people to be physically inactive. Next to each item on your list, write a suggestion for changing that factor for a healthier lifestyle.

2. **Developing an Activity Plan.** Develop a plan for an active lifestyle that includes at least 60 minutes of physical activity a day. Be sure to include activities that promote the three elements of fitness.

3. **Practicing Refusal Skills.** In a group, brainstorm ideas for saying no to drugs. List your ideas on a sheet of paper, then take turns presenting them to the class. Ask classmates to vote on the most effective refusal strategies.

Making Connections

1. **Science.** Using science-based information sources, research one of the illegal drugs discussed in this chapter. Learn about its short-term and long-term negative effects on the brain and body. Be prepared to present your findings to the class.

2. **Social Studies.** Find out what the federal government is doing to prevent the spread of STDs, including AIDS. Prepare a brief report on prevention programs and on their effects over the past few years.

Managing Your Life

Healthy Choices

Assess your current level of health and wellness based on what you have learned in this chapter. What changes could you make in your lifestyle to improve your health? Follow the chapter suggestions for setting realistic goals, tracking your progress, and staying motivated. Schedule time to assess your plan every two weeks and make any necessary changes.

Using Technology

1. **Video Presentation.** With a partner, use reliable sources of information to learn about effective warm-up and cool-down exercises. Choose several of the exercises to practice. Make a video demonstrating the exercises and explaining what each one achieves. Show your video to the class.

2. **Internet.** Visit the Web site of the National Eating Disorders Association or a similar organization. Find out more about one of the following topics: warning signs of eating disorders; effects on health; treatment options; what family and friends can do. Share your findings with the class.

Nutrient Needs

Key Terms

- nutrients
- carbohydrates
- fiber
- proteins
- amino acids
- saturated fats
- unsaturated fats
- trans fats
- cholesterol
- vitamins
- minerals

Objectives

- **Describe** the main functions of the six classes of nutrients.
- **Identify** foods that are good sources of each class of nutrient.
- **Explain** the purpose of Dietary Reference Intakes.
- **Compare** nutrient needs at different life stages.
- **Summarize** the special nutrition needs of athletes.

QUICK WRITE

Write a brief description of how you decide what to eat each day. Do you think your food choices are good for your health? Why or why not?

*W*hat are some of your favorite foods? Perhaps you enjoy biting into a crisp apple or sipping from a bowl of steaming chicken noodle soup. For good nutrition, make sure your diet—the sum of your food choices— includes a variety of healthful foods. Because different foods perform different functions, making wise food choices is essential to meeting your nutritional needs and ensuring good health. Learning about nutrition will help you establish healthful eating habits that will improve the quality of your life, now and in the future.

they all perform different functions. No single nutrient can do the work of another. Indeed, some nutrients rely on the presence of others to help them perform their tasks. Together, all the nutrients work as a team to give you energy and help your body systems run smoothly. See Fig. 34-1.

Nutrient Functions and Sources

Nutritionists—scientists who study food and its effects on the body—have identified a number of different nutrients. **Nutrients** are chemicals found in food that help the body work properly. You need nutrients to maintain good health and to fight disease. There are more than 40 key nutrients, which can be grouped into six classes: carbohydrates, proteins, fats, vitamins, minerals, and water. You need all of these nutrients because

Fig. 34-1. No single food can supply all the nutrients you need. For good health, you need a variety of different foods every day.

Carbohydrates

Carbohydrates are the nutrients that provide your body with ready energy. Grain products, vegetables, fruits, and dry beans and peas are high in carbohydrates. They also provide other nutrients, making them particularly valuable.

Carbohydrates are your body's most efficient fuel, so most of your body's energy supply should come from carbohydrates. If you don't eat enough carbohydrates, your body has to get energy from other nutrients or from its reserve supplies in body tissues. To keep your body functioning at its peak, you need carbohydrates throughout the day. See Fig. 34-2.

The two main categories of carbohydrates are starches and sugars. In addition, many foods that supply carbohydrates are also good sources of fiber.

Starches ~ Starches are called *complex carbohydrates*. As your body digests starches, it breaks them down into *glucose*, which is the major source of energy for your body. Rice, potatoes, bread, and pasta are examples of foods high in starch.

Sugars ~ Your body can also form glucose from the sugars, or *simple carbohydrates*, found in foods. Fruits, grain products, and milk are among the foods that provide natural sugars in addition to other nutrients.

Sugar that has been removed from its natural source and processed is called *refined sugar*. Table sugar is an example. Other types of refined sugars include corn sweeteners, corn syrup, dextrose, fructose, lactose, molasses, and honey. Refined sugars are also called *added sugars* because they are added during the preparation of foods like cakes, candy, cookies, soft drinks, and many processed foods. Added sugars are listed as ingredients on food labels. For good health, get most of your energy from starches and natural sugars instead of refined sugars.

Fiber ~ One of the benefits of eating certain carbohydrate foods is that they contain indigestible threadlike cells called **fiber**. Fiber is not really a nutrient, since it's not digested,

Fig. 34-2. Foods that are high in carbohydrates are a good source of energy. Besides the foods shown here, what are other good sources of carbohydrates?

but it performs several important jobs. For example, fiber helps move food through the digestive system and may reduce the risk of heart disease and cancer.

Fruits and vegetables, especially the peels and seeds, are good sources of fiber. Whole-grain cereals and breads are excellent sources of fiber because they use almost the entire grain seed, or kernel, and contain almost all of the grain's original nutrients. See Fig. 34-3.

Proteins

Proteins are the nutrients your body uses to build and repair body tissues. They are the basis of all your body's cells and form the major part of your hair, nails, and skin. Proteins are important for people of all ages, but especially for children and teens because they are growing.

When you eat foods containing proteins, your body breaks down the proteins into their chemical building blocks, which are called **amino acids**. The amino acids are then recombined in various ways to make up body tissues. Foods that provide all of the essential amino acids—such as meat, poultry, fish, eggs, and milk—are said to contain *complete protein*. Foods that provide some but not all of the essential amino acids— such as grains, vegetables, nuts, and seeds— provide *incomplete protein*.

People who do not eat the animal products that provide complete protein can still get all the essential amino acids. They do it by eating a variety of incomplete proteins. For example, beans and rice together provide the essential amino acids. So do dry beans or peas plus grains, nuts, or seeds. The incomplete proteins do not necessarily have to be

Fig. 34-3. Fiber is a necessary aid to digestion. The whole-grain bread in this sandwich is an excellent source of fiber.

combined in the same dish or meal. They just need to be eaten during the same day.

Fats

Fats are your body's most concentrated sources of energy. The body needs them for several reasons. Fats allow your body to transport and store certain other nutrients. They also help regulate body temperature and growth. After the body has used the fat it needs for these purposes, it stores the rest as body fat. Some body fat is needed to insulate the body, cushion vital organs, and serve as a reserve supply of energy.

Fat is naturally present in some foods, such as meat, fish, dairy products, and nuts. It is also used as an ingredient in salad dressings, cakes, cookies, and many other prepared foods.

Viewpoints

Using Nutrition News

You can't make informed decisions without information. Yet on the subject of nutrition, the news seems to change directions like a weathervane. How can you act on information like that?

Camille: I try to use the latest findings to plan what I eat, but sometimes I get confused. Every day, some new study seems to contradict an older one. First margarine was better for you because butter had cholesterol. Now butter is better because margarine has trans fats. Some people recommend a low-carbohydrate diet; others say you should cut back on fats and eat plenty of carbs. I'm starting to wonder who I can trust.

Danny: Scientists are learning so much about nutrition. Every piece of information helps us make better decisions. You have to expect that the "rules" of good nutrition will keep changing as people learn more about the human body and the roles of different nutrients. A lot of things we accept now probably sounded unbelievable at first. It's great that people keep making new discoveries about food.

Seeing Both Sides ~ How would you describe Camille's and Danny's individual attitudes toward nutrition news? Outline a practical approach to using nutrition news that reflects points the two hold in common.

Types of Fats ~ Foods contain different types of fats. **Saturated fats** are usually solid at room temperature. They are found mostly in animal products such as meat, milk, cheese, and butter. Tropical oils, such as coconut and palm oil, are also high in saturated fats. **Unsaturated fats** are usually liquid at room temperature. They are found mainly in oils from vegetables, nuts, and seeds, such as corn, olive, peanut, and sesame oils. See Fig. 34-4.

Trans fats (also called trans fatty acids) are a type of fat formed when food manufacturers turn liquid oils into solid fats in a

Fig. 34-4. All of these foods—butter, olives, avocado, vegetable oil, lard, and nuts—contain fats. Which ones contain saturated fats?

process known as *hydrogenation.* Saturated and trans fats can be found in some of the same foods. These foods include vegetable shortenings, hard margarines, crackers, candies, cookies, snack foods, fried foods, baked goods, salad dressings, and other processed foods made with partially hydrogenated vegetable oils.

Cholesterol ~ Saturated fats and trans fats are less desirable in the diet because they may lead to high levels of cholesterol in the blood. **Cholesterol** is a white, waxlike substance that plays a part in transporting and digesting fat. High blood cholesterol levels can lead to heart disease, high blood pressure, and other health problems. Most cholesterol is produced in the liver. It is also found in certain foods, including egg yolks and dairy products. Eating foods high in cholesterol can raise the levels of cholesterol in the blood. Eating too much saturated or trans fat can raise it even more.

Vitamins

Vitamins are nutrients that help your body function properly and process other nutrients. Even though you need them in only tiny amounts, they are essential to good health. Fig. 34-5 on the next page shows the functions and food sources for some of the major vitamins.

Not getting enough of certain vitamins can lead to a number of problems, including diseases of the eyes, skin, and bones. Getting too many vitamins can be harmful as well. The body is able to get rid of some of the unneeded vitamins, but others can build up to dangerous levels. The difference is determined by whether the vitamins are water soluble or fat soluble.

Water-soluble vitamins are easily absorbed and can move through the body dissolved in water. Since water is constantly lost from the body through urine and perspiration, you need fresh supplies of these vitamins every day. Excess amounts are not stored for later use. Vitamin C and the B vitamins are water soluble.

Vitamins A, D, E, and K are *fat-soluble vitamins.* They dissolve in fat and travel through the bloodstream in droplets of fat. They can be stored in body fat so that they are available when your body needs them. Excess amounts can build up to harmful levels, however. Too much vitamin A, for example, can cause nerve and liver damage.

Vitamins at a Glance

VITAMIN	FUNCTIONS	SOURCES
Vitamin A 	■ Builds good vision, healthy teeth and gums, and strong bones ■ Helps immune system resist infection	■ Eggs, liver, milk products *Foods that contain beta-carotene, which the body uses to make vitamin A:* ■ Yellow-orange fruits and vegetables, such as cantaloupes, apricots, carrots, and sweet potatoes ■ Dark green leafy vegetables, such as broccoli and spinach
B Vitamins: Thiamine (B_1), Riboflavin (B_2), Niacin, Vitamin B_6, Vitamin B_{12}, Folate (folic acid), Pantothenic acid, Biotin	■ Help nerve and brain tissue work well ■ Aid in digestion 	■ Milk products, meat, breads and cereals, dry beans and peas, dark green leafy vegetables, enriched cereals, fortified juices
Vitamin C 	■ Helps body build cells—aids in healing cuts and bruises ■ Helps form healthy teeth and gums and strong bones	■ Citrus fruits (such as oranges and grapefruits), strawberries, kiwi, cantaloupe, tomatoes, potatoes, broccoli, raw cabbage, bell peppers, plantains
Vitamin D	■ Helps body use minerals, such as calcium and phosphorus ■ Helps form strong bones and teeth	■ Your body makes it if skin is exposed to enough sunlight ■ Added to many milk products ■ Fatty fish such as salmon and mackerel
Vitamin E	■ Helps keep red blood cells healthy	■ Vegetable oils, grains, nuts, dark green leafy vegetables
Vitamin K	■ Helps blood to clot 	■ Broccoli and other dark green leafy vegetables, cauliflower, egg yolks, liver, wheat bran, wheat germ

Fig. 34-5. You need a variety of foods to get the vitamins you need. Which fruits and vegetables are good sources of vitamin A?

Minerals at a Glance

MINERAL	FUNCTIONS	SOURCES
Calcium	■ Builds and maintains healthy bones, teeth, and muscles ■ Keeps heartbeat regular ■ Helps blood clot normally	■ Dairy products, dark green leafy vegetables, canned fish with soft bones (such as sardines, salmon, and mackerel), fortified orange juice, fortified soy milk
Iron 	■ Builds red blood cells, which transport oxygen through body	■ Liver, spinach, meat, eggs, raisins, dry beans and peas, nuts, enriched grain products 
Phosphorus	■ Works with calcium to help build and maintain strong bones and teeth ■ Helps body obtain energy from other nutrients	■ Dairy products, meat, fish, poultry, dry beans and peas, whole-grain breads and cereals
Potassium	■ Regulates muscle contractions and transmission of nerve signals ■ Helps regulate fluid in cells ■ Works with sodium to regulate blood pressure	■ Oranges, bananas, dairy products, meat, poultry, fish 
Sodium	■ Helps regulate blood pressure ■ Helps regulate fluid balance in body	■ Table salt, processed foods
Magnesium 	■ Helps body build strong bones ■ Regulates nervous system and body temperature	■ Whole-grain cereals and breads, dry beans and peas, dark green leafy vegetables, nuts, seeds
Zinc	■ Is needed for proper growth ■ Affects senses of taste and smell ■ Helps wounds heal	■ Shellfish, meat, eggs, dairy products, whole-grain breads
Iodine	■ Needed for proper functioning of thyroid gland, which produces substances that help the body obtain energy from nutrients	■ Iodized salt, seafood 

Fig. 34-6. Minerals perform a variety of important functions. Which minerals work together to build and maintain strong bones and teeth?

Minerals

Minerals are nutrients that regulate body processes and that form parts of many tissues. Fig. 34-6 on the previous page shows the functions and food sources for some of the minerals you need. Your body contains large amounts of some minerals and tiny quantities of others. For example, calcium is the mineral that is present in the body in the largest quantities. Iron is present in only very small, or trace, amounts. Maintaining the proper levels of these minerals, as well as of other essential minerals, is vital to good health.

Calcium, along with phosphorous and magnesium, helps bones grow and is particularly important during adolescence. Maintaining healthy bones is also an ongoing process. People who don't get enough calcium are more likely to develop a condition called *osteoporosis*, or brittle bone disease, in their later years. Bones that have become brittle are more likely to fracture.

Iron is vital for building red blood cells. People who do not get enough iron may develop iron-deficiency anemia—a condition that results in lack of energy and low resistance to infections.

Water

Nearly 70 percent of your body weight is made up of water. Water is found in every cell and is the basic material of your blood. It transports nutrients throughout the body and carries away waste products. Water also helps move food through the digestive system and helps regulate the temperature of your body.

Your body loses 2 to 3 quarts of water a day, and you need to replace it. Water, juices, milk, and soups are healthy choices. Foods such as fruits and vegetables also provide small amounts of water. You need additional fluids in hot weather and when you exercise or do physical work. See Fig. 34-7.

Fig. 34-7. Getting enough fluids is especially important when you're outdoors in hot weather. Which of the foods at this picnic would help meet the body's need for water?

Assessing Nutrient Needs

You have learned that you need small amounts of vitamins and minerals and larger amounts of carbohydrates, proteins, and other nutrients. What happens if you don't get the nutrients that you need? A person who doesn't get an adequate supply of needed nutrients over a long period of time may develop a *nutrient deficiency*, or shortage of a nutrient. The symptoms of a nutrient deficiency vary depending on the nutrient that has been in short supply. Tooth decay, skin disorders, and fatigue are just a few of the conditions that can result from nutrient deficiencies. Getting too much of some nutrients, such as saturated fat, can also cause health problems.

Nutrition experts have studied the nutrient needs of males and females at different ages. Based on this knowledge, they have developed reference values for each nutrient. Collectively, the reference values are called Dietary Reference Intakes, or DRIs.

One of the DRIs is the Recommended Dietary Allowance (RDA). An RDA is the amount of a specific nutrient needed each day by the majority of healthy people of a specific age and gender. Another measure, known as Adequate Intake, or AI, is used for nutrients for which there is not yet enough scientific knowledge to establish an RDA. As its name suggests, an AI is an amount believed to be sufficient to meet daily needs.

Nutritionists and other health care professionals use the DRIs when advising patients on food choices. The food industry uses them when developing new products. The U.S. government uses them to shape national nutrition policies. In addition, the U.S. Food and Drug Administration uses DRIs as the basis for the Daily Values that are used in nutrition labeling.

DRIs are updated from time to time to reflect new findings. On page 741 in the Appendix, you will find a table of DRIs for specific nutrients.

More to Explore

Dietary Supplements

Most people can get all of the vitamins and minerals they need by eating a variety of foods. Therefore, most people don't need dietary supplements—extra vitamins and minerals in the form of pills, capsules, or powders.

Only under special circumstances are dietary supplements necessary. For example, a doctor might recommend dietary supplements for pregnant or nursing women who may need extra calcium and other nutrients. Supplements may also be advised for people who are taking certain medications, recovering from an illness, or following special diets.

If you think you need a dietary supplement, check with your doctor first. When using a supplement, be sure to follow the instructions on the label. Taking more than the recommended amount could cause health problems.

TEXT LINK≈

Daily Values and *nutrition labels* are discussed in detail in Chapter 37.

Changes in Nutrient Needs

Throughout the life span, good nutrition is essential for health. People of all ages need the same basic nutrients. However, the amounts needed vary at different ages. Teens, for example, need extra nutrients to fuel their growth and development. Life events and lifestyle also affect nutrient needs. Pregnant and nursing women have special nutrient needs, as do athletes and other highly active people. Understanding the benefits of nutrition and knowing what is appropriate at different life stages are keys to nutritional health throughout life.

- **Childhood.** During childhood, the body is growing rapidly, and activity levels are high. At each stage—infant, toddler, and preschooler—children need an increasing amount of food energy (measured in calories) to build body tissue and provide fuel for physical activity. For example, a 6-month-old infant needs about 850 calories per day, a 2-year-old about 1,200, and a 5-year-old about 1,500. Nutrient needs also change. For example, toddlers need large amounts of calcium and phosphorus to develop strong bones and teeth. Older preschoolers need more protein, more vitamins A, C, and K, and more magnesium and iodine than toddlers. Inadequate nutrients or calories in childhood can result in poor growth and decreased resistance to infection.

- **Adolescence.** Teens are growing rapidly and need even more energy than children do. Depending on their level of activity, teen males may need as many as 2,800 calories a day, and teen females may need 2,200 calories a day. Teens need more iron as they grow and build muscle. Once girls begin to menstruate, their need for iron increases. Teens also need extra calcium—as much as 1,300 milligrams a day—to build strong bones. See Fig. 34-8.

- **Adulthood.** As people get older, they are no longer growing, and some tend to become less active. For these reasons, most adults find they need fewer calories to maintain an appropriate weight. Those

Fig. 34-8. Teens need extra fuel to support their growth and energy. Most people need more nutrients during their teen years than at any other stage in their life.

who eat the same amounts of food as they did when they were still growing are likely to gain weight. While adults of all ages continue to need the same nutrients as children and teens, they need some in smaller amounts.

Pregnant and Nursing Women

Good nutrition is especially important during pregnancy. In general, pregnant women need an extra 300 calories per day for the last six months of pregnancy to supply enough energy for mother and fetus. They also need extra protein, vitamins, and minerals—especially calcium and iron. Poor nutrition during pregnancy, as well as the use of tobacco, alcohol, or other drugs, can harm the health of both mother and child.

Nursing mothers need an extra 500 calories per day. They also need additional vitamins and protein, as well as calcium. The higher the intake of nutrients, the more nutritious the breast milk will be and the healthier the mother and baby.

Nutrition for Athletes

Athletes who are actively training need the same nutrients as other people, but they need extra calories. No one food or nutrient builds muscle or increases speed, but complex carbohydrates—such as breads, pasta, rice, and starchy vegetables—are the best sources of the energy an athlete's body needs.

Physical activity also requires extra fluids, especially during hot weather. Drinking plenty of fluids prevents dehydration and heatstroke. Most fluids should be taken in as water. Fruit juices, low-fat milk, and foods with high water content, such as lettuce and oranges, are also good sources of extra fluid. See Fig. 34-9.

Many athletes wonder what they should eat before competition to improve their performance. Eating a meal three or four hours before competition is best because it gives the body time to digest the food. The meal should have a variety of foods and should be high in complex carbohydrates and low in fats.

There are many misconceptions about the nutritional needs of athletes. A common one is that athletes need to take supplements for extra protein. In fact, normal eating patterns meet athletes' protein needs. Furthermore, if athletes eat a balanced variety of nutritious foods, they do not need vitamin or mineral supplements or salt tablets.

Fig. 34-9. *Athletes need plenty of fluids to replace those lost during physical activity.* *What other nutritional requirements do athletes have?*

Chapter Summary

- Nutrients can be divided into six main classes: carbohydrates, proteins, fats, vitamins, minerals, and water.
- Most of your body's energy supply should come from carbohydrates.
- Proteins build and repair body tissues.
- Fats allow the body to transport and store other nutrients.
- Vitamins and minerals are needed in small amounts but perform vital functions.
- Nutritionists use Dietary Reference Intakes to assess the nutrient needs of people at different ages.
- The amounts of nutrients that people need vary through the life span.
- Pregnant and nursing women need extra calories, as do athletes.

Reviewing Key Terms & Ideas

1. In general, what are **nutrients**?
2. What is the main function of **carbohydrates**?
3. What is **fiber**? Why is it beneficial?
4. For what purposes does your body use **proteins**?
5. What are **amino acids**?
6. Why do you need fats in your diet?
7. What are the differences between **saturated fats**, **trans fats**, and **unsaturated fats**?
8. Why are people advised to limit the amount of **cholesterol** in their diet?
9. In general, what do **vitamins** do?
10. What are the basic functions of **minerals**?
11. Which minerals play a key role in building strong bones?
12. What jobs does water perform in your body?
13. Name four ways in which Dietary Reference Intakes are used.
14. Do teens generally need more or fewer calories than adults? Why?
15. What special nutrition needs do athletes have?

Thinking Critically

1. **Identifying Alternatives.** Some people have trouble digesting dairy products. What are the key nutrients found in dairy products? What are some other food sources of each of these nutrients?
2. **Distinguishing Fact from Opinion.** What recommendations about nutrition for athletes have you heard? Do you think they are facts or myths? Why? How could you find out for sure?

Applying Your Knowledge

1. **Sources of Nutrients.** Using magazine pictures or your own photos, make a visual display showing some of your favorite foods. Alongside each picture, list specific nutrients the food provides. Be sure to include foods that are good sources of each of the six classes of nutrients.

2. **Nutrition Through the Life Span.** In a small group, conduct research to learn more about the specific nutritional needs of either children, teens, young adults, middle-aged adults, older adults, pregnant women, or nursing mothers. Present your findings to the class. After all presentations have been given, discuss the similarities and differences in nutritional needs at each stage of the life span.

Making Connections

1. **Science.** Vitamins were discovered gradually as scientists investigated certain diseases and the role of foods in preventing them. Choose one of the vitamins and write a brief report explaining how it was discovered.

2. **Social Studies.** In some regions of the world, people continue to develop illnesses that result from nutrient deficiencies. Identify one such illness and learn more about it. What causes it? In what parts of the world is it a problem and why? What could be done to prevent it? Be prepared to report on your findings.

Managing Your Life

Nutrition Resources

New discoveries are constantly being made about nutrition. How can you stay up to date? Good management means knowing how to make the best use of the resources available to you. Make a list of resources that could help you obtain accurate, timely information about nutrition. Include human, material, and community resources. Explain why each resource would be helpful.

Using Technology

1. **Nutrition Analysis Tools.** A number of online or software tools are available to help people determine the nutrient content of the foods they eat and to compare their nutrient intake with recommended amounts. Choose one such tool and investigate its capabilities. Evaluate how user-friendly and useful it is.

2. **Internet.** Conduct an Internet search to determine the latest recommendations for daily fluid intake. Find out how much fluid is recommended for people of different ages and activity levels and the types of fluids that are suggested. Be sure that the sources you use are reliable. Share your findings with the class.

CHAPTER 35

Guidelines for Food Choices

- hunger
- appetite
- Dietary Guidelines for Americans
- enriched
- fortified
- nutrient-dense

Objectives

- Describe the physical, emotional, and social needs that food satisfies.
- Identify social and personal influences on food choices.
- Evaluate the reliability of food and nutrition information.
- Summarize the recommendations of the Dietary Guidelines for Americans.
- Demonstrate how to use MyPyramid to make daily food selections.

QUICK WRITE

What factors influence the foods that you choose each day? In a few paragraphs, explain what you think are the strongest influences on your food choices.

*F*or health and vitality, you need the right kinds of foods—foods that supply the right nutrients in the right amounts. Does your current eating plan do that? If you are like many people, you don't pay much attention to what you eat. It's easy to fall into the habit of eating what appeals to you, or what is available, without a second thought. Yet when you consider the role that nutrients play in providing energy and regulating body systems, you realize that food choices deserve your attention.

To make wise food choices, it helps to understand the broad role that food plays in your life. You should also be aware of the many influences on your food choices. Finally, you need reliable information that will help you choose healthful foods in the right amounts. This chapter will help you make good food choices based on sound nutritional guidelines.

Food Fills Many Needs

Humans don't just eat to live. Food has many purposes. Besides meeting basic physical needs and helping you stay healthy, food also helps to meet emotional and social needs.

Physical Needs

Eating the right foods helps your body perform vital functions. What you eat and drink helps your heart to beat, your temperature to remain normal, and your cuts and bruises to heal. Food also supplies the energy you need for daily activities, from automatic actions such as breathing and digesting to more demanding activities such as sports. See Fig. 35-1.

Food does more than keep your body functioning from one day to the next. It affects your health over a long period of time. Children who do not get adequate amounts of the right foods may experience growth problems and diseases of the bones and skin. Wise food choices during the teen

Fig. 35-1. *Everything you do takes energy—and that energy comes from the food you eat.*

and adult years help people avoid heart disease and other long-term health problems. At any age, a well-nourished body is better equipped to heal properly and combat disease than a poorly nourished one.

Your body tells you when it needs more food. If you go without eating for too long, you may hear your stomach growl or feel it contract, or you may get a headache. In other words, you feel hungry. **Hunger** is your body's physical signal that it is short of energy and needs food. Hunger is different from appetite. **Appetite** is a desire, rather than a need, to eat. Your appetite may be stimulated by the sight of a bowl of cherries or by the smell of baking bread. Having a good appetite is healthy. If you find food enjoyable, you're more likely to eat the food you need.

Fig. 35-2. Many people associate certain foods with certain emotions. What foods do you crave when you're feeling low?

Emotional Needs

Food satisfies emotional as well as physical needs. People start to make associations between food and feelings very early in life. Infants learn to associate feeding with physical contact and a sense of security. Such emotional links with food continue throughout life. You might, for example, crave hot chicken soup when you have a cold because that's what someone made for you when you were younger. You connect the food with the feeling of being loved and cared for. See Fig. 35-2.

Although there is an emotional element to the enjoyment of food, allowing emotions to control eating habits can be unhealthy. Some people turn to food when they are lonely, depressed, anxious, or bored. People who are sad or grieving may lose their appetite. Allowing negative emotions to control food intake can create health problems over time. You can avoid letting emotions rule your eating habits by being aware of the feelings that stimulate you to eat.

Social Needs

Do you enjoy going out for pizza with friends? Many people combine eating with the company of friends and family because both experiences are pleasurable. In such cases, food helps to meet people's social needs. For some busy families, mealtimes are the only occasions when the whole family can be together. For many workers, lunch is an important opportunity to discuss business or just to relax with coworkers.

Food also plays a role in maintaining social traditions. Many people enjoy turkey at Thanksgiving and cut into a cake on their birthday. Wedding receptions, religious holidays, and other special occasions may also be celebrated with special foods.

Influences on Food Choices

If you were to ask ten classmates what they ate yesterday, you'd probably get ten different answers. Each person is unique, and that is reflected in food choices as well as in personality. People's food choices are affected by both social and personal influences.

Social Influences

Several social factors influence food choices. They include your family; your cultural, ethnic, and religious background; the region you live in; your friends; and the media.

- **Family.** One of the greatest influences on how and what you eat is your family. Family preferences and eating patterns have influenced you since childhood. The foods that a family eats are also influenced by the family's food budget and by how much time the family has for preparing and eating meals. Many people imitate their family's eating patterns when they grow up and start their own families.

- **Cultural and ethnic background.** The United States is a nation of immigrants, and many people eat foods that originated in other parts of the world. Foods from many cultural and ethnic groups are available here—in people's homes, in restaurants, in supermarkets, and in specialty stores. See Fig. 35-3.

- **Religious customs.** Families often eat special foods on their religious holidays—lamb at Passover or egg dishes at Easter, for example. Religious rules may also forbid the eating of certain foods.

- **Regional traditions.** Although most foods can be found all over the United States, certain dishes are still associated with specific regions. Have you ever tried New England clam chowder, Texas barbecue, or Louisiana gumbo?

Fig. 35-3. No matter where you live, it's possible to buy foods from many different cultures. What kinds of ethnic foods have you tried?

Fig. 35-4. *If you had never tried sushi before, encouragement from a friend might make you more likely to sample it.* What foods have you learned about from friends?

- **Friends.** You might be introduced to new foods and to different styles of cooking by friends whose background is different from yours. When you eat out, friends may encourage you to try foods that are unfamiliar to you. See Fig. 35-4.

- **The media.** Magazines, newspapers, and television programs offer many suggestions for preparing food and eating for good health. Food is also advertised in these media. You may be tempted to try certain foods because the ads make them look inviting and appetizing.

Personal Influences

Personal influences on your food choices are unique to you. They have to do with the way you live, what you prefer, and your eating habits.

- **Lifestyle.** The patterns of your daily life influence what and when you eat. If you have a part-time job, you might not always have time for family meals. You may have to plan quick meals or eat out. Your food choices may also depend on whether you enjoy preparing and eating food or would rather spend your time on other activities.

- **Individual preferences.** You already know that you enjoy some foods more than others. Over time, you may discover new foods to add to your list of preferences. Some people enjoy trying new foods, while others prefer to eat only familiar favorites.

- **Habits.** Do you eat regular, balanced meals? Do you tend to skip meals and survive on snacks? Are you even aware of your eating habits? It's a good idea to become aware of the eating habits that you have. That way you can identify bad habits that involve poor food choices and replace them with good habits. If you develop good habits now, and make them part of your lifestyle, you could gain benefits for years to come.

Making Informed Food Choices

Making deliberate, well-informed food choices is an important part of taking responsibility for your health. With so much nutrition information available, though, how can you figure out which advice to follow? Learning how to evaluate nutrition information for accuracy and how to recognize food myths and fads are helpful first steps.

Evaluating Information

When evaluating food and nutrition information, the most important point to keep in mind is "consider the source." Where did the information come from? The most reliable sources include government agencies such as the Food and Drug Administration and nonprofit organizations such as the American Heart Association. If the organization or company providing the information is trying to sell a product, the information may be biased and therefore unreliable. Always check your sources and use critical thinking skills to determine which sources are trustworthy. See Fig. 35-5.

Recognizing Myths and Fads

Have you heard that chocolate causes acne, or that margarine contains less fat than butter? Although these statements might sound true, they are actually false. Like other types of myths, food myths are spread by word of mouth or through the media. To make informed food choices, you need to be able to separate the facts from the myths.

Be especially skeptical of fad diets that promise quick and easy weight loss. Some fad diets limit you to special diet bars or milk shakes. Others include large amounts of one nutrient, such as protein, but almost no others. Avoid any diet that excludes one or more of the major nutrients or that calls for eating 800 calories or less per day. Such diets do not provide enough vital nutrients. Also avoid diet pills that suppress the appetite—they can have harmful side effects.

Dietary Guidelines for Americans

Developed jointly by the USDA and the Department of Health and Human Services, the **Dietary Guidelines for Americans** offer science-based advice for making smart choices from every food group, finding balance between food and physical activity, and getting the most nutrition out of your calories. These guidelines are revised every five years and are designed to help your reach your best level of health.

Fig. 35-5. Lots of magazines include articles about food and nutrition. What clues would you look for when evaluating whether the information is reliable?

Aiming for Good Health

Good health involves making smart food choices and being physically active every day. Follow these guidelines to maintain or improve your level of good health:

- **Get enough nutrients within your calorie needs.** Choose a variety of foods and beverages packed with nutrients from the basic food groups. Just be sure to stay within your daily calorie needs. MyPyramid, as described on pages 514 and 515, can help you adopt a balanced eating plan.

- **Manage your weight.** Maintaining a healthy weight helps you live longer and reduces your risk for certain diseases. Balance the calories you consume from foods and beverages with calories used in physical activities. You may want to review the discussion of weight management in Chapter 33.

- **Be physically active each day.** Daily physical activity promotes health, well-being, and a healthy body weight. Try to include 60 minutes of moderate physical activity in your daily routine. Even simple changes—such as riding a bike instead of driving, or taking the stairs instead of the elevator—will make a difference. See Fig. 35-6.

- **Focus on key food groups.** No single food provides all the nutrients in the amounts you need. Choose a healthy eating plan that emphasizes whole grains, vegetables, fruits, and fat-free or low-fat milk and milk products. Foods made from grains provide your body with many essential nutrients, including vitamins, minerals, carbohydrates, and fiber. Examples of whole grain foods include whole wheat bread, brown rice, and oatmeal. Vegetables and fruits provide vitamins, minerals, fiber, and other important nutrients for good health. Eating a variety of fruits and vegetables every day will help you stay healthy and may reduce your risk of many chronic diseases. See Fig. 35-7.

- **Limit fats.** Choose a diet that is low in saturated fat and cholesterol and moderate in total fat. Dietary fats, especially saturated fats and cholesterol, can contribute to high blood pressure and heart disease. Within each food group, look for the low-fat choices, such as lean meats and poultry. Choose low-fat or skim milk and foods

TEXTLINK≈

You will learn more about *keeping foods safe to eat* in Chapter 38.

Fig. 35-6. Physical activity helps you look and feel better, manage stress, and maintain a healthy weight. What are some other possible benefits?

Fig. 35-7. Fruits and vegetables—especially dark orange and green ones—are packed with vital nutrients. What new-to-you fruits and vegetables would you like to try?

that are broiled or baked instead of fried. In addition, limit your intake of high-fat toppings, such as butter, sour cream, and oily salad dressings. Choose healthy oils.

- **Be choosy about carbohydrates.** Pair whole-grain carbohydrate foods, such as brown rice, with vegetables and beans. Choose other beverages and foods to moderate your intake of added sugars. No food is "bad" in itself, including sugar, but eating too much of some foods is a poor choice. Foods high in added sugar can lead to tooth decay as well as weight gain. Check the ingredients of the foods you eat—sucrose, glucose, maltose, lactose, fructose, and syrups are all forms of sugar.

- **Reduce sodium and boost potassium.** Sodium, which you get mainly from salt, plays an important part in controlling fluids and blood pressure in your body. It can also contribute to high blood pressure in some people. Choose foods that are low in salt, and try seasoning foods with herbs and spices instead of salt. In addition, eat plenty of potassium-rich foods and beverages, such as fruits and vegetables, to counteract the effects of sodium with high blood pressure.

- **Play it safe with food.** Keep food safe to eat from bacteria and hazards by knowing how to prepare, handle, and store food properly.

MyPyramid

MyPyramid, shown in Fig. 35-8, is a symbol and interactive food guidance system developed by the U.S. Department of Agriculture (USDA). It is designed to encourage you to make healthier food choices and to be active every day. It divides foods into five basic groups (plus oils) and arranges them in a pyramid shape with vertical color-bands of varying widths representing each food group. The color bands are wider at the base than they are at the top to show you that not all foods within a food group are equally healthful. For example, a baked sweet potato is a more healthful choice than French fries.

Foods from all groups are needed every day. The five groups are:

- **Grain group.** Foods in this group are the richest source of carbohydrates. They also provide B vitamins, vitamin E, iron, fats, incomplete proteins, and fiber. For the most nutritional value, select whole-grain, enriched, or fortified grain products. Whole-grain means that the natural nutrients were never removed. **Enriched** indicates that many of the nutrients lost in processing have been added back. **Fortified** indicates that specific nutrients have been added during processing.

- **Vegetable group.** Vegetables are valuable sources of carbohydrates and are high in fiber. They provide many important vitamins and minerals, including vitamins A and C, iron, and calcium. Choose fresh, frozen, canned, or dried vegetables, eaten raw or cooked, and vegetable juices.

- **Fruit group.** Fruits and 100 percent fruit juice contain many of the same nutrients as vegetables. They are good sources of fiber and carbohydrates and provide essential vitamins and minerals, especially vitamin A, vitamin C, and potassium. Choose fresh, frozen, canned, or dried fruits, eaten raw or cooked, and fruit juices.

- **Milk group.** Milk is a source of carbohydrates, fat, and protein. It is rich in

riboflavin, as well as vitamin A, and is often fortified with vitamin D. Drinking milk is an excellent way to get calcium and phosphorus. Yogurt and cheese are also nutritious choices.

- **Meat and beans group.** Meat, poultry, fish, dry beans and peas, eggs, nuts, and seeds are in this group. They are all sources of protein and B vitamins. These foods also provide vitamins A and E, iron, and other minerals. Many foods in this group contain saturated fats, though excess fat can be removed.

The narrowest color-band in MyPyramid represents oils. Although oils are needed for good health and to help the body absorb some nutrients, they are high in calories. Eat them sparingly.

Designing an eating plan based on the food groups is easy. You can adapt your choices to your own food preferences, eating patterns, family circumstances, and cultural traditions. Food combinations, such as lasagna, include foods from several groups.

How Much Food?

By entering your age, gender, and activity level into MyPyramid on the Internet, you can learn how many calories you need each day. For most females ages 14 to 18, the range is from 1800 to 2400 calories. For most males ages 14 to 18, the range is 2200 to 3200 calories.

Based on calorie level, MyPyramid tells how much food to eat from each food group. For example, a 17-year-old female who is moderately active needs 2000 calories daily from these amounts of food: 6 ounces of grains (half as whole grains); 2-1/2 cups of vegetables; 2 cups of fruits; 3 cups of milk; and 5-1/2 ounces of meat and beans. You can check MyPyramid to find out what's right for you.

Checking Up on Food Equivalents

MyPyramid measures vegetables, fruits, and milk in cups. Grains, meat, and beans are measured in ounces. If you eat a large orange, how does that equate to cups in the fruit group? Read below to find out. Check MyPyramid on the Internet for more equivalents.

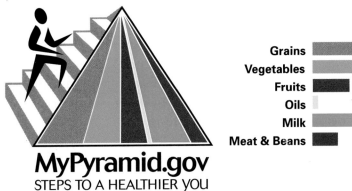

GRAIN GROUP

What equals 1 ounce?
- 1 slice of bread
- 1 cup of ready-to-eat cereal
- 1/2 cup of cooked rice, pasta, or cereal
- 1 ounce of dried pasta or rice

FRUIT GROUP

What equals 1 cup?
- 1 large orange (varies for different fruits)
- 1 cup of fresh (cut), frozen, or canned fruit
- 1/2 cup of dried fruit
- 1 cup of 100% fruit juice

VEGETABLE GROUP

What equals 1 cup?
- 2 cups of raw, leafy vegetable
- 1 cup of cooked or chopped raw vegetable
- 1 cup of vegetable juice

MILK GROUP

What equals 1 cup?
- 1 cup of milk or yogurt
- 1-1/2 ounces of natural cheese
- 2 ounces of processed cheese

MEAT & BEANS GROUP

What equals 1 ounce?
- 1 ounce of lean meat, poultry, or fish
- 1/4 cup of cooked dry beans or peas
- 1 egg
- 1 tablespoon of peanut butter
- 1/2 ounce of nuts or seeds

OILS

Oils are in many foods, such as nuts, fish, cooking oil, and salad dressings. Most teens need 5 or 6 teaspoons of oils, or the equivalent, per day.

How are oils counted?
- 1 tsp. of vegetable oil = 1 tsp.
- 1 Tbsp. of soft margarine = 2-1/2 tsp.
- 1 Tbsp. of mayonnaise = 2-1/2 tsp.
- 2 Tbsp. of Italian dressing = 2 tsp.

Fig. 35-8. MyPyramid is your easy-to-use guide to daily food choices and physical activities.

Once you know your MyPyramid numbers, you can compare the amounts you eat to what is recommended. Use the equivalents on page 515 as your guide. For example, if you eat an egg for breakfast, that counts as 1 ounce toward the total ounces you need from the meat and beans group. If you need 5-1/2 ounces in all, you have 4-1/2 ounces to go for the day. You don't need to measure and weigh everything. Learn to estimate as shown in Fig. 35-9

Choosing Wisely

When using MyPyramid, be sure to vary your choices within each food group. For example, enjoy many different types of vegetables rather than choosing the same two or three kinds all the time.

Choose plenty of low-fat, high-fiber, nutrient-dense foods. **Nutrient-dense** foods are low or moderate in calories and rich in important nutrients. In general, nutrient-dense foods are also low in fats and added sugars. Such foods include whole-grain products; fresh fruits and vegetables; legumes; lean meats, poultry, and fish; and dairy products. When choosing dairy products, read the labels and choose non-fat or low-fat varieties. Limit your intake of foods with low nutrient density, such as potato chips, soft drinks, and ice cream.

What Do Food Amounts Look Like?

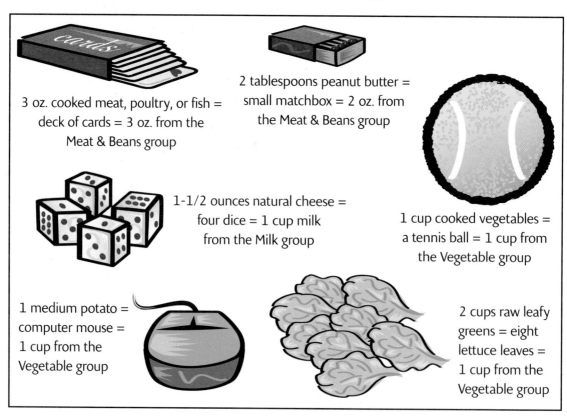

3 oz. cooked meat, poultry, or fish = deck of cards = 3 oz. from the Meat & Beans group

2 tablespoons peanut butter = small matchbox = 2 oz. from the Meat & Beans group

1-1/2 ounces natural cheese = four dice = 1 cup milk from the Milk group

1 cup cooked vegetables = a tennis ball = 1 cup from the Vegetable group

1 medium potato = computer mouse = 1 cup from the Vegetable group

2 cups raw leafy greens = eight lettuce leaves = 1 cup from the Vegetable group

Fig. 35-9. Keep these images in mind when you are counting your daily food amounts.

FINDING CREATIVE SOLUTIONS

Using Free Association

If you want to find a creative solution to a problem, you'll need to give your creativity a jump start. One useful technique for doing just that is called free association.

How It Works

You can use this technique whether you're working on a problem by yourself or in a group. Start by defining the problem in one or two words. Write them at the top of a sheet of paper. Then jot down any related words and phrases that pop into your head. For example, if you were free associating on the words *more active*, your list might include words and phrases like *jump, run, sweat, tired, fun, shoes, basketball*, and so on.

As you go through this process, don't pressure yourself to come up with a solution to your problem. The goal is simply to get your brain going in new directions. Write down everything that comes to mind, even if it seems as though you're getting off the subject. If you give your mind the freedom to roam, one of the words or phrases you come up with could eventually lead to the solution you're looking for.

Try It Out

Most people have some good eating habits and some that aren't so good. The problem with habits is that they aren't always easy to change. See if free association can help you come up with ideas for improving your own eating habits.

▶ **Your Turn** *Free associate on the words "good nutrition." Come up with as many words and phrases as you can. Then look back at your list. What ideas are sparked by the words and phrases you wrote down? Do any of them suggest ways you could improve your everyday food choices? Do any of them suggest reasons for some of the poor choices you make now?*

Evaluating Your Choices

You have the information you need to develop a healthy eating plan. Now you need to put it into practice. Start by evaluating your current eating habits. Do you tend to eat too much from one of the food groups and too little from another? If you need to make changes, do so gradually. Start by adding or cutting out an amount of food from one of the food groups. As each change becomes a habit, make another one, until you are following the pyramid guidelines. Then use them every day as your easy-to-follow road map to good nutrition.

Chapter Summary

- Food meets a variety of physical, emotional, and social needs.
- A person's food choices are affected by both social and personal influences.
- You can make informed food choices by evaluating nutrition information, avoiding food myths and fads, and following government nutrition guidelines.
- The Dietary Guidelines for Americans offer recommendations for better health.
- MyPyramid tells you how much to eat from the five food groups based on your calorie needs.
- To use MyPyramid effectively, pay attention to the amounts of food you eat, make wise selections from each food group, and balance calories consumed with those you burn through physical activity.

Reviewing Key Terms & Ideas

1. Briefly explain how food meets physical and emotional needs.
2. What is the difference between **hunger** and **appetite**?
3. How does food serve social needs?
4. Name three social influences and three personal influences on food choices.
5. What kinds of organizations offer the most reliable nutrition information?
6. List four recommendations from **Dietary Guidelines for Americans**.
7. Name the five food groups from **MyPyramid**, and identify one or more of the chief nutrients each group supplies.
8. Give an example of a food equivalent from each of the food groups.
9. What is the difference between **enriched** foods and **fortified** foods?
10. Why should you limit the amount of fats and oils you eat?
11. Explain the importance of amounts of food when following MyPyramid.
12. What does **nutrient-dense** mean? Give four examples of nutrient-dense foods.

Thinking Critically

1. **Drawing Conclusions.** Why do people need to be aware of the emotions that stimulate them to eat? How can they benefit from that awareness?
2. **Defending Your Position.** Do you think that MyPyramid is an effective tool for guiding daily food choices? Why or why not? Be prepared to defend your position to someone who holds the opposite view.

Applying Your Knowledge

1. **Evaluating Nutrition Information.** Find a newspaper or magazine article about a nutrition-related topic. Use critical thinking skills to evaluate the reliability of the article. Explain your conclusions.

2. **Applying the Dietary Guidelines.** List each of the Dietary Guidelines for Americans. Next to each guideline, name two steps you could take to improve your eating or physical activity habits. For example, next to "Limit added sugars," you might say, "Replace sugary snacks with more healthful choices."

3. **Making an Eating Plan.** Using MyPyramid and the Dietary Guidelines, devise an eating plan for you for one day. Include an explanation of how your plan follows the guidelines and recommendations.

Making Connections

1. **Science.** Use Internet or library resources to learn more about the processes of enriching and fortifying foods. Find out what kinds of foods are typically enriched or fortified, with what nutrients, and why. Summarize your findings in a brief report.

2. **Language Arts.** With a classmate, write an article for a nutrition magazine on one of the following topics: "The Truth About Saturated Fats" or "Sugar: The Inside Scoop." Include reasons for cutting back on saturated fat or sugar.

Managing Your Life

Changing Your Eating Habits

How do you rate your current eating habits in light of what you have learned in this chapter? Do you need to make some fundamental changes? You're more likely to be successful if you identify specific actions to take, then set priorities. Make a list of three eating habits that you would like to change. Beside each item, write a new habit that you would like to adopt instead. Number them in order of priority. Over the next few weeks, work on introducing these changes into your life gradually.

Using Technology

1. **Presentation Software.** Use appropriate software to create a presentation called "Are You Hungry?" that explains the difference between hunger and appetite. Use illustrations and explanatory text to help viewers understand how the hunger mechanism works and how appetite can persuade people to eat when they are not hungry.

2. **Photography.** Prepare a visual guide to reasonable serving sizes that will help you and your family follow pyramid guidelines. Prepare and photograph portions of a variety of foods from each food group. Use the photos to create a poster that you can display in your kitchen or dining room.

Planning Meals and Snacks

Key Terms

- eating patterns
- entrée
- convenience foods
- vegan
- food allergy
- food intolerance
- lactose intolerance

Objectives

- Explain the benefits of eating regular meals, especially breakfast.
- Give examples of healthful snacks.
- Identify factors to consider for successful meal planning.
- Give guidelines for eating healthful meals and snacks away from home.
- Describe special food needs of vegetarians, people with medical conditions, and children.

Make a list of your favorite snack foods. As you read this chapter, replace any low-nutrient snack choices on your list with more nutritious ones.

You have learned the basics of good nutrition. Now it's time to apply this knowledge to your own life. How do you approach making healthful food choices every day? When you reach for snacks, what choices do you make? What are the benefits of meal planning? How can you make nutritious food choices when you eat away from home? This chapter will explore answers to these and other questions about planning meals and snacks.

Nutrition Through the Day

You know that what you eat affects your health, but when and how often you eat affects it too. Do you often skip breakfast, eat on the run, or snack late at night? Your **eating patterns**, or daily routines for eating, have an effect on your energy level and overall health and fitness.

Eating patterns can vary depending on cultural traditions, family customs, and daily schedules. One common pattern is to have a relatively light breakfast and lunch, with dinner in the evening as the main meal. Another option is to have the main meal at midday and lighter meals in the morning and evening. One eating pattern is not necessarily better than another. What matters is that you have meals and snacks at regular intervals.

Skipping meals is not healthy and often leads to overeating and poor food choices later in the day.

Breakfast is particularly important. When you wake up, your body may have gone 10 to 15 hours without food. Nutrients that the body cannot store become depleted. Eating healthful foods in the morning restores these nutrients and energizes you for the day ahead. See Fig. 36-1.

Fig. 36-1. A healthful breakfast provides the fuel you need to start your day with energy. *What foods do you enjoy at breakfast?*

No matter where or when you eat, think of each food choice you make through the day as part of a balanced whole. Remember that the Dietary Guidelines and MyPyramid give you goals for your food choices and physical activity level. Try to plan ahead for meeting those goals. If you need two cups of fruit in a day, for instance, you could have one-half cup of banana slices on your cereal at breakfast, one cup of melon at lunch, and four ounces of pineapple juice as an afternoon snack. By planning, you won't let a day go by without getting the essential nutrients you need to stay healthy.

What if your day doesn't work out the way you predicted? Don't worry—you can adjust your plan as you go. For example, if you haven't had a serving of fruit by afternoon, grab an orange for an after-school snack and include fruit at dinner. If you munch on oil-popped, salted popcorn at a movie, make sure that your next meal is low in fat and sodium and get some exercise. With thought, creativity, and a basic knowledge of nutrition, you can make healthful food and activity choices every day.

Smart Snacking

Many teens, because they are active and growing rapidly, need more nutrients and calories than three meals a day can provide. Snacking is a good way to "refuel" when you need extra energy. The key is choosing the right snacks at the right time. See Fig. 36-2.

The best time to snack is midway between meals—not just before mealtime—so that you'll still be hungry for regular meals. The best reason to snack is because you're hungry. Try not to snack simply because you are bored or anxious.

For good nutrition, snack on a variety of low-fat, low-sugar, nutrient-dense foods. Remember that snacks count as part of your daily food total, along with breakfast, lunch, and dinner. You can use snacks to fill in gaps if you are short on the amounts you need from the five food groups. Here are a few healthful snack ideas. What food groups do they represent?

- Celery sticks with low-fat cream cheese and raisins.

- Whole-grain bread with peanut butter.

- Carrot sticks and other raw vegetables.

Fig. 36-2. The key to smart snacking is to choose nutritious foods. Why would fresh vegetables be a good choice?

- A slice of pizza with vegetable toppings.
- A banana, an apple, some grapes, or any other fruit.
- Plain popcorn.
- Dry-roasted, unsalted nuts.

Family Meals at Home

You may already be responsible for planning and preparing some of the meals your family eats at home. When you're living on your own, meal planning will become an even more useful skill. It's good to know how to plan a meal that everyone can enjoy. See Fig. 36-3.

Many families prefer to plan meals for several days, a week, or even a month at a time. Planning meals in advance has several benefits. Families who plan ahead are more likely to enjoy well-balanced, nutritious meals that are appetizing and attractive. Planning also enables families to satisfy everyone's needs and schedules while staying within their food budget.

Menu Planning Considerations

Meal planning begins with deciding on a menu, a list of foods that will be included in the meal. A common strategy is to first select an **entrée**, or main dish. Then you can select side dishes that work well with the main dish.

Several important factors need to be considered when planning a menu. They include family members' needs, your resources, nutrition, and meal appeal.

Fig. 36-3. *Family meals are a time to enjoy one another's company and share the events of the day. A well-planned meal adds to the enjoyment.*

Family Members' Needs ~ When planning meals for your family, you need to know:

- How many people will be eating at each meal? Do some require larger- or smaller-than-average servings?
- Will everyone be eating at the same time, or will food have to be kept warm or reheated later?
- What foods do family members especially like or dislike?
- Does anyone have dietary restrictions or other special food needs? If so, you'll need to accommodate them. Later in this chapter you'll read about planning meals for vegetarians, children, and people on medical diets.

Resources ~ As you plan meals, be realistic about your resources. Resources to consider include:

- **Time.** If you don't have much time, plan simple meals that involve few preparation steps and short cooking times.

- **Preparation skills.** If you're a beginning cook, plan meals that are easy to prepare using basic cooking skills. As you gain experience and confidence, you can begin to expand your skills by preparing more complicated dishes. See Fig. 36-4.

- **Money.** Plan your meals within the family food budget. Few people can afford to dine on steak and lobster every day.

Fortunately, it's not hard to plan nutritious, tasty meals using less expensive foods. You'll find tips for smart food shopping in the next chapter.

- **Supplies and equipment.** Before deciding on a menu, make sure you have or can get the foods and equipment you need. Remember that some foods are seasonal and are not available at all times. Check to see whether you need any special tools and equipment or whether you have something you can use as a substitute. If you don't have a wok, for example, you could use a regular skillet to make a stir-fry dish.

Nutrition ~ One of your goals for the meals you plan will be to provide good nutrition. As you know, good nutrition is vital to good health. Keep MyPyramid and the Dietary Guidelines in mind as you plan the menu. Make sure you include nutrient-dense foods from several food groups.

Meal Appeal ~ Meal appeal refers to the characteristics that make a meal attractive and appetizing. See Fig. 36-5.

When you plan meals, keep these characteristics in mind:

- **Color.** A meal with only one color is far less appealing than one with a variety of colors. Plan meals that include colorful fruits and vegetables.

Fig. 36-4. When planning a meal, be realistic about your skills. You can tackle more ambitious meals once you've learned the basics.

Fig. 36-5. *A successful meal should look as good as it tastes.* Which characteristics of meal appeal can you identify in this example?

- **Shape and size.** The shapes and sizes of foods can be varied for an appetizing look. Tomatoes can be cut into wedges, while peppers and carrots can be cut into strips. Grapes and parsley leaves can add visual interest.

- **Texture.** A variety of textures adds interest to a meal. A soft pasta, for example, might be combined with chewy vegetables and a crisp salad.

- **Flavor.** The right combination of flavors makes a meal more enjoyable. Combine the mild flavors of rice or pasta with the hotter and spicier flavors of curry or spaghetti sauce.

- **Temperature.** Consider varying the temperature of foods in a meal. A chilled salad and warm bread would go well with hot chili.

Preparation Options

As you plan your meals, consider not only what foods you want to include in the menu but also what options you have for purchasing and preparing them. For example, if you're planning to have burritos, you could order them from a restaurant, heat up frozen burritos, or make them yourself. Each option has benefits and drawbacks. Ordering burritos is the easiest option, but also the most expensive. Frozen burritos would save time, but might not be as tasty or nutritious as those you make yourself. What are the pros and cons of making homemade burritos?

Many preparation options involve **convenience foods**—foods that are partly prepared or ready-to-eat. Convenience foods can save you time and effort, but they are not always the best choice. Using them usually costs more than making a meal from scratch. Many convenience foods are high in sodium; some are high in fat or sugar. For good nutrition, limit your use of convenience foods or choose ones that are more healthful.

FINDING CREATIVE SOLUTIONS

Guessing, Checking, and Adjusting

Have you ever wondered how many times the Wright Brothers tinkered with their airplane design before their historic flight at Kitty Hawk in 1903? Experts in many walks of life, including cooking, often have to guess, check, and adjust before they resolve a problem or find the best solution.

How It Works

Guessing, checking, and adjusting is a way of experimenting to find solutions. You can use it to try different furniture arrangements, to create a new outfit, or to invent an interesting salad. Start by guessing how something will turn out. Put your guess into action, check the results, and determine what needs to be changed. Then, like a scientist, adjust one thing at a time to improve on your initial guess. If one adjustment doesn't work, try something else until you are satisfied with the result.

Try It Out

Assume that Sunday is rice casserole night at your home. Everyone expects this family favorite, made with rice, cheddar cheese, and canned cream of mushroom soup. Your creative impulse urges you to try something different. Maybe you can "touch up" the old recipe with a new twist.

▶ **Your Turn** *Suggest four changes you could make to add fresh appeal to the rice casserole over the next four weeks. How would you check the results of your changes? What adjustments might you make?*

Choosing Recipes

Many people like to vary the meals they make by following different recipes. A recipe gives you detailed instructions for preparing a particular dish. You can find recipes in cookbooks and in newspapers and magazines. The Internet is also a good source for recipes. At some Web sites, you can type in

the name of an ingredient, such as shrimp or apricots, and receive a list of recipes that use that item. Family and friends are also good sources of recipes. You might enjoy learning family recipes that you can eventually pass on to future generations.

When choosing a recipe, be sure to read it carefully. As when planning a menu, you'll need to consider your resources—the time available, your preparation skills, your food budget, and the supplies and equipment you have or can obtain.

Nutrition is also a consideration when choosing recipes. Try to choose recipes for foods that provide important nutrients and are low in fat, sugar, and salt. Some recipes include nutrition information that tells you the amount of calories and nutrients per serving. Sometimes you can modify a recipe to make it more healthful. For example, you could substitute fat-free sour cream for regular sour cream in a recipe for beef stroganoff.

TextLink≈

You can learn more about *recipes* in Chapter 39.

Eating Out

When you eat away from home, it can sometimes be challenging to make healthful food choices. Your selections may be limited, and you may not be able to find out the fat, sugar, or sodium content of a particular food. If you choose carefully, however, you will be able to enjoy tasty, healthful meals and snacks when you eat out. See Fig. 36-6.

Restaurant Meals

If you plan to eat in a restaurant, look for a place that has a large selection of menu items. The more choices you have, the easier it will be to find healthful foods. Then follow these tips for making healthful selections:

- To avoid excess fat, choose a main dish that is broiled, grilled, steamed, or baked instead of fried. If possible, ask to have your entrée prepared without added fat.

- Consider having soup and a dinner salad instead of an entrée. Broth- or tomato-based soups are lower in fat than creamed types.

- If portions are large, arrange to share a dish with a friend, or take some of the meal home for the next day.

- Order such side dishes as a baked potato and a tossed salad instead of french fries.

Fig. 36-6. Eating out is fun and, if you choose carefully, nutritious too. How can you make sure you get a healthful meal when you eat out?

- Choose fresh fruit for dessert. If you don't see fruit on the menu, ask whether it is available.

Eating at School

Today nutritionists plan many school lunch programs. They consider nutrition and follow government guidelines and recommendations. When you select your lunch from the offerings in the school cafeteria, keep in mind your daily nutrition requirements and other meals and snacks you will be having that day.

Fig. 36-7. If you make packed lunches for school, enjoy experimenting with healthful combinations of foods that you like.

If you bring food from home, here are ideas for packing nutritious lunches:

- For sandwiches, choose whole-grain breads such as whole-wheat, multigrain, rye, pumpernickel, or oatmeal.
- Instead of high-fat cheese and luncheon meats, choose sandwich fillings with less fat and sodium. You might try water-packed tuna; lean meat or poultry; chopped or shredded vegetables; mashed, cooked dry beans mixed with chili powder and dry mustard; or low-fat cottage cheese mixed with chopped fruit or vegetables. See Fig. 36-7.
- Instead of adding mayonnaise, ketchup, or other high-fat or high-sodium condiments to sandwiches, try lettuce, onion, tomatoes, or bean sprouts.
- Round out your lunch with low-fat milk or fruit juice and fresh fruit, plain popcorn, fig bars, or yogurt. Pass up the potato chips, soda, and cookies.

Vending Machines

Making healthful choices at a vending machine may be easy or impossible, depending on what the machine offers. Although some machines sell only candy and chips or soda, larger vending machines may provide more nutritious options. Consider these examples of good vending machine choices:

- If main dishes are offered, consider beef stew or vegetable soup. Although they are likely to be high in sodium, they are good sources of vitamin A.
- If the vending machine is refrigerated, you might find an apple or yogurt. An apple is high in fiber and has no fat. Yogurt is low in fat and sodium and provides calcium and riboflavin.

- Raisins, if available, are a healthful choice, with only 40 calories and a trace of fat and sodium.

Sometimes your only option may be vending machine choices that are high in sodium, fat, or sugar. In that case, make sure that the rest of the food you eat that day provides a better balance.

Meeting Individual Needs

Planning meals and snacks requires extra consideration when you, a family member, or a guest has special needs. Vegetarians, for example, need the same nutrients as everyone else, but must get them from an eating plan that excludes certain choices. The same is true of people who must avoid specific foods for medical reasons. Children's food needs differ from those of adults and vary depending on age. Understanding these individual needs makes it possible to plan nutritious, appealing meals and snacks for anyone.

Fig. 36-8. Vegetarian meals can include hearty soups, colorful stir-fries, and other nutritious dishes. *What vegetarian dishes have you tried?*

Vegetarian Food Choices

People may be vegetarians for religious, cultural, ethical, or health reasons. Vegetarian eating plans vary, but generally fit into one of the following categories:

- Eating only foods from plant sources—grain products, legumes (dry beans and peas), vegetables, fruits, nuts, and seeds. This is often called a **vegan** (VEE-gun) eating plan.
- Eating foods from plant sources *plus* milk products.
- Eating foods from plant sources *plus* eggs.

- Eating foods from plant sources *plus* both milk products and eggs.
- Eating vegetarian foods most of the time but occasionally eating meat, poultry, or fish.

A well-planned vegetarian eating plan offers the benefits of being low in fat and cholesterol and high in fiber. However, because their food choices include few or no foods from animal sources, vegetarians need to ensure that they get enough protein, vitamins, and minerals from other foods. See Fig. 36-8.

The key to a healthful vegetarian eating plan is variety. Here are some suggestions for how vegetarians can meet their needs for certain nutrients:

- **Protein.** Vegetarians can get complete protein by eating a variety of grain products, legumes, vegetables, and nuts each day. Each of these foods provides incomplete protein. Together they can supply all the essential amino acids your body needs. In addition, vegetarians who eat eggs and dairy foods get complete proteins from those sources.

- **Iron.** Enriched cereals and breads, dried fruits, dry beans, and dark green leafy vegetables are sources of iron. Foods rich in vitamin C help the body absorb iron.

- **Calcium.** Legumes and green leafy vegetables are good sources of this mineral. In addition, you can buy soy milk and orange juice that have been fortified with calcium.

Tofu—a versatile soy product—is a good source if it has been processed with calcium.

- **Vitamin D.** Vegetarians who don't drink milk can get vitamin D from fortified breakfast cereals and some soy beverages.

- **Vitamin B$_{12}$.** Fortified cereals and fortified soy products can supply this nutrient.

- **Zinc.** Good sources include whole grain foods, legumes, nuts, wheat germ, and tofu.

Food Allergies and Intolerances

Some people must avoid certain foods because of an allergy or intolerance. In the case of a **food allergy**, the body's immune system reacts to a particular food substance as though it were a foreign invader. When this food is eaten, the body produces substances that irritate the system. Common reactions include stomach pain, diarrhea, rashes, itching, swelling, or nasal congestion. In extreme cases, the reaction can be life-threatening.

Foods that most often cause allergic reactions include nuts, eggs, milk, wheat, shellfish, and soybeans. Once a food allergy is identified—either through allergy testing or by keeping a food diary—the food can be eliminated from the diet. Nutrients supplied by that food can be made up by substituting other foods.

People who have a **food intolerance** have trouble digesting a food or food component. Some people, for example, can't digest gluten, a protein found in wheat. They need to avoid foods that contain gluten. If they don't, they can experience a variety of problems such as diarrhea, anemia, bone pain, and muscle cramps.

Lactose intolerance is an inability to digest lactose, the form of sugar that is found in milk. When people with lactose intolerance drink milk, they may experience gas, bloating, abdominal pain, or diarrhea. To avoid the symptoms, they may need to limit the amount of milk in their diets or use special lactose-free milk products.

Other Medical Conditions

Some people need a special eating plan because of a medical condition such as heart disease or diabetes. In some cases, they must eliminate certain foods from their diet altogether. In other cases, they must pay attention to the balance of the foods that they eat.

Diabetes is a disorder in which the body cannot adequately control blood sugar levels. It is caused by inadequate production or use of the hormone insulin. To manage diabetes, people need to make careful food selections and get the right balance of food. Some need regular insulin injections. Diabetes is a lifelong condition for those who develop it early in life. Overweight and inactivity increase a person's chances of developing it later in life. Weight control is therefore an important factor in preventing diabetes.

Food for Children

If you've ever helped care for children, you probably already know that they have their own needs and preferences when it comes to food. When planning meals and snacks for children, caregivers need to know what is appropriate for each stage of development.

Infants obtain most of the energy and nutrients they need from formula or breast milk. Between four and six months, most infants can begin eating semisolid food such as rice cereal specially formulated for infants. Then caregivers can begin introducing solid

Fig. 36-9. Children who are encouraged to learn about food and help prepare meals are more likely to develop healthy eating habits. *How might you persuade a child to try new foods?*

foods—one at a time to check for allergic reactions. Strained, pureed vegetables come first, followed by fruits, and then cooked and pureed meats. At about eight or ten months, babies are ready for finger foods, such as soft toast, pieces of fruit, cooked vegetables, and cheese.

During the toddler, preschool, and elementary school years, children develop eating habits they are likely to carry into adulthood. Growth slows but activity levels usually increase, so nutrient and calorie needs are still relatively high. Caregivers can help children develop healthy eating habits by providing a variety of nutrient-dense foods and establishing regular, consistent meal patterns. Allowing children to help in the kitchen or doing simple cooking activities with them helps make learning about food and nutrition fun. See Fig. 36-9.

CHAPTER **36** *Review & Activities*

Chapter Summary

- A regular eating pattern that includes breakfast is best for overall nutrition and health.
- Healthful snacks help teens get the extra nutrients and calories they need each day.
- Several important factors need to be considered when planning the menu for a meal.
- Convenience foods expand your options for preparing meals.
- Sources of recipes include cookbooks, newspapers and magazines, the Internet, and family and friends.
- When eating away from home, take care to select healthful meals and snacks.
- Planning meals for vegetarians, people with medical conditions, and children requires special attention.

Reviewing Key Terms & Ideas

1. Why is it a good idea to follow a regular **eating pattern**?
2. Why is the first meal of the day particularly important?
3. What qualities do healthful snacks have? Give three examples of healthful snacks.
4. What does **entrée** mean?
5. What four factors do you need to consider when planning a meal?
6. Explain how time and preparation skills influence meal planning.
7. Name five qualities of food that you can vary to make an appealing meal.
8. What are two advantages and two disadvantages of using **convenience foods** in your meal plans?
9. Name three factors to consider when you choose a recipe.
10. List three suggestions for making healthful food choices in a restaurant.
11. What is a **vegan** eating plan? How can it supply complete protein?
12. What is the difference between a **food allergy** and a **food intolerance**?
13. What dietary adjustments does a person with **lactose intolerance** need to make and why?
14. Describe the process of introducing solid foods to an infant.

Thinking Critically

1. **Analyzing Behavior.** Think about when and why you snack. What situations or feelings, other than hunger, tend to trigger your "snack attacks"? Why?
2. **Understanding Cause and Effect.** What factors might explain why the number of meals eaten out has continued to rise in recent years? What are some ways in which this trend might impact health?

532 UNIT 8 *Wellness, Nutrition, and Food Choices*

Applying Your Knowledge

1. **Analyzing Eating Patterns**. For a week, keep a diary describing when and where you eat meals and snacks. At the end of the week, summarize your eating patterns. How might you improve them?

2. **Vending Machine Choices**. Take a survey of snacks available in vending machines in your school. What are the best and worst choices from a nutritional standpoint? Present a summary of your findings to the appropriate school staff. Include any suggestions you have for offering more healthful choices.

3. **Meal Planning for Individual Needs**. Assume that you are planning to invite three friends over to dinner. One is a vegetarian and one is lactose intolerant. Plan a menu that is appealing and accommodates their special needs.

Making Connections

1. **Social Studies**. Choose a country or culture and investigate the eating patterns typically found in it. How are they similar to and different from your own eating patterns? Prepare a report for the class.

2. **Math**. Find a recipe for a main dish that is also available as a convenience food. Estimate the recipe's cost per serving, based on the prices of the main ingredients. Also calculate the cost per serving of the convenience food. Estimate how much time each will take to prepare. Create a table of your results.

Managing Your Life

Planning Appealing Meals

You have learned how to vary certain characteristics of meals to create meal appeal. Put these ideas into practice by planning a series of appealing meals for your family. Start by listing some of the favorite foods of family members, then determine how you can integrate those foods into meals that have all the characteristics of meal appeal. Present your ideas to the class.

Using Technology

1. **Presentation Software.** Use appropriate software to create a brief presentation designed to motivate teens to eat breakfast. Use photos, drawings, and text to explain why people need breakfast and the problems encountered by breakfast skippers. Provide creative suggestions for quick, easy, nutritious breakfast foods, including some nontraditional choices and some that are portable.

2. **Internet.** Use reliable Internet sources to learn about the causes, incidence, and treatment of Type 2 diabetes. Prepare a report of your findings. Include information about healthful behaviors that would reduce a person's risk of diabetes.

CHAPTER 37

Shopping for Food

Key Terms

- unit price
- staples
- Daily Value
- "sell by" date
- perishable
- "use by" date
- expiration date
- pasteurized

Objectives

- **Explain** factors that affect food costs and the family food budget.
- **Discuss** strategies for saving money when shopping for food.
- **Give** guidelines for planning a food shopping trip.
- **Interpret** information provided on food labels.
- **Describe** how to judge the quality of various types of foods.

QUICK WRITE

Write a brief description of your current method for food shopping. As you read the chapter, make notes for improving your shopping strategies.

*Y*ou've probably been food shopping dozens of times, either alone or with someone in your household. Whether you're buying a week's worth of groceries or just picking up a few items, food shopping requires decision making at every step. You make some of the decisions ahead of time by determining what items you need and where you'll get them. You make other decisions in the store: Do the salad greens look fresh? Should I buy fresh, frozen, or canned green beans? Single-serving or family size? Which brand? The more knowledge you have, the easier and more successful your decision making will be. Smart shoppers know how to get the highest quality foods at the best prices.

Food Costs and Budgeting

Food is a significant expense in the family budget. Have you ever wondered why some foods cost more than others, or why food prices go up and down? To understand food prices, it helps to know something about how food gets to the store.

Most food begins at a farm, in the form of crops or livestock. From there it may be shipped to a processing center. After it's processed and packaged, it's shipped to your supermarket. All along the way, many people are involved in preparing and inspecting the food, advertising it, designing and manufacturing the packaging, storing the food, and selling it. See Fig. 37-1.

Fig. 37-1. Transportation—getting products from producer to retailer—is just one of the many factors that affect the price of food.

All the businesses involved in this process have to make money. When you buy a carton of yogurt or a box of cereal, you're paying not only for the raw materials but also for all the work that went into getting the food to your shopping cart.

Food costs fluctuate depending on supply and demand. When supplies are plentiful, prices tend to be lower. By the same token, prices go up when supplies are short. If a severe frost damages the citrus crop in Florida, you will probably see a corresponding increase in the price of Florida orange juice.

Viewpoints

Food Packaging

Some foods come with their own natural packaging: the banana has its peel; the coconut, its shell. For most foods, though, some kind of manufactured packaging is needed. How much packaging is enough?

Marcos: So much food packaging is unnecessary and wasteful. Manufacturers use two or more layers of wrapping, then put the wrapped food in a bigger box with flashy colors to make it stand out. All this stuff adds to the price of the food, and it just gets thrown away. Sure, some packaging materials are recyclable, but not everyone recycles. It's better to reduce the amount of packaging in the first place.

Kenzie: Without packaging, we'd have a lot fewer foods to choose from. Most of what we eat wouldn't keep long without some kind of protection, especially if it travels across the country. Without packaging, a lot of food would get wasted. And the more we rely on convenience foods, the more kinds of packaging we need. Besides, think of all the information on food packages. How would we decide whether to buy a food without reading the label?

Seeing Both Sides ~ Cite an example of food packaging that supports each point of view. What could food makers and supermarkets do to help reduce packaging waste without losing the benefits?

When you eat out, you add still more layers of costs to your food. You pay for not only the food itself but also the costs of preparing it, serving it, and cleaning up afterwards. Eating at home costs less because you do these tasks yourself. To stay within their budget, many families limit the number of times they eat out. They save restaurant meals for special occasions.

Most families expect to spend a certain amount on food each week. Their food budget depends on their income and the size of the family. Even the age of family members is a factor—growing teens need more food than older family members. Available time and food preparation skills also affect the food budget. A family that has the time and the skills to prepare home-cooked meals may spend less on food than one that relies more heavily on convenience foods.

Fig. 37-2. You can save money if you check supermarket ads for sales. What promotions do your local food stores use to attract business?

Money-Saving Strategies

Are you a skilled shopper? Some people spend significantly less on their grocery bills than others because they know how to save money. These strategies can help you make the most of your food budget:

- Take advantage of sales. Stores often have weekly specials on selected items. See Fig. 37-2.

- Use coupons for items that you buy regularly. You can find coupons in newspapers, advertising flyers, and on some product packages. Look for stores that double or triple a coupon's value.

- Buy a store brand or generic item when you have no real preference. They are generally less expensive than national-brand items and may be equal in quality.

- Plan meals around low-cost main dishes. For example, a main dish made with beans and rice is nutritious and costs much less than meat, poultry, or fish.

- Compare prices of different available forms of food, such as fresh, frozen, and canned.

- Use frequent customer cards that give discounts at the checkout counter.

Comparing Unit Prices

Another money-saving tip is to check unit prices. The **unit price** is the price per ounce, pound, or other unit of measure. This information makes it easy to compare the cost of products in different-sized packages to find the best buy. Unit prices are often displayed on labels attached to the front of the shelf where the item is found. If necessary, you can calculate the unit price yourself. Simply divide the total price by the number of ounces or other units.

Fig. 37-3. Before going shopping, check your supplies. If any items are running low, add them to your shopping list. What staples does your family like to keep on hand?

Making a Shopping List

The most important step in preparing to shop is to create a shopping list. Having a list helps ensure that you don't forget something. It also helps you avoid impulse buying, which can add to your shopping bill.

Begin your list by reviewing the ingredients you need for the menus you've planned. Also check your supplies of **staples**—basic food items you use regularly, such as flour, sugar, rice, and pasta. Since these items don't spoil easily, most people keep them on hand at all times. Complete your list with any other items you need, such as paper products, detergent, and perhaps frozen meals to have on hand for emergencies. If you have coupons, match them to the items on your list. See Fig. 37-3.

You'll save time in the store if you organize your shopping list. Group similar types of food together: fresh vegetables and fruits, pasta and grains, meats, and so on. Take a pen or pencil with you when you go shopping and check off each item as you place it in your cart. That way you'll be less likely to overlook something on the list.

Often—but not always—items in larger packages have a lower unit price. However, don't buy more than you can use. If you buy the large economy box of cereal but end up throwing half of it away after it goes stale, you haven't saved money.

Planning for Food Shopping

Any project goes better if you plan ahead, and that's certainly true of shopping. By planning ahead, you can make sure you get everything you need. That way you won't discover that you're out of a vital ingredient when you're preparing a meal. Planning also helps you save time and money.

Where to Shop

Some people buy all their groceries at a supermarket for the convenience of "one-stop shopping." Others buy different kinds of items in different places. They might buy fruits and vegetables at a farmers' market and meat at a butcher shop. Ethnic stores are likely to have items that are not available in a supermarket. People with large families may prefer to shop at warehouse stores that offer big savings on large quantities.

Convenience stores, most of which are open 24 hours a day, are handy if you need to pick up a few items. However, their prices are usually much higher than those in other stores, and the selection they offer is limited.

Where you shop will depend on your priorities. Remember that prices, quality, selection, and service can vary widely. To get the best deals, you may need to shop around. Whatever type of store you choose, evaluate cleanliness as well. Dirt, unpleasant odors, and evidence of pests are signs that you should shop elsewhere.

When to Shop

How often should you go food shopping? Some families prefer to make one large shopping trip every week or so, with a few quick trips in between to pick up items such as milk and bread. Other families prefer to make several small shopping trips every week so that they always have fresh ingredients on hand. In general, planning ahead and making fewer shopping trips is more likely to save you money.

No matter how often you shop, it's smart to go food shopping after you have eaten rather than before. If you shop for food when you're hungry, you may be tempted to buy items that look good but that you don't really need.

Reading Food Labels

Get into the habit of reading food labels when you're shopping for foods. They provide a wealth of information and enable you to judge the nutritional value of different food items. See Fig. 37-4.

Fig. 37-4. Food labels provide useful information that can help you compare products and get the nutrients you need.

Basic Label Information

The federal government requires full ingredient labeling on all processed, packaged foods. Almost every food label contains this basic information:

- The name of the food.
- The amount of the food, by weight or by volume.
- The name and address of the manufacturer, packer, or distributor.
- Ingredients listed in order by weight. The ingredient that weighs the most is listed first. By law, ingredients that might cause allergic reactions must be clearly identified on the label.

Nutrition Facts

Labels for many foods are required by law to provide nutrition information in a Nutrition Facts panel. You can use this information to compare the nutrients found in different food products. Fig. 37-5 shows how to interpret the information in a typical Nutrition Facts panel.

Notice that the panel gives the "% Daily Value" for many of the nutrients it lists. The **Daily Value** for each nutrient is a reference amount established by the U.S. government. Daily Values help you judge whether a food is high or low in a specific nutrient. You might not know offhand whether 13 grams of fat is a lot or a little, but knowing that it's 20 percent of the Daily Value for fat gives you a clearer picture.

Label Terms

Some product labels make claims about the food's nutrient content. By law, these claims must follow strict guidelines. Here are some examples:

- **Free.** For this term to be used, the food must contain only a trace amount (if any) of the specified nutrient. "Fat-free," for example, means the food contains almost no fat.
- **High.** To be "high in vitamin C," one serving of the food must provide at least 20 percent of the Daily Value for vitamin C.
- **Reduced or Less.** The food must contain 25 percent less of the specified nutrient than a similar food. You might find canned soups labeled "Reduced Sodium," for example.

Product Dating

Dates stamped or printed on food packages can help you judge freshness. You may see different types of dates on different types of products.

A **"sell by" date** indicates the last day a product may be sold. "Sell by" dates are usually found on products that are **perishable**, or spoil quickly, such as dairy products and meats. The date allows a reasonable amount of time for you to store and use the product at home.

A **"use by" date** is the last day a product is considered fresh. The label might say "Best if used by…." A food may still be safe to eat after this date, but its taste and nutritional quality may have suffered.

An **expiration date** indicates the last day a product should be eaten. After this date, the product may not be safe and should be discarded.

Understanding Nutrition Facts

SERVING INFORMATION. This area shows the serving size and the number of servings in the package. The calorie and nutrient amounts given below are for one serving of this size. Keep in mind that if you eat more (or less) than one standard serving, you'll get more (or less) calories and nutrients than shown.

Nutrition Facts

Serving Size   1 cup (228g)
Servings Per Container   2

Amount Per Serving

Calories   260   Calories from Fat 120

	% Daily Value*
Total Fat 13g	20%
Saturated Fat 5g	25%
Trans Fat 2g	
Cholesterol 30mg	10%
Sodium 660mg	28%
Total Carbohydrate 31g	10%
Dietary Fiber 0g	0%
Sugars 5g	
Protein 5g	

Vitamin A 4%		Vitamin C 2%	
Calcium 15%		Iron 4%	

*Percent Daily Values are based on a 2000 calorie diet. Your daily values may be higher or lower depending on your calorie needs:

		Calories:	2,000	2,500
Total Fat	Less than		65g	80g
Sat Fat	Less than		20g	25g
Cholesterol	Less than		300mg	300mg
Sodium	Less than		2,400mg	2,400mg
Total Carbohydrate			300g	375g
Dietary Fiber			25g	30g

Calories per gram:
Fat 9   ·   Carbohydrate 4   ·   Protein 4

CALORIE INFORMATION. The panel shows both the total number of calories in one serving and the number of calories that come from fat.

NUTRIENT AMOUNTS. The amount of each nutrient in one serving is given in grams or milligrams (metric units of weight).

PERCENT DAILY VALUE. Nutrient amounts are also listed as a percentage of the Daily Value reference amount. This helps you judge whether the food provides a lot or a little of each nutrient. As a quick rule of thumb, 5 percent or less is low; 20 percent or more is high.

DAILY VALUES EXPLANATION. This information shows you what the Daily Values for different nutrients are. The numbers in the column under "2,000" are Daily Values for a person who needs 2,000 calories a day. These numbers are used to calculate the Percent Daily Values above. Larger labels, like this one, also show Daily Values for a person who needs 2,500 calories a day. This helps you make adjustments based on your own calorie needs.

CONVERSION GUIDE. This helps you learn the number of calories in one gram of fat, carbohydrate, and protein.

Fig. 37-5. The Nutrition Facts panel found on almost all processed foods helps you make informed food choices for good nutrition.

Selecting Quality Foods

Have you noticed that some shoppers take time to choose carefully when they are buying food, whereas others just grab the nearest item? Those who choose carefully are more likely to be satisfied with their purchases. When you know what to look for and what to avoid, you'll get better quality for your money.

Fresh Fruits and Vegetables

You can find many types of fresh fruits and vegetables in the produce department. Some of the vitamins in fresh produce start to deteriorate after harvest, so choose fruits and vegetables that still look fresh and crisp.

Fruits and vegetables should also have a healthy color and no bruises, spots, or sticky areas. Choose fruit that is relatively heavy for its size—this usually indicates that the fruit will be juicy. Ripe fruits generally have more flavor than unripe ones. Fruit that is very soft to the touch, however, may be overripe. Since produce keeps its quality for only a short time, buy only the amount that you need.

You can buy most fruits and vegetables year round because they can be shipped from all over the world. However, some fruits and vegetables are more plentiful during their peak growing season. Fresh strawberries, for example, are in season in the early summer. When fruits and vegetables are in season, they are highest in quality and usually lower in price because they don't have to be shipped far. Get to know the peak seasons for produce in your region, and take advantage of good quality and good values. See Fig. 37-6.

Carrots, salad greens, and some other fresh vegetables are available cut and prewashed in sealed bags. These are convenient for meal preparation, but usually cost more than loose produce.

Fig. 37-6. Farmers' markets are a great place to find fresh fruits and vegetables in season. What are some of your favorites?

Meat, Poultry, Fish, and Eggs

When shopping for meat, it helps to know how you will cook it. If you want to cook meat in dry heat—by grilling, broiling, or roasting, for example—you'll need a cut that's naturally tender. Tender cuts of meat include those with *loin*, *rib*, or *round* in the name. Less tender—and less expensive—cuts include the shoulder, chuck, flank, and brisket. They are better suited to cooking methods such as stewing and braising. The long, slow cooking in moist heat helps tenderize them. Poultry and fish can generally be cooked in either dry or moist heat.

How can you judge the quality of meat, poultry, and fish? Here are some guidelines:

- Check the color of meat. Beef should be bright red; pork should be grayish-pink; lamb should be light or dark pink. Meat that looks brown and dry is probably not fresh.

- Poultry should look plump and meaty. The skin should be creamy white to yellow with no bruises.

- Fresh fish should have a mild smell, and the flesh should be firm when pressed.

- Tap the shells of live shellfish such as clams, mussels, and oysters. They should close tightly.

Before putting raw meat, poultry, or fish in your shopping cart, slip the package inside a plastic bag. If the package leaks or drips, the juices won't get on other foods in your cart.

Eggs come in different sizes, usually large and extra large. Most recipes are based on the large size. You might have a choice of white or brown eggs, and the brown ones may cost more. The two varieties are actually identical in terms of quality, taste, and nutri-

tional value. Whatever type of eggs you choose, open the carton and make sure they aren't cracked or broken.

Grain Products

In most supermarkets, you can choose from a wide variety of grain products, including breads, cereals, rice, and pasta. Whole-grain products, made from the entire grain kernel, are a good choice. They retain the grain's original nutrients and fiber. Examples include whole wheat bread, brown rice, and whole-grain breakfast cereals.

TIPS FOR Success

Choosing Lean Meat

Want to know which cuts of meat are lowest in fat? Here are some clues:

- Lean cuts include those with *round* or *loin* in the name.

- Beef is available in different grades, such as prime, choice, and select. Select is the leanest and least expensive of the three.

- Look for cuts with less *marbling*—the fine streaks of fat that you can see in the meat.

- Choose cuts that have little visible fat around the edges. You can trim the fat away before cooking, but why pay for it in the first place?

- When buying ground beef, check the label for fat content. It may have anywhere from 2 to 25 percent fat.

In contrast, when making grain products such as white bread or white rice, parts of the grain kernel are removed. In the process, some nutrients are lost too. *Enriched* grain products have nutrients put back in to replace those lost. Some grain products are *fortified*, meaning that additional nutrients, not in the original grain, have been added.

If you want whole-grain bread, check the ingredients list. "Wheat bread" isn't necessarily made with whole wheat. It could just be enriched bread with coloring added to make it darker brown.

Dairy Foods

When shopping for milk and other dairy foods, check the labels for fat content. If you want to restrict your fat intake, choose fat-free or low-fat milk instead of whole milk. Be sure you buy milk that has been **pasteurized**, treated by a process that kills harmful bacteria.

Reading labels is essential when choosing yogurt and ice cream, too. Like milk, these products may be fat-free or low-fat, but may still be high in calories because of added fruits and sugar. If you're concerned about calories, you might want to choose a fat-free yogurt with less sugar and add your own fresh fruit.

Shopping for cheese can be an adventure—there are so many varieties to choose from. They range from firm, aged cheeses, such as cheddar and parmesan, to soft, unripened types, such as cream cheese and cottage cheese. Over time you will discover the types of cheeses you prefer. Although most regular cheeses are high in fat, lower-fat versions are available. Always check that packaging is airtight.

Canned and Packaged Foods

Canned and packaged foods are convenient, but many are high in sodium. Some are also high in sugar or fat. Use the Nutrition Facts panel to help you make healthful choices. See Fig. 37-7.

Avoid buying cans that are bulging, dented, or rusty. Bulging or dented cans may contain dangerous bacteria. Rusty cans may be old, and may have rust on the inside as well. Also avoid any food packages that have been opened or damaged.

Frozen Foods

When selecting frozen foods, avoid packages that are soft or soggy because they may be thawing. Also avoid packages that are stained, covered with ice, or irregularly shaped. They may have thawed and refrozen, and the safety and quality of the food may have suffered. Wait until the end of your shopping trip to pick up frozen foods. That way they won't start to thaw in your cart.

Character **IN ACTION**

Supermarket Courtesy When you're buying food, be considerate of your fellow shoppers. As you ponder your choices, don't block the aisle with your cart. Handle produce gently to avoid damaging it. If you decide not to buy an item, return it to its proper place. Use the express checkout lane only if you have the correct number of items. What other examples of supermarket courtesy can you think of?

Fig. 37-7. You might want to look for canned foods that are lower in sodium or have less sugar. *How could you identify such products?*

Finishing Your Shopping

When you've made all your selections, it's time to enter the checkout line. Be sure to pay attention to the signs posted. Express lanes may allow only a limited number of items and no checks. Some supermarkets have self-scan lanes, where customers scan, bag, and pay for their items without the help of a cashier.

After you have paid for your purchases, return home right away. Store perishable items, including frozen foods, meats, and dairy products, as soon as you get home to avoid spoilage. If you planned well and selected items carefully when shopping, you'll have a kitchen stocked with healthful, tasty foods for enjoyable meals and snacks.

Chapter Summary

- Many factors affect the price of food, including shipping, processing, marketing, and supply and demand.

- Families can use money-saving strategies to stay within their food budget.

- A well-planned shopping list helps ensure that you get all the items you need.

- Where and how often you shop will depend on your priorities.

- Food labels provide information to help you judge the nutritional value and freshness of food products.

- Learning how to select quality foods will help ensure that you get the most value for your money.

Reviewing Key Terms & Ideas

1. How are food prices affected by supply and demand?

2. What factors influence the amount a family might spend on food each week?

3. Give four examples of strategies that can help people reduce their grocery bills.

4. What does **unit price** mean? How can it help you save money?

5. Why should you check your supplies of **staples** when preparing a shopping list?

6. How can you organize a shopping list to save time?

7. What are the pros and cons of convenience stores?

8. What should you consider when planning what time of day to shop? Why?

9. What is a **Daily Value** and what is its purpose?

10. Briefly describe five types of information found on a Nutrition Facts panel.

11. What is the difference between a **"sell by" date** and a **"use by" date** on a food package?

12. Why should you buy fruits and vegetables in season whenever possible?

13. How can you judge the quality of fresh fish?

14. If a package of pork is labeled "Loin Chop," what two assumptions can you make? Why?

15. What guidelines should you follow when selecting frozen foods?

Thinking Critically

1. **Making Generalizations.** How does advertising make it more difficult to stick to your food budget? How does it make it easier?

2. **Making Predictions.** What might happen if there were no guidelines for the use of label terms such as "free" and "reduced"?

Applying Your Knowledge

1. **Using Nutrition Facts**. Compare the Nutrition Facts panels for two ready-to-eat cereals. Explain which product you would choose on the basis of nutrition and why.

2. **Price Comparison**. Choose any six food items that you buy regularly, such as a certain brand and size of peanut butter. Compare prices from at least two food stores in your area. Record your findings in a chart. What conclusions can you draw?

Making Connections

1. **Math**. Calculate unit prices to determine which item in each pair would be more economical:

   ■ A 4-pound bag of sugar for $1.85 or a 5-pound bag for $2.09.

   ■ 12 ounces of macaroni for $1.09 or 7 ounces for 77 cents.

   ■ A gallon of milk for $2.89 or a half-gallon for $1.68.

   ■ A 2-ounce jar of chili powder for $2.59 or 1.25 ounces for $1.19.

2. **Science**. Investigate recent advances in food packaging technology. What innovative materials or methods are helping to keep food fresh longer? Report your findings.

Managing Your Life

Family Shopping List

Help your family get organized by creating a generic shopping list. Consult with family members to identify items that you regularly purchase when grocery shopping. Compile these into a list organized by the department or aisle of the store where you shop most often. Leave space under each heading for additional items to be added. Post copies of the list in the kitchen, and encourage family members to circle or write in items that need to be bought on the next shopping trip.

Using Technology

1. **Spreadsheet**. Use spreadsheet software to track your family's weekly food expenses in two categories: food from the store and food from restaurants. After setting up the spreadsheet, use receipts to enter the information for two weeks. Create graphs to compare the amounts spent each week in each category. Summarize the insights you gained from this activity.

2. **Online Food Shopping**. At some Web sites, you can shop for groceries and have them delivered to your home. Search on the term "food shopping" to find such a site. Explore the site to learn how it works. What advantages does online shopping offer? What are some disadvantages? When might you use online shopping and why?

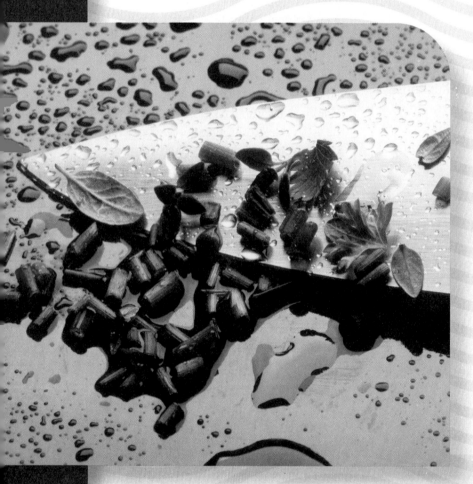

CHAPTER | 38

Safe Kitchen, Safe Food

Key Terms

- work triangle
- work centers
- foodborne illness
- cross-contamination
- rotation
- freezer burn

Objectives

- **Describe** how kitchens are equipped and organized.
- **Give guidelines** for preventing accidents and injuries in the kitchen.
- **Identify** ways to prevent foodborne illness.
- **Discuss** principles of safe food storage.

548

QUICK WRITE

Did you know that more accidents occur in the kitchen than in any other room of the home? Write down your thoughts about why this is true.

*W*hat comes to mind when you hear the word "kitchen"? Perhaps you think of delicious cooking smells, family members chopping and stirring, or people gathering to talk and eat. Pleasant associations like these help make a kitchen the "heart" of the home. To keep the kitchen a pleasant place, everyone who works in it must follow some basic safety rules. You need to know the proper way to use equipment and to store and prepare food. By learning and practicing safe habits, you can help prevent kitchen accidents and ensure that food is safe to eat.

Kitchen Basics

Working efficiently and safely in the kitchen starts with knowing something about how kitchens are equipped and organized. Meal preparation is much easier when a kitchen includes the basic equipment you need and is arranged efficiently. See Fig. 38-1.

Major Appliances

Kitchens are organized around major appliances. Almost all kitchens include a refrigerator and a range, or else a separate cooktop and oven. These are generally considered to be the bare essentials. Many kitchens also have a dishwasher, a microwave oven, and perhaps other major appliances.

Before using any major appliance, read the instruction manual. Follow the directions for proper use and care. They will help you make the best possible use of the appliance while keeping safety and energy efficiency in mind.

Fig. 38-1. Whether a kitchen is large or small, it can be a pleasure to work in. The key is to keep it clean and organized.

Small Appliances

There's a small appliance for almost every food preparation task. Electric mixers, food processors, blenders, electric skillets, and slow cookers are just a few examples. Before acquiring a small appliance, though, think carefully. How often would you really use it? How much time and energy would it save? Are those savings worth the money you would spend on the appliance, the space needed to store it, and the time needed to clean and maintain it? See Fig. 38-2.

Other Kitchen Equipment

A well-equipped kitchen also includes a variety of utensils—tools such as knives, cutting boards, measuring cups, pots, and pans. As with small appliances, consider your needs when buying utensils. While many specialized tools are available, you can accomplish most tasks using basic items. For example, if you don't have a cheese slicer, you can just use a knife.

Kitchen Organization

In order to prepare food efficiently, you need a clear path from the refrigerator to the sink to the range. These are the three points of the **work triangle**. If you drew a diagram of your kitchen and connected these three points, would the resulting triangle be long and skinny, or more evenly balanced? In an efficient kitchen, the distance between any two points of the triangle is not so long as to waste steps.

The arrangement of the major appliances also influences the location of **work centers**—organized areas where specific kitchen tasks are performed. The idea is to place all the items and supplies needed for a particular task in one area. A food storage center, for example, would logically be near the refrigerator. There you might keep storage containers, plastic storage bags, and other items you use for storing foods. A cooking center would be located near the range and include pots and pans, cooking tools, pot holders, and so on. When everything you need for a task is close at hand, you can work more efficiently.

Fig. 38-2. When deciding whether a small appliance is worth the money and the space, consider how often you will use it. What small kitchen appliances do you find most useful?

Fig. 38-3. Make a habit of following kitchen safety rules, such as using pot holders to handle hot items. When are people most likely to forget to follow the rules?

Preventing Kitchen Accidents

Knowledge is one of the most useful resources for working in a kitchen. Knowing what dangers might occur will help you avoid them. If you pay close attention to your work, develop careful work habits, and follow safety rules consistently, you can prevent most kitchen accidents. See Fig. 38-3.

Sources of Danger

When you stop to think about it, there are quite a few hazards in a typical kitchen. Knives are sharp, and an oven or range gets hot rapidly when it's turned on. Grease on the floor can cause you to slip and fall. Metal pots, pans, and tools can get hot very quickly. Even food can be so hot that it can burn.

Many electric appliances can cause shock if they have frayed cords, are used incorrectly, or are used near water. In addition, leaks from gas appliances, such as ranges, are very dangerous because they can cause explosions and fires.

Cleaning products stored in the kitchen can cause serious injuries. Many common cleaning agents are poisonous if they are swallowed. They can also cause irritation or injury if they splash into a person's eyes. These products can be particularly dangerous to young children, who are naturally curious.

Kitchen Safety Guidelines

To Prevent Cuts

- Always hold a knife by its handle. Cut by moving the knife blade away from your fingers. Use a cutting board.
- Wash knives separately from other dishes.
- Insert beaters or cutting blades into an appliance *before* plugging it in.
- Watch out for sharp edges on the lids and rims of opened cans.

To Prevent Burns and Scalding

- Use pot holders when handling hot items.
- Lift the far side of a pan's cover first so that the steam won't burn you.
- Keep pan handles turned in over the center of the range or over a counter so that the pans won't get knocked off the range.

To Prevent Fires

- Keep paper, cloth, and other flammable materials away from the range.
- Keep your sleeves and other parts of your clothing away from flames and hot burners. Tie back long hair.
- Clean all grease from the oven, cooktop, and vent above the burners.
- Keep a fire extinguisher handy.
- Smother a grease fire by turning off the heat source and covering the pan. Never use water.
- Turn all range or appliance controls to "Off" when you have finished cooking.
- Never turn on a gas range if you smell gas. Leave the building, call your gas company immediately, and follow their instructions.

To Prevent Electric Shocks

- Plug only one electric appliance into an outlet at a time.
- Unplug appliances when they are not in use. Pull on the plug, not on the cord.
- Keep electric appliances away from water. Don't touch them with wet hands.
- Don't use appliances with frayed cords.
- Don't drape cords over the edge of a counter.
- Don't stick metal objects such as knives or forks inside a toaster or other electric appliance.

To Prevent Falls

- Wipe up spills immediately.
- Stand on a ladder or step stool, not on a chair or box, to reach a high shelf.
- Never leave anything on the floor where someone might trip over it.

To Prevent Poisoning

- Store household chemicals well out of the reach of children. If necessary, secure cabinet doors with childproof latches or locks.
- Be sure all household chemicals are properly labeled.

Fig. 38-4. If you practice these safety rules regularly, they will become second nature to you. What can you add to the list?

Safety Precautions

The safety rules listed in Fig. 38-4 will help prevent cuts, burns, fires, electric shocks, and other serious injuries that can occur in the kitchen. The list is long, but learning and following these rules can help you, your family, and your friends and classmates prevent kitchen accidents.

Preventing Foodborne Illness

Foodborne illness, also known as food poisoning, is sickness that results from eating food that is unsafe to eat. Most foodborne illness occurs when food is contaminated with harmful bacteria. Bacteria are carried by people, insects, and objects. In small amounts, they generally cause no harm. When they are allowed to multiply, however, they become a health hazard. In general, bacteria are more likely to multiply in food that is not kept at the right temperature. See Fig. 38-5.

Many different kinds of bacteria can cause foodborne illness. *E. coli* bacteria, for example, are generally found in raw or undercooked ground meat, in contaminated water, and in unpasteurized milk. *Salmonella* bacteria are found in raw or undercooked poultry and eggs.

One of the most serious foodborne illnesses is botulism, which can be fatal. Improperly canned foods are the most common source of botulism. Never taste or eat food from a bulging or leaking can.

Practicing Cleanliness

You can prevent bacteria from spreading and multiplying by following basic food safety rules. One of them is to keep the kitchen, food, equipment, and yourself clean. Follow these guidelines:

- Wash your hands well before working with food and after using the restroom.
- Use hot, soapy water to wash tools, utensils, cutting boards, and other surfaces every time you prepare food.
- Use only clean dishcloths, sponges, and towels. Use separate towels for wiping dishes and drying your hands.
- Wash the tops of cans before you open them.
- Use a separate spoon, not your fingers, for tasting food. If the spoon has been used for tasting once, wash it thoroughly before using it again.
- Use a tissue when you sneeze or cough, and turn away from the food. Then wash your hands.

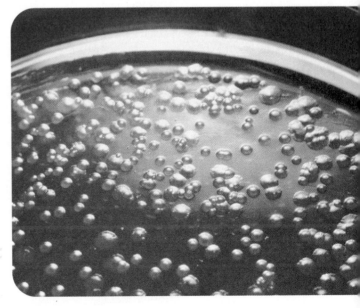

*Fig. 38-5. **Bacteria are much too small to be seen without a microscope, but they can make you very ill.***

- Keep your hair out of the food. If your hair is long, tie it back.

- Wash fresh fruits and vegetables thoroughly under cold, running water. See Fig. 38-6.

- Keep pets out of food preparation areas. Never allow cats to jump on countertops.

- Avoid touching the eating surfaces of plates, flatware, and glassware when you set the table.

Pests, such as flies, ants, cockroaches, and mice, are a concern because they carry dirt and bacteria that can contaminate foods and surfaces. Keeping the kitchen clean will help keep pests from showing up. If pests are a problem, choose a pest-control method that is effective and safe. Don't allow insecticides to come in contact with food or with surfaces, utensils, or containers that will touch food. If the pest problem persists, call a professional exterminator to deal with it.

Avoiding Cross-Contamination

Cross-contamination occurs when harmful bacteria are transferred from one food to another. Cross-contamination most commonly occurs when raw meat, poultry, or fish or their juices come in contact with other foods. For example, you could cause cross-contamination if you used a knife to cut raw meat and then used the same knife to cut vegetables without washing it first. Here are some guidelines for preventing cross-contamination:

- Make sure that raw meat, poultry, and fish are kept away from other foods at all times—in the shopping cart, in the refrigerator, and on countertops.

- Wash everything that has come into contact with raw meat, poultry, and fish in hot, soapy water before using it again. That includes cutting boards, knives and other utensils, countertops, and your hands.

- Place cooked food on a clean plate. Never use the same plate that held the raw food unless it has been washed thoroughly.

Fig. 38-6. Even if a fresh food item looks clean, you should still wash it carefully to remove any bacteria that might be present.

Controlling Temperatures

You can help prevent foodborne illness by keeping foods at the proper temperature when thawing, cooking, and serving them. A general rule to follow is "Keep hot foods hot and cold foods cold." Bacteria grow to dangerous levels most rapidly when they are exposed to temperatures between 40°F and 140°F. Fig. 38-7 shows safe and unsafe temperatures for handling food. The red zone indicates the danger zone. Avoid keeping perishable and cooked foods in this zone for more than two hours.

Thaw Foods Safely ~ Freezing food does not kill bacteria—it simply keeps bacteria from growing. When thawing frozen foods, take care to avoid the danger zone. The bacteria may still be alive and could grow to harmful levels. Never leave frozen meat, poultry, or fish on the countertop to thaw at room temperature. You can thaw frozen foods safely in the refrigerator if you allow plenty of time—many foods require a day or more. If faster thawing is needed, you could place the food in a leakproof plastic bag and submerge it in cold water. Another safe method is to use the defrost or low setting on the microwave oven. If you use the microwave method, be sure to cook the food immediately after you thaw it.

Cook Foods Thoroughly ~ Proper cooking ensures that foods reach a high enough temperature to kill harmful bacteria.

Temperature Guide to Food Safety

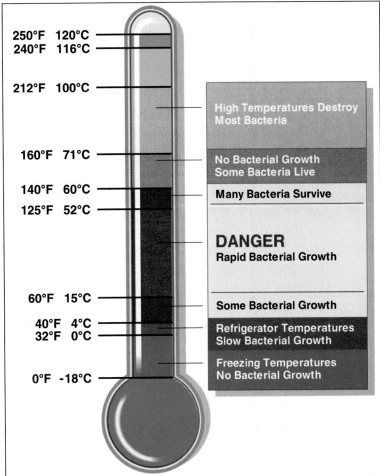

Fig. 38-7. To keep food safe to eat, keep it out of the danger zone.

You can't always tell whether food is done by looking at it. The best way to ensure that foods are cooked thoroughly is to check the internal temperature. You can use an oven-proof thermometer designed to stay in food while it's cooking or an instant-read thermometer that lets you quickly check the temperature after cooking.

Here are some examples of safe internal temperatures:

- Fish: 145°F
- Meats, egg dishes: 160°F
- Leftovers (reheating): 165°F
- Poultry pieces, ground poultry: 170°F
- Whole poultry: 180°F

Serve Foods Safely ~ Once food is cooked, keep it hot until it is served. Cold foods that spoil easily—such as milk, custard pies, or mixtures containing mayonnaise—should be kept cold. Never leave food sitting out for more than two hours at room temperature, or for more than one hour if the temperature is above 90°F. If you take food on a picnic, use insulated containers. Whether you eat outdoors or in, cover and refrigerate leftovers right away.

TIPS FOR *Success*

Safe Packed Lunches

Packed lunches than cannot be refrigerated need special handling. Follow these tips:

- Use an insulated lunch bag or tote to maintain temperatures.
- Keep cold drinks in a vacuum bottle. Refrigerate the bottle before filling it.
- Keep hot foods in a wide-mouthed vacuum bottle. Fill the bottle with hot water first. Let it stand while you heat the food to steaming hot. Pour the water out and put the food in.
- Freeze cold foods before you pack them. They will thaw by lunchtime and will help keep other foods cool.

Storing Food Safely

Storing food properly keeps it safe. It also saves money because less food is wasted. A general principle to follow with all food storage is "first in, first out." Set up a system of **rotation** so that older supplies are used before newer ones. For example, when you purchase a new carton of milk, place it behind the carton that is already in the refrigerator so that you will be sure to use the older milk first. Look for "sell by" and "use by" dates on food containers. Be sure to use up food before the "use by" date has passed or within a reasonable time after the "sell by" date.

Be sure to read labels and packages for storage instructions. The three main types of food storage are refrigerator, freezer, and dry storage.

Refrigerator Storage

The refrigerator is the place for many perishable foods, such as dairy products, eggs, meat, poultry, and fish. Some fresh fruits and vegetables are also usually stored in the refrigerator. Canned, bottled, and packaged foods may need to be refrigerated after opening. Foods can dry out quickly in the refrigerator, so use covered containers or wrap foods in foil or plastic. The temperature of the refrigerator should be kept between 32°F and 40°F. Fig. 38-8 lists the refrigerator storage times for some common foods.

Freezer Storage

Perishable foods that require long-term storage should be kept in the freezer. The temperature of the freezer should be maintained at 0°F or below. Foods that are bought frozen should be kept in their original con-

Refrigerator Storage Times

SAFE STORAGE TIME	FOODS
1 to 2 days	Poultry; fish and shellfish; ground meat; store-cooked convenience meals; variety meats (liver, kidneys, etc.); cream pies
3 to 5 days	Cold cuts (opened); fresh meats (not ground); leftover cooked meats and meat dishes; fully cooked ham slices; store-prepared salads
Up to 7 days	Milk, cream; cottage cheese; bacon; whole fully cooked ham; hard-cooked eggs; hot dogs (opened); smoked sausage; cakes and pies
Up to 3 weeks	Eggs; sour cream; hard cheese (opened); hard sausage
Up to 3 months	Butter; margarine; salsa (opened); salad dressing (opened)
6 months	Ham (unopened can); hard cheese (unopened)

Fig. 38-8. Some foods stay safe in the refrigerator longer than others. Have you ever left a forgotten item in your refrigerator too long? How could you keep this from happening again?

tainers. Foods that are frozen at home need special packaging to prevent **freezer burn**—a condition in which food dries out and loses flavor because of improper freezing. You can prevent freezer burn by using airtight containers, plastic freezer bags, heavy-duty foil, or freezer paper. When you prepare food for the freezer, be sure to include a label that states the contents, the number of servings, and the date of freezing. You can store foods safely in a freezer for periods ranging from 1 to 12 months. Most meats can be stored for 12 months; dairy products should be used within 6 months. Use a rotation system to ensure that you use older supplies first.

Dry Storage

Dry storage consists of kitchen cabinets or shelves where food remains at room temperature. It is suitable for many canned, bottled, and packaged goods. Some perishables, such as potatoes and onions, are best kept in a cool, dry place.

When organizing dry storage, avoid using shelves that are near or above heat sources, such as the range or a radiator. Also avoid areas that might get damp, such as an under-sink cabinet.

Unopened packages can be stored for weeks or even months. Once you open them, though, you may have to change your storage method. Leftover canned foods should be transferred to a storage container and refrigerated after opening. Foods such as cereals and crackers, which tend to go stale after opening, can remain at room temperature but should be placed in a storage container with a tight-fitting lid. Storing food properly helps you avoid waste and enjoy fresh, safe, good-tasting food.

Chapter Summary

- Kitchens are organized around major appliances.

- Before purchasing small appliances or utensils, consider whether you really need them.

- Kitchens with an efficient work triangle and well-organized work centers are easier to use.

- Following safety precautions will help prevent kitchen accidents and injuries such as cuts, burns, fires, and electric shocks.

- You can prevent foodborne illness by practicing cleanliness, avoiding cross-contamination, and controlling the temperatures of food.

- Proper storage keeps foods safe to eat.

- The three types of food storage areas are the refrigerator, freezer, and dry storage.

Reviewing Key Terms & Ideas

1. Give two examples each of major appliances, small appliances, and utensils found in a typical kitchen.

2. What kitchen components make up the **work triangle**? What is its significance?

3. Explain how **work centers** relate to kitchen organization.

4. Name three ways to prevent burns in the kitchen.

5. What actions can you take to prevent falls in the kitchen?

6. In general, what causes **foodborne illness**?

7. Name four cleanliness guidelines that can help prevent foodborne illness.

8. Why is it necessary to eliminate pests from the kitchen?

9. Why is **cross-contamination** a hazard? What do you need to do in order to prevent it?

10. What is the "danger zone" for food, and why is it called that?

11. How can you tell whether a hamburger has been cooked thoroughly? Be specific.

12. What is the function of a **rotation** system in food storage?

13. How should most perishable foods be stored?

14. What is **freezer burn**? How can it be prevented?

Thinking Critically

1. **Drawing Conclusions.** Why is it important to design the layout of a kitchen for efficiency? How might this contribute to safety?

2. **Understanding Cause and Effect.** Incidents of foodborne illnesses are often associated with outdoor meals and with meals for large numbers of people. What might explain this?

Applying Your Knowledge

1. **Small Appliances.** Brainstorm a list of small kitchen appliances. Decide which category you would put each appliance in: "Basic Necessity," "Nice to Have," or "Waste of Money." Be prepared to explain your reasons.

2. **Kitchen Efficiency.** Evaluate the way foods and utensils are stored in your kitchen. Think of ways you might rearrange these items to create more efficient work centers. Discuss your ideas with your family.

3. **Kitchen Safety.** Based on what you learned in this chapter, prepare a list of safety guidelines that you can post in your kitchen at home. Focus on practices that need improvement. Be sure to explain the reasons behind the guidelines.

Making Connections

1. **Science.** Besides bacteria, foodborne illness can be caused by viruses or parasites. Choose a specific foodborne illness microorganism and learn more about it. Where can it be found? What symptoms of illness does it cause? How can the illness be prevented?

2. **Social Studies.** Research how people in Colonial times kept food cool during hot weather. What other techniques did they have for preserving and storing food? Write a brief report on your findings.

Managing Your Life

Safety for All

Are you concerned about friends and relatives who don't follow some of the safety guidelines you have learned in this chapter? Help protect the people in your life by reviewing safe kitchen practices with them and helping them understand ways to protect themselves from accidents, injuries, and illness. Suggest changes they might need to make or equipment they might need to purchase, such as a fire extinguisher or a step stool. If necessary, help them rearrange work areas in their kitchen so that they are safer places to work.

Using Technology

1. **Web Page.** Create a "Guide to Food Safety" in Web browser (HTML) format. On the main page, outline the topics you will cover. Provide links to pages on which you give more information about each topic.

2. **Presentation Software.** Use appropriate software to create a presentation on cross-contamination. Give illustrations of practices that cause cross-contamination, such as chopping vegetables on a board used to cut raw meat. Include guidelines for avoiding cross-contamination.

Food Preparation Basics

Objectives

- **Identify** the basic information provided in recipes.
- **Describe** methods for measuring, cutting, and mixing ingredients.
- **Compare** different cooking techniques.
- **Explain** procedures for microwave cooking.
- **Create** a schedule for meal preparation.

QUICK WRITE

Write about your attitude toward cooking. Is it something you do only out of necessity? Is it something you enjoy? Why might you choose to prepare a meal yourself when so many other options are available?

*H*ave you ever watched a professional chef preparing a meal on a television cooking show? If so, you know that a lot of skill and knowledge go into food preparation. To get good results, you need to know what recipe terms mean, what equipment to use, and how to perform food preparation tasks correctly. This chapter will help you become familiar with terms and techniques used in food preparation. You can find additional information in cookbooks, on Web sites, and in other sources.

Recipes for Success

Recipes are road maps to successful food preparation. They provide you with all the information you need to make an array of tempting dishes, from apple crisp to zucchini soup. Following recipe directions carefully will help ensure that the meals you prepare are tasty and appealing. See Fig. 39-1.

What a Recipe Tells You

The information provided in a recipe may be arranged in several ways. In the most commonly used format, the ingredients are listed first, followed by the assembly directions. Another, less common, format combines the ingredients and directions. No matter how a recipe is organized, it should include certain basic information. Fig. 39-2 on the next page explains the main parts of a recipe.

Fig. 39-1. A recipe, like a road map, needs to be followed carefully. What might happen if you took a "detour"?

Reading a Recipe

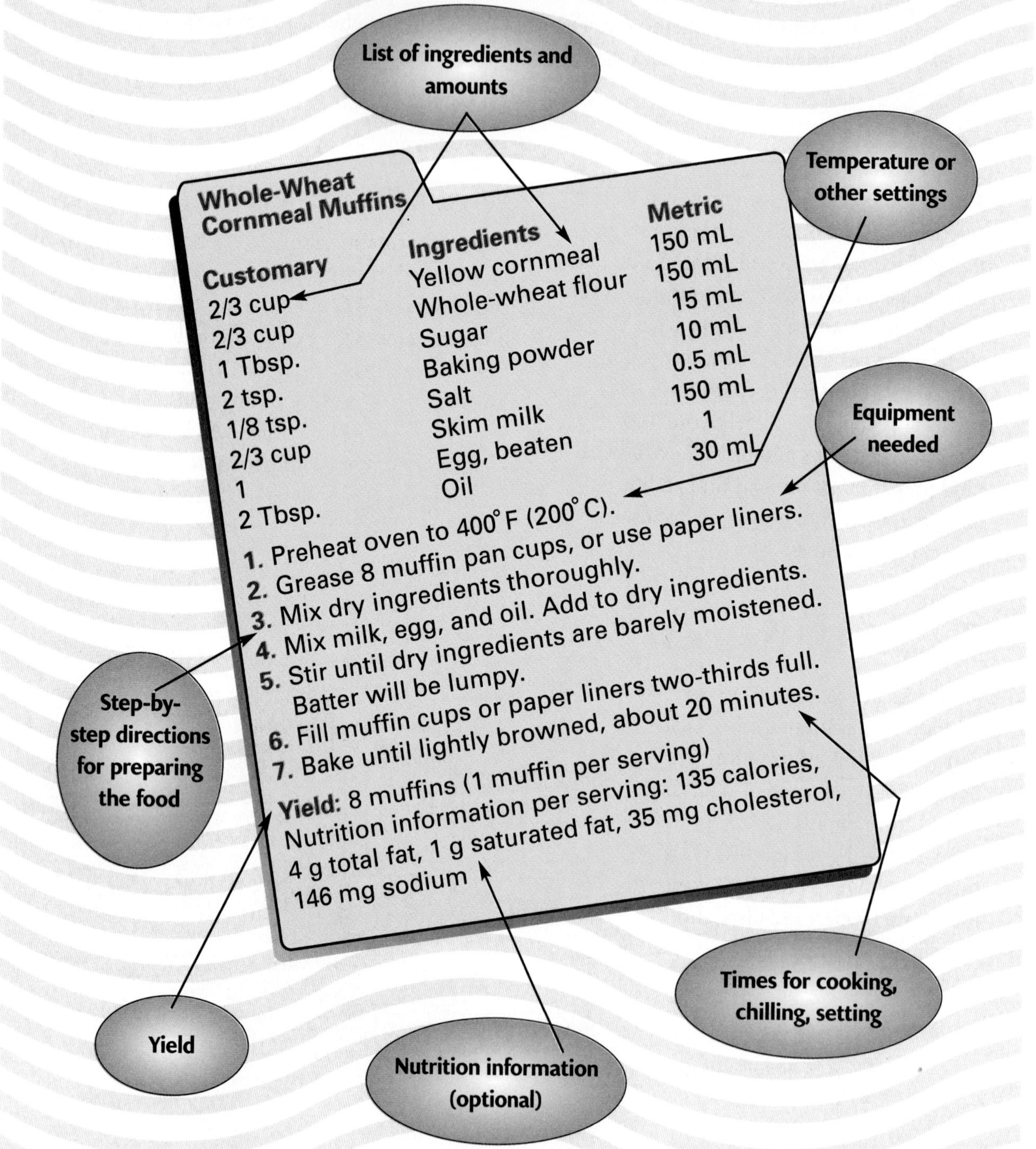

List of ingredients and amounts

Temperature or other settings

Equipment needed

Whole-Wheat Cornmeal Muffins

Customary	Ingredients	Metric
2/3 cup	Yellow cornmeal	150 mL
2/3 cup	Whole-wheat flour	150 mL
1 Tbsp.	Sugar	15 mL
2 tsp.	Baking powder	10 mL
1/8 tsp.	Salt	0.5 mL
2/3 cup	Skim milk	150 mL
1	Egg, beaten	1
2 Tbsp.	Oil	30 mL

1. Preheat oven to 400° F (200° C).
2. Grease 8 muffin pan cups, or use paper liners.
3. Mix dry ingredients thoroughly.
4. Mix milk, egg, and oil. Add to dry ingredients.
5. Stir until dry ingredients are barely moistened. Batter will be lumpy.
6. Fill muffin cups or paper liners two-thirds full.
7. Bake until lightly browned, about 20 minutes.

Yield: 8 muffins (1 muffin per serving)
Nutrition information per serving: 135 calories, 4 g total fat, 1 g saturated fat, 35 mg cholesterol, 146 mg sodium

Step-by-step directions for preparing the food

Yield

Nutrition information (optional)

Times for cooking, chilling, setting

Fig. 39-2. A well-written recipe offers all the information you need to prepare the dish you have chosen.

Fig. 39-3. *When you're making soup or stew, you might want to add or omit some ingredients to suit your taste.* What are other possible reasons for changing a recipe?

Using Recipes

Before using a recipe, read it carefully. Make sure you have all the ingredients on hand and that you understand the directions. For best results, follow the recipe directions exactly. This is especially good advice when you're a beginning cook or when you're using a particular recipe for the first time.

Once you gain more experience, you can be creative by varying recipes to suit your taste. Some types of recipes are more flexible than others. Recipes for certain baked products, such as breads and cakes, depend on exact proportions of ingredients. If you make changes, the product could end up with an unpleasant texture or other problems. It's easier to make creative changes to recipes for stews, salads, casseroles, and similar mixtures. See Fig. 39-3.

Sometimes you will want to prepare more or fewer servings of a recipe. You can use your math skills to change the **yield**—the amount of food the recipe makes. For example, suppose a recipe for pasta salad makes four servings, but you have six people to feed. Since you want to make 1½ times as much salad, multiply the amount of each ingredient by 1½. Of course, it might be easier to multiply all the ingredients by two and have leftovers! As with making other recipe changes, it's easier to change the yield for mixtures like salads than for baked goods.

Using Convenience Foods

Sometimes you may choose to save time by preparing mixes and other convenience foods rather than following a recipe. Read and follow the package directions carefully. Sometimes they will suggest variations for a touch of creativity.

You might want to combine convenience foods and fresh foods in some recipes. You could use a ready-made pie crust to make an apple pie, or you might use a combination of canned and fresh vegetables in vegetable soup. That way you combine the benefits of convenience foods and home cooking.

Measuring Techniques

Do you know the difference between a teaspoon and a tablespoon? How about the right way to measure flour? If you don't know how to measure ingredients accurately, recipes won't turn out the way you expect.

Units of Measure

Two different systems of measurement may be used to give the ingredient amounts in a recipe. The *customary system* is the standard system of measurement used in the United States. The *metric system* is the system of measurement used in most of the world. The metric system is also used by American scientists and health professionals.

Remember that the two measurement systems are just different ways of expressing the same amounts. Both systems include units for measuring **volume**—the amount of space taken up by an ingredient—and units for measuring weight. Fig. 39-4 shows common units of measure in each system.

Notice that in the customary system, the term *ounce* is used as a measure of weight as well as of volume. Remember that these two kinds of ounces are not the same. As a rule of thumb, if an ingredient is a liquid or if the measurement specifies fluid ounces, you can assume that ounces refer to volume. With solid foods, the same term most often refers to weight.

In working with recipes—especially when changing the yield—it's helpful to understand equivalents. An **equivalent measurement** is the same amount expressed using a different unit of measure. For example, 16 ounces is the same amount as 1 pound or about 500 grams. Fig. 39-5 lists some common equivalents.

Customary and Metric Units

TYPE OF MEASUREMENT	CUSTOMARY UNITS	METRIC UNITS
Volume	teaspoon (tsp.) tablespoon (Tbsp.) fluid ounce (fl. oz.) cup (c.) pint (pt.) quart (qt.) gallon (gal.)	milliliter (mL) liter (L)
Weight	ounce (oz.) pound (lb.)	gram (g) kilogram (kg)

Fig. 39-4. It's helpful to know how to measure using both the customary and metric systems. Which system do you think is easier to use? Why?

Equivalent Measurements

CUSTOMARY MEASURE	CUSTOMARY EQUIVALENT	METRIC EQUIVALENT (APPROX.)
1/4 tsp.		1 mL
1/2 tsp.		2 mL
1 tsp.		5 mL
1 Tbsp.	3 tsp.	15 mL
1/4 cup	4 Tbsp.	50 mL
1/3 cup	5⅓ Tbsp.	75 mL
1/2 cup	8 Tbsp.	125 mL
3/4 cup	12 Tbsp.	175 mL
1 cup	16 Tbsp. or 8 fl. oz.	250 mL
1 pt.	2 cups	500 mL
1 qt.	4 cups or 2 pt.	1000 mL or 1 L
1 gal.	4 qt.	4 L
1 lb.	16 oz.	500 g
2 lb.	32 oz.	1000 g or 1 kg

Fig. 39-5. Equivalents let you measure ingredients in more than one way. If a recipe called for 1½ pints of milk, how many cups would you measure?

Equipment for Measuring

To measure ingredients correctly, you need to use the right equipment in the right way. Basic equipment for measuring includes:

- A liquid measuring cup made of clear glass or plastic with markings on the side. It has a spout so you can measure and pour liquid ingredients without spilling them.
- A set of dry measuring cups in different sizes. They are used for dry or solid ingredients.
- A set of measuring spoons. These are used for small amounts of any ingredients.

Methods for Measuring

For accurate measurements, you need to follow the right procedures. Different measuring methods are used for different kinds of ingredients.

Dry Ingredients ~ Examples of dry ingredients include flour, sugar, baking powder, and spices. Select the correct size of dry measuring cup or measuring spoon. Hold it over waxed paper or over the ingredient's container to catch any spills. Fill the cup or spoon slightly higher than the brim, then use a knife or spatula to level it off even with the brim.

Fig. 39-6. Putting the measuring cup on a flat surface gives a more accurate measurement than holding it in your hand. **Why is this true?**

Always spoon flour gently into the measuring cup. If you dip the cup into the flour, the flour could pack down, giving you more than you need. When measuring brown sugar, spoon the sugar into a measuring cup and press it down firmly. Continue to add and pack down the sugar until the cup is full.

Solid Fats ~ You can measure solid fats such as butter, margarine, and shortening by spooning the fat into a dry measuring cup and packing it firmly. Level off the top, then scrape the fat out with a spatula. If you buy butter or similar fats in ¼ pound sticks, use the tablespoon markings on the wrappers to cut off the amount you need.

Liquid Ingredients ~ For small amounts of liquids, select the correct size of measuring spoon. Hold the spoon away from the bowl of other ingredients. That way, if any liquid spills, it won't fall into what you are making. Fill the spoon just to the brim.

For larger amounts, use a liquid measuring cup. Place it on a level surface and add the liquid. Check the measurement at eye level by crouching down and looking through the side of the cup. If necessary, pour some liquid out or add more until the liquid reaches the right mark on the cup. See Fig. 39-6.

Measuring by Weight ~ If a recipe specifies an amount by weight, use a kitchen scale. First place an appropriate empty container on the scale. Adjust the scale to read zero. Then add the ingredient to the container until the scale shows the correct amount. In some cases, you may not need a scale to measure by weight. The weights of many packaged foods are given on the label.

Cutting Techniques

Many food preparation tasks involve cutting food into smaller pieces. There are many different techniques for cutting food, ranging from slicing and dicing to peeling and shredding. By learning the terminology and practicing your skills, you can become an expert. Fig. 39-7 shows techniques for cutting foods.

Cutting Terms and Techniques

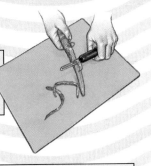

Pare. Use a paring knife or a peeler to cut away the skin of a fruit or vegetable. A peeler cuts a thinner layer, leaving more of the vitamins that are concentrated just under the skin.

Slice. Cut food into thin, flat pieces. Usually done with a sharp knife and a cutting board while steadying the food with one hand or with a fork. A food processor may be used to slice some foods.

Chop and mince. To chop food, cut it into small, irregular pieces. The recipe may tell you what size pieces you need— coarse, medium, or fine. To mince food, keep cutting until the pieces are as small as you can make them. You may also use a food processor for chopping and mincing.

Cube and dice. To cube or dice foods, cut them in three directions. First, slice the food. Next, stack the slices, and cut them first in one direction and then the other. To cube, make the cuts about 1/2 inch apart. To dice, make the cuts about 1/4 inch apart, or as specified in the recipe.

Puree. Use a food mill, food processor, or blender to mash food until it is smooth. Vegetables are usually cooked before being pureed.

Shred and grate. Use a grater to shred foods such as carrots and cheese. When you push the food firmly across the grater's large holes, fine shreds will fall away. Use a knife to shred foods such as lettuce and cabbage. A food processor—with the proper blade inserted—is useful for large shredding jobs. To grate food, make very small particles by rubbing the food against the small holes of the grater.

Fig. 39-7. When cutting food, you need to know which tool to use and what the terms mean.

Mixing Terms and Techniques

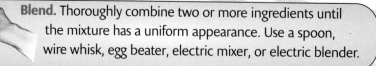

Blend. Thoroughly combine two or more ingredients until the mixture has a uniform appearance. Use a spoon, wire whisk, egg beater, electric mixer, or electric blender.

Stir. Mix slowly in a circular or figure-8 motion with a spoon or a wire whisk.

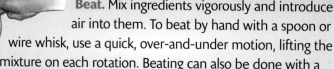

Beat. Mix ingredients vigorously and introduce air into them. To beat by hand with a spoon or wire whisk, use a quick, over-and-under motion, lifting the mixture on each rotation. Beating can also be done with a rotary beater or electric mixer.

Whip. Beat very rapidly, incorporating so much air as to increase the volume of the product. For example, whipped cream is twice the volume of the original heavy cream. Use a wire whisk, rotary beater, or electric mixer.

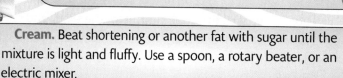

Cream. Beat shortening or another fat with sugar until the mixture is light and fluffy. Use a spoon, a rotary beater, or an electric mixer.

Fold. Use a spoon or rubber scraper to gently add an air-filled ingredient to a mixture. For example, you might fold whipped egg whites into cake batter. Gently cut down through the mixture and across the bottom. Then, without lifting the utensil out, bring some of the mixture up and over. Repeat until the ingredients are combined.

Cut in. Mix a solid fat with dry ingredients using a cutting motion. Use a pastry blender or two knives.

Toss. Tumble ingredients lightly together using a fork and spoon.

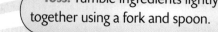

Fig. 39-8. Using the proper mixing techniques will help ensure that your recipe turns out right.

Mixing Techniques

Mixing or combining ingredients is another skill frequently used in food preparation. A recipe should clearly explain how and in what order to combine the ingredients. You might think that it doesn't matter how ingredients are combined, as long as they end up mixed together. Actually, the technique used can make a big difference in the results. Fig. 39-8 illustrates and describes mixing techniques.

Cooking Techniques

Cooking involves applying heat to foods. Most cooking techniques fall into one of three categories: cooking with moist heat, cooking with dry heat, or cooking with fat.

Cooking with Moist Heat

Moist heat cooking involves the use of liquids or steam to cook the food. Fig. 39-9 explains the different moist heat cooking methods.

Moist Heat Cooking Methods

Steaming can be done by boiling a small amount of water in a pan, then putting the food in a steamer basket that holds it above the water. Cover the pan and let the water continue to boil while the steam cooks the food. You can also use an electric steamer. When done properly, steaming retains most of the food's nutrients. Vegetables are often steamed.

Boiling means heating liquid at a high temperature so that bubbles rise continuously to the surface and break. A recipe might tell you to bring sauce to a boil or to cook noodles in boiling water. Most foods, however, should not be cooked in boiling liquid. Boiling can rob food of nutrients and cause it to overcook or break apart.

Simmering means heating liquid to a temperature just below the boiling point. Small bubbles should form, with some bubbles rising slowly to the surface. Vegetables are often cooked in simmering liquid. Fewer nutrients are lost than with boiling.

Poaching is cooking whole foods in a small amount of simmering liquid so that they keep their original shape. Poaching is appropriate for tender foods such as fish and eggs.

Braising involves browning food in a small amount of fat, then cooking it slowly in a small amount of simmering liquid until tender. This method is often used to cook large, less tender cuts of meat.

Stewing is similar to braising, but the food is cut into small pieces first. Stewing is used for less tender cuts of meat and for poultry, vegetables, and some fruits.

Pressure cooking requires a special airtight pot in which the food cooks quickly in very high temperatures. This method is appropriate for foods that take a long time to cook.

Fig. 39-9. Moist heat cooking involves hot liquid, steam, or a combination of the two. What are some advantages of moist heat cooking?

Foods such as rice and dry beans are cooked in moist heat so that they can absorb water and soften. Moist heat cooking is also a good choice for making meats, vegetables, and other foods tender. Moist heat helps flavors to blend, as when you make sauces and soups.

Cooking with Dry Heat

With **dry heat cooking**, the food is cooked uncovered without adding liquid. Foods cooked with dry heat get brown and crisp on the outside but remain moist and tender on the inside. The main dry heat cooking methods are roasting, baking, and broiling.

- **Roasting and baking** both mean cooking food uncovered in the oven. Many foods can be baked—breads, fruits and vegetables, cakes, cookies, pies, casseroles, and

fish, for example. The term *roasting* is used primarily to refer to large pieces of meat or poultry. Foods that are roasted or baked often have a crisp, brown crust and are tender and flavorful inside.

- **Broiling** means cooking food directly under or over a glowing heat source. When you use the broiler unit of an oven, you place the food on a broiler pan, which has slots that allow fat to drain away during cooking. Grilling food on an outdoor grill is another method of broiling. Broiling is often used for tender meats, such as steaks and hamburgers, and for poultry, fish, and some vegetables.

Cooking with Fat

Cooking with fat is a quick method that produces flavorful foods. However, it has the disadvantage of adding fat and calories to the food. When cooking with fat, choose oils that are low in saturated fats. Olive oil and canola oil are healthful cooking oils. Nonstick cooking spray is also a good choice. There are several methods for cooking with fat.

- **Sautéing** means cooking small pieces of food in a small amount of fat over low to medium heat. For example, a recipe might tell you to sauté chopped onions until they become soft and transparent. Stir the food occasionally as it sautés.

- **Panfrying** is a similar method for larger pieces of food, such as tender meats, fish, or eggs. While panfrying, you may need to turn the food so it cooks evenly.

- **Deep-fat frying** is cooking food by immersing it in hot fat. French fries and doughnuts are examples of deep-fat fried foods. This method of frying adds the most fat.

TIPS FOR *Success*

Making Do

If you don't have the right tool for a particular job, substituting is the answer. Try these ideas if you can't find a:

- **Peeler.** Use a sharp paring knife to remove the skins of firm fruits and vegetables.

- **Wire whisk.** Try a fork or rotary beater for beating eggs. To beat cake batter, use a long-handled spoon.

- **Sifter.** Use a fine mesh strainer to sift flour or other dry ingredients.

- **Pastry blender.** Try using two small knives to cut shortening into flour.

- **Stir-frying** involves stirring and cooking small pieces of food very quickly at high heat in very little fat. This method can be used for vegetables, meat, poultry, and fish. Because it uses less fat, stir-frying is a more healthful way to cook with fat than the other methods.

Microwave Cooking

Do you enjoy the convenience of microwave cooking? Because the microwave oven performs many cooking tasks faster than a conventional oven, you can cook a meal in minutes or prepare a snack in seconds. Microwave ovens are also cleaner and more economical to operate than conventional ovens.

Most microwave ovens are best suited for cooking relatively small amounts of food. Microwave ovens are also ideal for reheating cooked foods and defrosting frozen foods.

Microwave Cookware

Not all cookware is suitable for microwave cooking. Ceramic, glass, plastic, and paper containers are usually appropriate, but look for a label indicating that they are microwave-safe. Microwave-safe ceramic, glass, and plastic are unaffected by microwaves. They are also heat-resistant, so they don't crack or melt when the food becomes hot. Ceramic dishes that are not microwave-safe may shatter in a microwave oven. See Fig. 39-10.

Fig. 39-10. Before putting a dish or utensil in the microwave oven, make sure it is made of microwave-safe material. *What materials are safe for use in the microwave oven?*

Metal pans and bowls should *never* be used in a microwave oven. They may cause **arcing**, sparks that can damage the oven and start a fire. Some dishes have metallic trim or a metallic glaze, and they, too, should not be used. Avoid using recycled paper in a microwave oven, since it may include metal fragments.

Microwave Techniques

Because food heats up so quickly in a microwave oven, moisture also builds up rapidly. This may cause some foods to burst. Another concern is the possibility of uneven cooking. Special techniques help prevent these problems.

Stirring and Rotating ~ Microwaves penetrate food to a depth of about 1½ inches. The heat generated by the vibrating food molecules is then conducted toward the center of the food. That's why the center of food cooked in a microwave oven takes longer to cook than the outer edges.

Soups, stews, and other foods containing liquids heat evenly if you stir them occasionally. For best results, stir from the outer edge toward the center.

When food can't be stirred, it needs to be rotated. Most newer microwave ovens have a turntable that will do the job for you. If your microwave oven doesn't have a turntable, rotate the dish a quarter- or a half-turn partway through the cooking. This maneuver allows the microwaves to penetrate the food on all sides. In some cases, you might also need to rearrange food pieces or turn them over.

Covering ~ Most foods should be covered in a microwave oven to hold in moisture and prevent spattering. You may cover foods with several different materials, depending on how much moisture you want to hold in.

- Paper towels or napkins work well for covering bacon, sandwiches, and appetizers. Wrapping breads in paper towels prevents them from becoming soggy. Use towels that are marked "microwavable."

- Waxed paper is often used on casseroles to hold in some moisture while letting steam escape.

- Microwave-safe dishes with covers are ideal for vegetables and casseroles. They hold in more steam.

- Microwave-safe plastic wrap also holds in steam. To keep it from bursting, pierce the wrap or turn it back at one corner before starting to cook.

Puncturing ~ Foods that are encased in a skin or sealed in plastic should be pierced before they are placed in a microwave oven. Otherwise, steam will build up inside the food and cause it to burst. Piercing foods with a fork or making a small knife slit will prevent pressure buildup. Puncture whole potatoes, sausages, hot dogs, tomatoes, and apples, as well as vegetables that are to be cooked in plastic pouches. See Fig. 39-11.

Fig. 39-11. Puncturing prevents certain foods from bursting as they heat up. What causes them to burst?

Defrosting ~ A microwave oven is very convenient for defrosting frozen foods. Defrosting cuts down on meal preparation time and allows you to create and change menus easily. Also, you can prepare individual servings or whole meals ahead of time, freeze them, and then thaw and reheat them when you want to.

How long it takes a food to defrost depends on the size and density of the food and on the temperature at which it was frozen. Most microwave cookbooks provide a defrosting chart. Some models of microwave ovens have automatic defrost features that set the defrosting time and power level based on the food weight.

Standing Time ~ A mistake that many people make when cooking with a microwave oven is to ignore the standing time called for in a recipe. **Standing time** is the time allowed for the food to continue to cook after the microwave oven is turned off. As the food stands, the molecules inside it continue to vibrate and to cook it. Standing time is almost as important as cooking time to ensure that the food turns out properly.

Microwave Safety

For safety, follow these guidelines when using a microwave oven:

- Use pot holders when you remove food from a microwave oven. Heat from the food may pass into the container and make it hot. See Fig. 39-12.

Fig. 39-12. Many people don't realize that dishes of microwaved food can be hot enough to burn you. Always protect your hands with pot holders.

- When removing the cover from microwaved food, lift the side farthest away from you so that the escaping steam doesn't burn you.

- Don't use an extension cord with a microwave oven. The oven should be grounded with a three-prong plug and should not be on the same electrical circuit as other appliances.

- Keep your microwave oven clean and in good working order. Spattered food left on the inside walls will increase cooking time because it will absorb microwaves. If the door does not seal tightly or if the oven makes any unusual sound, call an authorized repair service.

Organizing Meal Preparation

Timing and efficiency are just as important to meal preparation as cooking skills are. When you're preparing a whole meal, you must figure out what needs to be done in what sequence so that all the food is ready at the same time. With careful planning and efficient techniques, you can put together a meal that everyone, including the cook, can enjoy. See Fig. 39-13.

Fig. 39-13. Working in the kitchen will go more smoothly if you organize the tasks that must be done.

Making a Schedule

Preparing several dishes so that they are ready at the same time can be tricky, but it gets easier with practice. Start by reading the recipe or package directions for each food on the menu. Make a list of all the tasks needed to prepare each. Then estimate how much time each task will take. It's best to allow a little more time than you think you will need.

To make a schedule, figure out the best sequence for doing all the tasks on your list. Try these suggestions:

- **Dovetail tasks.** Look for ways to **dovetail**, or overlap, tasks in order to save time. Perhaps you could prepare a salad while rice is cooking.
- **Group similar tasks.** For example, you might decide to chop all the vegetables for several different dishes at one time.
- **Prepare some items ahead of time.** Could you prepare and refrigerate a gelatin dessert the day before? Make things easier on yourself by getting a head start.

Once you've decided on the sequence of tasks, determine when you will need to start each task so that it's completed on time. If the total preparation time is 45 minutes and you plan to serve the meal at 6 p.m., you know you'll need to begin preparing the meal no later than 5:15.

Working Efficiently

Once you have your schedule, you're ready to prepare the meal. The process will go more smoothly if you:

- Clear the kitchen counters to give yourself room to work.

FINDING CREATIVE SOLUTIONS

Working Backward

To solve most problems, you have to not only choose a course of action but also plan the details of carrying it out. The more details there are to think about, the more overwhelming that process can be. If you're stuck at "Where do I start?"—not quite knowing how to get your plan off the ground—you may find that the best approach is to work backward.

How It Works

To work backward, start by visualizing the end of the process. Then work back step by step to figure out how to get there.

For example, suppose your committee is preparing a booklet to welcome new students to your school. The last step in the process might be to pick up the completed booklets from the copy shop. The step before that would be to drop off the pages that need to be copied and bound. What comes before that? You'll need to get each page ready, of course. Visualize what you want the end product to be like, then keep working backward to figure out how to create it.

Try It Out

You and a friend have volunteered to prepare a brunch for 10 people next Saturday at 11:00. The menu is pancakes, quiche, fresh fruit cups, coffee, and juice.

▶ **Your Turn** *Work backward to identify the steps in preparing the brunch. Estimate how long each step will take. Create a schedule showing when each task needs to be done, working backward from 11:00.*

- Assemble all the ingredients, utensils, and appliances you will need before you start.

- Check off each task in your schedule as you complete it.

- Clean up as you work. Rinse bowls, utensils, and pans immediately after using them. Then place them in hot, soapy water to soak until you can wash them.

If you're working with another person, take care not to get in each other's way. Use separate work areas, or alternate tasks at the sink or range. As you gain experience in the kitchen, you will become better at planning your time and working efficiently.

Chapter Summary

- A recipe provides the information you need to prepare a dish.
- Recipes should be followed carefully, but some allow for creative changes.
- Accurate measuring is a key to recipe success.
- A variety of techniques are used for cutting and mixing ingredients.
- Moist heat and dry heat cooking methods affect food in different ways.
- Cooking with fat produces flavorful foods but adds fat and calories.
- For successful microwave cooking, select the right cookware and use recommended techniques.
- A well-planned schedule and efficient work methods will help you organize meal preparation.

Reviewing Key Terms & Ideas

1. Name five types of information provided in a recipe.
2. What types of recipes are less easily changed? Why?
3. What does the **yield** of a recipe tell you?
4. Name a customary and a metric unit for measuring **volume**.
5. Give an **equivalent measurement** for 1/4 cup in the customary system and in the metric system.
6. Explain how you would measure a cup of flour and 1/2 cup of milk.
7. What is the difference between chopping and cubing?
8. How does beating affect a mixture?
9. Describe how to fold one ingredient into another.
10. Give three examples each of **moist heat cooking** and **dry heat cooking**.
11. Why is simmering often a better cooking method for vegetables than boiling?
12. Explain the difference between braising and baking.
13. What is **arcing** and what causes it?
14. Why do foods need to be stirred or rotated in the microwave oven?
15. What happens during **standing time**?
16. Why is it helpful to **dovetail** tasks?

Thinking Critically

1. **Understanding Cause and Effect.** Efforts to fully adopt the metric system in the United States have not been successful. What are some possible reasons?
2. **Defending Your Position.** If you had to choose between a microwave oven and a conventional oven for all your cooking, which would you choose and why?

Applying Your Knowledge

1. **Measuring Practice.** Working with a partner, take turns using standard measuring equipment to measure the following amounts: 2/3 cup water, 1/2 cup flour, 1/4 cup shortening, 12 oz. uncooked macaroni, and 1 teaspoon baking powder. Follow the techniques described in the chapter. Have your partner check your work.

2. **Organizing a Meal.** Choose one of your favorite meals that includes a main dish, vegetable, bread, and salad. Make a schedule that includes all the tasks needed to prepare the meal and ensures that the food will all be ready at the same time. If possible, carry out your plan to see how well it works.

Making Connections

1. **Math.** Read the recipe for Whole-Wheat Cornmeal Muffins in Fig. 39-2. Assume you need to make 24 muffins instead of 8. Calculate how much of each ingredient you will need, using customary measurements. Be sure to convert the results, as needed, into easily measured amounts using the equivalents given in Fig. 39-5.

2. **Social Studies.** What elements of the American lifestyle make microwave ovens so popular? In a small group, discuss the social and economic realities of family life that contribute to their widespread use.

Managing Your Life

Stocking Your Kitchen

It's not too soon to start planning for the kitchen equipment you will need when you move into a place of your own. Based on the kinds of meals that you expect to prepare, make a list of the bare essentials you will need. Include measuring equipment, cutting and mixing tools, pots and pans, and so on. You may want to ask friends and relatives for advice. After completing your list, rank the items in order of priority. Identify resources and strategies that could help you acquire the items within a limited budget. Make a plan for acquiring the items over a period of time, and begin putting it into action.

Using Technology

1. **Internet.** Explore some of the Web sites that offer online recipes. Compare the sites for ease of use, variety of recipes, clarity of instructions, and other characteristics that you feel are important. Share your findings with your classmates.

2. **Video.** Ask an experienced cook to work with you to create a video that demonstrates the cutting and mixing techniques described in the chapter. Ask the person to explain each technique as he or she shows it. Edit the video and arrange to show it to the class.

CHAPTER 40

Serving Meals

Objectives

- **Explain** the significance of sharing meals as a family.
- **Compare** ways in which meals can be served at home.
- **Demonstrate** how to set an attractive and well-ordered table.
- **Give** guidelines for mealtime etiquette.

QUICK WRITE

Write about what you enjoy most about family meals. What could you do to make mealtimes even more enjoyable?

A well-prepared meal does more than satisfy hunger and contribute to good nutrition. It should also be an enjoyable experience. While the flavor of the food is certainly part of that enjoyment, so is the pleasure of good company. Whether you're dining with family or friends, at home or away, look for ways to make meals more pleasant for everyone.

Sharing Meals

For many families, mealtime provides a valued opportunity to be together. At mealtime people can relax, talk about the day's events, share ideas, and enjoy one another's company. In today's busy world, it's not always possible to share a meal together every day. That makes it all the more important to enjoy mealtime when the family does have time to eat together. See Fig. 40-1.

Mealtimes bring other benefits too. Lessons that you learn from eating with your family can contribute to your success in social situations. Family dinners are a good place to learn how to participate in a group conversation, express interest in what others are saying, and show respect for the ideas and feelings of others.

Family mealtimes also provide an opportunity to establish healthful lifetime eating patterns. Studies show that relaxation while eating helps the digestive process. The pleasant atmosphere of a family meal can help you associate healthful food with enjoyment.

Fig. 40-1. Mealtimes give families an opportunity to spend time together and share news of the day. How does that help strengthen family relationships?

Every family has its own customs for serving and eating meals. They may be influenced by the family's lifestyle, ethnic background, religious beliefs, or family traditions. As you read about some mealtime customs that are common in the United States, remember that it's important to respect other customs too.

Character IN ACTION

Respecting Food Choices People choose foods based on their personal tastes, dietary needs, culture, customs, and beliefs. When eating with friends, don't make comments about their food choices, even if they seem strange to you. When you invite guests to a meal, ask them ahead of time if they have any special food needs or preferences. Give an example of a special dietary need and how you would accommodate it.

Serving Styles

Different families have different ways of serving meals. The serving style a family chooses may depend on the situation. These are the three most common serving styles:

- **Family style.** The food is brought to the table in serving dishes, which are passed from person to person. People can serve themselves the amount they want and can avoid any foods that they dislike. One disadvantage is that people may be tempted to overeat.

- **Plate style.** The food is placed on each person's plate in the kitchen, and the plates are then brought to the table. Food that has not been served can be kept hot in the kitchen until second helpings are offered. Plate style saves cleanup time because no serving dishes are used. It's also easier to control portion sizes.

- **Buffet style.** Bowls and platters of food are arranged on a serving table. Dinner plates are placed at one end, and people serve themselves as they walk along the table. They then find a place to sit down to eat their meal. This style of service is generally reserved for large gatherings when there is not enough seating for everyone at one table.

Setting the Table

Most families set the table in similar ways. Traditional rules for setting the table make it easy for you to know what to expect, no matter where you eat. You can add special touches for variety or to create a certain atmosphere.

Place Settings

Sit-down meals require individual place settings. A **place setting** is the arrangement of tableware that each person needs for a meal. Tableware for a simple place setting includes a plate, glass, napkin, and **flatware**—knife, fork, and spoon. Depending on the foods served, a place setting might also include more forks or spoons, a bread plate, a salad plate, another glass, and a cup and saucer. Fig. 40-2 shows how the tableware is arranged for a place setting.

Place Setting Arrangement

1. **Dinner plate.** Place in the center of each place setting, about 1 inch from the edge of the table.
2. **Knife.** Place immediately to the right of the dinner plate. The curved edge should face the plate.
3. **Spoon(s).** Place to the right of the knife. If there is more than one spoon, the one used first goes on the outside.
4. **Dinner fork.** Place immediately to the left of the dinner plate.
5. **Salad fork.** Place to the left of the dinner fork.
6. **Napkin.** Place to the left of the forks. You may want to use a napkin ring as shown. You can also fold the napkin in a rectangle and place it with the folded edge farthest from the forks.
7. **Salad plate.** Place above the forks. The bread plate, if there is one, goes to the left of the salad plate.
8. **Water glass.** Place just above the tip of the knife.
9. **Beverage glass.** Place to the right of the water glass and slightly forward.
10. **Cup and saucer.** Place to the right of the spoon(s).

Fig. 40-2. Correctly placed table setting items don't just look good; they are also convenient to use. Why might additional flatware be needed?

Special Touches

Many people like to add special touches to table settings to make holiday meals stand out. Even everyday meals can be made more special with a few touches that show that you care.

- **Table covering.** A tablecloth—clean, pressed, and hanging evenly around the table—adds elegance to a meal. Another option is to use place mats instead of a tablecloth.

- **Napkins.** Colorful napkins add a cheery touch to a table setting. Choose colors that coordinate with the table covering.

- **Table decoration.** A simple flower arrangement, or even a single cut flower in a bud vase, can make a meal more special. Alternatives to fresh flowers include silk flowers, a bowl of fresh fruit, or a plant.

TIPS FOR *Success*

Keep It Simple

When entertaining, keep it simple by following these tips:

- **Choose recipes that you know and trust. You will feel more confident and avoid unpleasant surprises.**

- **If you have one complicated recipe, keep the rest of the menu simple.**

- **Choose dishes that can be prepared in advance. Set the table ahead of time.**

- **Remember that a cheerful attitude and good company are the most important ingredients for a special meal.**

- **Lighting.** For special occasions, you may want to use candlelight for a dramatic effect. Place several candles in candleholders, or try floating votive candles in a bowl of water.

- **Music.** Soft background music can set a pleasant mood for dining. Make sure the volume is set on low, however, so that everyone can hear the conversation and people don't need to shout over the music.

Mealtime Etiquette

Etiquette refers to accepted rules of behavior in a particular culture. Mealtime etiquette is designed to make meals comfortable and enjoyable for everyone.

Etiquette is based on courtesy and respect. You show respect for others at mealtime through the way you look, the way you eat, and the way you talk. The good manners you practice at home will be an asset as you enjoy meals in social settings away from home.

Hygiene and Appearance

Good mealtime hygiene is important both for your own health and for the health of others. Always wash your hands before the meal. If you need to comb your hair or apply makeup, do it before you come to the table.

If you need to cough or sneeze, cover your mouth or nose with a handkerchief or napkin and turn away from the table. If the coughing or sneezing continues, excuse yourself from the table.

Table Manners

For the most part, good table manners are just common-sense courtesy. See Fig. 40-3. Here are some basic guidelines to keep in mind:

- Sit up straight at the table. Avoid resting your elbows on the table while you eat.

- Place your napkin on your lap. Keep it there except when you need to use it.

- If a serving dish is not within easy reach, ask for it to be passed to you. Don't reach in front of someone or across the table.

- Use the serving forks and spoons, not your own flatware, to serve yourself.

- Don't start eating until everyone has been served, unless a host urges you to start.

- If there are several forks or spoons and you're not sure which to use, start with the outermost one. Flatware for the first course is always farthest from the plate.

- Chew quietly with your mouth closed. Don't speak when your mouth is full.

- Break bread or rolls into small pieces with your hands.

- If you're having trouble getting food onto your fork or spoon, push it with a small piece of bread or your knife.

- If you're eating at someone's home and are not sure how to eat a particular food, watch to see what the host does.

- Signal that you have finished by placing your flatware across the center of your plate and your napkin to the left of the plate.

Fig. 40-3. Knowing basic table etiquette will help you feel at ease when visiting friends or eating out.

Conversation

Conversation is an important part of dining. Meals are a time for warmth and friendship, not for arguments or disputes. Discuss topics of interest to everyone, and avoid discussing unpleasant experiences.

When you're a guest in someone's home, thank your hosts before you leave. A special word of thanks for the food and hospitality is always appreciated. For some occasions, you might want to bring a simple gift for the hosts and send a note of thanks afterwards.

Restaurant Etiquette

Good manners are also important when eating out. When you enter a restaurant for the first time, look to see if it is an informal restaurant where guests seat themselves. Often a sign indicates whether someone will lead you to a seat.

When you are seated, review the menu. Ask the server any questions that you have about the food, such as how it is prepared or what ingredients are used. Some servers will read you a list of specials that are not printed on the menu.

If you need to get the attention of a server during the meal, speak in an ordinary voice as he or she passes your table. If the server is across the room, raise your hand to catch his or her eye.

After receiving the bill, review the list of items ordered and make sure the total is correct. If there has been a mistake, which sometimes happens, politely and quietly bring the error to the server's attention.

Tipping—giving extra money to servers in appreciation of good service—is customary in all restaurants that offer table service. Usually, 15 percent of the cost of the food (before taxes) is an acceptable tip. Many customers tip 20 percent in more expensive restaurants. Some restaurants automatically add a 15 or 18 percent tip to any check when there are six or more people at a table. See Fig. 40-4.

Fig. 40-4. A cash tip is often left on the table. If you use a credit card, you can add the tip to the total on the receipt if you prefer.

FINDING CREATIVE SOLUTIONS

Doing a Practice Run

"All the world's a stage," wrote William Shakespeare. The line serves as a reminder that for some of life's biggest "scenes," you can hold a dress rehearsal. Doing a practice run lets you identify and correct possible problems before the real "performance."

How It Works

When you have an important task or event coming up, think through all the steps that are involved, and then practice those steps ahead of time. That way, you can identify anything that might go wrong and take action to deal with it. As you practice, duplicate the conditions closely. Leave as little to chance as possible.

If you're preparing for a job interview, for example, practice getting to the interview location on time. Travel the route you will take in advance, at the time of day you'll take it. If you encounter any traffic jams, you can plan ways around them or allow more time for the journey. Similarly, if you want to make a new dessert for a friend's party, prepare the recipe at least once before then so that you can make sure it turns out well.

Doing a practice run is no guarantee against the unexpected. However, the better prepared you are for an event, the more likely it is that you will enjoy success.

Try It Out

One of your friends has invited his new girlfriend to dinner at a fancy restaurant. He wants to make a good impression, but he's had very little experience dining in that type of place. He asks for your help in getting ready for this important event.

▶ **Your Turn** *How could a practice run benefit your friend? Describe ways that you could help him rehearse to ensure an enjoyable evening.*

If you're with a group in a restaurant, try to decide ahead of time how you will handle the bill. If you want separate bills at the end of the meal, let the server know ahead of time. If you get one bill, decide how it will be divided. The easiest way may be to divide the total between the number of people at the table. This arrangement could be unfair, though, if some people ordered more expensive meals than others. Either way, one person should take responsibility for collecting the money, adding it up, and making sure the server receives the correct amount, including the tip.

Chapter Summary

- Sharing meals as a family has several benefits.
- Common serving styles for family meals include family style, plate style, and buffet style.
- Each item in a place setting goes in a specific place.
- Special touches help to make a table attractive and a meal memorable.
- Using good manners at mealtime allows everyone to have an enjoyable dining experience.
- Mealtime conversations should include topics of interest to everyone.
- Restaurant etiquette includes leaving a tip in appreciation of good service.

Reviewing Key Terms & Ideas

1. Identify three benefits of family mealtimes.
2. What is the difference between the family style and plate style of serving?
3. What is the purpose of a **place setting**?
4. What pieces of **flatware** are included in a simple place setting?
5. What is the proper location for a salad plate? A salad fork?
6. Give three examples of special touches you could use to make a table setting more attractive.
7. What is **etiquette**? What is it based on?
8. When dining with a group, when is it polite to start eating?
9. If there are several forks at your place, how can you tell which to use first?
10. How should you signal to your host that you have finished your meal?
11. Describe the proper way to get a server's attention in a restaurant.
12. What is the usual amount for tipping restaurant servers?

Thinking Critically

1. **Defending Your Position.** You have read that mealtime etiquette is designed to make meals comfortable and enjoyable. Some people might argue that etiquette guidelines have the opposite effect—they make people who don't know the rules feel awkward and uncomfortable. Which position do you support? Why?

2. **Identifying Alternatives.** Mealtime conversation should be pleasant and stay away from controversial topics. What are some possible topics of conversation that you could bring up when dining out with someone you don't know very well?

Applying Your Knowledge

1. **Designing a Table Setting.** With your family's permission, prepare a special table setting at home to demonstrate what you have learned about special touches in this chapter. When the meal is served, ask the family to give you feedback on your setting. What did they notice in particular? What ideas do they have for another kind of table setting?

2. **Table Manners.** Working in a group, write a skit in which the Goodmanners family and the Badmanners family are dining together in an elegant restaurant. Use your skit to demonstrate as many of the points of etiquette discussed in the chapter as possible. Include a server and other restaurant patrons if your group is large enough. Act out your scene for the class.

Making Connections

1. **Social Studies.** Use travel and tourism guides from the library or Internet to learn about mealtime etiquette in another culture. Find out about serving and eating customs, polite behavior, and any other details that a traveler would need to know. Share your findings with the class.

2. **Math.** Using the standard 15 percent rate, calculate the tip for family meals costing $22.45, $28.50, and $54.95. Round up to the nearest five cents.

Managing Your Life

Planning Family Meals

Does your family tend to eat on the run? Do busy schedules often get in the way of family meals? Arrange to meet with family members to discuss the idea of making mealtimes more special. Talk about ways you can adjust your schedules so that you can eat together as a family as often as possible. Also discuss ideas for improving the mealtime atmosphere. Perhaps you could take turns designing table settings with creative touches. Make a plan for one week. After you carry out your plan, meet again to evaluate how well it worked and make any necessary changes.

Using Technology

1. **Presentation Software.** Use appropriate software to prepare a presentation that gives guidelines for restaurant etiquette. Include advice about how to order, how to get the server's attention, how to calculate the tip, and so on.

2. **Photography.** Create and photograph several table settings that use different special touches to make them look attractive. Present your photos to the class. Explain what you were trying to achieve with each setting. Ask classmates to critique your efforts.

Career Options
Hospitality and Tourism

*I*t's the people who work in the hospitality and tourism industry who provide the services people use when they eat out, take a vacation, go on a business trip, or enjoy a ball game. Hospitality and tourism offer career opportunities for people of all levels of education and experience. This career cluster can be divided into three broad sectors: Food and Entertainment; Lodging; and Travel and Tourism. For most occupations in this cluster, employment opportunities are holding steady.

Main Employers

- Hotels
- Resorts
- Restaurants
- Airlines
- Cruise lines
- Theme parks
- Sports arenas
- Tour operators
- Convention centers

Hospitality and Tourism Job Opportunities

Industry Segment	Entry Level	Additional Education and/or Training	Advanced Education and/or Training
Food and Entertainment	▪ Kitchen Assistant ▪ Waiter/Waitress ▪ Food Preparation Worker ▪ Short-Order Cook ▪ Host/Hostess	▪ Chef ▪ Baker ▪ Dining Room Manager ▪ Social Director	▪ Food and Beverage Manager ▪ Executive Chef ▪ Catering Manager
Lodging	▪ Bellperson ▪ Front Desk Clerk ▪ Maid ▪ Laundry Worker ▪ Gift Shop Clerk	▪ Concierge ▪ Assistant Housekeeper ▪ Bell Captain ▪ Reservations Manager	▪ Executive Housekeeper ▪ Front Office Manager ▪ Hotel Manager
Travel and Tourism	▪ Taxi Driver ▪ Lifeguard ▪ Theme Park Worker ▪ Cruise Ship Worker	▪ Flight Attendant ▪ Travel Agent ▪ Ticket Agent ▪ Tour Guide	▪ Convention and Visitor Bureau Manager ▪ Cruise Director ▪ Recreation Director ▪ Tour Director

CAREER PATHS

Jim Mackie, **ASSISTANT CHEF**

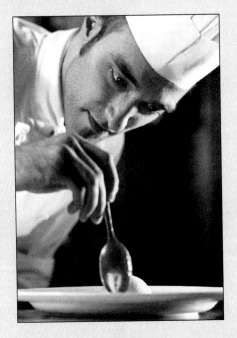

My parents love to cook, and when I was a small child I used to help them. By the time I was a teen, I was inventing some pretty awesome recipes. I set owning my own restaurant as my career goal.

After high school, I got a job in a local restaurant as a kitchen assistant. I helped prepare vegetables, make salads, and so on. It was fun to learn about what goes on behind the scenes. I also realized how much I *didn't* know about cooking, despite all those years I spent cooking with my parents.

To gain more experience and knowledge, I enrolled in two-year program at a culinary school. Classes included cooking techniques, nutrition, food costs, sanitation, and so on. As part of the program, I worked in some local restaurants to practice my new skills. My part-time job as a waiter helped me see things from the customer's point of view.

When I graduated, I was offered this job as an assistant chef. The restaurant has a great reputation. I'll probably be an assistant chef for five or six years, working at two or three different restaurants during that time. I'll learn how different chefs do their work and run their businesses. I'm still working toward saving enough money and gaining enough experience to start my own restaurant.

Check It *Out!*

Choose three hospitality and tourism occupations that interest you. Use print or online resources to find out about the working environment, conditions, and hours. Summarize your findings in a brief report.

589

UNIT 9

Clothing and Fashion Choices

CHAPTER 41

Creating Your Look

Key Terms

- status
- dress code
- wardrobe
- clothing inventory
- accessories

Objectives

- **Analyze** influences on clothing choices.
- **Interpret** appropriate dress for specific roles and occasions.
- **Discuss** management of family clothing needs across the life span.
- **Explain** factors to consider when evaluating your wardrobe.
- **Propose** options for recycling unwanted clothes and expanding your wardrobe.

592

QUICK WRITE

What do clothes mean to you? What messages can they send? What can they symbolize? Write a brief essay summarizing your thoughts.

Charlene called Rana over to look at the computer screen. "Isn't this cute?" said Charlene, pointing to a sweater on a popular retailer's Web site. "I think I'm going to order it."

"Hmm," thought Rana. The sweater had swirls of bright colors. It certainly wasn't something she would wear herself, but it did look like her friend's style. Rana and Charlene had a lot in common, yet they always respected each other's right to be different, too. That's one reason the two teens were such good friends.

The Impact of Clothing

What clothes are you wearing right now? Why did you choose them today? You may have spent a lot of time deciding what to wear, or you may have made your choice almost automatically. Either way, whether you realize it or not, there's more to clothing than what you see in the mirror.

Clothing plays many roles in your life—physical, emotional, and social. Physically, clothes are a basic need because they enhance comfort and safety. If that were clothing's only role, however, there wouldn't be so much variety in what people choose to wear. As you will see, clothing choices are influenced by emotional and social factors as well. In turn, the clothes you wear can influence how you feel about yourself, how others see you, and how you relate to others. See Fig. 41-1.

Fig. 41-1. *The way you feel about yourself may be reflected in the clothes you choose.* How might your clothes affect how you feel?

Dressing for Comfort and Protection

Before you get dressed each morning, do you check the weather report? Would you pack differently for a vacation at the beach than for a ski trip? Dressing appropriately for the climate and weather is essential for not only your comfort but also your health. That's especially true if you'll be outdoors. In hot weather, loose-fitting, loosely woven clothes help your body to cool itself by letting perspiration evaporate. In cold weather, protect yourself with layers of warm garments, a head covering, and gloves or mittens.

People also choose clothes for comfort and safety based on their activities. Some activities, such as many sports and certain jobs, require special safety apparel. Whether it's steel-toed shoes, safety glasses, or a hockey helmet, be sure to wear the appropriate items for your own protection. See Fig. 41-2.

Dressing to Express Yourself

The clothes you choose can express your personality, interests, and values. You may know people who combine colors and styles in unique ways as an expression of their creative, independent attitude. A sports fan wearing a baseball cap with a team logo demonstrates a personal interest. The same is true of pet lovers who own sweatshirts with dog or cat designs. Wearing a T-shirt promoting a charity event can tell others that you value that cause.

Clothes can reflect pride in cultural heritage, too. Thomas occasionally wears garments made of kente, a traditional African fabric. Alisa has made several skirts with print fabric from her native country, Honduras.

Clothing choices sometimes reveal how you feel about yourself. If you're unhappy, tired, or your self-esteem is low, you might not care much about the way you look. Other people might be able to guess your mood by looking at your appearance. On the other hand, certain clothing choices might send a signal that you're feeling cheerful and confident.

Some people use clothes as a way to communicate their **status**, or position in their peer group or in society. They feel it's important to wear expensive clothes with the "right" brand names to impress others. Their real purpose, however, may be to boost their own image of themselves. While there's no harm in wearing expensive brands if you can afford them, your clothes are not a good foundation on which to base your self-esteem.

When looking at clothing as an insight to personality or status, remember that it's only a clue at best. Judging people on the basis of their clothes alone is unfair and often inaccurate.

Dressing to Meet Expectations

When choosing what to wear, most people consider not only their own preferences but also expectations about what is considered customary and appropriate. These expectations vary depending on:

- **Societal standards and trends.** In any given society, there are certain unwritten rules about appropriate clothing. These ideas can change over time. Prior to the early 20th century, in America and other Western societies it was considered improper for women to wear pants. Today, pants are commonly worn by both men and women. More subtle changes in fashion trends occur from year to year, influencing what people wear.

- **Culture.** Clothing customs, like other aspects of society, vary in different cultures. Many people around the globe have adopted American-style dress to some extent, especially for business wear. Still, every culture retains unique, traditional clothing styles.

- **The situation or occasion.** Dressing appropriately for an event can make you feel confident and at ease. What if a teen went to his first homecoming dance wearing a suit and tie while the other guys wore khaki pants and sweaters? What if his date wore a sweater and skirt while the other girls wore long dresses? There's a good chance the teens would feel awkward all evening. It's not that one outfit is right and one is wrong for such an occasion.

What matters is the tradition that has been established. If you're not sure what's appropriate for a specific occasion, ask someone who is likely to know.

- **Roles.** Whether a particular outfit is considered appropriate also depends on the person's role. The president of a company might wear business suits to enhance her professional image. Although she could perform her job in jeans, her colleagues and clients might consider casual clothing inappropriate for her role. On the other hand, for a warehouse worker in the same company, jeans might be expected work attire.

- **Group identity.** Clothes can identify people as belonging to a certain group. Military uniforms are an obvious example, but there are also more subtle ones. Your

---

TIPS FOR *Success*

Dressing for Special Occasions

Not sure how to dress for the occasion? Here are some guidelines:

- It's customary to dress up for ceremonies such as graduations and weddings. The attire is often more formal for evening weddings than those held earlier in the day.

- Clothing appropriate for religious services varies considerably. When you plan to attend an unfamiliar service, ask about appropriate clothes ahead of time.

- Funeral customs also vary. In general, wearing conservative clothes in subdued colors shows respect.

peer group has adopted certain clothing styles that are seldom worn by people in your grandparents' generation. People use clothing to express membership in social groups of all kinds, positive and negative. Can you think of some examples?

Dress Codes ~ Most expectations about what to wear are not formal rules, but simply traditions passed on by example. However, it's likely that at some time in your life you'll be required to follow an official **dress code**, a set of rules describing required or appropriate clothing. Many schools and workplaces use dress codes to promote a desired atmosphere. See Fig. 41-3.

A dress code may specifically describe what should be worn. For example, an upscale restaurant might require its servers to wear black pants and crisp, white shirts with collars and long sleeves. In other cases, dress codes describe what *not* to wear. A school might outlaw shirts with inappropriate slogans or images, tank tops, and clothes that reveal too much. In addition to a dress code, rules may be set about other aspects of appearance. Employees might be required to shave facial hair, cover tattoos, and remove certain jewelry as a condition of employment.

You might not always see the need for a dress code or agree with its rules. However, as a student or employee, it's your responsibility to follow any dress code that's been set. In the long run, adapting to a dress code is usually less trouble than arguing about it or violating it.

Fig. 41-3. Some school dress codes require students to wear uniforms. What are some advantages of this approach?

Fig. 41-4. For a job interview, dress neatly and conservatively. You want the interviewer to remember you for your skills, not your inappropriate clothes.

How Others See You

Why should you pay attention to other people's expectations about clothing? Choosing appropriate clothes can help you make a good first impression. In a job interview, for example, dressing too casually or sloppily can decrease your chances of being hired. The interviewer may think that you aren't really interested in the job or doubt that you could project the right image when representing the company. See Fig. 41-4.

Dressing appropriately is also a good idea with people whom you already know. Toby likes to wear fashions that are, to say the least, unconventional. But at the party for his great-aunt's 80th birthday, Toby dressed conservatively—he even wore a tie. He explained the change this way: "I knew Aunt Jessie would be offended if I dressed the way I usually do. To me, it wasn't worth upsetting the people I care about just to wear certain clothes for a few hours. *I* decide how I dress, and I chose to wear something to make Aunt

Jessie happy. In the end, it's not so much what you wear as why you wear it."

Resolving Clothing Conflicts

When it comes to clothes, it's not always possible to please both yourself and others. Sometimes your desire for self-expression clashes with the expectations of others. Conflicts between teens and adults over clothing choices are nothing new. Many adults can look back to their teen years and remember wearing styles that their parents didn't like.

As you approach adulthood, you have a greater say in deciding what clothes to buy and wear, especially if you pay for them yourself. At the same time, however, your growing maturity means that you're better able to understand other points of view and recognize when a compromise is called for. Respecting parents' viewpoints about clothes can pave the way for a relationship that's more harmonious in other ways.

TEXTLINK≈

You may want to review the *conflict resolution* strategies explained in Chapter 18.

Clothing conflicts can also arise when your values differ from those of your friends. What if a group of your friends is dressing in a way that makes you feel uncomfortable? What if following a new fashion trend means buying clothes that you think are inappropriate, ugly, or overpriced? Some teens are so determined to become part of a certain crowd that they lose sight of who they are and what is important to them and their families. If you feel such pressure, ask yourself whether inclusion in a group is worth putting aside your beliefs and standards. With clothing, as with all choices, make a point of establishing your own priorities and acting on your own values.

Clothing for the Family

The clothing needs of individuals and families change through the life span. Meeting these changing needs requires careful consideration.

Clothing for Special Needs

There are many reasons why a family member might have special clothing needs. A child might have an arm or leg in a cast for a while. Perhaps an older family member uses a scooter to get around. Someone with arthritis may have difficulty with small buttons. Whatever a person's age or disability, he or she wants to look nice, feel comfortable, and be as independent as possible. When choosing clothes for those with limited mobility, keep these guidelines in mind:

- Two-piece outfits are easy to put on and take off. Garments that open in the front or have a large neck opening are helpful.

- Choose clothes that fit loosely enough for comfort but are not baggy. Avoid long, loose clothes that might cause a fall or become tangled in equipment.

- To help prevent falls, select flat shoes with nonslip soles.

- Clothes that must fit over a cast need to be wider. For garments that fit under a brace or cast, select a soft knit.

- If crutches will be used, choose longer shirts. Pockets make it easier to carry items.

- Slippery or smooth fabrics allow for easier transfer to and from a wheelchair or scooter.

Children need clothes that let them move freely during active play and are easy to care for. Clothes that are simple to put on and take off enable children to dress themselves. Children's clothes should also be free of hazards such as drawstrings that could get caught on playground equipment and cause an accident. Because children grow quickly, their clothing must be replaced frequently.

For adults, clothing needs vary depending on the types of work they do and their other activities. People of any age who have physical limitations may need clothing with special features for comfort and convenience.

Whatever the family's clothing needs, meeting them is a basic necessity, just like food and shelter. Families must manage their clothing expenses carefully by considering their resources, setting priorities, and establishing a budget.

In most families, the clothing budget is limited and must be shared by everyone. If one person overspends, then the others have to get by with less. You can show responsibility by taking care of the clothes you already have, by keeping your spending within agreed-upon limits, and by making wise clothing purchases. Even if you have your own money to spend on clothes, good management will leave more money in your pocket to spend another day or to put into savings.

Evaluating Your Wardrobe

Do you know anyone who has a closet full of great clothes, yet complains about having nothing to wear? The most likely explanation is that the person's **wardrobe**, or collection of clothes, doesn't meet his or her needs and wants. Taking the time to evaluate your wardrobe can help prevent this dilemma.

Fig. 41-5. It's easy to buy clothes on impulse and spend too much. When you see something you like, ask yourself, "Do I really need this?"

Assessing Needs and Wants

Part of good management is knowing the difference between your needs and wants. Clothing needs are those basic garments required for your daily routine—clothes for school, work, and activities. Wants are more likely to be based on emotions. You may *need* a certain number of pairs of pants to get you through the week. You may *want* pants in your favorite color or in step with the hottest trend. You will probably be most happy if your wardrobe reflects some of your wants as well as your needs. Remember, however, that needs come first. See Fig. 41-5.

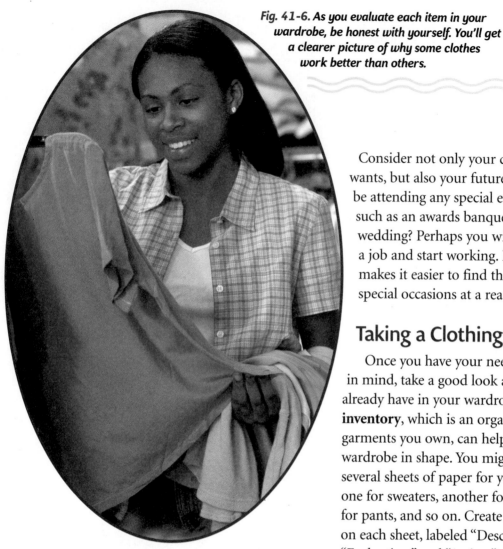

Fig. 41-6. As you evaluate each item in your wardrobe, be honest with yourself. You'll get a clearer picture of why some clothes work better than others.

Consider not only your current needs and wants, but also your future plans. Will you be attending any special events this year, such as an awards banquet or a relative's wedding? Perhaps you will interview for a job and start working. Planning ahead makes it easier to find the right outfit for special occasions at a reasonable price.

Taking a Clothing Inventory

Once you have your needs and wants in mind, take a good look at what you already have in your wardrobe. A **clothing inventory**, which is an organized list of the garments you own, can help you get your wardrobe in shape. You might want to use several sheets of paper for your inventory—one for sweaters, another for shirts, another for pants, and so on. Create three columns on each sheet, labeled "Description," "Evaluation," and "Action."

To start your inventory, pull out and examine one item at a time. On the appropriate sheet, jot down a brief description of the item, such as "brown corduroy."

In the next column, evaluate the item. You probably have favorite clothes that get worn again and again. There are many possible reasons why other items are seldom or never worn. Perhaps they're stained, wrinkled, or need repair. Some may be too tight, too loose, or too scratchy. Maybe you just don't like the way they look. Under "Evaluation," write down pros and cons of each item. See Fig. 41-6.

To identify your clothing needs, think about your daily life. Where do you go? What do you do? The types of clothes that you wear most often should make up most of your wardrobe. Mario, for example, goes to school and church and helps his brother with his lawn care business. He sings in the concert choir at school and likes to go hiking with friends on the weekends. Since jeans and other casual clothes work well for most of Mario's activities, they make up most of his wardrobe. However, Mario also has several dressier outfits for church and school concerts.

Finally, decide on your action plan for the item. Make your decision based on your evaluation of the garment.

- If the item is in good condition, you like it, and you wear it often, write "Keep" as your action plan.
- If the item isn't in good condition, decide whether the problem can be fixed. If so, jot down what repair is needed. Set a goal for completing it. Check off each repair as it's done.
- If the item doesn't fit, you don't like it, or you haven't worn it in a year or more, consider whether it can be redesigned. As you'll read later, there are many ways to give clothes a makeover.
- If the item can't be repaired or redesigned, write "Recycle" as your action plan and set the garment aside. Clearing out items that just aren't right for you will make room for pieces that work better.

Recycling Unwanted Clothes

What can you do with the clothes you no longer want? Although they don't belong in your wardrobe anymore, they may still be useful to you or someone else. Here are a few options:

- **Sell clothes** that are in good condition at a yard sale or consignment shop.
- **Give away clothes** to friends or relatives, or donate them to charity. Before you do, check the items over carefully to make sure they're clean and in good shape. See Fig. 41-7.
- **Reuse fabric** for sewing projects or other uses. You might use denim from old jeans to sew accessories for your room. Fabric squares in various colors and patterns can be made into a bright patchwork quilt. Worn-out clothes made of soft and absorbent fabric can be cut up to make cleaning cloths.

Fig. 41-7. If you and a friend both have clothes you no longer want, perhaps you can make a trade. Who else might want your old clothes?

Expanding Your Wardrobe

When you've completed your clothing inventory, take a look at what's left. How well does your collection of clothes fit the needs and wants you identified earlier? If you're like most people, you'll discover some gaps in your wardrobe.

Clothes are expensive, so it's likely that you won't be able to buy everything that you need right away. Fortunately, there are resources besides money that can help. Time, skills, creativity, friends and family members—even the clothes you already own—all can be resources for expanding your wardrobe.

Making New Combinations

If you feel like you keep wearing the same outfits over and over, perhaps you don't need more clothes—just more creativity in using the clothes you have. Experiment with new looks by mixing and matching different items. Combining clothes in new ways gives you a greater variety of outfits to choose from. This creates the illusion that your wardrobe is larger than it really is.

Using Accessories

Another way to give a new look to clothes you already own is with accessories. **Accessories** include items that enhance an outfit, such as belts, ties, scarves, hats, and jewelry. By adding, removing, or changing accessories, you can give an outfit a different look. For example, a tie or scarf could give everyday clothes a dressier look for work or a special event.

Fig. 41-8. Tie-dying is a fun way to add color and design to a shirt. *What creative ideas might you like to try?*

FINDING CREATIVE SOLUTIONS

Asking "Why?"

Before you can find a creative solution, you have to identify the roots of your problem. One technique for doing that is simple, but powerful—just ask "Why?"

How It Works

Start by writing down the situation that you're having trouble with—for example, "I'm having a hard time in math" or "I'm always running out of money by the weekend." Then ask yourself, "Why?" List all the reasons that you can. The idea isn't to assign blame, but to analyze the situation honestly. Next, go back to each of the reasons you wrote down and ask "Why?" again. You might want to draw a diagram with reasons splitting off from reasons, like the branches of a tree. Take the process as far as you can. Once you've identified the specific factors that are contributing to your problem, you're more likely to find solutions that will really work.

Try It Out

Matthew felt like he never had anything to wear. Before going shopping for more clothes, he decided to try making a "why" diagram. First he wrote down, "I have a hard time finding anything to wear in the morning. Why?" He thought of two answers: "Sometimes the things I pull out of the closet aren't in good shape" and "Sometimes I pull out something that's fine, but I can't find anything to wear with it."

▶ **Your Turn** *Finish Matthew's diagram. For every branch, ask "Why?" and try to come up with at least two possible answers. See how far you can break down the problem. What solutions can you think of?*

Redesigning Clothes

An effective and inexpensive way to expand your wardrobe is by redesigning older clothes. They might be from your own closet, hand-me-downs from a relative, or something you bought at a garage sale or thrift store. With creativity and a few supplies, you can convert old jeans, shirts, or jackets into truly unique garments.

Fabric and craft stores sell many products that can be used to embellish clothes. You can find various types of decorative buttons, beads, trims, and iron-on and sew-on appliqués. Fabric paints and dyes can add color or design to a garment. Before using an unfamiliar product on your clothes, always practice the technique on a scrap of fabric. See Fig. 41-8.

With basic sewing skills, you can redesign clothes you might not wear otherwise. You might turn jeans into shorts. If a garment is too loose or too long to be in style, it can be taken in or hemmed. If you don't know how to sew, find someone willing to help you learn.

Sewing New Clothes

Sewing skills can be used not only to update older outfits but to create new garments as well. Many teens and adults find that sewing is an enjoyable hobby. It allows you to create one-of-a-kind garments using your choice of patterns and fabrics. In some cases, sewing your own clothes costs less than buying them. Even when it doesn't, you can get better quality and fit. Chapter 45 focuses on basic sewing skills.

Trading and Sharing Clothes

Trading clothes with a sibling or friend is a no-cost way to expand your wardrobe. If you have clothes that are in good condition but that you seldom wear, perhaps you could offer them in exchange for a friend's unwanted item that you would really like. When trading with a friend, get parental approval first. A parent who paid for a leather coat might not think that exchanging it for a college sweatshirt is a fair trade.

Borrowing clothes can also be successful under the right circumstances. If you were invited to a "tropical island" theme party, you might ask to borrow a Hawaiian shirt from a family member. Many teens enjoy borrowing clothes from their friends. For some families this is an acceptable practice; for others it is not. Talk to your family and friends to make sure you understand what items are acceptable to borrow and for how long.

Renting Clothes

Clothes for special occasions—including costumes, uniforms, tuxedos, and sometimes formal gowns—are available from rental shops. Renting is a good option if the item will be worn only once or on rare occasions and would be expensive to buy.

Buying Clothes

The options already discussed can help reduce your need to buy new clothes. Still, after reviewing your clothing inventory and considering your options, you may decide to purchase some items.

Before you start shopping, make a plan for what you want to buy. Set priorities, ranking the garments that you need by importance. A shirt for your school uniform might rank #1 because you need it right now and would wear it often. A swimsuit that you wouldn't be wearing for months would have a lower priority.

Character IN ACTION

Respecting Others' Property If you borrow a garment, be sure to return it promptly and in good condition. It should be clean and free of any damage. Treating borrowed clothes even more carefully than your own shows respect and builds trust. Remember, too, that relationships involve both give and take. Try to reciprocate when the lender asks to borrow from you. Write a "Clothes Contract" to use the next time you borrow clothes.

You'll learn strategies for *shopping for clothes* in Chapter 43.

Suppose you know that you need two or three pairs of pants to replace ones that you've outgrown. Instead of just writing "pants" on your shopping list, think about exactly what you'll look for. What styles, colors, and fabrics would most enhance your wardrobe? As you plan, keep these ideas in mind:

- **Versatility.** Some garments are versatile enough to be used for more than one occasion. Perhaps the right outfit could be worn for religious services, graduation, and job interviews.

- **Mixing and matching.** Your wardrobe will go further if items can be mixed and matched with one another. Review your wardrobe inventory. What colors are in the clothes you already have? What items might you wear more often if you had something to go with them? To get the most from your wardrobe additions, plan to shop for items that coordinate with the clothes you already own. See Fig. 41-9.

Remember, you don't want to repeat the mistakes that caused some of your old clothes to end up crumpled in the back of your closet, unworn and unwanted. Take another look at the "Evaluation" column of your wardrobe inventory. If you don't like some of your current clothes, why not? What are the qualities that make other clothes your favorites? In the next chapter, you'll learn about design elements and principles that may help you answer those questions.

Fig. 41-9. *Try building a wardrobe around a few basic colors, like black and red. You'll be able to combine pieces in many different ways.*

Chapter Summary

- You may choose clothes for comfort and protection, to express yourself, or to meet the expectations of others.
- Appropriate clothing helps you make a good first impression.
- Conflicts over clothing choices may arise, but they can be resolved.
- Families must use management skills to meet their changing clothing needs.
- A clothing inventory can help you evaluate how well your current wardrobe meets your needs and wants.
- Look for ways to recycle garments that you no longer want.
- Buying new clothes is not the only way to expand your wardrobe.

Reviewing Key Terms & Ideas

1. Give three examples of choosing clothes for comfort and protection.
2. What is **status**? Explain how it relates to clothing choices.
3. How do societal standards and trends influence clothing choices?
4. How and why might an employer establish a **dress code**?
5. Give at least two examples of ways family members' clothing needs might change over time.
6. What three steps should families take to manage their clothing expenses?
7. What is the benefit of evaluating your **wardrobe**?
8. Describe the information found in a completed **clothing inventory**.
9. What should you consider when deciding whether to keep a garment that you already own?
10. Give an example of how **accessories** can change the look of an outfit.
11. Name three ways, other than buying clothes, to expand your wardrobe.

Thinking Critically

1. **Recognizing Assumptions.** Have you ever made an assumption about someone based on what he or she was wearing? What led you to make the assumption? Did it turn out to be true? Based on your clothes, what assumptions might others make about you? Why?
2. **Analyzing Viewpoints.** Describe an imaginary situation in which a teen and a parent have a conflict over clothing choices. What is the viewpoint of the teen? What is the viewpoint of the parent? How might they resolve their conflict?

Applying Your Knowledge

1. **Analyzing Influences**. Think of a specific outfit you wore in the last week. In writing, analyze the factors that influenced you to choose those clothes. Include factors that relate to the physical, emotional, and social roles of clothing.

2. **Dress for Success**. Imagine you're a finalist for a college scholarship and must give a presentation to the selection committee. Sketch or find a photo of the outfit you would wear. Describe why it would be appropriate for your role and the occasion.

Making Connections

1. **Social Studies**. In many cultures around the world, certain traditional clothing is worn on special occasions. Research and report on one example. On what occasions is it worn? What does the clothing signify or symbolize?

2. **Math**. At the library or online, locate the latest Consumer Expenditures Survey annual report from the Bureau of Labor Statistics. Find the table that lists consumer expenditures by category. For the most recent year shown, what is the average amount spent on apparel and services? Calculate what percentage of total average annual expenditures this represents. Draw conclusions about the impact of clothing expenses on the family budget.

Managing Your Life

Resources for Clothing Decisions

To build a wardrobe that works well for you, you'll need to make creative use of all your other resources. Write an analysis of specific resources you have that can help you dress well for less. Do you have the time and skills to make or redesign clothes? If you don't have the skills, what resources could help you develop them? Do you have a friend or family member who might be willing to share or trade clothes? Identify as many resources as you can. Then decide on three specific steps you will take to make the most of your resources.

Using Technology

1. **Spreadsheet.** Use a spreadsheet program to set up a clothing inventory. Enter several sample garments to show how the inventory spreadsheet would work. What are the advantages and disadvantages of an electronic inventory compared to a handwritten list?

2. **Internet.** Visit a Web site that features clothes that appeal to teens and young adults. Observe the types and styles of clothes featured. Then visit the Web site of a sewing pattern company. How do the clothing styles compare? How useful might sewing skills be as a means of expanding your wardrobe?

CHAPTER | 42

Fashion and Design

Key Terms

- fashion
- style
- target market
- illusion
- hue
- value
- shade
- tint
- intensity
- color schemes
- emphasis
- proportion

Objectives

- **Identify** and describe the main segments of the fashion industry.
- **Analyze** ways the fashion industry influences consumers.
- **Describe** elements and principles of design.
- **Demonstrate** knowledge of color terminology.
- **Choose** flattering clothing by applying the elements and principles of design.

608

Write a short, descriptive essay identifying your favorite color and explaining your choice. How does this color make you feel? How do you incorporate it into your life? Why do you think favorite colors are so individual?

"Look at this old picture of Dad," Nate said to his brother, Shaun. "I can't believe he actually wore that tie. And look at that jacket!"

Shaun replied, "I wouldn't be laughing too hard. Some of the clothes you wore five years ago aren't exactly in style anymore. Back then everybody wore them, but they'd look silly now."

Their father came in, holding something behind his back. "I've been meaning to ask you, Shaun—can I borrow this sometime?" With a teasing grin, he held up one of Shaun's wildly patterned shirts. "It looks a lot like the ones that were popular when I was your age."

Shaun looked at Nate and groaned. "You can have it, Dad. No offense, but I think I'll try for a different look!"

The Role of Fashion

Most people want to be fashionable, but what does that mean? In clothing, **fashion** refers to design characteristics that are popular at a certain point in time. The term "style" is frequently used when discussing fashion. A **style** is a distinctive form of a clothing item. Different styles have characteristics that distinguish them from one another. For instance, polo, rugby, and T-shirt are all *styles* of knit shirts. What pant styles are fashionable today?

What Influences Fashions?

Have you ever wondered where ideas for clothing designs and styles come from? You've probably seen pictures of tall, pencil-thin models on fashion runways. They model the creations of high-fashion designers who present their collections twice a year in cities such as New York, Paris, London, and Tokyo. See Fig. 42-1.

Fig. 42-1. One goal of high-fashion designers is to attract the attention of the media.

Some high-fashion designers specialize in unique, extravagant garments sold mainly to celebrities and others who can afford them. These fashions probably don't resemble the clothes worn by people in your hometown. Other designers create more affordable clothing collections for the general public. Some of these designers are known by name. You've probably seen sections in department stores devoted to a particular designer.

In addition, thousands of anonymous designers are employed by clothing manufacturers. They are responsible for designing most of the clothes you wear. While these designers stay aware of high fashion, they produce their own designs, perhaps incorporating shapes, fabrics, or details that are in step with fashion trends. Some are hired to create *knock-offs*, lower-cost imitations of popular fashion designers' creations.

Viewpoints

Trends and Friends

In a group of friends, are clothing trends ties that bind, or chains that confine? The answer to that question probably depends more on the friends than on the clothing.

Jared: My friends and I try to stay on top of fashion trends, and we like to wear the same styles. It's not just a case of going along with the crowd. Wearing the same styles and brands is one way of hanging together. It's like teammates who wear the same uniform, except with more room for your own personal taste.

Lindy: I could never wear something just because my friends do. I choose clothes that I feel good in and that express my personality. If that happens to be what my friends are wearing, fine. If not, no problem. Differences like that keep friendships interesting. We would bore each other if we all had the same tastes.

Seeing Both Sides ~ Do you view your own fashion choices mainly as a way to fit in or as a way to express individuality? Can the same clothing accomplish both goals? Explain.

Whatever they create, designers must pay attention to their **target market**, the consumers they plan to appeal to with their products. Successful designers keep in touch with lifestyle trends. Their designs may be inspired by popular movies, television shows, magazines, news events, travel, art exhibits, or ethnic or historical clothing.

The Fashion Industry

Designers are not the only people involved in creating clothing. The clothes you buy from the racks of your favorite stores are available only because of the coordinated efforts of many people. They, and the companies they work for, make up the fashion industry. See Fig. 42-2.

The fashion industry consists of four segments:

- **The textile industry.** This segment produces the fibers and fabrics that clothes are made from. Textile companies' fabric designers work on new fabrics a year or two before they appear in stores.

- **The apparel industry.** Apparel manufacturers employ designers to produce their brand's "look" for the season. The manufacturers then buy the fabric and mass produce their clothing collections. The apparel industry is sometimes known as the *rag trade* or *garment industry.*

- **Fashion merchandising.** This segment of the fashion industry sells apparel and accessories to consumers. Many types of retailers sell clothing, from department stores to catalog and Internet merchants. Some workers decide what fashions to offer for sale; others keep track of merchandise or assist customers.

- **Fashion promotion.** Experts in fashion promotion use ads and publicity photos to

Fig. 42-2. The textile industry turns fibers into fabrics. How might it influence the apparel industry?

influence consumers as a group. They may work for companies such as trade publications, ad agencies, and public relations firms.

The Influence of the Fashion Industry

How does the fashion industry affect you personally? For one thing, you are limited by what manufacturers decide to produce. Some years, for instance, it might be difficult to find a long, dark green cardigan sweater. Most sweaters that year might be short pullovers in pastel colors.

The designer system affects people economically and socially, too. Millions of consumers are willing to pay more because of a popular designer's name on their clothes. Manufacturers play on this desire for status by placing brand logos in visible places on clothes and accessories.

The fashion industry can also affect your image of yourself. By using models with certain physical characteristics, advertisers send the message that these features are the most desirable. While similar messages are found in other types of advertising, they are most powerful in the fashion industry because appearance is the main reason for buying clothing. Let your own values, rather than ads, influence your fashion decisions.

Elements of Design

Deciding what to buy and which clothes to wear together are some of the most common clothing decisions that you make. Smart choices aren't purely good luck. You can use the same basic elements of design that designers depend on to make their choices. If you study almost any garment carefully, you can pick out these elements: line, shape, space, texture, and color.

Line

The stripes on a sweater, a scoop neckline on a T-shirt, and the seams on jeans are examples of *line*. See Fig. 42-3.

As you look at a line, your eye tends to follow its direction: vertically, horizontally, or diagonally. A vertical line leads your eye up and down, giving a sense of strength. Horizontal lines lead your eye from side to side. They create a feeling of restfulness. Diagonal lines give the opposite effect, suggesting excitement and movement. The more slanted the line, the more excitement is created.

Lines may be straight, curved, or zigzag. Straight lines suggest a crisp, more formal look, while curved lines create a softer effect. With zigzag lines, the eye must keep changing direction, resulting in a feeling of drama.

Lines and Illusion ~ Designers often use line as a way to create an **illusion**, an image that fools the eye. They can de-emphasize or camouflage certain features of a person's figure by leading the eye in a specific direction.

Fig. 42-3. Lines can be created by the pattern of the fabric or the way the garment is constructed. What effect is created by the lines in this garment?

- **Vertical lines.** An unbroken vertical line can be used to give the illusion of more height and less width. However, vertical lines spaced far apart give the illusion of added width instead.

- **Horizontal lines.** Lines going across lead the eye from side to side, creating an illusion of width. However, when the stripes are far apart, the eye moves up and down instead.

Shape

The outline of a garment defines its *shape*, a second element of design. Most clothing can be categorized as having one of four basic shapes: natural, tubular, bell, or full. The shape of a garment can affect how the wearer looks. See Fig. 42-4.

Four Basic Clothing Shapes

Natural. Follows the body's outline. Emphasizes the natural waistline.

Tubular. Rectangular with no waistline. Vertical lines are dominant. Can make the wearer appear taller and slimmer.

Bell. Combines vertical and horizontal lines. Can add contours and make the wearer appear shorter.

Full. Has more horizontal and curved lines than the other shapes. Makes the body look larger.

Fig. 42-4. Learning to recognize basic clothing shapes can help you choose outfits that look good on you.

There may be more than one shape within a single garment. For example, in pants with flared legs, the top part of each leg is tubular and the flared bottom has a bell shape.

Garment shapes are influenced by fashion trends. If designers are emphasizing the tubular shape this season, consumers who look best in one of the other shapes may find shopping a challenge.

Space

Another element of design, *space*, refers to the area within the outline of a garment or outfit. Space can be divided by seams, buttons, pockets, decorative trim, or accessories. See Fig. 42-5.

Picture a simple black dress with a high neckline and no waistband. Now picture the same dress with large patch pockets and a contrasting belt. These features would divide the space of the dress into several distinct

areas, resulting in a different look. How would space be perceived when navy pants are worn with a white shirt versus when they are worn with a navy turtleneck?

Texture

Texture, the way a fabric looks and feels, is another element of design. Certain textures are associated with specific types of clothing. Casual wear often uses fabrics such as denim, corduroy, and bulky wools. These fabrics have textures very different from the smooth finish of a formal gown or tux. What type of fabric textures would you expect to find in biking or ski clothes? How do the functions of these garments affect texture choice?

Just as designers use line to create illusions, they can also use fabric textures. In general, nubby and bulky fabrics make a person look larger. Fabrics with a dull finish, such as denim and flannel, usually make the figure look smaller. Fabrics that shine draw attention.

Color

Of the five design elements, people usually notice color first when they look at a garment. Most people have a favorite color, and it's often one that looks good on them. Kayla loves blue because friends say it matches her eyes. Her friend Marta dresses in vivid colors that complement her coloring. Learning more about color can help you select clothes in colors that suit you and put outfits together in new ways.

Fig. 42-5. The seams, stitching, and pockets on this jacket are examples of how its designer chose to use space. How would the jacket look without these special features?

Understanding Color

Do you know the difference between a "hue" and a "shade"? Learning the terms associated with color will help you understand and discuss fashion color combinations more easily and accurately. These same color concepts and terms are also used in art and interior design.

A **hue** is a specific color that can be identified by name, such as green, red, or blue-violet. A diagram called the *color wheel* can help you understand how different hues are related. Study the color wheel shown in Fig. 42-6 to find the colors described below.

- **Primary colors**—red, yellow, and blue—are the basic colors. All other hues—hundreds of them—come from mixing the primary colors.

- **Secondary colors**—orange, green, and violet—are formed by mixing equal amounts of two primary colors. Orange, for example, is a mixture of red and yellow. It appears on the color wheel halfway between those hues.

- **Intermediate colors**—such as yellow-orange—are a mixture of a primary color and a secondary color.

Colors can be mixed in various amounts, resulting in an almost limitless number of hues. For example, by adding more blue to a blue-yellow mixture, you can create turquoise. Adding more yellow results in a brilliant yellow-green.

Black and white are *neutral colors* that don't appear on the color wheel. However, they can be used to change the **value**—the lightness or darkness—of a hue. Adding black to a hue results in a **shade**, a color

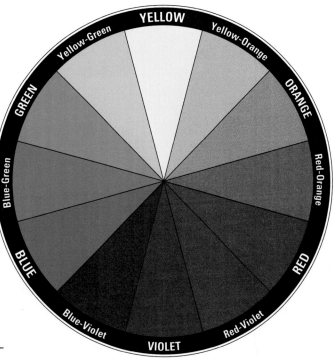

Fig. 42-6. The color wheel shows the relationship between primary, secondary, and intermediate colors.

darker in value. For instance, burgundy is a shade of red. Adding white results in a **tint**, a color lighter in value. Lavender is a tint of violet. Pastel colors are tints.

Intensity is used to describe the brightness or dullness of a color. Neon orange and lime green are bright—they're high in intensity. Navy blue and rust are examples of subdued colors that have low intensity. Intensity can be reduced by adding either gray (a mix of black and white) or the hue directly opposite on the color wheel.

The color wheel can help you choose color combinations that look good together. These combinations are called **color schemes**. Fig. 42-7 on the next page explains common color schemes.

Color Schemes

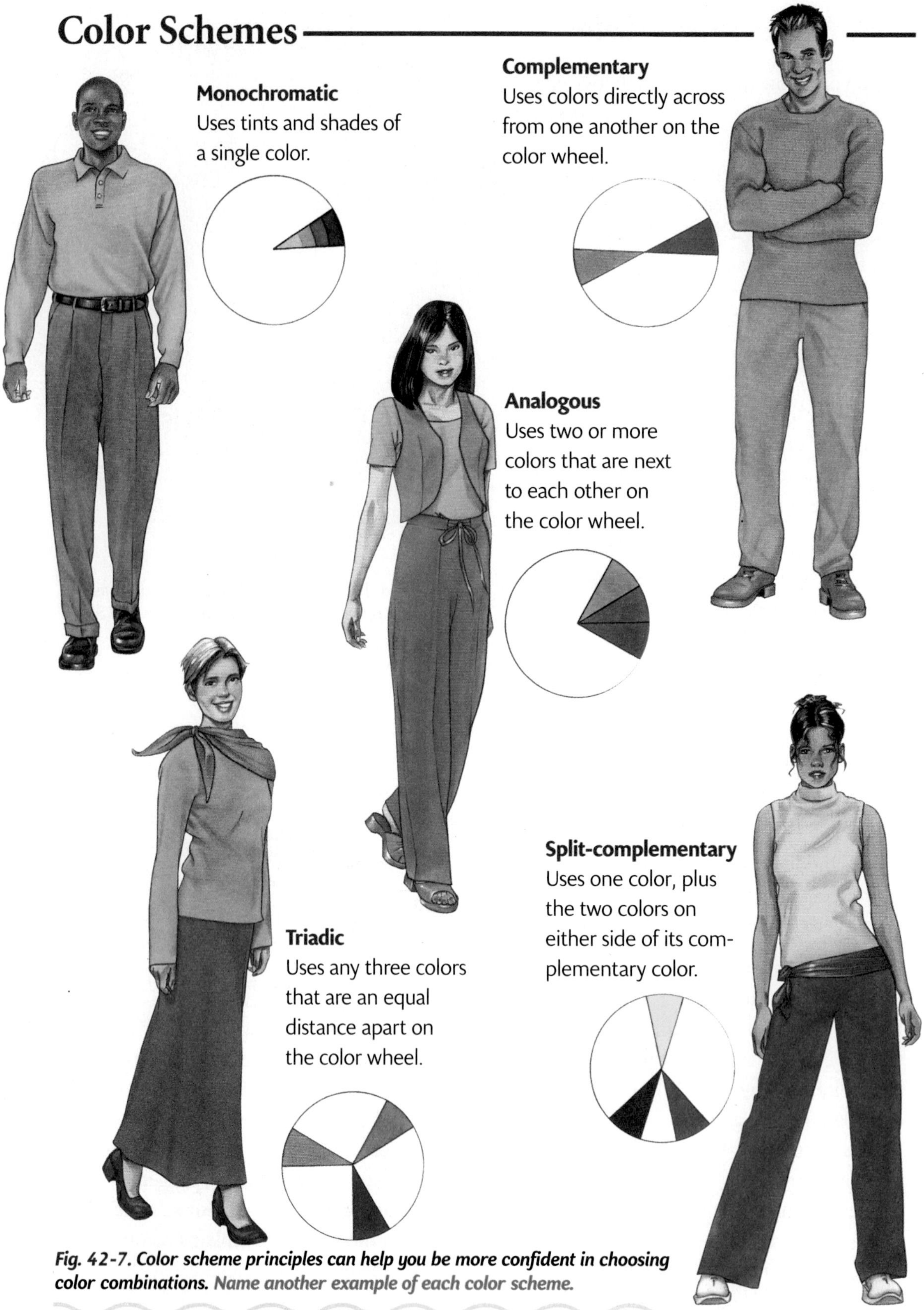

Monochromatic
Uses tints and shades of a single color.

Complementary
Uses colors directly across from one another on the color wheel.

Analogous
Uses two or more colors that are next to each other on the color wheel.

Triadic
Uses any three colors that are an equal distance apart on the color wheel.

Split-complementary
Uses one color, plus the two colors on either side of its complementary color.

Fig. 42-7. Color scheme principles can help you be more confident in choosing color combinations. Name another example of each color scheme.

The Visual Effects of Color

Like the other elements of design, color can be used to create illusions. Leon's aunt often wears black because she says it makes her look slimmer. In general, dark shades or black do make figures appear smaller than light tints or bright colors would.

Colors are often classified as "cool" or "warm" depending on the feelings they suggest. This characteristic can also create illusions. A jacket in a cool color—blue, green, or violet—would look smaller than the same jacket in a warm color—red, yellow, or orange. See Fig. 42-8.

Color can also create illusions. A one-color outfit gives the illusion of added height. Clothing separates with sharp contrasts—either in hue, value, or intensity—might make you look shorter.

TIPS FOR *Success*

Choosing the Best Colors for You

Wearing flattering colors will help you look and feel your best. To determine which colors are top choices for you:

- Stand in front of a mirror in natural daylight. Hold colored paper, fabric, or clothing under your chin. Look at as many colors, shades, and tints as possible. Which ones make you look better?

- Think back to compliments you have received when you wear clothes of certain colors.

- Learn more by reading a book about color analysis or locating a store that offers the service.

Because of the tones in your skin, hair, and eyes, certain colors will look better on you than others. Your best colors will make your complexion look healthier and your eyes sparkle. Less flattering colors can make your face look tired or your eyes appear dull. Check the "Tips for Success" feature above for suggestions that will help you determine which colors look best on you.

Fig. 42-8. Color is a powerful tool for enhancing your looks. Take the time to figure out what colors make you look your best.

Principles of Design

In addition to the elements of design, fashion designers use a set of artistic guidelines called the principles of design. These include emphasis, proportion, balance, and rhythm. Emphasis and proportion are most closely linked with clothing. Paying attention to these principles can help you achieve a wardrobe that helps you look your best.

Fig. 42-9. Emphasis can be used to focus attention where you want it. Here the contrasting shirt and tie draw attention to the face.

Emphasis

As a design principle, **emphasis** is the technique of drawing attention where you want it. When you look at an outfit, there's usually one aspect, called a *focal point*, that catches your eye first. By choosing the right focal point, you can draw attention away from figure traits that you want to minimize and toward areas that you want to highlight. For instance, a contrasting collar draws attention to the face.

When they create garments, designers add emphasis using color, line, texture, design details, and trims. When you're putting an outfit together, you can add emphasis of your own with accessories. A belt in a bright, contrasting hue can draw attention to the waist, for example. See Fig. 42-9.

Proportion

The way one part of a design relates in size to another part and to the whole design is known as **proportion**. Proportion in a suit would be the length of the jacket in relation to the length of the skirt or pants.

Designers know that unequal proportions are the most pleasing to the eye. That's why you would be unlikely to find a ladies' suit with the jacket and skirt measuring exactly the same length. A longer jacket and shorter skirt, or shorter jacket and longer skirt, would be more visually appealing. See Fig. 42-10.

Choose clothing that is in proportion to your own size. If you have a small frame, avoid clothes with overly large features such as pockets and jacket lapels. If your body frame is large, clothes with very small details or accessories would look out of proportion.

Balance and Rhythm

Fashion designers also pay attention to balance and rhythm. *Balance* involves giving equal weight to the spaces on both sides of an imaginary center line. The two sides don't have to be identical for the design to appear balanced. Balance helps create a feeling of stability.

The design principle of *rhythm* carries the eye through a regular pattern of design elements. For instance, on a blazer, the bottom of a pocket might have the same curve as the bottom of the front opening. Sometimes when outfits don't look "right," it's because they lack rhythm. For example, when plaids don't match at a visible seam, the rhythm of the pattern is broken.

The Impact of Design

As you acquire new garments and create outfits with clothing you already own, the elements and principles of design can help you look your best. Using them, you can create subtle illusions that you might not have thought possible. You can have confidence that your design choices will make a good impression on others. A well-chosen outfit can, for example, help you look capable and professional at a job interview.

There may be times when you choose to break some design rules and let your individuality take over. You might put colors or fabrics together that aren't likely

combinations. Experimenting with your creativity can be fun, but remember the elements and principles of design when planning for an important occasion. They are the keys to looking your best.

Fig. 42-10. Notice the effect of the jacket-to-pants proportion in these two examples. *Which is more pleasing? Why?*

Chapter Summary

- The fashion industry is made up of four main segments, all working together.
- The fashion industry has a strong influence on consumers, both individually and as a group.
- The elements of design include line, shape, space, texture, and color.
- The color wheel can help you understand color and choose pleasing color combinations.
- Principles of design include emphasis, proportion, balance, and rhythm.
- Effective use of the elements and principles of design can help you look your best.

Reviewing Key Terms & Ideas

1. Explain the difference between **fashions** and **styles**.
2. Identify the segments of the fashion industry and describe the functions of each.
3. What are some ways in which the fashion industry influences consumers?
4. How can line be used to make a person appear taller?
5. Name and describe the four basic clothing shapes.
6. What types of fabric textures are usually chosen for casual clothes?
7. Explain how **hue**, **value**, and **intensity** are related.
8. Give an example of a color that is a **tint**. How are tints created?
9. If you wanted to appear taller, what color shirt would you wear with blue jeans? Why?
10. What do **color schemes** help you do? Give an example of a complementary color scheme.
11. Explain how you can use **emphasis** to create outfits that look good on you.
12. What is meant by **proportion**? What type of proportion is most pleasing?

Thinking Critically

1. **Analyzing Effects.** How might clothing ads affect the self-concept and self-esteem of those who don't look like the models or wear the trendiest brands?
2. **Analyzing Behavior.** Why do many consumers want to buy new clothes when fashions change, even if the clothes they have could still be worn? How does the fashion industry take advantage of this?
3. **Identifying Alternatives.** If your favorite color was not flattering to you, how could you wear it and still look good?

Applying Your Knowledge

1. **Fashions Through Time.** Each of the four basic clothing shapes has been fashionable during certain periods of history. Using books or Web sites on historic fashion, find examples from four different time periods that clearly show the differences in shape. Create a display, labeling the shapes and dates.

2. **Color Schemes.** Describe and/or illustrate outfits that are good examples of each color scheme described in Fig. 42-7. Base your examples on clothing catalogs or ads, your own wardrobe, or outfits worn by friends and family members.

3. **Critiquing Fashions.** Design principles are not followed at all times. Make a picture collage of fashions that appear to contradict these artistic principles. Point out how they go against the guidelines.

Making Connections

1. **Science.** Using reference materials, prepare a report that briefly explains the relationship between color and light rays. Include these concepts in your report: spectrum, wavelengths, pigments, absorption, and reflection.

2. **Language Arts.** Study the language used by *copywriters* (advertising writers) to create excitement about new fashions. Find three fashion photos in a magazine or catalog and write your own descriptions of the outfits.

Managing Your Life

Making Informed Choices

A good manager uses information as a resource for making decisions—including clothing choices. Use what you have learned about design elements and principles to identify clothing features that would enhance your looks. For example, what garment shapes would look best on you? How might you use the principle of emphasis? Look through catalogs and magazines to find an outfit that incorporates at least three of your ideas. Write a paragraph explaining why the outfit is right for you. Attach a picture, labeling the outfit's flattering features. Before learning about design elements and principles, would you have chosen this outfit? Why or why not?

Using Technology

1. **Internet.** Conduct an Internet search to find articles about fashion trends for the upcoming season. Write a synopsis of what designers want people to be wearing in the next six months. Explain how you located the articles (for example, list key words used in your search).

2. **CAD.** Use a computer-aided design program to create your own fabric and/or fashion design. Share your design with the class.

CHAPTER 43

Shopping for Clothes

Key Terms

- irregulars
- seconds
- markdowns
- vintage clothes
- cost per wearing
- classics
- fads
- care label

Objectives

- **Describe** strategies for finding clothes at reasonable prices.
- **Calculate** the cost per wearing of a garment.
- **Distinguish** between clothing fads and classics.
- **Evaluate** clothes for fit and quality.
- **Give** guidelines for shopping responsibly.

QUICK WRITE

Suppose you have a $100 gift card from a clothing store, and you find a $100 item that appeals to you. Write about how you would decide whether it was worth using the entire gift card on that one item. Why might you keep shopping?

*R*afael likes to shop at trendy clothing stores. He's flattered when people admire his clothes, but he's puzzled because his friend Chet receives even more compliments than he does. Chet is a bargain hunter and often shops without actually buying anything. One time Chet told Rafael that his shirt was one his uncle had worn when he was in high school. Rafael asked his sister why people find Chet's clothes so appealing. What would you say if you joined their conversation?

Some of your beliefs about the best places to shop may actually be untrue. For instance, did you know it sometimes costs *more* to shop at a factory outlet store than at a local department store's sale? Instead of making assumptions about prices based on the type of store, see for yourself. Making a point of comparing clothing prices at different stores near you. You'll soon get to know which ones generally have the best selection and prices.

Managing Clothing Costs

It doesn't take an unlimited clothing budget to look your best. You might be surprised how little some well-dressed people spend on clothes. They use good taste and sharp shopping skills to achieve their own special look. As you'll see, there are many strategies that you and your family can use to help keep clothing costs under control.

Choosing Where to Shop

Trying out a variety of shopping options is one way you can achieve a great wardrobe on a budget. Clothing can be found at many types of stores, including department stores, discount stores, off-price retailers, and factory outlets. See Fig. 43-1.

Fig. 43-1. Clothing stores differ in the selection, prices, and services they offer.

Once you're familiar with prices in your area, you'll be able to recognize bargains when shopping away from home, too.

Here are more tips for choosing a place to shop for clothes:

- In addition to national brands, many department stores offer less expensive "private label" clothes made especially for them. Most have frequent sales, too.

- At discount stores, it pays to check items carefully. Garment quality and condition can vary greatly.

- Off-price retailers offer brand-name and designer merchandise at reduced prices, but they may not have the latest styles.

- At factory outlets, you may find items labeled **irregulars**. This means they have slight imperfections that are generally not noticeable and don't affect use or wear. For example, the color of a sweater might not be the exact shade that the manufacturer intended. Items labeled as **seconds** usually have more noticeable flaws, such as a small hole in the fabric. If you don't mind buying irregulars or seconds, you can save money.

TEXTLINK ≈

See Chapter 30 for more about *types of stores* and their characteristics.

Catalog and Online Shopping ~

Catalogs and online stores are convenient ways to shop for clothes. When comparing prices, remember that shipping charges are usually added. If you return an item, you probably won't get a refund of the shipping charges, and you may have to pay even higher charges for return shipping. Before placing an order, always read the company's return policy. This is especially important with clothes, since you can't try them on before you buy. See Fig. 43-2.

Sales and Markdowns

Paying attention to store sales and being patient waiting for them are two keys to stretching your clothing budget. Cherise's attitude is, "If I see a sweater or something I really want, I just wait for it to go on sale. I love to get a good deal. If someone else buys it before me, I just figure it wasn't meant to be and save that money for something else."

A look at store ads shows that there are many types of sales to help you save on clothing expenses. If you know you will need a new winter coat, you might buy one at a *preseason sale* when coats first arrive in August, or at a Labor Day *holiday sale*. Most stores have *clearance sales* of one season's clothes to make room for the next season's.

Fig. 43-2. Catalogs and Web sites offer expanded options and the convenience of shopping from home. What drawbacks should you keep in mind?

Coupon sales can be excellent times to buy. Look for coupons in the newspaper or your mail.

Most stores offer **markdowns**—permanent price reductions on specific items—year-round. The longer an item takes up space on a store rack, the more it is marked down. For instance, a $35.00 shirt might be marked down to $22.50. Sometimes stores advertise special sales that give customers an additional discount off the markdown price, such as an extra 25 percent off.

Used Clothes

Many people, especially parents with growing children, appreciate finding quality used clothes at bargain prices. Used items have usually had some wear, but "like-new" clothes that haven't been worn can also be found. Sources of preowned clothes include:

- **Consignment stores.** These stores operate by selling others' used clothes, then sharing the profits with the garments' owners. For instance, when Terri's shirt sold for $10.00 at Hannah's Hanger, Terri received $7.00 and the store kept $3.00. Most consignment stores carefully screen merchandise, resulting in relatively high quality.

- **Thrift stores.** Some nonprofit organizations sell donated clothes and other goods to the public through thrift stores. The proceeds of these stores are used for charitable projects.

- **Garage sales, yard sales, and rummage sales.** All of these can be terrific sources of preowned clothes. Some garments may be new with the price tags still attached. However, other clothes may be in poor condition.

- **Vintage clothing stores.** Shops specializing in **vintage clothes**—garments from a previous era, such as the 1930s or the 1970s—can be found in many cities and on the Internet. Vintage clothes can give a unique look to your outfits. Since high-quality vintage items are in demand, some prices may be comparable to new clothes or even higher. However, you might find vintage bargains at thrift stores or yard sales.

Whatever the source of preowned clothes, check them carefully before you buy. Look for stains, tears, and problems such as fading, missing buttons, or broken zippers. If you can make minor repairs yourself, you can get good clothes for less. Remember, though, that preowned items generally can't be returned or exchanged.

The Cost of Care

There's more to clothing costs than the amount marked on the price tag. As long as you own a garment, you'll need to care for it. If the garment can be washed along with other items, the cost of care is minimal—you'll simply toss the item into a load of laundry that you were doing anyway. Washing an item separately might cost just a few dollars a year. The costs of professional dry cleaning, on the other hand, can add up quickly. For example, if you have a wool sweater dry cleaned ten times at $4 per cleaning, then you've paid $40 in addition to the initial price of the sweater. When shopping, look for care instructions on garment labels and consider the impact on your budget. See Fig. 43-3.

Cost Per Wearing

Suppose you buy an outfit for $100 and wear it once. Now suppose you take the same $100 and buy clothes that you're able to wear twenty times. Which is the better buy? Although the cost is the same, the second outfit gives you "more bang for your buck."

This example illustrates the concept of **cost per wearing**—an estimate of how much you actually pay per use. To calculate cost per wearing, divide the total cost of the garment—including any cleaning costs—by the estimated number of wearings. In the example above, the second outfit costs only $5 per wearing ($100 ÷ 20). Of course, the first outfit is $100 per wearing.

Most of the time, you probably won't actually calculate the cost per wearing. Still, it's helpful to keep the principle of cost per wearing in mind. It tells you that:

- Buying a garment that you will wear often, or that will stay in style for many years, is money well spent.

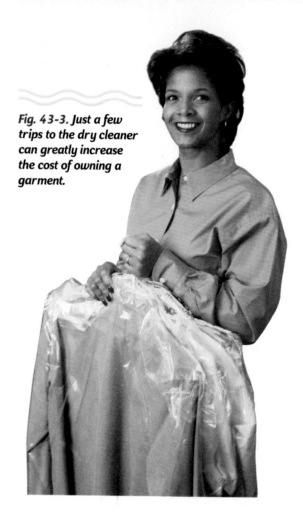

Fig. 43-3. *Just a few trips to the dry cleaner can greatly increase the cost of owning a garment.*

- Quality counts. An item that falls apart the first time you wash it is no bargain. A more expensive item may be a better buy if its higher quality means it will last longer.

Classics and Fads

When thinking about cost per wearing, consider how long a clothing item is likely to remain in style. Some styles are **classics**, styles that stay popular for a long time. Examples of classic styles are blazers, turtleneck sweaters, polo shirts, and traditional blue jeans.

At the other end of the spectrum, **fads** are styles that remain popular for only a short time. Pants with very narrow or very wide legs may appear in stores, then disappear. Certain bright colors and designs sometimes show up for just a single fashion season. Although fads can be fun, the fact that they come and go so quickly increases the cost per wearing. See Fig. 43-4.

Both classics and fads can have a place in your wardrobe. The key is to find ways to be in style without breaking your budget. If purple is hot this season, you might go for a purple T-shirt or socks rather than expensive purple shoes. When you see a new style that you like, try to recognize whether it's a fad and make your buying decisions accordingly.

Fig. 43-4. Fads are distinctive styles with a short life. Would you consider any of these garments a fad? Why or why not?

Evaluating Your Selection

Once you're considering a certain garment, how do you decide whether it would be a smart addition to your wardrobe? Start by reading labels, checking the fit, and checking the quality. Then you'll be able to evaluate the price and reach an informed decision.

Reading Tags and Labels

If you usually just check clothing tags for size and price, take a closer look. The tags and labels attached to clothes contain other valuable information about the garments. *Hangtags*—tags meant to be removed—often

give information such as the brand name, the size, any warranty, and a bar code. In addition, look for one or more sewn-in labels. By law, clothing manufacturers must provide certain information on these labels, including the manufacturer, the country where the item was made, the fiber content, and specific care instructions.

Fiber content is given as the percentage of each fiber by weight. As you'll learn in the next chapter, the fiber content can help you predict how well a garment will wear, whether it will wrinkle easily, and other qualities.

The sewn-in label that includes care instructions is often called a **care label**. It tells you how to keep the garment looking its best. See Fig. 43-5.

If you don't follow the care instructions, you may end up with a shrunken sweater or an entire load of laundry that turns pink. If you aren't willing to hand wash a shirt in cold water and hang it to dry as the label says, or to pay the extra costs that result from a "Dry Clean Only" label, don't buy that garment. Instead, choose one that can be machine washed and dried with similar clothes.

Checking the Fit

Do you skip trying on clothes before buying? A quick trip to the dressing room is time well spent. If a garment doesn't fit right, you probably won't wear it often. That means you will lose money or have to return it. Fig. 43-6 shows how to evaluate whether an item fits well.

Move around in the dressing room when you try a garment on. Sit down, reach up, and bend over. If you can't do any of these things easily—or if the garment sags, pulls, or gaps anywhere—it's not a proper fit. Even

Fig. 43-5. Checking the information on clothing labels and hangtags can help you choose clothes that fit your lifestyle.

when snugly fitting clothes are popular, avoid garments that are *too* tight. Clothes with a little breathing room look better and are more comfortable.

Finding Your Size ~ If you're not sure what size to try on, ask a knowledgeable sales clerk for advice. Clothing for females comes in various size categories, such as juniors, misses, and petites. Each is designed for different body proportions. For males, sizes are often given in measurements. For example, pants labeled 30 × 32 have a 30-inch waist and a 32-inch *inseam* (inside leg length). For both males and females, clothing is also found in letter sizes, such as M (medium) or XL (extra large).

You can't always rely on a certain number or letter as your size. One manufacturer's large may be no bigger than another's medium. In addition, the style of garment can greatly affect the fit.

Catalogs and online clothing sources usually provide detailed information about choosing the correct size based on body measurements. Still, individual garments vary, so be sure to check the return policy.

Checking for a Good Fit

Collar or Neckline. A collar or neckline that is too tight may restrict breathing or cause irritation. Collars that are too large feel uncomfortable.

Chest and Back. A garment should feel comfortable across your chest and back as you walk, sit, bend, and move your arms.

Shoulders. Most sleeves are designed to start at the edge of the shoulder. If too tight, they restrict arm movement.

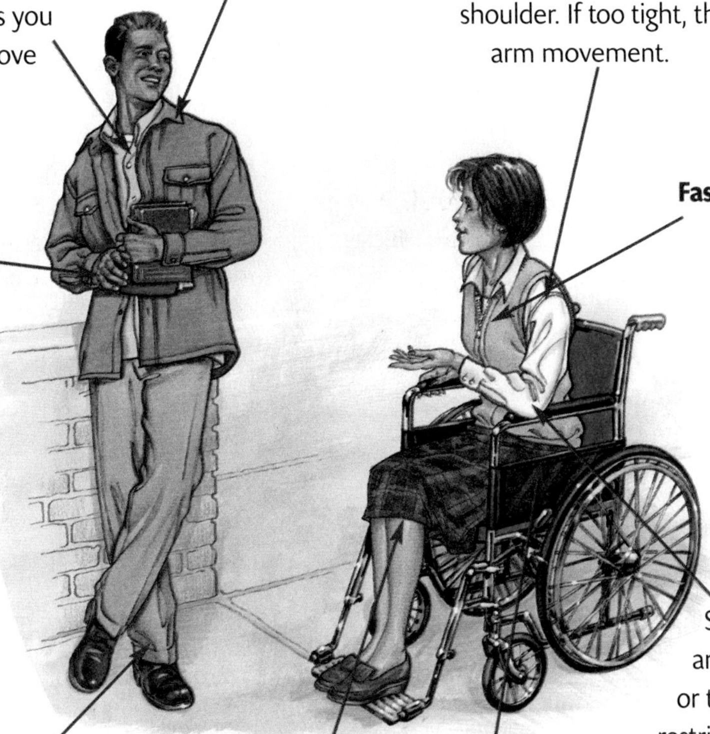

Fasteners. Zippers and buttons should not gap or pull as you move.

Waistband or Waistline. Clothes that are tight in the waist are uncomfortable. You should be able to slip your finger easily inside the waistband. Waistbands should be about 1 inch (2.5 cm) larger than your waist measurement.

Sleeves. Sleeves that are too short or too long can restrict movement or get in the way. Long sleeves should come to your wrists.

Pant Legs. The bottom edge of pant legs should break at the top of your shoes or feet.

Hemline. A garment's length should be appropriate for the item's proportions and its intended use. Garments that are too long or short restrict movement.

Hip Area. Pants and skirts should fit smoothly but allow the wearer to bend and sit comfortably.

Fig. 43-6. When you try on clothes, look for these signs of a good fit. Why should you try on clothes every time?

Checking Quality

Some shoppers are convinced that paying higher prices guarantees that clothes are top quality. That may be true some of the time, but it's definitely not true all of the time. To know whether you're getting your money's worth, you must be able to judge the quality of a garment. Fig. 43-7 shows points to check when judging quality.

Evaluating the Cost

Finally, evaluate the cost of the garment in relation to its quality and fit. Remember to consider the cost of care and the cost per wearing, not just the price tag. Before deciding to buy, ask yourself questions like these:

- How often am I likely to wear it?
- How long is it likely to fit and stay looking nice?
- Is the price appropriate for the level of quality?

- Could I save money by waiting for a sale or buying it elsewhere?
- Could I make it myself for less?
- Is the item worth spending this much of my clothing budget?

Shopping Responsibly

Consumers expect certain things when they shop—clean dressing rooms, friendly and fair treatment from employees, and good value for their money. As a shopper, you have certain responsibilities, too. Here are some rules for being a courteous and responsible shopper:

- Keep clothes clean when trying them on. Stores lose money on soiled merchandise.
- Remove any jewelry that might snag a garment.
- Treat garments as if they were your own. Remove them carefully from hangers. If a zipper or button is difficult to close, try on a larger size.
- Leave the dressing room in good condition. Put clothes back on hangers, and return them to their proper place or to the salesperson.
- If you must return or exchange a purchase, do so as soon as possible so it can be resold before markdowns are made. Take along your sales receipt to show the price of the item.

Character IN ACTION

Honesty in Buying Clothes Have you ever been tempted to buy an outfit, wear it once, and then return it? Some shoppers think this practice is harmless, but that's not true. Garments that show signs of having been worn can't be resold at their original price, so the store loses money. Returning garments isn't fair to other customers, either. When you pay for a new item, you expect to get one that hasn't been worn—and so do your fellow shoppers. What are some honest ways to obtain clothes for a special occasion without breaking your budget?

Evaluating a Garment's Quality

Care information. Check the garment labels for the fiber content and care information. Choose clothes made of easy-care fabrics.

Seams. A *seam* is the line of stitching that joins two pieces of a garment together. Stitching should be straight and smooth and secured at each end.

Wearing qualities. The tighter the knit or weave, the better the garment will hold its shape. Check the fiber content for durable fibers.

Trims. Are any trims (decorations sewn on the garment) attached neatly and smoothly?

Pattern. If the fabric has an evenly spaced pattern, such as a plaid or check, make sure the design is straight and even all around. The pattern should run in the same direction. Do lines match at seams?

Wrinkling. Grasp a handful of fabric, crush it in your hand, and release it. Do the wrinkles stay? If so, the garment is likely to wrinkle easily.

Fasteners. Are zippers sewn neatly, and do they slide smoothly? Button all buttons. Check buttonholes for accurate placement and secure stitching.

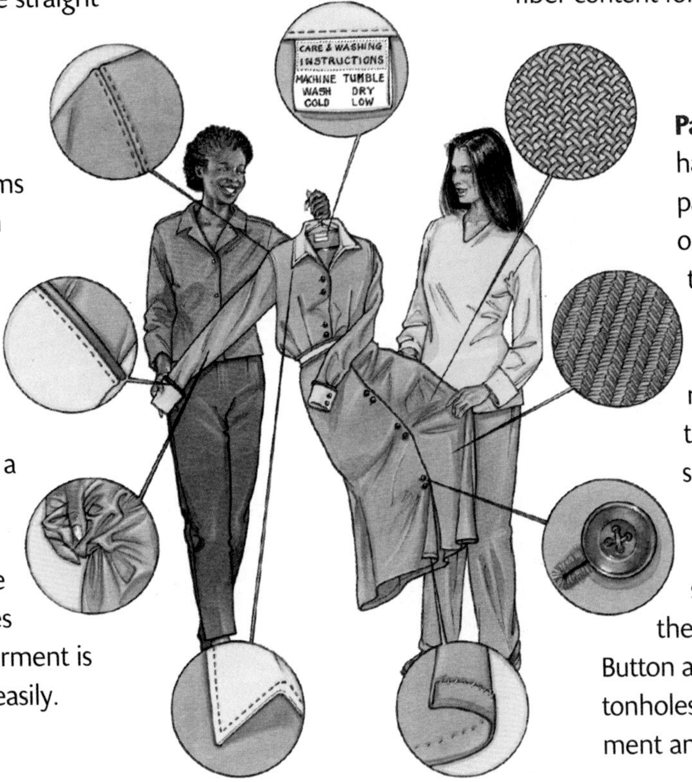

Corners and edges. Are the corners of collars and lapels flat and smooth? Some edges, such as necklines and armholes, often have *facings*. These extra pieces of fabric are sewn to outside edges, then turned to the inside to give a finished edge. Facings should lie flat and be anchored so they don't show.

Hem. The *hem* is the bottom edge of the fabric that is turned to the inside of the garment and sewn in place. Hemmed edges should be smooth. Unless decorative stitching is used, the hem should be invisible from the right side.

Fig. 43-7. To get the most for your money, look for the details that indicate clothes are well made.

Chapter Summary

- You can save money on clothes by choosing an economical place to shop, looking for sales and markdowns, and considering used clothes.
- The cost of care adds to a garment's cost per wearing.
- Recognizing whether styles are classics or fads can help you shop wisely.
- Hangtags and care labels provide useful information.
- Trying on a garment is the only sure way to know whether it fits properly.
- Check for a garment's quality by examining its fabric and construction.
- Evaluate a garment's cost before adding it to your wardrobe.
- You have a responsibility to treat merchandise carefully as you shop.

Reviewing Key Terms & Ideas

1. Assume you live near a department store, a discount store, and an off-price retailer. You want to shop at the one that offers the best selection and prices. How can you tell?
2. What is the difference between **irregulars** and **seconds**?
3. What are **markdowns**?
4. Name three possible sources of used clothes.
5. Would you look for **vintage clothes** at a rummage sale or a department store? Why?
6. How is **cost per wearing** calculated?
7. Would a wise shopper pay more for **classics** than **fads**? Give an example of each.
8. Why do you need to read the **care label** to understand the true cost of a garment?
9. Name five things you can learn about a garment by reading its hangtags and sewn-in labels.
10. Describe three signs that pants fit properly.
11. What quality points should you look for when examining a garment's seams?
12. How can you show responsibility when using a store's dressing room?

Thinking Critically

1. **Recognizing Assumptions.** What assumptions might consumers make about high-priced clothes with designer logos? Do you think these assumptions are justified? Why or why not?
2. **Making Generalizations.** Which general categories in an average teen's wardrobe would you expect to have the highest and lowest cost per wearing? Why?

Applying Your Knowledge

1. **Local Shopping.** Visit three stores in your area that sell clothes. If possible, choose three different types of retailers, such as a discount store, specialty store, and consignment shop. Describe the main differences in the stores and an advantage and disadvantage of each.

2. **Budget-Stretching Strategies.** Imagine you write a newsletter on money-saving tips for families with young children. Write an article suggesting strategies to help stretch clothing budgets.

3. **Evaluating Fit and Quality.** Try on a garment you already own. Evaluate the fit and quality as if it were for sale in a used clothing store. List the good and not-so-good points. How much would you pay for the garment? Why?

Making Connections

1. **Math.** Calculate the cost per wearing of two items of clothing you have purchased recently. Explain how you arrived at the total cost and the estimated number of wearings. Then show how each calculation changes if you wear the garment only half as much as you expect.

2. **Social Studies.** Find information about four clothing fads from history. Describe or sketch the fads and explain when and by whom they were worn. What characteristics do you think made them fads instead of classics?

Managing Your Life

Dressing Well for Less

Good managers know how to make the best use of their resources. That's true in any situation, including shopping for clothes. Use your management skills to devise a workable plan that would allow you to dress well for less. Consider your needs, your resources, and your shopping options. Write a paragraph describing your overall goal, then identify at least four specific actions you can take to reach it.

Using Technology

1. **Internet.** Find three online shopping sites that sell clothes. Compare the sites' features. How detailed are the product descriptions? What information do they provide about fabric content and care? What resources are available to help you find the right size? How do shipping costs and return policies compare? Write an article that summarizes your findings and makes recommendations for consumers.

2. **Web Page.** Create a "Guide to Shopping for Clothes" in Web browser (HTML) format. On the main page, outline the topics you will cover. Provide links to pages on which you give more information about each topic.

Fabrics and Their Care

Objectives

- **Compare** different types of fibers, fabric construction methods, and finishes.
- **Explain** the importance of proper clothing care.
- **Select** appropriate laundry methods.
- **Compare** options for dry cleaning clothes.
- **Describe** how to store clothes properly.

Think of a time when you couldn't wear what you planned because it wasn't clean or was wrinkled or needed repair. Write a brief analysis of what caused the problem. Did you have the skills to prevent it? If not, how could you acquire them?

"Shalonda, this must be the first time you've worn that shirt," said Danielle. She and her friend had bought identical shirts when they shopped together two weeks before. Danielle continued, "Just wait until you wash it! Mine's only been washed and dried once, but it shrank so much, I can't even wear it now!"

Shalonda was puzzled. Then she asked, "You didn't put it in the dryer, did you? I've washed mine twice, but I hung it up to dry and then touched it up with the iron."

Danielle began to realize she had herself to blame for her shrunken shirt. She hadn't read the care label, and had put the new shirt in the washer and dryer with some jeans. Now it was ruined, and she had wasted her money.

Properly cared for, clothes last longer and help you look your best. Taking care of your clothes starts with understanding what they are made of. Knowing the basics about fabrics and their care can also help you make better choices when you sew or shop for clothes.

Fibers and Yarns

The fabric in your clothing starts out as **fibers**, very fine, hairlike strands of various lengths. These fibers are twisted or grouped together to make **yarns**. Unlike knitting yarns, these yarns are usually thread-size. The yarns are then made into fabrics that become clothes, towels, and other textiles. See Fig. 44-1.

Information about fiber content can be found on the sewn-in care label of garments you buy. When you purchase fabric for sewing projects, look for a label at the end of the fabric bolt.

Fig. 44-1. Fibers are twisted together into yarns, which are then made into fabric.

Natural Fibers

The many types of fibers can be grouped into two categories: natural and manufactured. **Natural fibers** come from plants or animals. They include cotton, linen, wool, silk, and ramie. Each natural fiber has its own special characteristics, as shown in the chart below, Fig. 44-2.

In general, natural fibers absorb moisture and allow air to reach your skin. Clothing made from natural fibers is comfortable to wear, keeping you cool in warm weather and warm in cold weather. However, it often requires more care than clothing made from manufactured fibers.

Characteristics of Natural Fibers

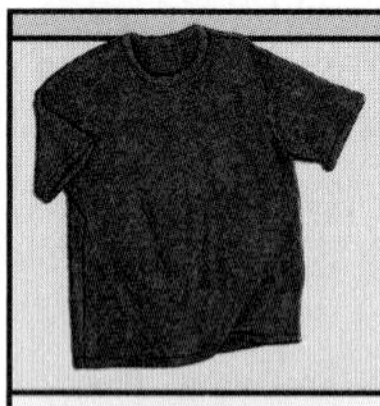	**Cotton.** Comes from the seedpod (or *boll*) of the cotton plant. Especially comfortable in hot weather. Strong and absorbent. Takes fabric finishes well. Shrinkage and wrinkling can be corrected with fabric finishes.
	**Linen.** Comes from the stalk of the flax plant. Stronger than cotton and very absorbent. Comfortable, but wrinkles easily and must be pressed with a very hot iron. Sometimes used for fashions with an unpressed look.
	**Wool.** Comes from the fleece of sheep. Warm because its fibers trap air. Wears well, resists wrinkles and abrasion, and repels water. Shrinks easily and is a favorite target of moths. Most must be dry cleaned. Can be made washable and moth resistant using special fabric finishes.
	**Silk.** Comes from fibers in the cocoon that the silkworm spins. Lightweight and flexible with a natural *luster* (shine). Resists wrinkling. May be dyed vivid colors. Can be damaged by perspiration, deodorant, and high ironing temperatures.
	**Ramie.** Comes from the stems of China grass. Especially strong with a natural luster. Absorbent, washable, and resists mildew and insects. Because of its stiff texture, is usually blended with other fibers.

Fig. 44-2. The most common natural fiber is cotton. What are some possible reasons?

Manufactured Fibers

Many of today's fabrics are made of **manufactured fibers**, those formed completely or in part by chemicals. Some, such as rayon and acetate, are made from natural wood chips and chemicals. Others, such as polyester, are composed entirely of chemicals. The chart below, Fig. 44-3, describes characteristics of six of the manufactured fibers.

Characteristics of Manufactured Fibers

	**Rayon.** Absorbent, soft, and comfortable. Drapes easily, but also wrinkles easily. May shrink, so dry cleaning is usually recommended.
	**Polyester.** Resists wrinkles and shrinking, but is not absorbent. Washable and dries fast, but attracts oily stains. Some fabrics tend to *pill*, or form tiny balls of fiber on the surface.
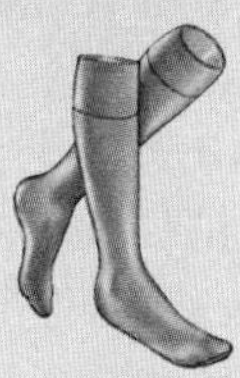	**Nylon.** Strong, lightweight, and holds its shape well. Not absorbent. Tends to collect static electricity. Washable and dries quickly, but is sensitive to heat. White nylon fabrics have a tendency to yellow.
	**Acrylic.** Soft, warm, and resists wrinkling. Should not be dried at high temperature. Fibers resist fading. Some pill, and static electricity can be a problem.
	**Acetate.** Looks like silk and drapes easily. May wrinkle and fade. Very sensitive to heat. Usually dry cleaned.
	**Spandex.** An elastic fiber often combined with other fibers. Bleach and high laundry temperatures should not be used.

Fig. 44-3. Rayon was the first manufactured fiber. Today there are more than 25 different kinds.

More to Explore

Lyocell: A Strong New Fiber

Textile manufacturers develop new fabrics on a regular basis, but it's even bigger news when a new *fiber* comes along. In 1996, lyocell became the first new fiber to be approved by the Federal Trade Commission in 30 years. It's a manufactured fiber made from the wood pulp of farm-grown trees. Tencel® is the trade name used by the company that developed lyocell. You may see others as well.

Lyocell has many appealing characteristics. It is:

- A strong fiber known for its luster and soft draping effect.

- More absorbent than cotton, but less absorbent than wool, linen, and rayon.

- Similar to cotton in that it "breathes" and is comfortable to wear.

Some lyocell fabrics may be laundered, but others must be dry cleaned. Like cotton, lyocell wrinkles and requires careful ironing to avoid scorching.

Manufacturers blend lyocell with natural and manufactured fibers, such as wool, silk, rayon, cotton, nylon, and polyester. Fabrics containing lyocell are used for clothing and products for the home. Since lyocell costs more than cotton, it is often found in relatively expensive garments.

Most manufactured fibers were created to replace or imitate natural fibers. Nylon, for instance, resembles silk. Acrylic takes the place of wool in some blankets and sweaters. An advantage of manufactured fibers is that many are easy to care for. Lyocell, a new manufactured fiber, is described on this page.

Yarns

Various types of yarns can be formed from fibers. Long, straight fibers usually create smooth, silky yarns. Short, curly fibers tend to make softer, fluffier yarns. The thickness of the yarn also depends on how tightly the fibers are spun together. The qualities of the fiber and yarn affect the wear and care of the fabric.

Often a yarn is made from two or more different fibers to take advantage of the best features of each. This is called a **blend**. You may have a shirt that is 60 percent polyester and 40 percent cotton, a common blend. It has the comfort and look of cotton, but often doesn't require ironing because of the high percentage of polyester.

Fabric Construction

Textile mills use several methods to make yarns into fabric. The two most common methods are weaving and knitting.

Woven Fabrics

Weaving involves interlacing two sets of yarns together at right angles. Woven fabrics generally hold their shape better and are stronger than knits. The type of weave, along with the characteristics of the fiber and yarn, helps determine whether the fabric is soft or

Types of Weaves

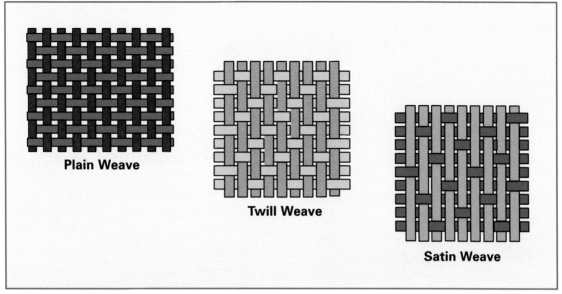

Plain Weave

Twill Weave

Satin Weave

Fig. 44-4. Notice the unique pattern of each weave. Which weave creates a diagonal line in the fabric? In which weave do yarns "float" on the surface, creating a smooth, shiny fabric?

crisp, smooth or textured. Fig. 44-4 illustrates three basic types of weaves—plain, twill, and satin. These basic weaves and their variations produce very different fabrics.

- **Plain weave** is the most common weave. You often see it in shirts and sheets.
- **Twill weave** produces fabrics, such as denim, that are stronger than those of plain weave.
- **Satin weave** produces smooth fabrics with a sheen, but they are less durable. Some blouses and evening apparel are made from this weave.

Knit Fabrics

Knit fabrics are constructed by pulling loops of yarn through other loops of yarn, creating interlocking rows. You probably have many clothes made from knit fabrics, such as T-shirts and sweaters. Many workout clothes are made from knit fabrics because knits stretch with movement and return to their original shape. Knit clothes are comfortable and don't wrinkle easily.

Other Fabric Construction Methods

In addition to woven and knit fabrics, some manufacturers produce fabric made in other ways. *Nonwoven fabrics*, such as felt, are made by matting or bonding fibers with heat, moisture, or adhesives. *Bonded fabrics* are created by fusing one fabric to another, making two layers. For water repellency, raincoats are often made of bonded fabric. *Quilted fabrics* are produced by putting a fluffy layer of batting between two layers of fabric. The layers are held together by decorative stitching or a special heat treatment.

Color and Other Finishes

Fabric finishes are any special treatments that improve the appearance, feel, or performance of the fabric. These range from adding color to making fabric water repellant.

Color or design can be added at various stages of the production process, from fiber to finished garment. Manufacturers use computers to achieve the exact colors they want.

Some fabrics and garments are **colorfast**, meaning that their color will remain the same over time. If a garment is not colorfast, its color may fade after repeated washings. The care label may say "Wash with like colors." Doing so will help prevent the dye that comes out of a non-colorfast garment from staining other clothes.

Some finishes make fabric look or feel more appealing. For instance, flannel is brushed to create softness by raising the fiber ends. Other finishes make a fabric shinier or crisper. Some add a special property such as wrinkle resistance or soil release. These finishes may be permanent or temporary.

Some children's clothing and sleepwear is treated to make it flame-resistant. Check the label to see whether the garment has this special finish. See Fig. 44-5.

Daily Clothing Care

Clothes that are properly cared for last longer. Taking care of your clothes protects your investment in your wardrobe and will help your family's clothing budget go farther.

Have you ever planned to wear a favorite outfit, but found when you pulled it out of the closet that it was stained, wrinkled, or had a missing button? You can avoid such unpleasant surprises by making clothing care a daily habit. At the end of each day, or whenever you change clothes, take a few moments to inspect the garments you've worn. If you see any stains, treat them promptly using the methods described later in this chapter. The sooner you treat stains, the greater your chances of removing them. Also look for any minor repairs that are needed and take care of them as soon as possible. You'll learn how to make simple repairs in Chapter 45.

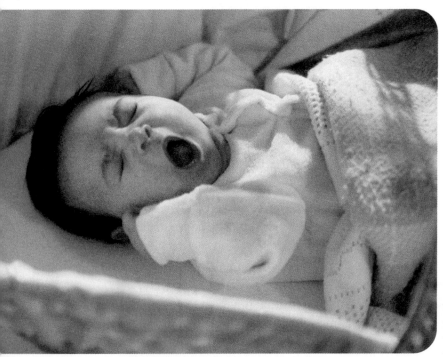

Fig. 44-5. Children's sleepwear is required by law to be either snug-fitting or flame-resistant. Why is flammability a concern with loose-fitting sleepwear?

If you don't need to take care of stains or repairs, decide what other care is needed. Put garments that need washing in a hamper until you're ready to do laundry. However, clothes don't always need to be washed or cleaned after every wearing. Sometimes you can just air out garments by hanging them outside the closet or draping them over a chair. Airing clothes between wearings helps eliminate odors. You might also need to brush off lint or press out wrinkles.

Once clothes are ready to wear again, put them where they belong. If you just heap them in a pile, they can easily become wrinkled, dirty, or damaged.

Cleaning Clothes

Shrunken shorts. Pink T-shirts that used to be white. Wrinkled and stiff blue jeans. All of these laundry problems can be avoided by following a few simple steps. The first step is to sort the clothes that need cleaning.

Sorting Clothes

As you prepare to do your own laundry or the family laundry, separate clothes into groups according to:

- **Care instructions.** Read the sewn-in care labels. Separate items that can be machine washed in warm water from those that need cold water, hand washing, or dry cleaning. Also look for special instructions, like "wash separately." See Fig. 44-6.
- **Color.** To keep colors true, separate whites and light colors from bright or dark colors.

- **Weight of items.** Separate heavyweight items from those that are more delicate.
- **Linting.** Items such as towels and rugs often produce a lot of lint. Separate them from items that lint might cling to, such as a pair of black slacks.
- **Amount of soil.** If some items are heavily soiled, such as a mud-stained ball uniform or greasy work clothes, wash them separately from lightly soiled clothes.

As you sort, prepare clothes for washing. Check pockets and remove all items. Close zippers and hook-and-loop fasteners. They can snag other garments.

Once you've sorted the laundry, you will have several piles. If a load has only a few items, try to delay laundering. Large loads are more efficient than small ones, saving detergent, water, and energy. Also remember to balance loads to prevent tangling. Laundering four sheets in one load guarantees that they will become tangled. Instead, launder fewer sheets with some pillowcases or garments.

Removing Stains

Stains on clothes are a very common problem. Removing most of them isn't difficult, especially when you act promptly. You have three opportunities to deal with stains:

- **As soon as you notice the stain.** Suppose that after lunch, you find a big spot of ketchup on the front of your shirt. You might be able to get most of it out by immediately rinsing the stain in cold water. You could also use a stain removal product in the form of a moist towelette made for such situations.

- **When you check your garments at the end of the day.** Soaking garments in plain cold water, or water mixed with detergent, eliminates many stains.

- **Just before you wash the garment.** Pretreating stains just before laundering can be done in several ways. One is to apply and rub a little detergent directly on the stain. Applying a prewash stain removal product is another option, especially for oily or greasy substances. Follow the package directions. Typically, you wait a few minutes to allow the product to work before laundering.

Various stain removal products are available. The package should tell you what types of stains the product is designed to remove.

With many stains, the *worst* thing you can do is to wash the garment in hot water and then dry it in a dryer. Heat sets many stains, making later removal difficult or impossible. If a stain remains after washing, air dry the garment, then treat the stain again.

Machine Washing

Once you've sorted laundry and pretreated stains, you can begin the wash cycle. If you're using a particular washer for the first time, ask for a quick lesson. Front-loading machines, for example, operate differently than standard top-loading machines. Here are general directions:

- **Step 1.** Select the water temperature appropriate for the items in the load. When two temperatures are listed, such as "warm/cold," it means the wash cycle will be warm and the rinse water will be cold. See Fig. 44-7.

- **Step 2.** Set the washer cycle for the type of load, such as regular, permanent press, or delicate. You also need to choose the length of the wash cycle. Lightly soiled clothes require less time to wash than dirtier clothes.

- **Step 3.** As the machine starts to fill with water, add detergent and any other laundry products according to package directions. Some machines have special dispensers for bleach and for liquid fabric softener.

- **Step 4.** When the detergent is mixed with the water, add the items being washed. Pile them in the washer loosely so they can move freely during the wash cycle. Loads that are overcrowded don't get as clean.

Fig. 44-7. Most automatic washers have similar control panels. This one lets you choose the temperature, water level, and wash cycle.

Fig. 44-8. Avoid twisting or wringing garments when hand washing. After rinsing, roll the garment in a towel to remove excess water.

Hand Washing

Some delicate garments are labeled "hand wash." You might also want to use this method when you have just one or two items to launder. Start by soaking the item in sudsy water. Then gently squeeze the suds through the garment. Drain the sink or basin and refill it with fresh water to rinse the garment. Repeat the rinse step until the water is free of suds. See Fig. 44-8.

Drying Clothes

Care labels usually tell how to dry garments. "Tumble dry" means the item can be dried by machine, but you can use a different method if you prefer. Some clothes must be line dried or dried flat.

- **Machine drying.** Select the temperature setting that best matches clothes' care labels. Some dryers have sensors to determine when clothes are dry. With others, you must set the drying time. Clean the lint filter before every load. Not only does this help clothes dry faster, but it's also essential for safety, since lint is very flammable. Remove dry clothes promptly so they don't wrinkle. Fold or hang them, smoothing areas such as collars and cuffs with your fingers.

- **Line drying.** Hanging laundry outside on a breezy day helps wrinkles disappear and clothes smell fresh. You can also air dry clothes indoors on hangers, a clothesline, or a drying rack. Air drying saves energy.

- **Drying flat.** Use this method when the care label recommends it. Such items may shrink or be damaged by the dryer, and they may stretch out of shape if line dried. For fastest drying, use a mesh drying rack that allows air to circulate. If you don't have such a rack, place the item on a thick towel, gently reshaping it. Turn the garment over every few hours, replacing the damp towel with a dry one.

Whatever method you use, dry clothes promptly. Wrinkles set when wet clothes are left in the washer. If left long enough, wet or damp clothes may develop **mildew**, a fungus that shows up as small black dots. They may also develop a sour odor that is difficult to remove. As you remove items from the washer, shake out each wet garment. This, too, helps minimize wrinkling.

Tonio dries his clothes in the dryer for 10 to 15 minutes to help remove wrinkles, then hangs them on hangers from the shower rod to finish drying. This technique usually eliminates the need for ironing. "When I realized that the lint from the dryer was actually fibers from my clothes, I started taking them out of the dryer early," he said. "I think my clothes last longer and look better this way."

Removing Wrinkles

No matter how carefully you wash and dry your clothes, some items will wrinkle. With an iron, you can quickly improve their appearance.

An iron is used for two different techniques. *Ironing* means sliding the iron over the fabric to smooth out wrinkles. It's used on sturdy fabrics, such as cotton. *Pressing* involves lifting the iron and setting it back down on the fabric. This technique is used on fabrics that may stretch, such as knits and wools. See Fig. 44-9.

Select the iron's heat setting based on the garment's fabric and care label. For a blend, such as polyester and cotton, choose the lowest suggested setting. An iron that is too hot can scorch, or even melt, clothes. Allow a few minutes for the iron to preheat to the chosen temperature.

When ironing a garment, start with small areas such as collar, cuffs, and then sleeves. Then iron the large flat areas, such as the back and fronts of a shirt.

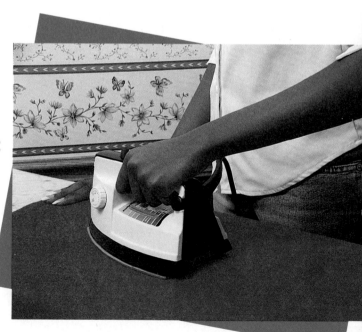

Fig. 44-9. An iron uses heat and pressure to remove wrinkles. Most irons also have a steam setting for fabrics that can withstand a higher temperature.

Dry Cleaning

Most families have some garments that must be dry cleaned. The dry cleaning process uses special chemicals, rather than water and detergent, to get clothes clean.

When you take garments to be commercially dry cleaned, point out any stains and try to identify what caused them. That will help the dry cleaner determine how to remove them.

There are two alternatives to commercial dry cleaning. Some coin-operated laundries have machines for dry cleaning. Dry cleaning kits to use with a dryer are also available. The kits contain premoistened cloths to place in a special bag with a few garments. After the garments tumble in the dryer for a specified time, you remove them promptly and hang them on hangers. The process works best with wool, rayon, silk, linen, and cotton knits. As with all laundry products, it's important to follow directions carefully.

Storing Clothes

Organized storage can save valuable time when you're rushing to get dressed. Storage methods also affect how clothes look and how long they last.

Use the best methods to keep clothes looking good and wrinkle-free. For hanging clothes, plastic or padded hangers are good choices. To prevent stretching, store knits folded rather than on hangers. Keep your closet and drawers organized by putting like items together. You might put all your T-shirts in the same drawer and hang all your slacks in one area of the closet. Avoid overcrowding—it causes wrinkles. Practicing smart storage strategies, as well as proper care, will help keep your clothes looking good for a long time.

Be sure clothes are stain-free before putting them away. Stains set with time, and some attract damaging insects. To prevent mildew from forming, make sure clothes are completely dry. Avoid storing clothing in damp, humid areas, such as a basement.

TIPS FOR *Success*

Maximizing Storage Space

Do you feel as though you never have enough storage space for your clothes? Try these ideas to make the most of the storage space you have.

- Save closet space with hangers designed to hold more than one garment.
- Install hooks or over-the-door racks for belts and other accessories.
- Store out-of-season and seldom used items in less convenient places. Try underbed storage containers or empty suitcases.

Chapter Summary

- Fibers are either natural or manufactured. Each fiber has its own characteristics.
- Fabrics can be woven, knit, or constructed in other ways.
- Fabric finishes are designed to improve fabric in some way.
- Taking proper care of clothes starts with inspecting them after wear.
- Stains can usually be removed if treated promptly.
- Pay attention to care label information when laundering clothes.
- Some clothes must be dry cleaned instead of laundered.
- Storing clothes correctly keeps them in good condition.

Reviewing Key Terms & Ideas

1. How are **fibers** related to **yarns**?
2. What is the key difference between **natural fibers** and **manufactured fibers**?
3. Name three natural and three manufactured fibers. List two characteristics of each.
4. What is a **blend**? Give an example.
5. Compare the construction and characteristics of woven and knit fabric.
6. Give four examples of different purposes for **fabric finishes**.
7. What are two advantages of **colorfast** fabrics?
8. Why is it important to take proper care of clothes?
9. Describe three ways to treat a stain.
10. Explain how to hand wash a garment.
11. What is **mildew**? When might it become a laundry problem?
12. Why should some garments be pressed rather than ironed?
13. How is dry cleaning different from regular laundering?
14. Describe how to store a wool sweater to keep it in the best possible condition.

Thinking Critically

1. **Identifying Alternatives.** Imagine that your job requires frequent week-long business trips. What types of fabrics would you choose for your business travel wardrobe and why? How would you keep clothes looking neat and clean while traveling?
2. **Understanding Cause and Effect.** What might happen if you tried to iron or press clothes without knowing the fiber content of the fabric?

Applying Your Knowledge

1. **Fiber Inventory.** Take an inventory of the types of fibers found in your clothing. Which two fibers were used most? What are some likely reasons?

2. **Selecting Laundry Methods.** Choose three washable items from your wardrobe, each with different care instructions. For each item, write down the care label information, then describe in detail the laundry procedures you would follow. Begin with sorting and end with removing wrinkles. Assume one item is stained with chocolate.

3. **Dry Cleaning Comparison.** Research the cost of having various garments cleaned by a local dry cleaner. Calculate the cost of cleaning the same garments at home with a dry cleaning kit. Compile the class results.

Making Connections

1. **Science.** Chemicals called phosphates used to be included in most laundry detergents, but that's no longer the case. Research the cleaning action and environmental impact of phosphates to find out why. Write a brief summary of your findings.

2. **Language Arts.** Create an interesting, informative brochure for college freshmen who will be doing their own laundry. Include a stain removal chart and laundry tips.

Managing Your Life

Streamlining Laundry Routines

If you're not already routinely doing laundry for yourself or your family, you will be someday. Like any household task, the laundry process can be made more efficient using management skills. Consider how the first two steps of the management process—planning and organizing—could help you reach the goal of saving time and energy when doing laundry. Brainstorm as many ideas as you can for making each step in the laundry process more efficient, both in your current situation and in the future when you're on your own. Share your ideas with your family. If family members agree, implement one or more of your ideas for a few weeks and evaluate the results.

Using Technology

1. **Internet.** Use the key words "closet organization" to see what products are on the market. Select five products that might be useful to you. Analyze their costs and benefits.

2. **Analyzing Technology.** Find out how EnergyGuide labels and the Energy Star program can help consumers choose laundry appliances that save energy. How does each work? Do you think these programs are easily used by consumers? Why or why not?

Sewing Basics

Key Terms

- bobbin
- serger
- notions
- grain
- pattern guide sheet
- alter
- staystitching
- facing

Objectives

- **Identify** the uses of basic sewing equipment and tools.
- **Give** guidelines for selecting a pattern and fabric.
- **Explain** key steps in altering and using a pattern.
- **Demonstrate** basic skills for constructing and repairing clothing.
- **Give** examples of simple clothing alterations.

QUICK WRITE

Write a few paragraphs expressing your thoughts about sewing. How could it be both a practical skill and a way to express your creativity? What, if any, sewing experience have you had?

*S*ewing is a great way to add to your wardrobe and change the look of your home. You can personalize clothes to fit your taste, shape, and size. Try sewing unique gifts for others. With sewing skills, you can also keep your clothes in good repair so you look your best.

Sewing Equipment

A sewing machine is a primary piece of equipment used for sewing projects. Some sewers also use a serger. If both are available, each is used for the tasks it does best.

The Sewing Machine

The sewing machine's main purpose is to sew fabric together to make clothes and other items. Various manufacturers make sewing machines, many with impressive special features. Some are computerized and can perform specialized tasks automatically. Many experienced sewers appreciate what these high-end machines are capable of doing. However, a more basic and less expensive sewing machine is easier to learn and works well for almost all sewing projects. See Fig. 45-1.

Fig. 45-1. Take time to practice threading and stitching anytime you use a different machine.

Most sewing machines have the same basic parts and controls. See Fig. 45-2 on the next page for a guide to typical parts of a sewing machine. If you have access to a machine, identify where these parts are located on it. Check the owner's manual for specific information about that machine's use and care.

Using a Sewing Machine

Before using a sewing machine, there are several simple skills you need to learn:

- **Winding a bobbin.** Machine sewing requires two sets of thread. The top thread comes from a spool on top of the machine. The bottom thread comes from

a **bobbin**, a small metal or plastic spool beneath the needle. At the beginning of a project, you usually must wind thread from the top spool onto the bobbin. Check the owner's manual for directions.

- **Threading the machine.** A sewing machine won't form stitches unless it has been threaded correctly. The spool of thread is placed on the spool pin, then the thread is run through a series of thread guides and finally through the needle.

Threading patterns differ by machine. Learn to correctly thread the machine you will use.

- **Choosing machine needles.** Select the sewing machine needle for a project according to the fabric to be sewn. There are two basic types of needles. *Universal needles* have a sharp point and are suitable for any fabric. *Ballpoint needles* have a rounded point and are designed for knit and stretch fabrics. Needle size is desig-nated by two different systems, but in

Sewing Machine Parts

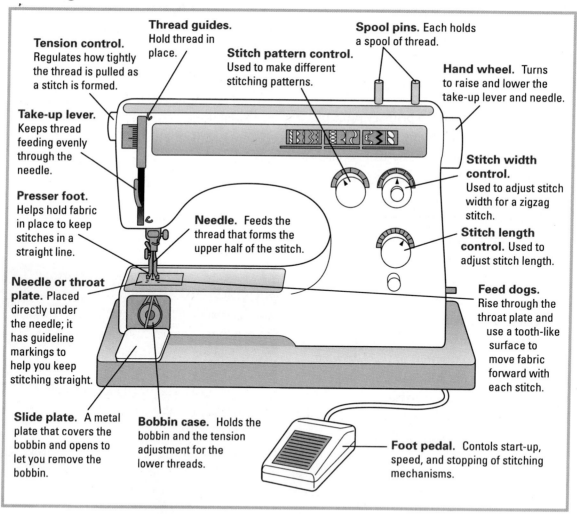

Tension control. Regulates how tightly the thread is pulled as a stitch is formed.

Thread guides. Hold thread in place.

Stitch pattern control. Used to make different stitching patterns.

Spool pins. Each holds a spool of thread.

Hand wheel. Turns to raise and lower the take-up lever and needle.

Take-up lever. Keeps thread feeding evenly through the needle.

Presser foot. Helps hold fabric in place to keep stitches in a straight line.

Needle. Feeds the thread that forms the upper half of the stitch.

Stitch width control. Used to adjust stitch width for a zigzag stitch.

Stitch length control. Used to adjust stitch length.

Needle or throat plate. Placed directly under the needle; it has guideline markings to help you keep stitching straight.

Feed dogs. Rise through the throat plate and use a tooth-like surface to move fabric forward with each stitch.

Slide plate. A metal plate that covers the bobbin and opens to let you remove the bobbin.

Bobbin case. Holds the bobbin and the tension adjustment for the lower threads.

Foot pedal. Contols start-up, speed, and stopping of stitching mechanisms.

Fig. 45-2. While sewing machines vary, they have the same basic parts.

both, a larger number indicates a heavier needle. Use a size 9 or 11 (70 or 75) for lightweight fabric, a size 14 (90) for a medium-weight fabric, and a size 16 or 18 (100 or 110) for heavy or thick fabrics. Experts recommend using a new needle for every major project.

Machine Stitching ~ In machine sewing, the fabric is moved from front to back by *feed dogs*, two small rows of metal teeth in the needle plate. A stitch is formed when the upper thread and needle pass through the fabric, catching the bobbin thread from below. When repeated, the process creates a row of stitching.

Use the machine controls to select the type of stitch and the length. Depending on the machine, stitch length is measured in millimeters or given as the number of stitches per inch. Some machines have many specialty stitches, but the four basic ones are shown in Fig. 45-3.

- **Regular stitch.** This is the stitch you will use most often, mainly to make the *seams* that join pieces of fabric together. Set the stitch length control at 10 to 12 stitches per inch or 2.5 to 2 millimeters. For heavy fabrics, lengthen the stitch slightly.

- **Basting stitch.** Use this long stitch to gather and to *baste*—hold pieces together temporarily. Set the length at 6 to 8 stitches per inch or 4 to 3.3 millimeters.

- **Reinforcement stitch.** This very short stitch helps prevent stretching and strengthens corners or points. Set the control at 16 stitches per inch or 1.5 millimeters.

- **Zigzag stitch.** Use this Z-shaped stitch to finish seams and edges, make buttonholes, and sew special seams. You can adjust both the width and length of stitches.

Basic Sewing Machine Stitches

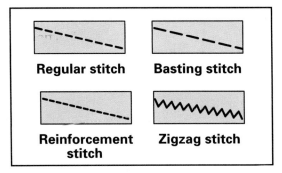

Regular stitch   **Basting stitch**

Reinforcement stitch   **Zigzag stitch**

Fig. 45-3. The four stitches shown are the ones used most often in machine sewing.

The Serger

A **serger** is a machine that sews, trims, and finishes the edge in one step. It's ideal for producing finished seams and very narrow rolled hems. Another use is to create stretchable seams. Usually, the serger is used for specialized tasks such as these, and the rest of the project is done with a sewing machine. However, some simple garments can be made entirely on a serger.

As you can see in Fig. 45-4 on the next page, a serger looks quite different from a sewing machine. It works differently, too. Sergers use two to five threads to make each stitch. Cutting knives trim seams to just the width of the stitches.

Sergers make two basic types of stitches. The *overlock* stitch, shown in Fig. 45-4, sews the fabric layers together, creates a finished edge, and trims away the excess fabric. The *overedge* stitch finishes the edge of a single layer of fabric. Many clothes you buy have serged seams or edges.

Overlock seam

Fig. 45-4. A serger's capabilities complement those of a sewing machine. For example, the overlock seam, shown above, is stitched, trimmed, and finished in one operation.

Sewing Tools

Besides a sewing machine, you will need a few tools of the trade. These include tools for measuring, cutting, and marking. You will also need pins, hand sewing needles, and a pincushion.

Fig. 45-5 shows tools commonly used in sewing projects. You will need at least one tool to cut fabric, one to measure, and one to transfer pattern markings to your fabric.

Preparing to Sew

Have you ever wanted to try a new fashion, but couldn't find what you wanted? Maybe you *were* able to find it, but you didn't like the way it fit or couldn't afford the price. Perhaps you would like new curtains or a pillow for your room. Sewing your own can be the answer.

As you will see, sewing is a step-by-step process. The more you sew, the more skillful you will become.

Sewing Tools

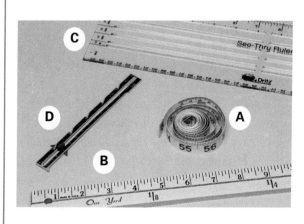

Measuring Tools

A. Tape measure. Flexible measuring tape used to take body measurements.

B. Yardstick. Used to measure fabric, mark grainlines, mark hems, and draw long lines.

C. Ruler. Clear plastic with $\frac{1}{8}$-inch markings. Used to measure and mark lines. Most are 12 inches long.

D. Sewing gauge. A 6-inch ruler with an adjustable sliding marker. Handy for measuring hems and seams.

Cutting Tools

E. Shears. Used to cut fabric. Have long blades and two handles that are shaped differently. Bent handles allow fabric to remain flat on the table while you cut.

F. Scissors. Smaller than shears. Both handles are the same shape. Used for trimming and clipping.

G. Seam ripper. Used to remove stitches. Has a sharp pointed end and a small blade to cut through stitches.

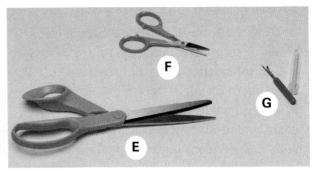

Marking Equipment

H. Tracing wheel and paper. Wheel resembles a small, saw-toothed pizza cutter. Used with tracing paper to transfer pattern marks to the fabric. One side of tracing paper is colored.

I. Tailor's chalk. Available in squares, pencils, or powdered chalk form. Can be used to mark most fabrics. The residue brushes off.

J. Fabric marking pen. Has ink that evaporates or can be washed away with cold water. Don't apply heat to marks before removing them.

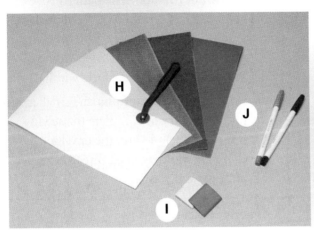

Other Basic Sewing Tools

K. Pins. Used to attach pattern pieces to fabric and hold layers of fabric together for sewing. Straight pins with colored glass heads are a good choice.

L. Needles. Carry the thread through fabric to form stitches. Different types are used for hand sewing and sewing machines. Sizes are identified by number, smaller numbers being finer.

M. Pin cushion. Holds pins and needles when not in use, keeping them safe and sharp.

N. Thimble. When sewing by hand, protects the finger as it pushes the needle through the fabric.

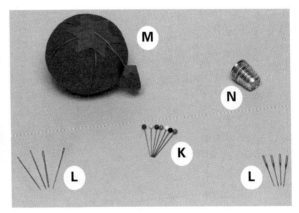

Fig. 45-5. The proper tools make sewing easier and the results more professional.

Finding Your Size and Pattern

Taking body measurements is essential for choosing the right pattern size. Your size usually differs from the size of clothes you buy. Pattern catalogs—available where fabric is sold and on the Internet—provide size charts and measuring instructions. For accuracy, you need someone to help take your measurements.

Pattern catalogs and pattern envelopes provide useful information to help you select an appropriate pattern. Fig. 45-6 shows the back of a typical pattern envelope. Check the envelope for:

- **Skill level.** Patterns with names such as "Quick and Easy" are good choices for beginners.

- **Photo or drawing.** The front of the envelope shows you what the finished garment or project looks like. Most patterns also show more than one *view*. For instance, the pattern might let you make both a tote bag and a cell phone case, or a shirt pattern might give you a choice of collar styles.

- **Description and design details.** Look for a written description of the pattern details and a drawing of the back of each view.

- **Fabric information.** The pattern envelope recommends certain types of fabric and advises against others. A yardage chart lists how much fabric to buy, depending on the view, the size, and the fabric width.

- **Notions.** A list of **notions**, the smaller supplies necessary to complete the sewing project, is included on the envelope. For example, you may need thread, a zipper, buttons, and elastic.

Pattern Envelope Back

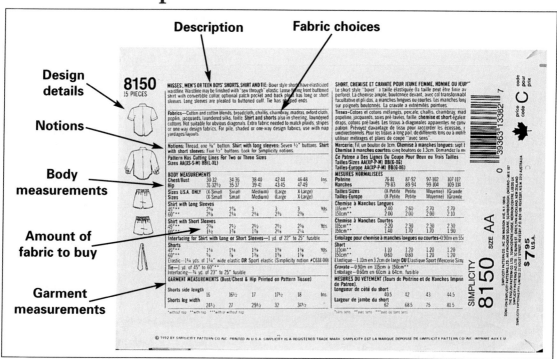

Fig. 45-6. The back of a pattern envelope provides information that's needed to start a project.

Pattern Guide Sheet

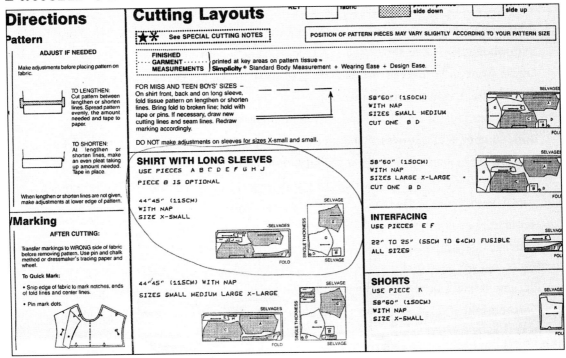

Directions

Pattern

ADJUST IF NEEDED

Make adjustments before placing pattern on fabric.

TO LENGTHEN: Cut pattern between lengthen or shorten lines. Spread pattern evenly, the amount needed and tape to paper.

TO SHORTEN: At lengthen or shorten lines, make an even pleat taking up amount needed. Tape in place.

When lengthen or shorten lines are not given, make adjustments at lower edge of pattern.

Marking

AFTER CUTTING:

Transfer markings to WRONG side of fabric before removing pattern. Use pin and chalk method or dressmaker's tracing paper and wheel.

To Quick Mark:

• Snip edge of fabric to mark notches, ends of fold lines and center lines.

• Pin mark dots.

Cutting Layouts

★ ★ See SPECIAL CUTTING NOTES

POSITION OF PATTERN PIECES MAY VARY SLIGHTLY ACCORDING TO YOUR PATTERN SIZE

FINISHED GARMENT MEASUREMENTS printed at key areas on pattern tissue = Simplicity® Standard Body Measurement + Wearing Ease + Design Ease.

FOR MISS AND TEEN BOYS' SIZES – On shirt front, back and on long sleeve, fold tissue pattern on lengthen or shorten lines. Bring fold to broken line; hold with tape or pins. If necessary, draw new cutting lines and seam lines. Redraw marking accordingly.

DO NOT make adjustments on sleeves for sizes X-small and small.

SHIRT WITH LONG SLEEVES
USE PIECES A B C D E F G H J
PIECE B IS OPTIONAL

44"45" (115CM) WITH NAP SIZE X-SMALL

44"45" (115CM) WITH NAP SIZES SMALL MEDIUM LARGE X-LARGE

58"60" (150CM) WITH NAP SIZES SMALL MEDIUM CUT ONE B D

58"60" (150CM) WITH NAP SIZES LARGE X-LARGE CUT ONE B D

INTERFACING
USE PIECES E F
22" TO 25" (55CM TO 64CM) FUSIBLE ALL SIZES

SHORTS
USE PIECE K
58"60" (150CM) WITH NAP SIZE X-SMALL

Fig. 45-7. *The pattern guide sheet tells how to lay out the pattern on the fabric and gives step-by-step construction directions for the project.*

Choosing and Preparing Fabric

Follow the fabric suggestions on the pattern envelope. A medium-weight fabric with a small, all-over print is a good choice for first projects. Until you have mastered basic skills, avoid slippery fabrics, stripes, plaids, and one-direction designs.

When fabric is laid on the cutting table and folded lengthwise, the *selvages* (finished side edges) should line up. If not, the **grain** of the fabric—the directions the lengthwise and crosswise yarns run—may not be at right angles. A garment made from off-grain fabric won't hang evenly and may twist to one side. If you need help checking the grain or have other questions, ask a staff member at the store.

Washable fabric should be washed and dried before it's used. That way, any shrinkage occurs before the item is made rather than afterward.

Using a Pattern

A typical pattern contains paper pattern pieces and a **pattern guide sheet**. This sheet gives specific instructions for cutting out and sewing the project.

On the guide sheet, find the *cutting layout* for the particular item or view you are making. It shows the best way to lay out the pattern pieces on your fabric. Cutting layouts often differ depending on the width of the fabric. For easy reference, circle the layout you will use. The guide sheet also provides step-by-step directions for each project and view on the pattern. Circle or highlight the steps you will need to complete. See Fig. 45-7.

Pattern Symbols and Lines

Adjustment line. Double line showing where the pattern may be lengthened or shortened.

Buttonholes. Lines that show their exact location and length.

Center front and center back. Solid lines that show the center of the garment.

Cutting line. The heavy outer line along which you cut.

Dart. A fold line, stitching lines, and dots (for matching).

Dots, squares, and triangles. Markings used for matching seams and construction details.

Fold line. Solid line showing where the fabric is to be folded.

Grainline. Heavy, straight line with arrows at each end to indicate how the pattern should be placed on the grain of the fabric.

Hemline. Solid line indicating the finished edge of the garment.

Notches. Diamond-shaped symbols along the cutting line that are used for matching fabric pieces that will be joined.

Placement line. Line showing the exact location of a pocket, fastener, zipper, or trim.

Place-on-fold bracket. Arrow with bent ends. Indicates that the pattern piece is to be placed along a fold of fabric.

Seam line or stitching line. Broken line usually ⅝ inch inside the cutting line.

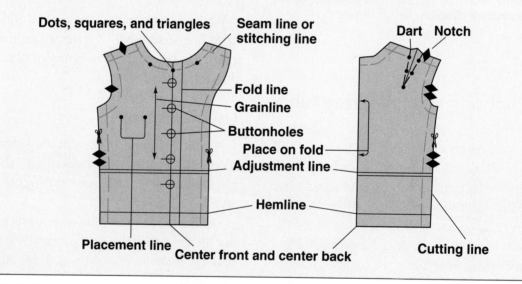

Fig. 45-8. Pattern symbols are your guide for assembling a project. Locate as many of these as you can on a real pattern.

Jake was making sport pants with an elastic waist. The guide sheet indicated that pattern pieces C and D were needed for this view. He unfolded the tissue pieces, cut those two pattern pieces apart from the others, and smoothed them out. The pattern he chose was designed for both men and women and had unisex sizes. When it was time to cut out the pattern pieces, Jake realized he would have to cut carefully on the cutting line designated for size Large. Just to be sure, he used a marker to highlight that solid line.

Fig. 45-8 shows common symbols and lines found on patterns. Learn to identify them and know their meanings.

Getting a Great Fit

If your body measurements are identical to the ones that apply to your pattern size, you are fortunate. For most people, at least one of the measurements is slightly larger or smaller. A small difference probably won't matter much in a loose-fitting garment.

However, for more fitted styles, you may need to **alter** your pattern—make changes to match your measurements.

Altering Length ~ Many garment patterns have length adjustment lines printed on the main pattern pieces. Look for double lines going across the pattern. Fig. 45-9 shows how to use the adjustment lines to lengthen or shorten a pattern. Pattern length can also be altered at the bottom edge.

Altering Width ~ With most patterns, you can alter width up to 2 inches. Suppose you're making pants and want to widen the legs, making each 1 inch bigger around. A pants leg has two seams (inseam and side seam), and each seam joins two pieces of fabric. This makes four places at which width will be added to each leg. Therefore, divide the total adjustment—1 inch—by four. The result, ¼ inch, is the amount of adjustment to make at each seam. On the pattern pieces, draw a new cutting line along each seam, ¼ inch outward from the original cutting line. To decrease width, draw the new line inside the original cutting line. See Fig. 45-10.

ALTERING LENGTH

Fig. 45-9. To lengthen, cut the pattern apart at the adjustment line and spread apart the extra amount needed. To shorten, make a fold on the adjustment line. The depth of the fold should be one-half the amount of excess length. Adjustments can also be made at the bottom edge.

ALTERING WIDTH

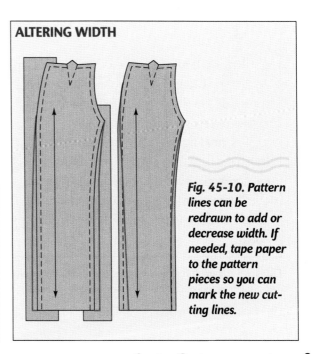

Fig. 45-10. Pattern lines can be redrawn to add or decrease width. If needed, tape paper to the pattern pieces so you can mark the new cutting lines.

Pattern Layout and Cutting

Positioning. Place the pattern pieces on the fabric as shown on the guide sheet. If pattern pieces are shaded on the cutting layout, place them printed side down. Start with pattern pieces to be placed along the fold line of the fabric. (Look for the "place on fold" symbol.) Pin the pieces along the fold line. Then lay out the remaining pattern pieces. Check that each pattern piece is on grain by measuring the distance from each end of the grainline arrow to the selvage. If the distances are not equal, adjust the piece and remeasure. Pin on the grainline arrow to hold the piece in place.

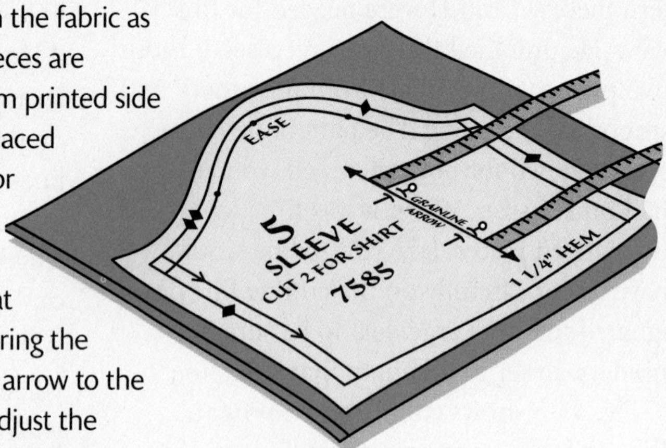

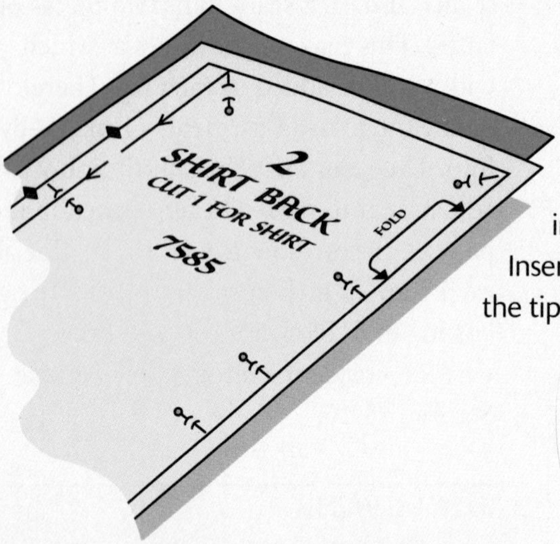

Pinning. Smooth out the pattern pieces. Start by pinning the corners of each piece diagonally. Then insert pins about every 6 inches along the edge of the pattern piece. Insert pins at right angles to the edge, keeping the tips of the pins within the cutting lines.

Cutting. Carefully check the pattern layout again before you cut. Using sharp shears, cut along the cutting line in the direction indicated by small arrows or tiny scissors. Use long, even strokes, holding the fabric flat with your free hand. Use the points of your shears to cut corners, curves, and notches. Always cut notches outward from the cutting line. Cut double and triple notches together as one long notch.

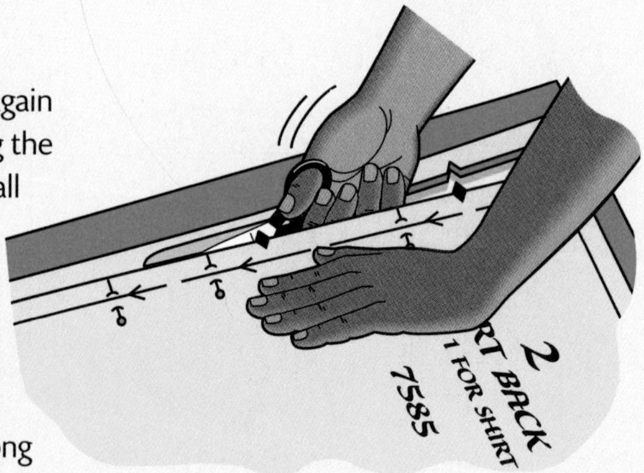

Fig. 45-11. Carefully position and pin the pattern pieces before you cut. What might be the result if grainlines were ignored when laying out pattern pieces?

Transferring Pattern Markings

- Choose a color of tracing paper that will make visible marks, but won't show through to the other side of the fabric.
- Slide the tracing paper under the pattern so the waxy, colored side is against the *wrong* side of the fabric. (For two layers of fabric, use two pieces of tracing paper or fold one in half.)
- Using a ruler as a guide, roll the tracing wheel once along the line that you want to mark. Mark dots with an X.

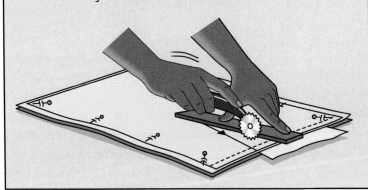

Fig. 45-12. There are several methods of transferring pattern markings to the fabric. One of the most common uses a tracing wheel and special tracing paper.

On multisize patterns, blend sizes by marking a gradual change from the cutting line of one size to another. For example, you might need a size Medium at the waist and size Large at the hips.

Pattern Layout and Cutting

Use a large, flat surface to lay pattern pieces out on your fabric. Refer to the pattern guide sheet for directions. The first step is to fold the fabric as shown on the cutting diagram. Be sure to note how the guide sheet indicates the right (exterior) and wrong (interior) sides of the fabric. Usually, you'll fold the fabric lengthwise with the right sides together. That brings the lengthwise finished edges together. Now you're ready to position the pattern pieces, pin the pattern to the fabric, and cut out the pattern. Fig. 45-11 illustrates these steps.

Marking Pattern Symbols

Before removing the pattern pieces from the fabric, you must transfer key construction symbols from the pattern to the *wrong* side of the fabric pieces. Darts, dots, placement lines, buttonholes, and other key locations are marked. Fig. 45-12 shows how to use tracing paper and a tracing wheel. Fabric-marking pens, tailor's chalk, pins, or thread may be used instead.

Machine Sewing Techniques

Most patterns include clear step-by-step sewing directions. Here are some basic machine sewing techniques you will use on many projects.

- **Directional stitching.** Throughout the sewing process, sew in the direction indicated by the small arrows on the pattern, usually from the wide to the narrow end.

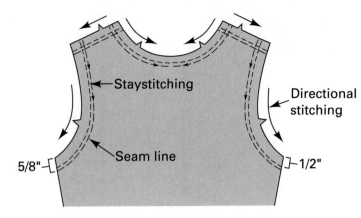

Staystitching

Directional
stitching

Seam line

5/8"

1/2"

Fig. 45-13. The staystitching on curved areas does not show in the finished garment. Notice the arrows that indicate directional stitching.

- **Staystitching.** Often, a first step is to staystitch curved areas to prevent them from stretching during the construction process. **Staystitching** is a row of regular machine stitches through a single layer of fabric. The stitching is placed ½ inch from the fabric edge. See Fig. 45-13.

- **Pinning seams.** A standard, or *plain,* seam is ⅝ inch wide. Place the two layers of fabric together with the right sides facing each other. Match any notches or dots. Pin the edges together with the pin points facing inward.

- **Stitching seams.** Position the fabric in the machine with the edge on the ⅝-inch mark. The ends of seams are secured by *backstitching* to prevent the seams from pulling apart. To backstitch, start with the needle about ½ inch forward of the seam end. Sew in reverse to the fabric edge, then forward the length of the seam. Remove each pin before sewing over it. Backstitch again at the other end of the seam. See Fig. 45-14.

- **Seam treatments.** After stitching, a seam is generally pressed open, with one side of the seam allowance pressed to each side. Sometimes seams need additional treatment before they are pressed. These techniques help seams lie flat and smooth by reducing their bulk. Fig. 45-15 shows how to trim, grade, clip, and notch seam allowances.

- **Facings.** A **facing** is a shaped piece of fabric used to finish the raw edge of a garment. Facings are typically found at necklines and armholes. On facings that have an inward curve, the seam allowance is clipped up to the staystitching so the seam will lie flat.

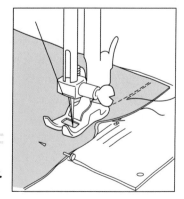

Fig. 45-14. The plain seam shown is the most common. Backstitching keeps seams from pulling apart.

Seam Treatments

Trimming. Trimming the seam allowance reduces its bulk.

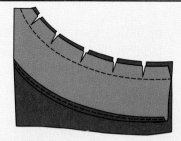

Clipping. Seams with inward curves may be clipped to the staystitching line.

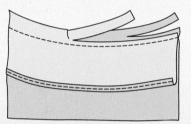

Grading. Grading is similar to trimming, but each layer is trimmed slightly longer, gradually reducing the bulk.

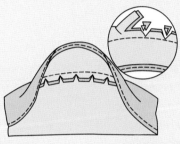

Notching. On outward curves, V-shaped pieces are clipped from the seam allowance.

Fig. 45-15. After seams are sewn, various techniques may be required. The pattern guide sheet tells when these techniques are needed.

Fig. 45-16. For darts, match the pattern markings and pin in place. Stitch from the wide end to the narrow end. Leave about 3 inches of extra thread at the end of the dart and tie a knot to secure the stitching.

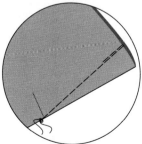

- **Darts**. Darts are used to give shape to a garment. The pattern markings indicate where to fold the fabric to make the triangular dart. Fig. 45-16 shows the techniques used in sewing a dart.

Depending on your project, you may use a variety of other sewing techniques, such as making gathers, sleeves, collars, or zippers. In addition to the pattern guide sheet, sewing books and classes can help you learn more advanced skills. Some Internet sites also explain and illustrate sewing techniques.

Hand Sewing Techniques

Hand sewing begins by threading a hand-sewing needle and knotting the end of one thread. Choose a needle with a smaller number for lightweight fabric and larger number for heavy fabric. Secure the knotted end to the fabric where it won't be visible, such as in a seam allowance.

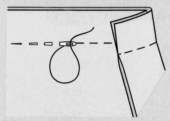

Running stitch. Use this simple stitch for sewing seams, basting, and gathering. Weave the needle in and out of the fabric several times, then pull the thread through. When sewing a seam, make small stitches about ¼ inch long. Make longer stitches for basting or gathering.

Hemming stitch. This slanted stitch is used frequently with a serged, taped, or zigzagged hem edge. Working from right to left, take a tiny stitch in the garment. Place the needle between the hem edge and the garment, then bring it up diagonally and out through the hem edge about ¼ inch from the first stitch. Continue spacing stitches about ¼ inch apart.

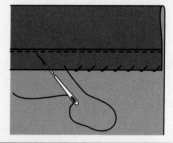

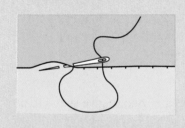

Slip stitch. This stitch is almost invisible. Use it to attach a turned-under edge, such as a folded-edge hem or pocket, to another piece of fabric. Insert the needle inside the fold of the fabric, bringing it out again about ¼ inch from the previous stitch. Pick up just one or two garment threads at the point where the needle emerges from the folded edge. Bring the needle back inside the fold and continue.

Blindstitch. This stitch is ideal for hems and to hold facings in place. Fold the edge of fabric back about ¼ inch. Take a small stitch in the garment or project, catching just a thread or two. Then take a tiny stitch above in the hem or facing. Don't pull the stitches tight. Form a very narrow zigzag stitch as you continue stitching.

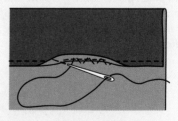

Fig. 45-17. Hand stitching can be used both for making items and for repairs. For example, you could use a small running stitch to repair a seam that's become unstitched.

Hand Sewing Techniques

Most project construction can be handled by a sewing machine. However, hand stitching is used for finishing steps on many projects. A variety of repairs can also be made by hand.

Fig. 45-17 describes four common hand stitches. If you are right-handed, it will probably seem natural to sew from right to left. Left-handed sewers usually work from left to right. Some people wear a thimble to protect the finger that pushes the needle through the fabric.

Hems

Some sewing projects call for hand hemming the bottom of a garment. For projects like a shirt, the pattern usually indicates where to fold up an edge to form a hem. For pants and skirts, the person who will wear the garment should try it on while a helper follows the steps below.

- **Pants.** Fold the fabric under so that the hem touches the top of the shoe in front and is about ½ inch longer in back. Pin the folded fabric in place.

- **Skirt or dress.** Determine the preferred length. Using a yardstick, measure the distance from there to the floor. Mark the hem line at that spot with chalk or a pin. Repeat the process every few inches around the skirt, making sure to measure the same distance from the floor each time. Fold the fabric under along the markings and pin in place. Check and adjust the length.

Once the hem has been pinned and the garment removed, decide on the desired depth of the turned-up fabric. Measure and mark that distance from the folded edge. Trim away excess fabric.

On woven fabrics, the cut edge of the turned-up fabric is finished in some way before the hem is hand stitched in place. If finishing is needed, options include:

- Zigzagging the edge with a sewing machine.

- Finishing the edge with a serger.

- Attaching seam tape or lace to the edge.

- Turning under the edge of lightweight fabric ¼ inch and pressing or stitching that fold, as shown in Fig. 45-18.

Fasteners

Most fasteners or closures—including buttons, snaps, and hooks and eyes—are attached by hand. Hook-and-loop tape is usually attached with machine stitching. For instructions for applying fasteners, check the package.

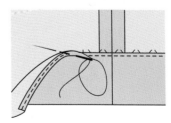

Fig. 45-18. The edge of this hem was folded and stitched by machine. It's being hand-stitched in place using a blindstitch, catching just a thread or two of the outside fabric. This makes the hem nearly invisible.

Everyone needs to be able to sew buttons. Fig. 45-19 shows how to attach the two types of buttons: sew-through and shank. Sew-through buttons have two or four visible holes. Instead of holes, shank buttons have a built-in loop, or *shank*, on the back.

If a button were sewn flat against a garment, there wouldn't be room to put it through a buttonhole. On a sew-through button, you must form a thread shank (something like a stem) between the button and fabric to allow space for buttoning. This space is built in on a shank button.

Making Repairs and Alterations

The basic machine- and hand-sewing skills you learn can be put to use on clothes you already own. Normal wear causes garment seams to tear, buttons to come off, and other problems. You may also want to make simple alterations to your clothes so they look different or fit better.

How to Attach Buttons

SEW-THROUGH BUTTON

Secure the thread to the underside of the garment at the exact button location. Bring the needle up through the fabric and one hole of the button. Lay a toothpick, or similar object, on top of the button between the holes. Bring the needle over the toothpick and down through a second hole. Make several more stitches to attach securely. For a four-hole button, repeat the process on the second pair of holes. End the stitches with the needle between the button and the fabric.

Next, remove the toothpick or pin, pull the button to the top, and wind the thread around the vertical threads under the button. Continue winding until the vertical threads are covered, forming a sturdy thread shank. Push the needle through to the underside of the fabric and secure it with a knot.

SHANK BUTTON

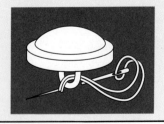

Secure the thread to the underside of the fabric at the button location. Sew a shank button in place with small stitches through the shank and into the fabric. Secure and knot the thread to the underside of the fabric.

Fig. 45-19. Build your skill by practicing on different types of buttons.

Simple Repairs

Check clothes after wearing for any needed repairs. It's best to make repairs before laundering clothes. Sewing on buttons or other fasteners is one common repair. Others include:

- **Repairing snags.** Knit fabric can easily develop a *snag*, a loop of yarn that has caught on something and been pulled to the outside. If the garment is puckered around the snag, gently stretch the fabric on each side to ease the snag back into place. Fig. 45-20 shows an easy technique to minimize a snag.

- **Mending seams.** When a seam comes apart, stitch it closed by machine or by hand.

- **Patching holes.** Fabric stores sell iron-on mending tape and patches. For dressier clothes, cut a small piece of fabric from the hem to use as a patch. Place it behind the hole. Turn under the raw edges of the hole, then use tiny stitches to secure the patch in place.

Altering Garments

Just as you can alter a pattern, existing clothes can be altered to change their fit or style. You could use the basic skills learned in this chapter to change a hemline, take in a seam, or move a button for a roomier waistline. Complicated alterations are better left to professionals or experienced sewers.

TIPS FOR *Success*

Sewing and Serging Safely

Sewing, like most hobbies, requires some safety precautions.

- Never sew over pins with your machine. A broken pin could cause injury.

- As you remove pins, put them in a pincushion, not in your mouth.

- Keep cutting tools closed when not in use.

- Pass sharp tools handle first.

- Store sewing tools safely.

- Sew at slow speed until you're used to the machine.

- Press and iron safely. Both heat and steam can burn. Unplug the iron when finished.

Fig. 45-20. Push a crochet hook through from the inside to the outside of the fabric at the site of the snag. Grasp the snag with the hook and pull it through to the inside where it won't be seen.

Chapter Summary

- Learning to sew begins with learning to use equipment and tools safely and appropriately.

- Before sewing, you must choose and prepare both a pattern and fabric.

- Patterns can be altered to customize the fit.

- Basic machine sewing techniques include directional stitching, staystitching, and making seams, facings, and darts.

- A variety of hand stitches are used for finishing steps, such as hems and fasteners.

- With basic sewing skills, you can make many simple repairs.

- Garments can be altered to change their fit or style.

Reviewing Key Terms & Ideas

1. Where is a **bobbin** located? What is its purpose?

2. Compare the uses of a sewing machine and a **serger**.

3. List five sewing tools and identify the purpose of each.

4. What should you do before deciding what size pattern to buy? Why?

5. Explain at least three ways the back of a pattern envelope can help a beginning sewer choose an appropriate project.

6. What are **notions**? Give three examples.

7. Describe how to check the **grain** when buying fabric and when laying out pattern pieces.

8. Give at least three examples of useful information found on a **pattern guide sheet**.

9. Explain how to alter a shirt pattern to increase the length.

10. Describe how to transfer pattern symbols to the fabric using tracing paper.

11. When making a sleeveless top, why might **staystitching** and a **facing** be used on the armholes?

12. Give one example of how you might **alter** a favorite garment to change its fit or style.

Thinking Critically

1. **Recognizing Assumptions.** Suppose a friend told you, "There's no reason I should learn how to sew." What assumptions might your friend be making? How would you respond?

2. **Predicting Consequences.** Choose any five specific recommendations given in this chapter. Predict what might happen if a beginning sewer ignored each one.

Applying Your Knowledge

1. **Testing Marking Tools.** Test different marking tools and methods on the wrong side of several fabric scraps. Evaluate the results. Are the marks visible? Do they show through to the other side? Are they easy to remove? Which method do you prefer and why?

2. **Seam Construction and Repair.** Using a sewing machine, sew together two fabric scraps by making a plain seam at least 10 inches long. Press the seam allowances open. Using small scissors or a seam ripper, snip the threads in a 2-inch section of the seam. Repair the seam by hand with a running stitch. Compare the strength and appearance of the machine and hand stitches.

Making Connections

1. **Math.** Choose a sewing project that interests you. Use the pattern envelope to determine the fabric and notions requirements. Shop for these items and calculate their cost. Create a chart showing the cost of each item and the total cost. Suggest ways that you might save money on the materials.

2. **Social Studies.** Choose an era of American history before 1960. Research typical clothes and how families obtained them during that time. What materials and techniques were used? Make a poster of your findings. As a class, make a clothing timeline using the posters.

Managing Your Life

Resource Tradeoffs

Sewing skills are a resource that can help you build and maintain your wardrobe. They can also come in handy for decorating your home or making gifts. As with all resources, however, using your sewing skills involves making trade-offs. Sewing takes time and requires that you invest in equipment and supplies. When are you willing to make these tradeoffs? Write a brief essay explaining how you would weigh time, money, and energy in deciding whether to sew an item yourself or purchase it.

Using Technology

1. **Internet.** Visit the Web site of a pattern manufacturer. Explore the resources available there. Write several paragraphs explaining how consumers can save time at the fabric store by visiting the company's Web site first.

2. **Video.** Watch a how-to video that teaches sewing skills. Write a review of the video. Were techniques clearly explained and demonstrated? What improvements can you suggest? What are the advantages and disadvantages of using a video compared to reading about sewing techniques in a book?

Career Options

Manufacturing and Engineering

Manufacturing and engineering have long been an important part of the economy. Workers produce the food people eat, the clothes they wear, the electronic equipment they buy, and the vehicles they drive. There are career opportunities for people of all levels of education and experience. The cluster can be divided into three broad sectors: Production and Operations; Metal Production; and Engineering. In this career cluster, employment opportunities vary significantly, depending on the specific area of manufacturing or engineering.

Main Employers

- Food processing industry
- Electronic equipment industry
- Motor vehicle industry
- Aerospace industry
- Apparel and textiles industries
- Chemical and pharmaceutical industries
- Printing and publishing industry

Manufacturing and Engineering Job Opportunities

Industry Segment	Entry Level	Additional Education and/or Training	Advanced Education and/or Training
Production and Operations	▪ Assembler ▪ Laborer ▪ Machine Operator	▪ Production Supervisor ▪ Instrument Maker ▪ Clothing Patternmaker ▪ Computer Technician	▪ Plant Manager ▪ Production Manager ▪ General Manager
Metal Production	▪ Machine Tool Operator ▪ Machine Tender ▪ Machine Setter	▪ Quality Control Technician ▪ Sheet Metal Worker ▪ Welding Technician	▪ Metallurgist ▪ Machine Shop Supervisor
Engineering	▪ Equipment Operator ▪ Measurement Technician	▪ Engineering Technician ▪ Engineering Research Assistant ▪ Inspector	▪ Civil Engineer ▪ Mechanical Engineer ▪ Electrical Engineer ▪ Industrial Engineer ▪ Aeronautical Engineer

The apparel industry is part of my heritage. My parents own a small but busy tailoring shop. They alter and repair clothes, and also create custom garments for their clients. At a very young age, I learned how to sew on a button and stitch a straight hem.

I dropped out of high school my senior year, thinking I could always work at the family shop. I did work there for a few years. It wasn't a bad job, but I grew bored with fixing zippers and shortening pants. I decided I really wanted to design clothes, not just alter them. That's when I found out that I couldn't apply to a design program without a high school diploma.

Right now, I'm working as a clothing patternmaker. I take a designer's original model of a garment and change it into individual pattern pieces. Using a computer, I outline the pieces and note the position of features such as buttonholes. Then I adjust the size of the pattern pieces so that garments of different sizes can be produced.

By going to school at night, I finished my high school equivalency diploma. Now I'm taking classes in design and computers at the local community college. It will take several more years before I can become a professional clothing designer. In the meantime, I get to work with designers every day, and I'm learning skills that will help me in the future.

Check It Out!

Choose one sector in this career cluster. Find three related occupations—one each level: entry, additional training, and advanced training. Find out what training or education is needed to advance from the entry-level position. Summarize your findings in a brief report.

UNIT 10

Housing and Transportation Choices

CHAPTER 46

Choosing a Place to Live

Key Terms

- security deposit
- mortgage
- condominium ownership
- cooperative ownership
- landlord
- tenant
- lease
- down payment
- closing costs

Objectives

- **Discuss** basic needs met by housing.
- **Identify** typical housing costs for renters and homeowners.
- **Describe** various types of housing.
- **Compare** the pros and cons of renting versus buying.
- **Explain** procedures for renting and buying housing.

QUICK WRITE

List six factors that will be important to you when you choose a place to live. Revise and add to your list as you read this chapter.

*W*ith graduation just a month away, Alyssa will soon be working as a nurse at a large hospital. She anticipates many changes as she enters this new stage of life, and she wants one of those changes to be her living arrangement. For the past two years, Alyssa has lived in an old house with three other nursing students. Although she has enjoyed many aspects of shared living, she feels more than ready to try living on her own. "It will be great to have my own space and to decorate it my own way," she says. "Now all I have to do is figure out how much I can afford and what my options are."

Housing Needs

Alyssa is looking forward to having a place she can call home. She knows that obtaining housing means more than simply "putting a roof over your head." Housing meets several distinct needs. It meets physical needs by providing shelter from the elements, a safe place for possessions, and space for personal activities. It meets emotional needs by providing privacy and an opportunity for personal expression. Housing also meets social needs. A home is a place to gather with family members and to welcome guests, and it can provide a feeling of belonging to a neighborhood or community.

While housing fulfills these basic needs for everyone, it can also fulfill individual needs that vary. People with disabilities have specific housing needs. Many homes today are designed to be as barrier-free as possible to accommodate both present and possible future needs of occupants and guests. Features such as wide doorways and hallways, adjustable-height shelves, and easy-to-operate fixtures make a home accessible and welcoming to all. See Fig. 46-1.

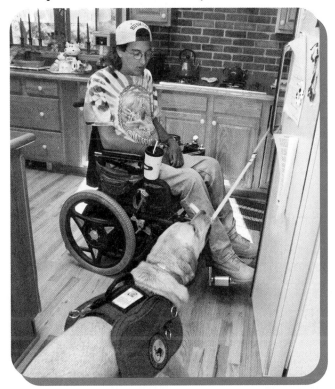

Fig. 46-1. Housing can meet a variety of individual needs. This home has been adapted to meet the needs of the owner and his canine helper.

Housing needs change over time and are often linked to life cycle stages. For example, how would the housing needs of a couple with three young children differ from those of a single 20-year-old or a retired couple?

Housing Expenses

Most people spend more money on housing than on any other single living expense. Several factors influence the cost of housing, including the size of the home and its location. Housing tends to cost more in rapidly growing areas of the country than in less popular regions. Even within a single community, costs vary among neighborhoods.

Before you begin to look for a place to live, you need to determine what you can afford. If you plan to rent, be aware that your rent is only part of what you will spend on housing. You also have to factor in the **security deposit**, a fee you must pay in advance to cover any damage you cause to the property. If you cause no damage, you should get the deposit back when you move out. You will probably have to pay for utilities such as gas, electric, water, phone, and cable, unless these are included in the rent. You may also need to buy furniture and appliances. In addition, you need to insure your possessions against theft or damage.

People who buy a home pay a monthly mortgage payment instead of rent. A **mortgage** is a long-term home loan. Like renters, homeowners must pay for utilities, furniture, and appliances. In addition, they must pay property taxes and, in some cases, homeowners' association fees. Homeowners also have maintenance costs and insurance expenses. Homeowner's insurance costs more than renter's insurance because it covers the building as well as everything in it.

More to Explore

Moving Expenses

When planning a move, be sure to include the moving expenses in your calculations. Here are some of the expenses you may have to budget for:

- Security deposit on a rental unit.
- Installation charges for telephone, Internet connection, and cable TV.
- Deposit for utilities such as gas, electric, and water.
- Cost of renting a truck or of hiring movers.
- Furnishings and window treatments to fit the new space.
- New driver's license if you move out of state.
- Increased vehicle insurance if you move to an area that has higher rates.

Housing Options

When Alyssa moves out of the house she is sharing, where will she go? Her first residence is likely to be an apartment, although there are other possibilities. In order to explore her options, she needs to know what her income will be. Then she can determine how much she will be able to spend on housing. A good general rule is to spend no more than one-third of gross pay on housing. People who commit more than that may not have enough left to cover food, clothing, and other necessities.

Renting or Buying

Alyssa's first decision will be whether to rent or buy. For most young people who are just starting out, buying is not an option. They usually don't have the money it takes to purchase a home.

The decision to rent or buy is not simply a financial one, however. Many young people are not ready to accept the responsibilities of home ownership. People who expect to move frequently may prefer the freedom that renting offers. Some people find that the advantages of renting outweigh those of ownership. You'll read more about the pros and cons of each option later in this chapter.

In spite of the advantages of renting, a large number of renters look upon it as a temporary arrangement. It gives them a place to live while they save toward buying a home. To save more quickly, many decide to share rented housing.

Sharing Housing

Alyssa hopes to live on her own, but when she figures out the costs, she may discover that she needs to share for a while longer. Housing expenses are a lot lower when two or three people share the rent or mortgage payments. Of course, sharing housing means sharing more than just the financial obligations. It also means sharing space. Some people enjoy the companionship of a roommate or two; others find that sharing is a total disaster. If you decide to share, think carefully about the person and the situation. Be will-

ing to make compromises as you work out the details of your living arrangement. See Fig. 46-2.

Living with a Roommate ~ The best way to make a shared living arrangement work is to agree on the ground rules before becoming roommates—even if you think you know the person very well. Don't wait until the roommate has moved in to discuss issues that might arise. Communicate your feelings about sharing expenses, space, food, and supplies.

Fig. 46-2. Cooperation and honest, but tactful, communication are the keys to successful shared living arrangements. What might happen if these skills were lacking?

Here are some topics to discuss with a potential roommate:

- **Finances.** Determine the total housing expense. Can the person afford to pay his or her share? How will bills be paid? Will you each be responsible for certain ones, or will you split all the bills?

- **Food and supplies.** Will you share food or keep separate food supplies? How about paper products and cleaning supplies?

- **Cleaning.** Do you have similar views on acceptable levels of clutter and cleanliness? How will cleaning tasks be divided?

- **Space.** Who gets the larger bedroom or the bedroom with its own bathroom? Who parks in the carport or garage?

- **Guests.** Are you each allowed to have overnight or weekend guests?

- **Consideration.** While you are sleeping or reading, is the roommate willing to keep the volume of music or TV low? Are you willing to take quick showers if you both need to get ready for work or school at the same time?

Living at Home ~ Recent years have seen a growing trend in living arrangements. More and more adult children are returning home to live with their parents. Sometimes it's a matter of economic necessity; other times the arrangement is simply convenient and practical. What situations can you think of that would result in this living arrangement?

Once children have been absent from home for a while, it can be difficult for parents to adjust to their return. It can also be challenging for the children to adapt to the new adult-to-adult relationship that they have with their parents. Cooperation and good communication are essential to making the arrangement work for everyone. Financial arrangements need to be agreed on ahead of time and, as with any sharing situation, everyone has to agree on the basic ground rules. See Fig. 46-3.

Fig. 46-3. When adult children return home to live with parents, everyone needs to make adjustments. This mother and son worked out a way to share the shopping, cooking, and chores.

Choosing a Location

Where would you like to live if you had the choice? Do you like the idea of fast-paced city life, or would you prefer a suburban neighborhood or a rural retreat? The three main types of locations—city, suburban, and rural—each have their pros and cons.

- **Cities.** Many cities offer great cultural, entertainment, and shopping opportunities, and city life can be exciting and stimulating. However, many cities are also crowded and noisy. Housing in major cities is often very expensive. You may have to pay as much for a one-bedroom apartment in a city as you would pay for a small house in the suburbs.

- **Suburban areas.** People who want access to a city without the drawbacks of city life often choose to live in the suburbs—the residential regions surrounding the city. They may take advantage of jobs and leisure activities in the city, but they can also enjoy being part of a more relaxed suburban community. See Fig. 46-4.

- **Rural areas.** People who want to live in a small community away from city life may choose a rural area. Rural areas may lack the excitement and conveniences of city life, but there is less noise and pollution, and people have easier access to outdoor pursuits.

Factors to Consider ~ Choosing a location is not as simple as deciding between city, suburb, or rural area. You also need to consider factors such as:

- **Familiarity.** You may want to stay in a location that is familiar and where you have family and friends. Many people enjoy the security of staying in the place they already call home.

Fig. 46-4. Although the offerings may not be as varied as in cities, suburbs do have their own entertainment and shopping opportunities. What other types of recreational activities might you find in a suburb?

- **Desire for change.** Others look forward to the challenge of change. They want a setting and lifestyle that is different from what they are used to.

- **Lifestyle considerations.** A person's career goals may require a move to a place where jobs are available. Workers also need to decide whether they want to live near their place of work or are willing to commute to work each day. People may be attracted to an area because of its climate, physical features, or low cost of living.

- **Practical considerations.** Transportation, shopping, and other practical issues can make one location more desirable than another. You might be able to take a bus to work from one location, for example, but for another you would need your own transportation.

Types of Housing

When you choose a type of housing, you need to consider both the structure and the type of ownership. In general, people choose different types of housing at different stages in their life. Their options are largely determined by their income, stage in the family life cycle, and their needs. Young adults just starting their career have a limited income and usually start by renting an apartment. After a few years, when they are established in their career and have more money, they may buy a small home. Married couples with two incomes have more options and may choose a larger home where they can raise a family. Older adults whose children have left home may decide to buy a smaller home that they can manage more easily.

Types of Housing Structures

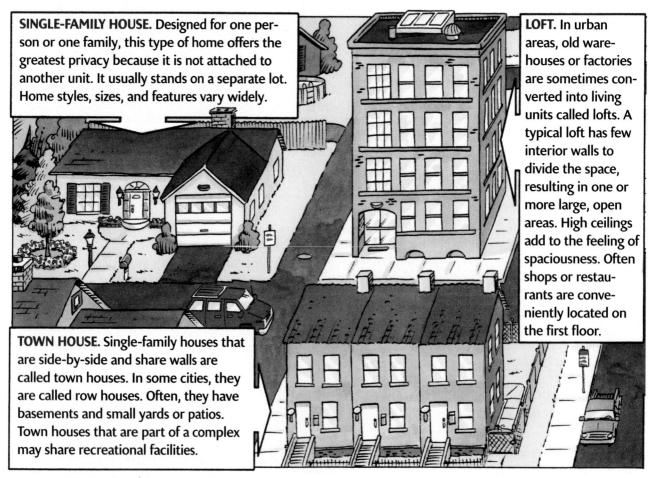

SINGLE-FAMILY HOUSE. Designed for one person or one family, this type of home offers the greatest privacy because it is not attached to another unit. It usually stands on a separate lot. Home styles, sizes, and features vary widely.

LOFT. In urban areas, old warehouses or factories are sometimes converted into living units called lofts. A typical loft has few interior walls to divide the space, resulting in one or more large, open areas. High ceilings add to the feeling of spaciousness. Often shops or restaurants are conveniently located on the first floor.

TOWN HOUSE. Single-family houses that are side-by-side and share walls are called town houses. In some cities, they are called row houses. Often, they have basements and small yards or patios. Town houses that are part of a complex may share recreational facilities.

Fig. 46-5. There's a home to suit everybody's needs and budget.

Types of Structures

Almost anywhere you go, many types of housing are available. Structures range from single units suitable for one family to large high-rise apartment buildings housing hundreds of people. Six of the most common types of structures are shown in Fig. 46-5.

Types of Ownership

All of the types of housing shown in Fig. 46-5 can be rented or owned. Ownership takes different forms, depending on the structure of the home. If you buy a single-family detached home set on its own lot, you own the building and the land. This is the traditional form of home ownership. If you buy a unit in a multiple-family complex,

such as an apartment or a town house, your ownership can take one of two forms:

- **Condominium ownership.** With **condominium ownership**, you own the unit that you buy and you share ownership of common areas, such as the hallways and grounds. In addition to paying for your unit, you pay a monthly fee to cover the cost of maintaining the common areas.

- **Cooperative ownership.** With **cooperative ownership**, you own stock in a corporation that owns the entire property and its grounds. The amount of stock you buy is in proportion to the size of the unit you occupy. When you purchase stock, you buy the right to occupy a particular unit, but you don't own the unit. You pay a

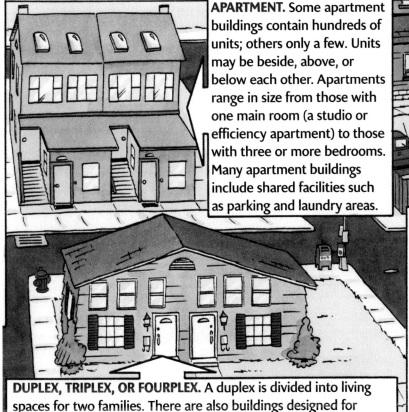

APARTMENT. Some apartment buildings contain hundreds of units; others only a few. Units may be beside, above, or below each other. Apartments range in size from those with one main room (a studio or efficiency apartment) to those with three or more bedrooms. Many apartment buildings include shared facilities such as parking and laundry areas.

MANUFACTURED HOME. A manufactured home is built at a factory, then moved by truck to a permanent site. The site may be on private property that belongs to the homeowner. Often, however, the homeowner rents lot space in a manufactured home "park." Manufactured homes are less expensive than other single-family homes, and most come with appliances and floor coverings. They can be an affordable way to become a first-time homeowner.

DUPLEX, TRIPLEX, OR FOURPLEX. A duplex is divided into living spaces for two families. There are also buildings designed for three families (triplex) or four families (fourplex). Each unit has its own outside entrance.

monthly fee that covers your share of all mortgage payments, maintenance expenses, and property taxes for the whole building. If you move, you sell your stock, not the unit.

In housing ads, you might see references to "condos" or "co-ops"—short for condominiums and cooperatives. People often use these terms to refer to the unit itself rather than the type of ownership. Also, some condominium owners rent out their units, which is why you might see an ad saying "condo for rent."

Fig. 46-6. One of the great benefits of renting is that you have fewer chores and more time to spend on activities that you enjoy. What other benefits of renting appeal to you?

Renting a Home

It's likely that your first home away from your family will be rented. When you rent a unit, you enter into an agreement with the **landlord**, the owner of the rental property. You become the **tenant**, or renter. Before you become a tenant, you should be aware of the pros and cons of renting. You also need to understand the rental process and your legal responsibilities.

Advantages of Renting

Rental housing comes in all shapes and sizes and may be furnished or unfurnished. Some key advantages of renting rather than owning a home include:

- **Fixed expenses.** Budgeting for housing is easy because there are no surprises. Tenants know what they will pay each month in rent. The costs of maintenance and improvements are the responsibility of the landlord.

- **Greater flexibility.** Renting is ideal for people who expect to move frequently or who are uncertain about where they want to settle. If they want to move, renters must give notice or wait until their rental agreement expires, but they don't have to worry about selling their home.

- **More free time.** Tenants need not spend time on repairs and maintenance tasks such as painting, yard work, and snow removal. See Fig. 46-6.

- **Lower insurance costs.** Renter's insurance costs considerably less than homeowner's insurance.

Disadvantages of Renting

Some of the drawbacks of renting include:

- **More restrictions.** Renters are restricted in the changes they can make to the property. They might not be allowed to paint or paper the walls, for example. Some landlords do not allow pets; others restrict the types of pets that tenants can have.

- **Financial drawbacks.** Unlike mortgage payments, which help you build ownership in the property, the money you spend on rent is simply gone. There are no tax advantages to renting, and the landlord may raise the rent at the end of each rental period.

- **Limited control.** Renters have little control over how the building is maintained and managed. Those who live in multiple-family buildings have no control over other tenants and may be bothered by their noise and clutter.

Selecting a Rental

When you choose a rental home, look beyond the floor plan and the way the home is decorated. Walk or drive around the neighborhood. Is the unit located in a safe area with a low crime rate? Is it convenient to work or school? Is public transportation close by? Use your senses. Your eyes, ears, and nose will give you a feeling for what it would be like to live there. Do the windows provide enough light? What is the view? Are common areas clean and free of trash? Listen for noises that will disturb you, and check for odors inside and outside.

Ask the landlord whether utilities are included in the rent. Find out about laundry facilities, parking, and security. The more you learn before choosing a rental home, the less likely you are to be disappointed.

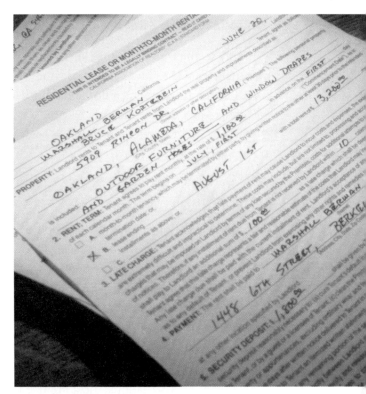

Fig. 46-7. *Before you sign a lease, make sure you understand exactly what the rent includes and does not include and what restrictions apply. Always get a receipt if you pay a security deposit.*

Signing a Lease

When you find a place you want to rent, you will need to fill out an application. Landlords want to know that you are reliable and able to pay the rent. They will check your credit history and verify your employment. Typically, tenants are then required to sign a **lease**, a legal document that specifies the rights and responsibilities of the landlord and tenant. You should read the lease carefully and ask questions about anything that you don't understand. See Fig. 46-7.

Most landlords require a security deposit—usually equal to one month's rent—when you sign a lease. Tenants with pets may be required to pay an additional pet deposit.

Buying a Home

It may seem far in the future, but you may eventually decide to buy a home of your own. Like renting, buying a home has both advantages and disadvantages.

Advantages of Buying

Here are some key advantages of being a homeowner:

- **Stability.** Owning a home gives people a feeling of putting down roots. They tend to develop a greater awareness of local government and business activities and of how those activities might affect their community.

- **Greater freedom.** Although some homeowners must follow guidelines set up by homeowners' associations, most are free to adapt their homes and yards to meet their individual needs and tastes. See Fig. 46-8.

- **Investment value.** A home is an investment. The cost of the home and the money put into maintaining it are not lost as they are with renting. If a home is well cared for, the owner can typically sell it for more than he or she paid for it.

- **Tax advantages.** Homeowners can deduct their property taxes and the interest on their mortgage from their federal income taxes.

Disadvantages of Buying

Some disadvantages of owning rather than renting housing include:

- **Unexpected expenses.** Although homeowners can plan for routine maintenance, some expenses, such as a broken furnace, can occur without warning.

- **Time spent on maintenance.** Maintaining a home takes a lot of time. In addition to the ongoing maintenance, tasks such as yard work, painting, and snow removal must be done as needed to protect the appearance and value of the home.

- **Reduced mobility.** Homeowners have less flexibility than renters when it comes to moving. The costs of buying and selling a home are high. You have to look upon home ownership as a long-term investment to make these costs worthwhile.

Fig. 46-8. Many homeowners enjoy creative activities such as gardening and decorating. Why does home ownership offer more freedom for these pursuits than renting does?

Fig. 46-9. An "Open House" sign means just that—the house is open for potential buyers to inspect. The agent selling the home will show you around and answer your questions.

Buying Procedures

If someday you begin to think about buying a home, the first step will be to determine your needs, wants, and price range. Then you can identify areas with homes that might be suitable. Be sure to evaluate the safety, convenience, and stability of any neighborhoods you're considering. To learn more about homes in a particular area, you might go to open houses. See Fig. 46-9.

Once you become serious about buying, you can look at available homes with a real estate agent. As the buyer, you do not pay the agent. Instead, he or she receives a percentage of the selling price from the person who is selling the home. Real estate agents provide many services for potential buyers, from finding homes that meet their needs to handling paperwork.

When you find a home you want to buy, the next step is to make an offer. Potential buyers often offer less than the asking price. The seller and buyer may then negotiate until they agree on the price and the offer is accepted. The next several weeks are spent preparing for the sale. The home is inspected, and the buyer arranges for financing. Finally, the sale is completed at a meeting called the *closing*.

Financial Considerations

Most people don't have enough money to buy a home outright, so they usually take out a mortgage and then pay back the loan in monthly installments. They also need enough money to pay the one-time costs involved in purchasing a home. One of these costs is the initial **down payment**, a portion of the purchase price that a buyer pays up front in cash. The down payment can range from 5 to 20 percent of the purchase price. Buyers must also pay **closing costs**—various fees due at the time of purchase.

Buying a home is a serious undertaking—usually the most significant purchase that anyone makes. Those who understand the process beforehand, and who prepare carefully, are more likely to find the home they want at a price they can afford.

Chapter Summary

- Housing fulfills a variety of basic and individual needs.
- The rent or mortgage payment is only part of the expense of housing.
- People who share housing need to compromise, cooperate, and communicate.
- The three main types of housing locations are city, suburban, and rural.

- Many types of housing structures are available.
- The three main types of home ownership are traditional, condominium, and cooperative ownership.
- If you rent a home, you should be aware of the pros and cons of renting and understand your legal responsibilities.
- Buying a home is a costly undertaking that requires careful preparation.

Reviewing Key Terms & Ideas

1. In what ways does housing meet basic human needs? Why do people's housing needs change over time?
2. What kinds of housing costs must a person budget for?
3. Explain the purpose of a **security deposit**.
4. What topics should you discuss with potential roommates?
5. What factors should be considered when choosing a location in which to live?
6. Briefly describe six common types of housing structures.
7. What are the key differences between traditional ownership, **condominium ownership**, and **cooperative ownership**?
8. Why do renters typically have more flexibility than homeowners?
9. What is the business relationship between a **landlord** and a **tenant**?

10. Name six things to look for or ask about when evaluating a rental unit.
11. What should you do before signing a **lease**? Why?
12. In what ways do homeowners have greater freedom than tenants?
13. Describe the steps that would take place if you found a home you wanted to buy.
14. What is the difference between a **down payment** and **closing costs**?

Thinking Critically

1. **Making Judgments.** What qualities would you look for in a roommate? Why? What ground rules would you want to establish?
2. **Drawing Conclusions.** Assume that you work for a large company and are being transferred to another city for three years. Would you rent or buy a home? Why?

Applying Your Knowledge

1. **Housing Choices.** Where do you hope to live when you leave your current home? Describe the location you would choose, and list the factors that are important to you. What kind of structure would best meet your requirements?

2. **Housing Costs.** Find out what it would cost to rent an apartment in your current community. Use classified ads or online advertising to get prices for one-bedroom and two-bedroom apartments. What is the average price of the two types of apartments? How much would you save on rent each month if you were to share a two-bedroom apartment?

Making Connections

1. **Math.** A new college graduate earns $2,100 a month. She is interested in a town house that rents for $625 per month. She estimates that utilities will average $140 per month. Renter's insurance costs $180 for one year. How much would she spend on housing each month? Based on what you learned in this chapter, can she afford to rent the town house? Explain.

2. **Social Studies.** How does geographic location affect the cost of housing? Use the Internet to identify the most and least expensive places to live in the United States. Prepare notes for a class discussion on the reasons for the difference in housing costs.

Managing Your Life

Estimating Housing Expenses

How much would it cost you to live in an apartment of your own? Assume that you will rent a one-bedroom apartment in your current community. Estimate the monthly rent (using an average for your area) and the monthly cost of electricity, gas, water, telephone, cable, and so on. Compare your estimates with those of your classmates. Prepare a final list with estimated costs that you can use when making future housing decisions.

Using Technology

1. **Internet.** Search the Web by entering the key words *moving expenses*. Look for a relocation calculator that enables you to determine the cost of moving from one city to another. What factors does the calculator take into account in determining cost? Make a chart showing sample costs, and share it with the class.

2. **Photography.** Look for examples of different types of housing structures in your community. Take an exterior photo of one example of each type that you find. In small groups, compile your photos into a visual display. Discuss your observations about the variety of housing in your community. Which types of housing seem to be most and least common? What are some possible reasons?

CHAPTER 47

Designing Living Space

Key Terms

- floor plan
- scale drawing
- traffic patterns
- proportion
- emphasis
- EnergyGuide label
- Energy Star label

Objectives

- **Create** a scale drawing of a room's floor plan.
- **Describe** the five elements of design and the effects that can be created with each.
- **Explain** how the principles of design apply to the design of a room.
- **Discuss** factors to consider when choosing furniture and appliances.
- **Suggest** strategies for meeting storage needs.

QUICK WRITE

Write a paragraph describing your ideal living room. What overall feeling would you want the room to express?

*E*ric felt excited as he looked around his new apartment. After living in a furnished room for a couple of years, he was eager to make this apartment an expression of his personality. The landlord had agreed that Eric could paint the walls, and she had even offered a discount on the first month's rent if Eric did the work himself.

As Eric was unloading boxes, the bed that he had ordered was delivered. Eric was surprised at how much space it took up. When he had planned the bedroom, he had pictured a desk by the window. Now he could see that a desk wouldn't fit anywhere in the bedroom. "I need to get organized before I buy anything else," thought Eric, "but I'm not sure where to start."

Organizing Your Space

To design a living space—whether it's one room or an entire home—start with the big picture. How much space do you have, and how is it organized? How do you want to use the space? Think about the activities that will take place there and how the space can be organized to accommodate them.

As you begin to plan, look through magazines that show different approaches to room design. Cut out pictures that appeal to you, whether it's because of the furniture arrangement, color scheme, accessories, or just a feeling or mood that the room conveys. This collection will become your reference as you organize your space and select your furniture. Notice what you like and dislike when you visit friends' homes, too. Gradually you'll gain ideas for what you want to accomplish with your own living space. See Fig. 47-1.

Fig. 47-1. Designing your living space can seem a little daunting at first, but once you get started you'll have lots of ideas.

Making a Floor Plan

A **floor plan** is a diagram that shows the main structural elements of a home or room. It can help you find the best way to arrange the furniture you have. If you're buying furniture, a floor plan can help you select pieces that will fit in the available space.

To make a floor plan of a room, begin by sketching the outline of the room's shape, as if you were looking down from the ceiling. Include walls, doors, windows, and other built-in features. Next, measure the room, including the width of doorways and windows. Write the measurements on your sketch.

To plan furniture placement, you need to draw your floor plan to scale. In a **scale drawing**, a given number of inches represents a given number of feet. A common scale is ¼ inch equals one foot. To use this scale, transfer your sketch to ¼-inch graph paper. Each foot you measured in the room is represented by one square on the graph paper. For example, to show a 12-foot-long wall, you would draw a line that extends 12 squares.

Use the same scale to make furniture templates. Measure the floor space each piece of furniture will take up. If you don't have the furniture yet, estimate its size. On a separate sheet of graph paper, draw the outlines of the furniture pieces. Label and cut them out to create templates. Now you can try out different arrangements by moving the templates around on the floor plan. That's much easier than moving the actual furniture. Fig. 47-2 shows a sample scale drawing of a room with furniture templates of the same scale.

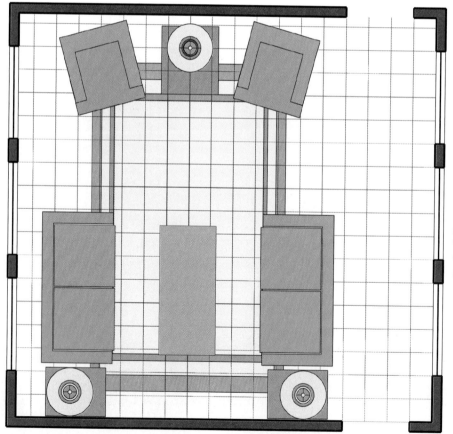

Fig. 47-2. Drawing a floor plan to scale and using cutout templates for furniture allows you to see exactly how items will fit in a room.

As you try different furniture arrangements, be sure to leave enough clearance space. For example, you need to leave space for doors and drawers to be opened and for chairs to be pushed back from a table or desk.

Considering Traffic Patterns

As you design your living space, you also need to consider **traffic patterns**, the routes people use to move through a room or from one part of a home to another. You want

FINDING CREATIVE SOLUTIONS

Taking a Break

Have you ever struggled with a problem for hours, only to find that the solution came to you later when you were taking a shower or walking the dog? That's because you'd given your brain a break. Some problems are like that. The solution comes when you almost stop looking for it.

How It Works

Like your body, your brain gets tired and performs poorly after working at a task too long. A difficult problem may seem unsolvable, or you may get fixed on a certain way of looking at it and be unable to see other possibilities. At times like this, taking a break can relieve tension and clear your head. Try going for a walk, listening to music, or washing dishes. Let the problem slip to the back of your mind. You may find that the solution will come to you when you least expect it. You might even want to try sleeping on it—a good night's sleep can recharge your creative "batteries."

Try It Out

From various relatives and rummage sales, Crystal had collected an assortment of furniture for her first apartment. Now she faced the challenge of fitting it into her living room. None of her floor plans worked. Every arrangement blocked the traffic pattern, discouraged conversation, or just looked bad. After two hours, Crystal was tempted to toss her floor plan and templates into the trash.

▶ **Your Turn** *What kinds of "take-a-break" activities would you suggest for Crystal? Think back over times in the past when you've dealt with a difficult problem. Make a list of the strategies you use when you need to give your brain a rest.*

people to be able to move freely from one area to another without walking around something.

When Antonia laid out her kitchen, she thought that her kitchen table would look great in the center of the room. She soon realized, though, that the table blocked the path from the refrigerator to the sink and that she had to walk around it dozens of times a day. After taking traffic patterns into account, Antonia found that it was far more convenient to place the table under a window instead.

Creating Different Areas

An effective strategy for organizing space is to create different areas for different purposes. You can do this by grouping furnishings and other items that you use at the same time. For example, a music area might have a CD player, CD storage, a comfortable chair or two, and lamps to provide soft lighting. A study area might include a desk, chair, bookcase, and desk lamp. See Fig. 47-3.

Creating different areas is also effective when people need to share space. Eduardo and Hector, for example, share a small apartment, and they each need an area with a desk and chair. Both thought the small sunroom off their living room was an ideal work area. They used a low, open bookcase to physically divide the space so that each of them would have a defined area to call his own.

Using Design Elements

On paper, Desirée's floor plan of her bedroom looked fine. She carried out her plan, but now that she looked at the room itself, it didn't look good at all. Desirée had allowed for adequate clearance space and a good traffic pattern. Why didn't it work?

No matter how good a floor plan is, paying attention to space alone will not achieve a good design. When designers plan a room, they also consider line, form, texture, and color. Paying attention to all five elements of design brings harmony to the design of a room.

Space

There are two aspects of space to consider—the size of the overall space and the arrangement of objects within that space. Different size spaces convey different feelings. Large open spaces give most people a sense of freedom. Too much empty space,

Fig. 47-3. One way to organize living space is to create different areas for specific activities. How has furniture been used to create different areas within this large room?

however, such as the space in an empty loft apartment, can seem barren and lonely. Well-designed small spaces can make people feel cozy and protected, but too little space can make people feel confined.

The furniture you choose and the way you arrange it can influence the effect of a room. When space is tight, limiting the number of furnishings will keep the room from appearing cramped and crowded. One way to limit furniture is to use pieces that serve more than one purpose, such as a storage unit with a pull-down desk. If you are dealing with a large space, try using a sofa, long tables, storage units, or even large plants to divide the space into two or three smaller areas. Another way to divide space is to arrange furniture into small clusters. To reinforce the idea of divided spaces, you might vary wall coverings or define different areas with distinct picture groupings.

Line

Every room comes with its own vertical and horizontal lines—the lines of windows and doorways, for example, and lines that mark the edges of a wall, floor, and ceiling. Shaped windows and arches may bring curved lines, while the slant of a staircase brings diagonal lines. Each of the four types of line helps create a certain feeling or image. Horizontal lines may create restful feelings, while vertical lines suggest action. Curved lines suggest grace and softness, while diagonal and zigzag lines convey excitement and movement. See Fig. 47-4.

The way line is used in a room can affect the way people see the space. Vertical lines—as in ceiling-to-floor drapes, tall bookcases, and tall windows—seem to add height to a

Fig. 47-4. Vertical, horizontal, curved, and diagonal lines all create different effects and feelings. What kinds of lines are dominant in this room design? What effect do they have?

room. In contrast, horizontal lines—such as low sofas and bookshelves—draw the eye around the room and create the illusion of greater width. You can combine different types of lines in any room. Awareness of line and of its overall effect will help you find a combination that works for you.

Form

Form refers to the shape and structure of solid objects. Some objects, such as beds and sofas, are large and bulky in form. Others, such as benches and end tables, may be small and delicate in form. When combining furniture in a room, it's important to choose forms that are in harmony with one another. For example, if you have a long, bulky sofa and are looking for a low table to place in front of it, choose one that's large and sturdy enough to blend with the sofa. In general, try to combine forms in a way that makes every item appear to fit well with the other items.

Texture

Texture refers to the appearance or feel of a surface. The texture of a surface may be rough or nubby or smooth. In some cases, texture is determined more by how an object looks than by how it actually feels. For example, modern printing technology makes it possible to produce wall coverings that look rough, even though they are actually smooth to the touch.

Texture influences the mood of a room. Plush, soft fabrics give a feeling of richness and comfort, while nubby, rough materials suggest ruggedness and stability. Metal, stone, and glass suggest coldness. Because the physical roughness or smoothness of a surface affects the way light is reflected, the texture of an object influences the way its color and size are perceived. When designing a room, you can use different textures to add variety and interest.

Color

Color is the most significant of the design elements and one that most people enjoy working with. You can express your personality and create a mood with color. In general, warm colors—yellows, oranges, and reds—tend to create a positive, energetic mood. Cool colors—blues and greens—can create a feeling of calm. Like texture, color can fool the eye. At the same distance, cool-

Fig. 47-5. Colors look different in different lighting. If you're choosing flooring, ask to borrow samples and see how they look in your home before you buy.

colored objects appear further away than warm-colored ones. You can make a small room appear larger by painting the walls a cool color.

The colors you choose when designing your living space will depend on your personality, the look you want to achieve, and the purpose of the rooms. Some people prefer cool, tranquil colors in a bedroom and warmer, more stimulating colors in a living room. Pay particular attention to the colors of expensive items, such as carpets and upholstered furniture, that you are likely to keep for a long time. See Fig. 47-5.

Using Design Principles

The principles of design are a set of guidelines for making the elements of design—space, line, form, texture, and color—work together in pleasing ways. The principles of design are proportion, balance, rhythm, emphasis, unity, and variety.

- **Proportion.** The way one part of a design relates in size to another part and to the whole design is known as **proportion**. Imagine a massive oak desk paired with a small wicker chair. Such a pairing would be out of proportion. A high-backed leather desk chair, on the other hand, would be in good proportion with the oak desk.

- **Balance.** This design principle involves giving equal weight to the spaces on both sides of an imaginary center line. In *symmetrical balance*, objects on each side of that line are mirror images of one another. In *asymmetrical balance*, the objects are unmatched but appear to have equal visual weight. See Fig. 47-6.

- **Rhythm.** The regular repetition of line, shape, color, or texture creates rhythm in design. Pictures hung at regular intervals, for example, create a rhythm that directs the eye to move in a natural flow from object to object. You can also achieve rhythm by using lines that radiate from a center point or by arranging objects to show a gradual increase or decrease in size.

- **Emphasis.** As a design principle, **emphasis** is the technique of drawing attention where you want it. For example, hanging a large, colorful art poster over a fireplace would draw the eye to that part of the room. The fireplace would become a focal point—a feature that stands out.

- **Unity.** When a design has unity, it creates the feeling that all objects in the room belong together. Furniture might have similar lines, for example, or similar colors might be used in drapes, pillows, and lampshades. A design that lacks unity can look cluttered and unattractive.

- **Variety.** Although rooms need unity, this is not to say that all items in a room should match. To achieve interest, you also need variety. Combining different, but compatible, styles and materials keeps the design from being boring. However, too much variety can create confusion.

Fig. 47-6. Balance can be symmetrical or asymmetrical. *Which type of balance do you see in this room design?*

Furnishing Your Home

The elements and principles of design can help you choose furniture and accessories. Knowing what look you want to achieve, and knowing how to achieve that look, will guide you in your choices. You will need to be patient, though. Most young adults have a limited amount of money to spend on furnishing their first home and can't achieve everything they want all at once. Still, with a little planning and creativity, you can create a comfortable living space that gives you great satisfaction.

Determining Priorities

Since you can't afford everything at once, examine your needs and wants and determine your priorities. For many people, a comfortable bed is a priority because everyone needs a good night's sleep. Beyond that, it depends on what is important to you. Beverly likes to cook and entertain, so one of her priorities is a dining table that seats at least six people. Cornell spends hours at his computer in the evening, so a computer console and a comfortable chair are high priorities for him. See Fig. 47-7.

Choosing Furniture

When choosing furniture, you have many options. With a limited budget, you may need to decide between buying lots of inexpensive items or getting by with just a few good quality pieces for a while. As with most choices, there are pros and cons to both. Inexpensive items let you furnish your home more quickly, but they may have to be replaced sooner.

Here are some additional options to consider when choosing furniture:

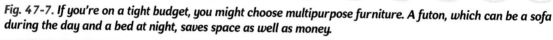

Fig. 47-7. If you're on a tight budget, you might choose multipurpose furniture. A futon, which can be a sofa during the day and a bed at night, saves space as well as money.

- **New furniture** may be very expensive, or it may be quite reasonable. The cost depends on the materials used and the quality of construction. Materials such as particle-board and plywood are less expensive than solid wood, but are often finished to look similar. You can also save money by buying furniture that you assemble yourself. Whatever type of furniture you buy, keep in mind that the sturdier and better constructed it is, the longer it will last.

- **Used furniture** that is well made may give you better quality than inexpensive new furniture. Even pieces that are in poor condition might be made usable with minor repairs. If the wood needs a new look, consider refinishing or painting it.

By painting old furniture, you can add color to a living space for very little cost. You can find used furniture in second-hand stores, or better yet, you may be able to acquire hand-me-downs from relatives.

- **Unfinished furniture** is wood furniture that has not been stained or painted. It's usually less expensive than finished furniture. Buying unfinished furniture and finishing it yourself allows you to customize the items to suit your taste and design scheme.

If your furniture budget is really limited, you can always improvise. You can make shelves with bricks and planks, for example, or place an old door on two filing cabinets to serve as a desk. Some people find that inexpensive outdoor furniture, such as a picnic table and two benches, works fine indoors until they can afford something better.

Using Accessories

Just as accessories such as a belt or jewelry add visual interest to an outfit, accessories in the home add visual appeal to a room. Some accessories, such as clocks, lamps, and books, serve a function. Others are strictly decorative. Examples of popular decorative accessories include pillows, candles, framed pictures, dried or silk flowers, and wall hangings.

You can use accessories to carry out the elements and principles of design in your living space and to express your personality. What's more, you can have fun in the process. Accessories don't have to cost a lot, and you can change them whenever you wish. Posters, for example, are inexpensive and can reflect interests such as music, art, or sports. As your interests change, or as you come up with new design ideas, you can buy or create new accessories.

TIPS FOR *Success*

Hanging Pictures

Pictures on a wall look so much better if you put some thought into their placement. Here are some suggestions:

- Hang large pictures so that their center is at eye level.

- Consider proportion. Don't hang a single tiny picture on a large wall or a very large poster above a small table.

- Design a grouping of smaller pictures by first tracing their outlines on paper. Cut out the pieces. Use tape to try various arrangements on the wall.

- When arranging pictures in a group, use an odd number of pictures. Place large pictures low in the grouping. Balance light and dark colors.

Choosing Appliances

If you need to buy a washer, dryer, refrigerator, or other major appliance, shop carefully. These are expensive items, so make sure the ones you choose have the right features for you. Just as you would for other furnishings, think about your needs and priorities before you buy. Also consider your possible future needs. Suppose, for example, that your apartment has space for only the smallest washer and dryer units. If you're planning to stay there for a couple of years or more, it might be wise to buy the small units. However, if you expect to move to a larger home soon, it makes more sense to put off the purchase.

To make informed purchasing decisions, follow these tips:

- Read unbiased reports and reviews that compare and rate various brands and models.

- Avoid models that are larger than you need or that have features you will not use.

- Examine the warranty and find out how you would get the item repaired, if needed.

- Compare new items with good-quality used items. For example, a new washer could cost more than $500, while a used one might be offered for $100.

- When comparing prices, take into account the cost to operate the appliance.

Most appliances are required by law to have an **EnergyGuide label** that shows the estimated annual energy consumption of that model. The black and yellow label also shows the range of energy use for similar models and the estimated yearly operating cost. Look also for the **Energy Star label**, a blue and green label indicating that a product meets government standards for energy efficiency. See Fig. 47-8.

Storage Solutions

As you work on a design for your living space, use your creativity to meet your storage needs. The best designs feature storage space that is convenient and accessible as well as attractive. Before you assess your

Fig. 47-8. These labels will help you save money in the long run. The EnergyGuide label is particularly useful for comparison shopping.

storage needs, go through the items you plan to store. Discard, recycle, or give away items you no longer need or want. Once you've eliminated unwanted items, follow these guidelines:

- **Group similar items together.** Store them in the same area so they will be easy to find. For example, place towels and bed linens together in a closet or storage unit.

- **Store often-used items within easy reach.** Avoid keeping something you use often on a high shelf or in a low drawer. On the other hand, store items that are seldom used in less accessible places, such as in a box under the bed or at the top of a closet.

- **Keep some items visible.** Storing objects in clear plastic containers, in wire-mesh baskets, or on open shelves helps you locate them easily.

- **Take advantage of unused space.** Install hooks or pegs on walls and doors, and use them to hang belts, ties, scarves, and other items. Hang a shoe rack on the back of a closet door. You could even hang baskets and other lightweight items from hooks in the ceiling. See Fig. 47-9.

- **Look for furniture with built-in storage.** You might find a bench with a seat that lifts up, for example, or a bed with drawers built into the base. You could use an old trunk as a coffee table and store out-of-season clothing inside it.

Sharing Living Space

Chances are you will share living space when you move into your first home. If you share with roommates, you'll need to take everyone's needs and wishes into account before making design decisions about common areas. People should not have to live

Fig. 47-9. "Vertical" storage on walls and doors uses space efficiently. *What unused space in your home could be put to use for storage?*

with color schemes they detest or with design schemes that make them feel uncomfortable in their own home.

Storage can be a sensitive area in shared living space. Take care to divide storage space fairly. If you decide to store like items together, such as CDs or books, label them so that each person can easily identify his or her own items.

Mostly, you need to show consideration and respect when sharing living space. You may have to wait until you have a place of your own before you can fully express your personality in your home design. Still, by working together and using the elements and principles of design, you and your roommates should be able to design a space that you all find pleasing.

Chapter Summary

- A floor plan and templates can help you plan furniture arrangements and traffic patterns.
- Pay attention to all five design elements when designing a living space.
- The principles of design will help you use the elements of design to best advantage.
- As you begin to furnish your living space, focus on your priorities.
- Accessories can help you add visual appeal to a room.
- Consider future needs as well as present needs when choosing appliances.
- When planning storage, focus on convenience and accessibility.

Reviewing Key Terms & Ideas

1. What does a **floor plan** look like?
2. What is a **scale drawing**? How does it help you arrange furniture?
3. Why do you need to consider **traffic patterns** when planning a room?
4. Compare the effects of having too much and too little empty space in a room.
5. What is the general effect of horizontal lines in a room design? Of zigzag lines?
6. Why is it important to pay attention to form when choosing furniture?
7. If you wanted the fabric on a chair to suggest ruggedness, what texture would you choose?
8. Which colors are warm and which are cool? What feelings does each convey?
9. How can you evaluate **proportion** in a design?
10. What creates rhythm in a design?
11. What is the purpose of **emphasis** in a design?
12. What are two advantages of buying unfinished furniture?
13. Why should you consider future as well as present needs when choosing appliances?
14. What do the **EnergyGuide label** and **Energy Star label** tell you?
15. What should you do before you begin to assess your storage needs?

Thinking Critically

1. **Making Predictions.** What might happen if you tried to design a room without knowing about the elements and principles of design?
2. **Defending Your Position.** Assume that you have a limited budget and must choose between used furniture and inexpensive new furniture. Which would you choose? Explain your reasons.

Applying Your Knowledge

1. **Drawing a Floor Plan.** Practice drawing a floor plan by making a sketch of your classroom or of one of the rooms in your home. Take measurements and then convert your floor plan into a scale drawing.

2. **Using Design Elements and Principles.** From home design magazines, cut out five illustrations of room designs that appeal to you. Attach labels to identify the design elements and principles that each illustration demonstrates. Be prepared to present your illustrations to the class and to explain how the elements and principles were used to create an effective design.

Making Connections

1. **Language Arts.** Write down each of the elements of design. Beside each element, list descriptive words that come to mind as you imagine how you might redesign your bedroom. After you complete your lists, put your thoughts together and write an overall description of the room.

2. **Social Studies.** Use reference materials to learn about traditional Japanese interior design. How might the furnishings, accessories, room arrangements, and other features of a traditionally designed home in Japan differ from typical homes in the United States? Share what you learn with the class.

Managing Your Life

Meeting Storage Needs

People tend to have more "stuff" these days than they used to, so storage can be a problem. If you get into the habit of paring down and organizing your possessions now, proper storage will become second nature to you. Make a plan to discard items you don't want, to store seldom-used or off-season items in less accessible places, and to store current items so that they are easy to find. As you carry out your plan, look for creative ways to use space and storage organizers.

Using Technology

1. **CAD.** Experiment with floor plans by using a computer-aided design (CAD) program. Choose two rooms and practice using the software to arrange furniture. Share your results with the class, explaining traffic patterns and any furniture clusters that you created.

2. **Video.** Arrange to watch an interior design television program with a group of classmates. Choose a show that features a makeover of a room. Afterwards, discuss with the group the results of the makeover. Describe the color scheme. Explain how the elements and principles of design were used. What were the greatest improvements? What techniques were used in order to save money?

CHAPTER 48

Home Care and Safety

Key Terms

- preventive maintenance
- carbon monoxide detector
- ground fault circuit interrupter (GFCI)

Objectives

- **Summarize** the benefits of caring for one's home.
- **Explain** ways to keep a home neat and clean.
- **Identify** preventive maintenance tasks.
- **Describe** strategies for preventing home accidents and preparing for emergencies.
- **Discuss** ways to promote community safety.

QUICK WRITE

List the tasks you already do regularly to keep your home clean and safe. As you read this chapter, identify actions that you should add to your list.

*T*ina looked frantically for her bus pass. It was often hard to find things in the apartment that she shared with two roommates. All three were busy students, taking full class loads and working part-time jobs. They didn't see housework as a high priority.

Tina remembered having her bus pass in the kitchen the night before. When she went there to look for it, one glance around the kitchen made her heart sink. The table and counters were loaded with books, magazines, unopened mail, empty food packages, grocery bags, and all sorts of other things. "This has got to change," thought Tina. "We'd better come up with a home care plan quick, before I lose anything else!"

Benefits of Home Care

Caring for a home means more than simply keeping things tidy. It means keeping the home clean, doing routine maintenance tasks, and taking action to prevent home accidents. Some people say they are too busy to care for their home or that they have more important ways to spend their time.

They don't realize that caring for a home actually saves time. Whether you're looking for a bus pass, a notebook, or a pair of shoes, you can find items more easily if you always put them in their proper place. Wouldn't you prefer to spend time doing something you enjoy instead of hunting for something that's misplaced? See Fig. 48-1.

Home care saves money, too. Caring for possessions makes them last longer and stay in better condition. It lowers the risk that you will damage something or throw it out by mistake.

Fig. 48-1. Your home doesn't have to be perfectly neat all the time. Just remember to put things away when you're finished using them. That way they won't get lost or damaged.

Yet another benefit of home care is that it improves your state of mind, your health, and your safety. A messy, disorganized home can make you feel anxious or depressed and may actually be dangerous. A clean and organized home, on the other hand, offers a more pleasant, more healthful, and safer environment. Besides, wouldn't you prefer to welcome friends into an inviting home that shows that you care about how you live?

Neatness and Cleanliness

Keeping a home neat and clean can become an everyday habit. By taking some simple steps each day, you can keep tasks manageable.

The Neatness Habit

You may need to work at it for a while, but if you make neatness a habit, it becomes second nature. Make a point of noticing current "un-neat" habits, such as flinging a coat over a chair when you come home. Get into the habit of hanging your coat up and doing other things that keep a home tidy. Here are some suggestions:

- Make your bed after you get up in the morning.
- Have a place for everything, and put things away as soon as you finish using them. Inexpensive storage boxes, crates, or shelves might be helpful. See Fig. 48-2.
- Sort mail the first time you look at it. Throw away junk mail, and place items that need your attention in a designated place.

Fig. 48-2. To organize a storage system, decide what needs to be stored, what kind of shelves or containers would work best, and where to put them. These shelves are both inexpensive and adjustable.

- Put newspapers and magazines in a recycling box when you finish reading them.
- Unload grocery bags as soon as you get home.
- When you change clothes, hang up items that don't need to be laundered. Use a hamper or bag for laundry and a separate basket for dry cleaning.
- Keep clutter to a minimum by getting rid of things you don't really need or want.

Establishing a Routine

Cleaning goes much faster if you establish a routine for doing tasks. Decide what needs to be done, who will do it, and how often.

For example, your routine for cleaning your bedroom each Saturday might include putting away clothes, changing sheets, dusting furniture, cleaning the floor, and polishing the mirror. Having a routine for every room simplifies home care and ensures that no part of the home is neglected.

A routine for cleaning is particularly important for people who share a home. Whether you live with roommates or with other family members, you need a system for sharing home care. Some people like to volunteer for a particular job because it's something they're good at or enjoy. Another approach is to divide the work on a room-by-room basis. Roommates sometimes select chores from a "job jar" or rotate cleaning tasks. Everybody should participate in cleaning, but individual abilities and health limits need to be taken into account.

Viewpoints

Storage Styles

"A place for everything and everything in its place" is a cardinal rule of organization. That's a very general guideline, however, with many possible variations.

Kevin: I find it's easier to get things done if projects and supplies are out where I can see them. If I try to be neat by hiding everything away, I tend to put things off or forget. Like if I need to fill out an application form, I put it on the desk in my room. I keep tools right where I use them most often—the broom and a mop are behind the kitchen door. It's faster and easier to grab them that way.

Shawna: To me, part of keeping a home looking nice is putting things away when you're not using them. Leaving school papers, cleaning supplies, and other stuff sitting out would be like leaving dishes on the counter after they're washed. Besides, if things are left out, they usually get moved or misplaced. Then it's more work to track them down when I need them.

Seeing Both Sides ~ Does everyone need to follow the same "rules" for organization? Why or why not? If family members have different storage styles, how might they reach a compromise?

Daily and Weekly Tasks

Households run more smoothly when cleaning chores are done on a regular basis. Some need to be done daily, some weekly, and some only occasionally. Here are some suggestions for daily activities that contribute to a clean home:

- Wash dishes.
- Wipe kitchen countertops, range, and sink.
- Sweep kitchen floor.
- Take out garbage as needed.

When it comes to weekly chores, you may choose to perform one job each day, or you may decide to do them all at one time. See Fig. 48-3.

Here are some tasks that you need to do weekly:

- Vacuum or sweep the floors.
- Shake out small rugs.
- Clean bathroom fixtures.
- Wash kitchen and bathroom floors.
- Dust the furniture and other objects.
- Change the bed linens.
- Do the laundry.

Jobs that need to be done only occasionally include washing windows, waxing floors, cleaning the refrigerator and oven, and cleaning ceiling fans and window blinds. In addition, many families do a thorough house cleaning every spring and fall as they prepare for summer and winter.

Cleaning Indoors

Television commercials might lead you to believe that you need a whole slew of machines and gadgets to keep a home clean. In fact, you just need a few basic items—and, of course, the discipline to use them. Those basic items include a vacuum, broom, cleaning cloths, sponge, bucket, and a few basic cleaning products. Follow these procedures for cleaning different areas inside your home:

- **Windows.** Apply a glass-cleaning product, then dry the windows with a clean cloth or with paper towels.

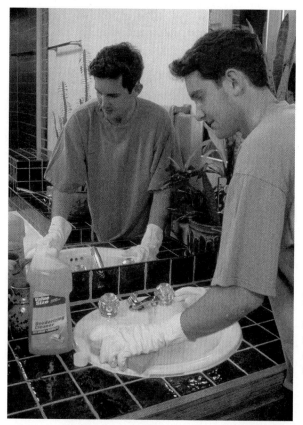

Fig. 48-3. For weekly chores, figure out a system that works for you. Would you prefer to do all chores at one time, or to spread them through the week?

- **Furniture.** Use a soft cloth or duster, with or without a dusting spray. Use furniture polish or wax occasionally to protect the wood. Vacuum upholstered furniture, and turn the cushions occasionally to ensure that the fabric wears evenly.

- **Floors.** Blot up spills immediately. Clean smooth floors with a broom or dust mop, then wash them using an appropriate cleaning product for the floor material. Vacuum carpeted floors.

- **Bathrooms.** Use a sponge or brush and cleanser to scrub the tub and shower. Rinse all surfaces thoroughly. Use cleanser or all-purpose cleaning spray on the basin, counter, and outside of the toilet. Use a toilet brush and disinfecting cleaner on the toilet bowl. Follow the directions on cleaning products carefully.

- **Walls and cabinets.** Use a sponge or cloth with an appropriate cleaning solution to wipe fingerprints and spots from walls, doors, switch plates, cabinets, and drawers.

Cleaning Outdoors

Maintaining the outdoor areas around your home will help your home look attractive and welcoming. The tasks you need to do will depend on the climate and on the type of home and yard you have. In general, keep the porch, patio, or balcony swept and tidy, and make sure walkways and driveways are free of clutter. Mow the lawn, rake leaves, and wash windows and screens as needed. If you live in a multifamily complex, some of these tasks might be done by maintenance staff. Even so, you share some of the responsibility for keeping outdoor areas tidy. Be sure you do your part to keep the area free of clutter and litter.

TIPS FOR *Success*

Save Cleaning Time

There are lots of things you can do to cut back on the time you spend cleaning. Here are some ideas:

- Keep dirt out of the home by placing doormats outside and inside every entrance.

- Remove outdoor shoes as soon as you arrive home.

- Clean up spills as soon as they occur. A fresh spill is easier to clean up than one that has had time to harden.

- Prevent soap scum from building up by wiping the tub, shower stall, and sink after each use.

- Wash dirty hands as soon as possible to avoid getting fingerprints on doors and other surfaces.

Preventive Maintenance

Have you heard the expression "Prevention is better than cure"? In health care, it means that it's better to prevent a disease than to treat it after it develops. The same is true of home care: it's better to prevent a problem than to fix it. **Preventive maintenance** means taking action to prevent problems or to keep minor problems from becoming major ones. Certain basic preventive maintenance tasks must be done to keep the home and its systems in good condition.

Fig. 48-4. Smoke detectors can save lives—but only if they work properly. Get into the habit of checking smoke detectors and replacing batteries every spring and fall.

Seasonal Tasks

In most situations, the following items need attention at least twice a year:

- **Furnace and air conditioner.** Clean or replace the filters at the end of the heating or cooling season and during periods of heavy use.

- **Smoke detectors.** Test to make sure they are working properly, and replace batteries as needed. Choose a regular time to do this, perhaps when the time changes in the fall and spring. See Fig. 48-4.

- **Water heater.** Turn off the power source, then drain water from the valve at the bottom until it runs clear. A buildup of sedi-ment shortens the life and efficiency of a water heater.

- **Refrigerator.** Vacuum the condenser coils to prevent overheating. Check the owner's manual for maintenance tips.

- **Garage.** Lubricate tracks of automatic garage door openers for smooth operation.

- **Gutters.** Clean leaves from gutters and downspouts in the fall and spring.

Annual Tasks

The following maintenance jobs should be done at least once a year. If you rent your home, find out who is responsible for doing them, you or your landlord.

- **Exterior.** In the spring, inspect the siding, paint, roof, and foundation for any problems.

- **Furnace and air conditioner.** Have a professional check the furnace in the fall. If you have air conditioning, have it inspected before periods of heavy use.

- **Fireplaces and wood-burning stoves.** To reduce the risk of fire, hire an expert to clean chimney flues once a year—twice a year if they are used often.

Other Tasks

Other maintenance tasks can be performed on an as-needed basis. Prevent drains from clogging by running a drain cleaner through them from time to time. Listen to the sounds of your home. If the refrigerator or water heater becomes noisy, have it checked to prevent a major breakdown. If a toilet starts to run continually, replace the flush mechanism. Every time you take action early to fix a minor problem, you prevent a major one from developing.

Preventing Home Accidents

An important part of home care involves keeping the home safe. Every year, millions of Americans are injured and thousands die in the very place where most people feel safest—in their home. The most common types of home accidents are falls, cuts, poisonings, electrical shocks, and burns. Most accidents that happen in the home could have been prevented. You can take responsibility for home safety by understanding potential dangers and taking steps to prevent accidents.

Preventing Falls

Falls are the leading cause of injuries and deaths in the home. Although children and older people fall most often, anyone can fall down the stairs or trip over an object. Falls are most likely to occur on cluttered or slippery surfaces. Most falls occur in bathrooms, in kitchens, and on stairs.

Follow these tips to minimize the risk of falling:

- Use a stepladder, not a chair, to reach high places. See Fig. 48-5.
- Keep toys and clutter off the floor in heavy traffic areas.
- Install safety gates at the top and bottom of stairs when toddlers are present.

- Keep rooms and hallways well lighted. Use night lights near stairs.
- Anchor throw rugs with carpet tape or nonskid mats.
- Arrange furniture to be out of the path of traffic.
- Wipe up spills immediately. Warn others when you have just washed or waxed a floor.
- Use a tub mat or adhesive strips on the bottom of the bathtub. Install grab rails for older family members.

Fig. 48-5. When you need to reach a high shelf, a stepladder is a sturdier and safer choice than a chair.

Preventing Cuts

Cuts from tools and equipment occur most often in the kitchen, in workrooms, and in outdoor areas. Always pay close attention to what you are doing when you use knives and other tools, and use the tools only as intended. See Fig. 48-6.

Here are some additional ways to prevent cuts:

- Store knives and kitchen tools with their handles toward the front of the drawer, or use a wooden knife block.
- Keep knives and scissors away from young children.
- Wear gloves and goggles when operating power tools. Store power tools and saws in a safe place, and cover the blades when they are not in use.

- Wear shoes with closed toes when operating a lawnmower or a trimmer.
- Unplug any tool or appliance before you try to adjust or fix it.

Preventing Poisonings

Most poisonings occur in the bathroom, kitchen, and bedroom. Young children are most at risk because they are naturally curious and don't always recognize danger. Medicines are a particular danger to children, who might think they are candy. To prevent children from gaining access to medicines, choose childproof containers and keep all medicines out of reach, preferably in locked cabinets. Be sure that children don't have access to any medicines that are kept in a purse, backpack, or bedside table.

Fig. 48-6. Even simple kitchen tasks require that you pay close attention to what you're doing. *What precautions would you take to keep from cutting yourself when making a salad?*

Fig. 48-7. A GFCI monitors the flow of current to an appliance. If it senses a change in current, it shuts off the flow of electricity. You can use the reset button to restore power.

Be aware of other poisons that are kept in or around your home. They might include cleaning products, gasoline, kerosene, fertilizer, paint and paint thinner, and insect and weed killers. Use locks or childproof latches to secure all cabinets and drawers that contain poisons. Be sure to keep all poisonous products in their original containers.

Poisonings can also occur when certain gases are inhaled. Carbon monoxide is an odorless, extremely poisonous gas that can be produced by defective gas appliances such as a furnace, heater, fireplace, or water heater. All gas heating devices should be checked regularly. If your home has such appliances, you should also install a **carbon monoxide detector**, a device that sounds an alarm when a dangerous level of carbon monoxide is reached.

Preventing Electrical Shocks

Most electrical shocks occur because of problems with plugs, outlets, wiring, and extension cords and because of improper use of appliances. Follow these precautions to prevent electrical shocks:

- **Plugs and outlets.** Inspect electrical cords for loose plugs or exposed wiring. When there are children in the home, use outlet covers. In kitchens and bathrooms, you can install special protective devices. A **ground fault circuit interrupter (GFCI)** is a device used near plumbing or water

to guard against electrical shock. A GFCI can be a special wall outlet or a portable unit attached to an appliance cord. See Fig. 48-7.

- **Extension cords.** To prevent circuit overload and the fires that can result, avoid plugging too many appliances into the same outlet. Instead, consider using power strips or extension cords to distribute the load to two or more outlets. Keep all electrical cords out of areas where people might trip on them, but don't place them under rugs or carpets.

- **Appliances.** To avoid electrical shock, never use electrical appliances with wet hands or while standing on a wet surface. Never use appliances in the bathtub or when there is water in the sink—they might fall in and cause electrocution. Make sure appliance cords are well covered with insulation and not frayed. Unplug small appliances when they are not in use.

Preventing Fires and Burns

Many of the guidelines for preventing electrical shocks will also help prevent fires and burns. In addition, you can reduce the risk of fires by being especially careful when using matches and candles. Make sure that no one in your home smokes in bed. Before throwing burned matches away, be sure they are properly extinguished. Don't place candles near anything that could catch fire or in a place where they could be knocked over easily. Never leave lighted candles in an empty room. If you have candles in a bedroom, make sure you put them out before you go to sleep.

If you use a portable space heater, place it well away from furniture, drapes, and anything else that could catch fire. Always follow the manufacturer's directions, and never leave the heater unattended.

As you might expect, the kitchen is the area where most fires and burns occur. Actions that you can take to prevent fires and burns in the kitchen are discussed in Chapter 38. Be particularly careful in the kitchen when young children are present. Turn pot handles toward the center of the range, and be aware that children don't necessarily know what is hot and could burn them. If you smell gas in your home, leave immediately and call the gas company from a neighbor's home.

Fig. 48-8. Several types of fire extinguishers are available, each effective on a different type of fire. Read the instructions on the label carefully.

Preparing for Emergencies

A gas leak is one kind of emergency that can happen in a home. Fire is another. You need to know what kinds of emergencies might happen in your home and prepare for them in advance. That includes weather-related emergencies—such as hurricanes, tornadoes, floods, or major snowstorms—that can occur in the region where you live.

Here are some general measures you can take to prepare for emergencies:

- Keep fire extinguishers in the kitchen and garage, and learn how to operate them. See Fig. 48-8.
- Install smoke detectors on every level of your home.
- Develop a fire escape plan with family members, and practice using it.

Fig. 48-9. Getting to know your neighbors contributes to community safety. What else could you do to help keep your community safe?

- Practice any recommended procedures for the disasters that might occur in your region.

- Assemble a disaster preparedness kit that includes a flashlight, battery-operated radio, candles, spare batteries, a first aid kit, bottled water, and canned food.

- Find and label shut-off valves for water, electricity, and gas. Learn how to operate them.

- Keep telephone numbers for the police, fire department, ambulance service, hospital, and poison control center next to each phone in your home.

Community Safety

Keeping your home safe and preparing for emergencies show that you are responsible. You can also show responsibility by contributing to the safety of your community. Everyone benefits when people do their part to keep their community safe.

You can start by getting to know your neighbors. If you know who belongs in your neighborhood, you'll find it easier to spot suspicious activity by strangers. You'll also know which neighbors may need assistance if there is an emergency. See Fig. 48-9.

Help to keep your neighborhood safe by paying attention to what is going on around you. If you see unfamiliar parked vehicles, groups of strangers loitering, or cars driving slowly through the neighborhood, stay extra alert. If you see suspicious activity, call the police.

You might want to organize or join a Neighborhood Watch program in your community. These programs have been effective in promoting safety and preventing crime. Some Neighborhood Watch groups have extended their role to focus also on emergency preparedness and terrorism alertness. Communities that work together to protect themselves in these ways feel reassured that everybody is looking out for everyone else.

Chapter Summary

- A clean and organized home saves time and money and is safer and healthier.
- Make neatness a habit, and establish routines for cleaning.
- You don't need a lot of gadgets for cleaning—just a few basic items.
- Maintaining outdoor areas helps a home look attractive and welcoming.
- Preventive maintenance keeps systems running smoothly and alerts you to any problems.
- Know when, where, and how home accidents are most likely to occur, and take action to prevent them.
- Prepare for the emergencies that are most likely to happen in your home.
- Contribute to safety in your community by being observant.

Reviewing Key Terms & Ideas

1. How does caring for a home save time and money?
2. What is the advantage of making neatness a habit?
3. Describe three different ways roommates might divide cleaning tasks.
4. What cleaning tasks need to be done every day?
5. Give five examples of weekly cleaning chores.
6. What basic items do you need for cleaning a home?
7. What is the purpose of **preventive maintenance**?
8. What can you learn by listening to the sounds of your home?
9. Name three guidelines for preventing falls and three for preventing cuts.
10. How does a **carbon monoxide detector** help protect people?
11. What is a **ground fault circuit interrupter (GFCI)**? In what rooms are these devices needed?
12. What items should you include in a disaster preparedness kit?
13. What actions can you take to promote safety in your community?

Thinking Critically

1. **Understanding Cause and Effect.** Reread the opening paragraph of this chapter. Why was the apartment in such a mess? How did the mess affect the roommates? What solutions can you suggest?
2. **Making Predictions.** What kinds of weather emergencies are most likely to occur in the region where you live? How can you prepare for them?

Applying Your Knowledge

1. **Preventive Maintenance.** With your family, make a list of the preventive maintenance tasks that should be performed in your home. Offer to take responsibility for one or more of these tasks or to help other family members carry them out.

2. **Planning Escape Routes.** Draw a floor plan of your home that shows the location of doors, windows, stairways, and outside fire escapes. Then work with family members to diagram a plan for escape in the event of a fire. If possible, indicate two ways to reach the ground from every room.

Making Connections

1. **Language Arts.** Create slogans that might encourage people to keep their home clean and tidy. Share your ideas with your classmates. Choose one of the slogans and use it as the theme of a poster. Place the poster somewhere in your home where everyone can be encouraged by it.

2. **Science.** Research the health risks that have been attributed to the presence of mold in a home. Write a report on causes of mold, effects on health, and clean-up and prevention strategies.

Managing Your Life

Developing Good Habits

You've learned that if you make neatness a habit it becomes second nature to you. Now is the time to adopt the habit. Over the next few days, notice "un-neat" habits that need improvement. Do you fail to make your bed in the morning? Do you leave papers lying on your desk? Do you throw clothes over a chair? Write down the habits that you need to work on. Beside each item on your list, write "I want to get into the habit of ..." and complete the thought. Use your list to guide your actions.

Using Technology

1. **Internet.** Surf the Web for sites that offer tips on cleaning and maintaining your home. Write down six of the most helpful ideas that you find, and share them with your classmates.

2. **Desktop Publishing.** Compile your cleaning tips, along with those shared by classmates, into a helpful booklet. If a digital camera or a scanner is available, include photos that illustrate the steps involved in some of the processes.

Choosing Transportation

Objectives

- **Compare** transportation options.
- **Summarize** costs of vehicle ownership.
- **Describe** steps in the process of buying a vehicle.
- **Distinguish** between various types of auto insurance coverage.
- **Identify** vehicle maintenance tasks that an individual can perform.

Write down your thoughts about why some people don't use public transportation, even when it's available. What could be done to persuade more people to leave their cars at home?

"I have to find another way to get to school," Tynice told her friend, Felix. "It's been great getting rides with my neighbor, but she's transferring to a four-year college next semester. I could always take the bus, of course, but that wouldn't always be convenient. Maybe I should look into buying a car of my own."

"Do you know how much it costs to run a car?" asked Felix.

"Well, a used car like yours wouldn't cost too much, would it?" said Tynice.

"You might be in for an unpleasant surprise," warned Felix. "Buying the car is only part of the story. You also have to insure it and maintain it. When you look into what's involved, you might decide that taking the bus is a pretty good idea after all."

Transportation Options

How do you get to school, to your friends' places, or to shopping centers? After you graduate, how will you get to work or classes? Depending on where you need to go, you might walk, ride a bike, drive a car, or get a ride with a friend or family member. Perhaps taking a bus, commuter train, or subway is an option where you live. See Fig. 49-1.

When deciding how you will get to work or school, compare the cost and convenience of different options. As Tynice will learn, using a bus may be less convenient than having a car, but it's a lot less expensive.

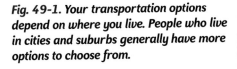

Fig. 49-1. Your transportation options depend on where you live. People who live in cities and suburbs generally have more options to choose from.

Using Mass Transit

People who live in or near a large city often use **mass transit**, public transportation systems designed to carry large numbers of people. Every day millions of Americans use buses, subways, trains, and even boats to get from place to place. See Fig. 49-2.

Mass transit systems bring numerous benefits, both to the people who use them and to society as a whole. Compared to using your own vehicle, mass transit:

- **Costs less.** Mass transit fares are often lower than the cost of gas, parking, tolls, and maintenance.
- **Saves time.** Trains and subways can often get passengers to their destination faster than cars because they don't get held up in traffic jams. Unlike drivers, passengers can use the time to read, write, or even take a nap.

- **Reduces stress.** Passengers don't experience the stress associated with driving, especially in heavy traffic or bad weather.
- **Reduces congestion.** Using mass transit reduces the number of vehicles on the roads.
- **Saves energy.** Mass transit uses much less energy per passenger.
- **Reduces pollution.** Fewer vehicles on the roads means less air pollution from exhaust systems.

Even though mass transit offers these benefits, many people use their own vehicles instead. They may prefer the greater flexibility that their own transportation provides, or they may dislike the crowded conditions of public transportation. Some people have no choice: living in communities that have no mass transit, they need their own transportation in order to get anywhere. Overall, the number of Americans who use mass transit is very small compared with the number who drive alone or with others.

Fig. 49-2. Mass transit systems, such as this ferry service, offer benefits to individuals and communities. What mass transit options are available in your community?

Using Your Own Vehicle

The main advantage of driving alone in your own vehicle is convenience. You leave when you are ready, and you have the flexibility to change your route or your schedule as you wish. The disadvantage for society is that every car on the road adds to traffic congestion, air pollution, and the consumption of scarce fuels. For you personally, the main disadvantage is that driving probably costs more than other options. It may also be more time consuming and stressful.

Other Options

Sharing a vehicle with others is another transportation option. **Carpools**, arrangements in which a group of people commute together by car, save money and reduce the number of vehicles on the roads. In some carpools, the same person drives every day, and the passengers help pay expenses. In others, the participants take turns driving their vehicles. Some communities encourage carpooling by setting aside express lanes on highways for vehicles carrying two or more people. See Fig. 49-3.

If bicycling is a practical and safe option for you, it's certainly worth considering. It provides exercise, is inexpensive, and does not harm the environment. Some communities have created special bike paths to keep bikers safe and encourage bicycle use.

Getting Your Own Vehicle

If, after considering your options, you decide to get a vehicle of your own, you need to do some careful research. Buying a vehicle is a major step that involves a lot of money. It's worth taking the time to understand all that is involved so that you can make an informed decision.

What Will It Cost?

Few people can afford a brand new car when they buy their first vehicle. Most start out by buying a used car. Used cars range in price from a few hundred to many thousands of dollars. When figuring out what your vehicle will cost you, though, you need to consider more than the price of the vehicle itself. Additional expenses include:

Fig. 49-3. By encouraging more people to carpool, communities hope to reduce pollution and traffic congestion. What are some other benefits of carpooling?

Fig. 49-4. *When figuring out the cost of owning a vehicle, factor in the cost of running it as well as buying it.* What factors would affect the amount you would spend on gasoline?

- **Insurance.** Auto insurance rates for young drivers can be high, even if you buy an inexpensive car. Insurance is discussed in detail later in this chapter.

- **Fuel.** The amount you spend on fuel will depend on the number of miles you drive and on the fuel efficiency of your vehicle. See Fig. 49-4.

- **Parking and tolls.** Daily tolls and parking fees can add up to significant amounts over time.

- **Maintenance and repairs.** Regular maintenance keeps a vehicle working properly. Most vehicles need repairs from time to time. In general, the older the vehicle, the more repairs it will need.

How Will You Pay?

Unless you can afford to pay cash for a vehicle, you will need to arrange financing terms. You may have a choice of taking out a loan or leasing a vehicle.

- **Arranging a loan.** Most people make a down payment by paying a portion of the purchase price up front in cash. They then take out a loan for the remaining amount and pay it back in monthly installments. Loans can be arranged through a bank, credit union, or auto dealership. Typical auto loan periods range from 36 to 60 months. After you make your final payment, you receive the **title**, a legal document showing who owns the vehicle. The vehicle is then yours to do with as you like—you can keep it, sell it, or trade it in for another vehicle.

- **Leasing.** This option is for new vehicles only. When you **lease**, you pay a monthly fee in exchange for exclusive use of a vehicle for a specific length of time, such as three years. The leasing company owns the vehicle, not you. When the lease period is over, you must return the vehicle or make other financing arrangements. Some leases specify the number of miles you may drive during the lease period and charge a penalty for additional miles.

If you're in the market for a new car, look into the pros and cons of buying versus leasing. Lease payments may be lower than monthly loan payments, but at the end of the lease period you have nothing to show for the money you have paid out. In the long run, leasing is generally more expensive than buying. However, it depends on how you plan to use the vehicle, how much driving you expect to do, and how long you want to keep the vehicle.

The Purchasing Process

Buying your first vehicle is a major step—probably the biggest financial decision so far in your life. Start by figuring out what you can afford to pay, taking into account all the costs of vehicle ownership. That will help you determine whether to shop for a new or a used vehicle.

If you're like most people, you would prefer a new vehicle. Consider, however, that even the smallest, most basic new car is very expensive. A similar vehicle that is just two or three years old and in good condition would be nearly as nice and cost thousands less. Many dealers offer used vehicles that have been checked over thoroughly and come with a warranty.

Whether you buy new or used, do your homework. Learning all that you can before you start shopping will help you get the right vehicle at the right price.

Doing Your Research

Once you know roughly what you can afford to pay, think about what you need in a vehicle. How much driving do you expect to do, and in what road and traffic conditions? Will you use your vehicle for long trips? For carpooling? Do you need space for tools, sports equipment, or other bulky items? Your answers will help you identify vehicles that meet your needs.

Makes and Models ~ Car buyers' magazines and online sites provide plenty of information about different vehicles. By learning about the reliability, safety features, fuel economy, and performance of makes and models in your price range, you'll be able to narrow down your choices and identify vehicles that interest you. At that point, you might want to visit some dealerships to find and inspect the vehicles on your list. See Fig. 49-5.

Fig. 49-5. If you've done your research before you start shopping for a vehicle, you'll be able to focus on models that meet your needs.

FINDING CREATIVE SOLUTIONS

Restating the Problem

If you can't find a solution to a problem, maybe the difficulty lies in how you defined the problem to begin with. Restating the problem can help you approach it from a different angle.

How It Works

If the problem doesn't seem solvable the way you originally defined it, take another look at it. Ask yourself what needs, wants, goals, and priorities lie behind the situation. Then see if you can restate the problem in a way that *is* solvable.

Suppose, for example, that you haven't been able to find a part-time job. Ask yourself, "Why is this a problem?" If the answer is that you need the money, then you might restate the problem as "How can I earn extra money?" That could lead to some new ideas, such as having a garage sale or starting a dog-walking business. On the other hand, you might restate the problem as "How can I gain work experience to put on my résumé?" In that case, you might consider looking for volunteer opportunities. Either way, restating the problem opens doors to options that you had not considered before.

Try It Out

Trekking from one auto dealer to another, Kirk wonders why all the cars he likes cost so much. There's no way he can stretch his limited budget to cover more than a basic model, especially when he considers maintenance and insurance expenses.

▶ **Your Turn** *How do you think Kirk would describe his problem? Restate the problem in a way that focuses on solvable aspects. What new options does this generate?*

Prices ~ How do you know whether the price a seller is asking for a used vehicle is reasonable? You can check the vehicle's **book value**—the estimated value of a specific make, model, and year. Book values are available online or in the Kelley *Blue Book*, which you can buy in a bookstore or borrow from the library. Different prices are given based on factors such as the mileage and overall condition of the vehicle. You might also check the classified ads in your local paper to see what prices are being asked for vehicles that interest you.

If you're shopping for a new vehicle, magazines and online sources can tell you the manufacturer's suggested retail price (MSRP) of specific models. Note that this is not necessarily the price you'll pay. For one thing, there are likely to be additional charges for options and other extras; on the other hand, it's often possible to negotiate a lower price. Still, the MSRP will give you an idea of the vehicle's price in comparison to others.

Shopping for the Best Vehicle

Once you've done your research, you're ready to look for specific vehicles for sale. You can look in classified ads, on the Internet, and at dealerships. Prepare a list of questions to ask when you call about an advertised vehicle. If a vehicle sounds promising, arrange to see it. Inspect the exterior and interior carefully. See Fig. 49-6.

Be especially observant when inspecting a used vehicle. Look for signs of damage or previous repairs. You may want to arrange for a mechanic to check over the vehicle.

If you're still interested, take the vehicle for a test drive. You may need to inspect and test drive several vehicles before you find one that you want to buy. Don't let anyone pressure you into buying before you are ready. It's worth waiting until you find the best vehicle for you.

Getting the Best Price

Most sellers inflate their asking price because they expect buyers to negotiate. Classified ads for used cars often state "or best offer," which means the seller will consider taking less than the asking price. Dealerships, too, will often accept less than the **sticker price**—the dealer's initial asking price as shown on the sticker attached to the vehicle. You could save a lot of money by offering a lower price and then negotiating with the seller until you reach agreement.

You'll be able to negotiate more confidently if you gather information ahead of time. Use sources such as the Kelley *Blue Book* and *Consumer Reports* to determine what you can realistically expect to pay. If you're buying a new vehicle, find out the dealer's *invoice price*—the price the dealer probably paid the manufacturer for the vehicle. The difference between this amount and the sticker price is your negotiating room.

Whether you're buying a new or used vehicle, decide ahead of time on the highest price you're willing to pay. Don't let anyone pressure you into buying until you are comfortable with the price.

Fig. 49-6. When inspecting a vehicle, check how easy it is to reach all the controls and see all the gauges. What else should you evaluate?

Understanding Auto Insurance

If you drive a vehicle, you need auto insurance. Most auto insurance policies combine several types of coverage. Fig. 49-7 summarizes the main types that are available.

Liability coverage is required by law in most states. Collision and comprehensive coverage are not required by law, but are sometimes required for a new car loan. The other types of coverage are required in some, but not all, states. An insurance agent can advise you on the amount and types of coverage that you should have.

Choosing Coverage Options

Buying auto insurance is complex. You have a wide range of options to choose from, and each option has a price. If you think you will be buying a vehicle, do your insurance homework ahead of time. Once you determine your insurance needs and wants, you will be able to compare the rates offered by different insurance companies.

The most important aspect of auto insurance is liability coverage. If you have an accident and cause injury or damage to other people or their property, your liability insurance will cover the claims against you. You may be tempted to buy the minimum required coverage. Remember, though, that medical expenses resulting from an accident can be very high. Ask an insurance agent to suggest suitable liability coverage.

Should you pay for collision and comprehensive coverage, which would compensate you for damage to your own vehicle? A lot depends on the value and age of the vehicle. For a new or relatively new vehicle, you need this insurance. For an older vehicle, though, it may not be worth it. The insurance com-pany won't pay more than the vehicle is worth, and repair bills, even to an old car, can be costly. You could end up paying more for the insurance than you would ever receive if you filed a claim.

How Rates Are Assessed

Insurance companies base their rates on statistics. They try to predict the risk that a specific individual will file a claim. If the company determines that the risk is high, it will charge more for coverage. Drivers under age 25, for example, are responsible for more accidents than older drivers, so they are charged higher rates for auto insurance. Other factors that influence auto insurance costs include your gender, marital status, where you live, and the age and type of vehicle you drive.

Over time, your driving record will also be considered. Safe drivers who have had no accidents may have lower insurance rates.

Character IN ACTION

Responsible Driving When you're at the wheel of a vehicle, you are responsible for your own safety and for that of your passengers and other road users. Keep your eyes on the road, and stay focused and alert. Don't use a cell phone while you are driving, and don't let passengers, food, or music distract you. Always wear your safety belt and insist that passengers wear theirs. If you have young children in the vehicle, make sure they are properly secured in approved safety seats. Describe strategies for preventing passengers from distracting you when you are driving.

Types of Auto Insurance Coverage

TYPE	WHAT IT COVERS
Collision	Covers repairs to your vehicle if you have a traffic accident. Will not pay out more than the value of your vehicle.
Comprehensive	Covers damage caused by events other than a traffic accident, such as fire, theft, vandalism, and hail.
Liability	Property damage liability covers damage that your vehicle causes to someone else's vehicle or property. Bodily injury liability covers medical expenses related to injuries suffered by others.
Medical payments or personal injury	Covers medical expenses if you or your passengers are injured in an auto accident.
Uninsured/under-insured motorists	Covers damage or injury to you, your passengers, or your vehicle caused by a driver who has no insurance or insufficient insurance.

Fig. 49-7. Different types of insurance coverage focus on different needs. *Which type would compensate you if your vehicle were stolen?*

Maintaining Your Vehicle

Your vehicle will last longer, and will cost you less in repairs, if you maintain it properly. Every new vehicle comes with an owner's manual that explains its features and provides a maintenance schedule. If you buy a used car, you may receive the owner's manual. If not, contact the manufacturer and ask for one. Following the manufacturer's recommendations for maintenance is a good way to keep your vehicle running smoothly.

You'll need a reliable service facility to perform at least some of the maintenance tasks for your vehicle. Ask other drivers for recommendations.

Since service can be costly, you may want to perform some maintenance tasks yourself. Have a knowledgeable person teach you the basic tasks, or take a class. Here are some of the items that you could take care of:

- **Windshield washer fluid.** Check the level of the fluid regularly. Replace as necessary.

- **Tire pressure.** Use a tire pressure gauge to check tires monthly. If they are below the level recommended in your manual, add air. Underinflated tires wear out faster and reduce fuel efficiency.

- **Engine oil.** Check the oil level each time you refuel. Keeping the oil at the correct level protects the engine. Replace the oil at the recommended intervals. Once every 3,000 to 5,000 miles is typical.

- **Fluid levels.** Check the transmission fluid and brake fluid when you change the oil.

- **Lights.** Ask someone to help you make sure that your lights and signals work when you turn them on and off.

Chapter Summary

- Transportation options are determined by where you live and where you want to go.
- Using mass transit brings benefits to individuals and to society.
- Owning a vehicle involves many expenses in addition to the purchase price.
- To pay for a vehicle, you might take out a loan or, if the vehicle is new, lease it.
- Learning all that you can before shopping for a vehicle will help you get the right vehicle at the right price.
- Before buying auto insurance, examine the options and decide on the types and amounts of coverage you want.
- You can save on maintenance costs by doing some basic tasks yourself.

Reviewing Key Terms & Ideas

1. Name some examples of **mass transit**. What advantages does mass transit offer over driving your own vehicle?
2. What are two types of **carpool** arrangements?
3. In addition to the down payment, what costs do you have to budget for when you buy a car?
4. At what point do you receive the **title** to a vehicle that you purchase? What does this signify?
5. When researching makes and models of vehicles, what kinds of information should you gather?
6. Where can you find a vehicle's **book value**, and how does it help you?
7. Where will you find a vehicle's **sticker price**? Why should you offer less than the asking price?
8. What are the main differences between liability, comprehensive, and collision coverage? Which type is required by most states?
9. Why are drivers under age 25 generally charged more for auto insurance than older drivers?
10. Identify four maintenance tasks that vehicle owners should be able to perform.

Thinking Critically

1. **Making Predictions.** Do you think more people would use public transportation if the price of gasoline were to rise significantly? Why or why not?
2. **Identifying Alternatives.** Assume that you prefer the idea of buying a new car, but you can't afford collision coverage as well as the car payments. What risk do you run? What are some alternative strategies you might look into?

Applying Your Knowledge

1. **Public Transportation.** Investigate the availability and cost of using mass transit in your community or region. Choose a destination, and compare the cost of a single ride versus a pass for a certain time frame or number of trips.

2. **Insurance.** Learn more about insurance rates for young drivers. Create an imaginary teen vehicle owner. Give this person an age and gender, choose a make and model of vehicle, and decide on the types and amounts of coverage. Use the Internet to research rates. Compare your findings with those of your classmates.

Making Connections

1. **Math.** Figure out what your weekly fuel costs would be if you owned a vehicle that got 30 miles to the gallon, if you had to drive 25 miles each way to work five days a week, and drove an additional 150 miles a week for errands and social activities. Use current gasoline prices to make your calculations.

2. **Social Studies.** It has been said that the automobile was one of the most significant inventions in American history. Research and summarize how it changed the American way of life and what effects it had on the U.S. economy.

Managing Your Life

Organizing a Carpool

If you don't regularly carpool now, you might someday when you need to commute to a job. Develop a plan that you could use to organize a carpool with two or three other people. Explain how you would go about finding the other members. Then identify issues that the group would need to agree on, such as who will drive, how expenses will be shared, how long the group should wait for a member who is late, and what music, if any, to listen to. Explain how the group could come to agreement on these issues. Keep your plan for future use.

Using Technology

1. **Audio.** Write and record a mock radio advertisement highlighting the benefits of taking mass transit. As you develop your script, consider the reasons that some people might avoid public transportation. Use your finished product to attempt to change their views.

2. **Internet.** Visit a Web site devoted to helping consumers who are shopping for new and used vehicles. Make a list of at least six helpful tools found on the Web site. Experiment with the interactive tools and calculators. Give an example of what you learned from each.

Protecting the Environment

Key Terms

- global environment
- renewable resources
- nonrenewable resources
- conservation
- biodegradable
- precycling
- recycled-content products

Objectives

- Explain concerns about the global environment.
- Describe the roles of governments and individuals in protecting the environment.
- Identify ways to conserve energy and water.
- Give examples of ways to reduce, reuse, and recycle waste products.

List the actions you already take to protect the environment. As you read the chapter, write down additional measures that you could take.

*A*llison and Ned sat glumly on the porch. They had just come back from a disappointing fishing trip to a nearby river. As Ned glanced through the local newspaper, Allison sighed, "I wonder why somebody put up all those 'No Fishing' signs. We've always been allowed to fish there before."

"This may be the reason," said Ned, pointing to an article in the paper. "It says here that there was some kind of equipment failure at a factory in Neston that caused harmful substances to be released into the river. They've had to shut down the plant while they make repairs."

"But Neston is at least 20 miles from here. It's not even in our state!"

"Yes, but it's upriver from us, and pollution doesn't stop at borders," said Ned.

Concerns About the Environment

Water, air, and land make up our environment. Without these natural resources, life would not be possible. The quality of our environment affects the quality of life. Yet for many years, people have been polluting, wasting, and otherwise misusing the very elements that keep them alive. See Fig. 50-1.

As Allison and Ned learned, events in one town, state, or country can affect much broader areas. All local environments are parts of the whole **global environment**—the life support systems of the whole planet. To protect the world's human, animal, and plant life, everyone must work together to solve global environmental problems. The most challenging problems are diminishing natural resources and increasing pollution.

Fig. 50-1. The quality of the environment affects everyone's quality of life. That's why it's so important to protect the earth's natural resources.

Diminishing Natural Resources

The world's natural resources can be divided into two broad categories: renewable and nonrenewable. **Renewable resources**, such as plants, trees, and soil, replace themselves naturally over time. **Nonrenewable resources** cannot be replaced once they are used. Fossil fuels such as coal, oil, and natural gas are examples of nonrenewable resources. If people continue to rely on fossil fuels for heating, energy production, and transportation, supplies could run dangerously low.

Because there are limited supplies of nonrenewable resources, active conservation is necessary. **Conservation** is the careful management and protection of natural resources. The challenge in managing natural resources is to meet present-day needs without sacrificing the well-being of citizens in the future.

Most conservation efforts focus on using fewer nonrenewable resources. One strategy is to use renewable resources instead. Governments and industries continue to investigate alternative forms of energy that harness the power of wind, waves, and the sun. Wind farms, such as the one shown in Fig. 50-2, are becoming a common sight in some places.

Increasing Pollution

What exactly is pollution? In simple terms, it is the presence of harmful substances in the environment. Some pollution occurs naturally, as when a volcano erupts. Most pollution, however, is caused by people. Industrial nations are responsible for most of the world's pollution. Industry, automobiles, intensive agriculture, and other human activities all release pollutants into the environment. Each type of pollution—of air, water, and land—has harmful effects.

Fig. 50-2. Wind turbines look like huge airplane propellers. One wind turbine may provide energy for as many as 200 homes.

- **Air pollution** occurs when harmful gases and chemicals are released into the air. Breathing polluted air has been linked to medical conditions ranging from asthma and bronchitis to cancer and damage to the nervous system. Air pollution is also linked to wider environmental concerns such as global warming, acid rain, and the depletion of the earth's protective ozone layer. Like water pollution, air pollution can affect areas far from the source of the pollution.

- **Water pollution** comes from chemicals and other waste products that make their way into groundwater or rivers. Water is categorized as a renewable resource, yet the supply is limited. Only about 1 percent of the planet's water is fresh water. Polluted water can kill fish and other forms of marine life and can cause serious health problems for humans. Once polluted, water is difficult and costly to clean.

- **Land pollution** results from the disposal of household and industrial waste. Most solid waste goes to landfills—huge pits where the wastes are dumped and buried. The landfills in some areas are filling up, and there is a shortage of available land for additional landfills. See Fig. 50-3.

Fig. 50-3. Large cities often transport products to landfills in rural areas. *What can you do to minimize the garbage that your family contributes to landfills?*

Taking Responsibility

Protecting the global environment and finding solutions to environmental problems is a vast and complex challenge. There are no quick and easy solutions. People all over the world must work together to protect resources, deal with existing problems, and prevent future catastrophes. The United States already works with many other countries to limit waste and control pollution.

Within the United States, numerous programs have been established at the federal, state, and local levels to protect the environment. The Clean Water Act and Clean Air Act, for example, regulate the amount of pollution-causing substances that can be discharged into the water and air. Other acts ban the use of certain harmful chemicals and set controls on the exhaust emissions from vehicles.

It's easy to assume that governments will take care of environmental problems, but governments cannot do it by themselves. People must be willing to go along with government rulings and to participate in efforts to protect the environment. Read on to discover some of the many ways that individuals can make a difference.

Fig. 50-4. Adding insulation to exterior walls and attics can prevent heat loss and save energy.

Conserving Energy

When you take steps to conserve energy, you help reduce the demand for fossil fuels so that the supply of these nonrenewable resources will last longer. You also help reduce the air pollution that results when fossil fuels are burned.

How much energy does your family use? The answer depends on factors such as the size of your family, the age and condition of your home, and the climate where you live. Heating and cooling, water heaters, refrigeration, and laundry appliances consume most of the energy used in the typical home. Lighting, cooking, computers, appliances, and entertainment account for the rest. The energy used for transportation depends on where you live and your family's general lifestyle. If your family is like most, you can save energy by following some basic conservation measures.

Heating and Cooling

Heating systems, air conditioners, and water heaters use a lot of energy, so they are good targets for conservation efforts. One way to conserve energy used for heating and cooling is to make some basic home improvements. These improvements include sealing joints in ductwork to stop leaks, installing weather stripping around doors and windows, and adding insulation to the attic. See Fig. 50-4.

In addition, you can conserve energy just by making a few simple changes in your everyday habits. Follow these suggestions to conserve energy and cut fuel bills:

- During cold weather, set the thermostat no higher than 68°F while people are home. Lower the thermostat even more at night and when no one will be home for four hours or more.

- Stay warm by wearing an extra layer of clothing.

- In warm weather, use fans instead of an air conditioner when possible. Fans use less energy.

- When running central air conditioning, set the thermostat to no more than 15 degrees below the outside temperature. Never set it lower than 78°F.

- Close off rooms that are not being used by shutting the door and closing any vents and registers. Keep closet doors closed throughout the home.

- Use window coverings to help control temperature. On cold days, open blinds or draperies on the sunny side of the home; close them when the sun sets. On hot days, keep the sunshine out and your home cooler by closing drapes and shades.

- If you have a fireplace, close the damper when it is not in use. This will prevent warm air from escaping up the chimney.

- Keep your water heater set at "normal" or 120°F. Wrap insulation around the water heater and the pipes that lead to it. The insulation will save additional energy by holding in the heat.

- Use hot water sparingly. Wash clothes in warm or cold water, and use cold water to rinse.

Appliances and Lighting

When you're at home today, check to see how many appliances are running needlessly. Is a television playing to an empty room? Is a fan cooling a room that nobody is using? You can save energy simply by switching off electrical appliances when you are not using them. Here are some additional energy-saving tips for appliances:

- **Refrigerator.** Don't browse. Get what you need and promptly close the door.

- **Dishwasher.** Run the dishwasher only when you have a full load. Use the energy-saver cycle.

- **Oven.** Avoid using the oven in hot weather. Use a microwave oven or toaster oven for heating small quantities of food. Avoid opening the oven when food is cooking.

- **Washer and dryer.** Save laundry until you have a full load. Run the dryer only as long as necessary. Be sure to clean the lint filter after each load.

You can take a major step toward saving energy by choosing energy-efficient appliances. When shopping for appliances, take time to compare the EnergyGuide labels,

Why Energy Star?

The Energy Star program was introduced by the U.S. Environmental Protection Agency (EPA). It's a voluntary labeling system designed to identify energy-efficient products. Originally used on computers and monitors, the label can now be found on appliances, office equipment, home electronics, and more. Here are some examples of how Energy Star products compare in energy usage to other similar models:

- Energy Star lighting uses 66 percent less energy.

- Energy Star refrigerators use 26 percent less energy.

- Energy Star washers use 38 percent less energy and less water.

- Energy Star televisions use 24 percent less energy.

- Energy Star audio systems use 69 percent less energy.

Buying products that have earned the Energy Star label not only helps the environment but also reduces your energy bills. Be sure to look for the label when you shop.

Fig. 50-5. With low emissions and high gas mileage, hybrid electric vehicles (HEVs) cause less pollution than traditional cars, and they cost less to run.

which estimate the cost of running the appliance for one year. Also look for an Energy Star label on major appliances.

When it comes to lighting, get into the habit of turning off lights when you are not using them. Don't keep several lights on in a room if you need just one near where you are sitting. You might also replace standard bulbs with compact fluorescent bulbs that use less energy and last longer.

Transportation

Driving alone to school or work is the least energy efficient form of transportation. Taking mass transit, carpooling, and riding a bicycle are three ways to conserve energy and reduce air pollution. When a car is necessary, choose a vehicle that has good fuel economy. The more miles to the gallon a vehicle gets, the less fuel needs to be used.

The size of a vehicle and its engine determine the gas mileage that you can expect.

Trucks, sport utility vehicles, and large cars generally require the most fuel. Hybrid electric vehicles, or HEVs, are a relatively new type of vehicle that achieves superior fuel economy. See Fig. 50-5.

Conserving Water

If you live in an area affected by water shortages, you probably already know how to conserve water. Even if you live in an area where water is plentiful, you can do your part to conserve water. Conserving water saves energy and ensures that there is an adequate supply for everyone. Follow these suggestions to conserve water:

- Take a quick shower instead of a bath. A typical bath uses at least 20 gallons of water; a five-minute shower uses 8 to 12 gallons.

- Install low-flow showerheads and faucet aerators. You will use only about half as much water, but the water will feel as though it's running full force.

- Don't let water run continuously while you brush your teeth, shave, or shower. Instead, run water only when you need it.

- When washing dishes, fill a dishpan or sink for washing and another for rinsing. Washing and rinsing dishes under continuously running water wastes about 30 gallons of water per meal.

- Fix dripping faucets and other water leaks promptly.

- Don't overwater your lawn or garden. If you water with sprinklers, use them during early morning hours. Choose plants that thrive in your region without frequent watering.

- To keep water cleaner, use **biodegradable** detergents. They are formulated to break down easily in the environment.

- Don't put hazardous wastes, such as used engine oil, down the drain or into storm sewers.

Reducing Waste

You have grown up with the slogan "Reduce, Reuse, and Recycle." How well are you putting that slogan into practice? American families continue to generate enormous amounts of waste that must be sent to landfills. As you read the suggestions that follow, identify the changes that could be made in your home to reduce the amount of waste that your family generates.

Reduce

You can reduce waste by making environmentally responsible consumer choices. This practice is often called **precycling**. In the grocery store, for example, avoid items with excess packaging. Look for products with minimal packaging or those in packages that you can reuse or recycle, such as glass bottles. Your choices will send a signal to manufacturers, influencing their packaging designs in the future. Here are some additional suggestions for reducing waste:

- Bring your own cloth or plastic bags to take your groceries home. Use them over and over again.

- Buy items that you use frequently in large quantities to cut down on packaging.

- Buy foods such as dried fruits and grains from bulk containers whenever possible. See Fig. 50-6.

Fig. 50-6. When you buy from bulk bins, you avoid unnecessary packaging and take only the quantity you need. *What items could your family buy in bulk?*

- Cut down on single-use disposable products, such as plastic and paper cups and plates.
- Reuse lunch bags and water bottles.
- Rent or borrow items that you use only occasionally.

Reuse

The night before trash is picked up in Ernesto's neighborhood, the residents set useful items by the curbside. Ernesto has seen a computer monitor, old patio chairs, a barbecue grill, even a guitar and drum kit. By morning, the unwanted items are usually gone. Whether the recipients needed the items for their own use or hoped to sell them, the end result is a win for the environment. The item is reused and stays out of the landfill.

Every time you reuse items, you cut down on the need to discard and replace them. For example, instead of buying special boxes to store photographs and keepsakes, Liz makes her own by covering shoe boxes with fabric remnants. Perhaps you could save used printer paper and use the back of it for jotting down notes or shopping lists. What are some other ideas for reusing everyday items in your home?

Another way to reuse is to share. For example, instead of disposing of leftover paint or varnish, pass it on to a friend who can use it. Give household items and clothing to someone you know or to charitable groups that will distribute them to people who can use them. Find out whether your library accepts used books. Nursing homes, primary schools, and organizations such as Scout troops and 4-H clubs may appreciate your old greeting cards for use in craft projects.

Fig. 50-7. Everyone in the family can get in the habit of recycling. How does the recycling program in your community work? How can you encourage others to participate?

Recycle

Recycling involves changing an item in some way so that the materials in it can be used again. Aluminum cans, for example, can be melted down and made into sheets of aluminum that can be used for additional cans. Many communities have programs for recycling aluminum, paper, plastics, and glass. See Fig. 50-7.

Recycling has three main advantages: it conserves energy, it conserves natural resources, and it helps reduce waste. Thanks to individual and community efforts, millions of tons of items that might have ended up in landfills have been made into something useful instead.

If your community has a recycling program, be sure you and your family make full use of it. Look for other opportunities to recycle, too. You might find businesses or organizations in your community that collect items such as used plastic bags, batteries, or printer cartridges for recycling.

Other Ways to Help

What else can you do to help protect the environment? Here are some ideas:

- **Choose recycled-content products.** For recycling to be successful, there must be a market for the products made with recovered materials. Manufacturers produce thousands of **recycled-content products**, items made partially or totally from materials that might have ended up in a landfill. The products range from plastic lumber and deck furniture to egg cartons and paper towels. Products made from

Fig. 50-8. *This symbol tells you that you can recycle the product. A similar symbol, using three arrows inside a circle, tells you that a product is made at least partly of recycled materials.*

recovered materials and products that can be recycled are both marked by symbols. See Fig. 50-8.

- **Get involved.** Stay informed by following environmental issues at the community, state, national, and international levels. Consider donating some of your time to supporting worthwhile environmental organizations.

- **Show that you care.** Let your everyday actions demonstrate your commitment. The example you set will have a positive effect on classmates, friends, and family members. When you see others taking responsibility for the environment, show that you support them. Everything you do counts.

Chapter Summary

- Everyone must work together to solve global environmental problems.
- Renewable resources can replace themselves over time; nonrenewable resources cannot.
- Active conservation is needed to protect natural resources.
- Pollution of the air, water, and land results mainly from human activities.
- Energy conservation reduces fuel consumption and cuts back on air pollution.
- You can conserve energy and water by paying attention to your usage patterns and changing wasteful habits.
- You can cut back on waste by reducing, reusing, and recycling.

Reviewing Key Terms & Ideas

1. What is the **global environment**? Why do local environments affect it?
2. Give three examples of **nonrenewable resources**.
3. Why do people need to be concerned about **conservation**?
4. What are some of the harmful effects of air pollution?
5. Give two examples of U.S. environmental protection laws.
6. Explain why protecting the environment is the responsibility of individuals as well as governments.
7. What systems and appliances use the most energy in a typical home?
8. Explain how you can save energy when doing the laundry.
9. Name three ways to conserve water.
10. What is the advantage of **biodegradable** detergents?
11. What does **precycling** involve? Give two examples.
12. What is the difference between reusing items and recycling them? Give examples of how each can help the environment.
13. What are **recycled-content products**? How can you recognize them?

Thinking Critically

1. **Understanding Cause and Effect.** What can happen if some nations agree to follow strict environmental guidelines while others don't?
2. **Defending Your Position.** Of the conservation measures discussed in this chapter, which do you think could bring about the greatest benefit to the environment if everyone practiced it? Be prepared to defend your choice.

Applying Your Knowledge

1. **Conserve Energy.** Work with a small group to identify ways in which your school might be wasting energy. List specific actions that teachers, students, school administrators, and other workers could take to conserve energy. Write your recommendations in a proposal and submit it to the appropriate school administrators.

2. **Reduce Waste.** With family members, discuss specific ways to reduce the amount of waste your family throws out each week. Encourage everyone to contribute ideas. Choose the three best suggestions by taking a vote. Carry them out for one week, then evaluate how effective they were.

Making Connections

1. **Language Arts.** Find a poem or short essay that expresses concern for the natural environment. Share it with the class.

2. **Science.** In a small group, research the effects of water pollution. Choose a specific lake, river, or other body of water that has been polluted. Find out what caused the pollution and how it affected plant and animal life. What has been done to clean up the pollution? Prepare a report on your findings.

Managing Your Life

Taking Responsibility

Find out how you can become actively involved in environmental protection efforts in your community. Investigate existing programs run by the state and local government, public utilities, industry, and environmental organizations. Share your findings with friends and family, and encourage all of them to get involved in protecting the environment.

Using Technology

1. **Internet.** Visit the Web site of the Environmental Protection Agency. Find the page on which you can enter your zip code to find environmental information about your community. Summarize the types of information that are available, and list three facts you learned about your community from this Web site.

2. **Web Page.** Look for Web sites where local or state government departments or agencies provide information to help citizens protect the environment. Create a page in Web browser (HTML) format that provides links to, and descriptions of, the sites you found.

Career Options
Housing and Construction

*E*very time you see a building going up or a "For Sale" sign, you are seeing the housing and construction industries in action. Workers in this career cluster design, construct, and sell buildings of all types—from houses to schools to factories. There are opportunities for people of all levels of education and experience. This career cluster can be divided into two broad sectors: the housing sector, and construction and maintenance. Job opportunities for most occupations in this career cluster are expected to be excellent.

Main Employers

- Real estate companies
- Home furnishing stores
- Hardware stores
- Home equipment stores
- Department stores
- Interior design companies
- Construction companies

Housing and Construction Job Opportunities

Industry Segment	Entry Level	Additional Education and/or Training	Advanced Education and/or Training
Housing	▪ Cleaner ▪ Real Estate Clerk ▪ Home Furnishings Salesperson ▪ Home Appliance Salesperson	▪ Real Estate Salesperson ▪ Lighting Specialist ▪ Landscape Gardener ▪ Merchandise Display Worker ▪ Home Inspector ▪ Kitchen Planner	▪ Interior Designer ▪ Furniture Designer ▪ Landscape Architect
Construction and Maintenance	▪ Laborer ▪ Bricklayer ▪ Painter ▪ Plasterer ▪ Roofer	▪ Building Contractor ▪ Carpenter ▪ Electrician ▪ Plumber ▪ Heavy Equipment Operator	▪ Architect ▪ Building Inspector ▪ Construction Supervisor ▪ Surveyor

CAREER PATHS — Amy Kwan, INTERIOR DESIGNER

During my senior year in high school, most of my friends seemed to have their career goals all figured out. I didn't. While they went on to college, I took a job as a receptionist in a doctor's office. Within two years, I was promoted to office manager.

I liked my job but always felt something was missing. One day when I was rearranging the furniture in the waiting room at the doctor's office (for the fourth time), my co-worker jokingly said that I should be an interior designer. I suddenly realized that was work I would love.

I enrolled in college and started taking night classes in art and design. The doctor I worked for was very supportive and let me work fewer hours so that I had time to study. It took six years of going to school part-time to get my interior design degree, but I made it!

Today, I specialize in interior design for the health care industry. My colleagues and I have designed interiors for a hospital, an assisted-living facility, and even a few doctors' offices. We prepare drawings and layouts, design lighting, and select color schemes. We also choose the furniture, fabrics, window treatments, and floor coverings. It's especially important to make these spaces comfortable for patients as they deal with health care issues.

Check It Out!

Select one occupation each from the housing industry and the construction and maintenance industry. Use print and online sources to research the job outlook, estimated annual earnings, and advancement opportunities for each occupation. Create a chart comparing the two.

Family, Career and Community Leaders of America, Inc. (FCCLA) is a national student organization for students enrolled in family and consumer sciences courses in grades 6–12. Involvement in FCCLA offers members the opportunity to develop life skills, expand their leadership potential, and explore careers. FCCLA promotes personal growth and offers members opportunities to participate in a number of individual and chapter programs that strengthen life skills, including the following.

Power of One

Power of One helps students find and use their personal power by setting and achieving goals. Members complete projects on improving personal traits, getting along with family members, exploring career options, developing leadership qualities, and speaking out for FCCLA.

Peer Education Programs

Through peer education programs, FCCLA provides opportunities for personal, family, and community outreach. For example:

- *Families First* helps students gain skills to become strong family members.
- *Financial Fitness* involves young people in making, saving, and spending money wisely.
- *Student Body* helps students learn to eat right, be fit, and make healthy choices.

Community Service

FCCLA helps members strengthen their contributions to their community through this program. Students develop, plan, carry out, and evaluate projects that improve the quality of life in their communities.

Leadership Programs

FCCLA offers two leadership programs.

- *Dynamic Leadership* offers activities and project ideas that help students learn to model good character, solve problems, foster relationships, manage conflict, and build teams.
- *Leaders at Work* recognizes FCCLA members who create projects to strengthen leadership skills on the job in one of six career areas related to Family and Consumer Sciences.

Career Connection

This FCCLA program helps members target career goals. Students focus on six aspects of career development: Plug In to Careers, Sign On to the Career Connection, Program Career Steps, Link Up to Jobs, Access Skills for Career Success, and Integrate Work and Life.

STAR Events

Students Taking Action with Recognition (STAR) Events are competitive events in which FCCLA members are recognized for proficiency in individual and chapter projects, leadership skills, and career preparation. *STAR Event* categories include:

- Illustrated Talk
- Interpersonal Communications
- Career Investigation
- Job Interview
- Entrepreneurship
- Focus on Children
- Early Childhood
- Applied Technology
- Culinary Arts
- Hospitality
- National Programs of Action
- Parliamentary Procedure
- Chapter Service Project Display
- Chapter Service Project Manual
- Chapter Showcase Display
- Chapter Showcase Manual

> **For more information, contact FCCLA:**
> http://www.fcclainc.org

Daily Values and DRIs for Teens

Daily Values are standard values developed by the Food and Drug Administration (FDA) for use on food labels. They help you judge whether a food is high or low in a specific nutrient.

Dietary Reference Intakes (DRIs) are used by nutrition professionals. They give nutrient reference amounts for specific ages and genders. Only the amounts for teens are included here.

The DRIs include four types of nutrient reference values. Most of the values listed below are **Recommended Dietary Allowances (RDAs)**. An RDA is the daily amount of a nutrient that will meet the needs of nearly all healthy people. For some nutrients, there is not yet enough data to establish an RDA. In that case, the value listed is an **Adequate Intake (AI)**, an amount believed to be adequate.

Nutrient	Daily Value	Dietary Reference Intake (RDA or AI)			
		Males 9-13	**Males 14-18**	**Females 9-13**	**Females 14-18**
Protein	50 g**	34 g	52 g	34 g	46 g
Carbohydrate (total)	300 g**	130 g	130 g	130 g	130 g
Fiber	25 g	31 g	38 g	26 g	26 g
Fat (total)	65 g**	*	*	*	*
Saturated fat	20 g**	*	*	*	*
Cholesterol	300 mg	*	*	*	*
Vitamin A	5,000 IU (875 µg RE)	600 µg RAE	900 µg RAE	600 µg RAE	700 µg RAE
Thiamin	1.5 mg	0.9 mg	1.2 mg	0.9 mg	1.0 mg
Riboflavin	1.7 mg	0.9 mg	1.3 mg	0.9 mg	1.0 mg
Niacin	20 mg NE	12 mg NE	16 mg NE	12 mg NE	14 mg NE
Vitamin B_6	2 mg	1.0 mg	1.3 mg	1.0 mg	1.2 mg
Vitamin B_{12}	6 µg	1.8 µg	2.4 µg	1.8 µg	2.4 µg
Folate	400 µg	300 µg DFE	400 µg DFE	300 µg DFE	400 µg DFE
Biotin	300 µg	20 µg	25 µg	20 µg	25 µg
Pantothenic acid	10 mg	4 mg	5 mg	4 mg	5 mg
Vitamin C	60 mg	45 mg	75 mg	45 mg	65 mg
Vitamin D	400 IU (6.5 µg)	5 µg	5 µg	5 µg	5 µg
Vitamin E	30 IU (9 mg α-TE)	11 mg α-TE	15 mg α-TE	11 mg α-TE	15 mg α-TE
Vitamin K	80 µg	60 µg	75 µg	60 µg	75 µg
Calcium	1,000 mg	1,300 mg	1,300 mg	1,300 mg	1,300 mg
Copper	2 mg	700 µg	890 µg	700 µg	890 µg
Iodine	150 µg	120 µg	150 µg	120 µg	150 µg
Iron	18 mg	8 mg	11 mg	8 mg	15 mg
Magnesium	400 mg	240 mg	410 mg	240 mg	360 mg
Phosphorus	1,000 mg	1,250 mg	1,250 mg	1,250 mg	1,250 mg
Potassium	3,500 mg	4,500 mg	4,700 mg	4,500 mg	4,700 mg
Selenium	70 µg	40 µg	55 µg	40 µg	55 µg
Sodium	2,400 mg	1,500 mg	1,500 mg	1,500 mg	1,500 mg
Zinc	15 mg	8 mg	11 mg	8 mg	9 mg

* No value established **Based on a diet of 2,000 calories per day

Key to nutrient measures

g	gram
mg	milligram (1000 mg = 1 g)
µg	microgram (1000 µg = 1 mg; 1,000,000 µg = 1 g)
IU	International Unit (an old measure of vitamin activity)
RAE	retinol activity equivalents (a measure of Vitamin A activity)
NE	niacin equivalents (a measure of niacin activity)
DFE	dietary folate equivalents (a measure of folate activity)
α-TE	alpha-tocopherol equivalents (a measure of Vitamin E activity)

Milk, Yogurt, and Cheese Group

	Amount	Cal-ories	Car-bohy-drates (g)	Fat (g)	Pro-tein (g)	Cal-cium (mg)	Iron (mg)	Vita-min A (RE)	Vita-min C (mg)	Cho-les-terol (mg)	Sodium (mg)
Cheese, American process	1 oz/28 g	105	Tr	9	6	174	0.1	82	0	27	406
Cheese, Cheddar	1 oz/28 g	115	Tr	9	7	204	0.2	86	0	30	176
Cheese, cottage, creamed	¹/₂ c/125 ml	112	0.1	5	14	67.5	0.15	54	Tr	17	455
Cheese, cottage, dry	¹/₂ c/125 ml	62.5	0.5	Tr	12.5	23	0.15	6	0	5	10
Chocolate milk	1 c/250 ml	210	26	8	8	280	0.6	73	2	31	149
Ice cream, 16% fat	¹/₂ c/125 ml	175	16	12	2	75.5	0.05	110	5	30	58
Milk, whole	1 c/250 ml	150	11	8	8	291	0.1	76	2	33	120
Milk, reduced-fat 2%	1 c/250 ml	121	12	5	8	297	0.1	139	2	18	122
Milk, fat-free (skim)	1 c/250 ml	85	12	Tr	8	302	0.1	149	2	4	126
Yogurt, fruit	1 c/250 ml	230	42	3	10	343	0.2	25	21	10	133
Yogurt, plain, fat-free	1 c/250 ml	125	17	Tr	13	452	0.2	5	2	4	174
Yogurt, plain, whole milk	1 c/250 ml	140	11	7	8	274	0.1	68	1	29	105
Yogurt, frozen, low-fat	¹/₂ c/125 ml	110	24	0	3	100	0	0	0	0	50

Meat, Poultry, Fish, Dry Beans, Eggs, and Nuts Group

	Amount	Cal-ories	Car-bohy-drates (g)	Fat (g)	Pro-tein (g)	Cal-cium (mg)	Iron (mg)	Vita-min A (RE)	Vita-min C (mg)	Cho-les-terol (mg)	Sodium (mg)
Bacon, fried crisp	3 slices	110	Tr	9	4	2	0.3	0	10	16	303
Beef, lean (roasted)	3 oz/85 g	220	0	13	25	5	2.8	Tr	0	81	43
Beef, hamburger, lean	3 oz/85 g	230	0	16	21	9	2.1	Tr	0	76	70
Chicken (roasted) (¹/₂ breast)	3 oz/85 g	140	0	3	27	13	0.9	5	0	73	64
Chicken (fried) (¹/₂ breast)	3.5 oz/98 g	220	1	9	31	16	1.2	15	0	87	74
Eggs (hard-cooked)	1 egg	80	1	6	6	25	0.6	84	0	213	62
Egg substitutes	¹/₄ cup/50 ml	30	1	0	6	20	1	0	0	0	100
Fish, flounder (baked)	3 oz/85 g	80	0	1	17	13	0.3	10	1	59	101
Ham, boiled (1 slice)	1 oz/28 g	65	0	6	5	3	0.8	0	0	16	375
Kidney beans (red beans)	1 c/250 ml	230	42	1	15	74	4.6	1	0	0	968
Lamb leg (roasted)	3 oz/85 g	205	0	13	22	8	1.7	0	0	78	57
Lentils	1 c/250 ml	210	39	Tr	16	50	4.2	4	0	0	26

Food	Amount										
Nuts, peanuts, salted	1 c/250 ml	840	27	72	37	107	3	0	0	0	626
Nuts, walnuts	1 c/250 ml	785	19	74	17	113	2.9	15	0	0	12
Peanut butter	2 T/30 ml	190	6	16	8	10	0.6	0	0	0	150
Peas, dried, split	1 c/250 ml	230	42	1	16	22	3.4	8	0	0	26
Pork (roasted)	3 oz/85 g	275	0	19	24	3	0.7	3	0	84	61
Sardines	3 oz/85 g	175	0	9	20	372	2.5	56	0	85	425
Seeds, sunflower (dry, hulled)	1/2 c/120 g	405	14.5	34.5	17.5	87	5.15	35	0	0	Tr
Tofu	1 piece, 2 1/2" x 3 1/2" x 1"	85	1	5	9	108	2.3	0	0	0	8
Tuna, canned in oil	3 oz/85 g	170	0	7	24	7	1.6	20	0	55	303
Turkey, dark meat (roasted)	3 oz/85 g	175	0	7	26	0	2.0	0	0	72	67
Veal cutlet	3 oz/85 g	185	0	9	23	9	2.7	0	0	109	56
Fruit Group											
Apple	1 (2 3/4"/63 mm)	80	20	1	Tr	10	0.4	7	6	0	Tr
Apricots	3 med.	55	14	Tr	1	18	0.5	277	11	0	1
Banana	1 med.	100	26	Tr	2	10	0.8	9	12	0	1
Blueberries	1 c/250 ml	90	22	1	1	22	1.5	15	20	0	9
Cantaloupe	1/2 melon	80	20	Tr	2	38	1.1	861	90	0	24
Dates	10 dates	220	58	Tr	0.25	47	2.4	4	0	0	Tr
Grapefruit juice	1/4 c/60 ml	25	6	Tr	Tr	6	0.05	Tr	24	0	1
Grapes, seedless	10 grapes	35	9	Tr	1	6	0.2	4	2	0	1
Orange	1 (3"/76 mm)	65	16	Tr	0.5	54	0.5	27	66	0	Tr
Orange juice (from concentrate)	1/4 c/60 ml	30	7.25	Tr	1	6	0.1	19	30	0	2
Peach, peeled	1 (2 1/2"/63 mm)	40	10	Tr	1	9	0.5	47	7	0	Tr
Pear, Bartlett	1 (2 1/2"/63 mm)	100	25	1	1	13	0.5	3	7	0	Tr
Pineapple, cubed, raw	1 c/250 ml	80	21	Tr	1	26	0.5	4	26	0	2
Prunes, dried	4 med.	110	29	Tr	1	22	1.7	97	1	0	2
Raisins (snack package)	1/2 oz/14 g	40	11	Tr	Tr	9	0.5	Tr	Tr	0	2
Vegetable Group											
Beans, green, raw	1 c/250 ml	45	7	Tr	2	63	0.8	83	15	0	4
Bean sprouts	1 c/250 ml	35	7	Tr	4	20	1.4	2	20	0	6
Broccoli	1 c/250 ml	40	7	Tr	5	71	1.2	218	140	0	17
Cabbage, shredded	1 c/250 ml	15	4	Tr	1	34	0.03	9	33	0	13
Carrot, raw	1 stick	30	7	Tr	Tr	27	0.5	2,025	6	0	25
Celery, raw	3 stalks	15	6	Tr	5	48	0.3	15	12	0	105
Corn, sweet kernels	1 c/250 ml	130	31	1	5	5	0.3	41	8	0	8
Lettuce, iceberg	1/4 head	20	2.6	Tr	0.8	18	0.45	44	5	0	12

(Continued on next page)

Appendix 743

TABLE OF FOOD VALUES (Continued)

	Amount	Cal-ories	Car-bohy-drates (g)	Fat (g)	Pro-tein (g)	Cal-cium (mg)	Iron (mg)	Vita-min A (RE)	Vita-min C (mg)	Cho-les-terol (mg)	Sodium (mg)
Peas, green, frozen	1 c/250 ml	125	19	Tr	0.8	30	2.3	107	21	0	139
Pepper, green sweet, raw	1 med.	15	4	Tr	1	7	0.5	39	94	0	2
Potato, baked	1 med.	145	33	Tr	4	8	1.1	0	20	0	8
Potatoes, french fried	10 pieces	155	18	7	2	9	0.7	0	5	0	108
Spinach	1 c/250 ml	40	6	Tr	5	245	4	1,474	18	0	126
Tomatoes, canned	1 c/250 ml	50	10	Tr	2	62	1.2	145	41	0	391
Tomato, raw	1 med.	25	6	Tr	1	9	0.6	139	28	0	10
Tomato juice	1 c/250 ml	40	10	Tr	2	22	1.6	136	29	0	881
Bread, Cereal, Rice, and Pasta Group											
Bagel	1 med.	200	43	2	7	29	1.8	0	0	0	245
Bread, white enriched	1 slice	70	13	1	2	21	0.6	Tr	Tr	0	129
Bread, whole-wheat	1 slice	65	14	1	3	24	0.8	0	Tr	0	180
Bread, pumpernickel	1 slice	80	17	Tr	3	27	0.8	0	0	0	177
Corn flakes, fortified	1 c/250 ml	95	21	Tr	2	V	V	V	13	0	V
Crackers, saltines	4 crackers	50	8	1	1	2	0.5	0	0	0	165
English muffin, plain, enriched	1 muffin	140	25	1	5	96	1.7	0	0	0	378
Egg noodles, enriched	1 c/250 ml	200	37	2	7	16	1.4	110	0	50	3
Granola cereal w/ raisins and nuts	⅓ c	125	38	5	3	18	0.9	2	0	0	58
Oatmeal, instant (flavored)	1 packet	160	26	2	5	168	6.7	460	0	0	254
Pasta, enriched, cooked	1 c/250 ml	190	39	1	7	14	1.4	0	0	0	1
Pita bread	1 pita	165	32	1	6	49	1.4	0	0	0	339
Rice, instant, enriched, cooked	1 c/250 ml	180	40	Tr	4	5	1.3	0	0	0	0
Rice, enriched, cooked	1 c/250 ml	185	41	Tr	4	33	1.4	0	0	0	0
Rice, puffed, whole-grain	1 c/250 ml	60	13	Tr	1	3	0.3	0	0	0	0
Wheat flakes, fortified	1 c/250 ml	105	24	Tr	3	43	4.5	375	16	0	354
Wheat, puffed, whole-grain	1 c/250 ml	55	12	Tr	2	4	0.6	0	0	0	0
Wheat, shredded, whole-grain	1 lg. biscuit	90	20	1	3	11	1.2	0	0	0	3

Fats, Oils, and Sweets

Food	Amount										
Butter	1 T/15 ml	100	Tr	12	Tr	3	Tr	106	0	31	116
Cheese, cream	1 oz/28 g	100	0.2	10	2	23	0.3	124	0	31	84
Cream, heavy	1 T/15 ml	80	0.1	6	Tr	10	Tr	63	Tr	21	6
Cream, light	1 T/15 ml	30	1	3	Tr	14	Tr	44	Tr	10	6
Cream, sour	1 T/15 ml	25	1	3	Tr	14	Tr	23	Tr	5	6
Honey	1 T/15 ml	65	17	0	Tr	1	0.1	0	Tr		1
Margarine, regular	1 T/15 ml	100	Tr	12	Tr	3	Tr	139	0	0	132
Mayonnaise	1 T/15 ml	100	Tr	11	Tr	3	0.1	12	10	8	80
Oil, corn	1 T/15 ml	125	0	14	0	0	0	10	0	0	0
Salad dressing, Italian	1 T/15 ml	80	1	9	Tr	1	Tr	3	0	0	162
Salad dressing, Italian, low-calorie	1 T/15 ml	5	Tr	1	Tr	Tr	Tr	Tr	10	0	136
Sugar	1 T/12 ml	45	12	0	0	0	Tr	0	0		Tr

Combinations/Miscellaneous

Food	Amount										
Chili with beans	1 c, canned	340	30	16	19	82	4.3	15	8	28	1,354
Doughnuts, glazed	1 doughnut	235	22	13	4	17	1.4	Tr	0	21	222
Pierogies	3 pierogies	180	34	2	6	0	0	0	0	15	340
Pizza, cheese	1 slice	290	22	9	15	220	1.6	106	2	56	699
Popcorn, plain	1 c/250 ml	25	5	Tr	1	1	0.2	0	0	0	0
Taco	1 taco	195	18	11	9	109	1.2	57	1	21	456
Veggie burger (made w/ brown rice, oats, mushrooms, mozzarella cheese)	1 burger	140	Tr	2.5	8	Tr	2	Tr	10	0	180

Note: All fruits and vegetables fresh unless noted. Vegetables fresh cooked unless noted. Metric equivalents are approximate.

Key: g = gram. ml = milliliter. oz = ounce. c = cup. T = tablespoon. Tr—Nutrient present in trace amounts. V—Varies by brand; consult label. Information about nutrients in other foods can be found on the "Nutrition Facts" panels on food packages.

Glossary

401(k) plan A type of retirement plan in which employee contributions are deducted from each paycheck, reducing the amount of income tax owed. (Ch. 31)

A

abstinence Refusing to engage in high-risk behavior, including sexual activity and the use of tobacco, alcohol, and other drugs. (Ch. 2, 22, 33)

abuse A situation in which one person threatens the physical or mental health of another. (Ch. 20)

accessories Items that enhance an outfit, such as belts, ties, scarves, hats, and jewelry. (Ch. 41)

accountable Willing to accept the consequences of your actions and words. (Ch. 4)

active listening Concentrating on what is said so that you understand and remember the message. (Ch. 15)

active play Play involving physical activities that employ large motor skills. (Ch. 26)

addictive Causing a mental or physical dependence that leads users to crave regular doses of a substance. (Ch. 33)

aerobic activities Sustained, rhythmic activities that improve the efficiency of your heart and lungs. (Ch. 33)

age appropriate Suited to a child's developmental stage. (Ch. 26)

aggressive Overly forceful and pushy. (Ch. 15)

alcoholism A disease in which a person develops a physical and mental need for alcohol. (Ch. 20)

alter To make changes in a garment or pattern pieces to match your measurements. (Ch. 45)

amino acids The chemical building blocks of proteins. (Ch. 34)

annual percentage rate (APR) The annual rate of interest that a creditor charges for using credit. (Ch. 32)

anorexia nervosa An eating disorder that involves an extreme urge to lose weight by starving oneself. (Ch. 33)

appetite A desire, rather than a need, to eat. (Ch. 35)

apprenticeship A training program that combines classroom instruction with on-the-job learning. (Ch. 9)

aptitudes Natural talents that you were born with. (Ch. 10)

arcing Sparking that can occur when metal objects are used in a microwave oven. It can damage the oven and start a fire. (Ch. 39)

assertive Able to express your ideas and opinions firmly and with confidence. (Ch. 15)

attention span The length of time someone is able to concentrate on one task without losing interest. (Ch. 26)

authority figures People who have the right and responsibility to influence your behavior. (Ch. 14)

B

bait and switch A deceptive practice in which a retailer lures shoppers to the store by advertising an unusually low-priced item that it has no intention of selling, then tries to persuade shoppers to buy a higher-priced item. (Ch. 29)

baking Cooking food uncovered in the oven. Also called *roasting*. (Ch. 39)

beat To mix ingredients vigorously and introduce air into them. (Ch. 39)

binge eating disorder An eating disorder that involves compulsive overeating. (Ch. 33)

biodegradable Formulated to break down easily in the environment. (Ch. 50)

blend 1. To thoroughly combine two or more ingredients until the mixture has a uniform appearance. (Ch. 39) 2. A yarn or fabric made from two or more different fibers. (Ch. 44)

blended family The type of family formed when a single parent remarries. Blended families can include children of each spouse, plus new children of the couple. (Ch. 19)

bobbin A small metal or plastic spool beneath the needle of a sewing machine; holds one of the two threads that form the stitches. (Ch. 45)

body image The mental concept you have of your physical appearance. (Ch. 33)

body language A person's posture, facial expressions, gestures, and way of moving. (Ch. 15)

boiling Heating liquid at a high temperature so that bubbles rise continuously to the surface and break. (Ch. 39)

bonded Covered by an agreement that provides protection against financial loss. For example, a person you hire to make repairs to your home should be bonded. (Ch. 30)

bonds Certificates of debt; a type of investment. (Ch. 31)

book value The estimated value of a specific make, model, and year of vehicle. (Ch. 49)

braising Browning food in a small amount of fat, then cooking it slowly in a small amount of simmering liquid until tender. (Ch. 39)

broiling Cooking food directly under or over a glowing heat source. (Ch. 39)

budget A plan for spending and saving money. (Ch. 7)

bulimia An eating disorder that involves bouts of extreme overeating followed by attempts to get rid of the food eaten. (Ch. 33)

calories Units used to measure the energy that you get from food and that you use for physical activity. (Ch. 33)

carbohydrates The nutrients that provide your body with ready energy. (Ch. 34)

carbon monoxide detector A device that sounds an alarm when a dangerous level of carbon monoxide is reached. (Ch. 48)

career A series of related jobs in a particular field. (Ch. 9)

career cluster A group of occupations that have certain characteristics in common. (Ch. 10)

career path The steps you take to reach your career goal. (Ch. 9)

career plan A plan for the career path that you will follow. (Ch. 10)

caregiver Anyone who provides care for an infant or young child, or for an older adult or a person with a disability who needs assistance. (Ch. 25)

care label On a clothing item, a sewn-in label that includes care instructions. (Ch. 43)

carpools Arrangements in which a group of people commute together by car. (Ch. 49)

certificate of deposit (CD) An investment in which you deposit money with a financial institution for a specified period of time and receive an agreed-upon interest rate in return. (Ch. 31)

chain letter An e-mail or mail message that encourages people to send copies of the message to additional people, along with money. (Ch. 28)

character Moral strength and integrity. (Ch. 3)

childproofing Identifying potential hazards in the home and taking steps to keep them from causing harm. (Ch. 25)

cholesterol A white, waxlike substance that plays a part in transporting and digesting fat. (Ch. 34)

chop To cut food into small, irregular pieces. (Ch. 39)

classics Clothing styles that stay popular for a long time. (Ch. 43)

clique A small, exclusive group that restricts who can join. (Ch. 21)

closing costs Various fees due at the time the purchase of a home is finalized. (Ch. 46)

clothing inventory An organized list of the garments you own. (Ch. 41)

collaboration Cooperative efforts by a group of people. (Ch. 4)

colorfast Having color that will remain the same over time. (Ch. 44)

color schemes Color combinations that look good together. (Ch. 42)

communication The process of sending and receiving messages between people. (Ch. 15)

compensation package The combination of pay and any additional benefits offered by an employer. (Ch. 11)

competence Having the qualities and the skills needed to perform a task or participate fully in an activity. (Ch. 1)

condominium ownership A form of ownership for units in a multiple-family complex. Each person owns his or her own unit and shares ownership of common areas such as hallways and grounds. (Ch. 46)

conflict A clash among people who have opposing ideas or interests. (Ch. 18)

consensus Agreement by the entire group. (Ch. 16)

conservation The careful management and protection of natural resources. (Ch. 50)

constructive criticism Feedback that suggests ways you can learn and improve. (Ch. 12, 23)

consumer Someone who buys and uses products and services. (Ch. 28)

context All of the conditions surrounding a problem or situation. (Ch. 6)

contingency plans Alternative courses of action that could help you overcome potential obstacles. (Ch. 5)

continuing education Courses geared toward working adults. (Ch. 12)

convenience foods Foods that are partly prepared or ready to eat. (Ch. 36)

cooperative ownership A form of ownership for units in a multiple-family complex. Each person owns stock in a corporation that owns the entire property and its grounds. (Ch. 46)

cooperative play Play that involves interacting with other children in small groups. (Ch. 24)

copyright Legal rights given to the people and companies that produce original works. (Ch. 8)

cost per wearing An estimate of how much you pay for a clothing item per use. (Ch. 43)

cover letter A brief letter that you send along with a résumé in order to introduce yourself to a potential employer. (Ch. 11)

CPR Cardiopulmonary resuscitation; a first aid technique that combines rescue breathing with chest compressions. (Ch. 25)

cream To beat shortening or another fat with sugar until the mixture is light and fluffy. (Ch. 39)

credit An arrangement in which you receive money, goods, or services now and promise to pay for them in the future. (Ch. 32)

credit history A pattern of past behavior in paying debts. (Ch. 32)

credit limit The maximum amount of credit that a creditor will extend to you. (Ch. 32)

creditors Organizations that extend credit, such as banks, finance companies, and stores. (Ch. 32)

credit rating An evaluation of a consumer's credit history. (Ch. 32)

credit report A record of a particular consumer's credit transactions and payment patterns. (Ch. 32)

crisis An event or situation that overwhelms usual coping methods and causes severe stress. (Ch. 20)

critical thinking Applying reasoning strategies in order to make sound judgments. (Ch. 8)

cross-contamination The transfer of harmful bacteria from one food to another. (Ch. 38)

cube To cut food into evenly sized pieces that are about ½ inch on each side. (Ch. 39)

custody Legally assigned responsibility for making decisions that affect children and providing for their care. (Ch. 20)

cut in To mix a solid fat, such as shortening, with dry ingredients using a cutting motion. (Ch. 39)

D

Daily Value A nutrient reference amount established by the U.S. government for use on food labels. (Ch. 37)

deadline A time or date by which a task must be completed. (Ch. 7)

debit card A card that deducts the cost of purchases from the user's account at the time of purchase. (Ch. 31)

decision-making process A six-step procedure for making thoughtful choices. (Ch. 6)

deductible A set amount that the holder of an insurance policy must pay for each loss before the insurance company pays out. (Ch. 31)

deep-fat frying Cooking food by immersing it in hot fat. (Ch. 39)

defensive driving Taking steps to minimize the chances of an accident. (Ch. 2)

dehydration Excessive loss of body fluids. (Ch. 33)

delegate To assign tasks to other team members. (Ch. 16)

developmental tasks Skills and abilities that are mastered as part of the maturing process. (Ch. 24)

dice To cut food into evenly sized pieces that are about ¼ inch or less on each side. (Ch. 39)

Dietary Guidelines for Americans Science-based advice for making smart choices from every food group, finding balance between food and physical activity, and getting the most nutrition out of your calories. (Ch. 35)

direct mail advertising The practice of delivering ads to consumers' homes by mail. (Ch. 29)

discrimination Treating certain people differently as a result of prejudice. (Ch. 14)

diversity Variety. (Ch. 21)

dovetail To overlap activities in order to save time. (Ch. 7, 39)

down payment A portion of the purchase price that a buyer pays up front in cash. (Ch. 46)

downsizing Laying workers off in order to reduce costs. (Ch. 9)

dress code A set of rules describing required or appropriate clothing. (Ch. 41)

dry heat cooking Cooking food uncovered without adding liquid. (Ch. 39)

E

eating disorders Extreme eating behaviors that can lead to serious health problems and even death. (Ch. 33)

eating patterns Daily routines for eating. (Ch. 36)

embryo A developing baby during the first eight weeks of pregnancy. (Ch. 24)

emotional maturity The ability to understand and act on one's emotions in ways that are appropriate for an adult level of development. (Ch. 27)

emphasis The technique of drawing attention where you want it. (Ch. 42, 47)

employability skills The skills that help you fit into the workplace and be a valuable team player. (Ch. 9)

endorse To give approval to a product in an advertisement. (Ch. 29)

EnergyGuide label A black and yellow label found on appliances. It shows the estimated annual energy consumption of that model, the range of energy use for similar models, and the estimated yearly operating cost. (Ch. 47)

Energy Star label A blue and green label indicating that a product meets government standards for energy efficiency. (Ch. 47)

enriched Term indicating that many of the nutrients lost in processing a food have been added back. (Ch. 35)

entrée Main dish. (Ch. 36)

entrepreneur Someone who sets up and operates a business. (Ch. 9)

environment Everything that surrounds you. (Ch. 24)

equivalent measurement A way to express same amount using a different unit of measure. (Ch. 39)

ethical leadership Leadership based on moral principles. (Ch. 16)

ethics The principles and values that guide the way you live. (Ch. 3, 6)

etiquette Accepted rules of behavior in a particular culture. (Ch. 40)

expectations The wants and needs a person hopes to gain from a relationship. (Ch. 14)

expenses The items that you spend your money on. (Ch. 7)

expiration date The last day a product should be eaten. (Ch. 37)

extended family A larger family group including not only parents and their children but also grandparents, uncles, aunts, and cousins. (Ch. 19)

eye contact Direct visual contact with another person's eyes. (Ch. 15)

eye-hand coordination The ability to make precise movements with the hands in relation to what the eyes see. (Ch. 24)

F

fabric finishes Special treatments that improve the appearance, feel, or performance of fabric. (Ch. 44)

facing A shaped piece of fabric used to finish the raw edge of a garment. (Ch. 45)

fads Clothing styles that remain popular for only a short time. (Ch. 43)

family life cycle A process of growth and change that families go through over the years. (Ch. 19)

fashion Design characteristics that are popular at a certain point in time. (Ch. 42)

feedback A response that lets a speaker know that the listener is trying to understand the message being delivered. (Ch. 15)

fetus A developing baby from the ninth week of pregnancy until birth. (Ch. 24)

fiber Indigestible threadlike cells found in certain foods that contain carbohydrates. (Ch. 34)

fibers Very fine, hairlike strands of various lengths that are combined to create the yarns used to make fabrics. (Ch. 44)

finance charges Costs incurred when using credit, including interest and any additional fees. (Ch. 32)

first aid Emergency care or treatment given right away to an ill or injured person. (Ch. 25)

flatware Knives, forks, and spoons. (Ch. 40)

flexibility Willingness to adapt to new or changing requirements. (Ch. 12)

flextime A system that allows workers to choose when they will begin and end their working day. (Ch. 13)

floor plan A diagram that shows the main structural elements of a home or room. (Ch. 47)

fold To use a spoon or rubber scraper to gently add an air-filled ingredient to a mixture. (Ch. 39)

food allergy Condition in which the body's immune system reacts to a particular food substance as though it were a foreign invader. (Ch. 36)

foodborne illness Sickness that results from eating food that is unsafe to eat. (Ch. 38)

food intolerance Condition in which a person has trouble digesting a food or food component. (Ch. 36)

fortified Term indicating that specific nutrients have been added to a food during processing. (Ch. 35)

fraud Deceitful conduct for personal gain. (Ch. 28)

freezer burn A condition in which food dries out and loses flavor because of improper freezing. (Ch. 38)

G

global economy The way national economies around the world are linked by trade. (Ch. 9)

global environment The life support systems of the whole planet. (Ch. 50)

grain The directions in which the lengthwise and crosswise threads of a fabric run. (Ch. 45)

grate To cut food into very small particles by rubbing it against the small holes of a grater. (Ch. 39)

grief The sorrow caused by the death of a loved one and the emotional adjustment to that loss. (Ch. 20)

gross pay The total amount of your earnings before deductions are taken out. (Ch. 31)

ground fault circuit interrupter (GFCI) A device used near plumbing or water to guard against electrical shock. (Ch. 48)

groupthink A faulty decision-making process caused by a strong desire for group agreement. (Ch. 16)

H

harassment Persistent annoying, hostile behavior directed at a specific person. (Ch. 21)

heredity The set of characteristics that you inherit from your parents and ancestors. (Ch. 24)

hormones Natural chemicals that are released within the body and affect its systems. (Ch. 24)

hue A specific color that can be identified by name, such as green, red, or blue-violet. (Ch. 42)

hunger Your body's physical signal that it is short of energy and needs food. (Ch. 35)

I

identity theft The illegal use of an individual's personal information. (Ch. 8, 28)

illusion An image that fools the eye. (Ch. 42)

"I" messages Statements in which you say how you feel and what you think rather than criticizing someone else. (Ch. 15)

immunizations Vaccines that prevent specific diseases. (Ch. 25)

impulse buying Making unplanned purchases with little or no thought. (Ch. 30)

income The money you take in and have available to spend. (Ch. 7)

individual retirement account (IRA) A plan that enables workers and their spouses to set aside money for retirement. (Ch. 31)

infatuation An intense romantic attraction. (Ch. 22)

infomercials Television or radio ads that last 30 minutes or more and are designed to seem like regular programming. Also called *paid programming.* (Ch. 29)

initiative Willingness to do what needs to be done without being asked. (Ch. 12, 23)

intensity The brightness or dullness of a color. (Ch. 42)

interest A fee paid for the opportunity to use someone else's money. (Ch. 31)

internship Short-term work for little or no pay in exchange for an opportunity to work and learn. (Ch. 9)

investing Committing money in the hope that it will make more money over time. (Ch. 31)

irregulars Items offered for sale that are slightly imperfect. (Ch. 30, 43)

J K L

job leads Information about specific job openings. (Ch. 11)

job shadowing Spending time in the workplace with someone who has a job that interests you. (Ch. 10)

job sharing An arrangement in which two part-time workers share one full-time job. (Ch. 13)

joint custody An arrangement in which divorced parents share legal responsibility for their children. (Ch. 20)

lactose intolerance An inability to digest lactose, the form of sugar that is found in milk. (Ch. 36)

landlord The owner of rental property. (Ch. 46)

large motor skills Physical skills that use the large muscles in the arms and legs. (Ch. 24)

leadership Direction and motivation that helps a team or group achieve its goals. (Ch. 4, 16)

leadership style A leader's pattern of behavior when directing a team. (Ch. 16)

lease 1. A legal document that specifies the rights and responsibilities of a landlord and tenant. (Ch. 46) 2. An arrangement in which you pay a monthly fee in exchange for exclusive use of a vehicle for a specific length of time, such as three years. (Ch. 49)

lifestyle The way you live. (Ch. 9)

long-term goal Something you plan to accomplish months or years from now. (Ch. 5)

low birth weight A condition in which an infant weighs less than 5½ pounds at birth. (Ch. 27)

M

manufactured fibers Fibers formed completely or in part by chemicals. (Ch. 44)

markdowns Permanent price reductions on specific items. (Ch. 43)

mass transit Public transportation systems designed to carry large numbers of people. (Ch. 49)

media Channels of mass communication, such as newspapers, magazines, radio, television, movies, and Web sites. (Ch. 6, 17, 29)

mediation The process of settling a dispute with the help of an impartial third party. (Ch. 18)

mentor Someone who acts as a teacher and a guide. (Ch. 3, 12)

mildew A fungus that shows up as small black dots. (Ch. 44)

mince To cut food into irregular pieces that are as small as possible. (Ch. 39)

minerals Nutrients that regulate body processes and that form parts of many tissues. (Ch. 34)

mixed message A message in which your words and body language don't communicate the same thing. (Ch. 15)

moist heat cooking Using hot liquids or steam to cook food. (Ch. 39)

money market account A type of savings account that pays a higher interest rate because the financial institution invests the money you deposit. (Ch. 31)

mortgage A long-term home loan. (Ch. 46)

mutual fund A group of investments held in common by many individual investors. (Ch. 31)

NO

natural fibers Fibers that come from plants or animals. (Ch. 44)

neglect The failure of parents to meet a child's basic needs. Can also occur when the basic needs of others who require care, such as some elderly or disabled people, are not met. (Ch. 20)

net pay The amount you actually receive in your paycheck after deductions are taken out. (Ch. 31)

networking Using personal contacts to find a job. (Ch. 11)

nonrenewable resources Natural resources that cannot be replaced once they are used. (Ch. 50)

nonverbal communication The process of sending messages without words through the use of facial expressions and gestures. (Ch. 15)

notions The smaller supplies necessary to complete a sewing project. (Ch. 45)

nuclear family The most basic family form, consisting of a husband, wife, and their children. (Ch. 19)

nurture To provide the care and attention needed to promote development. (Ch. 19, 26)

nutrient-dense Term describing foods that are low or moderate in calories and rich in important nutrients. (Ch. 35)

nutrients Chemicals found in food that help the body work properly. (Ch. 34)

obsolete Out of date and no longer useful. (Ch. 8)

outsourcing Contracting out certain tasks to other companies. Done by many businesses in order to cut costs. (Ch. 9)

overscheduling Trying to accomplish too many things in a limited amount of time. (Ch. 7)

P Q

panfrying Cooking food in a small amount of fat over low to medium heat. (Ch. 39)

parallel play Play that takes place alongside other children but not with them. (Ch. 24)

pare To cut away the skin of a fruit or vegetable using a paring knife or a peeler. (Ch. 39)

parenting Providing care, guidance, and support in order to promote a child's development. (Ch. 25)

passive Tending to keep your opinions to yourself and to give in to the influence of others. (Ch. 15)

pasteurized Treated by a process that kills harmful bacteria. (Ch. 37)

pattern guide sheet A sheet included with a sewing pattern that gives specific instructions for cutting out and sewing the project. (Ch. 45)

peer education A program based on the principle of teens teaching teens. (Ch. 18)

peer mediation A process in which specially trained students help other students resolve conflicts peacefully. (Ch. 18)

peer pressure The influence of people in your own age group. (Ch. 3, 17)

perishable Tending to spoil quickly. (Ch. 37)

persevere To work patiently to overcome challenges. (Ch. 1)

personal boundaries Limits you set for yourself based on your values and priorities. (Ch. 13)

personal growth The process of working toward your potential. (Ch. 1)

personality The combination of characteristics that makes you different from every other person. (Ch. 1)

personal standard A rule or principle you set for yourself that guides your behavior. (Ch. 3)

place setting The arrangement of tableware that each person needs for a meal. (Ch. 40)

plagiarism Taking part of another person's original work and using it as if it were your own work. (Ch. 8)

poaching Cooking whole foods in a small amount of simmering liquid so that they keep their original shape. (Ch. 39)

portfolio A collection of work samples that demonstrate your skills. (Ch. 11)

potential The capability of becoming more than you are right now. (Ch. 1)

practical problem A complex situation that has many aspects, involves making several interrelated choices, and requires thinking about values and ethics. (Ch. 6)

precycling Making environmentally responsible consumer choices. (Ch. 50)

prejudice An unfair or biased attitude toward an individual or group. (Ch. 14)

premature Born before 37 weeks of development. (Ch. 27)

prenatal Before birth. (Ch. 24)

pressure cooking Using a special airtight pot to cook food quickly at a very high temperature. (Ch. 39)

preventive maintenance Taking action to prevent problems or to keep minor problems from becoming major ones. (Ch. 48)

principal The original amount of money borrowed. (Ch. 32)

prioritize To decide which goals and activities are most important to you. (Ch. 5)

proactive Able to take initiative; willing to anticipate future decisions or problems and take action. (Ch. 3, 6)

procrastination The tendency to put off doing something until later. (Ch. 1, 17)

proportion The way one part of a design relates in size to another part and to the whole design. (Ch. 42, 47)

proteins The nutrients your body uses to build and repair body tissues. (Ch. 34)

puree To mash food until it is smooth. (Ch. 39)

pyramid scheme A get-rich-quick plan based on recruiting more and more participants. (Ch. 28)

quiet play Play involving activities that engage the mind and use small motor skills. (Ch. 26)

rebate A refund of part of the purchase price of a product. (Ch. 30)

reciprocity A mutual exchange in which each person gives as well as receives. (Ch. 21)

reconcile To bring a bank statement and your own record of transactions into agreement. (Ch. 31)

recycled-content products Items made partially or totally from materials that might have ended up in a landfill. (Ch. 50)

redress The right to seek legal remedy when laws are violated. (Ch. 28)

references The names of people that potential employers can contact to learn more about you. (Ch. 11)

reflexes Automatic, involuntary responses. (Ch. 24)

refusal skills Techniques for resisting negative peer pressure. (Ch. 17)

relationships The connections you have with other people. (Ch. 14)

renewable resources Natural resources that replace themselves over time. (Ch. 50)

resilient Able to recover from or adjust to change or misfortune. (Ch. 1)

resource Something you can use to achieve a goal. (Ch. 5)

resourceful Able to use creative problem solving to manage available resources wisely. (Ch. 5)

respite care Temporary care that relieves caregivers of their responsibilities for a short period of time. (Ch. 25)

résumé A written summary of a job seeker's work experience, education, skills, and interests. (Ch. 11)

return policy A retailer's rules for returning or exchanging merchandise. (Ch. 28)

rivalry A situation in which people compete against each other to gain an advantage. (Ch. 23)

roasting Cooking food uncovered in the oven. Also called *baking*. (Ch. 39)

role conflict A situation that occurs when one of your roles has a significant negative impact on another role. (Ch. 13)

role model A person who sets an example for others. (Ch. 16)

roles The parts you play when you interact with others. (Ch. 2)

rotation A system in which older supplies are used before newer ones. (Ch. 38)

saturated fats Fats that are usually solid at room temperature. (Ch. 34)

sautéing Cooking small pieces of food in a small amount of fat over low to medium heat, stirring occasionally. (Ch. 39)

scale drawing A drawing in which a given number of inches represents a given number of feet. (Ch. 47)

seconds Items offered for sale that have noticeable flaws. (Ch. 30, 43)

security deposit A fee that a renter must pay in advance to cover any damage he or she might later cause to the property. (Ch. 46)

self-concept The way you see yourself. Also called *self-image* or *identity*. (Ch. 1)

self-esteem The value or importance you place on yourself. (Ch. 1)

"sell by" date The last day a product may be sold. (Ch. 37)

serger A machine that sews, trims, and finishes the edge of a seam in one step. (Ch. 45)

service learning Taking what you learn in the classroom and using it to meet a community need. (Ch. 4)

sexual harassment Annoying behavior of a sexual nature. (Ch. 21)

sexually transmitted diseases (STDs) Diseases that are spread through sexual contact. (Ch. 22, 33)

shade A darker color created by adding black to a hue. (Ch. 42)

shoplifting The theft of merchandise from a store by shoppers. (Ch. 28)

short-term goal Something you want to accomplish soon. (Ch. 5)

shred To cut or tear food into thin strips. (Ch. 39)

simmering Heating liquid to a temperature just below the boiling point. (Ch. 39)

single-parent family A family headed by one parent. (Ch. 19)

slice To cut food into thin, flat pieces. (Ch. 39)

small claims court A court in which claims under a certain amount are settled by a judge. (Ch. 28)

small motor skills Physical skills that use the small muscles of the hands and fingers. (Ch. 24)

sociability The quality of behaving in a friendly manner and enjoying other people's company. (Ch. 23)

socialization The process of learning how to interact with other people. (Ch. 19)

standing time Time during which food continues to cook after microwaving. (Ch. 39)

staples Basic food items you use regularly, such as flour, sugar, rice, and pasta. (Ch. 37)

status Position in a peer group or in society. (Ch. 41)

staystitching A row of regular machine stitches through a single layer of fabric; helps curved areas hold their shape. (Ch. 45)

steaming Cooking food over, but not in, boiling water. (Ch. 39)

stereotype A belief that all people in a particular group have the same qualities or act the same. (Ch. 14, 23)

stewing Cooking small pieces of food in a small amount of simmering liquid. (Ch. 39)

sticker price The dealer's initial asking price as shown on the sticker attached to a vehicle. (Ch. 49)

stir To mix slowly in a circular or figure-8 motion with a spoon or a wire whisk. (Ch. 39)

stir-frying Stirring and cooking small pieces of food very quickly at high heat in very little fat. (Ch. 39)

stock Ownership interest in a company; a type of investment. (Ch. 31)

stress Your body's response when you feel overwhelmed by responsibilities and demands. (Ch. 2)

style A distinctive form of a clothing item. (Ch. 42)

substance abuse The use of illegal drugs or the misuse of legal drugs or substances. (Ch. 20, 33)

support system All the people and organizations a person or family can turn to for help. (Ch. 13, 19)

T

tact The quality of knowing what to do or say in order to avoid offending others. (Ch. 23)

target market The consumers that the makers of a product plan to appeal to. (Ch. 42)

teamwork The process of working with others to achieve a common goal. (Ch. 16)

technology The application of science to help people meet their needs and wants. (Ch. 8)

telecommute To work from home using communication links to the job. (Ch. 13)

tenant Someone who rents property from its owner. (Ch. 46)

testimonials Positive statements about a product based on personal experience. (Ch. 29)

tint A lighter color created by adding white to a hue. (Ch. 42)

title A legal document showing who owns a vehicle. (Ch. 49)

tolerance Respect for other people's beliefs and customs. (Ch. 14)

toss To tumble ingredients lightly together using a fork and spoon. (Ch. 39)

traffic patterns The routes people use to move through a room or from one part of a home to another. (Ch. 47)

trans fats A type of fat formed when food manufacturers turn liquid oils into solid fats. (Ch. 34)

U V

unit price The price per ounce, pound, or other unit of measure. (Ch. 37)

unsaturated fats Fats that are usually liquid at room temperature. (Ch. 34)

"use by" date The last day a product is considered fresh. (Ch. 37)

value The lightness or darkness of a color. (Ch. 42)

values Beliefs and ideas about what is important. (Ch. 3)

vegan (VEE-gun) A type of vegetarian eating plan in which only foods from plant sources are eaten. (Ch. 36)

verbal communication The process of sending messages with words. (Ch. 15)

vintage clothes Garments from a previous era, such as the 1930s or the 1970s. (Ch. 43)

vitamins Nutrients that help your body function properly and process other nutrients. (Ch. 34)

volume The amount of space taken up by an ingredient. (Ch. 39)

W X Y Z

wardrobe A collection of clothes. (Ch. 41)

warranty A guarantee that provides protection against faulty products. (Ch. 30)

wellness An approach to life that emphasizes taking positive steps toward overall good health. (Ch. 2, 33)

whip To beat very rapidly, incorporating so much air as to increase the volume of the product. (Ch. 39)

win-win solution A solution that benefits everyone involved and has no real drawbacks for anyone. (Ch. 18)

work centers Organized areas where specific kitchen tasks are performed. (Ch. 38)

work ethic A sense of obligation to work hard and to complete tasks efficiently and well. (Ch. 12)

workplace culture The attitudes, behavior, habits, and expectations of a company's owners and employees. (Ch. 12)

work triangle The path in a kitchen from the refrigerator to the sink to the range. (Ch. 38)

yarns Fibers that have been twisted or grouped together. (Ch. 44)

yield The amount of food a recipe makes. (Ch. 39)

Credits

Cover and Interior Design:
Squarecrow Creative Group

Cover Photo:
Vote Photography

Articulate Graphics: 446, 448, 450, 451, 463, 467
Artsville: 498, 499
Marshal Berman: 681
Keith Berry: 394, 634
Arnold & Brown: 141
Bradley University: Todd Buchanan 102
Ken Clubb: 370, 567, 568, 613, 616, 629, 631, 636, 637
Comstock: 483
Corbis: 20, 30, 72, 105, 125, 131, 133, 147, 197, 292, 309, 325, 351, 378, 414, 473, 512, 626/Paul Barton 14, 194, 263, 472, 627; Joe Bator 367; Nathan Benn 77; Bettmann 284; Ed Bock 112, 408, 435; BSPI 635; Stephanie Cardinale 609; Dean Conger 670; Jim Craigmyle 368, 612; Davy Crockett 402; Dex Images 354; Dharma 78; George Diebold 110; Anne Domdey 318; Randy Duchaine 535; ER Productions 126; Randy Faris 27; Jon Feingersh 339; Firefly 11, 415; FK Photo 51; Charles Gupton 88, 320, 380, 600; John Henley 7, 83, 111, 156, 262, 465, 485; Walter Hodges 391; Ted Horowitz 44, 553; Huewitz Creative 355, 553; JDC/LWA 386; Ronnie Kaufman 198, 299, 379, 500; Michael Kellar 328; Sharie Kennedy/LWA 173; Charles Krebs 348; Rob Lewine 140, 279, 335, 523; James Leynse 97; Lightscapes Photography 726; Yang Liu 113; Don Mason 441; Roy McMahon 640, 687; Rich Meyer 404, 417; Richard T. Nowitz 356; Gabe Palmer 93; Jose Luis Pelaez 86, 87, 161, 324, 333, 345, 365, 593; Todd Pearson 382; Photographer's Choice 420; David Raynor 421; Rob & Sass 397; Bob Rowan/Progressive Images 344; Chuck Savage 66, 163, 447, 474, 677; Lawrence M. Sawyer 617; Norbert Schaeffer 321; Ariel Skelley 26; 64, 227, 298, 371, 385, 477; Tom Stewart 7, 37, 82, 101, 107, 114, 117, 127, 157, 158, 289, 303, 307, 357, 373; David Stoecklin 594; Dan Tardif/LWA 361, 409, 456; William Taufic 440, 669; Francisco Villaflor 100; Wartenberg Press 252; Douglas Whyte 590; Larry Williams 424; Stephen Wilstead/LWA 395; Jeff Zaruba 427
Owens Corning: 730
Luis Degado: 709
Envision: Mark Ferri 12, 495, 521; Lisa Koenig 508; Steve Needham 12, 493, 494, 497, 522; Madeline Poiss 542
Curt Fischer: 549
David R. Frazier Photolibrary: 136, 183, 738
Tim Fuller: 275, 566, 581, 739
Ann Garvin: 30, 550, 572, 573, 601, 643, 649
Getty Images: Daniel Allan 462; Ty Allison 53; Tony Anderson 310, 592; Anderson-Ross 38, 85, 131, 200; Jim Arbogast 278; Daniel Arsenault 266; Barros & Barros 201; Benelux Press 225; Nathan Bilow 238; Kareem Black 69; Botanica 686; Larry Bray 69; Gary Buss 457; Peter Cade 208, 721; Mary Jane Cardenas 11, 444; Chabruken 90; Flip Chalfont 217; Ron Chapple 80; Paul Cheslev 9, 281; Color Day Production 71, 264; Cosmo Condina 715; Robert E. Daemmrich 239; Dax Images 10; Ghislain & Marie David de Lessy 121, 220, 242; Digital Vision 240, 611; Richard Drury 187; Steve Dunwell 233; Denis Felix 128 ; Fisher-Thatcher 336; Jules Frazier 479; G&J Images 179; Rob Gage 213; Tony Garcia 672; Suzanne & Nick Geary 430; Glanstep 334; Kim Golding 406; Holy Harris 138; Philip Lee Harvey 210; Jack Hollinsworth 481; Tony Hopewell 714; Tipp Howell 487; Howard Huang 203; Billy Hustace 226; Janeart Inc. 195; Zigy Kaluzney 265, 315

Zigy Kaluzney 265, 315 392; Kaluzny-Thatcher 282; Vicky Kasala 271; Michael Krasowitz 271; Seth Kushar 130; Klaus Lahnstein 588; Erica Lanzer 296; Tony Latham 701; Clarissa Leahy 285; David Leahy 589; Pat LeCroix 5, 62; Catherine Lederer 28; Lifestock 182; Ian Logan 36; Bill Losh 364; Rita Maas 520; Machan 142; Ebbie May 178; William McKellar 700; Ryan McVay 28, 99, 137, 146, 235, 293; Doug Menuez 143; Arnos Morgan 221; Jonathan Morgan 476; Kevin Morris 234; Muldowney 84; Steve Niedorf 57; Erin Patrick O'Brien 234; Gabe Palmer 455; Kevin Patterson 228; Lori Adamsky Peek 400; PhotoDisc 22, 25, 29, 33, 45, 50, 55, 76, 92, 98, 159, 168, 202, 207, 209, 219, 231, 280, 283, 286, 311, 346, 387, 401, 507, 511, 619, 668; Photographer's Choice 23, 420; Javier Pierni 211; Andreas Pollok 185, 624; Cal Posey 274; Jon Riley 416; Marc Romanelli 65; Spencer Rowell 268, 359; Rubberball Productions 619; Nicholas Russell 230; Andy Sacks 151; John Sann 395; Ian Shaw 81, 596; Dan Sherwood 6, 96; Harry Sieplinga/HMS 124; Stephen Simpson 329; Chad Slattery 301; Don Smetzer 229; Brendan Smialowsky 454; Duncan Smith 191; Phillip Spears 190; Dan Stewart 6; SW Productions 8, 9, 40, 98, 224, 245, 253, 255, 256, 306, 319 502, 692; Thinkstock 59, 218, 283 390; Paul Thomas 254, 332; Patrisha Thomson 212; Arthur Tilley 52; Bob Torrez 276; Frederick Tousche 119; Penny Tweedie 313; Alexander Walter 149; Anne Marie Weber 221; Angela Wyant 584; Yellow Dog Productions 216, 623; David Young-Wolff 39, 63, 73, 247, 719

Image Works: Bob Daemmrich 708; David Lassman/Syracuse Newspaper 673

Index Stock: Stewart Cohen 144; Gary Conner 445; Jim Corwin 717; Katie Dietz 153; Steve Dunwell 413; Mark Gibson 648; Bill Lai 527; Patricia Barry Levy 162; Medio Images 43; Chris Minerva 716; SW Production 622

Ken Karp: 614

Ken Lax: 605, 618

Lofasofa: 694

Mallon: 334

Masterfile: Andrew McKim 693

Kevin May: 46, 696, 707

Mishima: 372, 602

Morgan-Cain: 555

Photodisc: 15, 145 (Steve Cole), 186, 283, 387, 496, 510, 536, 610, 682, 683, 690, 691, 697, 703, 711, 727, 728, 729, 734

Photoedit: Bill Aron 452, 484, 509, 545; Michelle D. Bridwell 551, 571; Myrleen Ferguson Cate 528; Mary Kate Denny 10, 383; Tony Freeman 360, 411, 432, 478, 680; Robert W. Ginn 423; Spencer Grant 384, 538; Christina Kennedy 537; Dennis MacDonald 16, 513; Michael Newman 489, 539, 583, 597, 718; Clayton Sharrard 733; Stephen Skjold 169; Don Smetzer 676; Dana White 706; David Young-Wolff 175, 295, 300, 338, 433, 438, 459, 503, 524, 528, 529, 531, 554, 561, 563, 574, 579

Schulte Corp.: 702

Stockfood: Fotokia, 506; Dennis Gottlieb 13, 560; Sian Irvine 492; John Montana 578; Jim Scherer 534; Elizabeth Watt 525; Zabert 548

J. J. Stoecker: 215, 482, 650, 651, 658, 659, 735

Superstock: 340, 469; Steve Dahlman 374; Richard Heinrein 322

Randy Sutter: 675

Toyota: 732

Underwriters' Laboratory: 437

USDA: 515

U.S. Environmental Protection Agency: 696

Vote Photography: 599, 628, 641, 642, 644, 652, 653

Donald Wardlaw, Architect, ATA: 688

Dana White Productions: 104, 114, 129, 176, 287, 349, 350, 405, 422, 431, 704

Ron Zalme: 678-679

Index